Watsonia

Watsonia
A Writing Life

Don Watson

Black Inc.

Published by Black Inc.,
an imprint of Schwartz Books Pty Ltd
Level 1, 221 Drummond Street
Carlton VIC 3053, Australia
enquiries@blackincbooks.com
www.blackincbooks.com

9781760642792 (hardback)
9781743821596 (ebook)

A catalogue record for this book is available from the National Library of Australia

Cover design by John Warwicker
Text design and typesetting by Marilyn de Castro

The following chapters have been excerpted from larger works: "Gough Whitlam",
from *Not Just for This Life: Gough Whitlam Remembered*, edited by W. Guest and G. Gray
(NewSouth Publishing and University of New South Wales Press, 2016); reproduced by
permission of NewSouth Publishing / "Spin doctrines", from *Gobbledygook: How Clichés, Sludge
and Management-Speak Are Strangling Our Public Language* (Atlantic Books, 2004); reproduced by
permission of Atlantic Books / "There it is again", from *There It Is Again: Selected Non-Fiction*
(Vintage, 2017); reproduced by permission of Penguin Random House Australia / "Brian
Fitzpatrick", from *Brian Fitzpatrick: A Radical Life* (Hale & Iremonger, 1979) / "A Highlander on
the Australian frontier", from *New Edinburgh Review Anthology*, edited by J. Campbell (Polygon
Books, 1982); reproduced by permission of Polygon Books through PLSclear / "Mark
Twain", from *The Wayward Tourist: Mark Twain's Adventures in Australia* (Melbourne University
Publishing, 2007); reproduced by permission of Melbourne University Publishing /
"On indignation", from *On Indignation* (Hachette Australia, 2020); reproduced by permission
of Hachette Australia / "The Gippsland frontier", from *The Ash Range* by L. Duggan (Pan Books
Australia Pty Ltd, 1987) / "A 'paradigm' shift", from *Death Sentences: How Clichés, Weasel Words,
and Management-Speak Are Strangling Public Language* (Gotham Books, 2005) / "Recollections:
Afterword", from *Recollections of a Bleeding Heart: A Portrait of Paul Keating PM* (Random House
Australia, 2011) / "Caledonia Australis revisited", from *Caledonia Australis: A Scottish Highlander
on the Frontier of Australia* (Random House Australia, 2009) / "Memory and imagination", from
Armidale '42: A Survivor's Account by C. Madigan and J. Senbergs (Macmillan 1999) / "Lingering
memories of monster kicks at Loch", from *The Greatest Game*, edited by R. Fitzgerald and
K. Spillman (William Heinemann Australia 1988) / "Andrew Chapman", from *Political Vision:
A Photographic Journey Through Australian Politics* by A. Chapman (Echo, 2015)

Every effort has been made to trace copyright holders and obtain their permission
for the use of copyright material. The publisher apologises for any errors or omissions
and would be grateful if notified of any corrections that should be incorporated in
future reprints or editions of this book.

Contents

Introduction   1

BEGINNINGS

The Gippsland frontier   15

Occasional address   20

Journey to the Outer Hebrides   25

A "paradigm shift"   27

Oscar and the ALP   33

LEADERS AND LEADERSHIP

Gough Whitlam   43

From Hawke to eternity   45

Paul Keating: Garibaldi in an Armani suit   48

Recollections: Afterword   69

John Howard's guilty secret   79

Julia Gillard and political leadership in Australia   82

In praise of Tony Windsor   86

Tony Abbott: My fellow Australians   90

The mystery of Malcolm Turnbull   93

Leaders and dung beetles   98

AUSTRALIAN TRADITIONS

Once a jolly lifestyle   107

A toast to the postmodern republic   113

Rethinking the republic   120

The joke after God   127

Judaeo-Christian mateship   132

Anzac Day   135

Meanjin's noble failure   143

Rabbit syndrome   152

All the way with Donald J?   193

THE WORDS TO SAY IT

Teaching English   201

The public language   208

Spin doctrines   214

Iconography   223

The conservative crusade against the ABC   227

There it is again: Or a short history of cant   232

Freudenberg: A time to remember   236

"Use your brains"   241

AUSTRALIAN HISTORY

Stories light and dark   249

Manning Clark   266

Geoffrey Blainey   272

Brian Fitzpatrick   279

Liberalism, capitalism — and revolution?   283

A Highlander on the Australian frontier   289

Caledonia Australis revisited   300

Memory and imagination   312

Cassocks among the tussocks   318

INJUSTICE AND IDEOLOGY

The "war" on terror   325

The East Timor problem   332

A never-never land for sense   337

Revolutions past   345

Sport and Nature

A demigod called Don	355
Steve Waugh: Why we loved the other PM	361
The turf	364
Ken Hunter: Like a vertical greyhound	375
Lingering memories of monster kicks at Loch	378
Seasonally adjusted	382
Possums, rabbits and the society of birds	389

America

The 310 to Drippin' Springs	399
Faith, freedom and Katrina	407
Once upon a time in America	419
Enemy within	435
American carnage	493

Writing and Art

Mark Twain: The wayward tourist	507
Jan Senbergs	525
Andrew Chapman: Political vision	529
Prometheus and the pen	532

Epilogue

On indignation	541
On optimism	555
Acknowledgements	561

Introduction

Human actions are essentially very delicate phenomena, many aspects of which elude mathematical measurement.

—Marc Bloch

I NEVER SET OUT TO be a writer, but drifted into it. In a different time, in my father's day, for instance, I might have ended up a swagman. As a boy I briefly fancied the navy, but that lasted no longer than my religious phase. My plans for a career as a travelling salesman or a detective can be put down to teenage hormonal imbalance; the derangement passed eventually, but the urge to wander lingered.

I would have been a happy wanderer, and happier still if free of any compulsion to write about the experience. But wandering excites thinking and the back and forth of observing and imagining, and, if you are not careful, this can lead to writing. The customs are related by marriage. Wordsworth wrote 387 poems, and, according to Thomas De Quincy, he walked upwards of 180,000 miles while doing so. "Sauntered" was the term Wordsworth used in *The Prelude*: "like a river murmuring / And talking to itself when all things else / Are still". He walked to discover not only his thoughts but his words, and walking gave a rhythm to them.

Though there have been some, such as Max Beerbohm, who thought walking the silliest thing any intelligent being could do, I'm with Wordsworth – and Plato, Aristotle, Montaigne, Rousseau and Nietzsche, who all found walking an indispensable mental aid. George Santayana went so far as to say locomotion was the key to human intelligence. But most human beings have been content to walk and think without adding to their lives the burden of written composition. I could saunter many delightful miles in the time it often takes me to find the right word, and many more again before I can construct a decent sentence. Writing is hard labour, and harder still when it feels unnecessary. My unrelenting ploughboy genes haul me towards the pleasures of intercourse with life on the planet. In forty years my body, sensing extinction I've no doubt, has never stopped resenting the stillness that writing requires.

As for my mind, so long as some part of it resists the writer's flimsy assumption that his thoughts are worth recording, it might as well be in cahoots with my body. When a bulging disc is not tormenting me, it is a voice reminding me of *real* writers in my bookshelves and begging me to throw in the towel. And the truth is, lock me in a cell for a fortnight and offer me *Middlemarch* or a pencil and pad for recording my thoughts, and I'll take the book. Offer me something that I can bounce off a wall, and I'll take that as well.

The lurking apprehension that I am unsuited to this occupation has always preyed on my endeavour. The first answer to the curse, when I can remember it, is to remind myself that farming does not come easily to all farmers, and that not everyone who farms wants to be a farmer. Few are those able to choose their vocation, and fewer still those who choose the right one. So long as I remember this, I do not need a psychotherapist or Marcus Aurelius. By both instruction and example, my father and mother taught me we all must make the best of whatever hand life deals us. Thus advised, a writer needs nothing more to overcome self-doubt except an ego that's at least sporadically capable of putting up a fight, including the one with his father or mother.

This motley collection might suggest to the reader, as it suggests to me, that I've never known what kind of writer I am. But I *would* claim to have learned what kind of writer I am not: not brave or hardy enough, I suspect, to be a frontline journalist like Victor Serge or Robert Fisk. To wander is one thing; to be shot at another. I am not a poet, sadly; or a novelist, just as sadly – I write novels in my head but can't take myself seriously when I try to write them down. I don't have the mind for philosophy, either.

I would accept the quotidian "wordsmith" if the politicians and business types who use the term to describe their writers did not imagine writing and thinking in a kind of feudal arrangement, wherein they, at the apex, do the thinking, and the writers, down among the yeomanry, the wordsmithing. That set-up would be agreeable enough if words and ideas were independent of each other, or if language were the servant of thought and not its midwife. The two are entangled and only sometimes can we say which came first. This is *one* thing I've learned about writing. The idea we start with will very often become a different idea the moment we try to write it down. The more we write, the more the originating thought splits and morphs into other ideas. It is another, related, phenomenon to discover the true subject and our view of it only after several drafts.

I would settle on "journeyman": these pieces are the work of a journeyman learning and, if nothing else, growing more conscientious the longer he persists. And because writers need it as much as anybody else, it's as well to acknowledge, as Joseph Conrad did when he'd survived the dreads and learned to be a man in the Gulf of Siam, that "one's best efforts were seconded by a run of luck".

I am fairly sure that writing becomes seductive to young brains when, somewhere in the amygdala, by chance, the beat of language attaches itself to the primal emotions and becomes a means of their expression. Evidence for this might be found in *Romeo and Juliet* or *Cyrano de Bergerac*, but equally in the speeches of a Martin Luther King Jr or Pericles. If your life is going to depend on writing, you are lucky if haunting and seductive language is put before you when you're young and rumbling with passions that nothing *but* language can temper or express. Then, if you have to walk a distance each day, or have a little watercourse to follow, and in your head the physical and mental landscapes merge, dumb urges swirl with Lear's torments or the puzzles of Huck Finn and combine like atoms; and, though you may not know it and though you may still end up a swagman or in commerce, the ground is being prepared for writing. It was my luck to have all of that, and a wonderful teacher or two.

The first of my more sustained intellectual efforts was also fortified by luck. Influenced in varying degrees by the Vietnam War, some inspiring history lecturers and the rise and fall of Gough Whitlam, I became what the politer members of my family would call "a bit of a radical" (and the less polite, at best, "a flamin' idiot"). I've no doubt that oedipal rebellion was also active in my conversion to a kind of socialism just short of revolutionary. And though I knew him only through his writing and surviving friends, I think it very likely that the left historian, civil libertarian, radical publicist and heavy drinker Brian Fitzpatrick, in addition to being the subject of my doctorate, bore aspects of a surrogate father – or at least a renegade uncle. It is even possible that a romantic reading of Fitzpatrick's outsider status and lifelong resistance to the colonising tendencies of Melbourne orthodoxy played some part in my decision to quit academia for freelancing. I was susceptible to both the graceful ironies of his prose and the radical nationalist conceit that Australian history inclined by nature towards egalitarian social progress, and the political task, therefore, was to get the present in lockstep with that inclination.

That was where I'd landed, roughly speaking: in the bottomless canyons of history with all the victims and underdogs. By "with" them, of course, I mean "on their side". I was much more often "with" other people who were on their side and believed history arced in the direction of justice for all – not in heaven, but on earth. Yet though I was a socialist of sorts, my behaviour lent less support to revolutionary theory than to Oscar Wilde's belief that socialism was doomed to failure because people would not be willing to give up their evenings. I am fairly sure it is for this reason, more than any other, that I have never joined a political party.

Though the term "progressive" was not then in fashion, it would have done for me. I was on the side of progress. But progress for a radical socialist is not the same as progress for an advocate of free enterprise or a progress association. And that's the least of it. Progress – or "going forward", as we say nowadays – is no more natural to the human condition than is staying put, or even retreating. We are historical in the sum of our parts, and if our primal instincts incline us to violence, jealousy and revenge, all the greater is our need for history, culture and art, the stored knowledge of human genius, altruism and cooperation. Sometimes the masses rise up with a vision of the future, but just as often they revolt in defence of what they have or imagine they once had, or what tradition tells them. The past might oppress and mystify us, and in the hands of some historians it might bore us silly, but it also informs, enchants and binds us. I've been beached in this contradiction for as long as I can remember – possibly we all are – and in one way or another I suspect it has provoked a lot of what I've written.

As a young historian, the fashion for "history from below" impressed itself upon me. I was in awe of E.P. Thompson and his *The Making of the English Working Class*, and the other giant of those days, Eric Hobsbawm. Both were Marxists (Hobsbawm, bewilderingly, a communist to the end). Labour history interested me, but not enough to write it, and while I enjoyed Marx's gripping polemics, I did not have the mind for Marxist theory, or any other kind. The "ethnographic" historian Greg Dening had already subverted me, anyway – though it was years before I realised what he had done. I remember reading something by Isaac Deutscher that also corroded my radical certainties: it was to the effect that while they might not approve of Stalin's purges, good historians could understand them. This led me to wonder if the more we "understand" such enormities, the weaker grows our impulse to condemn them. The notion was less than blindingly original, but it was around this time – the early '80s – that I stumbled into the liberal camp, where no one can be free of contradiction. Or condescension, I discovered. Something in the creed, perhaps its roots in both Christianity and the Enlightenment, lends itself to oppressive moral vanity.

It was around the same time that I read two books that are unalike in everything but their sympathy for the underdog. One, by the Oxford historian Christopher Hill, concerns the English religious rebels of the seventeenth century. It is called *The World Turned Upside Down*. I had no interest in seventeenth-century British history and don't know how I came to read it, but I found myself gripped by a history book as never before. It was more than the subject matter: Hill's way of working the voices of insanely brave religious radicals into the raw material of history brought multitudinous life to his story and a pulse as strong as a great novel's. He, too, was a Marxist, I discovered later, but reading him would tell you only that he had abundant sympathy for the human condition. Impressed though I was with the rebels, the book had less effect on my politics than on the way I wanted to write.

There is no one way to describe *One Hundred Years of Solitude*, but among many other things it is the story of Latin America told from the point of view of the colonised, rather than the colonisers. Political as such a story must be – and as its author was – the book transcends politics. As fairy-tale or myth it reinvents history. ("What is history but a fable agreed upon?") Historians instinctively seek to construct the past on rational foundations, and they are ill-suited to dealing with "the despairs, the rages, the impulsive acts, the sudden revulsions of feeling" in human history, as another hero of mine, Marc Bloch, put it. For me, the irresistible hold of *One Hundred Years of Solitude* consisted almost entirely in the way Gabriel García Márquez finds liberating wonders in the same reality that historians pass over or render lifeless. *Finds*, not invents. As he said, "We have had to ask but little of imagination, for our crucial problem has been a lack of conventional means to render our lives believable". At this point we see that Hill and García Márquez are not so unalike. They meet on the never-ending frontiers of reportage.

As history abounds in irony, I was drawn to it. Too much so, I came to realise. But how could it be otherwise? The rural humour of my childhood was laced with the irony that is inevitable when human ambition meets implacable Nature. Steele Rudd and Job both were full of irony. So was the Sermon on the Mount. Marx couldn't resist it. Nor could Mark Twain, Trotsky, Voltaire, Tolstoy, Wilde, Balzac, Orwell and Camus. Paul Fussell's *The Great War and Modern Memory* put irony at the centre of twentieth-century literary sensibility. Postmodernism put an ironic spell on the universe. It was in everything I read or saw: Godard, Truffaut, Hitchcock and film noir. (In arthouse cinemas a special kind of knowing laugh evolved among the cognoscenti.) Irony lent drollness to political commitment in Claud Cockburn's memoir of the 1930s, *In Time of Trouble*, which beguiled me. It was the wheel on which Bruce Petty's genius turned. It was at the core of the new wave of Australian plays, novels and films, as it had been in Australian literature since Henry Lawson and *The Fortunes of Richard Mahony*. European conquest welled with tragic irony, nowhere more tragically (and sometimes ludicrously) than in stories of Victorian explorers on this and other continents. I fell for the great ones: Richard Burton, Mungo Park, Charles Doughty, Leichhardt, Sturt, Stuart, Ernest Giles. I wrote a book called *Caledonia Australis* that concerned a minor explorer but a major irony.

Apart from an extravagantly illustrated history for children, I didn't write another book for nearly twenty years. In the inner-Melbourne scene of the '80s, amid too much drinking, New Left thinking collided with Old Left Labor, feminism with the patriarchy, multiculturalism with the Anglo-Celtic inheritance, historical revisionism with historical convenience, and seriousness with football and satire. There was a near surfeit of comedy. While the Americans were taking themselves far too seriously, going to church and inventing things like the internet, we were divining the limits of irony. I stopped writing history to write for Max Gillies's satirical television and stage shows, and the many one-off corporate gigs he did in the guise of Bob Hawke. The prime minister offered limitless potential for send-ups, and not only because of his charismatic alpha-male persona. Here was his Labor government, deregulating the economy, stripping away protections, selling public assets, punishing fraternal state governments and lauding the wonders of the marketplace. Hawke hung out with corporate heavyweights and spivs. His treasurer cruised around in Zegna suits and had a taste for Gustav Mahler and ormolu clocks. Labor's apostasies needed a contortionist to front them, and Hawke was the man. He dredged every emotion, deployed every gesture and intonation, strained every facial fibre and just about every verbal convention to do it. You had to love him – and the nation did.

It was at the high point of the Hawke years that I took up writing speeches for the Victorian premier John Cain. Having spent most of the postwar years out of office, Labor in the 1980s and '90s was determined to graft a new story on the nation's mind. First for Cain and then for Paul Keating, I was one of the elves employed at that task. There was the story of economic reform that might have looked a bit like Thatcherism, but when allied to Labor's social policy would make all Australians both richer and more secure. There was the story of Labor as the party of the fair go, of social improvement, nation-building and national independence. And then, inferentially, there was the story of the government's opponents: somnolent and moth-eaten and living in the past or, as occasion demanded, mad-eyed, Ayn Randian zealots bent on abolishing all that was fair and decent in the country's traditions. To borrow a line of Manning Clark's that Paul Keating came to use, Labor people were the enlargers of life, the lovers; their opponents were the straiteners and punishers.

Around 1985, Tim Robertson and I began writing a play based on Clark's *A History of Australia*. Clark wrote history in the idealist tradition, from a perspective owing much to Dostoyevsky, D.H. Lawrence and the King James Bible. He was more interested in good and evil, grand unifying ideas and kinks in the human character, than politics, parties or mass movements of any kind. Though Clark would be the ringmaster, we set out to do something that owed more to E.P. Thompson's "history from below" or to the Annales school of French historians than to his magisterial perspective: something in the rough-and-tumble, democratic mould of Ariane Mnouchkine and Théâtre du Soleil's *1789*. The show would be staged in a vast, open space, such as the Melbourne or Sydney Showgrounds' pavilions, and combine theatre, circus, song, agitprop and all the radical energy of the Australian theatre renaissance. But, for reasons that in their elusiveness and invincibility mirror those of many historical catastrophes, the show ended up the very opposite of our intention: a musical, in Melbourne's Princess Theatre, during a heatwave, competing with *Cats*.

Bob Hawke came to opening night. He sat just in front of me and laughed merrily. It was a pretty merry show all in all: merriment and melancholy in equal measure and, for all the darkness and anguish rendered, we thought it good-hearted, funny and true to generally shared traditions. But the show bombed in devastating fashion, in part because of a bizarre five-page (and front-page) shellacking from Rupert Murdoch's newspapers. The blitz proclaimed the arrival of the culture wars.

In time the heart-sinking debacle of the show shrank to the size of a sore point, but the culture wars became a permanent and increasingly depressing feature of Australian public life. It seemed the country couldn't live without the organising principles of the Cold War. The philosopher R.G. Collingwood thanked God for reactionaries because they clarified the issues, but nothing was clarified by the right-wing culture warriors. Years after his death in 1991, the horde was still pursuing Manning Clark as if to purge him from the national memory. They pursued historians whose work assumed that the triumphs of European settlement were robust enough to survive the evidence of massacres and other instances of cruelty and devastation that spoke of a dark side in our history, as if to say that Australia's European history is, or must be made, unblemished. They went after scientists who warned about climate change, and even after science itself. They condemned the High Court when it determined that native title had survived the invasion of the continent; and they declared it a day of shame when, at considerable political cost to the Keating government, an accommodation was reached with miners, graziers and Indigenous people and the Court's decision was passed into law. They went after the ABC, and trade unions, and people seeking asylum, and environmentalists, and they did not hesitate to cultivate fear and loath-ing wherever it was useful to their cause, though the cause itself remained obscure. The more the conservative worldview mutated into a wondrous assemblage of loud and unlikely reactionaries, the more the years of the Cold War, which was at least a clash of genuine values, looked like spring-time for democracy.

Some rearrangement of the political landscape was to be expected during Australia's transition from a nation that constructed its self-understanding in racial and imperial terms to one that was judged by how successfully it found its own way in the world.

Liberalism lives on but is under fire everywhere and often with good cause. So long as every issue is made divisive – and social media and the Murdoch press assure this – liberals will be provoked and depressed unto exhaustion. They will be provoked over matters that are funda-mental to the survival of democracy and the planet, and they will be provoked over the legacy of Captain Cook. They will veer into the thickets of political correctness. They will state the case for personal and group identity and grievance even if their truculence impinges on the effort for the common good and fuels reactionary causes. They will give in to tribalism. Yet liberalism, even in all its barely assimilable vari-ants, is the indispensable creed. And, like the indispensable nation, it is forever fighting not only enemies without but many within, including its own inherent contradictions.

Soon after Hurricane Katrina, I went wandering in the United States. I had gone there on a book tour to promote *Death Sentence*, a short book that is often mistaken for a treatise on good grammar and plain English, but which, like the tracts that followed, was really in the nature of a pebble thrown at the unstoppable tide of managerialism and the stupefying language it has visited upon the world. In the next few years I went back to the United States several times, and if things had fallen differently I might still be wandering there. I cannot quite explain its attraction. Platitudes of the "humanity in all its best and worst dimen-sions" variety will not do. It's possible the effect might have owed more to the pleasures of wandering than to the places I wandered in – but I loved the US. There is something inherently epic about it: it is epic even in its mundaneness. Yet approachable. It offers itself, asks you to become part of it, to know it. It beckons. I never spent a day there without feeling I was following a thread, that I was in the middle of a story that I half knew; and, what was more, with every turn I took, I knew I was passing other stories by. The United States intrigued me not because the place was different to everything I knew, but because, like a dream or déjà vu, it was never more than one remove from something familiar.

It was also terrible. So much of the United States spoke of human achievement and much else of immanent regression. The experience confirmed me in my old social democratic convictions. In the brute greed, the gross inequality, the patriotic belligerence and obeisance, the crumbling infrastructure, the provincial ignorance and the elite's ignorance of the provinces, the paranoia, the religious manias, the ugliness, and in the incessant lunatic shouting of Fox News and the mad dogs of the radio, you could see what happens when venality governs the public debate and ideas of social improvement are traduced and abandoned. The full horror is only arriving now, but even in 2005 it was possible to see that liberal democracy, in all its varieties, had been harried out of sight.

In Australia it is not so much a case of what we've lost as what we've failed to gain. Many of the articles that follow are spun on this sentiment, though I confess a few do touch on the losses and some on what we're losing now. No intelligent being is immune to melancholy: without it hope would be just foolishness. The past looms as large as any future we can imagine or predict, dogging us, begging to be understood. Were we to interrogate it now, among things we've never dreamed of we might discover what Australians believed not very long ago: that the effort to create a tolerably fair and just society is, if not the guiding principle, then a defining element of Australian democracy and an essential counterweight to doctrines of unrestrained self-interest or corporate force. I admit this reading of our history bears hallmarks of my tribal affiliations, but conservatives – true conservatives – might also see merit in it. It's not a socialist utopia but Australia we're defending, and the reasons for hope.

Yet it would be a pity to fight all your life for democratic socialism but never see a golden whistler or hear low breathings in the bush. We don't have to be drawn into culture wars. Politics is not compulsory. To be sure, it is not easy to resist the adrenaline rush of moral indignation, to stop conceiving stratagems and designing or anticipating ambush.

But for sanity's sake, we sometimes need to cut the tethers to the tribe and *decommit*. Stop getting riled. Why waste your mind and all the potential of your senses on your enemies? A walk need not end up in a tract. Or even a poem. But it will at least open the way to seeing things that are beyond words.

BEGINNINGS

The Gippsland frontier

UNTIL VERY RECENTLY I HAD not realised that Gippsland was an idea as well as a place. I presume the idea of Gippsland dawned on me slowly because I grew up there and it presented itself to me as simply existing. It may well be that what I saw was what Gippsland was. On this reading Gippsland is primarily a kitchen with a view of a tank and cypresses. It is then a privet hedge, a lavatory, a fowl house, a pine tree, a cow shed, a watercourse, the weaner paddock and the back hill with the big gum tree and the eagle's nest.

But it always comes back to the kitchen and the porridge and the scone and the Anzac biscuit. The red dog always lay under the stove in a storm.

In *south* Gippsland there was a winter smell and a summer one. In winter it was the smell of very wet earth, damp jumpers and rancid milk on rubber boots in the porch. In the summer it was the smell of hot hay.

God it was hot carting hay. Young people these days don't know what hard work is. That's a fair sort of fact now and it was an unassailable fact then.

We always knew the past meant work. Work. Real work. Work you might possibly be able to imagine but never equal. You looked at the forearms of the older generation and there was no denying it. Like legs of mutton. Hands as big and hard as housebricks. Each finger as thick as a schoolteacher's wrist.

You knew the land on which you kicked the football had once been bluegum forest. There were still a few big museum pieces to remind you. A patch of hazels on a hillside and the blackwoods by the roadside were proof of the middle tier. Their cover gone, tree ferns in the gullies baked to a slow death.

The blue gums had been two hundred feet high at least. They had been felled with crosscut saws and burnt, or split with an axe and wedges into posts. One man or perhaps two did all this – teenage brothers did it. They did it all by hand. The harvest was done by hand, the cows milked by hand, the cream separated by hand.

But how to live in the face of pioneering virtue? How to redeem yourself through work when all the work's been done? I mean the mighty work. Your body might ache from exertion but they had worked harder by far. You can labour away with your axe all morning but it's pathetic in comparison. Look at the size of your chips. Bloody puny little things. You could eat your dinner off one of your father's. One chip of his keeps the stove going all night.

It's the same "cutting rubbish". You can't match the calm, relentless efficiency of his work. He labours in a state of grace. Blackberries, bracken, thistles (variegated, Scotch, shore, Californian and milk), burr, barley grass and snake, all fall beneath his fernhook. He pulls the ragwort without changing stride and bends to larvicide a burrow. He moves across the hillface as if he'd been doing it for a hundred generations. You'd swear he was solar-powered. And you hack away gracelessly with your face red – and the thought forms itself, "I will be an internationally renowned cricket player and trumpeter and I will return to Gippsland in middle age with my nose thumbed. How mean all this is! When I am eighteen, no sixteen, I will say goodbye, by cripes".

Snake! A bloody snake! Hack, thump. Eyes full of blood. Bits of red-bellied snake everywhere. Surely it's time to knock off. Of course there were more snakes in those days – their days I mean.

Snakes were a significant element in Gippsland bonding. Red-bellies, yellow-bellies, copperheads and tigers, we killed them with fernhooks, shovels and hoes. A piece of plain wire was very good, particularly on rough ground. There were Gippslanders who could grab them by the tail and crack them like whips. Returning from a Presbyterian Ladies' Guild meeting one Wednesday afternoon, Mrs McIntosh of Wild Dog Valley stood upon a five-foot copperhead at her front porch. She ran its head through with her hatpin, as I recall. In the Strzelecki Ranges, where the roads are narrow, windy and precipitous, the practice of skidding the back wheel on snakes caused more than one spectacular fatality. Boiling water was poured down their hideaways while extended families gathered at the ready with all manner of implements, including shotguns. We told jokes about snakes and played jokes with dead ones. Long into the nights we yarned about them. Deep in the Gippsland subconscious there lay coiled a snake. Had it been a Catholic province, I believe there would have been an annual festival.

But Gippsland did not have such things. A potato festival evolved at Koo Wee Rup, it is true, and in recent years the town of Korumburra has held a festival of the giant earthworm. It is not Rio, however. Gippsland is not quirky. They scotch all fancy and display there. They root out evil and prize the very normal.

The idea of Gippsland is the idea of normal. That is what pioneering is – the quest for normality, a set of unwritten rules by which a community lives. This is a radical enterprise, particularly when you realise what that normality encompasses. Here are some potted examples which make a mockery of the belief so often expressed in Gippsland, and doubtless elsewhere, that one day things will "get back to normal".

Gippsland was first explored by a pious Calvinist from the Catholic isle of Barra, and a Polish sub-mountebank who was knighted for philanthropy in the Irish famine and who died, a friend by then of Florence Nightingale and William Gladstone, in Savile Row.

Among Gippsland's early settlers was the hereditary clan chief Glengarry, whose garb and weaponry in the colonies had him on at least one occasion taken for a bushranger.

In its first decade of white settlement three languages were spoken in the Gippsland bush – English in its various forms, the several dialects of the Kurnai tribes (who had been there for at least fifteen thousand years) and Scots Gaelic. It was commonly alleged that a prominent Gaelic speaker, Ronald Macalister, was eaten by some Aborigines, and bloody massacres ensued.

The dispossession of the Aborigines and the manner of it was described by a melancholy English settler as one of the darkest chapters in the annals of history, a description which might have echoed Glencoe and Culloden in the minds of the Highlanders who were engaged in the rampage.

In the frontier period of Gippsland's history the Highlanders and others made free with their fantasies and found them turned into reality.

(The frontier might be described as a place where imagination and reality meet.) These Gippsland gentlemen dreamed of vast domains thickly populated with cattle, sheep and horses – all on a scale quite unimaginable to their fathers. They got them all. They fancied secure tenure and great houses and servants. They got them too.

They also fancied women, but in the first decade there were none to speak of except Aboriginal women. So they took them, but were not satisfied. Being gentlemen, they craved respectable white women, and from this craving came the White Woman of Gippsland – a woman held captive by the Kurnai, held in bondage, forced to bear the children of heathens. It was really too much for any decent man to contemplate. So the blacks were hunted down and killed, or kidnapped and held to ransom. At the end of it all, when the gentlemen of Gippsland had consolidated their assets and become MPs, JPs and paragons of respectability, the Crown Lands Commissioner who had seen it all declared in private that the White Woman of Gippsland was in all likelihood a concoction of the settlers' imaginations. At the moment when Gippslanders were pronouncing themselves responsible for a triumph of civilisation over barbarism (it was happening all over the Empire) they locked away the imagination which had made it possible. They also locked away their memories, of course – who would have believed them anyway? – and substituted a patina of Victorian heroics. This was very normal.

Those same frontiersmen founded a pioneering legend of virtue which was subsequently expanded and improved – but never revised – by a generation of selectors. These poorer folk had more humble ambitions but greater obstacles in the way of their achievement. They had to work even harder than the original pioneers. And they had to clean up their mess – the thistles, ragwort, burrs and rabbits. The selectors cut farms out of bluegum and mountain-ash forests in a labour that now looks superhuman. The children worked as hard as the adults. They did this not simply to make a living – that was something which could have been done much more easily in the cities. They did it to achieve what they imagined would be dignity and respectability. Some of them would have called it grace.

The pioneering legend made harsh demands. It said, quite unnecessarily under the circumstances, you must work with your body on the land and in the kitchen to an extent at least comparable to those who came before you. It also said you must be loyal in roughly equal proportions to the British Crown and the land your forefathers tamed. In fact it said Australia and the Crown were damn near indivisible. The whole place had been settled with Britain in mind, and only a cur would betray that heritage. So it was said you must fight in British wars wherever they occur – even in Palestine, Turkey and Egypt.

It was nothing short of normal to do so. For it all came down to the defence of the tank stand outside the kitchen, didn't it? There is a Norman Lindsay poster from World War I illustrating precisely this. It boiled down to the defence of one's right to lead a normal life. People in those days looked forward to things getting back to normal after the war. With that imperative in their minds they were not at all impressed by the wonder of what was going on. You need to step outside Gippsland to see the marvels inside. Laurie Duggan, an insider who has been out, has opened the great familiar Gippsland door a little wider. In these pages readers from Bunyip to Mallacoota will see familiar things but they will see in them something remarkable and quirky. Readers beyond Gippsland's borders will recognise it even more readily because they have a broader view. Neither quirkiness nor grace can be readily seen close up or in a plate of Anzacs. *The Ash Range*, however, helps us see. For a start it tells us that an extraordinary thing has happened in this part of the world – history.

Introduction, Laurie Duggan, *The Ash Range*, 1987

Occasional address

THIS GREAT AND UNEXPECTED HONOUR is the more gratifying for coming from the university of which I was a foundation student several hundred years ago.

I've not had a lot of luck with these sorts of things. When I graduated from La Trobe, hordes of student Maoists were gathered in the undergrowth outside the windows of the hall, pressing their noses against the glass and shouting things like "Marxism! Leninism! Mao Tse-tung thought!" and "Archibald Glenn war criminal!" Sir Archibald Glenn was the chancellor of the university, and we were in the dining room of the college named after him.

Some of those Maoists had been friends of mine. Just a couple of years earlier they had been law-abiding students at a liberal university all but purpose-built for them, the sons and daughters of conscientious rural and working-class Victorians. We had all demonstrated against the Vietnam War.

But now they were fanatics, devoted to a man and an ideology that a decade earlier had cost the lives of forty million people and to a revolution bent on destroying not just every trace of Western civilisation in China, but Chinese civilisation as well. It rather spoiled the afternoon, especially for the parents, some of whom had travelled from the Mallee to see their offspring graduate.

A few years later, on the day I was awarded my doctorate, Monash University bestowed an LLD on the wonderful poet Judith Wright. To meet

---

A version of a graduation speech given to students at La Trobe University in 2018.

her was one of the great privileges of my life, and I imagined her occasional address would soar and delve like her poetry. But instead of telling us about the human heart or the flight of birds, she talked about photocopiers. She spoke of the injustice done to authors who received nothing when their works were copied on these newfangled machines. We could tell she had a point, but a graduation ceremony did not feel like the right time to make it.

I will try to do better.

Some of you will have read Roald Dahl's *Fantastic Mr Fox* – or perhaps you saw Wes Anderson's film version. If you have, you will remember the moment – pivotal in a million melodramas – when the hero is cornered and must find some means of escape. Mr Fox is cornered by his wife. He's been stealing chickens again, and as a consequence of this indulgence, this folly, his family is now facing annihilation.

You promised to give it up, she says.

I know, he says. And he knows it means curtains for the marriage and, what's worse, for the love and respect of the vixen he adores.

Why, she asks? Why?

He comes up with a doozy.

Because I'm a wild animal, he says.

It's pathetic, really. After all, she's a wild animal too. She sighs in despair at the outrageous gall of it, and even though she knows that what he's really done is forgive himself, she forgives him too.

I might come back to this.

I have a friend who says I am too interested in politics. He says I waste my time on it. He's quite a distinguished friend. A writer. He's had an audience with the Queen, so I have to take him seriously. I was once within touching distance of the Queen – but I knew better.

My friend says he's more interested in literature and philosophy and art than politics.

I say to him, I'm interested in literature and philosophy and art too – and in science and horse racing for that matter, but so what? There's room for all those interests in a life well-lived.

But, he says, you would have more time for the really important things if you spent less time thinking about politics and sounding off about them to anyone who'll listen. Get off your soapbox.

I ignore the slur. I say, The reason you pretend to be uninterested in politics is that democracy does not suit your worldview. Lobbed in your unconscious is a childish yearning for a feudal arrangement in which you – by virtue of your interest in literature, art and philosophy – are a lord, if not a prince.

He accuses me of an ad hominem attack, typical of politics.

I say he's wrong – my point goes to motive as much as character.

You see how we've run headlong into quicksand. I know I'm right, but I also know I'll never persuade him to see the truth about himself. That to do so would oblige him to see either that he lacks self-knowledge or that he's a humbug. I value his friendship too much to go that far.

I know he values our friendship as much as I do. That's why he says, Let's talk about cricket.

He knows nothing about cricket, but I'm not going to tell him that either.

The thing is, I do hate politics, I tell him. I hate the grip it has on my mind and on my moods.

If I were honest, I would also have to concede this to him: if I had ignored politics these last fifty years I would not now be in danger of dying without having read hundreds of books I want to read; without having arrived at a coherent position on the meaning of existence; without having understood black holes, or how a bird flies or a spider spins its web. A million other things I will never know. I might have learned to play a guitar and to speak Russian if I had given up politics for just a couple of those fifty years. It is because of politics that I will die as ignorant as a sheep or an insect about the reasons why I lived. Remember this – these are the things you will regret at the end. Not the things you did, but the time you wasted.

And all for what, my friend says. Has anything you have ever thought or done in politics changed the world at all?

Not a skerrick, I have to say.

It's true. Even when I was close to political power and could join in the euphoria of public policy-making and public life, all we did was overturned or compromised, and all the fine justifications we gave for doing what we did were traduced or mocked to oblivion.

My friend has me cornered. Yet I have also cornered myself. Like Fantastic Mr Fox, I am desperate.

I say, I cannot give up politics because I'm a political animal.

We all are.

If the first instinct of all living things is to survive, the second one is to organise. And that concerns power: who will wield it and how, and in whose interests? On this depends my survival. And my family's survival. Not only my survival, but my dignity, the circumstances in which I live, my life chances. Decency depends on the political choices we make.

One way or another, everything depends on politics. Why would I not be interested? How could I not be interested?

My friend says: If, as you say, politics is part of our natures, that only means it is something to overcome. It is in our natures to eat one another. The bones of our prehistoric forebears have human toothmarks in them.

The raison d'être of civilisation, I can hear him saying, the actual reason for it, is to defend us against nature. Freud said it, and in *nature* he surely included *our* natures.

He thinks he's won. I'm to believe that it's a mark of the civilised individual to be above politics.

But he hasn't won. I'll tell you why.

About ten years ago my friend had a heart attack, and not only was his life saved, but it didn't cost him a penny. Why? Because forty years ago a political party – faction-ridden, hidebound and full of flaws – came up with Medicare, and defended it against all attacks for a decade until at last the enemy gave up. It was down to politics.

So is the scheme by which authors are now paid each year for works that have been photocopied. Judith Wright had something to do with this. She also had a great deal to do with saving the Great Barrier Reef from the Queensland government's plans to issue leases for oil exploration.

And so is this place a product of political imagination and effort – it was a conservative government that allowed liberal, enlightened minds to conceive it and bring it into being.

So please – don't recoil from politics. Read everything you can – twice or three times if it's good; be curious; turn off your screens for two hours every day and learn to play the guitar, or to sing, or to study the habits of birds or mushrooms. Become accountants, lawyers or consultants, or whatever is congenial to you and earns a living. But stay interested, and when you think you're wise enough, tough enough and you believe enough, consider getting involved. Your survival – the world's survival – depends on it.

Congratulations and good luck.

Occasional address, La Trobe University,
16 May 2018

Journey to the Outer Hebrides

ONE NIGHT IN THE WINTER of 1980 I took a ferry to the windswept, Gaelic-speaking isle of Barra in the Outer Hebrides. I was looking for traces of Angus McMillan, a venerated Australian pioneer. Born and raised on Skye, McMillan had moved to Barra with his family as a young man and left the famished isle for Australia in 1837.

The other guest in the hotel wore an eyepatch. He let me finish my soup, then said in a velvety burr: "You'll be Donald Watson". He didn't say how he knew; just that he'd heard I was coming. "You'll be catching the boat to Vatersay after the priest returns in the morning", he said.

Through my room's window next day, I saw the priest on the boat as it passed Kisimul Castle in the bay. I was on the jetty when he came back.

On Vatersay, where not a hundred people lived, in a stone cottage smelling violently of urine, a ragged old man gave me a cup of tea while his wife, a renowned shenachie, searched her memory's vaults and said the McMillans likely lived near the little mill. Yes, that was where I should go, the mill.

One stone wall was all that remained of it. Wind whipped the machair and, lone wall aside, you could easily believe there had been no one there since the Vikings.

My new friend said, "In the morning you'll be taking the launch to South Uist. You'll stay with my father". His father was the doctor.

The man steering the boat across the dark swell called out, "Over the next wave!" and picked up a shotgun from the floor. We went up the wave, and coming down the other side an eider duck was bobbing. Our pilot held the tiller steady with his knee and shot the bird. At once his dog jumped overboard and fetched it.

The doctor was a gentle man with snowy hair, a collector of local songs and stories. That evening we drank some whisky with a friend of his, another historian of the Hebrides. But neither of them knew anything about my Angus.

"You'll be getting a lift to Benbecula in the morning", the doctor said, and of course it came to pass. Wearing new green gumboots bought in London, I walked across the causeway in rain so heavy it was hard to find air to breathe.

In Lochmaddy, I waited three days for the storm to ease and the Skye ferry to come in. A performing bear had escaped and the hotel patrons begged the publican not to send them out into the dark at closing time.

The ferry came at last and strolling on the deck I came upon the doctor. He seemed to be expecting me. "You'll come to stay in my cottage", he said. "And you'll borrow my car and see the glen where your man was raised". And that afternoon I stood in the empty, silent glen.

There was no sign of McMillan, of course. But the thought came to me that the melancholy of these depopulated scenes might be a clue to his character and the story I needed to tell. And I wondered if my hosts had played the Muse to help me find it.

Qantas Magazine, 2019

A "paradigm shift"

THIS BOOK WAS NOT WRITTEN by a linguist on behalf of the language, or by a grammarian on behalf of grammar. I am not qualified for either of those enterprises. The book is written from my experience as a writer and a reader, and if it is written on behalf of anyone, it is the people who have to write and read and listen to our public language every day of their lives. It is an argument on behalf of what these days are called the stakeholders. For four years, I was the Australian prime minister's speechwriter, and for four years before that I combined writing speeches for a state premier with writing political satire for a comedian. I wrote on history and politics in the newspapers. Now and then, I wrote speeches for corporate chief executives. I wrote – or rewrote – company brochures and in-house training manuals. I gave occasional seminars on writing for government departments, corporate communications teams and conferences of schoolteachers. In all these places I came across language that was all but dead and people who seemed willing to join in its destruction. Over fifteen years, I saw the plague accelerate and spread from the private to the public realms, from the global to the local, to churches and to schools, where, at eleven years of age, my granddaughter was required to prepare her very own personal mission statement, and at age twelve wrote her first English essay in PowerPoint. My grievance, I confess, is personal.

The earliest symptoms of what became a permanent gripe showed up in the last half of the 1980s when I was working for the premier.

First published as the preface to *Death Sentences: How Clichés, Weasel Words, and Management Speak are Strangling Public Language*.

It was then I found I could not understand the information sent me by government officials for turning into speeches. I wondered if the job required a better mind than mine to grasp the concepts underlying politics and public policy. But it was the language of those public servants' briefs: it worked on me like too much Valium. One paragraph and my mind swam, consciousness drifted. Whatever thoughts the words contained, I could not reach them: I could not understand because I could not make myself interested.

Around the same time, while moonlighting with a multinational chemical company, I came across Total Quality Management (TQM). I was curious about TQM and I believed the people who told me about the wonders it worked in companies. But when asked to write it in attractive or plain English I did not know how. I could not distinguish the thoughts from the phrases in which they came. As one cannot separate cement from cement, one cannot say "a structured system for satisfying internal and external customers and suppliers by integrating the business environment, continuous improvement, and breakthroughs with development, improvement, and maintenance cycles while changing organisational culture" without saying "structured system", "satisfying internal and external customers", "integrating the business environment", "continuous improvement", and so on. In this language the only thing left to a writer is to shuffle the phrases and experiment with verbs. So you will see, for instance, that in its mission statement the guided missile manufacturer BAE Systems prefers *delighting* its customers to *satisfying* them.

In time, I learned that this was the beauty of management jargon, the unbreakable code. Anyone could write it and, with a little practice, speak it, and just to write or speak the stuff was to prove you were professional: so professional that every underling who could not crack the code must imitate you. The miracle was that once you knew a dozen or so "key" or "core" terms, once you were "focused" on them, thought was scarcely necessary. In fact, writing like this was best done, and perhaps could *only* be done, without thinking at all.

I took the job with the prime minister, and in his office became aware that the now customer-focused and service-driven federal bureaucracy had added TQM and other management jargon to its own traditionally plentiful store. It was in these years that my grievance became a small obsession. I came to loathe "enhanced", "vibrant" and "commitment", to name just three. It was like getting fleas off a dog, but in the end "enhanced", "vibrant" and "commitment" were all but abolished.

Resistance was in vain, of course. The Information Revolution came in on top of the Management Revolution. The Technological Revolution tumbled in with both of them. Economies were global. Markets were free, at least ideologically speaking. The unstoppable tide washed into all the corners of our lives. The local library got a mission statement; the church called its mission to the poor "excellence in hospitality"; the kindergarten became outcomes-based; and, entering into the spirit of marketing and focus groups, politics turned "values-based" and worked primarily in messages. Much that we used to call society became the economy, and, being an *information* economy, language was drafted to its service. Everywhere – public and private, all levels of government and all government agencies, the military, schools, health, politics, media – the language was coopted, hacked about, gutted. Worlds of meaning – the cultural equivalent of many lakes, rainforests and species – disappeared. And hardly a voice was heard protesting.

When this book was published in Australia, no one, including its author, expected it to sell many more than the first print run of five thousand copies. That was almost two years ago, when it was well known that books about language sold only to specialists and pedants. Now we know otherwise. The fashion may not last as long as books about celebrities or terrorism, but just now it is possible for books about language to become number-one bestsellers. Tens of thousands of people buy them; and it seems that for each ten thousand, two hundred or so are inspired to write letters to the author, and of those a dozen or so invite him to speak at a conference or give a lecture of some kind. Books about language now oblige their authors to hire assistants and start websites. They get them thinking about writing sequels. There can only be one reason for this gratifying clamour: far more people than we thought cherish the language, and the evidence of its decay dismays them.

A year and a half after the book was published in Australia, the letters still arrive. They come from people obliged to use management language in their jobs with big corporations, small companies and all kinds of government departments, including departments of education; from teachers who are compelled to instruct children in language none of them understands; from people who, by some Orwellian fiat, have become "customers" and "stakeholders" – even "valued" customers and "valued" stakeholders – and cannot stand it anymore. They come from people who hear something sinister in the anesthetising jargon of management and politics, and from people who read it as a symptom of decline in culture, morality and democracy.

Some of the letters are anecdotal, and some recommend to me the writings of Karl Kraus, who believed the abuse of language was a moral crime, or of Martin Heidegger, who believed that "our being is founded in language". Heidegger's point is that our being cannot be founded in modern technical or "calculative" language, or the kind that aims at "uniform accessibility of everything to everyone". This is a fair description of contemporary public language, and, when he insists that such language undermines aesthetics, morality and being, Heidegger might be trying to make the same point in theory that many of my correspondents make with their stories from experience. I mean people such as those who say they worked for years in jobs concerned with "communications" without ever quite understanding what they were doing. The teachers who can no longer write students' reports, but instead must tick the box next to the "calculative", "outcomes-based" description that they guess comes closest to their own assessment of each child's progress – or rather the child's "essential learnings and key competencies". ("Outcomes", by the way, "describe what students learn about and what they do, as a result of the teaching and learning in the course".) Or the man who said that on the day he had to leave his old father in a nursing home, the most difficult thing to bear was not the parting or the three-hour wait in the foyer, but the mission statement on the wall: the sign proclaiming, WE WILL EXCEED ALL YOUR EXPECTATIONS. It drove him mad then, and it still drives him mad.

Some of these reports from the front line are sad, despairing letters; others are ironic and derisive. There are letters from schoolchildren and from people who have been "downsized" or "rightsized" or "structurally adjusted". A few write thinking they have recognised a fellow curmudgeon. I expected more of these, and more from folk wanting to correct my grammar. What I did not expect was so much gratitude. Never did a writer feel more appreciated. They tell me that they now feel less alone, that they had for so long thought they were the only ones, in the government department, on the bank's communications team, at the human resources conference, in the school staffroom, or on the board of the library who could not understand what their colleagues were saying – and whatever they did make of it sounded like baloney.

Today someone writes to say that while proofreading the annual report of a large welfare agency he came upon this sentence: "The ensuing months saw the creative development of a comprehensive suite of collateral including envelopes, business cards, letterheads, and design templates". It is not the punctuation or the grammar that concerns him, but rather the stationery described as a "comprehensive suite of collateral", the "ensuing months" (they "ensued" from a "branding conference"), the "creative" element. It's the pomposity of the thing, the loss of proportion, the folly of it. My correspondent wrote in the margin of the document, "What does this mean?" A manager sent it back with a note attached: "It's corporate language". He was not offering an apology or an excuse, but a justification, as if "corporate language" were a requirement of incorporation, or as if it fulfilled a duty as doctors once thought it did to write prescriptions in Latin.

Lawyers might make a more instructive comparison. Law used to be the foundation of public language, but now management is. Legal language can be arcane, obscure and pompous, but management language is much worse. There is a provenance to law that management lacks, and it is capable of elegance and force. The lawyer Abraham Lincoln will do for evidence of this. Legal language at least has its roots in the same ground as the language the rest of us speak. But management language is newfangled in root and branch and rarely sounds like anything but hokum.

It is thus well suited to politics and the media and to what Eric Alterman last year called in *The Nation* the "post-truth political environment". Management-speak is a great gap-filler. It is hollow, pompous and modern in just the right proportions. Its leaden phrases makes the vapid sound concrete, and obscures the thoughts that inspired them from listener and speaker, reader and writer alike. There is no better instrument than management jargon to soften us up for the "post-truth political environment".

If we get used to business calling every little change a new paradigm or a paradigm shift, we might not be as frightened as we should be when presidents announce that the world's greatest democracy is now governed by a new paradigm. When "enhanced" has been exhausted of all meaning by a decade of overuse, we might be less inclined to wonder what is meant by "enhanced interrogation techniques". When we are accustomed to corporations of all kinds telling us they are dedicated equally to delighting their clients and being "values-based", who will smell hypocrisy or danger when politicians tell us that they are too? If we believe the words of mission statements, or don't believe them but see the point, what won't we believe or see the point in? When the everyday words of the workplace are hollow and stripped of meaning, it is certain that they will become the words used in politics. That is the deepest concern. Of course one is for the language: for plainness and elegance and genius, especially the genius of the vernacular. But one is equally for the democracy and the quality of mind that language serves and expresses, and upon which democracies depend.

Preface, *Death Sentences* (US edition), 2005

Oscar and the ALP

OSCAR WILDE NEVER HAD MUCH clout in Australian politics. Paul Keating had a soft spot for him, but many of his old colleagues would think this typically contrary of their former leader, and consistent with his wilful lack of interest in team games and the American Civil War. It is true that Wilde was a bit of a dandy and as unsuited to the Australian political climate as he was to Reading Gaol. Yet so long as he is not taken literally (seriously, yes, but *never* literally), there are rousing thoughts in Wilde for people who imagine more humane and honourable societies.

Labor will resist, of course. Australian Labor was born pragmatic and "sans doctrines". No theorists, including Marx, ever got a grip on it. Likewise revolutionaries and martyrs, foreign or domestic: Labor never fell for them. If the term "socialist" ever described the party, it always meant different things to different parts of it. "Democratic socialist" or "social democratic" have been picked up from time to time, but soon put down again; probably because they smell of Europe, doctrine and theorising. They are all there, or have been at different times; but all of them combined have had probably less influence than the orthodoxies of Jesus Christ and J.M. Keynes.

Labor's deepest instincts are gradualist and its affections patriotic. The party has housed radicals and mavericks and had periodic hot romantic flushes, but it was born at the same time and under the same utilitarian star as the country itself.

So what sort of party is it? It's a *Labor* party, the political or parliamentary wing of the labour *movement*. And it's an *Australian* Labor Party, which means it's a federal creature and as sentimental about the nation as it is about the workers. It's the ALP: a broad church or extended family in which ideals of improvement, fellowship and philanthropy live in perpetual struggle with personal ambition and factions and hatreds of almost Balkan depth and mystery.

The national dimension of ALP ideology is something its critics too often forget. From the beginning, the party joined social improvement with nation-building and national security, and it remains an unshakeable fact of its existence. The balance is essential to political success, and so is the inspiration that each side provides. By the time Bob Hawke's race was run, critical sections of the electorate had come to despise, perhaps even more than economic rationalism and its arcane, pitiless language, the sanctimony with which the politically correct commended Labor's social policies, as if all moral virtue and political possibility existed in "access and equity" or "rich multicultural diversity".

As prime minister, Paul Keating's "nation-building" economics, independent foreign policy and republican push helped to loosen at least their rhetorical grip and restore the balance of the party. He did the national thing and the "helping hand" thing in pretty well equal measure. And for two or three years it succeeded.

There was something of the same divide in Labor's recent hideous leadership contest. Beneath Beazley's "I can beat John Howard" mantra was the national security ticket, while Simon Crean recited social policy as if he'd been expressly told to go out there and drive us mad – what Australians are really interested in is health, education and saving the Murray. As usual both of them were telling us what the people wanted. As usual they did not tell us in any persuasive or even vaguely interesting way what they believed.

All who aspire to the leadership these days have at least one belief, and they have it in common. They believe in the polling. They draw different inferences, but they believe in it as passionately as they believe in anything in the world. They believe in staying on the message that the polls determine. And all seem to have decided in the present affluence that, be it ever so myopic, misinformed, prejudiced or disagreeable sometimes, what the people take to be self-interest must in no way be offended.

Imagining half-mistakenly that socialism might bring about similar material conditions, Wilde asked what would happen to the human soul when folk were secure and pain and necessity no longer governed human life.

It was a good question for socialists then and, since free markets delivered about three-fifths of the deal that socialism failed to, it remains a good question for Labor now. On the face of it, Wilde's answer was much more like a neoliberal's than an old socialist's: he saw the prospect of universal personal security as an opportunity for unprecedented individual expression and fulfilment.

But before our local Tories rush to get him on their think tank, Wilde was a neo-Hellenist, which is a very different thing to a neoconservative or a neoliberal. Wilde was for art. For pleasure. He loathed virtually everything that neocons love or depend on, including the state (and let no one tell you that neocons don't love state power), the media, public opinion, sentimentality and the "sickly cant about duty". For old Oscar it was not a question of what human beings can have, but of what they can be. It wasn't about security, but boundless possibility.

Forget for now that the present affluence might not be as extensive or as permanent as it looks, or that personal security is not for everyone another word for happiness. Wilde warned about the tyranny of the people, which he said was as brutal as the tyranny of Popes and Princes. The tyranny, of course, is exercised over themselves; or, rather, over their potential as individuals. "They have marred themselves by imitation of their superiors", he said. He imagined the state and the press as the agents of this tyranny. He knew from brutal personal experience that, combined with public opinion, they could destroy anyone who broke the rules. He did *not* know about opinion polls and focus groups.

He was an innocent in politics, but certain depressing themes in the history of the twentieth century suggest that Wilde's analysis was pretty right. It is a pity that more old socialists didn't listen. And modern Labor could do worse than listen now.

It must be gratifying to echo the people's voice as your focus groups define it. The tactic might encourage you to think that in this way you make yourself a servant of the people's will; a blessed state because it feels both honourable and savvy. But in so far as this "will" is defined by polls, and polls are much influenced by interpretations of events that are substantially those of the government and the media, and not influenced by any creed of your own because you have substituted polls for original thought, just whose "will" are you obeying? A loose reading of the Wildean argument would tell us that, far from acting in the people's interest or their own, Labor's poll-driven politics connives in the oppression of both.

If Labor fancies that through obedience to polls it is less the servant and more the *incarnation* of this confected general will, much the same applies: it has only joined the people in "imitating their superiors", which is to say those who wield power over the people, including the government and its most influential thinkers and supporters. With this strategy, Labor imitates those whose great effort in life is to oppose them in every way they can.

We citizens are obliged to ask much the same question about "the people" that Wilde asked. He asked, "Who told them to exercise authority?" We might add, "Who are they, that they should have authority over the rest of us?" Their authority might not be "blind, deaf, hideous, grotesque, tragic, amusing, serious and obscene", as Wilde said it was: but "narrow, short-sighted, uninformed and actually hostile to the public and national interest" are all possible. It might be prejudiced or mad. For all we know these people might be the type who would put Oscar Wilde in jail, or children behind razor wire at Woomera.

They "called up the street ... and the street has dispatched" them, Max Weber said about the German revolutionaries Karl Liebknecht and Rosa Luxemburg after they were murdered. We might wonder if there are not postmodern equivalents. Of course you can't ignore the polls, but if you make yourself their dummy you will look at best characterless and silly, at worst downright craven. In your earnest demonstrations of respect for the people and their wishes, they see a lack of self-respect. You bring yourself into contempt. You will be dispatched.

Here is Wilde again. "But the past is of no importance. The present is of no importance. It is with the future that we have to deal. For the past is what man should not have been. The present is what man ought not to be." The future, he says, is "what artists are", a notion that will not recommend itself to any political party. But Labor must try not to be pedantic. It really must. Wilde means that an affluent future contains an opportunity for happiness. To "think anew", Lincoln used to say. It is the possibilities we need to dwell on, even the possibility of changing human nature. Wilde says that the only thing we really know about human nature is that it changes.

Labor needs to think this way. Perhaps a "change" in human nature *is* stretching things, but it has to play to the better side of it. Kim Beazley was perfectly Wildean last election night when he talked about the better angels of our nature. So why, every other day in the election cycle, bury it like a bone on the dark side? One day you won't be able to find it.

More than a plan or a strategy or a tactic, Labor needs a philosophy. Nothing comprehensive: just a few sentences that reveal what it thinks about the way things are. Calwell did it in 1965 when he declared against the war in Vietnam. He lost the election but that decision helped set Labor up for years. Whitlam did it when he talked about national possibilities in 1972. Hawke did it when he talked about summits and accords in the interests of national reconciliation. "Language most shows a man", Ben Jonson said: "Speak, that I may see thee". Labor needs to speak.

The difference between Labor and its opponents has always consisted in this. The successful conservatives like Menzies – and now Howard – spoke to a philosophy. So did Deakin in his prime. Curtin, Chifley, Whitlam, Hawke and Keating spoke in the same way for Labor, though with each the terms were different. The two who won elections from Opposition, Whitlam and Hawke, both embodied a set of ideas about the future of Australia. They had words for thought and belief. And through those words they revealed a bit of what someone noticed in Abraham Lincoln some years before the Civil War: "a vein of sentiment", he called it, and he thought it might take Lincoln a long way in public life. Joined to astute reading of public opinion, it did.

For seven years Labor has read public opinion and lost the vein of sentiment. It has not had the words. Few outside the party and not so many in it could tell you what it is they think. They seem to think only what they think the people think. In all this recycled focus-group opinion, people who have had a passion for Labor all their life no longer see in it any of their own sentiments and beliefs. It is not just the more notorious compromises, or the disaster of Knowledge Nation, or the gruesome leadership struggle. What hurts more is that while Labor has been picking its way through the polls, Australia has become a different place.

This is the radical consequence of poll-driven politics. You lack definition. You say: I have a plan. I have a policy. I have what Australians want. You don't say what you hold to, but instead offer your take on what your audience holds to. You don't define your intellectual position, even though it means next time you tell them what you intend to do they'll know *why*. They need that much to believe you.

Oscar Wilde can no more give them the words for that than he can give them the policies; but Wilde sounds a lot more modern than Labor has sounded for years. He talks about individualism *and* unselfishness; a love of tolerance and a loathing of cant and sentimentality; sympathy with suffering and an even greater sympathy with happiness; delight in the social, and hatred of arbitrary authority. He talks about defining yourself by your future.

This last is a very good idea for Australia. It ought to be Labor's idea, and until quite recently it was. But they are *all* good starting points, especially if taken together with the recommendation that any plans should ignore existing conditions – because "it is exactly the existing conditions that one objects to".

A weekend retreat in this frame of mind might have a marvellous cleansing effect. It might oblige federal Labor to see that in pursuit of the existing mean average Australian reality – the battling, aspirational, non-chattering, family Australian – it has become a rarefied almost-unrecognisable extension of it, as a garden gnome is to a suburban garden. A highly professional gnome, no doubt, but just as inarticulate and inspiring only to a few. And this is not the worst of it: the worst of it is that Labor only *looks* like the gnome and is judged to be the gnome, while the real gnomes look like the government.

I went to a lot of ALP functions last year, in every state. At one of them in northern New South Wales, a man who was not a member of any chattering class asked rhetorically: isn't it true that if Kim Beazley had confronted Howard more forcefully over the refugees he would still have lost but he would also still be leader and people would be joining the party not leaving it? The room applauded. I don't know if the man's inferences were right, but every time I repeated his question at other ALP gatherings, it was greeted in the same way. Without exception.

Perhaps they were *all Wildeans*. They didn't look like it. And they didn't look like they were about to abandon the country to its enemies. They seemed like typically Labor people: more typical and just as patriotic as many of the people who compose its public face. No doubt they hadn't been shown the polling. But had they been, I suspect they would have said: What would you have us follow – what we believe or what these other people believe? If those meetings were anything to go by, the irony was positively thunderous: in trying to connect with some abstract representation of the people's will, Labor had stopped connecting with itself. What could be less utilitarian? You want to plug in, but you're not a plug anymore. You're just a wish.

It won't help to argue about the decision to give way to vicious, and viciously manipulated, public opinion in the last election campaign. In letting go of their initial "principled" stand, Labor only continued the strategy of "finessing" their way back to power. It would be nonetheless unwise to fool themselves that no choice existed, or that they were the first to suffer such savage opprobrium. Evatt got at least as bad for opposing the bill to ban the Communist Party, and Calwell was treated no better over Vietnam. They paid a political price: but Hawke was paid a dividend for refusing to compromise on Asian immigration; Keating won an election with the republic, reconciliation and an explicitly social democratic program on full show; and Jeff Kennett was not punished for telling Pauline Hanson that she was not welcome in Victoria.

Virtue is optional and not its own reward, but it does help with definition. Labor might start defining itself by declaring itself once and *forever* unequivocally opposed to the present policy on refugees from dictatorships. It might call itself what essentially it must be to win by means other than default, a social democratic party. It could declare that *it* will relentlessly oppose the drift to vassalage, with or without a deputy's badge. It can do any, all or none of these things, but it must say what it thinks about the country. This is what a national party does.

If an Irish genius shines no light for them, perhaps a French one will. Alexis de Tocqueville visited the United States in one of those times when "societies come to rest and the human race seems to draw breath". It was a good time for small parties, not great parties.

And what was a great party? "What I term great political parties", he wrote, "are those committed to principles rather than their consequences, to general considerations rather than to individual cases, to ideas and not to men. These parties generally have more noble characteristics, more generous enthusiasms, more genuine convictions, a more open and bold approach than the others".

That is not all Tocqueville says about great parties, but it is all Labor needs to remember. Labor cannot be a small party. If it is not a great party, it is not a party at all.

The Bulletin, 2003

LEADERS AND
LEADERSHIP

Gough Whitlam

ONE DAY IN THE COURSE of the post-dismissal election campaign, Gough Whitlam addressed the fuming multitudes in the Melbourne CBD. I walked into the city with Ian Turner, the ex-AIF, ex-communist radical nationalist, labour historian, popular culture commentator, hairy, charismatic academic guru and snuff-taking bon viveur who was then supervising my thesis. Turner was an influential player in the centre unity faction of the state ALP. He had helped hold the Victorian branch of the ALP together after Whitlam's federal intervention. He had lived a lot of the history of the postwar left and was a walking, talking expression of its newfangled multifarious future.

Much as I admired Ian Turner, I seem to recall that in my case the rage Whitlam had asked us to maintain was cooled by the need of any young left-wing radical to be not too impressed by the ex–prime minister's reformist policies, or too shocked by his sacking. He had over-stepped the rules of the Establishment and affronted the Americans. Did people expect polite applause?

I don't recall a single thing that Whitlam said that day, just the boom-ing patrician voice and the boiling devotion of the crowd. And coming away galvanised. Gough Whitlam was the first and only politician of his time to make our hearts quicken. He gave some of us our first inkling that the Australian Labor Party could be a nation-changing party – whatever that notion might consist of – and a vehicle for a generation's patriotic hopes. The conversion was not instantaneous, but after that day in the centre of Melbourne I was never the same again.

Insofar as they made him confrontational and defiant, Whitlam's vanities were as valuable a part of his legacy as his legislative program, or anything he did in foreign policy. There had always been principle and courage and dogma in the Labor Party, but Whitlam lent it a new character. And instead of casting back to the party's history, Whitlam got it making history in the here and now. If hubris brought him down, it was also what got the ALP motoring again. His successors came determined not to repeat the mistakes of the Whitlam government: to proceed more cautiously, to take the people with them, to foster reconciliation and negotiation, to be better at economics than their opponents. But they brought, as well, a fortifying moral purpose that only such a thing as the dismissal could give them. Unalike though they were in both substance and style, the Hawke and Keating governments grew green on the bones of 1975.

Though I had talked to him on the phone three or four times, I did not meet Gough Whitlam until one evening in 2001 when he turned up to an evening talk I was giving at the University of Western Sydney. With half a dozen others we went out to a local Greek restaurant and stayed talking till midnight. He was funny, curious and entirely free of rancour and recrimination or any sign of megalomania; the nearest thing you could ever see to a political leader's state of grace.

From *Not Just for This Life: Gough Whitlam Remembered*,
edited by Wendy Guest and Gary Gray, 2016

From Hawke to eternity

THE PRIME MINISTER IS TALKING about a fifth term. Let's be frank about it. Let's say that which modesty forbids him to say. He's seeking immortality.

The first hint of this came last year when one of his biographers, Blanche d'Alpuget, observed that his chest had caved in. Nothing less. The prime minister was concave from the waist up. He was burnt out. It seemed to d'Alpuget that the old cockerel of yesteryear was headed for the Colonel's kitchen. Taxidermist, she might have said.

It was not the first or the last time that Bob Hawke has been portrayed as crowing on the rim of history's dustbin. Three months ago there were reports that he had given up: the demise of his government was assured and he had accepted that. Both before then and since, it has been said that the man was a mere cipher. Keating's doormat. Six months ago serious people were saying he was mad.

It turns out neither stuffing nor embalming are on the agenda at present. Bob Hawke is nothing if not an active man. And nothing if not Australian. We're not talking of his speech, his unquestionable patriotism, his love of sport and mates, or the way he puts one in mind of certain burrowing marsupials. None of the clichés.

We're talking about something weird. Weird in the way Australian acacias and eucalypts are weird. They need a bushfire to regenerate. They need to be burnt out. He is a kind of wattle pod. Sure, he vanishes: so do the wattles. So do those little fish in the Australian desert. But they come back when it rains.

Hawke is a piece of Australian natural history – the centre of his popularity is a strangely familiar atavism. Why should we be surprised, then, if he thinks immortality is a possibility? It is his nature to be mythic.

For most of us, the pilots' strike has been a pain in the bum. For the prime minister it's an opportunity to be Bert Hinkler. He told us he had been trained as a pilot. He talked about time "at the stick" as if he had been in a cockpit all his life. Hansard does not confirm the report that at one point, when the Speaker asked him if he would like to table the document, he replied, "Roger. Over and out". But if he had shown us his tin legs we would not have been surprised.

We're looking at a legend in the making. You can see it in the emblematic gestures. He seems to hold the smile for longer. It's not just his instinct for a photo opportunity. He's looking for the timeless moment. When he raises one eyebrow these days, he looks very much like an omniscient goanna. When he raises both eyebrows, turns his head on one side and scratches the back of his neck, you'd swear he was a wallaby. He is becoming a figure in a landscape.

He is no longer looking for a spot in the history books. That much is well and truly assured. There is no shortage of iconographic Hawke material. He's in Madame Tussauds. There's a statue at Bordertown. His head has been the mould for wine casks. He's not after these things. It's not a biographer he wants, or a portraitist. He wants a figurative painter.

When Paul Keating talks about the "big picture", it's just possible that Bob Hawke is pondering the most appropriate place and the most appropriate form he might take in it. Will he be set in Arcady, like a brushed-up swaggie? Will the suburbs of the toiling masses convey a richer message? Will he be some kind of angel and, if so, on what angle to the firmament, what expression should he adopt, on whom or what should his gaze rest? Or will he be Ned Kelly, but, unlike Nolan's Kelly, with his head screwed on the right way?

What could be more pragmatic than this effort to not die? It's a very old favourite with just about everyone. The crowd will love it and the closer he gets to pulling off this stupendous feat the more it will feel like the act of a spoilsport to vote for anyone else. Who knows, going for a fifth term might be all that's needed to get a fourth. We have a prime minister with an eye on eternity and a leader of the Opposition with a chronic incapacity to be convincingly born. It's epoch-making stuff.

Yet the stakes are high for Mr Hawke. He may indeed be the first Australian prime minister to join the creatures of the Dreaming. But by the end of a fifth term, even a fourth, there is also a good chance that he will be less of a living legend than a gargoyle. Remember Billy Hughes?

But we should be less worried about what this process will do to Mr Hawke than what it will do to us. Remember Bob Menzies? Substantially a creature of his own boyhood imagination, Menzies painted himself into the mental landscape of this country so thoroughly that his fantasies became ours, his satisfaction ours, what should have been his embarrassment ours – and when he became inert and ridiculous so did we. It could happen with Hawke: if he were to stay another eight years, sometime in the 1990s the country might well sail into very still waters and stay there. For that's what myths do – they immobilise the world.

Yet no one should predict anything where Bob Hawke is concerned. He is the most protean of politicians and the chances are that the genius of nature will provide him with the wherewithal to spend many more years at the stick without putting the nation into a stupor.

Sunday Herald Sun, 24 September 1989

Paul Keating: Garibaldi in an Armani suit

IN 1993 A DELEGATION CAME to Parliament House to show the prime minister and his advisers some new technology – information technology. It was the internet. They showed us as Stephenson might have shown the King his steam engine. One of them did front of house, demonstrating to all who passed how with this new device he could "pull up" documents from the Library of Congress onto his screen. He "pulled up" a letter from the Soviet archives – a letter from Lenin ordering the execution of some kulaks. In recent years, the letter has been frequently quoted as evidence that the architect of the Russian Revolution was a cruel sociopath, and Stalin less an aberration than his natural heir. Whether you accept this interpretation or not, it is a significant letter. The man who "pulled up" the letter needed no convincing. As we read it on the screen and wondered how it had got there, he said – "I don't know who this Lenin guy was but he sure didn't like those kulaks". In our different ways we all bring a little bit of ignorance to history and add it to the pile. He might not have known who Lenin was, but he had grasped much better than us the part in history his machine was about to play.

I am going to talk about the Keating government, and Paul Keating, in particular, because I worked for him. I am not going to talk about everything that government did, or tell you everything I think or know about its leader. You need not fear that I am going to give you a history of the Keating government, or spend an hour of your time in praise or condemnation of it or him. I am going to talk about Keating and history and what this might tell us about history and modern politics. The anecdote is by way of setting Paul Keating as prime minister in his time – which some people called the end of history.

As a subject of study and as a component of general knowledge and public debate, history has lost massive ground in the past twenty years or so. Both here and in the United States, the word "crisis" is freely used to describe the pedagogical failure of history teaching and the gathering wave of ignorance about history in broader society. Australian history has been in particularly dramatic decline. This was the main reason for the Keating government's effort to reinstate the teaching of civics. Not that we thought civics would lead students back to the pleasures and possibilities of history; ignorance of history is more than ignorance of significant facts. But it was a start, and we thought it might lead on to something with the states, which are responsible for education. The Carr government, to its great credit, has gone further and pushed history back into schools and public life. In that sense at least, history is bound to judge the Carr government kindly.

Things are not so flash elsewhere, although six or seven years ago they were probably worse. Then it seemed Australia might be the first, if not the only, country to lend credibility to the claims of Francis Fukuyama that with the collapse of the communist economies we were on the threshold of the end of history. Yet the experience of the Keating government tends to suggest the opposite (as one would expect – for everything in Fukuyama's book there is something to contradict it): since 1992, when Keating first questioned a version of history which prevailed in some conservative circles, the subject has been at or near the centre of political debate, at times rivalling the economy, which in the '80s Keating made the indisputable "main game", even the "sacred narrative" – but that term won't do because it is a synonym for myth.

It should not occasion much surprise that history demonstrated such a capacity to stir the passions. Much more remarkable is its decline. History has contrived somehow to end up in its own dustbin. Yet history is nothing less than the whole human drama; it is pretty well anything we want it to be. To make it boring and irrelevant is a phenomenal achievement and one for which the history profession has to take a lot of credit. But of course much else conspires to defeat history in the information age – a million other stories furiously compete, narrow vocationalism rules the roost, training is everything, economists who were once safely stowed in cupboards and spoke only at certain times of the year now run the debates, our imagination lies elsewhere. On the frontiers of a long technology-driven revolution such as this one, perhaps history was bound to be a straggler or abandoned like the Drover's Wife.

There are good reasons why the young might pass the subject up. They do not want to inherit their identity – money, yes, but not who they are. If they think history is boring it may be a sign that the Oedipal reflex is working. It is more worrying for history if our children reject it because they think it is unknowable. Their experience, and maybe their education, might tell them that meaning is elusive, subjective, ephemeral and ambiguous, and pursuing it is a waste of time. Yet, while this attitude may cause concern among historians and give rise to furious denunciations of postmodernism, they can hardly think the problem is a new one. On the contrary, they have had to deal with it since their subject was first thought of.

Historians' despair need not prove fatal. It's like the Irishman and the anthropologist who asks him if he believes in fairies. He says, "No! no! Of course not. But they're there". Young people might deny history, but it's there. We know it will remain in the psyche, churning away even in those who think it's boring and irrelevant.

Perhaps historians need to recognise that what they do fulfill is a sort of primal need. The need for stories is buried deep in our psychology, maybe in our DNA, like our desire for salt, which a scientist I know says derives from our beginnings in the sea – it's a hedonic craving, which means it's nearly irresistible, even when we know it clogs our arteries and kills us.

History is a bit like that. It's a contradictory drive. On the one hand there's a pull towards the lost past and our desire to preserve it in myth and memory. For these reasons we construct our sacred narratives. Also for these reasons, some of us feel a pang of gloom when we see an abandoned house, the image Freud associates with mourning. If melancholy and mourning are part of the human condition, so is history. And both of them can be as fatal as salt.

On the other hand there is the desire to make our own history – to pull down what is offensive to our modern eye, or no longer useful or profitable, and to make our own mark. Like capitalism – we destroy so we can invent and renew. Like someone not wanting to look back, someone escaping from memory. There is Proust and there is progress. In the midst of one the other rears its head.

This paradox was alive in Paul Keating – his melancholy seemed to exist in proportion to his drive for change and renewal. He would re-design Australia on a drink coaster, launch brutal assaults on traditions, mock his opponents' attachments to the past – and every time he went to Cairns he'd groan and curse at what had been done to the architecture on the shoreline.

He liked neoclassical architecture and furniture because it was – remember – "eternally smart". I suspect he liked neoclassical economics for the same reason – for its simple lines. The Japanese beam, those buildings of Jefferson's in Washington – the things that will last forever, like the Labor Party, the Church of Rome and the message of Christ. I think the word "eternal" is essential to understanding Paul Keating.

That may be why he never lacked resolve when it came to change. He was connected to tradition – Australian, Labor, Irish, Catholic, Sydney, family – and he knew the value of it but, as Paul Kelly once said, he was "unburdened by the dead hand of the past".

> Keating brought to caucus and machine politics the disciplined infal-libility of his Catholicism. Dressed with the smart severity of a Jesuit, he slid along the parliamentary lobbies carrying ambition as an altar boy cradles his missal, reflexes sharpened to strike heretics.

Judging what was dispensable and what was for keeps was not such a hard question for Keating. He could go on changing and inventing and never fear the thread would break.

I am writing a book about the Keating government, or more accurately, Paul Keating's prime ministership, or even more accurately, Paul Keating and his prime ministership. I find the task produces these same paradoxical responses in me. It is astonishing to me that the documents of just six years ago provoke the kind of feelings Freud associates with the sight of an abandoned house. At the same time it often seems as if nothing separates us from those few years, that essentially the project is continuing, we are still having the arguments and we want to win them as much as ever. The task of doing Keating – even doing him slowly – is a hard one. I suspect it always has been.

As history students we were taught to never stray far from the evidence. We were taught how to assess the value of documents, even read between the lines; how to analyse them – and how to construct a convincing narrative. We learned that history is a very complex undertaking. But the most perfect mystery of the discipline, in any of its variations, is unlikely to save the historian who takes on modern politics.

What, for instance, do we make of a record which is written by journalists and politicians, mediated by television and radio? There is something always heroic about historians' assumptions – and those of journalists for that matter: three quarters of a century after Heisenberg established the uncertainty principle in physics, a century after Cézanne brought the same principle to painting landscapes, we march on as if reality can be described with an eye and an ear and a pen. In one of his columns in 1992, Gerard Henderson wrote that Paul Kelly's account of Australian politics in the '80s, *The End of Certainty*, was a tour de force of a kind, but it suffered from being "written in the hothouse, in-bred atmosphere of Parliament House" and was "not history in the established sense", and "by its very nature, it cannot hope to be definitive". It's hard to argue with his case, but the question remains, who *could* write the definitive history? A historian in the established sense? I doubt it.

It is obvious that a government cannot succeed if the media is concertedly against it. It is said less often, but it's equally true that a government is halfway to extinction if it blames the media for its misfortunes. This is all part of the exhausting, fiendish embrace of politics and the media: your most imaginative thoughts will be traduced, your noblest deeds scoffed at, your effort unrecognised; in fulfilment of their "vision" requirement you will announce your intention to create a pretty little postmodern republic in the South Seas, and to prove you are compassionate and wise you will offer to build a sophisticated safety net around the robust free market economy they asked for – and your policy speech will be headlined "Pork barrel republic!" But if you rail and shout, you're gone. Take them with you when you pay the nation's respects to the martyrs of Hellfire Pass, and on the very railway where the thousands died they will shove a microphone under your nose and ask you about the latest current account figures. In the interests of regional stability and improving the current account figures you go and make friends with those on whom your predecessors made war, and the journalists will hound you about not going to a place in Vietnam where a dozen Aussies died and at dusk they'll sneak off into the jungle to get a picture of "The graves Keating wouldn't visit!"

But be seen to complain and they will skewer you, and your opponents will suddenly feel lighthearted and go around whistling and mocking, even if as little as a week ago they were privately crying foul themselves. Because they know the media will say that a political leader who turns on them is the leader of a government in decay, a leader who has grown arrogant and out of touch. And their office will divide in two – between those saying, "Stop laughing, the pendulum could at any moment swing back through the wall and brain us", and those who say, "All the more reason to laugh and sing now".

In a way the media is right: a government which blames them hasn't learned the lesson of Job – to grin and bear it. For the media may be likened unto God and bad weather – it may seem unreasonable and cruel, but a person looks a fool ranting at it, and gains nothing.

He looks twice the fool when, soon after, the pendulum does swing and he finds himself having to quickly affect an attitude of basking in the reflected glow of his opponents being barbecued. Not that anyone will really notice – that's the other thing about modem politics, the attention span is about 7.5 seconds, unjogged memory about 7.5 days and diminishing yearly. What political leaders have to keep telling themselves is that they will get unjust critical reviews and also unjust favourable ones – and in this at least they are no different to large groups of other people, including footballers, jockeys and novelists. They need to accommodate the notion that even when the media story is not the true story, it is the only story that matters, because nothing in politics is real unless the media says so – and one of the two major parties tags along with the idea.

They have to plough on – even in the knowledge that if their strategy is too plainly directed at massaging the media they will be accused of cynical manipulation and subverting policy to tawdry political purposes; and if their strategy ignores the media or offends it they will be charged with being secretive and undemocratic or, worse, with political naivety and incompetence and being unfit to play the game. Ask John Hewson.

It is not just that meaning in politics is dependent on media interpretation. That has been the case for a very long time. And it is not new for the media to attract a range of human types, from the near-depraved to the flawlessly principled and bright – which is a compass no wider than the community and the parliament can boast. What *is* new is the pervasiveness of the media. It is in everything. It's not the fourth estate but the range on which we all ride, the whole environment, and politicians must decide very quickly if they'll be a raptor or a rabbit. The politicians who survive and prosper must of necessity know the steps to the dance. While they may complain to journalists and editors on the telephone, they can't step away from it without stepping away from reality. It's a tar baby embrace.

The American commentator Jonathan Schell says that the people of the United States now see politicians and journalists as a single class – a new leviathan of the "rich, famous and powerful who are divorced from the lives of ordinary people and indifferent to their concerns". In Australia this trend might not be so advanced but the same symptoms can be seen – in the last Victorian election, for example. Schell says this perceived merging of politics and the media has expanded the gap which exists in any democracy between those who participate fully and those who only participate in elections. This gap used to be filled by political parties and civic bodies, including trade unions. All these are shrinking. And the widening gap is filled by a sense of powerlessness, disenchantment – and talkback radio shows which heighten these feelings and add to them demands and expectations which are often the antithesis of good policy.

Political parties now monitor and analyse the calls to talkback radio, as well as the opinion polls and focus groups. If in all other circumstances politicians are expected to be honest, on talkback the audience demands sycophancy and self-abasement. On the John Laws program in 1995 a caller declared that in her part of the world women were having children for the sole purpose of claiming government benefits. Unable to persuade her that this was not a convincing reason to abolish the benefits, Keating finally exclaimed, "What do people want?" It was a costly mistake that confirmed the perception of Keating as arrogant and out of touch, not to say wilful and undisciplined.

Meanwhile the temptation of flakiness grows stronger: governments construct policies in line with carefully monitored public expectations, which in office they must abandon or compromise. This meets another public expectation, that politicians are weak-brained and cannot be trusted. And the loathing grows. It is, as Schell says, a *folie à deux*.

The journalists clean up on both the swings and the roundabouts. For weeks in 1993 many of them urged the second Keating government to do the responsible policy thing and drop the tax cuts promised in the 1992 One Nation economic statement. The government *did* the responsible thing and paid half, with half to follow. The media came at him, blazing with self-righteous fury, and labelled Keating a liar.

How a historian can be expected to read this diabolically difficult game of politics I don't know. I'm with that old deconstructionist Lord Melbourne, who a century and a half ago said, "I wish I was sure of anything as Tom Macaulay is of everything". In addition to all the difficulties which have made practical people in the past say the historical enterprise is bunk, there are too many layers of motive and meaning to allow anyone who is not part of the game to know how it is played. Politicians and hard-nosed insiders of fabled acumen don't always read it well themselves. The Willis letters are a case in point.

It won't stop people trying to find their way through, of course. Postmodern commentators make sporadic forays into interpretation that sometimes sound tantalisingly like the truth; but not the truth that matters. What is the use to a speechwriter to have the death of the author proclaimed? Psychoanalytic approaches are attempted and not without bringing enlightenment, but neither politicians nor the media will buy it as a significant factor in anything. Angry neoconservatives and left-liberals shout at the gates, sustained by the heat of their convictions but getting no nearer the light, for they don't know the "reality" of things. They all get their moments and no one is going to make them pay for it.

Where does that leave the poor old empirical historians whose discipline holds them to account – or at least is meant to? It didn't matter much to the historian who wrote the entry on the republic in the *Oxford Companion to Australian History*. "In the 1990s", it says, "Paul Keating and his speechwriter, Don Watson, revived the patriotic nationalist republicanism of Henry Lawson, as if the only authentic Australians were those who wanted to separate from Britain". So much for sticking to the evidence. There are times when you have to admit that Henry Ford was on to something. There are times when you think events can only be described by those who lived through them.

I don't know how modern political history can be written by anyone who has not actually lived inside the organism. As a hundred bad books attest, it is not a sufficient condition, but it is almost certainly a necessary one. It is not the whole story or the only one and it relies on uncertain memory and testimony of self-interested witnesses, but *The End of Certainty* is possibly as great a work of Australian history as anything to come from the academy in the last twenty-five years. It helps that Kelly is a formidable writer, but he couldn't have done it without having been there in the hothouse.

You can write credibly about football and art without having played at any of them. Politics is different. Modern politics is a game in which all day, every day words are conceived, written, uttered and translated into instant images which are then written about again and translated into more images – and the context and motivation for each is different, and necessarily the meaning each time is different, though it may be disguised to sound or look the same, or even disguised to look different when it is really the same.

And the media – like a pack of dogs, or a herd of cows – come rattling up to Five Ways, saying. "Which way? Which way? Where's the story? Which way?" And one says "This way!" And they all follow. Except, say, Alan Ramsey or Laurie Oakes or Michelle Grattan, who wander off down their own roads – and soon we hear the distant voices of the pack returning, saying – "What's Laurie doing? What's Ramsey's angle?" But never saying, of course, "We went the wrong way".

The problem for constructing a convincing narrative for modern politics is that everyone – every politician and every journalist – is in the business of constructing and deconstructing convincing narratives daily. When you decide who won the news that night, or at the end of the week, what you're really measuring is whose story was best. Did your story survive? What is the history of this week? Of this morning?

What writer can accurately measure the difference, or say if what the media ran with was what the speaker intended, and if the doorstop was in any case a means of drawing attention away from something less palatable, or to steal the limelight from an Opposition statement later in the day. And who knows if more influential than anything said or reported was a curl in the politician's lip, an impression he gave of weariness or arrogance, or something else that did not register with the press or any poll or focus group? Why did hundreds of ecstatic schoolgirls mob Keating one day in the 1996 campaign? What had they seen that no one else had?

To state the bleeding obvious – the written record, the documents left for historians to study if they survive the shredder and the widespread

indifference to posterity, will reveal what was said but not what was sig-
nified. They won't capture anything like the whole drama – which often
resembled the advertisement in which a skier comes hurtling, yodel-
ling out of the mountains and, in a flurry of legs, arms and snow, crashes
through the roof of a bar and with a smile asks the waiter for a beer. It
never fails to make me think of Keating arriving at the Press Club or in
the House for Question Time. But that's an ad – you don't see the whole
drama on the news and current affairs shows, and what you do see brings
you not much closer to the truth of the matter.

And then there's the radio the next day. What the hosts will make of
a politician's performance is another imponderable, as is what the audience will make of the radio shows – you see one friend at the weekend
and he tells you you're going well, you see another who listens to another
station, or watches *A Current Affair*, or her mother does, and she says your
bloke's letting the Japanese cut down all the old growth forests for koala
meat! He's a fiend! You ought to be ashamed! And you go back to work
thinking what a great simplifier of things the Cold War was and that
Fukuyama was right after all – the great issues must have been settled.

I don't know how in future the general histories will be written –
from inside or outside. The major work on the 1996 election is Pamela
Williams's *The Victory*. For want of much else, most of the reviews treated
it as the definitive work, the last word, and so, presumably, did the
many people who bought and read it. In truth, much of it strikes me
as excellent – but not the parts I know about. Williams makes damning personal remarks about Keating on the evidence of one, possibly
two, not disinterested people. Labor's national secretary, Gary Gray, told
Williams that Keating was mentally unstable. To say that his evidence
was "flimsy" and her use of it "questionable" is to be more than generous. No self-respecting historian could countenance her method. But
a self-respecting historian is unlikely to ever strike Williams from the
record – though someone might one day make the point that Winston
Churchill was lucky he didn't have Gary Gray around.

History may not be at an end, but it certainly doesn't seem set for a big
win. Do we now say that there is no objective truth that can be known?
Perhaps there never was, which is what Lord Melbourne seemed to be

saying about Macaulay 150 years ago? Of course history has always been problematic. In any democratic society it is bound to be argued about. But it's fair to say, I think, that it has never worn so many disguises. Never have there been so many stories from which to choose.

We need a story, don't we? We need our own story. Read a child a familiar bedtime story – and change it. Put the fox up in the rafters and the hen circling on the floor. Make the first bowl of porridge just right, the second one too hot. The child will pick it up at once, and correct it for you, possibly angrily. This is the first flowering of political correctness. In its most basic form that is perhaps what history is. It's much the same with adults – and much the same with politics. Don't you dare change the story.

It was storytelling which made Paul Keating such an effective reformer in the 1980s. I don't mean the art of sugar-coating, or even putting a spin on things – though there was plenty of that no doubt. I mean Keating made a drama out of the economy and he put the whole population in the theatre, even sometimes on the stage. He was centre-stage, of course; if you've got Fred Astaire in your cast you don't leave him shuffling aimlessly down the back. Sure, he was boasting when he said he had the markets in one pocket and the ACTU in the other, and the governor of the Reserve Bank under his wing, and this person doing these tricks, and someone else doing others – but it was more than a boast. It was an image of confluence and energy – or synergy if you like. Each Budget came as another act in the drama, players were given roles, pulled off and reprimanded as object lessons if they didn't perform according to the text. He got the crowd barracking.

And he invented a language. He once said that he had spent years making words into "hammers". Sometimes these hammers were for beating people on the head. More often they were to make an indelible mark, so that the ideas would stick. That's how he educated the country in the necessity of economic reform.

He knew that he was replacing one story with another – the story of protection and regulation and reliance on commodities with the story which began when the dollar was floated and the financial markets were deregulated. The first story ended in the decline in the terms of trade, underdeveloped and antiquated manufacturing, increasingly futile and perilous attempts to ride on the sheep's back or on each new upswing in commodity prices. We all remember it – we could sing it in our sleep. This he liked to characterise as the Menzies story – with references to Qualcast mowers and Morphy Richards toasters. The second story was all about opening the place up, giving it a future, getting it up and running, lifting exports as a proportion of GDP from 14 per cent to 23 per cent – you'll remember that story too.

This is what he was reminding the press gallery about on that night at the National Press Club when he compared himself to Placido Domingo and signalled his challenge to Bob Hawke. He was reminding them that he always gave value to the business of streaming the economics and politics together. That night he also reminded the press that they had been an essential part of it: "I hope that we can continue between us, spinning the tale, the great tale of Australian economic change, and wrapping it up in interesting ways, with interesting phrases and interesting words".

As treasurer, Paul Keating wrote history as he went. He told the press that they could attach themselves to John Hewson if they liked. But Hewson would never "lift economics and politics to an art form". By art form he meant storytelling, or something tantamount to history.

The Placido Domingo references and the implications for Hawke's leadership have obscured some significant larger elements in that off-the-cuff speech. He talked about more than economics; about lingering empire attitudes in Australia and South Africa, for instance. And how we Australians had too rarely run the place according to our own lights; how we'd never sat down and written a constitution "which a couple of hundred years later could be as fresh as the day it was written". "We occupy a continent", he said, "and we're one nation, and we're basically a European nation, changing now to adapt to the region".

In those words can be glimpsed the kernel of the expanded story he told in the course of his prime ministership, the one which when it was thrown up against the "sacred narrative" of the Menzies years caused grave offence – both real and feigned. No one wrote the Domingo speech for him – it was in his head. People who think Keating constructed his view of history to suit his political needs in 1992 should go back to that 1990 speech and, even further, to the 1970s, when he assailed the Fraser government for continuing to think in colonial terms about the Asian countries. There is a consistent pattern to his thought.

Abraham Lincoln was unequivocal: "As our case is new, so we must think anew and act anew", he said. Could this be a justification for rewriting history? Or a motto for good government which abandons the myths and pieties by which inaction – and political correctness – is justified? Lincoln knew his history and how to use it. How does he begin the Gettysburg Address? With history – "four score and seven years ago ..." It promises to be as platitudinous as any old Anzac Day address. In the great tradition of pious emptiness it pays familiar homage to the founding fathers of the republic. But then, in a silky shift of gears, it becomes revolutionary – the Gettysburg Address calls up history to demand a change.

And what did his opponents say about it? They said he was rewriting history. *The Chicago Times* said he had misstated the cause for which the soldiers at Gettysburg gave their lives and "libel[led] the statesmen who founded the government. They were men possessing too much self-respect to declare that negroes were their equal". Lincoln, they said, had turned the words of the founding fathers into things they did not mean. How come no one now says that the Gettysburg Address is politically correct?

In *An Intimate History of Humanity*, Theodore Zeldin writes: "To have a new version of the future, it is always necessary to have a new version of the past". He is not advocating the application of the airbrush. He is saying that as much as we need the stories by which we know ourselves and secure ourselves in the cosmos, we also need to invent and renew ourselves. We need to balance the opposing forces.

For all Keating's hard work in the '80s, when he got the prime ministership in 1991 he needed to renew himself and his government. The original title for the economic statement by which the government defined its attack on the recession was not One Nation, but Renewing Australia. (One Nation seemed such a good name at the time.) But the recession had not only knocked the stuffing out of the economy; for the time being, it had deprived the whole Labor reform program of legitimacy. As the author of that program, it had deprived Keating of legitimacy too. This was not what he had promised. It was a chapter from another book.

You can see the attempt to make the recession a legitimate part of the story in that remark about having to have it, which haunted his whole prime ministership. Perhaps he should have said *it is my melancholy duty to inform you that the world is going into recession and therefore Australia has also gone into recession.* How many in the population – or the press gallery – would have known he had borrowed it from Bob Menzies?

There were plenty who wanted him to apologise, to stand in the stocks of talkback radio and have those words thrown back at him – those words he had made into hammers. Jana Wendt conducted a show trial in his absence. But Keating had no bent for self-abasement. Instead he and the government came up with a statement which contained some carefully disguised old-fashioned Keynesian solutions, and equally old-fashioned messages of national strength and bonding and the realisation of dreams first dreamed one hundred years ago. By 1992 the Keating government had a new story – and the polls showed it was back in the hunt.

Fukuyama had just written *The End of History and the Last Man.* With the death of communism, he said, liberalism had achieved a Nietzschean final triumph. Ideology was dead – again. There was no longer any reason for any other isms at all: no elite for absolutism, no trade unions for socialism, no nations for nationalism. The end of history means the end of the political: ideologies, values and derring-do will be replaced by economics and technology and consumerism. Three years after One Nation, one year after Working Nation, in the same year as Creative Nation, the Japanese whiz Kenichi Ohmae published a big-selling book called *The End of the Nation State.* So what on earth was this specimen of a Last Man doing running around talking about republics and new flags and new senses of national purpose, and asserting some new national role in the region, and bringing forth grand new programs for the new Australia of his imagination, all trumpeting the word "nation", and reviving civics for heaven's sake!? And what was he doing stirring up a hornet's nest about the wars, and biffing Britain and Bob Menzies? The Last Man, according to Fukuyama, was meant to be a dismal creature – an inhabitant of a liberal democracy when all are agreed on liberal democracy and have nothing to dispute but money and possessions. Without ideals, heroism or creative urges, the Last Man is Mediocre Man – or, if you like, a colourless nerd. Yet Keating was acting like some kind of Garibaldi in an Armani suit.

Political reality does tend to ignore intellectual fashion. The first and most pressing reality for Keating was to restart the economy. The second was to puncture Fightback and its author, Opposition leader

John Hewson. The third was to throw off the dark spectre – the recession. He discovered in the course of that first year that the second objective was his best answer to the third. One Nation was to deal with the first problem and give him the basis for an argument with the second.

But one other problem remained; namely, that, even in the best of times, economics is too barren a landscape for a prime minister to live in. Paul Keating needed something more human and more vivid – something half as rich as Menzies's tapestry of traditions, symbols, bogeys and signs of progress would do. And Providence being more wonderful than any other theory, it so happened that John Hewson knew nothing of such things and was only at home on economic turf. By softening economic policy at some of the edges – in car industry tariffs, for example – he led John Hewson into a policy billabong and, leaving him there, paddled furiously for the mainstream.

Before this, when all the debate, understandably, was about unemployment, and the Budget deficit, and the current account and the prospects for growth, and – even as that word was mentioned – the threat of another inflationary boom and another recession, Keating inserted, of all things, some history. He decided that a new perspective on the future required a new perspective on the past.

To the economic commentators, and all those he had instructed in the reform story, this was blasphemy. He'd jumped the monastery fence. John Hewson thought telling the Queen that Australia was going its own way showed a lack of respect. And then when Keating lambasted the Opposition for their sycophantic attachment to Britain, imperial honours, protected industries, sheep and Morphy Richards toasters – even after Britain deserted us for Europe, and failed to defend Singapore and wouldn't give us back our troops – there was a terrible roar of protest which echoed all the way to the London tabloids.

There had to be an explanation: it was because he was Irish; it was because he wanted a political diversion; it was because of Jack Lang; it was because he didn't have a proper education; it was because he was getting advice from some ning-nong with a dingo's degree in history.

It was the Singapore reference which offended most. In fact it is difficult to find a respectable history, including that by Winston Churchill, which does not fundamentally support Keating's interpretation. Gerard Henderson found Robert O'Neill to say it was not so. But Guy Wint and Peter Calvocoressi, Basil Liddell Hart, Paul Hasluck, E.M. Andrews, Coral Bell, David Horner, Hank Nelson and Bill Gammage say it more or less was. As for it being an Irish Catholic Labor version of history, it was pretty well identical to the version I got growing up in a Scottish Protestant rural conservative household. I've heard it said by people wearing RSL badges, at least after a beer or two has gone down.

Yet it was as if Keating had torn the sacred text, changed the words in the bedtime story – as if he had no right to speak on such subjects, as if he could not know. Anyway, what did history have to do with a prime minister? The RSL accused him of heresy, if not treason. Three years later the letters were still coming in. In 1995 I tracked down the author of an article in an RSL branch newsletter which claimed that Keating had said British soldiers were cowards who had run away at Singapore. He was having his lunch when I telephoned. I asked him where he got this idea. He said a friend had told him he thought he'd read it somewhere or heard it on the radio or something.

It was difficult for Keating not to talk about history. He couldn't advocate a republic or a new flag without talking about it. When the High Court put Mabo on his plate he was obliged to talk about it. He couldn't set things up for the centenary of Federation without saying a word or two about history. And, although hardly anyone seemed to notice, his government coincided with the fiftieth anniversary of the last four years of World War II. He hadn't chosen to make all the speeches of commemoration at all those war graves and over at the Memorial – he was obliged to.

He could have delivered more conventional speeches: there have been many wars in history and they have produced any amount of eloquent sentiments for a prime minister to choose from, and any amount of platitudes that doubtless once had meaning, but were now useful only in the way that a door sausage is useful and about as stimulating. But Keating believed he had a responsibility to invest the wars with contemporary meaning. He thought the sacrifice of Australians would cease to be understood if that link could not be made, if the word "sacrifice" drifted towards cliché.

He went to Kokoda and, forewarning no one, fell to his knees and kissed the ground at the base of the monument. The press came running to his advisers asking who had put him up to this astonishing gesture.

No one had. Later he talked to the children who had sung the national anthem and waved little Australian flags they had made at school. Keating patted one of them on the head. A sound boom picked up what he said. On the news that night we heard him say to the little boy, "Don't worry, son, we'll get you a new one of those". The patriots shrieked. At Bomana cemetery he said that the soldiers who lay there had died "not in defence of the old world, but the new world. Their world". In headlines twice as big as the event the cry went up that Keating was discriminating between the fallen.

I would like to know if Geoffrey Blainey agrees with Theodore Zeldin. I think he must. Geoffrey Blainey has always understood the need to reinterpret the past and he has never shied away from the challenge. He is a master storyteller – a kind of shenachie – who can tell an old story in words we in the present can understand and even feel. He can also change a story and get away with it. It was Blainey, after all, who offered a radical reinterpretation of Australia's European foundations, a new theory about distance as a prime influence on our development, a treatise on war which suggested among other things that the Japanese had had their reasons.

But Geoffrey Blainey came after Keating savagely. Blainey said Keating had "done deep harm by altering the facts of history to support his political campaign". He said Keating had appointed himself as the nation's "wandering lecturer in history". He said he had been "impetuous" and "silly" and he had "blundered" in.

Other historians welcomed Keating's contribution, though Geoffrey Bolton was reported as saying that there was "a worry when politicians interpret the past". It is not hard to see the dangers Bolton is pointing to – we don't want our politicians telling us what we should believe about the past. It is at least as dangerous, probably, as historians telling us what we should believe about the present. However there remains the difficulty (which Bolton of course recognises) of effecting some kind of constitutional lobotomy on our leaders. And it does create problems for speechwriters, so much of life being a dialogue with the past, so many electors wanting politicians in their speeches to recognise what has happened to them. It is the most powerful thing in a speech, this touching on people's experience. It pulls them into the country's story, it makes it a shared emotion. And often it has a useful humanising effect on the politician. We could go back to only talking about economics, but then some of us might go back to the British Isles.

Such nice considerations buttered no parsnips with Dame Leonie Kramer. On reading a transcript of an address Keating gave on Anzac Day, 1992, in Port Moresby, she fulminated in *The Sydney Morning Herald* against his "sentimental clichés" and "rhetorical flourishes". When he said that Anzac "does not confer on us a duty to see that the world stands still", she said: "Who in their right mind would suggest that the world stands still? The nature of existence is change". And who in their right mind would argue with that, or feel the need to say it? Except I thought Lévi-Strauss had a point when he said that myths and legends had the capacity to make the world stand still, in a manner of speaking.

Kramer was particularly incensed by the passage in Keating's speech which contained the words "Australia looks to America, free of any pangs as to our traditional links or kinship with the United Kingdom". She responded fiercely: "Why can we not acknowledge the common sense of turning to the US for help without discarding our origins, which in any case we share with the US?" Well, yes. But it does appear that Kramer thought the offending words were Keating's. They were, of course, famously Curtin's.

As Curtin is not in a position to defend himself, let me offer an answer on his behalf: he was not discarding our origins, and he knew he needed to acknowledge the past. He needed, in a sense, to bless it before passing on. He also needed to stare it down for the power that it had. When you read about Curtin in those days it is very obvious that he knew just how momentous his actions were. That was one reason why it took so much out of him. Curtin was giving us what we have a right to expect of political leaders but do not always get – a decision. Courage. Leadership.

If anyone wants another reason why he said he was turning to the United States "free of any pangs" about our spiritual ties to Britain – consider the possibility that there was some anger in his words. And the possibility that this anger was shared by Menzies and by Casey, because assurances had been given in London, and these turned out to be hollow. Menzies lamented to the high commissioner in London, Stanley Melbourne Bruce, that he was being urged to send Australian troops to the Middle East not only by Anthony Eden, but by "old soldiers". That is, by the past, by the legend of World War I. Allan Martin quotes him in a letter to Bruce: "If only a kindly Providence would remove from the active political scene a few minds which are heavily indoctrinated by the 'old soldiers' and by the 'Versailles' point of view". Menzies, Martin tells us, said that he had to remind his critics that "this is not 1914".

Perhaps the world does stand still, after all. Just as it moves under us sometimes.

The point is made not to dispute the value of the contribution Australian soldiers made in the Middle East or anywhere else. It's only to show that the most cultivated adults can be as prone to fury as any toddler when the words of a favourite story are changed.

When, as president of the United States, Lyndon Johnson became a tribune and battering ram for civil rights and the elimination of poverty, his old supporters were shocked. "Why, Lyndon why?", they cried. "You never held these views before!" "I wasn't president then", he replied. To be fair, it must have been a shock to hear Paul Keating weighing into history. This was the person who, Third Empire clocks apart, had done nothing but tear tradition down in the previous decade. That's if you count heavily protected industry, regulated financial markets, fixed exchange rates, declining terms of trade and centralised wage-fixing as traditions.

Power does corrupt – sometimes it corrupts our perfect view of people. So Paul Keating wore a smart suit and believed that neoclassical economics was the main game, and frequently talked about it as if it could only be played to the exclusion of everything else. Jack Lang wore a smart suit. Rex Connor believed economics was the main game. But Rex Connor believed we should buy back the farm. Keating didn't. And Jack Lang carried a Gladstone bag in which he kept, in neat pockets, a shaving brush, a pencil, a tape measure, a diary and a KLG spark plug. I never saw Keating with such a thing – though he is a meticulous packer just the same.

There were commentators who felt that Keating's interest in history was too sudden to be anything other than political opportunism. There were some who felt that because he lacked a formal training in history he could not be right about it – so when he got his figures wrong at a door-stop interview in France or drifted into hyperbole or parody, they savaged him. Suddenly history became the knowable, verifiable, unarguable, immutable thing that everyone who has ever practised the discipline, and everyone who has ever read it seriously, knows it cannot be.

This is a very small part of any history of the Keating government. For me, the story has shifted in the past three years. In the aftermath of the 1996 election it was about how the election had been lost. I don't know the answer to that. I have read at least twenty good reasons and thought of a dozen or so myself. But I still don't know. The most satisfactory argument remains a line in *Middlemarch*: "It always remains true that if we had been greater, circumstances would have been less strong against us".

I have a feeling that politicians of the Keating mould are just now out of date. They are power politicians. It comes from the Catholic Church, the Labor Party and an uncluttered mind. Carl von Clausewitz, Henry Kissinger and Ulysses S. Grant are of the same mould. These days, however, the surveys show that people don't respect power in their leaders, but want to be "empowered" themselves. They want respect.

Most writing about politics is about power – who won or lost, who is angling for a coup. It is always a better story than policy. It's addictive. It might not do a lot for sales if a book about Keating concerns itself too much with the policy effort – the effort to find an independent role in Asia before it was too late, finding some strategy to cope with the information revolution, dealing with the new social imperatives created by an efficient growth economy which seemed to shed jobs as fast it created them, globalisation, Mabo, the republic, the decline in regional Australia.

The evidence of four and a quarter years in politics would fill half a dozen mechanics' halls, and that's not counting the electronic stuff and how it looked and sounded. Or the stuff in memories. I don't know how a historian or any other commentator is meant to cope. Yet they try: not long after the 1996 election, I read a newspaper column by McKenzie Wark which argues that Don Russell and Don Watson were typical of their generation: good on ideas but with little concern for detail. With the greatest respect, I don't think Wark knows what details are.

Being a simple empiricist at heart I keep going back to my first meeting with Keating. It wasn't arrogance or pride I was presented with – but melancholy. He was like a man with a sad fixation about what had been lost. That quality was there, on and off, all the way through. For an adviser or a speechwriter it could be worrying – but for a historian it was constant encouragement.

Lecture for the History Council of
New South Wales, 20 September 1999

Recollections: Afterword

Paul Keating let me know what he thought about this book a few days before the launch; on the night itself in the Sydney Town Hall he let the audience know – not everything (some bits were reserved for me alone), but enough to leave them in no doubt about his loathing. The book was launched by Noel Pearson, who when he had read it told me he thought it was a "love story". I confess to wondering sometimes if therein lay a piece of the problem. A few years later Pearson wrote about the "darkest and barely restrained dudgeon" of Keating's mood that night, and the "variously erudite, humorous, vicious and thoroughly mesmerising black performance" with which I was "surgically pinned to the wall". I would take issue with "surgically": it struck me as more a shillelagh than a knife.

After saying nothing more in public for the best part of a decade, last year Keating wrote an article in which, coopting to his case a remark alleged of Graham Freudenberg, he charged me with breaking "the contract". I knew what he meant by this "contract" – it is the common understanding that political leaders own their speeches regardless of who writes them – but I could not see how I had broken it. I agree with the "contract" and have affirmed it a hundred times on public platforms, including a couple shared with Freudenberg, the great Labor speech-writer and historian who also believes in it. Prime ministers decide what they will say and what they won't, they fire the bullets or throw the streamers and bear the consequences. I don't recall Paul Keating ever

First published in the tenth-anniversary edition of *Recollections of a Bleeding Heart: A Portrait of Paul Keating PM*.

uttering a word that he did not want to utter. Under the "contract" all of them are his and he is welcome to them.

The occasion for his sudden assault last year was an article in *The Sydney Morning Herald* which reported comments I made about the speech Keating delivered in Redfern Park in 1993. When the *Herald* reporter phoned, as usual I told him that he should speak to Keating. But you wrote it, said the reporter. I was his speechwriter, I said, but it is Keating's speech. I *explained* the "contract". I have no recording of the conversation, but I am confident that I went on to say, as I say in the book, no other senior politician in the Labor Party would have delivered it – not as he did, without changing a word. No one else had the personal conviction and political courage in the same measure. My saying this, Keating said, was "condescending". To a certain kind of ego, in certain circumstances, it might be: to another kind, I'd venture it is no more than a statement of two discrete facts: that we thought the same way, and he had the mettle to say what he thought.

I spoke to Graham Freudenberg and he too was surprised that Paul Keating thought I had "broken the contract". Perhaps it was something in the way my remarks were reported, but from his article it seems he has come to believe that because the speech was his under the "contract" he had actually written it. Either that, or the matter of the speech was a surrogate for deeper grievances. Whatever the case, I cannot alter the fact that one dark night I wrote it. That was not to put words in his mouth, but to put them on a page: for him to use as he saw fit, as he would any other form of advice. In a political office a speech is advice formally composed. An offering. Whether he used all or some or none of it was entirely Keating's pigeon.

History devours millions, raises and lays on acolytes to so few. Why would any man who has enjoyed all the privilege and exhilaration of the highest office be so tormented by the thought it might go down in history that his words – no less than Kennedy's and Reagan's, Whitlam's and Hawke's – did not in every case scuttle from his own hand, or that from time to time he misread the signs or needed help to read them? Why *not* might be more the question. And if that is troubling, why not be agitated by a listing and imperfect monument like this book?

Paul Keating called *Recollections* the "black box recorder" of his prime ministership. Though he meant to illustrate my failure, this remains the nicest thing he said about it and I have been tempted to infer that at least I did a fair job of getting down the last words of the government before it crashed in flames. The "black box" was a good metaphor and useful for his caustic purposes, but it came from an outraged misreading of the book. A black box recorder records as God might: everything, with an omnipresent and objective ear. This I lack. The book was no black box for the only slightly less obvious reason that anyone writing history (or a speech) has to sift and select evidence, find a structure, a voice, a tone – the key in which the story's told. Anyone telling a story has first to decide what the story is going to be, and then how to tell it. All storytellers worth their salt know that if you try to tell everything you will wind up telling nothing. They all know that the story you tell is determined by the angle from which you look at the events. The angle determines where the light falls. Change the angle and you change the story. Paul Keating will know this: he has a strong claim to being the greatest storyteller Australian politics has seen.

I prefer a different metaphorical machine: not a black box, but a hand-held camera. In this book the camera is focused on Keating in the main, but not to the exclusion of the people who worked for him, or the contest of ideologies, the germination and defence of ideas, the moods, the psychology and the clamour of the daily life of the prime minister's office in which they were all engaged. It sees not only what was done, but what, for better or worse, was not done. What was started and not finished. What opportunities we grasped and what we missed. Who won the battles and who lamented those they lost. What was willed and what pure chance. The camera could not be everywhere, only where I took it – in and out of offices, cars, planes, hotels – and only when I remembered to switch it on, only when the words and images were clear enough. And then I added a voiceover, to create the context. I wasn't thinking of a camera at the time, but that's how I think of it now.

I don't have a single image of Paul Keating writing a speech. He delivered some ad lib, certainly; but the great majority were written for him. I have many images of him marking up drafts – at his desk and, just as often, in the car, on the way to whatever was the occasion for the speech. I can picture him deleting (sometimes with apologies and occasionally with belligerence), adding his own lines, instructing me in the realities of the case, drawing the big picture, checking with Don Russell or

Allan Gyngell or any one of a dozen other people – taking ownership of the speeches. Not just of the word, but the ideas. Speechwriters do have ideas; at least they ought to, because they cannot write in any useful way without them. I saw Keating take intellectual and political possession of speeches, but one was as likely to see him pruning the wisteria in the prime minister's courtyard as to see him *writing* them. I wrote most, and Allan Gyngell, Ashton Calvert and John Edwards wrote the remainder: just as Graham Freudenberg wrote the majority of Whitlam's and many of Hawke's. And a long line of advisers "wrote" other stories including the political one – as insiders always have, both for superior politicians like Keating and dismal ones like Billy McMahon.

But for good or bad, and regardless of whether he brought intellect and strength to the task or dullness and pusillanimity, whether he bravely led or followed bleating, the politics and the story belong to the prime minister. It is the way politics and government work in this country. They work in other ways as well, but this is the way I saw them work, and that, after long consideration, is what I chose to write about.

A sometime historian who made a living from freelance writing was bound to keep a diary, and I did – and made it known. When the government fell and everyone went off to new jobs, I went back to my old one. I had the makings of a book, but for three years I didn't have the will – or, as it happened, the wherewithal to write it.

I began writing *Recollections* at the ANU's Humanities Research Centre in the summer of 1999. Canberra was the usual hell for agoraphobics: boundless sky and unfilled space; the nation's ghosts camped in mausoleums by an artificial billabong; the living, invisible shiny-bums in Parliament House, observing their protocols half-buried in a hill. The campus was a vacant field, except for the Pakistani scholars who gathered every day in the adjacent flat to watch the one-day cricket. Their voices and Richie Benaud's and the rest of Kerry Packer's scout troop mixed with the calls of the currawongs and mudlarks. No doubt the birds were hanging out around the flagpole over at Parliament House too: the birds and the sky and the weird seductive emptiness are the only things that place shares with the rest of Australia. "It's all happening!" Bill Lawry shouted every hour or so.

But there was nothing happening in the nation's capital. Nothing you could see, at least. That's the way it is in Canberra: it all happens, but out of sight. With the shining light of the mighty bush outside, everything happens in that anaemic and unnatural glow inside. It's an unnatural city. And an insider's city, of course.

My problem was the voice. Who was speaking: a historian, an insider or both? The story of the insider was personal, close and unfinished. I was still living it. So was Paul Keating. In those days we often lived it together, on the phone mainly. The closeness of these events might be why I began writing from the magisterial position: to establish the distance necessary to lend the story the stature of magisterial history, and the insider the stature of a historian. The position demanded that the author hide the signs he had been in the vicinity when the events described occurred. Other insiders have written their accounts in this way and managed to satisfy more readers than the subject and his least demanding admirers. There are fine books by participants who, for the sake of seeming objectivity, have backed out of the room or taken up a position on the ceiling. Hagiographies, the subject's self-reverence projected through another's mouth, are not inevitable. But it remains that the elevated or omniscient third-person narrative demands an artificial logic for events that are often random and subjective: and when participants in those events do this, the most skilful and unflinching practitioners risk losing some of the truth – and the life – of the politics to which they were privy.

Whatever advantages an insider may gain from elevating his perspective, I could not find life among them. After trying for months to translate first-person experience and perspective into third-person narrative, I began to think that my efforts had a little in common with Graham Freudenberg's *A Certain Grandeur* and Stephen Mills's *The Hawke Years*, and even a little with Norman Mailer's *The Armies of the Night*, but much more with whatever it is that makes policemen address the media like zombies programmed by a malignant spirit. I wondered if an insider-cum-historian, with a collegial story, threatened egos and precious reputations to protect, might become less of a witness to the subject than a proxy for it.

Just before I left the HRC I gave an afternoon seminar. Afterwards, the formidable professor of history F.B. Smith approached and said, first, that watching him as prime minister he had often wondered if Paul Keating was depressed, then that he doubted if he would read the book that I proposed to write. I do not recall his reasons with much clarity, but I think he felt that books written by political participants are invariably *parti pris* and, especially when they are written so soon after the events they purport to describe, should not be taken seriously. If he did not actually say it, I think he might also have found them dull and inconsequential. But had I thought of annotating and publishing the diary I had mentioned in the seminar? asked Professor Smith. He would not read the book I was proposing, he said, but a diary was a different matter. I had not thought of it, but I saw his point.

For a fortnight or so I took the idea seriously. A diary has qualities of immediacy and authenticity that secondary accounts cannot match, and it is an often alarming corrective and stimulus to memory. Yet useful as the diary was, both as a record of daily events and a window onto my feelings about them, it was so far from being the whole story no amount of annotating could make up the difference. Some of it was of a purely private nature and some concerned matters that for reasons of legality or good faith could not be published; add to this the ephemera, repetitions, self-indulgence and baloney which would have to go and it would be as if, instead of *Moby-Dick*, we had been left with Ishmael's daybook. But Barry Smith's radical suggestion led me to decide the book should be written much as the diary was: from where I had been, at that angle, on the deck of the *Pequod*, not halfway up the mast or trailing in a whaleboat.

I would not pretend to have had no role or point of view beyond that of silent witness or amanuensis. I did not decide this because I wanted to claim more for myself or anybody else, or to say that it was in the prime minister's office that everything of significance was decided. It was to put what I knew – the office – at the centre of the action. I had not been in caucus or Cabinet or thousands of other meetings; I had had nothing to do with Keating as treasurer. Not having experienced events in person is of course no barrier to conventional history; and had I not been in Keating's office, that option would have been open to me, as it remains now for any other historian. But because I *had* been in the office, I felt no better equipped to attempt a conventional history of Paul Keating's prime ministership than Keating himself was.

The veneer of a disinterested narrative might go some way to meeting the requirements of an unwritten clause in that unwritten contract of Paul Keating's, which in essence is one between the writer and the history he witnessed; but there is no such contract and, if there were, a self-respecting citizen invited to work in a political office would no more sign up to it than to one requiring that his tongue be drilled before returning to society. As much as they might stray towards believing it is their right and duty, history's great actors cannot lay down the terms of good history. They may prefer the elevated vantage point for the elevated authority and tone it grants the story of their lives, but elevation doesn't guarantee the quality of observation, the sympathy and curiosity of the reader, or the judgement of posterity.

Take William Manchester's decidedly magisterial two-volume biography of Winston Churchill, one of Paul Keating's favourite books. There was Christopher Hitchens declaring the other day that Churchill "probably has no more hagiographic chronicler than William Manchester". And yet, as Hitchens wrote, on one matter (that of Churchill's attachment to Edward VIII) the hagiographer not only acknowledges a profound misjudgement on Churchill's part, but "virtually gives up on his hero for an entire chapter". The same Manchester found room within his paean to describe Churchill's heroic drinking habits, his chronic depression and his deeply eccentric personal behaviour which led colleagues and bystanders to declare him "unstable". If you can't trust your hagiographer with such things …? Except that Churchill is the more singular because of them – and more likely to see what others can't, and do what others quail from. The best political leaders are often made of unusual stuff, and the most rudimentary psychology tells us it is no accident.

Others have fair claim on the economic transformation of Australia, Bill Kelty, Bob Hawke and two or three Treasury officials among them; but Paul Keating's so-called "big picture" vision, his political courage, the requisite luck and his gift for storytelling have earned him most of the credit. Certainly no one did more to bring about the successful economy we now enjoy. But history just will not behave. If this transformation not only brought economic growth and prosperity, but in some cases laid the ground for the debasement of political debate to tin-eared sloganeering and second-hand managerialism, should he not share the credit for that as well?

To whose account shall we put it if the new "competitive" economy spawned multitudes of competitive narcissists who crowd the verges of the lily pond, and Labor parties abandon not just their beliefs but their brains to satisfy their sovereign needs or vanities, and even frame their education policy for narcissists (My School)?

It is not such a long bow: just as Keating's political demise prompted a new generation of Labor politicians to discard big-picture politics for poll-driven caution, the subtle transition from society to economy did its bit to stifle the things from which he drew his strength, his inspiration and his language. A Labor movement of spirit and character, for instance: one with an idea and a story big enough to at least sometimes break the political culture's anaesthetising grip; one that might attract more individuals of character and independent mind, and fewer of the kind he recently labelled "populist sickos".

For as much as Paul Keating's career is inseparable from the economic revolution of the '80s and '90s, he also embodied its opposite. He was the poet and aesthete of the side. It was Keating who championed the new economy in animating and often irresistible metaphors. And, as prime minister, it was Keating who insisted that while the economy was the main game, it was not the only game. What made Keating rare in politics then, and would make him a genuine freak now, was his ear: I don't mean for music, but for language. He lived in the language, not as a pedant does, but in a visceral, intuitive way. Language – and music – kept alive in him the essential understanding now largely lost among our leaders that, as well as economics and politics and management and polling, there is a poetic key to human reality.

As in other things, in this he was old-fashioned, if not downright pre-industrial. He was all for the new – new economy, new money, new alliances, new eras, new republics – and he was also for the old: for Schinkel's architecture and ormolu clocks. This was not simply a matter of taste; it was the Keating persona. It was who he was, and no one who knew him, much less who wrote about him, could ignore it. These traits did not always make for flawless politics or predictable behaviour (that is what we have now), but it did make him exceptional: the brilliance when it showed came as much from this temperament as it did from his political nous or his grasp of policy, and if ever there is a Keating legend it will come from the same sources. Not the political animal, the economic rationalist or the technocrat, but the contours and eruptions of his mind, his ego (his "I") set him apart. All the others I could admire or learn from, but the last defined him, and, right or wrong, it defines him in this book.

If in *Recollections* there is too much of my "I" and not enough of his, if the grand vision lacks definition, if I am too personal or too critical or wrong, there is always the autobiographical option. Whitlam, Hawke and Howard have done it. So recently did Malcolm Fraser. And last year Blanche d'Alpuget added to Bob Hawke's own take on his government her second biography of him. It is hard to say which is greater: the service such books do to the reputation of their subjects, or the degree of offence they give to their former colleagues. It's possible that in the broader sweep of things – broader, say, than sales in the first year – they do little of consequence in either category. The exercise cannot be other than self-serving to some degree, and transparently so. Yet, if anyone could transcend this obvious shortcoming it is Keating. Two large-scale biographical works, two or three smaller ones, David Love's *Unfinished Business*, a hit musical – the coverage of his life and career has been, as they say in finance, non-trivial; and yet who would wonder if he thought it a bit slapdash, ambiguous, incomplete? I hope the one *he* writes is as big as *War and Peace* and at the end he is able to say what Tolstoy said when he finished: that his book "is what the author wished, and was able to express in the form in which it is expressed".

Blanche d'Alpuget told me that there are people in the Labor Party who believe my book was an act of "treachery". She did not say if it was two or two hundred people but, whatever their number, in almost a decade only Paul Keating has said the same to me. I have no doubt he expected a different kind of book and because, very near the publication date, someone who knows him as well as I once did urged me not to show him the manuscript, saying it would never be my book or the book it should be if I did, I know Paul felt I had deliberately deceived him. Though I wish he did not think this, I remain grateful for the mutual friend's advice.

Yet it has been painful to live with his accusation. If he feels betrayed, I have to concede the possibility that I betrayed him. In that case, I can only hope that one day he will realise the betrayal had nothing to do with spite or neglect of his feelings, but with reasons concerning the business of writing that are no less compelling to a writer than reasons arising from politics are to a politician. It was not for want of admiration or loyalty or gratitude that I did not write a book that pleased him.

It comes down to the fact that everyone who sets out to write history must be free to decide how he will do it. It can't be any other way.

I regret only a few things more deeply than Paul Keating's belief that he was betrayed by this book, but if I had written it according to his lights rather than mine, from any angle other than mine, I would have betrayed myself; and, for want of a more clinical term, history – the bit I saw at least – would have been betrayed as well.

Afterword, *Recollections of a Bleeding Heart*, 2011

John Howard's guilty secret

LATE IN 1992, KOREAN, CHINESE and Filipino women, and an Australian of Dutch birth, assembled in Tokyo to tell Japanese political leaders of detestable treatment they endured as "comfort women" for Japanese officers in World War II. The Australian woman was reported as saying afterwards that she did not hate the Japanese or want revenge, but she wanted them to admit the truth. She said she wanted reconciliation.

We can presume John Howard would be on the women's side in this. So why does he behave like the leaders of Japan?

The prime minister appears to see himself as a kind of Canute dutifully keeping the tide of white guilt at bay. Talk about hubris. The notion of cross-generational guilt to which he declares himself doggedly opposed runs in the very roots of his own culture. In the Old Testament it is because the sins of the fathers will be visited on the children that we are advised against wrongdoing. In Shakespeare the evil that men do lives after them. It has been a given from the Greeks to Freud. But Howard reckons he can hold it off.

Some commentators insist he is sincere in his belief that there can be no such thing as "cross-generational guilt". We may conclude from his recent visits to Gallipoli and the battlefields of France that he is no less sincere in believing there is such a thing as cross-generational pride. And cross-generational memory and mourning, which is why we say "lest we forget" on Anzac Day. And he would no doubt concede that from such feelings spring concepts like faith and duty and noble actions to go with them. But not from guilt apparently – though from guilt might come, say, restitution, understanding, reconciliation. Not for certain, but one would think it was worth a try.

It is hard to see why Howard admits some cross-generational emotions and not others. Let us assume he is, as his supporters say, sincere in this and sticking to his guns. Some of humanity's worst crimes have been committed out of sincere belief and in the name of sticking to one's guns – Goebbels's speeches are models of the kind. Howard is not disposed to commit crimes against humanity, but sincerely believing something and sticking to one's guns is proof against nothing, including meanness and stupidity.

And that is the point – Howard is not stupid. Sincere and dogged he may be, but that is no reason to imagine he is not also calculating. Indeed the big thing to know about John Howard is that he is one smart fellow – which is why when he tells us he won't be a party to "cross-generational guilt", of itself a dumb idea, we can assume he is being clever.

As clever as he was when he kicked the republic into touch. As calculating as he was when he gave a wink and a nod to the sentiments that coagulated around One Nation. As smart as he tried to be when he did the same thing with anti-Asian sentiment in the late '80s. These last two were much more than nods in the direction of prejudice. They were bait for otherwise fair-minded voters with more pressing matters on their minds than these.

They were also bait for his political opponents. If ever they accuse him of condoning prejudice, he will be on the airwaves in a trice and sounding highly principled and angry – which makes the bait more tempting because he's raised it to higher ground.

It hasn't all been easy for Howard. He almost certainly underestimated Aboriginal leaders who, as members of the previous government could have told him, are just as smart and hard-nosed as he is. The man he put in charge of ATSIC turned on him. The governor-general has opposed him, and now the Australian of the Year is frustrated. Even a few brave members of his own party stood up to him briefly.

This resistance has forced a few strategic adjustments and a change in his tone, but the unspoken objective is unchanged. He won't sink reconciliation, but he'll run it aground. And if he can't run it aground, he'll knock the rudder off it and make it sail in circles until he drains the lake – he won't kill reconciliation, but he'll deny it what it needs to live.

He will use every means available to him, including the most powerful, which is public opinion. He will use the people against it. To make a mean argument sound like a democratic one, he will call some people "mainstream" and others elites; and he will say he's doing the will of the "mainstream" as if he's just doing his democratic duty.

Howard was playing to public opinion when he refused to take a stand against mandatory sentencing. He was attempting to manipulate public opinion with the claim that not enough Aboriginal children were stolen to constitute a generation, and when he traduced historians of the racial frontier in Australia as members of a "black armband" school who worked in a "guilt industry". Like the one about cross-generational guilt, these are dumb arguments in every sense except Howard's political ones.

He employs the same tactic with the idea of a treaty. He says it will be "divisive", which is plain silly on the face of it, except it's a fair guess that Howard is wondering if it might not be the answer to his prayers about reconciliation. Of course a treaty will be divisive, because one way or another – including the now familiar way of refusing to lead – Howard will see to it. He has already begun. He has laid the bait for Kim Beazley.

Howard says he now wants to get on to the practical side of reconciliation – things such as health, employment and education. His predecessor said the same thing the first time he addressed the reconciliation council. But Paul Keating, like nearly everybody else, recognised that addressing the matters of land and history were minimum preconditions for addressing the practical side of things in ways that might, at long last, work.

There will never be practical solutions where there is no basis of justice or trust. It is possible that Howard cannot understand this, but it is not likely.

The real giveaway is not the word "sorry" but the concept of "guilt". As much as he talks about it, it is not guilt that Howard is being asked to acknowledge.

It is truth. He calls it "guilt" because he can't say he will not acknowledge the truth. Of course he acknowledges that evil things happened in the past, but every other word and gesture is calculated to leave the significance, if not the actuality, of these events contestable. "But good things happened as well", he says, as if anyone ever said they didn't. It's effective, but it's also puerile. It diminishes the country.

The Age, 2 June 2000

Julia Gillard and political leadership in Australia

IT IS NOW ALL BUT universally agreed that the Australian Labor Party is a near ruin, ruled body and soul by factional bosses and opinion pollsters. To the public the party presents the spectacle of governance either by faceless men, or by men with unappealing faces. These bosses decide Labor's leaders, Labor's candidates, Labor's policies and Labor's tactics. Finding they are mere spectators with no more influence on the direction of policy than unaligned Australian voters, unaligned is what hordes of party members have chosen to become.

As the bosses' grip grows tighter, the membership declines and branches fold. Recently, the stalwart senator John Faulkner used the word "anaemia" to describe his party's present condition. Leaping to his side, Kevin Rudd, who was deposed in a factional putsch last year, declared the factions were a "cancer". The former New South Wales Labor minister Rod Cavalier said they were "killing" the party and that, in much of Australia, Labor was "stone-cold dead". The factional leaders deny all this, of course, but why are voters flocking elsewhere? Why, even when the party is standing for something (such as a mining tax or a carbon tax), is it perceived as standing for nothing, or for less than the Greens or GetUp! stand for, or as unlikely to stand for it any longer than is politically expedient? Why was their last campaign derisory in almost every detail? Why does Bob Brown feel able to say the Greens will soon be the major party of reform?

It is possible, however, to agree with Faulkner's judgement and with the broad sweep of media opinion since he came forth with it, and yet suspect that, while this is not the wrong tree, there is another one to bark up. The other one is that uncommon combination of sound and imaginative policy with articulate politicians of character, which, along with a lot of baloney, tends to go under the heading of "leadership". Indeed, for all its legends of grassroots organisation and democratic trailblazing, the party's history is no less a story of leaders strong enough to drag a creaking and complaining Labor movement with them. In the modern era, think of Whitlam, Hawke and Keating: albeit with interventions, they led by force of personality and big ideas, and the factions either made themselves useful and followed willingly or were dragged along by the undertow. More recently, until the awful inner child took hold of him, they followed Kevin Rudd.

The point can be made by watching Julia Gillard in two television appearances: a Monday night ABC interview with Chris Uhlmann, which she managed expertly, and an address to the nation the day before, which was feckless and embarrassing. In the interview she was assured, unhesitating, in command of the policy detail and alert to the political traps. There were the sharply ordered intelligence and the equal instincts for advantage and danger of a serious political animal. But in her address she hinged her usual pedantry to confected inflections and a wildly veering tone: one moment defiant, the next didactic, the next ingratiating. It was like watching a bad method actor. No meaning could survive such a performance.

To be fair, Gillard is not the first prime minister to struggle in the first twelve months of office, and she has had more against her than any of the others. Less well known than Hawke, Keating, Howard and even Rudd were when they ascended, she has also had to contend with the facts of a hung parliament and being a woman in the role. Every day has been a struggle for legitimacy. All this, plus a hostile tabloid press and radio, and an outrageously unprincipled and unchecked opponent; her most bitter enemies have to concede she wants for nothing in resilience and steel.

Of course she has made some of her own problems and given the public reason to doubt her honesty. But there never was a successful politician who did not have avowals to live down and embarrassments to hide. Politics is a game played with two sticks of equal length – principle and pragmatism – and successful politicians are those who wield them well in combination: so well, in some outstanding cases, that folk give up trying to tell one from the other and roll over. What the German sociologist Max Weber called "charismatic authority" is partly made of this. And it's what Julia Gillard so far lacks in spades. The problem is not a want of sincerity or conviction, but any means of exercising or displaying them.

Now, it might be that the Labor Party is beyond salvation by any leader. And just as possible that politics itself is too far gone to produce a leader capable of testing the proposition. To borrow something else from Weber, while passionate conviction and shrewd pragmatism are characteristics of great political leaders, what really distinguishes them is their detachment – not their proximity to the electorate but their distance from it. The natural posture for a politician has always been "chief among equals". But modern media does not allow this. Now it is at best "equal among equals" and commonly last or least among them. Listen to talkback, watch Q&A, tune into the internet and ask where the power and respect lies. Who lays strongest claim to the record, the knowledge and the authority, charismatic or otherwise? Not the leaders. Most of what used to be theirs is shared between the host and the audience, for whom pretty well any opinion is as good as another. The politicians scramble for the residue.

Every day they do what they used only to do in election campaigns. There is Tony Abbott, aspiring prime minister, in a hard hat or gauze one, staring down a mine, fiddling with a tractor, filleting a fish. The people are sovereign, he says. To hell with the sovereignty of scientific facts: popular opinion will determine if the earth is warming and what to do about it – just as it determined the answer to polio and the movement of the planets. There was Prime Minister Rudd, tin-eared and ineffably graceless but a mind to be reckoned with – where else should we see him every day but surrounded by babies or hospital patients? And there is Julia Gillard, prime minister of the Commonwealth, daily risking her dignity in the nation's malls and school grounds, confessing her insecurities at the National Press Club, bringing herself close to tears as she asks to be understood, surrendering to the maw of magazine culture and afternoon television, and taking the office with her. The Oprahisation of Australian politics is now pretty well complete.

No generation of Labor leaders has been so devoted to opinion polls as this one, yet it is doubtful if any has been more inept at moving opinion when it needed to. Perhaps the organisation is too rancid to attract, or (*vide* Lindsay Tanner) retain, the talent from which leaders might be drawn. It could just as well be that such leaders as it has, though capable negotiators and effective scrappers, are victims of dodgy political fashions that in time will fade.

The other possibility is that the wretchedness of Gillard signifies a more general upheaval in the social and political setting. The clichés, the tortured and oppressive cadences are habits of the language she was raised in. Demotic it may be, but this language carries only the shallowest meaning. The phrases are not to inform or inspire the audience but merely to echo it and satisfy its narcissism. The spin the public loathes is made expressly for them.

So it is with contemporary politics: not enough formal culture remains to support a well-made argument over a fallacy, or a speech over a slogan. The art is lost for want of belief in it. Which might be why, when called on to make the case for something as bold, complex and remote from immediate gratification as a carbon tax, an old codger such as John Hewson makes the case with twice the force of anyone in the Labor government.

The Monthly, August 2011

In praise of Tony Windsor

The Hon. Tony Windsor
Member for New England
Tamworth

Dear Mr Windsor,

I can find no elegant way of saying this, so I will use plain terms: I have a kind of crush on you. Don't worry, I'm not after a date or anything. I won't be stalking you round the hills of New England. It's more the sort of crush I had on James Stewart after I saw *The Man Who Shot Liberty Valance*, or Yves Montand whenever he played a resistance fighter. It's a political kind of crush.

I know when it started, to the day. I was at a cattle sale up your way – not to buy or sell, only to look. You and Rob Oakeshott had just signed up with Julia Gillard, and many of the men in moleskins would have thrown you in the river and held you under with their cattle prods. The bulls were all Angus and all black; the buyers were all farmers and all in R.M. Williams – boots, trousers, shirts and hats. I believe some of their socks and underwear were R.M.W. Bulls being bulls, they were all snorting and pawing the ground like Barnaby Joyce, but compared to the farmers they were cool reason itself.

I might have it wrong, but one way or another I thought you were telling the electors of New England that they should get that creaking, maudlin, passive-aggressive bush romance out of their heads and start bringing to politics the same sort of acumen that got them into crop rotation and no-till farming. Much as Labor gave up the socialisation objective and calling each other "Comrade", you wanted them to give up their habitual allegiance to the major conservative parties and feeling hard done by all the time. As Labor found that there were all sorts of creative combinations to be forged while managing a capitalist economy, a less reflexive and herd-like approach in rural politics might not only produce material rewards for farming enterprise and effort, it might also see those fine rural values we hear so much about actually get a foothold in the nation itself. Your constituents looked at a hung parliament with a Labor prime minister and could see only misery. But you, sir, saw opportunity.

Shocking as it was to do a deal with the Labor devil, your deeper offence was to break ranks with the herd. The best way to turn intelligent human beings into dumb animals is to fire up the herd instinct. It works in war and football, and it works in politics. The union (including the farmers union) makes us strong, but it can also make us forget our capacity for rational thought. The same goes for mateship, in some ways the dopiest union of all. You committed heresy, and for that you got what Socrates got – poison: "vitriol" you called it at your last press conference. Your wife was given it, too, you said. It turns out that a lot of bushies – as they call themselves nowadays – are just as consumed by a sense of their own virtue as everybody else. All they want is a fair go and someone to blame.

And think what they have to blame you for! All those millions for hospitals, roads and universities; all that investment in the national broadband network, climate research, clean energy, agriculture; all the concrete expression of regional policy that usually receives only lip service. Has anyone done more to bring the regions into the national story and the national future? It was unbearable for them! Then there's the Murray–Darling Basin Plan you did much to modify and bring about: it seems to come down fairly solidly on the side of farmers.

Now you're gone, the natural National Party order will be restored in New England, if any order built around a cultivated hysteric like Barnaby Joyce can be called natural. But New England is the smaller element in the loss the country suffered when you decided to leave after the final spill. With hacked limbs and Labor blood all over the stage, it was like the last scene in *Julius Caesar*; but bad as it was to lose Gillard and Greg Combet and some of the others, losing you felt worse.

A good bloke lost as collateral damage, people are saying. If that is all we can make of it, we will only deepen the folly. You could be the dead-set best bloke in history and be no loss at all. What matters is that you were a good politician: good enough to be the measure of what's missing in modern politics.

I mean the qualities that the media no longer much values or, in its more extreme and youthful forms, even recognises, and which the major parties only sometimes reward. Not "the vision thing" – though I suspect you have one – but the dependable, intelligent, worldly, unbreakable *character* thing, on which democratic politics and our faith in it depend. This is more than "good blokeism" – or "good sheilaism". It is having good judgement, including the judgement of others' character. It means hearing and representing the people, but neither aping them nor manipulating them; nor being only for them, whatever the broader interest; nor telling them only what they want to hear, or only the messages that your spin doctors reckon they must hear to the exclusion of both the demands of intellect and the refinements of civilised discourse.

You reminded us that a good politician is more than the confection of a good media manager. You had force without it. In fact you showed us that a lot of what passes for media management is really something got up for the satisfaction of media managers. Julia Gillard had a media manager, and no doubt a very able and up-to-date one, but I'm sure there were days, if not whole weeks, when it would have made no difference if she had employed a billy goat or the auctioneer at the cattle sale.

Every time I heard you in the media, I found myself in a remarkable state of listening. Not wincing or groaning or cursing, or desperately seeking some less enervating experience. You made the others look and sound like early-model robots. Speech is humanity's "connective tissue", as your fellow New Englander, the historian Alan Atkinson, once explained. By heeding this simple fact about language, you also heeded a simple one about democracy and public life: that insofar as they depend on knowledge, trust and engagement, they depend on language. You spoke as good politicians used to: as if your brain was working at the same time as your voice and governing what you said. You sounded thoughtful, considered and frank. You sounded *interesting*.

A year or so after the Walgett Bull Sale, in the midst of the uproar over the Murray–Darling Basin Plan, I went to a meeting of farmers just outside Mildura. The hats were smaller, but the mood was much the same. Some of them were ropeable, and I imagine it was for good reason, but none of them was ropeable enough for the man who is going to replace you in New England. There was Joyce, screeching like a galah going home at dusk. It is "the whole aim of practical politics", H.L. Mencken said, to frighten people with imaginary hobgoblins and make them "clamorous to be led to safety". He was on the money, as usual. Yet word has it that a lot of New Englanders have come around, and you would have beaten Joyce at the next election. There is the saddest thing: not only will a base politician replace a good one, but the lesson you taught by your example, that democracies need not be governed by hobgoblinry, is much less likely to be learned.

Might you not change your mind?

Yours in faint hope,
Don Watson

The Monthly, August 2013

Tony Abbott:
My fellow Australians

AT THIS TIME OF THE YEAR, my sleep is a cavalcade of dreams. Too much family stirs the mental pot. One thing leads to another and the next minute Tony Abbott appears, sitting backwards on a bicycle and wearing an Australia Day T-shirt, a proxy for some oppressive childhood memory no doubt. He goes at a good clip along an avenue of gums and shadows, pedalling round corners without so much as a rearward glance, and still managing to talk. "I have a resting heart rate of thirty beats per minute. To put that in perspective, a resting crocodile's is twenty-eight. Malcolm Turnbull's is seventy-six on a good day. Even John Howard never clocked less than seventy."

He is winding up a steep hill now, through a forest, standing on the pedals – don't ask me how.

"The more regularly one drives up the pulse, the more it falls at rest. With brutal exercise I have recorded rates that are the human equivalent of an Etruscan shrew.

"To rip through the rind of comfortable existence and enter the lowest deep of pain is my pleasure. I am an endorphin addict. It is how I know myself. Without exercise – at a dinner, for instance, or reading a briefing paper – I struggle to remain convinced that I am not hibernating like a python in a cave.

"Only when I exercise do I feel truly alive; yet the more I exercise, the less alive I feel when I am not. It is the paradox of my existence."

At that point he shoots down a fire track, and I wake and dictate all this into my smartphone. Once asleep again, I find him in a forest clearing, standing bow-legged on an old-growth tree stump and spouting to a gathering of lyrebirds. With his blue swimmers visible beneath a tattered toga, he might be the prophet Isaiah, but for some reason Thomas the Tank Engine also comes to mind.

"My fellow Australians," he says. "Today we celebrate Australia's remarkable progress from convict settlement to the great nation in which we live today. Surely no people on the planet have more reason to be joyous.

"How magnificent we are! What a future lies before us! What a past behind! We must remain true to our Judaeo-Christian values, and steadfast and fearless as the Anzacs. Great challenges lie ahead – the Budget challenge, the education challenge, the national broadband challenge, the arrival of Their Royal Highnesses the Duke and Duchess of Cambridge and Prince George in April.

"Let us now resolve to pay any price, bear any burden, meet any hardship, to make sure we can't think of anything else while they are here.

"By all accounts Prince William is a keen adventurer like myself, and I have already invited him to join me in an ironman contest and to go a few rounds in the ring. I urge you to flock and fawn and hang your flags up and down the land. Buy the souvenirs and mags. Leave them in no doubt that the sun will never set on your affection; that you would rather die than live without them.

"The future king and queen will have scarcely left our shores when we begin the centenary of the outbreak of World War I. And, as if that were not enough excitement for one year, nine months later we have the centenary of the landing at Gallipoli. What else can one say but 'Yippee'?"

The lyrebirds oblige. The forest resounds with their mimicry. And he goes on.

"Of course it goes without saying that these last two are solemn events. We should not commemorate historical episodes that saw the deaths of millions with the unbridled gaiety we bring to Australia Day, which – putting aside the destruction of an ancient civilisation and a legacy of rank injustice, suffering and despair – commemorates an event that caused the deaths of comparatively few. A couple of hundred thousand perhaps, if you count the disease and alcohol and so on, over several generations. Maybe half a million – tops.

"That is a good many more than the sixty thousand Australians killed in World War I. I know. I can count. But what are we supposed to do – get out the black armbands again, and bow our heads and fill our hearts with awe and sorrow every 26 January? Not on your Nellie. That's what we do on Anzac Day.

"Yes, there is a downside to our history. In much of life there is a downside. It comes with the upside. You can see that in the example of my heart rate. Difficult things happen sometimes. Besides, many of the deaths were not deliberately inflicted: the worst we could say of most of them is that they were careless; incidental, as it were, to the colonial and national projects on which the furtherance of our Judaeo-Christian values depend. Most of them were no one's fault, really. And frankly, some of them were their own fault, partly, frankly. And unlike the Anzacs, they were defending no one's freedom or values, or the Australian way of life – unless you count their own. It's chalk and cheese – well, chalk anyway."

At this point, silence descends on the gully. All birdsong stops. The leaves of the trees cease to rustle in the high breezes.

"It's all relative, you see. It's all a matter of context. It ain't necessarily so, and all that. What's important is not truth so much as …"

And here he hesitates, and a preternatural and nightmarish grin takes possession of his face. His eyes roll back and beads of sweat bubble on his brow. When at last the grin has gone, he exhales and mutters, "Sorry, just stretching my glutes". And he continues:

"There is no need to go into the micro details of history. The important thing is not to politicise these commemorations. Under my government, Christopher Pyne – a bravura example of Western civilisation and Judaeo-Christian Anzac values if ever there was one – will put a stop to the rewriting of history by postmodern, multicultural, left-wing relativists. We will decide what we know of history, and the circumstances in which we know it. We will make an end of it."

The Sydney Morning Herald, 25 January 2014

The mystery of
Malcolm Turnbull

"All joy wants eternity", Nietzsche said, speaking of woe and eternal recurrence. And, "we all get carried out in the end", Paul Keating said, speaking of prime ministers. Politics affords joy to a very few and extinction to everyone. The few, longing for eternity as they do, are generally the least prepared for death and suffer grievously when it comes.

How could we not love politics? A little different each time, but the same heartache and revenge over and over.

Sometime back in the 1990s, when Bronwyn Bishop was cantering around the country in an improbable and alarming effort to lead the Liberal Party, I recall someone (not Bob Ellis, I think it was Malcolm Turnbull) saying there was once a time when, among Liberal lawyers, only a silk could entertain such an aspiration. But now, so far had the party fallen, in his view, any old solicitor could bestride the thing. And of course, it came to pass, though not in the person of Ms Bishop. This was about the time when, by many reports, Malcolm Turnbull was seriously thinking of hitching his old Volvo to the Labor Party.

Well, it took its time, but the rightful order has been at last restored. He might have come via Goldman Sachs (in this financial age, an all but obligatory detour for the smartest cookies), but a silk is back in charge. (Well, he would have been one if Kerry Packer hadn't called.) And the joy is so palpable at the Lodge that the whole country seems a bit in love – even if he's the proverbial daffodil on a dunghill. Even if the once great silken party is now so torn by factions that the new leader has to tell them they don't exist and then weather their guffaws. Even if he will soon have Barnaby Joyce filling in for him whenever he goes abroad or takes a holiday. Even if he's obliged to deny his own beliefs and make the case for reactionary causes against which he has defined himself and devoted part of his life to overthrowing, and must appease the authors of them. Even if he has inherited the rubble of his predecessor, and even if he knows that he will be stalked forever by the Revenant, grim and rictus, himself his own dungeon, keeping his wound green and feeding his thirst for retribution.

Not to rain prematurely on his joyous parade, but might we wonder if the spectre of eternal return does not haunt the prime minister. Does he find himself thinking that, like the sailor from whom he takes his second name, he, Malcolm Bligh Turnbull, is the only man on whom he can depend? In bed at night, or in a cabinet meeting, might it not creep into his mind that William Bligh woke one day to find that he was commander not of a ship but of a drifting lifeboat, and thereafter could not contemplate his companions without a sense of insult creeping in his veins or look away if he wanted to avoid being sconed with an oar?

William Bligh had no choice, of course: just row and row. And then see revenge exacted on the mutineers, and then suffer mutiny again, and see revenge again. Unrelenting and unalterable, at every turn Mr Bligh was never anyone but himself. But Mr Turnbull, having just realised the deepest yearnings of the self, seems not to be himself at all.

Think of it. Under the *Border Force Act 2015*, up to two years' jail for speaking out against abuses on Nauru and Manus Island; under the new ASIO laws, up to ten years' jail for reporting on special intelligence operations, even botched ones, ever; under the same national security laws, virtually unrestricted surveillance of computer data; under the re-instated Australian Building and Construction Commission, denials of basic civil liberties. Wouldn't the barrister of *Spycatcher* days have torn it all to pieces? Meanwhile, the believer in science and an emissions trading scheme is joined with the non-believers and the vested interests in denial; the man who believes in "agility" and "innovation", "brilliant young men and women" and the "frontiers of change" watches a new CEO take a hatchet to CSIRO climate science, and apes the example of his predecessor on education policy and lets Gonski languish. The republican of the '90s is joined with the monarchists; the believer in same-sex marriage leads those who loathe the idea, and is tied by them to a crazy plebiscite; the ideological bedfellow of Barack Obama and Hillary Clinton is in bed with the mob who bedded down with George W. Bush and are disposed to line up with his mad-dog Republican successors. The man who defended Gillian Triggs when Tony Abbott mugged her now defends the rigid (and repellent) policy she opposes.

Of course, compromise sits equally with ambition and belief at the heart of politics. But it is almost impossible to believe that Malcolm Bligh Turnbull wants to go down as nothing more than a great compromiser or, worse, as a prime minister who puddled around in the politics and dodged the real tests of power – the ones that turn the country in the direction that on principle you think it ought to take. Interviewed by Barrie Cassidy in early February, he poured us another warm bath. It was like watching Bob Hawke in the prime of his contentment, fangs withdrawn and brimming with the spirit of Westminster collegiality and consultation. There was the policy on the one hand and the politics on the other, and you had to do the policy first and then the politics, the prime minister said. You'd swear he understood the Mysteries, that all we needed was some of his reason and optimism and we'd have unicorns again.

Not that anyone should think the approach can't yield decisive results. The PM told Cassidy that he had pretty well ruled out increasing the GST on policy grounds without even getting to the politics, which we can be fairly sure would have ruled it out if policy considerations hadn't. That's a result, to be sure – especially for the leader of the Opposition and the federal treasurer, who had to return to base just when they were getting airborne. By contrast, a land tax, the PM said, would pass the policy test but fail the politics, so that could be ruled out too.

The essential difference between Hawke and the Turnbull we are presently watching is that, for all his reconciliations with business, the Great Reconciliator never let us think he was anything but Labor: a pragmatic and reformed kind of Labor in which a concern for the workers and a concern for the profit share were one and indivisible, but Labor just the same. If you could not always see his fangs, you could sense them. John Howard managed much the same effect, but like Hawke his roots were in older times.

By comparison, Malcolm Turnbull, in so many ways a perfect fit for the modern cosmos, is in danger of sounding deracinated. Of contemporary politics, Carmen Lawrence wrote recently, "We're invited to take part in an elaborate game, one in which the players face off as deadly opponents when they are, in reality, largely indistinguishable". The less there is to distinguish the players, the more deeply they feel a need to affect profound differences. Abbott went so far with this the electorate reckoned he was loopy. Turnbull distinguished himself in more measured terms. "This will be a thoroughly Liberal government", he said on the night he took the prize. *The Guardian* spelled it "liberal", a mistake but also a measure of the hope his election brought to liberals as well as Liberals. It's possible he meant to blur the distinction, to satisfy not only the baying reactionaries in the Coalition but also a political centre desperate for calm and light.

"It will be a thoroughly Liberal government, committed to freedom, the individual and the market", he said, as if the old refrain still serves a distinguishing purpose that a commitment to universal happiness or rhinoceroses does not. Would any among a couple of million unaffiliated and undecided voters have been less happy if he'd said he was committed to a fair go for all? If he had stepped from a different meeting to say that he would be leading a thoroughly *Labor* government, committed to freedom, the individual and the market, would they have noticed an anomaly?

Which makes the hypothetical question irresistible: does he sometimes ask himself, what if, all those years ago, he had chosen Labor, or Labor him? After, say, a death struggle with Kevin Rudd to replace Kim Beazley in 2006? Or after Simon Crean in 2003? Or more recently: called up to lead Labor from the backbenches to which, Churchill-like, he had retreated after Abbott brought him down? Would he be more at home now?

Just think: Labor gets Neoliberal Man, a brilliant advocate, proven in modern business and technology, and the chap most likely to draw its way all those "knowledge workers" the unions failed to charm. Of course, he has to put up with the CFMEU and a few other rough outfits, but he doesn't have the National Party braying from the stalls. He has a party room a persuasive liberal reformer can carry in the main: he'll carry it on climate, on the republic, on education, Indigenous recognition, same-sex marriage – win an election and he could carry it on pretty well anything, and bright young things will be joining up to follow him into the future. He makes the Labor Party the social democratic party it must one day become, and, surfing on the swell, like Alfred Deakin in the first years of the Commonwealth, leads Australia to the spirited, open (and, yes, innovative) social democracy of Labor's late twentieth-century dream.

He gets carried out to be sure, but in a coffin inscribed "Malcolm Bligh Turnbull: Labor hero and maker of twenty-first-century Australia". Eternity after all.

In barren times we can be forgiven our little fantasies. The question is, which fantasy? The fantasy of the Saviour that might have been? Or the fantasy of the Saviour that never was? We should know by Christmas.

The Monthly, March 2016

Leaders and dung beetles

*My brother thinks he's a chicken — we'd try to talk him out of it,
but we need the eggs.*

—Groucho Marx

IN 1982 JOHN CAIN LED the Labor Party to the Victorian government benches for the first time in a generation. The state branch, a long-running fiasco, took the first steps towards becoming something like Victoria's natural party of government. Victoria re-emerged as the nation's most progressive state, and Melbourne became a much buzzier organism – not New York, but open, spirited and alive. If Melbourne is now regularly judged the world's "most liveable" city, and political conservatives think Victoria is Australia's Massachusetts, much of the credit must go to John Cain.

As the obituaries since his death in December have uniformly declared, Cain was a man of stern integrity and self-restraint. In the era of the long lunch, the premier occasionally took time off to eat a pie in the Fitzroy Gardens café. On aeroplanes, he walked through the business class rows of federal public servants and corporate honchos relishing their newly deregulated environment, to his seat in economy at the back. When a Brisbane hotel receptionist told him he and his wife Nancye were in the executive suite, he demanded a downgrade. "We'll have the same kind of room as him", he said, indicating me.

These were the days when some Labor leaders were in love with money and the newly moneyed. Cain could not hide his distaste. He kept his distance from the spivs, banned professional lobbyists, and declared that so long as he was premier there would be no casinos to play host to criminals and clean up the proceeds of crime, and no poker machines either.

As if moral principles were incompatible with laughter, portraits of Cain almost always ignore his sense of humour – he did fund the first Melbourne Comedy Festival – and understate the fillip he gave the good life. Had Jeff Kennett decriminalised prostitution and transformed Melbourne by reforming the licensing and retail trading laws, it would have been put down to his neoliberal philosophy. Cain did it because it was sound economics and enlarged society. He abolished offensive social barriers to women less because they offended feminist opinion and more because sporting clubs excluding half the population from the public land they occupied outraged democratic standards.

In a similar vein, Cain's insistence on strictly separating private interest from public duty (puzzling as that idea now seems), and his loathing for all forms of sleaze (also puzzling), should not be allowed to obscure the other principles he exercised as premier: his stress on policy development; his effort to create an independent and answerable public service; his openness to ideas; his sturdy belief in Labor's duty to the commons and the people.

He won three elections for Labor; then, undermined by duck-shovers and deadbeats, incompetents, cowboys and people besotted with power, sectional interest and the dogmas of economic rationalism, he resigned. Most of the worst blows he suffered were meted out, directly or indirectly, by members of his own party. And within three weeks of his resignation it was his own party that opened the way for a casino.

In the three decades after he resigned, John Cain all but vanished from the public mind. People old enough to remember his craggy face and signature overcoat might have recognised him when the tennis was on at Melbourne Park, the precinct for which he was pre-eminently responsible, or around the State Library that he nurtured and defended, or at the University of Melbourne, where he was a visiting fellow and critic of its corporate philosophy.

He was a man of the people, but no populist. He never sought the spotlight, never became a media blowhard, never a regular at meritocratic gatherings with all those AO epicorms of the bunyip aristocracy sprouting from their lapels. He was never in the honours lists – when they were offered he turned them down.

Even in his own day, some thought Cain's rigorous observance of propriety a little quaint. Now it would be an object of wonder. Where would the government hide Angus Taylor or George Christensen? Barnaby Joyce? Where would they hide the Nationals – as a bloc? Or the politicians and their advisers who step unblushingly from their ministerial office to the fossil-fuel corporations, arms manufacturers, media organisations and other outfits to whom, as our elected representatives, they granted government contracts or other favours? Or dozens of party donors, staffers, MPs and failed candidates appointed to $400,000-a-year positions on the Administrative Appeals Tribunal? Or the minister and her advisers who dispersed $100 million in sports grants to marginal electorates, and sizeable chunks of it to such necessitous outfits as Perth's Applecross Tennis Club and the Royal Adelaide Golf Club? And then there's Crown Casino. Our polity would be unrecognisable. Where would the prime minister hide the former coal industry executives presently residing in his office, the coal industry donors to his party, the coal industry connections in his ministry?

For that matter, imagine if even a few of John Cain's principles had prevailed against the ideological juggernaut that cast him as a Keynesian relic. Maybe a more sceptical view of markets, a more selective approach to selling public enterprises, might have caused us to shy at the corporate state. We might have seen less government money being shovelled the way of crooked education and healthcare providers; less water being sold for no decent purpose; fewer politicians being bought; more communities intact. More policy – including climate policy – less marketing.

The belated tributes after he died were heartening testimony to Cain's character and accomplishments. Yet to be reminded of his sterling qualities was also to be reminded of our curious inability to elect people like him.

Consider our last three prime ministers – last four, if you're inclined, but it's hardly fair. Alone or collectively, for devotion to public service, courageous leadership, strenuous commitment to good policy and measurable achievement, how do they compare to Cain?

Tony Abbott was a real trick of a PM, but who can remember a single useful thing he did, any profit the country got for electing him to the job? The second of the trio, manically dogged by the first, never overcame either his reactionary opponents or the impression that he loved his high office too much to risk it in a decisive battle with the enemy. And now, before we have time to decide if that judgement is fair, or to weigh the consequences for the country, he's back on *Q&A*, bobbing along in the same stream of consciousness, blithely singing of himself and lesser mortals, beguiling some, maybe, but leaving others trying to mortar his narrative to what they can recall – and wondering if their minds are going. He was the prime minister for a while, wasn't he? Yes, of course, after whatshisname, the weirdo on the bike.

And now there's Morrison from marketing: plodding in the ashes, searching for words or gestures to show, despite Hawaii, that he understands. But he's an adman: the purpose of his professional existence has never been to find meaning or confront it, but to invent it. The meaning of a grieving woman and weary firefighter declining to take his proffered hand, for instance. He takes their hands anyway, not to hold and comfort them, but to compel them to comfort *him*. He turns his back and looks for a more likely customer. That's the trouble with these disaster scenarios: even the most rudimentary market segmentation goes out the window. No sociographics. If a bloke's got no idea what kind of customer he's targeting, what's he meant to say?

He says he understands his absence has caused us some "anxiety". Not offence, bafflement or antipathy – anxiety. On social media he releases a select résumé of his government's good works in the form of a Liberal Party advertisement set to a musical pulse, a jingle. And he tells the Australian cricket team that when they're out there batting and bowling they're doing something that's like fighting fires, or the firefighters are doing something that's like batting and bowling, or, whatever, the two activities are related.

> Whether they're started by lightning storms or whatever the cause may be, our firefighters and all of those have come behind them to support them, whether they're volunteering on the front line or behind the scenes in a great volunteer effort, it is something that will happen against the backdrop of this test match.

If no other good comes out of the emergency, in future there will be no excuse for thinking marketing is some kind of science.

At some point in any interview with the prime minister one is liable to be reminded of a dung beetle: he starts with nothing much at all and by unstoppable single-minded exertion he pushes it through every interrogative thicket and every hurdle of logic and evidence until he's created a ball of bullshit several times his own size. Forget what he's said at other times, what stunts he's pulled, ignore the fudges, ask not where consistency, truth and substance lie: he will drown out his doubters in a storm of platitudes and shameless demotic saws. What he says may be off the point, beside the point or have no point at all, but sooner or later it *becomes* the point.

Some of us recall the PM expressing his concern that Greta Thunberg's warnings about climate change might unnecessarily alarm and depress young people. The young, he said, are entitled to imagine a happier future. Just how he reconciled this admirable concern with his church's belief in the (very fiery) End Times that await all creatures young and old, he never explained. But no matter. Despite so many indications to the contrary, he says he has never denied the reality of climate change and its effects, including the effects on the past several months of bushfires, in the course of which, we may presume, many young people found it impossible not to imagine an alarming and depressing future.

Yet it turns out the government has been busily reducing emissions from the get-go, even back when Abbott was running the show, and when Scott Morrison went into parliament with a lump of coal. The European Union is dedicating a quarter of its budget to tackling climate change. BlackRock, the world's biggest funds manager, is getting out of thermal coal. The Bank for International Settlements is telling the RBA that central banks might have to be "climate rescuers of last resort" and "buy a large set of carbon-intensive assets". For his part, our prime minister will allow our emissions reduction targets to "evolve". That's the plan. That and improving our "resilience and adaptation". What's more, in a sort of customer-care commitment, he's sworn to "keep us safe". All, of course, "without a carbon tax, without putting up electricity prices and without shutting down traditional industries upon which regional Australians depend for their very livelihood".

Now, we might not see in his strategy an answer to the threat our planet faces. But we're not in marketing, he is.

And whatever the record may show, he had a perfectly amiable conversation with the lady in Cobargo. And that was not *thermal* coal he took into the House. It was non-thermal. That's if it was coal at all, and not just a rock one of his advisers painted.

Loyal customers that we are, why wouldn't we believe him?

The Monthly, February 2020

AUSTRALIAN
TRADITIONS

Once a jolly lifestyle

EARLY IN THE NEW YEAR I entered a hairdressing salon in the main street of the Victorian Wimmera town of Horsham (not "Hers and Sirs" but the one next to it, if ever you're looking). At 9.30 in the morning the place was empty, and in no time the hairdresser was fluffing the hair around my ears in the familiar way of her profession, and I was about to say, in the familiar way of the country, "Hot, isn't it, but I suppose we should expect it at this time of the year". But before I could begin she said, "So, how's your day been so far?"

There was a time – a very long time – when country people rarely asked more of another human being than how he or she was going. In this same time there was often a whiff of damp hay, dogs or sweat about country schoolrooms, churches and picture theatres. Country people – this was before they were called rural and regional Australians – were the living embodiments of their work and environment, somehow even of their faith. They were as seals are to rocks and owls to the night, the elemental Australians.

Media celebrity has had some say in revising the ideal from, say, a sheep shearer to a crocodile wrestler. But a much more general and probably unstoppable change is underway too. The country, you see, is going forwards, which is to say it has joined up with the rest of the economy, the rest of the economy has joined up with the global economy, and when that happens "So, how's your day been so far?" becomes pretty well mandatory. It is the standard greeting of all customer-focused businesses, worldwide, and the world now includes the Wimmera. For hairdressers it is doubtless as much part of their training as scissor technique. As I left this hair-care centre of excellence I thanked her.

"Not a problem," she replied, "have a nice day".

Cruise control and empty roads create a state of mindlessness that is perfect for getting round Australia. Think of a Fred Williams or Arthur Streeton if you will – or in the Wimmera, Sidney Nolan – but the pleasure is in not thinking. Thinking is a form of resistance. Let the emptiness swallow you alive. Time and the miles will simply fly by.

Yet enough remains in the Australian countryside to occasionally disturb the driver's trance. A glimpse of a house in ruins can do it; a tank toppled off its stand, an overgrown domestic fence or fowl yard can provoke the subversive thought that something once happened here. What we see now was once something else. Children slept beneath that collapsed roof, were conceived beneath it, climbed in the shattered cypress.

You know it is the quaking of your own childhood that the house in ruins provokes, and the empty schools and halls remind you of the thin, brief shadow your own life throws. A glimpse of rusted iron and flaking weatherboard can hollow you out for half an hour. Or it can set you thinking of the ping-pong that was played inside that hall, the dances, weddings, meetings, baby shows, the young men gathering to enlist for wars. You can suddenly find your mind in full-blown worship of these ancestors: the prodigious work they did and their children never thanked them for; the faith no longer comprehended; the lives lived with no certainty of reward or sense of entitlement.

Those old halls with the broken pine trees round them speak for vanished communities and their secular spirit in the same way that the abandoned churches stand for an age when people, though they rarely got excited about it, practised religion in the hope of salvation and, if not that, for the good it did their souls, its restraining force and the pure energy it mined. Along with work, cooperation and religion were the eternal verities and the conditions of success. Those public buildings might now be forlorn monuments to these beliefs, but for the people who built them they were also the reward, the proof of their devotions.

It was natural for pioneer communities to erect the essential markers of civilisation's progress, and the pioneering went on long after those inveterate builders, the Victorians, had departed. The Great War demanded monuments and every second hamlet got one. They will last as long as the civilisation, unmistakable evidence of a strange, Homeric event and the myth it engendered. We should genuflect twice every time we pass one; the first time for the dead and the second for the builders who imagined something permanent, secular and noble.

The Great War also demanded postwar settlement schemes, which created new communities, and wherever they survived up went public buildings. The halls, libraries and mechanics institutes, post offices, churches, banks, butter factories, grandstands, rail stations, wheat silos and war memorials – just about everything that is substantial in form and meaning – were built before World War II. And apart from swimming pools just about everything built after it is gimcrack and suburban.

Put the difference down to the spirit of an imperial, pioneering age when stone, bricks, skill and labour were much cheaper. Wherever the need occurs and funds allow, no doubt public buildings still get built. But it is rare to see a modern one of imposing substance or of deeper meaning than a shopping mall, perhaps with a McDonald's in the middle puffing the fumes of frying oil into the air. The absence of substance or any sign of an aesthetic also exemplifies an age – our own, the one ruled by market ideology and private taste. Market ideology deplores public investment. It rearranges the cosmos on postmodern lines. Those old banks, courthouses, post offices and churches now do for hairdressers, beauty salons, pancake parlours, estate agents (known in some places as "lifestyle merchants") and people exercising various lifestyle options. No one can miss the irony, and nor should we miss the fact beneath it – that the first language of the postmodern is accounting.

There are no less than eighteen hairdressers in Horsham (population thirteen thousand), and in January local ABC radio reported that the shire intended to teach them drought counselling. They have "a one-on-one relationship for half an hour to an hour and it's important that they know how to listen and respond", a shire spokeswoman said. It seems when your customers are going through a drought – or, one assumes, a flood, bushfire or locust plague – it is not enough to ask them how their day has been so far. It might seem curious that the man on the land must now have the spiritual as well as the physical comforts all farmers since Job have had to do without. But much more radical is the idea that people need to be trained before they can take a sympathetic interest in their neighbours. Soon there will be diplomas in it, diplomas of mateship, perhaps. The cost, of course, will have to go on the price of the haircut.

Hairdressers occupy the old Bank of New South Wales building in the once grand Murray River town of Echuca. They have adopted the familiar marketing strategy of keeping a blackboard on the street outside and every day writing on it a homily or maxim of their own invention, much as Cicero might have done had he been in retailing. The one I saw in January was perhaps a taste of what the counsel farmers can expect next time they go in for a tint. It said: "Never put limits on yourself. Just be free at all costs". It must be that the booze got to Henry Lawson before he could think of that.

This is the bush, the mighty bush; crucible of the nation's spirit, imagination and binding beliefs. The legends were born in these places. Mateship was born here, and Anzac was born of mateship they say. So were Carbine, Bradman, the Drover's Wife, John Curtin and Black Jack McEwen: all children of the bush and all chips off the country's block, because, as the legend says and our media and leaders would very often have us believe, it was from the bush that Australia's character and traditions came.

Some readers might remember a few of them: a collective rather than individualistic ethos; an aversion to boasters; an outlook more fatalistic than optimistic; laconic, sceptical in most things, practical, more inclined to admire physical than intellectual prowess and achievement. In all but the last of these traits our New World society was believed to be different to the American one. Readers might note as well that Australia's traditional "values" in no way resemble the values of what contemporary commentators and successful political parties call "values-based" politics, which is said to be the most suitable variety in the current social climate.

As far as it is possible to tell with such an abstract term, "values-based" politics is concerned with other abstractions such as religion, the proper role and entitlements of fathers, the entitlements of the unborn child, the entitlements of the born ones, lifelong entitlements and what are called lifestyle choices. In vain will our political leaders and their ideologues search the *Bulletin* school, the collected works of Paterson and Lawson, Weary Dunlop's memoirs, the school readers, Mary Grant Bruce or the words of "Waltzing Matilda" for any sign of such "values". Too bad, we might say if they got on with their "values-based" politics and left the ancestor worship to those who know they have them. But they won't, of course.

Despite all the evidence to the contrary, they'll pretend that mateship is alive and readily seen in the nation's juice bars, that it is more than a male thing, that it has something to do with what the media and politicians would have us believe is a unique determination to save our homes from bushfires, and that it has nothing whatever to do with trade unionism, the welfare state or any species of big government. They will make themselves and their words heirs to mateship, or any other traditional "value" they can convert to the narcissistic prism essential to marketing and personal enlightenment. Who can say for certain that the swagman's defiant leap into the billabong should not be understood as a lifestyle decision? A values-based decision? It is tempting to believe that they are wasting their time; that you cannot invent or reinvent tradition. But you can, of course. You just need to say the same things often enough, starting with the ones who don't know better and shutting up the ones who do.

That life in the country is sweeter and richer in choice than it used to be is not a reason for the rest of us to feel gloomy. Why should the gentle breezes of airheaded aspirationalism caress only the suburban dweller? May they all be cabled to the World Wide Web until, in the name of individualism, freedom and choice, the dream of sameness is made real. Not a problem. May they plant the nation's cereal crop while watching Foxtel in the air-conditioned cabins of their mobile power plants. But deliver us from the refrain about traditions. Spare us the sacrilege.

In Wentworth, at the junction of the Darling and the Murray, a little grey Ferguson tractor has been hoist high on a pole to memorialise the heroic little machines that in the 1950s saved the town from floods. When I first looked up at it, a kookaburra was sitting on the steering wheel. It's impossible not to like Wentworth, with its old jail, its tractor worship and its junkyard museum. By these small gestures a town says it is a town, a conscious culture, a place with a memory. And Wentworth seems to say it as it should be said in the bush, without taking itself too seriously.

You go down to the Wentworth Club for tea and eat your steak and chips and out the window, pink in the sunset, the Darling flows on its immortal course. A cormorant crouches on a dead branch and hangs its wings out to dry. Downstairs young couples are playing the machines and older ones are dancing evening three-steps nose to nose. It is Austral bliss. But on the big TV in the dining lounge *A Current Affair* is covering the tsunami. Ray Martin and his team are up there in devastated Aceh and Phuket and the message keeps coming at us: our Aussie generosity is awesome and unmatched; it's amazing how we Aussies pitch in when there's a crisis; it's the Aussie way, the Aussie spirit, and Aussie tradition akin to mateship and our long history of fighting affliction.

It can only be to make us feel good, as if we need to feel dividends from kindness. As if, unlike the people who lived in those crumbling houses by the roadsides, and the people who built those public halls, we can't do things or face things without this constant stroking, without reward. We need the warmth of mutual self-congratulation, to see ourselves in everything, to be wrapped in the story of our life's progress every day. We need to be customers, valued customers. So we always have an answer to that question — "How's your day been so far?"

The Monthly, May 2005

A toast to the postmodern republic

WHEN YOU WRITE SPEECHES FOR other people for a living, any audience is a good audience. I address walls and poultry: I stand on a wheelbarrow and give after-dinner speeches as the moon rises over the fowl yard.

I say, Eight and a half generations of you fowls I have known. I've seen the entire landscape change. The remnants of the forest struck by lightning and disappear. The rabbits go. I've seen Melbourne spread out to Cranbourne. I've known eight prime ministers – one of them personally – several wars and droughts, three recessions. The family has been here since the first two came in chains in 1790. I say to them – and imagine the tears running down their beaks like perspiration on the nose of a Baptist when he's telling a fib – I say to them, After all this, when you have seen the age of the fence posts, the ruins of farms which are after all as much ruins as the ruins of ancient Greece, and the human cost the same, surely this country has been through enough, seen enough conquest and dispossession, bushfire, drought and flood, triumph and tragedy, experiment and disaster, epidemic and recovery; surely it has been a sufficiently legitimate human response in the last two hundred years. Surely, I say to them, Australia can be a republic.

The chooks treat it as a diversion, of course. They get on with the main game. They are pragmatists. Why change it if it works, they reckon, and tilt their heads back and let the water run down their throats. They reckon it's not important. They're like *The New York Times* reporter who told me on Australia Day while we stood on the lawns at Admiralty House and watched the ferries on the harbour and George Dreyfus played the cursed theme from *Rush* – she said, But it's not important, is it?

I said, but I've been here for eight generations. They came in there – and I pointed – on a little stinking ship, and were at once packed off to Norfolk Island and flogged no doubt. All for stealing a hanky. The last overseas-born ancestor came here in 1870. When can I say it *is* important?

It's not as important as the foreign debt, she said.

It *is* the foreign debt, I said. It is the balance of payments. It is the trade-weighted index. It is everything.

Well, it's not everything, of course. But it is a lot more than a diversion. It is of immense psychological importance: as it helped restore the faith of the Labor Party in the last twelve months, I think it will revive our faith in Australia and in ourselves.

It is central to our competitiveness, to our posture and status abroad, especially in Asia. My interest in an Australian republic lapsed for a long time in the '80s; it was revived by the experience of three months in Japan. It was often very difficult to describe to students who one was or make a case for being taken seriously, without actually appearing to stand for something, and without a brand name, a corporate logo other than a stuffed koala and a Union Jack.

Already in the last twelve months the prime minister's avowal of the republic has raised the level of interest in Australia among Asian countries. I have no doubt it has raised the level of respect. I think in a very short time it will be seen to have raised the level of our *self*-respect. It certainly improves our prospects. When people said the republic will not create one new job, they were very likely wrong.

The republic can be an important agent of national cohesion and strength. It can play a defining role. It can be both the packaging and the contents. These are the obvious things to say – the things about how important a sense of identity is. How much it enlivens us and lifts our self-esteem when we have a sense of who we are and where we fit in the story. How much it helps to *have* a story. I imagine there is no one here who hasn't thought about these things; on the other hand, I imagine there are quite a few who have stood in the queue for hours at Heathrow while people from the United States, Europe and the Middle East are ushered through, and you wonder what advantages they have earned from Britain that we have not.

I mean, the fact is that sensible Brits have long wished that we'd clear out, and the longer we've hung around the house like an overgrown

adolescent the *more* they have wished it. Less like an adolescent than a dod-
dering old bachelor uncle – the Uncle Dick of the imperial family. And
they are right. The inability to leave a room when it is time to go is common to juveniles, dunderheads and ingratiating bores. The longer we hang
around curtseying and fawning and mimicking, the more justifiable will be
the contempt heaped upon us in *The Spectator*, *The Times* and the tabloids.

Getting there will be principally a contest against ourselves, against
our innate and healthy desire to deflate, and our less healthy one to
shoot down hope and belief. It will mean we will have to overcome our
huge reservoirs of envy. The envy between cities. Between town and
country. Between classes. We might have to put aside individual greed.
You see how *all* the deadly sins – with the possible exception of lust –
are anathema to the making of a republic.

So, to some extent, is one of our best qualities an obstacle: I mean
our pragmatism. Insofar as pragmatism rarely sees any sense in looking
beyond the next potential problem, or changing what apparently works,
it will hinder our efforts to create the republic. A republic needs vision,
after all.

And yet I think that pragmatism will also *help* – because it *always* helps
to have a grasp of reality. More than that, I suspect, pragmatism will substantially *define* the federal republic of Australia. The best way to explain
this might be if I attempt to creatively diverge.

It is an extraordinary privilege to work in an election campaign. You
see your country a bit like an impressionist painter might have seen it.
You see glimpses of life – and a few hours later you can't remember
where it was you saw it. It's a landscape of dots, with scarcely any connecting lines.

You stand in a club in northern New South Wales; this is territory Barry Humphries has not yet discovered. Whole Noddy lands of
self-funded retirees. God's great waiting room. Five hundred men and
women, fifty-five and above, playing bingo in the morning. Thirteen,
twenty-seven, one hundred and three, dog's leg on toast-bingo. Meat
platter. It is a life of daily prizes. Outside, the bowling greens. And a man
on a mechanical roller whizzing silently backwards and forwards. This is
the land where all men wear Bermuda socks and shorts – and the women
all seem to be bigger than the men.

And a man beside me says: I always say, look at it this way.

Here is our pragmatist.

This is the best country in the world, he says. And this is the best town in the country. And this is the best place in the town. So – arms extended, a schooner at the end of one – What have you got? he says. You've got the best spot on earth. You're standing on it. Right here – looking at the floor. And he tilts his head back and lets the beer run down his throat.

And the bingo caller is saying thirty-four, twenty-nine, one hundred and six, cabbage roll, bingo. Veggie hamper. And the bloke on the roller is going sideways, backwards, forwards. And there's not a soul in the district – perhaps one or two – who knows anything about the families whose names appear on the World War I roll of honour in the town hall. But at least it's there.

Or you find yourself in an RSL club in Adelaide or a hall in Whyalla, or a picnic in Perth, or a tent by an ethanol factory near Nowra. Or a pie shop. And you fly from one to the other, and you happen to look up from your stir-fried chilli new-fashioned pork, served with a West Australian chardonnay by the men and women of the RAAF, and out the window the sun is setting on Uluru and all you can say is, What a bloody great rock!

Sometime in the course of the last five weeks I got a taxi across the Sydney Harbour Bridge, and the driver was a Bangladeshi. He told me that he was happy. He'd been all over the world and Sydney, he'd decided, was the best place in the world to live. What he earned as a taxi driver kept five families alive in Bangladesh. And all the other Bangladeshi taxi drivers in Sydney did the same.

And from the window of the hotel you could look down on Circular Quay and watch Japanese tourists watching while white Australians played the didgeridoo and Aboriginal Australians danced where Henry Lawson used to sit and tell stories for the price of a beer.

And the last taxi driver out of Sydney on the day after the election was a Brazilian. He told me not to go to Brazil because the poverty would shock me. He was listening to a tape – of brilliant, mad Brazilian music which seemed to dart around in your hair – and I said, Who is playing this? And he said, Don Burrows.

Somewhere along the way I was told the story of the refugee who sailed into Melbourne at the end of the 1940s, and he saw our wharfies and he said he knew at once that he had found freedom because it was plain from their demeanour that nothing would get them to goosestep. Twenty years later, of course, he knew that nothing would get them to do a lot of other things.

And someone else – a Catholic priest – told me in a pub on the day of the election that he had been in Cambridge for eight months and he was just back, and Johnny Tapp was calling a race at Warwick Farm – and he said, God I love that sound. It's the Australian national anthem.

All these little episodes I offer as a means of saying that whatever shape the federal republic of Australia takes, there will be something unstructured, if not *deconstructed*, about it. I imagine it as aleatory, impressionistic, figurative, eclectic, bebop. I'm only just game enough to say it: it might be the first postmodern republic.

I mean a republic that exalts the nation less than the way of life. Whose principal value is tolerance rather than conformity, difference rather than uniformity. Whose outlook is unambiguously Australian, and yet is more worldly and international than republics like the United States or France or Germany or Ireland. With humanist and even some romantic traditions, but not schmalz, false sentiment and fascism.

I have this sense that the pragmatism and dogmatic gradualism which delayed the moment for so long might end up serving us brilliantly. That we're going to have the chance to be reborn out of the reach of those nineteenth- and twentieth-century tyrannies of all kinds – including, as it turns out, the market fetish and greed of the '80s.

It's silly: I know you're not meant to have these kinds of thoughts in Australia. But it's marvellous what a win does for your confidence.

There was an article on the election by Jamie Button in *Time* magazine the other day, in which he quoted another article in the US magazine *Harper's* last year. The writer in *Harper's* had said that the era of the great plans was over for now. The twentieth century, after all, was littered with their failures: Gallipoli, the Third Reich, the Soviet Union, Fightback, Fightback Mark II.

The American said the new politics would most likely be much more concerned with the everyday lives of people and it would be expressed in the rather banal language of kindness, unselfishness, care. This was a comfort after a year in which the Australian government, I think, was to some extent reconnected to popular sentiment, feeling and need.

I began by saying that surely we are old enough, grown-up enough, have been through enough, to create a federal republic of Australia. There are any number of other arguments for it. But let me finish with the matter of our age.

The great myth about Australia is that we are young. We're not. Not only is this the oldest continent and Aboriginal Australia the oldest society on earth, this white Australia, or multicultural Australia, or whatever you like to call it, is also old. It's as old as the cultures from which we all came; but why be so apologetic? A hundred year ago, Henry Lawson could say, "I am Australian – I know no other land". And still you will hear Australians say, But we're European. There is still this reluctance among so many Australians to take themselves on their own terms.

This seems to me both a symptom and a cause of our endemic elderliness. This need to identify with the parent culture, this desire to imitate it. And it's another way in which we're old: we've been clogged up since birth with elderliness. For generations we were governed by people – men mainly – who were culturally conditioned to age prematurely. They're still around; you can see it in the young Liberals. They're the sort of people whose principal ambition from the age of seven is to be like their fathers. And this mimicry of wisdom and maturity becomes their primary skill. And it's this, expressed through so many mediums including the political one, that has held us up for so long.

It didn't matter that a lot of us felt everything about our lives here and nothing about elsewhere. That the signs we read are Australian signs – I have this thing about fence posts. Lately, I can't see an old falling-down fence without dissolving in a soup of nostalgia. It is a sharp pain. It's the story they tell in one swift signal to the organs: of lives passed, effort and failure, success maybe. That's what I meant at the start: the perfect and entirely sufficient argument for a federal republic of Australia is that it tells the story of what we've been through. It validates our experience. But it's better than that, it validates what we are and what we are doing now.

An extraordinary opportunity exists for us now as we undertake the biggest economic changes in our history, as we learn to cope with the social problems they create, and as we reorient ourselves in the world: as we do these things, we still have the option, unlike every other country, to redefine ourselves. We still have the option of a new, inclusive nation of Australia. We still have this pragmatic, republican option.

The truth is, we were born old. The creation of a federal republic of Australia will be the moment at which we become young.

Speech given at Mietta's, Melbourne, April 1993

Rethinking the republic

ONE DAY IN THE EARLY 1990s a package was delivered to the prime minister's office where I was then working. It must have looked like an arts or cultural sort of package, because arts and cultural sorts of things fell into my unofficial portfolio. Inside it I found a tape recording of the song "I Am Australian" (aka "I Am, You Are, We Are, etc."), together with the lyrics and a letter urging Prime Minister Keating to promote the song somehow, perhaps even to "launch" it as the *national* song. Shameful as it may now seem, upon listening to the tape I decided not to bother the prime minister with it. His musical taste was broad enough to encompass Mahler and limbo dancing, but, it being part of an adviser's job to protect his employer from frivolous or distasteful requests, I composed a respectful note of thanks, and put the package and its contents in the filing cabinet. I also seem to recall saying to someone that we all should hope the thing never escaped like The Blob into the public arena.

How could I get it so wrong? How could a republican working for a republican prime minister, patriotic and in love with the land, an advocate of an open, inclusive, multicultural Australia, conscious of history and believing in reconciliation with Indigenous people, recoil from the musical expression of these sentiments? And how could someone in a job requiring cultural awareness fail to see that the song would swell millions of Australian hearts, and that, twenty-five years after he dumped it in his filing cabinet, he would be singing it with several hundred fellow republicans at a dinner for the cause in Melbourne's Royal Exhibition Building?

Well, to begin with, there was the word "Australian". The song's refrain seemed to demand abandoning the diphthong before the "n" and pronouncing two syllables, or at least one and a half, as "I am

Austrayl-ee-an" (or for those who think the "l" an affectation, "Austray-ya-an"). This prospect, though gruesome, was yet not enough to wish the whole project to oblivion.

The second thing was the solipsism: remember it was being proposed as a national *song*, not as an anthem. But unlike this new song, Australia's national (and in my view, irreplaceable) song is not about the singer, not directly. It's about someone else, a manic depressive or Camusian outsider under a coolibah tree, a near-mythical other in a near-mythical place. So too are "Jerusalem", "Scots Wha Hae", "Oh Shenandoah" and "Londonderry Air" about other people and other events. These songs come down to the listener on a mnemonic thread. They touch emotions latent in ancestral memory, rendering them timeless. Such patriotism as they inspire is subjective and random, expressed at a melancholy, often poetic remove.

By contrast the lyrics of the new song were instructional: impeccably multicultural, historically conscious and generous to all, but evocative mainly of a civics lesson or a business card. We are haunted by certain words and melodies, no matter how often we hear them. This song could *de*haunt an entire nation. Even had all the rest been lovely, it would still be cursed by the dumb self-regard in that refrain, "I am Australian". Imagine, an Australian lost in the jungles of Burma or a prison in Istanbul singing "I am, you are" and so on. It almost invites retribution.

The narrative was reasonable: we *are* many (well, a fair few) and we *are* one (well, several really, taking the states and territories into consideration), and with a little poetic licence we can allow that – one or many – Australians are descended from Bennelong and Ned Kelly and Uluru and the Drover's Wife and red dust and umpteen distant lands, and we may as well be proud of it. The song assures us that the whole national project, plus the sixty thousand years of Indigenous civilisation, perhaps even the several billion years before that, and the climate and soil and the propensity of the land to parch, flood and burn, through hard work, migration and epic phenomena had all come down to "I", "You" and "We". In the course of this banality, poetic licence must expire. And that's before "I", "You" and "We" become, in our mind's eye, The Seekers. And they, for all the prettiness of Judith Durham's soprano, come down to three blokes in suits and ties, or just one, a Liberal MP plucking a double bass.

So when we found ourselves obliged to stand by our chairs and sing that song last year, who knows if it was the patriot or churl who wanted to bellow "Down came a jumbuck"? But this was a night when everyone had to be singing from the same sheet, and the sheet said "I am, You are, We are Australi-an". It seems this will be the battle hymn of the republic, and all believers must at least mouth the words.

This republican hopes to die or at least go deaf before the song assumes that status, or worse, as some folk such as Jeff Kennett recommend, becomes the national *anthem*. This republican will never accept that it "actually embodies the soul of Australia", as Jeff believes. Just the same, the republican moment in Melbourne did demand a reassessment. This republican has been obliged to concede the possibility that he recoiled not only because the song reduced Australia to a suburban parody but also because it was excruciating evidence that *we*, and the great national project upon which we believed we had embarked, could be diluted into such thin gruel.

Bill Shorten and Peter FitzSimons spoke with eloquent conviction at that dinner. It was not their fault that some of us went home wondering if the cause was worth pursuing after all. But the song made us wonder if we knew what the cause *was*.

We know patriotism is at the bottom of it: how can we reconcile our proud egalitarian spirit with a hereditary monarch, with *any* hereditary monarch, much less one who lives in another country on the other side of the world? Yet the very first thing republicans should do is shun the idea that they are more patriotic, more egalitarian or more Australian than the monarchists. The notion is demonstrably false and a quicksand for the republican argument. Nationalism is a protean sentiment: remember the monarchist John Howard, choking on almost infantile pique as he handed out medals to a victorious English rugby team. That's the other problem with the patriotic component of the cause: because it so easily turns into jingoism and narrow-mindedness, patriotism is as much an enemy of the republic as a friend. A sense of humour might be more useful.

But where is the passion to come from? Republican movements have generally been an expression of the desire for freedom and justice. "Taxation without representation is tyranny" is an old take on this human urge. "That the world might finally be the place for all and not the private property of those who have the colour and filth of money" is a more recent one, from Mexico. Sadly, for a movement traditionally requiring romance and enfilading language if not machine guns and martyrs, in our quest Zapatista talk will have no more purchase than the insurgent pamphleteer of the American Revolution Tom Paine. We have no tyranny to oppose. "Democracy! Liberty! Justice!" – Get a life why don't you! As for the colour and filth of money, our prime minister, erstwhile republican and Goldman Sachs dealmaker, has the answer ready: it's just the "politics of envy". And with that he orders the drawbridge raised.

In truth, in a world filling with tyrants, Queen Elizabeth II and her descendants represent a sort of anti-tyranny. *They* would never speak of the politics of envy. Of whom are you fonder, the Queen or Peter Cosgrove? Own up – whose passing will touch you more? How to cast off an outfit so benign? When Elizabeth is gone, some republicans say, then we can strike. Bob Hawke was saying it twenty-five years ago, but still she totters to and fro. And when he finally ascends who is going to kneecap poor old Charles, that gentle democratic socialist and organic farmer? The first run at an Australian republic was made when the British monarchy was in the horrors and the US republic was aglow with the tech boom. Now the old Queen is a living legend, her grandsons are marrying into Hollywood, and their radiant wives, children and fiancées burnish the royal breastplate every day. British democracy might be in a hole and chewing its own tail, but not the British monarchy. Meanwhile the US republic has elected to the quasi-monarchical position of president a man who for decency and gravitas – and possibly for sanity – compares unfavourably with King George III. Is there a country on earth with more anomalies than the United States?

We are unfettered and in no sense tyrannised. Our successes, like our failures, are all our own. Our democracy works imperfectly well, and it is hard to see how any of its practical imperfections would be remedied by going republican. A head of state elected by popular vote might well make it less perfect and, by imbuing him or her with more authority, less of a democracy. First time round, Paul Keating argued that a republic would signal to the world, and especially the postcolonial Asia-Pacific, that Australia was altogether free of its colonial origins and engaged with the region on its own terms. We would be no one's deputy or vicar.

But a deputy was the very thing John Howard thought we should be, and a deputy he made us. These days it is not the trappings or condescension of the British Empire that compromise our independence, but the agenda of the American one. And that, we can be certain, an Australian republic will not change.

So it's the anomaly. "End the anomaly" is our catchcry. Midnight Oil can get to work on it. But the monarchy is not the only anomaly we live with, and having the Union Jack in the corner of our flag is not the only other one. Women are half of the population but occupy very few positions of power, including only thirteen of the seventy-six government seats. That's an anomaly. The Liberal Party is a conservative party with many powerful members who despise liberals, and those who don't despise them regularly act as if they do. That's a bit of an anomaly, isn't it? The Labor Party is more of a liberal party, but 50 per cent of the power in it is held by trade unions whose members comprise less than 15 per cent of the workforce: the party is equally a vehicle for people of public spirit and bold progressive ideas and people who are meretricious hacks and absolute rotters. It is enough to say of the National Party that a republic will not abolish it.

Every day, in all manner of ways, we profess love for this country and yet continue to wreak destruction upon it. Our leaders speak of innovation and the boundless opportunities of the new, and then, in obedience to the old, march into parliament wielding lumps of coal. We're democratic, but not sufficiently so to grant an advisory voice to Indigenous people, or independence to the public broadcaster, or to care much when we learn the prime minister gave $1.75 million of his own money to an election campaign his side won by a veritable whisker. (But that would be the politics of envy again.)

Like people and their transitional objects, countries stumble along and bring anomalies with them. Our professed belief in the "fair go for all" could be called anomalous on many counts, and would be all the more so if "meritocracy" became an official Australian value, enshrined in a preamble to the Constitution, as the republican Benjamin T. Jones recently recommended. That the monarchy is not a meritocracy doesn't make meritocracy a good idea. Give someone a promotion and a million-dollar salary on Monday and by Tuesday she'll believe in meritocracy – *that's* what makes it a good idea. Sixty years ago the philosopher Michael Young came up with the term as a pejorative. Among other things, he pointed out that, for all its egregious flaws, at least feudalism didn't tell the poor that personal inadequacy was the cause of their miserable condition. Meritocracy is the name our neoliberal lords of condescension go by. It is as much the antithesis of the fair go as a hereditary monarchy. At a time of dismal politicians and stupendous inequalities of wealth in the democracies, the masses might take some persuading that it should be a core national value. To insert it in the Constitution as something we "hold dear" would not only be an anomaly but also a gift for mischievous monarchists. Just imagine, they might say, if sixty-five years ago Britons had been asked to elect someone as their head of state, on merit. And after a top head-hunting firm had scoured the world and proposed, say, ten meritorious candidates for consideration, would they have appointed someone better than the woman who inherited the job?

Paul Keating's idea for an Australian republic was the grander for its modesty and minimalism. No trumpet blasts, no marching, no hands on hearts while the anthem played, no flag waving – unless it was a new flag, without the Union Jack and with the blue washed out a bit, more the colour of our skies. As the continuing link to the British monarchy was an accident of history, an Australian republic would come into existence as nothing more than a rational corrective act. It would be the candle on the top of the democracy, the light of the nation's conscious identity. Our republic would not come forth as others had, a new nation-state born in a necessarily violent act of anti-colonialism, but drift in as an end-of-history sort of republic, a postmodern republic.

But Keating's republic was much more than the desire to shunt the monarchy up a siding. Can there be anyone who has not heard it by now? It was inseparable from a grand and subtle vision of a country with a creative voice in the world and the region, uncompromised by old attachments or current alliances; of an open and tolerant multiculturalism; a modern, resilient economy alive to the unprecedented opportunities on offer in the region; an extended social democracy, aware of its flaws and with the will to repair them. Thus would Australia at last realise its potential and become the mistress of its destiny. This was a republic with a purpose, one essential to our broader ambitions.

Yet at its core lay something visceral: not causeless or stupid, nor beyond explanation, but out of the reach of intellect or consciousness and just as essential. For those of us close enough to feel it, there *was* a spark in common with Tom Paine. Minimalist it might have been, but attached to a grand strategic vision Keating's republic touched off the elusive longing for self-possession which Federation and the monarchy, that otherwise harmless barnacle on the body politic, offended. And for a moment politics took flight.

It crashed, of course. The Keating republic went awry. John Howard, another accident of history, saw to that — though he can't take all the credit. No doubt the next big republican push can learn from the mistakes of that campaign. But it would be a much greater mistake to untether the movement from other, greater national aspirations. The republic should be rooted in a broader quest, much of it articulated twenty-five years ago, much more waiting to find expression.

To do otherwise, to put all the effort into manoeuvring the republic through the affections and prejudices of the populace, risks ending up with either a monarchy or a republic that we don't want, and gaining nothing else on the way through, except perhaps a national song of self-approval, a hymn on the old theme of what we are, not what we could be.

The Monthly, April 2018

The joke after God

ANYONE WHO SAW LAST YEAR'S Sydney production of Jack Hibberd's great bucolic play *A Stretch of the Imagination* – and anyone who saw the box office figures – had to face a single sad fact. There is no longer an audience in Australia for rural humour. There is no longer an audience which can comprehend extended reference to the natural world, or a joke with a provenance extending beyond the city, the suburbs or the last twenty years. Rural humour in Australia is as good as dead. Lousy films and television with idiotic rural stereotypes have assisted in its demise, but this is by no means the main reason. Rural humour died with the decline of the natural elements in our lives. Its basis was the contest between humanity and the elements on the march to civilisation. It died at the conclusion of the march, along with God as we used to know Him.

Rural humour derives from the experience of impotence and incompetence in the face of the elements. It involves animals – we will call animals elements for the purposes of the argument and because, some readers will recall, it was God who created them on the fifth day. Rural humour concerns dogs of genius and great savagery, dogs in hats and boots, simple-minded dogs, dogs with dynamite, wild cows and bulls, mishaps in castration procedures, peculiarly clever sheep, possums in chimneys and tanks, wombats, bandicoots and kangaroos. It concerns roosters, including ventriloquial roosters, goannas and snakes. Snakes and dogs are without doubt the major animal actors in rural humour, although in Queensland, where much in life is inverted, crocodiles and cane toads play leading roles.

Birds, particularly the parrot family, the emu and lyrebird (a solitary bushland stand-up comic and mime), are brilliantly represented in the rural comic genre. Even vegetables play a part in areas where the topsoil is substantial enough to support them. I have heard a tale of an avalanche of pumpkins – the entire crop was lost and an old man's hip was broken, but great merriment was had at the time and for years afterwards. Similarly, potatoes have been a source of humour through good years and bad. Soft fruit and apples, having the capacity to fall, have served us well. There are few jokes about greens.

Animal jokes sometimes have an anthropomorphic gist, but more often they are based on the simple premise that there is something unnatural about a wild animal in a kitchen. Or a dead animal in a kitchen. Many jokes involve unsuccessful attempts to exterminate animals. Remember Dave (or was it Joe?) dressing up as a kangaroo and hopping off into the maize paddock with a butcher's knife. Of course you don't, and it is likely you have forgotten or never heard the hilarious tales of calamities in the pursuit of rabbits with guns, gas, poison, smoke and ferrets. It is very easy to forget the ferret – and the fox, and the hen and the duck. And mice, single and in plagues.

Another element in rural humour derives from counterposing poverty and gentility, or necessity and gentility. This is predominantly a Protestant form of humour I suspect. The stories concern parsons preaching on dung floors. They are about maintaining dignity when rats are scurrying audibly in the walls: dead cats or possums in the ceiling on the day of the Ladies Guild luncheon.

Finally in the pantheon, there are those intractable elements: a tree or stump, heat, cold, wind, rain, fog and gravity. The famous "Stop Laughing. This is serious!" cartoon is a city joke about gravity with a million rural antecedents. It is when you consider the elements that you realise how ludicrous the rural stereotypes of modern film and television are. For there is no national farmer. The traditions of a mountainous or hilly region will be quite different from those of the Mallee or Western Plains. Objects roll in hilly areas. There will therefore be jokes about runaway jinkers, logs, milk cans and pumpkins. In flat areas the difficulty is to make them roll. Low as opposed to high horizons, climate, land use and natural vegetation all alter both the rural type and the type of joke.

But the basic elements remain the same. You will find them in Lawson, Paterson (a master of the hill joke) and Rudd, and in George Wallace as well. Wallace performed to city folk for the most part, but he maintained the themes of rural humour. He danced brilliantly but, unlike his Hollywood counterparts, with his shirt hanging out and the cuffs of his trousers over his heels. Sure, many Hollywood performers did the same, but Wallace danced as if he wasn't sure that he should be and as if he expected something to go wrong. Gravity was his enemy. Just when he was beginning to look good he would fall down.

Defeat is the essence of Australian rural humour. It is nature mocking our intentions. Consider the kookaburra laughing at the selector with his axe or his wife going after blackfish for their tea. Rural humour is the solitary figure – or the entire family – wrestling with the stump in the front paddock. Or the storm which one night blew the lavatory clean off the new schoolteacher's wife. It is Providence – unknowable, irascible, capricious Providence. In the Australian bush God was a satirist.

In America, at least in Hollywood, He was too often an ingenuous creep. Hollywood was a huge lie, as we know. Party to the American creed of manifest destiny, it lied most spectacularly about Providence or fate. There is no humour in manifest destiny unless it is not fulfilled, unless it goes wrong. *San Francisco*, for instance, was a film about Providence, and the love of a spiv for a soprano and a priest. (This by the way is one of the worst features of films about Providence. They have ministers of religion in them. There is nothing less funny than a minister or priest attempting drollery.)

In Australia, *The Squatter's Daughter*, made in the 1930s to something suspiciously like a Hollywood formula, also had an element of Providence but was emphatically not funny. The 1930s films of the old Steele Rudd stories contained the same debilitating measure of Hollywood pap, which turned laconic pioneers into half-witted bumpkins with a redeeming vision of the future.

These films reinvoked nationalism of the worst kind. They laid to rest all the lessons of the Great War, which had gone some way to replacing the notion that Providence was on the side of nations with the much healthier and credible conception that it was indiscriminate and gratuitous. It is only the latter interpretation which allows for humour in the face of disaster. It is Providence according to people not priests. The point to be learned is that we need the Allwise Disposer but we should not trust Him. And the same with generals.

We need God for humour, for without Him we fall prey to scientific understandings of people, animals and elements. The scientific assessment of our daily lives is death to humour. Have you read anything funny in *Cleo*, in *Forum*, in Masters and Johnson or books on diet management? There is nothing amusing about human perfection.

The spectacle of American athletes praying before and after every contest is truly revolting, particularly as they invariably win. What we need is not an Australian team which prays, or any other team which prays: what we need is for the Americans to continue to pray, and while they are praying, we need a good bolt of lightning. Then we will see that God is the maker of all things, including jokes.

Now it is a fact that God makes no written reference to comedy in our lives. Many of His characters have brilliant lines which you would give your right arm to have thought up yourself. Jesus's ripostes were often masterful. Some of the Old Testament is suggestive of rural hilarity – "By much slothfulness the building decayeth, and by idleness of hands the roof droppeth through" – and there is no attempt to deny our capacity or right to cackle and sing – "A feast is made for laughter and wine maketh merry" – but no one in his right mind would argue that the Bible is funny.

The word "humour" does not appear in Brown's definitive and voluminous *A Dictionary of the Holy Bible*, published in the eighteenth century when the Word was exceedingly well-studied in some quarters of the British Isles. Where "humour" might have appeared we have instead "humble", which consists of having "low thoughts of ourselves, and a deep sense of our unworthiness and weakness, and our walking accordingly"; and "hunger", which of course is "an *earnest* desire after food" (my emphasis). Nor is there anything under "joke", "comedy" or "gag".

There are some these days – I suppose there have always been some – who argue that God created the *whole thing* as a joke. This is a fallacy. The truth is that God meant us to *learn* humour, to discover it as we discovered at various stages the motion of the planets, gravity, gold and sin. For God is the Great Revealer, isn't He? And He created the elements and frequently put them at odds with us. Did He not? And He created the animals. Of that there is no doubt. Look under "beast" in Brown's *A Dictionary of the Bible* and you will find a very long entry indeed: "a living creature, devoid of rational consciousness, appointed for the service of man, and to ornament the universe". See how the joke is buried away – "devoid of rational consciousness" yet "appointed for the service of man" – there is the nub of laughter through a thousand rural civilisations.

On either side of beast we will find further support for our thesis. Bears: "their skull is thin, but firm, and contains a considerable quantity of brain, whence perhaps they are so sagacious". And so fierce and unpredictable? And bees: David's armies are likened to bees, "how readily they followed the hiss, the call of Divine Providence". And beetles, and beeves and behemoths. In the 1840s a behemoth was used by a settler to clear scrub in Gippsland, Victoria. Predictably the local farmers leant on the fence and laughed.

Plainly there is a revealed correlation between the death of God and the dying of humour. It is not that God was funny. But His presence was essential to create His opposite – the world run imperfectly by men and women. The world in which irony consists of the elements, not people, mocking our good intentions.

There is no going back, by the way. Those hippy literati will not find a sense of humour hobby farming on the south coast. It's not something you can take on board with a house cow and a grant. It will take generations, a flood, a drought and possibly a Fall.

We need a revival. We need more evangelists on the road. I mean real evangelists and a real God: not those unctuous neophytes and suburban lay preachers with their nice God. We need fiery preachers with a fiery God. Man and God in hot competition. Only then can we be assured that one day something funny will happen to those honey-tongued hypocrites in the United States athletics team. It will be very unpleasant for them you can be sure. And the irony will be – the really funny part – they won't know what hit them.

Meanjin, Winter 1986

Judaeo-Christian mateship

FROM THE EXPERIENCE OF AUSTRALIAN men at war and otherwise in extremis, the creed of mateship took on a sacred quality that is not to be mocked or belittled. That is why prime ministers should not make idiotic claims for it. If you want to kill mateship, make it a cliché. If you want to subvert it, render it an article of the national faith where it can invite ridicule. If bringing it into contempt is your aim, utter it as a mantra as you go about doing the opposite of the few precious things it stands for.

The creed itself is not immutable, but elements of it are. To begin with, it's masculine. If we must have national values and mateship must be counted among them, it is a national value for men only.

But not all men. Most men in relatively normal circumstances will settle for friendship, with which humanity made do for many years before mateship. But the cult of mateship has its origins and its most eloquent expression in circumstances that were not normal: most famously, among soldiers at war and bushmen in the bush.

These were men without women: not "good women" at least, and where there were not even bad women (which is to say prostitutes and "gins") there was, as one nineteenth-century settler put it, "alas ... the sin for which God destroyed the doomed cities".

The idea that there is something homosexual about mateship is a familiar sacrilege that we need not entertain. But we do need to recognise that the meaning of the word "mateship" is plainest when it describes the attachments and the needs of men struggling in a common cause. In simple terms, while mateship might justly be applied to relations between shearers or miners during a strike or lockout, it is a corruption in a day spa. The second definitive element of mateship is collectivism. It is an ethos of mutual aid and support, and no more compatible with a creed of self-interest or what today is called aspirationalism than liberalism is with fascism.

This is why, despite the efforts of politicians, talkback hosts and other purveyors of popular fantasy, mateship is now all but obsolete. It is not suited to the times. The segregation of men and women and the divisions of class do not exist as they once did, and it is not in the nature of modern warfare to create the episodes that might give it a second wind. Trade unions that have some claim to be expressions of the creed are declining, and may well be snuffed out by a government that professes faith in mateship.

It also happens that we are less provincial. Exposure to the world likely makes us less inclined to believe that loyalty to friends is an exclusive Australian principle. Americans talk of sticking by their buddies, the English by their chums. Europeans have been familiar with the concept for some time now. It is not unknown among the people who live in Africa. Why, even our own Aborigines seem to have grasped the idea.

Mateship was born about the same time as Australia's racial laws, which, it is worth remembering, predated Germany's by forty or fifty years and outlived them by another twenty-five. It is not of itself xenophobic, but seems happy in that kind of company. This might be why the PM fancies its chances in the present environment. But what he encourages is less mateship than mateshipism. This requires little more than calling everyone "mate" and ascribing everything that's good and true to that "peculiarly Australian value of mateship". Anything more in a postmodern world is probably psychosis.

The prime minister's own education minister must have been aware of this when he decided that the second of his nine values for schoolchildren should be: "Seek to accomplish something worthy or admirable, try hard, pursue excellence". Brendan Nelson must know that to pursue this perfectly reasonable (some might say breathtakingly fatuous) ambition often requires that we ditch less inspired or dull-witted mates. Nor does mateship allow us freely to cast off mates who have no respect for the minister's other eight values, which include honesty, integrity and tolerance. It is no accident that the creed is often professed among both the criminal and political classes.

That's the other unchanging thing with mateship. Essential and ennobling as it has been in some dire moments of our history, in ordinary times it is a bulwark of mediocrity and slumming. Can this be why we hear so much about it from our prime minister?

Well, he can't go on forever. When Peter Costello is prime minister we can expect less mateship and more your Judaeo-Christian/Chicago School of Economics national values. Mind you, anyone who can put that package together can probably squeeze in mateship as well. Look out for a kind of trickle-down mateship.

And then there's the possibility that, consistent with his devotion to mateship, John Howard will outsmart his treasurer, who is not a mate of his, and engineer the elevation of his minister for foreign affairs, who is a great mate. Now there's a prospect: perhaps only when Alexander Downer is prime minister and telling us to practise mateship will we give it up forever.

The Age, 2 September 2005

Anzac Day

BROADCASTING FROM THE MCG ON Anzac Day a few years back, as the din that always follows the minute's silence and reveille died away, a football commentator remarked with great reverence upon the sacrifices made to defend "our lifestyle". Greater love hath no man than this, that he would lay down his lifestyle for his friends.

In a world as virtual as it is real, where choice seems almost infinite and valued above all things and gratification is never more than a few keystrokes away, the words "life" and "lifestyle" have become all but interchangeable. Lifestyle is life accented with dreams, aspirations and entitlements, life with multitudes of choices, life going forward – *enhanced* life. A minute's searching on the web reveals the extent of it: there are lifestyle condoms, lifestyle butchers, lifestyle shops, lifestyle properties and even lifestyle funerals. There is a lifestyle TV channel, a Lifestyle navy and an army lifestyle. The food and drink, clothing, health, sex, security and shelter that all previous generations considered the necessities of life are today necessities of life*style*.

In countries like our own it seems possible that, relative to lifestyle, life has less meaning than it used to. Life is for people accustomed to scarcity, risk and struggle – for losers, if you like; lifestyle is for those who live in apparent perennial abundance and are determined to have a slice of it.

In the midst of lifestyle we are, nonetheless, still in death. We love our fallen with unbending devotion. Bookshops devote whole stands to new books on Australians in the Great War and others since. Thousands of young Australians gather every year at Gallipoli to observe the Anzac rituals with the solemnity of an age much more dutiful than their own.

While some trek to the Dardanelles, thousands more attend Anzac Day services at home. Our leaders, who have never fired a shot or had one fired at them, fashion platitudes to suit the task of tying sacrifice and slaughter to a prescriptive set of contemporary Australian values. "We are fighting now for the same values the Anzacs fought for in 1915", John Howard said at the funeral of the last Gallipoli veteran, in 2002. These values he named as "courage, valour, mateship, decency ... a willingness as a nation to do the right thing, whatever the cost".

He may as well have emptied his old sock drawer on the cenotaph — but war always did encourage vapouring in non-combatants. To be sure, every good Australian soldier holds with courage, valour, mateship, decency and doing the right thing. But, had they been asked, good Turkish and German soldiers would have held with them too. Sitting in his trench in Belgium, Corporal Hitler would have held with them, along with all the good British, French, Russian and American soldiers fighting on our side. If the meaning of Anzac is to be found in these values, our legend has hardly an original feather to fly with.

In truth, the soldiers went to the Great War much as soldiers always have: for all manner of reasons, personal as well as patriotic. And, as always, as much as they fought *for* something, they fought *against* what they took the other to be. They were *for* Australia and the British race and the British Empire, and they were *against* Germany and the German race and German imperial ambitions. As Bill Gammage found in his classic study of their letters, *The Broken Years*, "By 1914 most young Australians had thoroughly learnt an adherence to war, race, and glory ..." They knew where their duty lay because they had been taught it, and they looked forward to getting the can-opener into the Turk and the Hun.

Forty years or so ago, Australians' relationship with Anzac was less assured. Whatever spirit had possessed the old soldiers on the battlefields of Gallipoli, Belgium and France, on Anzac Days it seemed to consist in roughly equal measure of sad reflection and even sadder jingoism; of men haunted by the experience of war and men bent on crushing any deviation from the nation's xenophobic norms. Anzac was a great day in the nation's life. It was also the day when tensions in the nation's (male) psyche bared themselves a little, and it was this that attracted the playwrights.

Now the original Anzacs are dead and the survivors of World War II are all in a mellower stage of life, this ambivalence has faded. The old soldiers have reached from the grave and regained their grip on the country. Schoolchildren learn flag-flying and "positive" Australian history. They are told what the modern military is told when it departs for foreign wars: that the values of the Anzacs are the eternal values of Australia (and its alliances), that we fight in Iraq and elsewhere against terror for these values and that to deviate from them is to be less than Australian.

Yet if we take seriously the many soldiers who have written memorably on war, values seem to have nothing to do with it. The seminal French historian Marc Bloch knew a lot about war and not only because he had made intensive studies of it. He led a platoon on the Western Front in World War I; aged fifty-three, he fought against the invading Germans in 1940; and until his capture, torture and execution by the Gestapo in 1944, he was a leader of the French Resistance. It is recorded that his last words were *"Vive la France!"* Yet in his memoir of the Great War, he wrote: "I believe that few soldiers, except the most noble or intelligent, think of their country while conducting themselves bravely; they are much more often guided by a sense of personal honour, which is very strong when it is reinforced by the group".

Bloch having been a short French-Jewish intellectual, the Australian World War I historian and Anzac auteur C.E.W. Bean might have thought of him much as he thought of the German-Jewish general Sir John Monash — which is to say, not much. But Bloch knew at least as much about war — and patriotism — as Bean, and Bean could have no argument with his conclusion. For in describing what makes his beloved *poilu*, the common man, an uncommonly brave soldier and a member of a brave battalion, and how one depends upon the other, Bloch may as well be describing Bean's Anzacs. It was for the honour of their battalions that those brave Australian (and other) soldiers often said they fought; it was to their battalions that they felt the deepest loyalty; and it was in the battalion, "our father and our mother of unforgettable years", that the legend took shape.

In his memoirs, the Civil War general and American president Ulysses S. Grant wrote in a vein similar to Bloch's. Grant did not believe the nation should celebrate the anniversaries of victory or mourn those of defeat. War was too complex a business, the behaviour of men too ambivalent and contradictory, and the reporting too unreliable to be reduced to anything that could be semaphored with a flag or a cliché. "Truthful history" was the best tribute a nation could pay: history that did "full credit to the courage, endurance and soldierly ability of the American citizen, no matter what section of the country he hailed from, or in what ranks he fought".

Grant's memoirs contain brilliant descriptions of battlefield strategy and, unlike Bean's, graphic accounts of men's heads and limbs being suddenly torn from their bodies. But in Grant you won't find any values beyond military values, unless you take his condemnation of those who whipped up the frenzy for war as a condemnation of their values. He fought in one war, the Mexican War, for a cause he despised, and in another, the Civil War, against a cause he thought "one of the worst for which a people ever fought". But Grant was the least sanctimonious of memoirists. He did not dwell on causes, good or bad, but on what the situation required. As much as he admired his own, he admired the Mexican and Rebel soldiers for the qualities that are admirable in *all* soldiers: for how well they fought, how well they faced death, what moral heights they rose to. From Homer on, all good writing about war shares this admiration and wonder: it is the outlook that allowed the expatriate Australian Frederic Manning to write in one of the very best novels to come out of World War I, *Her Privates We*, that the slaughter was "magnificent" – as a "moral effort".

There are many good reasons to be wary of military legends, especially those that have escaped the exploits from which they descend. They can be used, for instance, to propel a country into futile and destructive wars. They can do a lot to keep a population stupid, or encourage them to live in the belief that they possess unique values which are not in fact unique and which they do not in fact possess. They can create a collective consciousness bound by falsehood and even fantasy: such that new generations lose touch with the fact that people from other countries fought just as bravely and with equal effect and paid an equal price; or come to think, as John Howard appeared to, that the legend and truthful history are the same thing. In fact, any truthful history of the Anzacs would contain countless examples of men who went to war for reasons more mundane or self-interested than patriotic, along with ample evidence that they were notorious for killing prisoners and wounded enemy soldiers, for "ratting" the enemy and for "souveniring" from the enemy dead. As Gammage says – and Grandad's letters slyly reveal – "many of them" killed "brutally, savagely and unnecessarily". Great warriors frequently do.

No one would want the country to forget the wars or fail to honour those who died in them. No historian can think it possible that a war in which 60,000 of the 330,000 volunteers died and whose effects still wash down through families and communities *could* be forgotten, or begrudge Les Carlyon the hordes of readers his epic books attract. No one can read them and no one can stand on those battlefields and regret the fact of Anzac Day.

The feelings are no doubt sincere. The ceremonies continue to be moving, the rituals as rich in meaning as they were at the beginning. But what is being remembered on this day of remembrance? Anzac Day began as a day for the soldiers who returned to remember those who did not. This was a principle in keeping with what countless soldiers have written down the years: that only those who have been in battle can know what it is like, that the experience of war demands things of a human being that no other experience does and creates one who is different in certain ways. It creates bonds of a certain kind.

It is inevitable and no bad thing, necessarily, that Anzac Day has been taken up by people who don't have the soldiers' experience. But the day's been second-guessed. The more politicians and media commentators talk of the values of Anzac Day, traduce it for convenient contemporary instruction and daub themselves with the soldiers' moral courage, the more like a kitsch religion it becomes.

If we want to keep the pathos free of politics, the bravery unconfused with acts performed in a swimming pool or on a football field, the sacrifice *kept* sacred and not submerged in the narcissistic puddle of modern lifestyle, we need to take the Anzacs not for idealised images of ourselves, but for what they were. Which is to say, soldiers: colonial soldiers, educated to believe in the cause of the British Empire and trained to do their duty at any cost. They were not some preconscious version of us, and if they fought on behalf of our modern lifestyle or our national identity, it was only incidental. Study them and they will disappoint our vanity. Search for the heart of Anzac and we might not recognise it.

The American philosopher William James was a man of peace: not a pacifist but an opponent of the militarists who around the turn of the last century were as hyperactive in America as they were in Europe. By 1906 he had decided that the only way to win the argument with the war-mongers was to "enter more deeply" into their point of view. We should begin, he said, by conceding the military virtues: discipline, duty, honour, "intrepidity", "contempt of softness, surrender of private interest, obedience to command". "All the qualities of a man acquire dignity when he knows that the service of the collectivity that owns him needs him." This much of the militarists' point of view the anti-militarists should allow – and then they should propose, instead of war, its "moral equivalent".

This moral equivalent, in James's scheme, would be "a conscription of the whole youthful population, to form for a certain number of years a part of the army enlisted against *Nature*". The rich no less than the poor would be sent to the mines, factories, fields, the fishing fleets; to build roads and tunnels and skyscrapers; to wash clothes and dishes and windows. Thus "the injustice would tend to be evened out, and numerous other goods to the Commonwealth would follow". Youth – gilded and ungilded – would "get the childishness knocked out of them", without having life knocked out of them as well. They would be made better citizens, society would prosper – and militarists would no longer be able to say that only war can bring out the best in humanity. It was a fair point then and an even fairer one now, when American administrations fight their wars with poor economic conscripts and private armies while the middle classes get on with their lifestyles.

We might think about it too. If we must see the Anzacs as our saviours, the wellspring of our identity and soul, let us enter into a more honest relationship with them. We may as well turn Amish as try to lead the lives they led; nor can we go to any kind of war resembling the one they fought. But we could recreate the civilian militias in which, after 1910, they had been obliged to serve – everyone from the age of twelve to twenty-six. With a few modifications, we could do it again. Women and non-"British" residents must not be left out this time, and fifty is the new thirty, after all. So let's say every Australian between the ages of eighteen and forty-eight could be, for a time equal to the average tour in World War I, a civilian Anzac.

Let those who are suited to soldiering learn how to do it. Let those who are not engage in the moral equivalent, submitting to military rigour not in a war *against* Nature as James recommended, but *for* it. Let battalions of citizen soldiers answer the bugle calls of climate change and environmental degradation. They can fight erosion, salt and evaporation. Let rabbits, cane toads, water buffalo, mynah birds, carp and pigs be their enemy: arm them against every feral animal, and let them deal with the corpses. Send them to fight against blackberries and willows on the banks of the streams, the forests and gullies. Give them tanks, solar panels and recycling devices to install. Let them plant trees. By all these works they will be drawn closer to the land from which in legend the Anzacs came, the apotheosis of the bushman and the pioneer.

Formed into battalions and platoons, they can supplement the ranks of firefighters and other emergency services; they can be the coast-guard; they can supply essential human care to the aged, the infirm, the lonely, addicted and homeless. In remote Indigenous communities they can meet the chronic need for well-motivated administrators, builders, plumbers, mechanics, health workers and horticulturalists, replace criminally neglectful bureaucrats and parasitic contractors, and teach such basic skills to the inhabitants. Let the citizen militias do it; and in doing so learn from Indigenous Australians some of their knowledge of the place. They can volunteer for their service abroad, especially among the underdeveloped countries of our region, and do wonders for the dispossessed and our country's reputation.

The deeds of such a citizen militia might transform environments and bring hope to despairing communities. But if the Anzac myth holds good, the more radical effect will be on the people serving. They will pick up skills, gain experience of discipline, lose weight, and learn something of duty and what it means to sacrifice; the chances are that few of them will face death and have to give up their lives, but they will *all* have to give up their lifestyles.

For at least two years every maturing Australian will be separated from the supports or dysfunction of family and enter into a situation where the fortunes of birth, and privileges of wealth and school, will count for nothing. Children will be liberated from the ambitions their parents have for them, and parents from their needful children. They will be cut off from shopping. All other lifestyle addictions, including career résumés, will be abandoned. Every draftee will be obliged to trade at least a portion of his or her narcissistic self-possession for the interests of the group and the common moral effort. And all the while they will be coming to more nearly know what they mean when they say "Lest We Forget".

Legends are never like the people who believe them, of course, or for that matter the people who made them. But a people truly devoted to a legend will be willing to prove the truth of it in experience. We could put the proposition to the vote: "Are you in favour of the government, in the spirit of Anzac and its values, having the power to compel all men and women between the ages of eighteen and forty-eight to sacrifice their lifestyles and serve the Commonwealth for a period of not less than two years?"

It's an outrageous idea, of course, and no one should take it seriously. The cost alone is unthinkable. Then again, we might get a better return than we got on sixty thousand dead from a population of four million. (That's not counting the wounded, those who died young and those who were traumatised for the rest of their lives, with consequences passed on to their children.) And weird though it is to think in these times that the country needs regimenting, it might not be as weird as taking into the twenty-first century a legend of warrior mates with which the society has about as much in common as Kevin Rudd has with Dad Rudd and Brendan Nelson with the vice-admiral of the same surname.

The Monthly, May 2008

Meanjin's noble failure

IT WAS ALWAYS GOING TO be a formidable task: what with our notorious philistinism, our "crass materialism", our "suburban mentality", if
you like. And there was our endemic "cultural immaturity": we were not
yet, it was well known, a "full-blown civilisation". As relationships with
mothers nearly always are, ours with Britain was maddeningly ambiguous, for it was at once the infection and the prophylactic. The British
diminished and enlarged us; they were parasite and host. There seemed
to be no answer, no end: Singapore had failed to sever the connection,
and even Suez only seemed to make it stronger. Were we destined to be
never more than half a country?

Still, it had to be admitted that the British connection was a lot less
offensive than the damnable influence of the Yanks with their Comics,
and their Cowboys and Indians, and their Cold War. To defend ourselves
against this invasion what did we have? A bush legend and the ABC?
What good was a bush legend when everyone was living in the suburbs which were as if created in a conspiracy against the mind, against
memory – against culture? What good was a public broadcaster if the
government – the wrong government – interfered?

Menzies bought the lot, of course; he made a meal of suburbia, British
philistinism, American commercialism; served it up to Australians for
the best part of a generation; left them addicts of royalty and the punt.
Who would ever have believed in 1941 that twenty years on Australia
would be even more supine and less identifiably "Australian"?

First published as a review of *The Temperament of Generations: Fifty Years of Writing in
Meanjin*, edited by Jenny Lee, Philip Mead and Gerald Murnane.

Certainly not the people who gathered around the new critical quarterly *Meanjin*. There's another problem – "critical": it was very nearly impossible to be a critic without breaching that golden rule of a youthful culture – no pissing in your own backyard. Not that rules meant anything to people like Barry Humphries and all the rest who decamped to London: they went right on saying all those things which in Melbourne were kept to the privacy of the pub or the post.

It was enough to make a man cranky. Enough to make him feel he was surrounded by ingrates. And enough to make anyone think twice before saying that, for all the vipers in its natural environment, all the obstacles to its survival and growth, for all its great service to our intellectual life, *Meanjin* has a little to answer for: that on more than one significant issue it was wrongheaded, that its direction was sometimes askew, that it harrowed the same infertile ground for too long. Stirring and impressive as much in this collection is, we are left thinking, "Is that all?", and find ourselves comparing it unfavourably with, say, three issues of *The New York Review of Books*.

One thinks twice because *Meanjin* was always an imaginative undertaking, heroic in its way, and they have all been honourable men and women who served. None was more heroic, of course, than C.B. Christesen, and nothing in this review or any other could deny the magnitude of his contribution to Australian letters and Australian writers.* Criticism, especially criticism from within liberal ranks, is a bit like kicking an old pioneer in the main street. One shudders to think what might happen if, when they howled, "But *Meanjin's* not commercial!", "It's not *The New Yorker*", "It's not comparable!", we came straight out with it and asked why not? Why, after fifty years, is *Meanjin* unknown to all but a handful of Australians? Why is it so profoundly without influence in the cultural and political life of this country? Why has its best quality always been essentially archival? Why in the cultural life of Australia is *Meanjin* not so much a prime mover as a Wolseley? We're bound to ask these questions because, surely, after fifty years we can no longer

---

*   The same could just as well be said of the late poet and critic Dorothy Green, which makes her absence from *The Temperament of Generations* quite remarkable. There are some strange omissions by any standards, and none stranger, even after reading the editors' explanation, than *Meanjin's* coverage of the visual arts.

assume that the blame lies with the philistines.

Meanjin, after all, always sought a wide influence. Its editor and contributors not infrequently lamented the demise, ideologically speaking, of the old *Bulletin*, and it's not unreasonable to surmise that *Meanjin* by intention or otherwise might have filled the gap. Certainly, from the start it hitched one wheel of the wagon to the democratic literary star, and another of course to the political left. *Meanjin* wanted to be popular. While Jim Davidson may reach for his pop gun when he hears the word popular culture, as he says in an interview for this collection, he did once talk about a *Meanjin* tram; and those interviews he conducted were first conceived as a device for selling the magazine – as the *Playboy* Interview sells *Playboy* to people who find the other stuff too dull. None of the four editors was ever going to complain about selling too many copies of the journal. So what does it sell? How many people do read it? Two thousand?

Viewed in this harshly quantitative light something more than irony might be seen in a juxtaposition of C.B. Christesen's persistent and desperate pleas for money in the 1950s with Vance Palmer's condemnation of commercialism in his almost famous 1941 article, "Battle". *Meanjin* liberals – we'll call them all liberals for now – loathed money. Here's Palmer fulminating against the stuff:

> Even our towns … the main street cluttered with shops, the million dollar town hall, the droves of men and women intent on nothing but buying or selling, the suburban retreats of rich drapers! Very little to show the presence of a people with a common purpose or a rich sense of life.

Very little to show much understanding of people or economics either. First among the great Australian traditions *Meanjin* carried on was a form of puritanism: thou shalt not be a shopkeeper, thou shalt not read *The Phantom* or bet on the dogs, thou shalt not write funny stuff (with the exception of a Dal Stivens's short story about cricket not one joke appears in this volume), or about sex or psychoanalysis – there is nothing in this measure of the life of the mind in Australia to suggest that Freud and Jung had lived and died in the twentieth century.

It is not entirely facetious to say that *Meanjin* might have been better off all round if it had vigorously *cultivated* a few rich drapers: for it's possible all that government, university and other institutional funding circumscribed its thought and operations. That is not to say "interfered" in any profound way – it was not the cultural equivalent of American investment in Australia. It was more like British investment – as we imagined it at least – more disposed to benign atrophy and hardening of the arteries. It encouraged the view that "culture" was good for you, like eating your crusts.

No doubt it will be argued that the journal *had* to be a branch office of the University of Melbourne. It was probably inevitable, in any case, that the milieu from which it sprang would be predominantly and increasingly academic. That was the tendency in Australian scholarship and letters – which meant that there was a fair amount of desiccation on the one hand and at least an equal quota of silliness on the other. *Meanjin* did not have to directly reflect this for the consequences to be obvious. Happily enough, the editors had enough good sense not to allow the thing to become a vehicle for the more precious academicians of old Parkville or the dizzier Marxists of Clayton and Bundoora. But avoiding extremes of academic or political fashion by itself does not put you in the mainstream. And that is what is absent from *Meanjin*, the sense, at *any* time, that it was living in average contentment with the here and now of this society. Try as they might, the *Meanjin* constellation did not like the way things were or the way they were going. For they liked neither the middle class nor the marketplace, and tenured as they were, they had neither a wish nor a need to understand them.

Really, they should have paid a little more unprejudiced attention to those droves of townspeople buying and selling. They might have discovered that there was more pleasure there, and more of the elements of the good society than they ever imagined. It is among them, after all, that your Runyons and Galbraiths are found; and your sponsors, and, just imagine, your private joint venturers. Who knows, *Meanjin* might also have turned up a wider market there. And if they found none of these at all, at least they would have discovered the foundations and the fodder of the liberal democracy in which they said they believed.

But they didn't believe in capitalism. They were communists, many of them; and socialists of different hues, as well as what came to be known in the Liberal Era as small "l" liberals. They all had in common the belief that capitalism was necessarily selfish and exploitative, hostile to tradition and antithetical to culture. Possibly they were right to believe this; but by ascending to heights of sensibility above the pong of crass commercialism, the magazine was at birth cut off not only from many of the riches, but much of the reality, of Australian life. To quote a small but poignant example: in 1968, I am reliably informed, a story by Murray Bail only found its way onto the pages of *Meanjin* after all brand names had been excised.

From this Olympian eminence America was bound to look vulgar. *Meanjin's* interests have indeed "always been broadly cultural and political", as Judith Brett said in an editorial in 1984: yet rarely so broad as to encompass the United States – not at least in a way which betrayed any affection for the place, or anything it stood for, or anything it has done. A perusal of the *Meanjin Index* to 1965 reveals no more writing about or from America than the Soviet Union, and a large part of the American was criticism of McCarthyism. The first major article on the United States in *The Temperament of Generations* is an "exploration of the dark side of rock culture" by Craig McGregor in 1971. Sure enough, in it he concludes that what America (and the world) needed "right now" was a revolution.

Hindsight screams – could they have got it more wrong? Here was a liberal magazine seemingly more hostile to Disneyland than the Gulag. Bernard Smith's defence of *Meanjin* in 1960 on liberal intellectual grounds was justified: all such defences are. But so was Vincent Buckley right to say that on the face of it *Meanjin* was pro-communist. The "unarmed truth" of Nina Christesen's 1974 review of *The Gulag Archipelago* was available much earlier – even before Geoffrey Serle, as guest editor, condemned Soviet communism for the first time in *Meanjin's* pages in 1957.

But more disaster was to follow: just when the Old Left was getting over its folly, along came the New Left, a bigger folly with less excuse. When Christesen looked around to see what the younger generation was doing he got theories of alienation, exhortations to revolution, and, among the various articles of Marcusian and Althusserian faith, "More lies are told to this generation than to any previous", and "democratic capitalist society provides one of the most effective forms of domination yet devised". The new generation worked over the previous one, looking for sustenance and echoing the old concerns. Where Vance Palmer had inveighed against the mindlessness and mammon-worship of the suburbs, now Tim Rowse upbraided the likes of Hugh Stretton for failing to see through to the exploitation and struggle they disguised and the revolutionary socialism that was needed.

There is a temptation, particularly among we onetime Marxist academics, to treat it all with the wisdom of the historicist. The Cold War did make it difficult for a person of principle to change colours publicly. There did appear to be a golden seam of socialism flowing from the last century, and it did appear to be the ideal on which a truly Australian democracy could be built. How *could* it be sustained in the face of American mass culture? And how could a liberal magazine be truly liberal if it succumbed, or even appeared to succumb, to McCarthyism; particularly in view of the fact that a lot of the best literature and art was coming from communists and fellow travellers? By the 1970s Australian democracy *had* withered: we *were* supine, racist and xenophobic. It is not at all difficult to find a historical explanation for what the historically uninformed would surely consider anomalies – it never is, if you know how.

But we are talking about the appropriateness of responses, and *Meanjin*'s response invites the same judgement as anyone else's. Not only are we entitled to ask why not a single liberal was heard to speak against the Soviet Union in the pages of *Meanjin* until 1957, we've a right to suggest that it was an error which compromised the journal's integrity and relinquished the opportunity to advance liberal democratic thought and culture. With hindsight it would seem that in this essential regard *Meanjin* did not take its own brief seriously.

Had it done so, a few other things might have followed. For instance we might have found more than a cultural nightmare and a political monster in the United States. We might have found that not only was there something in American art, literature and film but in the American idea of freedom. American politics and American intellectual life simply had more to offer us than *Meanjin*'s pages would indicate. For a start, and most obviously, they offered us the 1776 answer to the British problem and with it, who knows, the cultural cringe. One need not actually believe in the potential for an Australian republic; the desideratum is enough to remove most of the paralysing postcolonial ambivalence. The same position firmly held also radically alters the perception, half truism and half untruth, of Australia as "culturally immature". So long as we remained attached to Britain we had to conceive of ourselves as a foundling, albeit an aggressive adolescent. Yet we were also old before our time:

a clone of the old country in the New World. Menzies made of the country a conundrum, a sort of ratbag Canada: it is hard to see in retrospect why *Meanjin* didn't make itself simply liberal democratic republican.

Perhaps it's best to simply blame the Communist Party. For it's true, as that uncommonly cheerful magazine editor Stephen Murray-Smith once said, that if you take them out of Australian history certain radical possibilities immediately present themselves. There is no split in the Labor movement. No Menzies era. No socialist realism. No waste of many of the best minds of two generations. No moving of the debate about what this country might be to the bizarre theatre of the Cold War. No *Quadrant* as we know it. Imagine – literature and art unsullied by the party line, and the parameters of politics no less than the limits of democracy. That, in retrospect, should have been the ground *Meanjin* made its own.

The same Stephen Murray-Smith was also given to saying occasionally that *Meanjin* editors should stop complaining about the lack of money, recognition and understanding they were accorded, and begin to see that there was a privilege and, if only they'd let it happen, a pleasure, attached to the position. It's not clear why some *Meanjin* editors, perfectly reasonable and amiable in any other sphere, grew so crusty and peevish when their hands gripped the joystick of the journal. It might have more to do with the vehicle than the driver: for, while it always looked like a lean and independent quarterly of influence, and no doubt encouraged the sensation in those who drove it that it *was* an influential independent quarterly, and might even be said to *be* one, it was more accurately a thing – half beauty-spot, half boil – on the bum of the University of Melbourne, signifying next to nothing in the broader body politic. It was attached to the centre yet it could not have been further from it.

"I'm hanged if you can wring the neck of an Idea", Clem Christesen said in 1955. Perhaps not, but there are more ways of killing a cat: it can become an *idée fixe*, or an institution, a thing – and it can also die of natural causes. An idea can become a grand illusion, which may be why Clem Christesen's story as conveyed here in his beseeching, ranting letters appears so pathetic; why he could say in a letter to Jim Cairns in 1973: "I'm not known. The journal is not known … it's time I retired before I begin to feel too bloody bitter". Perhaps it is also why his retirement was such a tortuous and bizarre affair.

Dare we say he should have gone earlier, and *Meanjin* with him? Even though the *Meanjins* after him have all maintained their quota of truth, beauty, import and innovation? Jim Davidson was an exceptional editor, buzzing with ideas, blazing new songlines, puffing life into an intelligentsia which all but stopped breathing after 1975. He should have had *The Age* – and Judith Brett, *New Idea* – or at least something with the potential to reach ten thousand readers. There is no question, Davidson, Brett and Lee all put their stamp on *Meanjin*, but nothing could put *Meanjin's* stamp on Australia.

"Small" is the key to it – it might be attached to a leviathan, but *Meanjin* remains a little magazine, and like all the others it is predisposed to the atmosphere of the ghetto. It has always – and the more so when freelancers like the Palmers and Brian Fitzpatrick went – been something of a salon wherein various academics projected their own alienation on to an oblivious world outside. Had Christesen thrown it in after twenty years, he would have left a legacy which was more truly the temperament of his generation, or at least that considerable portion of it who read *Meanjin* in those days. And the world for his successors might have been more of an oyster than a shell.

You can kill an idea but not when it's become an institution: *Meanjin* lived too long. Whatever his successors intended, Christesen's *Meanjin* ruled: it was constitutionally incapable of the necessary change – that being nothing more or less than the sort of change which made people read it. As it is, *Meanjin* is the epitome of the kind of publication which, having no audience for so long, long since lost the ability to write for one, and, having no contact with the world, shows no sign of wanting to engage with it.

There is memorable and momentous writing here, of course – the Palmers, Clark, Hope, Fitzgerald, Porter, Hibberd, Harwood, Marjorie Barnard's ground-breaking piece on Patrick White, Harry Heseltine's great case for the existence of an unselfconscious modernity in Australian literature – but this goes without saying. Over the years much of the best writing, and not a few of the better ideas, *have* first appeared in *Meanjin*. But that, this book reminds us sometimes, is the pity of it.

"We had only to admit we were part of mankind", said Nettie Palmer in an essay on literary nationalism in a 1944 *Meanjin*. That seems to be a very worthwhile goal, and there is no doubt that *Meanjin* has done much good in pursuit of it. But to what extent is a magazine which is still institutionally supported and selling a couple of thousand copies after fifty years "part of mankind"? Can it still claim, if it ever could, to be a reflection of the "temperament of generations", when Palmer almost certainly had a much bigger audience in 1944 than Alec McHoul had for a piece on the United States in November 1990? Can a magazine turn its back on the driving forces and imperatives of its own culture and its own political system and still hold to Nettie Palmer's creed? The answer is surely no.

If we are to go by McHoul's article, the last in the collection, we might conclude that the temperament of generations has scarcely changed. For while every lamentable thing Alec McHoul has to say about the United States is probably true, there is more than that. More to the United States, more to capitalist democracies of any stripe, including our own. More to mankind, to use the Palmer grandiloquence. More, I'd venture, than *Meanjin* could ever allow and still remain *Meanjin*.

Jenny Lee tells us that when she took over *Meanjin* in 1987 Stephen Murray-Smith summoned her to lunch and told her that her success was vital to the future of Australian culture. One hesitates to contradict such a wise head. But it is difficult to see how a culture is vitally changed or preserved by institutions which have little to do with it. It is a New Zealand approach to international influence. Nor does history seem to be on the side of Murray-Smith. The tradition has not held: the things which Clem Christesen and Vance Palmer loved, those rural values and the ABC among them, have not been enough to sustain the culture beyond the first one hundred years. In 1891 *The Bulletin* was booming and a republic was in the air. In 1991 *Meanjin* is a shadow on a street in Carlton and it seems likely that the federation will soon have to decide to whom it offers up its sovereignty – Brussels, Tokyo or Washington. Maybe then we will recognise that *Meanjin* long ago joined the ranks of noble failures on which this place was built.

Scripsi, vol. 7, no. 1, 1991

Rabbit syndrome

America is beyond power, it acts as in a dream, as a face of God.
Wherever America is, there is freedom, and wherever America is not,
madness rules with chains, darkness strangles millions. Beneath her
patient bombers, paradise is possible.

—John Updike, *Rabbit Redux*

From a certain angle the most terrifying thing in the world is your own
life, the fact that it's yours and nobody else's.

—John Updike, *Rabbit is Rich*

IN 1901 THE CITY FATHERS of Bendigo, Victoria, purchased for their
public gallery an oil by Albert Charles Taylor entitled *Gentlemen, the Queen*.
Painted in 1894 it portrays, as one would expect, a bevy of whiskery British officers, resplendent in monocles and red uniforms, standing round a
dinner table with their glasses raised in the royal toast. It is a portrait of
the high Victorian Empire: the spirit is collective and triumphant – if to
the jaundiced postcolonial eye also smug, effete and goatish. The ritual
formality seems to say, as modern football coaches do, if you keep to the
game plan nothing can defeat you. You will have setbacks, the occasional
Kabul or Khartoum, but if you keep to the fundamentals you will end
up with an empire whose like has not been seen since time began. The
officers immortalised in the painting are profoundly conscious of this.

Around a corner of the same gallery hangs a 1901 portrait by Hugh Ramsay of one "Charles Schneider Esq. of Cincinnati USA". Mr Schneider is clear-eyed and clean-shaven, impeccably groomed, unambiguously masculine, confident, whole. Ramsay captured in his subject that untrammelled look Americans give the world, as if to say, "I am of the republic. I do not know doubt. I am sufficient". Mr Schneider could only come from the United States. "God has predestinated, mankind expects, great things from our race; and great things we feel in our souls ..." Like the men in the first painting, he represents an empire: the American empire, which, like the British one, saw itself as blessed by Providence and fulfilling nothing less than its "Manifest Destiny". Schneider and the British officers are all in a sense frontiersmen, people on the limits of imperial expansion. But the differences could not be more obvious. It is not just the contrast between Mr Schneider's rugged individualism and the formal collectivity of the British: his "can do" opposed to their "must do". It's a matter of consciousness. The British know they are imperialists and they have uniforms, rituals, a vast literature, a queen, a "natural dogma" to speak for that fact; though his country has recently fought and won an expansionary war with Spain and is making a determined territory-swallowing drive into the Asia-Pacific, though it subscribes to an imperial doctrine and is indeed an imperial power, Mr Schneider knows only that he is an American.

The Americans of Charles Schneider's Gilded Age were less inclined to talk about an American empire than an American marketplace. The distinction has proved a little confusing over the years, as it did for some of its early exemplars. Explaining the idea in 1899, Francis B. Thurber of the United States Export Association succeeded in sounding at once confused and very like a modern corporate boss or politician: "I do not believe in imperialism ... but I do believe in a policy of expansion which will give us the control of some markets which will be a steppingstone to others in a wider zone of influence which such control would enable us to exercise". Thurber's was one voice in a chorus demanding that the United States elbow its way into suitable places for dumping the national surplus, but he shared the widely held view that imperialism, at least on the British model, was un-American. Its being British was one reason for not liking it. The possession of colonies was repellent to the republic. Yet there were economic imperatives and these inevitably became political imperatives, and from the union was born – or reborn – the peculiarly American idea that what was good for American commerce was good for human liberty and happiness, wherever the necessary critical mass of consumers happened to be gathered – in China and Japan, for instance. And what with the way of geopolitics, and the behaviour of natives, it sometimes proved necessary to follow Kipling's advice to take up the white man's burden and actually *impose* a bit of influence in some parts; like Cuba and Puerto Rico and the Philippines and some of those islands out there in the Pacific. *Annexation* might be necessary in some cases, and if one truly believed in free commerce (and what true American did not?) one would not flinch from that prospect, especially as each and every means of commercial expansion meant extending the domain of US "national thought" as well. Furthermore, goddamnit, that same course would extend less evil and more progress to the natives of these countries according to the "principles of humanity" on which American commerce rests in the first place. If, in the pursuit of their legitimate interests (surplus dumping, for instance), American citizens or American trade or commerce were injured by some "unjust, cruel and despotic rule", their government would "take a hand in the correction of the evil". But there were to be no songs of empire. It was asserting a country's right to take its produce to market, nothing more and nothing less. It was a *God-given* right, literally, under the doctrine of Manifest Destiny.

That doctrine has endured, though the name and the details have changed: the Truman Doctrine, the Eisenhower Doctrine, the Johnson Doctrine, the Nixon Doctrine and Pax Americana. These were "only extensions of the Monroe Doctrine", I.F. Stone, the radical Washington publicist, insisted in the days of Vietnam. "We have long been an imperialistic people", he said and it was "poppycock" pretending Vietnam was an exception. Many have marched up to the US embassy chanting slogans about US imperialism. But inside they wouldn't hear of it. It has been the same for a century and a half. They "plague South America in the name of liberty", Simon Bolivar complained.

In the hundred years since the painting of Schneider and the purchase of *Gentlemen ...* Australia has floated between the two worlds of these paintings. Each of them receding and looming according to their interests and our desires. It was always hard to say which one we ought to paddle towards.

These days we are in no doubt about it: we are America's deputy and trusty as they come. Ask not whether this is an honourable destiny and a fitting conclusion to a century of nationhood; it is a *fait accompli*, both sides of politics broadly agree upon it, the question is inadmissible. If we wish, we may attempt to tease out a little of the character of the sheriff; not with the intention of passing judgement on the relationship or on our mighty friend, but with the notion that looking at America might reflect some light on this country and on the options open to us. What is appropriate behaviour in the context of our relationship? We look at America as Gaul – or somewhere more far-flung – might have looked at Rome, as a cat might look at a king. The writer is no expert on American habits or history. He has made only brief visits to America and has never lived there. His knowledge of foreign policy is rudimentary. But for the apparent presumption of his writing this essay he begs to be excused. Like all other Australians he has lived with the Americans all his life. He also knows a few Americans who have lived here for many years and, with the best possible will, it cannot be said that they know much about Australia. It is true that Alexis de Tocqueville, who is quoted here several times and whose *On Democracy in America* is enjoying a remarkable revival as a source of almost transcendent wisdom on the subject, wrote from the experience of a nine-month whirlwind tour. It is also true that Mark Twain spent much more time in Australia than I have spent on any one journey to America and he concluded that South Australia was a working-man's paradise. My case rests.

2.

And let us always remember that with ourselves, almost for the first time in the history of the earth, national selfishness is unbounded philanthropy; for we can not do a good to America but we give alms to the world.

—Henry Melville, *White Jacket*

As children growing up in the 1950s we were not encouraged to like the Americans. They saved Australia in the Coral Sea and we were not to forget it. They were to be preferred to the Russians and Chinese, and any other communists or Asians – that went without saying. We enjoyed most of those Rodgers and Hammerstein musicals. By the age of ten I think I knew the words to most of *Oklahoma!* and much of *South Pacific*, along with many songs by Harry Belafonte, Guy Mitchell, Elvis Presley, Bing Crosby and Peggy Lee. Soon after, bumptiously, I took to American jazz. It is unprecedented, surely, but so universal and thoroughgoing in Australian experience that it goes unremarked – almost all the songs of our youth were those of another culture, all the rhythms and beats, all the sentiments. It is hard to say which is the more astonishing – that America filled this basic need almost exclusively, or that America had such a genius for pleasure and invention. When suffering fits of anti-Americanism it is always helpful to try to imagine the world without those songs: no Cole Porter or Irving Berlin or Fats Waller or Gershwin or Kern or Rodgers or Hart. No Billie Holiday, no blues, no rhythm and blues, no Patsy Cline. Just George Formby and Rolf Harris. Or no Frank Capra and Billy Wilder for that matter. Think of the void in our imagining without Monroe or Brando or *Psycho* or *Vertigo*. No Cecil B. DeMille.

In their early teens, my father tells me, he and his brother ran seven miles after milking the cows to see *The Ten Commandments*. That must have been the mid-1920s. Thirty years later we trooped in with him to see the waters part in Technicolor and CinemaScope. The Americans coloured in the world and enlarged it. Britain remained our anchor, but the sea was turning American. We laughed at the Marx Brothers, Danny Kaye and Judy Holliday, liked Cary Grant and Katharine Hepburn, adored Grace Kelly – the princess they longed to have, we thought. We tolerated westerns, mainly I suspect because they made a heroic context for the kind of rural pioneering from which we ourselves were only recently removed. (Heroic, but watching Alan Ladd chopping at the tree stump in *Shane* we also laughed.) Certain American faces were irresistible: it is even possible that we hoped our own would evolve into something resembling Gary Cooper's or Gregory Peck's, and that behind the cragginess the same laconic rectitude and sexual magnetism would shine. As for the annihilation of the Indian nations, who were we to protest?

In general we felt at home with the Americans, so long as they were showing their wholesome side. We thought it wise to be friends with them, though it was mainly in the way one is friendly with relations. It was a mantra of one's elders that deep down the Americans envied us our Queen. They would not admit it, of course – being such an unnatural thing, an English-speaking republic, they had to defend it – but you could tell, we reckoned, that they regretted their revolutionary turning. That was why they were so predisposed to boastfulness and rank consumerism – it was compensatory behaviour. Our analysis had something in common with Bob Menzies's observation in the 1930s that any American who has "remotely any English, Scotch or Irish blood … tells you about it right away". Essentially they were distant cousins, Calvinistic like ourselves, yet even that appeared to be in name only. I seem to remember the family filing out of *Cat on a Hot Tin Roof* well before the end of the first reel. It was impossible to believe that Big Daddy and my father were both Presbyterians. It was unimaginable that we would ever sink to such depths of self-indulgence, such rank confessions. The differences more than the similarities struck us as remarkable, and of all the differences the most disturbing was their dark side.

The B-grade flicks (not that we knew, but they included classics of film noir) that played in the first half of every program at the country picture theatre where we went had too much shadow and menace. Why would you want to make films about such sleaze? Why dig it up? I would be forever haunted by the image of Gloria Grahame with her face wrapped in bandages after Lee Marvin, whose moll she played, threw boiling coffee over her. It was the sort of thing that happened in America, and not just because there was always boiling coffee around. And whisky, for heaven's sake – they drank it like tea. And mumbling narcissists (known as method actors) with sallow faces and weak chins whom we did not like; nor did we like films whose themes were juvenile alienation and rebellion and those underground torrents of obsession, horror, lust and violence flowing directly to that everlasting hell over which, it is said, the New England Puritans imagined their lives suspended. If, poor souls, they were condemned by their history to play out forever the unresolved drama of their forebears' twisted imagination, we were sorry but it was not to our taste. The United States had been and remained our saviour, but it did not mean we approved of their Manichean mindset, or enjoyed the oppression of their wealth and ego, or the seeming chaos of their appetites. Even their wholesomeness seemed a little *too* wholesome sometimes: I fancy we suspected it owed less to a love of virtue than an unhealthy awareness of depravity.

More than anything we loathed their war films. You would have thought no one else on the Allied side had fired a shot. Not only did they claim to have won the war single-handed, they changed the context to suit themselves. It was as if they really thought that they had been the only ones to resist the evil, and the only ones who knew what evil was. But of course that is probably the deepest thought in the culture. In *Air Force One*, a recent Hollywood blockbuster directed by a German with his tongue firmly in his cheek, the leader of a terrorist squad (played by the English actor Gary Oldman) takes control of the president's jet and declares he will kill everyone including the president's wife and children unless his demands are met. Oldman delivers a persuasive denunciation of America's role in the ruin of modern Russia. No person of average intelligence could fail to acknowledge that he has at least a reasonable case; but the Americans, especially the president (Harrison Ford), are in no mood to debate – even for a moment. To be American in this world is to be beyond the reach of others' reason – Air Force One, the president, his wife and staff are all of themselves good. Interlopers are vandals, demons, creatures of Evil. And indeed they *are* in this case, but it is still a Monroe Doctrine by another name. "Does anybody deny the right of this government", President Cleveland asked rhetorically, "in the interest of humanity, in the interest of the business of this world and the race, to say, 'You must put an end to this condition, or we shall compel you to do so'?" Of course they didn't. After a life-and-death struggle with the terrorist leader, the president (who fights with the warrior-like vigour one expects of a middle-aged American president), assisted by the First Lady, at last gains the upper hand and kicks the evil one into space with the words, "Get off my plane".

The old American war films (like Stephen Spielberg's more recent one, *Saving Private Ryan*) had none of the spirit of *Air Force One*, of course. Those films fulfilled the insatiable American need to make every battle a contest between personifications of Good and Evil absolutely conceived – and one that Good wins narrowly. (Victories over Satan are rare and against the odds, and the thought may lurk in the American mind that alone in the world their country has achieved it.) Everything is reducible to the universal human-interest story. *Schindler's List*, a film about the Holocaust by Stephen Spielberg, is in some mysterious way a human-interest story. On CNN the end of the world will be treated as a human-interest story, and, as with Spielberg's war and Spielberg's Holocaust, watching it happen we will feel that America owns this as well.

We were always very dark on the Americans after we had seen one of their war films. Of course we knew they had been reluctant starters on both occasions, and had only turned on the evil when it turned on them. We didn't have the figures, of course, but they would not have surprised us: the country that won the war lost something short of half a million soldiers (and a handful of civilians), while Britain lost almost as many soldiers and more than sixty thousand civilians. The Russians lost twenty-four million, the Chinese twenty million. The Americans provided the materials and munitions, and for their sacrifices – though more for their strength – we were grateful, always, and no less grateful because we knew that they grew richer from that war. But from their films we concluded they neither knew the facts of others' histories nor cared to find out. Nothing could induce them to recognise the sacrifice of others. "It was a good war", says Mrs Smith to Harry Angstrom in John Updike's *Rabbit Run*: "It wasn't like the first. It was ours to win and we won it". They say it to this day. Tom Wolfe was saying it – belligerently – in *Harper's* millennium edition last year. It is less the preposterousness of the claim than the way it confirms that the American mind has bone where in normal people there is space for another's reality. In truth those films seemed more gormless than sinister. They confirmed our view that the Americans had many of the characteristics of children, and that some of the worst things they did were the result of innocence. Yet it still felt like imperialism; an assault not only on common sense and knowledge, but also on our dignity and sovereignty.

British films we thought more truthful and honourable. Indeed, reduced to its bare bones, our film criticism came down to the following three categories: true story, based on fact, far-fetched. The British rated highly in the first two, the American product tended to congregate around the last. We also believed, despite much evidence to the contrary, that the Americans lacked a sense of humour, at least one of British standards. They lacked I RONY and, notwithstanding their propensity to spin tales that were far-fetched, took themselves altogether TOO SERIOUSLY. But then the British, who had always written their own war histories as if all Commonwealth troops were "British", withdrew east of Suez and joined up with Europe. What were we to do? Make our own films?

There was one very good reason why we put up with the American and British films – we were embarrassed by our own. And we were right to be. Much else made us cringe, and much has been written about it, but the only point to make here is that we cringed to Britain, not the United States. Our publishing and literary taste was largely determined in Britain, our graduates studied in British universities, our intellectual and creative talents expatriated themselves to Britain, we continued to think of ourselves as essentially British and our upper and educated classes faithfully imitated theirs. In the 1950s when the Australian architect Robin Boyd complained bitterly about the excruciating "Cockneyesque whine" of the Australian accent, it was "visiting Englishmen" he was worried about displeasing, and he was not suggesting an Americanesque accent instead.

Culturally speaking, Britain, not the United States, was our Mecca and our measure. Even as we eagerly joined with the United States in the Vietnam conflict, saw the American share in investment and control of our industries creep up on the British, and succumbed to American popular culture, it was to Britain that we looked for culture and meaning. Indeed we looked there as a way of balancing the American influence. For some of the influential middle class – even in my own non-middle-class childhood environment – the British connection was the best prophylactic in an increasingly American world. It even enabled us to look down on the Americans for being the philistines they were. It was not just a matter of their economic imperialism. It was a cultural position. So deep did this belief run that not only the left but also our liberal intellectuals and literati (gathered for instance round the otherwise noble journal *Meanjin*) were much more often to be heard damning Washington and Disneyland than Moscow and the Gulag. So unremitting was their loathing of American films, television and advertising and the popular culture they imagined it reflected, that it seems very likely they also loathed Americans.

Of course we did not give up without a fight. We got our own TV industry going and grafted it on the two great imported streams. From time to time we made a fuss about the local cultural product, even when it sent us up mercilessly – indeed this seemed to be the way we liked it. We found all sorts of ways to pretend we were upright and firmly on our own two feet, but in truth we bent over the barrel and were willing to bend further as occasion demanded. The reality of our actual position being fairly loathsome, such advertisements as we wrote for ourselves were essentially disguises. As it had been with the British, so it became with the Americans: the culture was a carapace to hide the truth from ourselves and others. We were as shrill and brash as the Americans sometimes, though not with their naivety: with us it was the opposite, a spirit corrupted by the weakness of our position in the world and our dependence on powerful friends. Lurking behind our self-confidence were anxiety and shame.

Unable to conceive of any independent strategy in Asia after the British withdrawal, we egged on the Americans in Vietnam and sent the army in to fight for them, as "mercenaries" as one veteran recently said. We had no say in the conduct of the war, and appeared not to want any. Because the Americans were conscripting their young men for the war, we conscripted ours – as many as we could afford to train, through a ballot that was unconscionable but convenient. While Australian soldiers fought in Vietnam, at home other Australians demonstrated against the war. *We* knew the Americans were imperialists even if the Americans did not. Never had there been less reason to believe in communism, but anti-Americanism managed to turns hordes of bright young people into Marxists, Leninists, Maoists, Trotskyists and anarchists – revolutionaries. America being multitudinous and market-supple, Americans provided most of the music for the revolution. And the clothing, hair and lifestyles, heroes, role models, buzzwords, artwork, poetry, novels, journalism and comic books. Mao and Ho Chi Minh somehow became anti-authoritarian figures, to be admired at the same time as one read Ken Kesey and lived like the Merry Pranksters. What great days they were. Add marijuana, LSD and sexual liberation, and the mind of the average opponent of American imperialism had something of the atmosphere of a Saigon bar.

3.

The big Mouseketeer has appeared, Jimmie, a grown man who wears
circular black ears. Rabbit watches him attentively; he respects him.
He expects to learn something from him helpful in his own line of work,
which is demonstrating a kitchen gadget in several five-and-dime stores
around Brewer . . . Jimmy sets aside his smile and guitar and says straight
out through the glass "Know Thyself, a wise old Greek once said.
Know thyself. Now what does this mean, boys and girls?"

—John Updike, *Rabbit Run*

John Updike's Rabbit quartet is on one reading a denunciation of American society as merciless and foetid as anything written about Rome or
Babylon. It began in 1960 with *Rabbit Run*. Harry "Rabbit" Angstrom,
high-school basketball hero, flees one night from his pregnant "poor
dumb mutt" of a wife, Janice, his two-year-old son and their home in
Brewer, Pennsylvania. He drives the dreadful highways to West Virginia;
from nowhere to nowhere. But he can't quite do it, so he goes back; back
to Brewer, and his old basketball coach, the egregious Tothero, who intro-
duces him to the prostitute Ruth. Ruth turns out to be just about the
only person of any moral density in the whole saga (unless it is Thelma,
an unloved friend's wife who loves Harry, who is dying of lupus, whom
he sodomises on request, of whom he says to her husband at her funeral,
"She was a fantastic lay"). Alas, Rabbit leaves Ruth, rising from her bed in
the middle of the night when the minister (with whom he regularly plays
golf) rings to tell him that Janice is in labour. Fourteen years later Janice
leaves Harry for a Greek car salesman, and Harry sets up house with
their son, Nelson, and an eighteen-year-old teenage junkie whose body
he shares with Skeeter, a messianic Negro. He runs the gamut of '70s
decadence and Reaganite reaction. He reads, almost exclusively, *Consumer
Reports*, and its verdicts form the staple of his conversation. He is a man
of almost incredible crassness. His sexual obsession is inexhaustible and
highly tuned. Nothing else comes close to exercising his imagination like
the merest suggestion of nipples or pussy. He stops thinking of female
possibility only when survival instincts compel some other thought –
to sell a Toyota, watch television, eat salted peanuts or improve his golf

swing. (Rabbit has a little in common with Homer Simpson.) Or to indulge in some second-hand patriotism – Pop, if you like, to the Mom of his pudenda fantasies. Rabbit is a Christian, Updike makes a point of telling us early in the first book.

But we get the feeling that Rabbit has some greatness in him. His instincts are sure, even if his thinking is not. Life and death might frighten him, but no earthly being does. His love of the female body, while obsessive, is unrestrained and marvellous in the detail of observation. He glories in it. From these reflections and others about Toyota Corollas and salted peanuts we are left in no doubt that he is both sentient and conscious. And Rabbit has an occasional intimation about death and the human condition that defies his platitudinous myopia and brainlessness and puts him well clear of the lower primates. Open-heart surgery and angioplasty can't save Rabbit: he eats himself to death, dying on a suburban basketball court in his mid-fifties, trying to recapture youth's glories forty pounds above a healthy weight. He could go no other way, unless it was on the golf course, or in the middle of that other addiction of the American male, a blow job.

The Rabbit books may be read in various ways – for example, as a ruthless dissection of the male psyche (Rabbit is outrageous but never less than familiar); as a satire on the human condition or modern American life; as an unsentimental but ultimately forgiving domestic portrait; as an elegy for the soul of America, torn between God and Nature, a sort of visceral proof that American commerce was, as Perry Miller said, "conceived in the bed of religion". Updike steps into the "woeful putre-faction" the old Puritan preachers saw at the centre of New England life, but not to judge as they did, only to describe or to laugh or to join the general melancholy. He does not need to judge, it is enough that he sees. He sees the hollowness at the centre, the door closed to possibility. "Your life has no reflective content," Jill, Rabbit's eighteen-year-old lay, tells him. "It's all instinct and when your instinct lets you down, you have nothing to trust. That's what makes you cynical. Cynicism is tired prag-matism. Pragmatism suited a certain moment here, the frontier moment, it did the work very wastefully and ruthlessly but it did it." But it's no longer useful. "You carry an old God with you, and an angry old patri-otism", she says. Jill burns to death in Rabbit's house while he stands outside and watches with his disintegrating twelve-year-old.

Ruth, the abandoned lover, is more direct – she calls him "Mr Death himself. You're not just nothing, you're worse than nothing". So Rabbit, "a typical good-hearted, imperialist racist", his body a decaying vessel poisoned by fast food and wasted potential, his imagination dimmed by prejudice and television, running on ignorance and fear, smears with shit those few things which are pure, Ruth says, and echoes the emptiness Updike sees at the core of America.

Naturally Rabbit has been equated with Uncle Sam himself. He is coarse, philistine and provincial; he is alienated from the land, religion and history, from his children, his imagination and his potential. Like a real rabbit he lives by his appetites for sex and food, and like a real American he tries to fill the remaining space with golf, daiquiris and dreams of a house with a sunken living room: the small objects to which, if the pursuit of happiness is to mean anything and a democracy is to work, the soul clings. "One does not see anything until one sees its beauty", Oscar Wilde said. Poor Rabbit sees beauty only in ass or a three-pointer – and money which he associates with ass in any case. He reunites with his wife for the convenience of her father's money and a job at his Toyota agency. Taking advantage of a surge in gold prices after the Russian invasion of Afghanistan, he buys bullion, spreads it on the matrimonial bed and he and the mutt rut like rabbits in it. It's the unexamined life – worse the un*imagined* life – taken to its highest point. So it was inevitable that the Rabbit quartet would be called "a powerful critique of America".

It is not, of course, a critique we have to accept, any more than we are obliged to take George W. Bush as representative of the American mind. The truth could lie anywhere between the president and Gore Vidal and other perennially disenchanted American souls. Foreign critics of the United States should not kid themselves: no scorn of theirs will match what Americans say about themselves. "If you find so much that is unworthy of reverence in the United States, then why do you live here?" H.L. Mencken asked himself. "Why do men go to zoos?" he replied.

Nowhere else are the words "free" and "freedom" so pervasive. Their anthem proclaims the land of the free, and no patriotic American speech fails to mention it. And in many ways, no doubt, it is a remarkably free country. Australians make much less of the idea, taking it more for granted, perhaps because Britain for so long seemed to guarantee it. The absence of the word from our public rhetoric and popular writing, relative to America at least, may also be due in part to a first half-century when a significant proportion of the population was *not* free. Upon their emancipation, convicts in Australia calculated that it was not in their interests to draw attention to the past by singing songs of freedom, unlike black Americans who were in no position to hide the fact that they had once been slaves. Like "The Star-Spangled Banner", "Advance Australia Fair" declares that we are free, but the observation is granted no more status than the one in the next line that the country is an island. The Americans, of course, are less "girt by sea", but, even if they were girt entirely, it is doubtful they would feel constrained to say so in their national anthem.

It is without doubt the strangest country when it comes to politics. For all their unequivocal love of freedom, the idea of it seems to produce in Americans a good deal of fear. In the citadel of freedom, the child of the enlightenment, the word "liberal" now carries the same meaning as its opposite. Desperate to avoid branding, candidates for office weave and dart and burrow in all directions, for to be identified as a "liberal" today is rather like being tagged "communist" a generation ago. In 1996 Lewis Lapham, the essayist and editor of *Harper's*, noted the publication of a book by Robert H. Bork, a Yale law professor nominated by Ronald Reagan for the Supreme Court and in 1996 a regular guest on the major American talk shows. The book, called *Slouching Towards Gomorrah*, was a jeremiad from one who, in his own words, "detests modern liberalism and all its works". For modern liberalism, read multiculturalists, radical feminists, homosexual activists, black extremists, intellectual "nihilists" and various other categories of people consumed by hatred and "contempt for American society". This diatribe sounds familiar to our own ears, of course, accustomed as they now are to the abuse of "elites", special interest groups, black armband historians, pushy blacks and chattering classes. But it is much more pungent in its American context, where it comes with slavering endorsements from the Christian Coalition and various influential right-wingers. *Slouching Towards Gomorrah* quickly hit the bestseller lists. Lapham noted its resemblance to medieval millenarian tracts, with its lists of modern "liberals" as the equivalents of tenth-century associates of Satan. Most remarkable was Bork's wish to jettison the Enlightenment in which the republic was created and re-create the United States as a Puritan theocracy.

The book was published in the same week as the Taliban seized control of most of Afghanistan, an irony that Lapham did not fail to note. He doubted if the Taliban had read Bork, yet even without him, "they seemed to know how to go about the great task of putting an end to the nonsense of liberty and equality".

We need not accept such acerbic views of America. We can agree with any of the more favourable assessments: that it is the best society yet achieved in an imperfect world, through to the one revived in recent times casting America as the repository of Good in the war against Evil – from Homer Simpson to Ned Flanders next door if you will. Of course, just the other day those now most fervently casting it as Good were saying it was sunk in Evil, and for the same people the city of the Twin Towers was the proof of it. New York was Gomorrah on the Hudson.

But who are we to talk if American politics is full of contradictions? We vilify people fleeing from the tyranny we are fighting. Whether we think America is essentially good or positively bad does not matter in the end: it is very likely both – it contains multitudes, as Walt Whitman said of himself. What matters is that Australia exhibits negative traits of culture and personality very like those we and others see exhibited in the United States. Perhaps Rabbit is a metaphor that Updike never intended: a distant metaphor for the soul of Australia, the country which, like Rabbit, recoils in fear from the insight that its life is its own and no one else's, and changes the angle to accommodate its fear. The country that tries but cannot leave the safety of an unsatisfying union (not the British, nor the Americans) and abandons anything more challenging even when it knows that fulfilment lies there. Whose imagination works only in fits and starts, flutters into life under the impulse of certain stimuli and then settles back into the familiar and second-hand. That, if recent indications can be trusted, is losing the capacity that Rabbit wonders at in women – the "strange way they have … of really caring about somebody beyond themselves". The country that declares itself the luckiest and best on earth and listens avidly to shock jocks abusing anyone who suggests otherwise while all the time telling us how bad it is; whose appetite for crap is bottomless; that talks high principles but values pragmatism and practises unqualified self-interest; substitutes platitudes for wisdom; suffers the same Protestant curse but without the fires of hell to warm it. That seeks shelter beneath those American bombers and just now shows every sign that it will find its definition there: huddling rabbit-like, never venturing too far from the burrow.

Whether this is consequent on prolonged exposure to the United States, or to our ranking as eager ally and client state, is difficult to say. Our flaws may be endemic, their likeness to Rabbit Angstrom's mere coincidence. But it is too much of a coincidence, surely, and too much bad luck that we should get more of the flaws and less of the strengths. Would that we had an Updike; or a Melville; or a Mark Twain. Has anyone documented the Australian condition as they have the American? Is the Australian condition sufficient to such talents, or even capable of producing them? Would that we had the Americans' confidence. A small portion of their inventiveness. Just one of their best universities or research institutes. Two of their best five hundred companies. Some of their instinct for philanthropy. Some of their genius. If just five or ten per cent of their immigrants had chosen Australia instead. Would that we had been so open and so civilised. Note that we are not asking for their rivers and plains, or any other natural advantages – just small things, but reflections of a spirit that they have abundantly and we, along with most other countries, seem to lack.

And, yes, they did win the war – at least it could not have been won without them. And with the Marshall Plan they saved Western Europe. Saved it? They made it. And they did save Australia. Just as they saved millions in accordance with the sentiment expressed on the Statue of Liberty. They have been a mighty force for freedom. Flawed, contradictory, murderous, outrageous; yet what empire in history was less malevolent? Which one did more good works? And imagine the world without Louis Armstrong. And if none of this persuades you, resort to the relativities – think of Eastern Europe, North Korea as opposed to South. A visit to the border north of Seoul in the early '90s was instructive: before reaching it one received instruction from a Strangelovian American officer in terms that were a poor parody of Kubrick's film. "Do not taunt or by any gesture even inadvertently provoke the communist soldiers on the other side of the parallel. Remember you are a TARGET." It would be hilarious if his demeanour had not been *comparatively* sane and his words essentially true. On the other side lunatic propaganda blared from loudspeakers, benighted soldiers strutted around trying to affect, and quite possibly feeling, the belligerence of true communists towards the capitalist enemy. If our side feels a bit like Hollywood, on the other side lie real madness, real ignorance and, one cannot help sensing, real evil. Whatever we might say about the Americans we need never be in any doubt, not so far anyway, that it is both wise and proper to be on their side in the greater swim of things.

4.

Maximum fine in 1829 for teaching an African-American living in Georgia to read or write — $500.

Ratio [in 2000] of the number of pupils per teacher in Michigan's schools to the number of inmates per guard in its prisons: 18:5.

—Harper's Index, Fall 2001

Our government makes no sense unless it is founded on a deeply held religious faith, and I don't care what it is.

—Dwight Eisenhower

The question is, however, what is the wise and proper way to be on their side? It might help to begin by recognising how little we have in common with them, how unalike we are, what distant cousins. Occasionally there have been signs of real affinity between our leaders. But whatever genuine affections existed between Holt and Johnson, the relationship between the two countries concerned little more than the Vietnam War and it was all one way. Hawke and George Bush had something going between them: but beyond the Gulf War, what sustained it? Perhaps uniquely, Keating and Clinton found common ground on a raft of issues and a genuine liking for each other. Their first meeting in Washington was remarkable not only for the obvious warmth between them, but because it was based on a shared policy vision, both international and domestic. They agreed broadly on health and education policy, on political strategies for social democratic parties, on trade liberalisation and the extension of APEC. It was a meeting of new Democrat and Labor minds at which Australia actually brought to the table something of weight for both sides. Doubtless my bias is showing, but it had rarely if ever been like this before, and certainly it has not been like it since.

Much responsibility for the failure attaches to Australian leaders without enough ideas, gumption or force of personality to impress this country's interests or philosophy upon the leadership of the most powerful nation on earth. How could APEC and Australia's role in it be allowed to slide as it has in the past five years? No doubt it got harder with Clinton later in his presidency, and harder still with George W. Bush; but just as surely the will to keep the Americans engaged with what *we* thought, especially what we thought about the region, dramatically faded. Perhaps the words and gestures were not intended to convey so plainly our change of heart, our mental baulk at the regional challenge; perhaps this was *exactly* what was intended. You only have to think like a deputy to look like a deputy, and look like a deputy long enough and one day they'll pin a badge on you and tell you to shut up and do as you're told. Too late then to discover your independence if the sheriff asks for something that it is not in your interests or nature to give. Too late to insist that you represent more than the sheriff's interests. Too late if you raise your gaze one day and see something weird or sinister lurking in the sheriff's eyes.

The Americans are different. Or should we say that we are? There are the obvious measures. We do not hang, fatally inject, gas, electrocute or shoot people found guilty of murder. The Americans do it to hundreds every year. Were we to engage in capital punishment, it is unlikely we would long entertain the idea that the general public had a right or a need to *witness* executions. The Americans take the idea very seriously. It is probably true that if the matter were to be determined by a popular vote, capital punishment would be reinstated in most if not all the states of Australia. But we do not determine it this way. There is no great clamour to execute criminals, and were there to be, an even greater clamour would oppose it. We read of Americans executing their fellow citizens, hear otherwise enlightened Americans supporting the procedure; see images on television of the devices they employ, the prisoner walking to the chair or table; and some of us think these people are not like us, *fundamentally*. There's something cruel and ghoulish about them. They missed a stage in the progress of Western civilisation. If it happens in China, it does not surprise: we don't expect the Chinese to be like us. We don't expect it of some European countries, yet the abolition of capital punishment is a condition of membership of the European Union. We tend to assume the Americans are progressing on the same intellectual and moral plane; and then we hear on the TV that sage Gary Cooper lookalike, Executive Assistant District Attorney Jack McCoy of *Law and Order*, urging the death penalty for some poor sod avarice or anger got the better of. Bill Clinton also thinks (or has been known to feign to think) capital punishment is an essential ingredient of a criminal justice system. He agrees with us about a public health system and a public education system and human rights and free trade in the Asia-Pacific; and he is also so ardent (and cynical) an executioner we read that in pursuit of popular approval, as governor of Arkansas, he went out of his way to be in his home state on the day a long-time inhabitant of death row, who had suffered brain damage, was put to death. This is so gross that it reminds us of (though it bears no comparison to) Stalin playing cat and mouse with his victims or Hitler repeatedly watching films of participants in the 1944 "Officers' Plot" being executed. It reminds us of every tyrant and debauchee who never learned reason or restraint. And the present incumbent? We read that during his term as governor of Texas more than a hundred people were executed.

Then there are the guns. Charlton Heston, another one of the granite-faced Americans of the '50s, Moses in the Technicolor *Ten Commandments*, turns out to be a paranoid macho screwball. They are *mad* about guns, as mad as any people on earth about them. And there is not just the violence, there's the accompanying theme of revenge that runs through the movie culture. As if they still take the Old Testament literally. We live for the most part with the comforting belief – so comforting we are barely conscious of it – that they are a lot like us, these Americans we see on TV and in the movies and read about in the papers so much we think we know them as well as we know ourselves. They're a bit whacky, of course, but on the whole they are clever and civilised. Then suddenly a news item jolts us, or some scrap of information from the internet or *Harper's* Index, and for a moment they seem to have more in common with an Albanian blood cult than with our own civilisation. Very often the news coming out of America suggests that the theocracy to which Robert H. Bork wants to return never went away.

It's not a theocracy, of course; and religion, though it wields an unusual influence, is not the nub of it. It's the history of the place – English, French and Spanish, the whole caboodle. Not just the history but what they have made of it. It is also the Mohawk, Mohicans, Cherokee, Nez Perce, Comanches, Apaches and Sioux. There was war of a kind on the Australian frontier. There was bloodshed and cruelty, but it did not sear itself into the founding myths and the national psyche like two centuries of Indian wars did in America. Indeed the Indian wars got themselves more thoroughly into Australian psyches than any conflict with the Aborigines did. For those of us who as children read *Tom Sawyer*, *The Last of the Mohicans* and *Ned in the Woods*, terror took an American shape in our brains long before we saw John Wayne hunting Natalie Wood and the Indians out west in *The Searchers*.

The frontier in Australian history was a very different thing. Russel Ward famously argued that unlike America, where the spirit that emerged was individualistic, the conditions of the Australian frontier produced mateship, unions, a collectivist ethos. In fact the term itself was scarcely used – a "frontier" was per se American and it meant a place of violence. We were raised to believe that the Aborigines hardly put up a fight and therefore little force was needed to remove them. It was a kind of anti-myth, a story without heroes or villains, save Daisy Bates, a missionary who might have been both, a story without influence on the national character. The whole episode of settlement came to us as essentially passive and lacking in drama. As children we were *not* entirely quarantined from the cruelty inflicted upon Aboriginal Australians, nor from moral judgement; but what had been swept under the carpet was left there. It was when a new generation of scholars began sweeping it into view that a new generation of thought police stepped in and denounced "black armband" history – meaning immoderate, bad, even unpatriotic history. The Americans romanticised their frontier wars, made myths from them, as usual turned their Manichean lenses on them, but they did not on the whole adopt this odious anti-intellectualism – it was a long while ago, why dig up the past? For all its myth-making, Hollywood has examined the American frontier with more intelligence and imagination than the Australian film industry has, and with a deeper concern for its meaning and consequences. The view for years now has been essentially revisionist. Even John Ford made amends to Native Americans with *Cheyenne Autumn*, a film local culture warriors would likely call "black armband" history.

In Australia, for all the efforts of Henry Reynolds (and of his opponents, for that matter), the national mind has never been so numb to the reality and the meaning of the frontier – or so uninterested. We wallow in comforting platitudes enlivened recently by occasional spats about the numbers killed in massacres. The effect of these arguments is first to polarise our history along the same ideological lines as divide our politics, and second to extinguish interest in the subject. These days some Australians are determined to believe that very few Aborigines were killed, while perhaps as many (with more credibility, I would maintain) are just as set on a great number. Meanwhile, a third, much larger complement grows increasingly conscientious in not giving a damn. Far from enlightening us or even making us think or feel something about these seminal events, the debate over the last few years has ground into confusion and such comforting platitudes from the highest reaches of power as, "I don't think Australians want to dwell on all the bad things". And those that do want to dwell on them, or escape such noxious pap, if they wish may turn to the latest book about Ned Kelly, the only nineteenth-century Australian still more than half-alive in the public imagination.

Americans may turn to Cormac McCarthy or Larry McMurtry; or, for instance, to any one of several film treatments of Jesse James and Billy the Kid. When they do they find psychologically complex, historically imaginative, subtle, savage, uncompromising takes on their history that Australians ought to envy. One of Hollywood's great gifts to the world was imagined history. Hollywood understood that the past was a field to be cultivated by interpretation, and had the studios been asked they might have agreed with Carlyle that the history of the world was but the biography of great men. The results have been often hilariously or nauseatingly bad, but they have also given Americans at the very least an impression of the past, even an engagement with it, relatively free of the constraints of "period". Look at the various screen takes on Billy the Kid; from Arthur Penn's to Marlon Brando's to Sam Peckinpah's to Gore Vidal's. It has to be healthy for a country to turn its heroes and villains upside down and shake them, to see what secrets they hold. Here, where fact-grubbing has always been at war with the imagination, notwithstanding Sydney Nolan's Kelly series of paintings, we have been less successful at creating a vigorous and imaginative relationship with our history.

It is not just their history but what they have made of it that sets America apart. Compare with the notion of black armband history the portrait of the Old West in decay in *The Wild Bunch*. *The Wild Bunch* celebrates the "bad things". It mourns *their* passing, not the "innocence" they destroy. In this way it is a very good history lesson of a particular kind. No doubt there are people who "do not want to dwell on the bad things in the past", but that does not mean they should not be made to. If "most Australians" or the "great majority of Australians" do not want to dwell on them, it could be because not enough bad things have been put in front of them. Perhaps that's why, when they see a real live bad thing, like a sinking boat loaded with refugees, they recoil in fear. Perhaps they need a Cormac McCarthy to write about the bad things, to show them that history confronted raw and unexpurgated yields dividends of poetry and awareness, and without fatal damage to a nation's cohesion or psyche. Or perhaps they need Comanches, "a legion of horribles … gaudy and grotesque with daubings like a company of mounted clowns, death hilarious, all howling in a barbarous tongue riding down upon them like a horde from hell …"

When the Frenchman Tocqueville visited the United States in the 1830s, the "religious atmosphere of the country" was the first thing that struck him. Not everyone agreed; many, including Emerson, thought religion was in decline and running shallower than before. But it ran infinitely deeper in America than it did in Australia, and in very different ways. Pious and orderly minds, when they surveyed Australia in the 1830s, perceived a worrying absence of religious observance. To this they ascribed most of the moral shortcomings of the people. Among other remedies the abolition of the convict system and the importation of upright single women were suggested. Although the colonial churches were very busy, and the now abandoned, crumbling or depleted churches of Australian town and country still speak glumly for this activity, the ministers wondered even then if religion amounted to much in the parishioners' hearts. "Practical paganism" and its genteel relation "moral enlightenment" prevailed and really they always have. Nothing in Australia prompted the rise of Mormons and Millerites and those countless other sects whose descendants are still at work on modern American television and in modern American politics 160 years later. There was no spontaneous "awakening" of the kind that gripped the American commercial classes in 1858, bringing them together in prayer and persuading all but the most cynical that God and commerce could be mixed. We Australians can add "under God" to a constitutional preamble, and even begin to use the name as freely as it is used in American public discourse, but that will not give us a religious mind. Few Australians will ever believe their country was "formed by God" as Americans believe of the republic. We will not unite in prayer. And it is difficult to foresee a day when our head of state, seemingly programmed to play out the old Puritan drama once again, confesses to a breakfast prayer meeting of leading clergy that he is liar and a fornicator and begs the forgiveness of the Lord and the nation.

In modern America no political leader can afford not to believe in God as defined by Christianity, for the very good reason that an extraordinary preponderance of the voting population does. Surveys consistently reveal that well over half of Americans believe in heaven and hell. By contrast, less than half agree with the basic proposition of evolution that human beings developed from earlier animal species; and it is possible that one of the people to disagree with this proposition is George W. Bush. The president favours the teaching of both Darwinism and Creationism in schools.

In Australia the decline of traditional religion did not cause so much thrashing about and there were far fewer visitations. No evangelical movement offered a serious challenge. The Protestant and Catholic churches staged their sectarian battles within the familiar guidelines. They vigorously exercised what political influence they could, but rarely broached the lines separating church and state. No one could speak credibly of theocracy. Nietzsche's announcement that God was dead met with the same general equanimity. Alfred Deakin and a little late nineteenth-century theosophy aside, they were less inclined to imparadise their hearts than their hearths: they put their faith in gradual socialism and topped it up with beer, irony and racism. With religion as with the marketplace, Australians did not rush after the main chance so fervently. That's how Americans seemed to us when we were growing up – too much public soul-searching and emoting, too obviously the salesmen of the world, too inclined to do things to excess. There were certain boundaries they seemed not to recognise.

This country was born of a very different union and soldered together not in a fiery furnace but through a protracted series of lawyers' meetings. Its originating documents are entirely without poetry or inspiration, or even an overriding principle; the principles, indeed, are *under*riding. A fondness for freedom does not need to be spelt out. We are British. Life, liberty and the pursuit of happiness – ditto. The Australian constitution is a statute of the British parliament, creating under the crown of the United Kingdom a Commonwealth, the six colonies as states, and a common market. The guarantees of liberties numbered two: religious tolerance, but only under the Commonwealth and not the states; and freedom from discrimination, but only for residents of one state when in another. Few contemporary Australians know anything about their constitution and fewer still could say which principles it takes for granted. This may be no bad thing, of course. It helps to keep the gap between rhetoric and reality within manageable limits. We are spared much overblown oratory and this helps keep hypocrisy to a manageable level.

Even fewer traces of high purpose attended the foundation of colonial Australia. It was no flight from tyranny to Paradise, try as some officers might to give it a Miltonic dimension and others to detect the hand of Providence. The colony was born purebred British, an outhouse of the old country consequent upon the Americans defeating her in the War of Independence. Several of the early officials of New South Wales, including governors, had fought against the American revolutionaries. Some thought "American" when they thought "revolutionary" or "republican" or "loud upstart". These men ran a prison. Not a free settlement, a place like pre-revolutionary America where a host of political ideas noisily competed, nor a religious refuge; but a place of punishment and, for some time, religious persecution: a place whose gentry were determined to establish an outrageously privileged land-owning aristocracy, and by 1850 had gone a long way towards achieving their ambition. If what happens in infancy has anything to do with it, the Americans are not our natural allies but much more like our enemies. Twenty-five years after the foundation of the colony, before the settlers had found their way so much as a hundred miles west, before they had seen what the continent looked like, the Americans were waging another war against the British.

The French stayed anchored outside the heads while the Union Jack was raised in Sydney Cove; in America they had a large slice of the continent and much influence on American political philosophy and on American strategic thinking. The Americans also had Spain to deal with. The United States began life as a multicultural society. They had more than two centuries of slavery, from which white Americans grew fat, and a civil war that saved the union and emancipated the slaves at the cost of more than half a million lives. But such were the racial horrors that followed, some wondered if black Americans weren't better off before emancipation; and the robber baron capitalism of Gould, Morgan and the Rockefellers that "dethroned God and set up a shekel in His place" (in Mark Twain's words) made some of America's better souls look back to antebellum America as a serene and just age.

But in case we should get on our high horse, it is also true that Teddy Roosevelt, self-styled hero of the "emotional classes" in their war with "Economic Man", welcomed a Negro to the White House and appointed a Jew to his cabinet. At that time Australia's founders were drafting the legislative expression of White Australia.

A recitation of these generally well-known facts is only useful to remind us how different we are; how strangely insignificant and unformed compared to the American experience of wars, awakenings and contendings. There is some kind of measure to be found in the faces of Sherman and Grant, literate, brutal soldier-statesmen of the republic. You don't see those kinds of faces among the fathers of Australian federation. Explorers make another useful comparison. Burke and Wills, Giles, Warburton, Sturt and Stuart found a dead heart in the centre of the continent and the further west they went the worse it got. Their experience gave the country legends whose main themes were irony and fatalism, hard-luck stories. Traversing the land from east to west Lewis and Clark found majesty and riches beyond measure and gave Americans yet more reason to glow with confidence and believe that they were blessed.

Even by the end of the nineteenth century the Americans did not *need* the rest of the world, beyond the purposes of commerce. The United States *was* the world; all a man like Charles Schneider of Cincinnati needed to know, or a boy like Huck Finn needed to discover. George W. Bush might look and sound to us like the dimwit he probably is, but Americans have not cared about how they looked in the world since Jefferson went to Paris. It's why so often when you meet them overseas or hear them talking, you can't help but feel that in the American mind the rest of the world exists as something extraneous to real life.

Turn-of-the-century immigration to America is a mirror image of the same phenomenon. Why should America take on the sensibilities of the rest of the world when the rest of the world wanted to be American? The millions of people who rolled through Ellis Island in the last decade of the old century and the first decades of the new did not come as part of a plan for a multicultural society. They were simply swallowed up by forces more powerful than xenophobia, prejudice, eugenics or any petty human motive for exclusion. They delivered to the United States unstoppable energy, mass, genius, character, hardship, cheap labour, another vast chapter in the American story. The lesson of immigration – through Ellis Island or Station Pier (or Christmas Island) – is always courage. It takes courage for the immigrants to come. It takes courage to take them in. And countries that take them gain courage from doing so.

America's proximity to Europe obviously gave it a great advantage over Australia in the contest for migrants. So too, perhaps, the fact that one destination was a flourishing republic and the other a British colony constructed from a jail. No person in his right mind would choose a jail over a republic; just as no one in possession of the facts would choose a British ship over an American. The republic also had the advantage of attracting people from all corners of Europe, including the British Isles; people who, when they arrived, were less inclined than were British migrants to Australia to think their stay was temporary or a home away from home. Is it possible that American immigrants more decisively cut the painter with home and were quicker to become American citizens and patriots? For the first hundred and fifty years of Australia's existence the effort was always at least partly to merge Australia's culture, economy, political structure and strategic interest with Britain's. As late as the 1930s R.G. Menzies was putting the case in London. Did Britain feel, he asked his hosts: "that its sons and brothers, one might almost say its sons and lovers, in Australia, are its own flesh and blood, or does it regard them as 'remittance men'?" The answer, which Menzies said would determine our mutual relations, "not merely for the next five years, but for the next five hundred years", is much less interesting than the question. Menzies was – at this stage of his life at least – tending to obsessiveness about blood. "Also we will make promise so long as the blood endures ..." he wrote on the bottom of one of his speeches. He imagined that the "sixty million people who ought to be in Australia tomorrow" could be at once the answer to Britain's social ills and the key to Australia playing "the part that we ought to play in the future of the British race". It was a theme he returned to repeatedly – Australia was like a son grown to adulthood, and seeking now to play a useful part in the British family. It was not a mercantile relationship but a blood relationship. He could not imagine any surer source of strength than this Britishness, this feeling that "my strength is yours".

There was Menzies's British blend and there was America's hybrid energy. No one can safely say which was the more valuable boatload, but a survey of, say, Australia's most successful postwar entrepreneurs, does suggest that it was not only the tyranny of distance that cost Australia the sort of vigour America enjoyed, but also our colonial status for the first century and our colonial mentality for much of the second.

Great oratory and high principle have always ridden shotgun on American self-interest. The American republic grew with God, the Constitution and the Declaration of Independence to guide it (and, after the Civil War, Lincoln's Gettysburg Address). The Australian colonies, if any single guiding light can be discerned at all, trekked manfully towards a "New Britannia in another world". During the Civil War, Her Majesty declared a position of strict neutrality and Australian colonial governments naturally followed suit. Nevertheless, when the confederate raider *Shenandoah* turned up in Port Phillip to land prisoners and take on crew, thousands of citizens went down to the water's edge and cheered her sailors. And a squad of the local elite took the ship's captain and his officers to the Melbourne Club and cheered them too. It is by no means certain that either show of enthusiasm indicated support for the rebel cause over the union, or even approval of the *Shenandoah's* notorious exploits in the Pacific. (By the end of the war she had plundered or destroyed thirty-six ships.) It was probably enough that she was American.

It was generally our way with the Americans. Twenty-five years earlier Charles Wilkes and two ships from the United States Exploring Expedition, a vast scientific and imperialistic enterprise surveying the Pacific, slipped into Sydney Harbour. Wilkes told his hosts how easily he might have ransacked the place, so poor were its defences. The colonial gentry of New South Wales were only too pleased to show them around. When the US Navy, known as the Great White Fleet, arrived in 1908,

Sydney crowds were positively jubilant. We might find them strange and not have a clue what stratagem or interest lay behind their occasional appearances, and we would deny that our response should be taken as admiration or sympathy for the republican course they had taken, but we loved to see them. No doubt it had much to do with our isolation and the comfort of seeing powerful English-speaking white men in this part of the world. But perhaps it was also rather like the way we found their music irresistible, the absence of inhibition, the love of display, their unembarrassed attitude to wealth, the way Fred Astaire and Judy Garland make you feel when they sing "We'll Walk down the Avenue". It is possible that somewhere in our minds we saw in these Americans the people we might have been.

By the time the Australian colonies federated, the United States was a century-old republic and a burgeoning imperial power. While Australians scratched together a constitution in the midst of a drought, a rabbit plague, an economic depression and a British war in South Africa, the Americans lived in a gilded age. Having learned the secret of electricity from Edison and the "secret of combination" from J.P. Morgan at about the same time, the country powered along like a locomotive. The effect was compound, especially as they also knew the secret of the tariff. Soon they learned too the secret of the alternating current in motors (from a Serbian immigrant) and the secret of advertising and the secret of clubs, cabals and plutocracy. American business took everything before it, including the American labour movement.

Remarkable as it now seems, we who went to school in the conservative, anti-communist '50s and '60s were taught the history of Australian labour. We learned about the rise of the trade unions and the Labor parties, as if it were inseparable from the rise of democracy. It was a legitimate, even heroic, part of Australian history. American labour never achieved the same status in American history. Had it been taught to Americans as it was taught to us, it would have been, as well as labour history, the history of staggering graft and corruption, spies, stooges and thugs, and the Winchester rifle and the baseball bat as instruments of political oppression; the history of Pinkerton Detective Agency whose employees in 1892, according to one historian, outnumbered the nation's standing army. It would have been, as they say, the downside – including the downside of mass immigration.

The more obvious presence of labour history in the story we were taught reflects not only our different experience but also different political values. In 1890s America, business, while brutally cracking the head of any worker in whom class consciousness was forming, gloated that it was "gradually subverting the power of the politician and rendering him subservient to its purposes". In Australia, Labor was incorporated into the system so thoroughly it formed one side of politics and the parliaments and one side of the political, social and industrial equation, and has done ever since. From the start both sides of politics agreed on the need for government intervention in the economy and society, including machinery to regulate the wages and conditions of labour. The consensus, described by Paul Kelly as the "Australian Settlement", was meliorist. Only recently has this broken down in the face of, first, financial deregulation and, more recently, labour market deregulation. Some might lament this and some might even hope to restore the government's role. It is unlikely that much can or will ever be done to reverse this process. The most useful thing is to recognise that in taking these decisions we took the biggest step we have ever taken towards the American social model. And this has profound implications for how we conceive of Australia and how we make it cohere.

5.

His vote is the desire of the politician — indeed, it is the very breath
of the politician's being; the parliament exists to do the will of the
workingman, and the Government exists to exercise it.

—Mark Twain on Australia, 1897

The difficulty to think at the end of the day
When the shapeless shadow covers the sun
And nothing is left except light on your fur ...

—Wallace Stevens, "A Rabbit as King
of the Ghosts", quoted in *Rabbit is Rich*

The missing part in Rabbit's life is what he does with those little bits that feed the soul. Feed the mouth he can manage, though even that can go begging when Janice screws up with the meal. The lusts he can feed, in mind if not always in body. But what is there for the soul? And how does he get it? Not that we would want to change him into a liberal academic, a Brahmin or a union leader – he's cute the way he is. As Thelma says, he's "lovely".

For our purposes the vacancy for which Rabbit stands was the one left by the death of God and the inadequacy of all replacements. Rabbit is the problem anticipated by Tocqueville: if you replace God with humanism and monarchs with the sovereignty of the people, to what will faith adhere? The answer was supposed to be, in part, a national ideal: democracy itself and all its heroes and history and rhetoric, its symbols, songs and flags. "I have never had a feeling politically that did not spring from the sentiments embodied in the Declaration of Independence", Lincoln once said. All these sentiments Americans have in abundance and work feverishly to maintain: the sacred texts of Jefferson and Lincoln worked over and over again, all the way down to that address delivered by George W. Bush to the joint sitting of Congress after the September 11 attack, which Ollie North, no less, within hours declared on CNN to be one of the greatest American speeches. The Americans long ago developed a natural dogma for the country and still breed up leaders who can regurgitate it at will.

But it was never enough by itself. That's where the little things make their entrance; the voluntary life of the nation that Tocqueville believed was essential if democracy was not to turn into tyranny. He meant in particular those associations that fill the gap between the people and the executive power: the churches, the lodges, unions, interest groups and clubs (Rabbit and Janice have their golf club). With the exception of the golf club, all these have seriously withered, but gardens, sunrooms, sunken living rooms and ten times more than even Rabbit, much less Tocqueville, could have imagined are there in models to suit every taste and pocket. All investments in ease and comfort for oneself and family are proof against despair and anarchy. How will a person fill his days? This is what the political question comes down to. How will the people or the nation advance? is academic by comparison. Our leaders now appear to understand this as a matter of political instinct. It is the stuff of politics as well as commerce. But the doctrine must accommodate a kind of paradox: whole-hearted pursuit of self-interest and ease and comfort is a step closer to American "individualism" and a step away from Australian "collectivism", "battlers" and the catchphrase no Australian politician can resist, the "fair go". Not even resort to such fabulous mantras as "the greatest share-holding democracy in the world" will alter the trajectory. And so long as the little things that feed the soul, from Nike to the news, come straight out of the American blender, more and more of our days will be filled like Rabbit's.

Unfortunately, the equation is far from perfect. The blessings of a democracy, even one deemed sacred, do not satisfy everyone. People, especially Americans it seems, still pin their hopes on whatever can be made to seem *more* sacred: new, renovated and crank religions, nature and Thoreau, witch-hunts, conspiracy theories including those involving extra-terrestrial visitations (for which the FBI has a separate website), hallucinogens, the Body, the Mind, product brands.

> One Sabbath morn, as heavenward
> White Mountain tourists slowly spurred,
> On every rock, to their dismay,
> They read the legend all the way –
> SAPOLIO.

Sapolio was a brand of soap and Bret Harte wrote the verse about it in 1876. A century later, far from satirising them, Harry Angstrom is as addicted to comparing product brands as he is to comparing the different shapes and textures of different women's pubic thatch. It is by a process of comparison that he reaches the conclusion that America must be the happiest place on earth. And by the very same process we often hear Australians talk themselves into the same conclusion. In the course of an election campaign I was told by a man in a northern rivers town that, as Australia was the greatest country in the world, and this was the best town in Australia, and the bar of the Leagues Club where we stood at eleven a.m. in the morning while everyone was playing bingo was the best place in town, the square of maroon carpet on which we stood was the best square of carpet in the world. In fact these variations on Rabbit's reflection assume greater significance in Australia because, with little else to render "sacred" after the fair go and Gallipoli, the thought itself is one of the tablets of natural Aussie dogma.

Therein, surely, lies the problem – or one of them. What is there to sacralise? Who is there to inhabit the pantheon? The very nature of our history, our traditional agnosticism and the national character we so admire in ourselves militate against heroes. So our leaders are left saying that Donald Bradman is the greatest Australian – a leader of eleven men, who could use a bat like no other before or since, but could not bowl. An Australian Rabbit might put Bradman front and centre in his pantheon, but the American one would know that Babe Ruth and Jack Nicklaus don't belong with Lincoln. Harry knows there is something beyond sport and sex; he just can't concentrate for long enough to find it.

Who else goes in? The last man standing from World War I? Phar Lap? John Curtin, and Menzies for balance? And what words are there to sing or recite or work over as the Americans do, so that every speech echoes Gettysburg? Henry Lawson has had his day and will not endure like Mark Twain – or Kipling for that matter. Henry Handel Richardson is admired principally by the "elites". Patrick White came too late, and is too difficult and writes more in reaction to Australia than on behalf of it. It is not because great deeds have not been done: it is that they do not amount to something articulate and powerful enough for the nation to gather around.

I can think of no better expression of this curious national inadequacy than the occasion of the first Keith Murdoch lecture in Melbourne this year. The speech, delivered by Keith Murdoch's son, Rupert, an American citizen, in the main concerned the Australian government's failure to spend enough on education and research. One could only applaud the sentiment; it is a scandalously poor record. But Murdoch's measure of this failure was entirely economic and comparative – as if he knew that his old countrymen only respond to their shortcomings when they are compared to the strengths of the Finns. Just as dispiritingly, not once did he mention the possibilities for personal growth and fulfilment, the advance of useful knowledge or the improvement of communities that for most of human history have been thought to inhere in education. Apparently not anymore – education is a means of human capital formation.

Sharing the stage for the oration, spotlit in a glass case, was the armour worn by Ned Kelly; and when it was over guests were treated to a reading of Kelly's barmy "Jerilderie Letter", accompanied by Irish singing, dancing and mock punch-ups, and Nellie Melba warbling gorgeously. It was not that it was not done well, but it *was* a wonder it was done at all, there, at a fundraiser for the State Library of Victoria, to go with a speech about education, and much as it hurts to say this – that it was being done *again*.

The inadequacy of funding for education and research that Murdoch noted (he did not comment on the distribution of funding) is much more worrying than the lack of a sacred text or rites that the floor show somehow underlined. The lack of a decent research and education system *and* the presence of an expatriate modern media equivalent of John Pierpont Morgan to tell us about it is more worrying still – but it is possibly the fate of postcolonial societies to go on welcoming eminent foreigners and expatriates like royalty long after we have forgotten the reason for doing it.

All countries need a sacred story, or at least all peoples do. This country has a sacred story up to 1945 or so, even 1965. As with most other new-world countries it does not satisfy the indigenous people and won't until the story of their dispossession is persuasively included in it. Neither the present government, nor the present Opposition should it one day form a government, are likely to seriously attempt this: the government because it covets the votes of bigots and ignoramuses thinly disguised as "battlers" and is led by a man who refuses to believe the Aboriginal story or its legitimacy as Australian history; the Opposition because it just covets the votes. As a consequence many non-Aboriginal Australians will also find the story less than sacred or true, and with this disenchantment will go other articles of national faith. The pity of this is greater because, even without the Aboriginal component, the story is powerful and moving. It tells of a flourishing democracy, sentimentally, and in some important ways formally, attached to Great Britain, a continent tamed by hard work and ingenuity, not as it turned out to establish a new Britannia in another world but an Anglo-Saxon society of a distinctive Australian character; with sound institutions, a spirit of social progress, a facility to battle through, a loveable tendency to larrikinism, good sportsmen and even better soldiers. Gallipoli was the making of it, then the battlefields of France. There *was* an Australian pantheon emerging, and the war memorials built between the wars were a powerful and imaginative expression of it. Tobruk and Kokoda and Changi are bound to become part of the story if it can be kept alive.

A modest new memorial on the perimeter of the new Parliament House has a view of the mountains and plains under that huge Canberra sky. The inscription says, "Look around you, these are the things they believed in". This was the other part of the sacred text thus far – the love of the land and the prospect of owning a bit of it. It's the dream romanticised and sentimentalised by Henry Lawson in *Reedy River* and Banjo Paterson in *Clancy of the Overflow* – the open-air democracy. But the inscription tells a sadder tale. In fact, of all the memorials in Australia I think this new one is the most poignant. What catches in the throat is the past tense – it is the verbal equivalent of a distant crow or magpie. Those Australians did believe in something, and they died for it. That much of the text is sacred, and like the land itself it belongs as much to the good people of Carlton and Balmain as it does to John Howard or Les Murray or R.M. Williams and the good people of the bush who get around in his moleskins.

The problem is it's over. It does not connect in the way it once did. The American sacred story is also essentially over, but it connects through the Declaration, the flag, the republic and the ringing familiar words. To outsiders it's a little repellent and a long way from the truth, but it works, it stays alive. The Australian story does not work anymore, or not well enough at least to hang the modern story on. A point has been reached where the words "fair go", "Gallipoli" and "show me a better country if you don't like this one" just don't do the job. The flag and the monarchy have reached a similar point. The existing panoply of symbols and mantras excludes too many people and too much of what has happened since the war – the migrants, Vietnam, the increase in the educated population, the beneficiaries and victims of the new economy, the new roles for women and new awareness of their roles in the past, a new awareness of the land. Australia now contains multitudes that the legend cannot accommodate. So long as our leaders ply the legend as if it *can* accommodate them, the further we drift from the truth about ourselves. It is quite possible to win political contests without confronting this truth, or by encouraging all sorts of false sentiment or turning ignorance and resentment to advantage. But the country loses. At times in our postwar history, our political imagination has matched the social and economic forces working on the nation and its consciousness. There have been times when the future became the main interest. But each time the bird was caught, stilled. Just now it might as well be dead.

If the country has a problem, so has John Howard. He has been trying to stuff a pluralist, postmodern bird into a pre-modern cage. The bird won't go. It's not that it won't fit, but rather that it's not a bird. It's no one thing. It's our multitudes. During his years in Opposition he called forth a class of people he called "battlers" – ciphers or ghosts of the pre-1945 Australia with echoes of the Depression, the forgotten people of R.G. Menzies, the diggers of World War I and the goldfields, cobbers. And as the battlers were glorified, another nebulous class was vilified. These were the "elites". It gave the battlers better definition to encourage images of effete, opinionated bleeding hearts chattering on the pavements while real people did the work and battled. Labor leapt on the idea like a sloth falling from a tree and soon they too were praising the "battlers" who loathed them, and loathing the chatterers who would lay down their lives for them. Strange to dismiss from your ranks the educated, the open-minded, the moderately thoughtful and reflective – and brand them for good measure. The archetypes of this political strategy are authoritarian, which is to say brutal and stupid. With both parties employing it here, the value of the tactic in a liberal democracy is hard to judge. Can we call it a success if one party wins with it and the other loses? On the other hand, it seems fairly certain that few benefits will flow to the country itself in the long term – and few to the political parties, dare we say. On the contrary, the effect has been to give ignorance at least the same value as education, likewise bigotry and tolerance, creativity and crassness, past realities and the present one. Much that a country – and a society – needs, including the capacity to imagine, to regenerate and reinvent itself, has been discounted. It's a strategy to honour every Rabbit in Australia.

In conjunction with eccentric policy priorities like half-strangling the ABC and suffocating the universities, it is also a policy to imitate the original Rabbit. That is to say, to imitate the hole in America. Harry Angstrom lives the American dream and finds it hollow at the centre, much as President Bush's war on terrorism speech was hollow at the centre – platitudes, phrases whose meaning had been leached out of them, tacked together like a henhouse, to borrow from George Orwell. Rabbit finds, and his life gives expression to the discovery, that the same thing has happened to religion – they have taken God out of it; as they took the individual out of individualism and put conformity in its place; as they took labour out of capitalism, liberalism out of enlightenment, the world out of worldliness and the taste out of food. Rabbit doesn't get it. The Americans don't get it. Watch CNN for half an hour – or even more alarming, Fox News – and try not to say, "They don't get it". And what is almost beyond understanding, this from a country of matchless resources and institutions and ideals and genius.

6.

Far better it is to dare mighty things, to win glorious triumphs, even though checkered by failure, than to take rank with those poor spirits who neither enjoy much nor suffer much, because they live in the gray twilight that knows not victory nor defeat.

—Theodore Roosevelt, 1899

Only occasionally is an American leader as frank as Grover Cleveland was back in 1896. "[We] have a concern with [Cuba] which is by no means of a wholly sentimental or philanthropic character", he said. His words captured something about America that should help us see more truly the nature of our position and, more importantly, encourage us to think about what it might be in a decade or two. The same might be said of Teddy Roosevelt, the most gung-ho of all American presidents. He is quoted by way of advocating that, saddled as we are with the Americans one way or another, we make the best of it and don't go like Rabbit shambling towards the void. This country does have choices. One of them is to follow the United States as if her motives really are wholly sentimental or philanthropic; the other is to be as clear-eyed and self-interested as they are about things. Even if both positions produced the same material result, there is still more to be said for pursuing the second one because more dignity and less of the grey twilight attaches to it.

The second course, being based on a realistic assessment of the American position, might lead us to a more realistic – and fruitful – assessment of our own. Let us say, for instance, that we make it a rule of life with our ally that we attempt to emulate only the greatness in American society, we still cannot recreate the history from which the greatness sprang, and we would not want to. (We can have their music but not their slaves.) We know that our material and human resources cannot compare to theirs. In fact we are so unlike each other, it is almost impossible to think of anything they do that we could do as well while remaining consistent with our character. Their tradition of great benefactions to public institutions, for instance, conflicts with our tradition of reliance on government funding – and while it is possible to increase the proportion of private to public in this country, there is also a danger that any success will be seized on by governments keen to rid themselves of yet more obligations to society. It is true the very rich in Australia don't put as much back as they do in America, but perhaps they don't take as much out. On a more abstract plane, we could aim to be as full of confidence and hope as they are, but only at the risk of losing that weary fatalism by means of which we understand each other and charm the world. We could wave the flag like they do, but it's a loathsome habit and, in any case, the flag is not all ours. Imitation is too close to flattery and flattery makes us look like flunkies.

Better to avoid what we *don't like* in the Americans, and here Rabbit provides a useful negative example. Take his patriotism: it is mainly vapid because patriotism nearly always is, and American patriotism is particularly vapid. All patriotism looks backwards, and with a distorting mirror. Lacking both their history and their myths as well as any satisfactory "sacred text", we could do the sensible thing – we could make the guiding principles of Australia its diversity and pluralism, its inorganicness, the *absence* of oppressive and constraining symbols (the flag and the monarchy, for example, are meaningless), and seize the chance to create a postmodern republic or a "republic of opportunity" as Guy Rundle called it in the last Quarterly Essay – and a very civilised society. Australia is as much a lifestyle as it is a nation – we should make the nation in that image. As for the sacred text, the natural dogma, the ruling ideology – let it be the old one, but let it also be whatever exists now and whatever we have in mind for the future. Oscar Wilde, who loathed the "materialising spirit" he saw in America, wrote in *The Soul of Man under Socialism*: "It is with the future that we have to deal. For the past is what man should not have been. The present is what man ought not to be. The future is what artists are". It is a more useful philosophy now than it was when he thought of it. For artist, read imagination and creativity, and then read just about any American whiz on the future. The whizzes are in tune with Wilde: those two commodities of artists (if not artists themselves), plus skills and knowledge, will be like diamonds. An Australia whose guiding principle was possibility, and that valued intelligence and skill more than it has in recent years, might actually revive the sentiment last uttered a century ago – that, with America, it was the hope of humankind.

The same kind of Australia would also return to the position of just a few years back when it maintained a healthy friendship with the United States while engaging vigorously with the countries of Asia. Our security does not appear to be more assured in proportion to our retreat from that policy, but our horizons do seem to be lower, and with them our sense of possibility less tangible. Again it feels like the Rabbit syndrome: camped by the burrow or halfway down it. And as night follows day, timidity becomes fear and fear becomes hostility, and with so much feeling pumping in our own veins, suddenly we can't or don't imagine what's happening in others, even though their distress is obvious and much greater than ours. Acts unconscionable to generous, confident and brave people – that is to say, people more like Australians four or five years ago – become justifiable and necessary.

Emptiness is the great danger. If the little things that feed the soul are the same here as they were in Rabbit's Brewster, Penn., c.1985, then we are headed for mediocrity and have no hope of delivering on our promise. Perhaps we can feed our souls with stock market shares and new technology and Gatorade, but there are signs that both sides of politics now sense that something more is needed. This sense may have arisen from the experience of tramping round the fading provinces and towns, hearing people repeatedly state their need to be useful as individuals and as communities. It was one of the lessons of politics: how a prevailing ideology shuts out the oldest, most rudimentary observations about society and human nature, and even when they are clearly pointed out will not permit them to enter. After years in denial it transpires that there is such a thing as a need for recognition after all; and also a need to be useful to one's fellows or at least to oneself. Individual and community effort is undoubtedly the key to meeting these needs, but governments that want to build a bridge back to the people will find a useful part to play. For those who do, the possibilities are almost infinite. But we should not expect too much too soon; it takes a long time to turn around a train of thought. Until that happens we can expect the federal government to pursue whatever policies they reckon match the idea of turning Australia into "the greatest shareholding democracy in the world". It is a sterling ambition, but constitutes such a narrow and perverse definition of democracy as to be either impossible to achieve or pointless. It is also very like making the Declaration of Independence the foundation of your belief and then shrinking from the word "liberal".

7.

Let us have faith that right makes might, and in that faith, let us, to the end, dare to do our duty as we understand it.

—Abraham Lincoln, 27 February 1860

Refugees frighten us. Reconciliation with Aborigines, native title, a republic – these things consistently prove too much for us. If Australia cannot face the truth that its life is its own and no one else's, then we should deal with the fear. It will not do to weld the negative and reactionary sentiments in the community into some kind of ideological truncheon to wave at intruders and frighten off internal opposition. We can't piece this mood together with the modern pluralist society *and* try to make it all cohere around the bathos of very old men and a semi-mythic military catastrophe in Turkey. If it has in fact been calculated that this refurbished fantasy is good politics or the best we can do with the place, if this is to be our disposition and identity, the best we can imagine, it must be a symptom of a greater need. And if that need is security, and we no longer want to find it on our own, there is but one remedy. Far better than playing America's deputy in South-East Asia, a region from whose forums we are comprehensively excluded, let us petition for inclusion in the American union. Demand it.

We are not disposed to live alone, obviously, so let us live with them. Would we have less respect in the world? No, we would have more, and we would have much more respect in Washington – we would have Congressmen, possibly even cabinet members. Think of what we would gain. More dignity, more influence and more peace of mind. It's all upside, surely. No more fifty-cent dollars. No more current account nightmare. We can amortise the debt. Let us integrate fully with the world's biggest economy and take our place under the missile shield. If they'll go to war over New York, they'll go to war over every state. It's much better than ANZUS. No agonising foreign policy decisions, no more excruciating arguments about the national identity. The cultural cringe ends the day we join. We're talking freedom here – a bloodless revolution and one straight out of the end-of-history handbook.

We should put it to them straight, like a business deal. It's not as if there's no upside for them. They get a state instead of a colony. They can go on pretending they're not imperialists, but we won't have to go on pretending our soul's our own. It's win–win if ever there was such a thing. Frankly it's hard to see a better idea coming up this side of 2010 – and if we wait any longer than that there'll be no deal to strike. We'll be begging them to have us.

That's the first option. It means jettisoning both the republic and the monarchy – which happens to be another argument for doing it. Should the republicans Costello or Crean become prime minister, there will be something weird and contradictory about backing out of Asia and into the deputy's role and urging a republic at the same time. But this is not the only reason why a republic is less attractive than it used to be. The "irritable patriotism" exemplified by Hanson and swallowed up by Howard, the new xenophobia and meanness, the retreat to Fortress Australia, all bode badly for a republic. The chances are it would reflect this mood. The new Australia might be too much like the old one created with a White Australia policy and other more easily understood phobias a century ago. The symmetry is too striking, the risk too great: particularly as the people continue to resolutely oppose appointing the head of state by any method other than popular election. This would so change the character of Australian democracy and so politicise the head of state that large numbers of republicans could not vote for it. Seeing the truth of this might save the country from the ultimate Americanisation – a White House – but imagine if it didn't. Far from the light and liberating republic on offer in the '90s, with power more diffuse and openness a byword, we will find ourselves with power more concentrated and the present xenophobia and tinny nationalism enshrined in it. The republic, remember, was to put the icing on the cake: it was to confirm the best in us, not the worst.

There remains the option of the status quo, insofar as it can be called that while Britain hurries to look more like an American vassal than we do. In view of the souring of Australia the monarchy is not such a bad option anymore. It is a timid course, but Australians just now *are* timid, as well as cantankerous, and the timid are more likely to vote away their liberties. Something as silly as the present arrangement is appropriate in the present circumstances, even if we wake up one morning and find Charles and Camilla on our throne. It's a pity they come from where they do, that's all. If only they were American it would be perfect. Bill Clinton comes to mind.

Quarterly Essay, November 2001

All the way with Donald J?

THE MATERIAL BENEFITS OF AUSTRALIA'S alliance with the United States are too many and too great to throw away – even on days when we cannot recall what they are. It is the bedrock of our security. Let's concede this much to the people who design our foreign policy, and to the people gathered like woodlice in the think tanks, and the media commentators who comment on their thinking – the foreign policy elite. The US alliance is the first premise, the one unchanging thing, the fixed star.

We know that the idea of an alliance or anything of the kind remaining "fixed" runs counter to the example of history, where nothing ever has been. The same goes for what is called in high circles the "current international environment". The current international environment, much like all international environments preceding this one, is decidedly *unfixed* – or "fluid", as they call it. But deeper consideration, far from undoing the logic of the alliance, actually reaffirms its usefulness. For in a fluid environment it is to something fixed, like a gatepost or a telephone pole, that sensible people cling even if the fluid rises and more promising things float by.

This desire to hang on, this condition of *stuckness*, is doubtless one reason why the US alliance remains almost as much an article of faith with the common people as it does with the best and the brightest. We are all heirs to the same primordial instinct, whether we have connections in Washington or not. So long as it is fixed we are fixed.

Seeing our American cousins down here has always heartened us: not just in the Cold War and the Pacific War but also way back in 1908, when at Alfred Deakin's invitation the Great White Fleet of the US Navy arrived to proclaim amid the local rapture that we were not the only white people in this part of the world. It turned out that Washington's imperial interests in the Pacific made a nice match with our anxieties about it, a better one indeed than Britain's interests did. The logic of the alliance was apparent even then: the Yanks would have our back if ever Whitehall gave up on us. It was a rehearsal for 1942, the big jump imagined. The enthusiastic welcome, Deakin said, was in part due to Australians' "blood affection for the Americans", but in larger part to their "distrust of the yellow races".

As there is with the nation itself, there is a racist gene in the alliance, specifically an anti-Asian one, but it's so far back in our evolution no one notices anymore – except possibly Asians. And should any Asian country raise the matter, our chaps can readily point to the polyglot composition of our population and migrant flows to demonstrate that the xenophobia of Australia's formative first seventy or eighty years is well behind us.

Not that anyone in Asia hobnobbing with our foreign policy elite would immediately notice much change in the racial profile; or anyone who deals with our business leaders and defence chiefs; or anyone who watches the national parliament. We might be "in" Asia, as Paul Keating said a quarter of a century ago, but Asia is still not quite in us. The United States is "in" us, and will remain so "till the crack of doom", as Robert Menzies said, and didn't leave a lot of room for anyone else. No matter: as business is business, diplomacy is diplomacy. Smarts are smarts. We can balance our interests. There is no need to choose. Each relationship can be dealt with on its own terms. We can deal firmly and creatively with a towering and pervasive Chinese presence in the region and yet maintain the alliance with our old friend and partner and cousin, buddy and mate, with whom we share so many values.

One bows before this wisdom in advance. They're not called elite for nothing. They know their stuff. Dare we suggest, however, that the US alliance looks more and more like their Pascalian wager: should it happen one day that no reasoning or evidence compels us to believe in it, prudence dictates that we continue to do so just in case. But since China is *the* country of our future, it seems neither particularly logical nor prudent to be always dragging into the room this evidence of our inextinguishable and non-negotiable loyalty to a rival country, thus lending to the Chinese relationship a permanent aspect of ambivalence, a perceptible signal that we are not quite who we say we are. Yet to believe otherwise requires us to think that we can treat one relationship as special and the other, of at least equal importance, as merely necessary; and that it matters not to the necessary party if we present as a country in full possession of its mind and negotiating its own interests in good faith, or as someone else's deputy or lapdog.

Viewed from another angle, just now the alliance has a lot in common with that moment in 1908 when an old empire with one set of interests in the region waxed furious that we should, if only momentarily, embrace a likely newcomer with interests better suited to our own. But that was a choice between one protector and another, and even then it took us several decades (and a couple of wars) to make the call. Could we now bear to tell the Americans, in words akin to John Curtin's, that "free of any pangs as to our traditional links" to Washington in future we would be looking to ourselves?

Can we ever overcome our fear of abandonment, the national syndrome exhaustively surveyed from different viewpoints by Allan Gyngell, David Walker and others, that propels us into the arms of powerful friends? Maybe not. The fear is primal, the infant's fear: if we're not over it by this stage, we might never be.

Now the country in whose embrace we have for so long found comfort is itself – once more – in the grip of fear: "nameless, unreasoning, unjustified" fear, as F.D.R. described it all those years ago. Being the world's sole superpower, the Americans have no more powerful friend to fly to. They are galvanised instead by exceptionalist fantasies, comforted by regenerative frontier myths of conquest and revenge. They hide their fear in an almighty military and security apparatus beyond the reach of democratic control or oversight. As the British did in their full flush of empire, they wage never-ending war in distant places far from public view. Land, sea and air, space and cyberspace, only "full spectrum dominance" – the whole dang universe – will do.

Donald Trump is the present spokesman for this derangement, the fear's instrument and its preposterous embodiment. Trump is a racist, an ignoramus, a huckster and a creep. The human face of our US ally is contemptuous of human rights, the free press and any democratic norm or diplomatic protocol that doesn't suit him, or which he thinks can be trashed to his political advantage. In addition to the trade war he recently started, the United States under Trump's "America First" banner has handed China undreamed of high ground and momentous strategic gifts by retreating from its role as Asia's security provider. The Trans-Pacific Partnership on which Australian governments set so much store, Trump knocked on the head. He flirts with authoritarian thugs while attacking, mocking and undermining democratic allies and institutions of the so-called rules-based international order. He has demolished truth, or what was left of it. He may even be Vladimir Putin's stooge.

Not everything about him, or even most of what he's done, demands an ally's reproach. He has not bombed Hanoi, which brought Gough Whitlam out against Nixon, or invaded Iraq, which got Mark Latham making rude noises. But he has done enough, surely, to make the silence from Canberra something to wonder at. Some of the commentators are showing signs of startlement, and tell us Trump is causing alarm, but the prime minister and his colleagues are mute. Perhaps we can put it down to sage diplomacy, to the diplomats' traditional insistence that these things are best done behind the scenes, or to a more sophisticated idea of loyalty than the rest of us maintain. Even allowing a role for half-honourable motives or sensible pragmatism – or a wish to avoid comparisons with Mark Latham – we're entitled to ask if the refusal of the government and the Opposition to express any kind of disquiet on the nation's behalf is best explained by the alliance: not in a literal sense, but a psychological one.

The terms of the alliance did not oblige us to join the Americans in Iraq, but long before that calamitous adventure it had morphed into a "whither thou goest ..." sense of obligation and brotherly co-dependence. Fraternal duty, it seems, meant more than any rational assessment of US motives, some of which were peculiar to the toxic cabal surrounding George W. Bush and had nothing to do with Australia's interests. The same sentiment made it much less likely that John Howard or those around him would see through the folly or, if they did, call it for what it was.

Now, having been told all our lives that the United States is the guarantor of security in our region, and of free trade, order and liberal democracy everywhere, and having come to mainly believe it, we see daily unmistakable signs that Trump is pulling it all apart. And such good allies are we – such mates – we dare not speak.

Mateship can do that. It can stunt your growth and narrow your awareness of possibility. It can make you a bit stupid; especially if you're the weaker one, it can make you a bit poodly, inclined to silence even when your mate turns out to be a psychopath. Mates can destroy us. The alliance mutated. It has become a sort of opiate. Feeding on anxiety, prejudice and apathy, among other human frailties, it lives more opulently in our brains than it ever did on paper. It has taken possession of us when it's self-possession that we need.

The Monthly, August 2018

THE WORDS TO SAY IT

Teaching English

I'M IMPRESSED BY THE TITLE of this conference. Teaching English for social change is in a sense wonderfully old-fashioned – it sounds like La Trobe University thirty years ago, when all teaching had to be for social change. Every breath had to be for social change. One ate, drank, smoked and formed intimate relationships for social change.

I don't know how you teach English for social change – at least in the sense that the old La Trobe Labor Club meant it. But I'm glad some people are determined on the notion that language and literature have social utility.

I have this idea too. I came to the conclusion over the four years I spent in Canberra that if we could improve the standard of written communication in the Commonwealth public service by say 25 per cent – I mean nothing more than making the language direct, active and clear – it would significantly lift the morale and happiness of all government employees and quite possibly raise GDP by as much as 2 per cent.

You see I think we ought to try to unclog Australia's language. I don't mean to be reprimanding, curmudgeonly or pedantic about it. Too often that is how the guardians of language behave. Often I think they could not live in a country whose citizens were equal to them in their command of grammar – that correcting other people is a sort of snobbish addiction. The effect is counterproductive, of course – it means they can

---

A version of a speech given at "Still Points, Turning Worlds: Teaching English for Social Change", the 1999 conference of the Victorian Association for the Teaching of English.

be safely ignored. It may even encourage a perverse ideological justification for crummy English.

I'm not sure that language should be a matter of standards anyway. I think the best approach is less lofty. Why not simply say – wouldn't you be happier if you could write what is on your mind, say what you mean, and if other people liked hearing you speak? Wouldn't you like to sound like a babbling brook? Like the Irish at their best?

For political reasons we need to connect language to happiness and economics. Especially economics. Modern governments take notice of economics. It will be painful. We will have to give up a few hostages. Stop worrying about some of the egregious but unstoppable fashions – let them say "empowerment" until they're sick of it. Give up on the words whose meaning is irretrievably lost – "disinterested" now means "uninterested". If I say I am here as a *dis*interested observer, people will think I'm not interested and say – so why bother to come? It's not an argument worth having.

Stop worrying about split infinitives. Bob Hawke worried about split infinitives. Apparently, he was like a terrier about them. Yet for all this fastidiousness, when speaking off the cuff, he embarked on his sentences like a mad man with a club in a dark room – he bumped and crashed around for so long his listeners became more interested in the possibility of his escape than in what he was saying. When he emerged triumphantly into the light, they cheered with relief and exultation, but without having a clue what he'd been talking about.

Bob Hawke was the longest-serving Labor prime minister in our history and the second longest of any stamp. He led a competent and often imaginative government. His use of the language made it easier to lampoon him, but it didn't hold back his career, or the nation's progress, to any perceptible degree.

We need to get this thing in perspective. That our language is going through a horror stretch is undeniable and worrying. But faulty syntax and the misuse of words – the "standards" which are so often talked about – will not lead us to ruin. And there are some things we can't do much to change or stop. Modern education, modern media, modern politics – none of these allow for perfection or even the faintest possibility of it. Put yourself in the politician's position when he has to stare down a lens and answer an unanswerable question without a second's notice. Put yourself in your child's position, subjected to hours of entertainment conducted in the American vernacular – or in the teacher's position, confronted by children like this.

But we should not give up the fight. When he saw errant apostrophes on a memorial to Australian soldiers which had been erected by the Australian government on a battlefield in France, the writer Frank Moorhouse rang the prime minister's office to complain – at once, from a phone booth somewhere in Picardy. It was an exemplary thing to do, if only to protect the French from our plague.

Possessive apostrophes have run wild like rabbits, and only a lunatic would suggest that we should not try to halt their progress. But eternal vigilance and endless complaints will not make them go away. The pragmatic solution, the smart thing, is to abolish them altogether. Sadness is better than chaos.

While we're at it we might give up on any suggestion that language is, or ought to be, governed by immutable rules or that it should be immune to transmogrification. Better to adopt a welcoming demeanour when common speech approaches, even when it comes distorted and ugly, or like messages on a shortwave radio out of the deputy prime minister's mouth. Rex Hunt, on balance, is probably good for the language.

What is *bad* for the language is the dry rot of officialise and corporate speak at the centre of it. This sort of thing, from a prime ministerial address a few years ago: "Negotiations and persuasion are just as important in maintaining agreement and focus for the significant reforms which we have reached agreement about".

From the Department of Finance in 1995: "Given the within year and budget time flexibility accorded to the science agencies in the determination of resource allocation from within their global budget, a multi-parameter approach to maintaining the agencies budgets in real terms is not appropriate".

From the Australia Council in the early '90s: "The Council's emphasis on grants will continue to be of great importance in ensuring the ongoing viability of the arts in Australia. However, support at the demand end of the spectrum has the potential to provide multiplier benefits for artists which grants alone cannot provide".

It dulls the brain like chloroform. No one can confidently say what it means on first hearing or reading. And it's not an exception – it's a core sample of the language. People who write like this cannot be happy.

A new senator wrote the other day: "I have flagged with the Government my involvement to assist in resolving the issues that are impeding reconciliation. I would like to progress discussions with Indigenous people to set in process the parameters for reconciliation".

Not very long ago the ruling classes mocked or winced at the grammar and accent of ordinary Australians. Now the ruling language is laughable. *At this point in time all issues are progressed in terms of a language which is not appropriate to the overall strategy of achieving enhanced outcomes for all Australians.*

This is sad. What happens every day in those places where clarity is most essential, where the language most needs life and meaning, approaches tragedy.

You see I never wanted to be a Frank Devine or a Max Harris – a grump. But years now of writing speeches from briefs delivered to me by public service departments and agencies, or in some cases from large corporations, and listening to speeches, as I realise I have done since I was very young – all this has made me conscious of a great and widening cultural void.

Take my word for it – people in many government departments and in private industry do not know what they are saying to each other. Instead, every day they exchange dead things. You can see it in many of the words they use. For instance, I don't think I ever received a brief between 1992 and 1996 which did not contain the words "commitment" and "enhance".

I broke my vow to never write another speech last month and did one for the head of a major statutory authority. They reworked my draft to put it in language with which, they said, the speaker felt comfortable. I looked at the last line first – and there was the word "commitment".

I didn't look any further. "Commitment" is the worst kind of politician's word. To say I am committed to something means neither that I believe it – or else I'd say "I believe", not "I am committed" – nor that I will do it – or else I would.

"Enhance" can mean anything, which is why it's so popular with people who have lost the ability to say what they mean. Once we might have said improve or illuminate or accelerate, or lengthen, broaden or make hairier – any one of scores of verbs. Now we say "enhance". We enhance our competitiveness. We enhance our chances, our hair colour, our children.

Verbs are the key. I want a National Verb Retrieval Day. I want a moratorium on "enhance", "commitment", "in terms of" and "impacted"; and I want a massacre of clichés, principally "rich cultural diversity", "enhanced competitiveness", "this is a great country", "the lucky country" and the "tyranny of distance".

If we forbade the use of these words we would be forced to think of others. I know there's something Calvinist about it – but we could attach rewards and celebrations at the end of it all. These words are like dummies, they are a substitute for thinking and feeling. They reveal nothing, excite nothing and discourage inquiry.

Politicians, whose grammatical shortcoming should generally be excused, cannot be forgiven for stuffing us with dead words and phrases rendered meaningless by overuse. I don't mind if Paul Keating or John Howard misuse the word "fulsome" or mess up their syntax under pressure from the media or in parliament. But no leader can be forgiven giving us the same stale fish every Anzac Day or in the wake of great tragedies or triumphs.

We're entitled to quiz our politicians about the words they use in the same way we quiz them about their economic figures and projections or their travel allowances or their memory of cabinet meetings. What do you mean "innocent"? Did you feel innocent before that happened, and less innocent now? Where's your evidence? What do you mean the "supreme sacrifice"?

Much good writing and speaking of course comes from the heart – which is all the more reason why they shouldn't be allowed to *pretend* that it does. Is it any less a lie than bodgy Budget projections or fiddled travel allowance forms?

Verbs are good because it's much harder to cheat with them. That's why they're so scarce. You have to think about a verb. They're doing words. If you stop using doing words, chances are you'll stop doing. Anything. That's why I want a verb day. It would create a vast surge of mental activity – we could write on every wall what George Eliot says in *Middlemarch*: "We have got to exert ourselves a little to keep sane and call things by the names other people call them by".

An even better wall hanging for all those preparing to write – a book or a letter or an essay or memo – might be the words of Ulysses S. Grant. Grant led the Union armies to victory in the American Civil War, and later became president. In about 1880 someone borrowed and lost Grant's lifetime savings. Encouraged by Mark Twain, to recover his financial position he consented to write his memoirs. Just as he began, his doctor diagnosed terminal cancer. In great pain he wrote the 250,000-word memoirs in twelve months – and died. The memoirs sold massively and recovered the Grant finances for his family. John Keegan describes them as "the most revelatory autobiography of high command to exist in any language". Edmund Wilson said they are as great as the Commentaries of Julius Caesar. And before his death Grant said this: "a verb is anything that signifies to be; to do or to suffer. I signify all three". Grant wrote with verbs – he was after all a doing man. He could not command armies in battle without verbs, and so he could not describe what happened without them.

Asked how he managed his astonishing feat of memory, intellect and articulation, he uttered these wonderful words: "When I put my pen to paper I did not know the first word that I should make use of … I only knew what was in my mind, and I wished to express it clearly, so that there could be no mistaking it".

So – the first rule of writing is humility in the face of the task. It is terribly hard and unforgiving. I think anybody who writes anything should be encouraged to think of the craft they will need – we should teach writing, not creative writing, just writing. Whatever the subject, in the end they have to write it. Don't they? They have to know what is in their minds and wish to express it clearly so there is no mistaking it.

The second rule is don't even try to write until you have something in your mind. You do need an active mind to write. Grant was recreating. But he couldn't just spill it out, it had to come forth in a shape and with an order to it.

I would tell young writers to practise humility and thinking. You need a point of view to write but not one that obscures the thing you're trying to describe, that closes the possibilities and mysteries. You need sympathy to write. You need to be able to imagine how others feel.

Half of it *is* feeling. How well you feel, hear and see is half of it. I think writers should practise listening both to noise and to silence. And to your own voice. I talk the words as I write. And I read them aloud for rhythm. If there's no rhythm there's probably something wrong with the reasoning. And read other books aloud. I like reading so much now, I don't know why I bother writing. I wouldn't write if I could afford not to. I would only read. I'd ask people to read the Bible aloud, and Cervantes and Montaigne and García Márquez and Patrick White, Coleridge and Seamus Heaney. So they hear the power of that marriage – language and thought.

Speech given at the "Still Points, Turning Worlds"
English teachers' conference, Melbourne, July 1999

The public language

ENGLISH IS AN ACCOMMODATING LANGUAGE. What with the Normans, the colonies, the Industrial Revolution, the information revolution, the New English Bible, globalism, multiculturalism, it grows from umpteen roots and is forever changing – or "going pear-shaped" to use the current expression. There are also the Americans who went out on their own somewhat – and, according to Dr Johnson, infected English with a "tract of corruption". They created their own rhetorical tradition and made English, like much else they contacted, including entire peoples, peculiarly reflections of themselves. "England and America are two countries separated by a common language", George Bernard Shaw is supposed to have said. And when we hear George W. Bush and Tony Blair we know how accurate that observation was.

But the long view suggests it is best not to worry too much. We might as well admonish Shakespeare for adding hundreds of new words when he found the language could not support his literary ambitions. Appalled by the "decay" of English, Johnson compiled a dictionary that he hoped might make words "permanent, like the things they denote". His dictionary was marvellous but his hope was vain.

Pronunciation and meaning have shifted as often as the words themselves. In the last quarter of the eighteenth century, just as New South Wales was founded, Britain's new wealthy decided they could put a social gap between themselves and those on whom they sat by establishing new rules of pronunciation and vocabulary. To choose one from hundreds of other consequences of this enterprise, *vermin* became the word by which rats and other unwholesome creatures would be known in England (and Sydney). Across the Atlantic, the good folks having recently decided they didn't hold with English ways, they stuck with *varmints* – and *varmints* they have hunted to this day.

As a child, Samuel Lysons was taught, like all the Lysons before him, to mute the "h" in *humble, hospital* and *herbs*. But in the 1860s in *Our Vulgar Tongue* he complained that now he was expected to pronounce the "h" in these words and mute it in others where for centuries it had been audible. You can hardly blame him for grizzling, or Henry Parkes and others of his generation who never figured out the formula for "h"s.

Samuel Johnson's curmudgeonly descendants still lurk in the letters page of our newspapers, waiting to smite any author of a split infinitive or unfamiliar word or phrase. This year, in a couple of letters clogged with rage, I was savaged for using the words *methodology* and *historiography* – though in keeping with Johnson's dictum they denoted accurately what I meant and, with almost three centuries' residence in English dictionaries between them, have a reasonable claim to permanence. The pedants should be writing to the ABC to tell them not to say the prime minister "has refuted allegations". But even when they're right these people miss the point. We could spend every waking hour fuming about the misused words, misplaced apostrophes, misquoted homilies and epithets.

This week I heard a politician say that he liked "to get up the goat" of his opponent. Flying home I heard the same usage satirised in an episode of *Kath and Kim*. Who knows who came first? Many Australians under forty speak with the same rising inflection we hear in our soap operas. It excruciates the rest of us who learned from our forebears only the laconic descending mumble, and the new style is worse for being joined to Americanisms. A majority of the young prefer *butt* to *bum*, and more and more kick *ass* instead of *arse*. Children and teenagers tell me that the supermarket *is on Smith Street* when I have always thought it was *in* it. If I object they say there's no need to *holler* at them. They ask, like the Americans, "Are you done?" when they want to know if I have finished my tea. I wait nervously for the day when a granddaughter takes my glass and tells me she doesn't hold with drinking. But it is important to try not to care too much.

Education will be useful but it won't hold back the tide. Imitation is much the stronger element for the very good reason illustrated by the parrot, that imitation is linked to survival. Imagine you are a parrot in the White House, or within earshot – and who is not? We have to cope with this:

And if the values are good enough for our people they ought to be good enough for others, not in a way to impose because these are God-given values. These aren't United States-created values. These are values of freedom and the human condition and mothers loving their children.

The words are at once startling and confounding, and it's possible that the president was startled and confounded as he said them. It is as if by the imperfect power of speech he has inadvertently strayed into self-analysis and discovered all the contradictions of the American mind in the one afternoon. The Monroe Doctrine is in there in embryonic form, the traditional ambivalence about the imperial mission, the vision thing, the mother thing – and, above all, the thing about one indivisible republic under God. President Bush finds himself attempting to unravel a central strand in American orthodoxy – the strand of Providence, the belief that America is governed through God, and that God-given values and United States–created values are the same. And, it stands to reason, values don't come any better than this – people ought to be grateful for chrissakes. Naturally, it's the president's prose, not the strand, that comes apart.

Who knows what side of the American equation George W. Bush comes down on: Jeffersonian secularism or the theocratic strain? It is possible he does not know himself. John Ashcroft, his attorney-general, knows, however. We need look no further than his rendition of his own song "Let the Eagle Soar". No rational person can hear this without wondering (a) how he became attorney-general, (b) if we are not in even greater danger than we thought, (c) why the faithful always think that singing helps, and (d) if belief in God can only be maintained at fundamentalist pitch by a sort of Promethean urge to set something *against* God, by way of proving His power, or perhaps just a need for Him.

The president's reflections on matters pertaining to power offer little enlightenment or comfort – but because we do not want to be excluded and think survival depends on imitation, we can be sure that something like them will be parroted in Canberra. The question is, can we do it and keep our dignity? "Confident action that will yield positive results", President Bush says, "provides a kind of slipstream into which reluctant nations and leaders can get behind and show themselves that there has been – you know, something positive has happened toward peace".

It must be possible to fight international terrorism and tyranny and still keep a halfway decent grip on the language. It might even be necessary. We tried hard but dropped off along with the rest of the world – Tony Blair apart – when the president talked about an "axis of evil". There was first the logical problem that the three countries said to form the axis are not connected in any way that constitutes an axis; at least not as described by any of the seven definitions of *axis* in the *American Heritage Dictionary*. What the phrase has instead of anything remotely like logic or truth is a cultural ring to it, an echo of the good old days; it sounds like the sort of thing a man should go after with a gun. A varmint in other words, or rather three of them – and who can say if, in some future edition of the *AHD*, *three or more varmints randomly arranged* will not be an eighth definition of *axis*.

Perhaps that is why the axis of evil sounded splendid to conservative America and barmy to just about everyone else. Most people might accept "evil" as apt enough when we speak about Saddam or North Korea or September 11 or the former Soviet empire, notwithstanding the obvious objection that it is a very select list in a very naughty world. But the axis of evil was just too American: too much like a sounding of its own depths, wherein lie witches, masked men with shotguns, evil angels and angels of the elect. Words have that power.

In David Ireland's novel *The Glass Canoe*, a sociologist ponders a footballer in his local pub, and asks how an inarticulate brute whose ordinary powers of thought are barely adequate to his own survival can display on a rugby field the mental agility of a genius. How can he at full tilt anticipate in an instant not just the first reactions of his opponents but the second and the third, a whole sequence of them, and compute in that instant the strategy that will leave them looking like *fools*? It's a conundrum of the same order as one attributed to Orson Welles when he addressed a small audience somewhere in America: after outlining his accomplishments he is supposed to have said, "Strange isn't it – how many of me and how few of you?" Why can Marcel Proust write a sentence of several hundred words that readers remember for the rest of their lives, yet a corporate or political leader writing of something more important than a madeleine or a pot of asparagus-scented urine finds himself immediately, as Thomas Hobbes put it, "entangled in words, as a bird in lime-twigs; the more he struggles, the more belimed".

Why is it, for instance, that for style, sentiment and truth, nothing our leaders have said about death in the last death-filled eighteen months has approached "It comes equally to us all, and makes us all equal when it comes?" It seems as fit now as it was when it was written four hundred years ago. Why have people who claim they owe so much to him taken grandiosity from Lincoln's language, but not the power in it? Put aside the political reflections and all the other wonders of the Gettysburg Address: he says, "The brave men, living and dead, who struggled here ..."Read it *aloud*. It's the "struggled" that strikes the nerve ends. It's a familiar word, hackneyed in some contexts but visceral in *this* one. Imagine if he had said "fought", "clashed", "risked their lives", "paid the ultimate price", "demonstrated their commitment". Lincoln must have wanted a word to say that it was terrible, terribly human. Not a memorable word, but a word that would make the thing it denoted memorable – for, as he says a moment later, the world will not "long remember what we say here, but it can never forget what they did here".

All verbs have inherent force. A well-chosen one like Lincoln's can be extraordinarily powerful. We don't hear verbs much these days. They try to master or inspire us with clichés, catchphrases and commitment to everything that to their tin ears sounds great. We don't understand or even hear them properly. We don't care – partly because their words anaesthetise us, partly because like parrots we're interested mainly in the gesture and not the meaning.

Fifty years ago Orwell and Spender among others noted how the language of communism dulled the senses of its adherents and hid the lies. Spender remembered the way in which good citizens were exhorted to have "certain socially useful qualities: industry, hatred, perhaps purity ... in a word those which made for the utmost devotion to the cause. One did not need charity, pity, tolerance, humility, truth, personal loyalty". Now in the private sector words like "commitment" and "accountability" are the watchwords for staff devotion to the cause, and they have been substituted for precisely the same qualities Spender noticed missing in communism. The words vanish with the things they signify – "wisdom", "decency", "civility": you will not find them in a corporate document of any kind. They're as rare as verbs. In the same way, companies (and political parties) talk of their "strategic initiatives" and "key values" to the absolute exclusion of "imagination", "foresight", "gumption", "belief".

These words have all but gone from the language of commerce, politics and the public service.

Of course it is beyond our leaders to write like John Donne or Abraham Lincoln, and we should hope fervently that they don't try. But that is no reason not to call on the language, which is no different to saying the lessons recorded in the culture, in life. We don't because in public life the language has never been held in less regard – not in Donne's time, Johnson's, Lincoln's or George Orwell's. It withers in the dungeons of the technocratic mind. It has no place in the media. In politics it lacks all qualifications for the main game. Instead we get "a commitment to ensuring the ongoing viability" of parrot droppings.

Lincoln is not the only example of a politician with a feel for language. President Grant fought in two wars, the Mexican and the Civil War. Out of the first, the United States, with the imperial throttle wide open, acquired Texas. In his *Personal Memoirs* Grant condemned both the annexation and the war. The army he commanded won the Civil War for the Union. But he believed the war could have been avoided *if* the "poor white trash" of the South, with no interest in slavery and nothing to gain from secession, had not been incited into fighting by that class who did have interests and felt they had "a sort of divine right to control public affairs". Grant was much more than soldier: his powers of reasoning and language were equally impressive. His description of the way he went about his memoirs was remarkably like Hobbes's first principle of speech – "to transferre our Mentall Discourse, into Verbal: or the Trayne of our Thoughts, into a Trayne of Words". Grant's trains led him to the conclusion that there *would* have been no secession (and no war) "if there had been a fair and calm expression of opinion, unbiased by threats, and if the ballot of one legal voter had counted for as much as that of any other. But there was no calm discussion of the question".

Today's war party might have a case as strong as Grant's, but perhaps we should wait until they can put it into words like his before we are persuaded.

The Bulletin, 12 November 2002

Spin doctrines

PUBLIC LANGUAGE CONFRONTS MOST OF us every day of our lives, but rarely when we are with friends or family. Not yet, at least. It is not the language in which we address lovers, postmen, children or pets. So far.

True, in the households of young professionals they will say, sometimes, that the new dog "adds alpha to their lifestyle", that they need "closure" with their orthodontist or mother, that they are "empowered" by their Nikes. There is seepage from the public to the private. But that's all it is. "At this point in time." We hope.

But it may be worse than it seems, much worse. What if the dejection we feel upon hearing the US president speak, or receiving a letter from a bank or a government department, were symptoms of permanent and accelerating decline? Martin Amis might be right. "The professionalization of ordinary existence: this is the enemy within." Language, after all, defines ordinary existence. "Speak, that I may see thee." It's how we know each other.

Public language is the language of public life: the language of politics, business and civil service. It is official, formal, sometimes elevated language. It is the language of leaders more than the led, managers rather than the managed. It takes very different forms: from shapely rhetoric to shapeless, enervating sludge. But in every case, for good or ill, it is the language of power and influence. What our duties are, for whom we should vote, which mobile phone plan we should take up: in all these contexts the public language rules.

As power and influence are pervasive, so is its language: we hear and read it at the highest levels and at the lowest. And, while it begins with the powerful, the weak are often obliged to speak it: to recite it, imitate it and, in the information age, work with it. "Even politicians speak / truths of value to the weak", Auden said. Believing as they do that we all need something, even if we don't know it, marketing people would agree.

The influence of marketing shows itself in advertising and commerce, where we would expect to find it, and in politics and war, where its presence might surprise us. Marketing goes wherever the media goes and the media goes pretty well everywhere, including war zones, which means wars require media management and marketing like everything else. "Embedded journalists" or "embeds" were born of this requirement, and so were many words, including "attriting", a new one for killing and maiming.

The same *professionalised* language exists in politics because increasing numbers of politicians are *professionals*. Many have management and marketing training and experience behind them. In Donald Rumsfeld's speech, one can even hear clear traces of EST, the seminal Californian variety of Large Group Awareness Training. EST made popular the word "closure", and the concept – or craze – of "self-actualisation". It spread word of Human Potential, which created vast luxurious fields for the consultancy industry. EST's mixture of Zen, Scientology, Dianetics, Maslow, Gestalt, Napoleon Hill and Dale Carnegie had a significant influence on the strand of management that murders language more efficiently than any other, Human Resources (HR).

By adopting HR policies and various associated creeds, including Knowledge Management and Neuro Linguistic Programming, educational institutions and other organisations, created to provide enlightenment, assistance and care, are speaking a language that dulls the senses and cannot express sentiment. They speak a dead language. They take on the same management and accounting principles as private companies created to make profits. They take on the same consultants, and consultants are the plague rats of the language virus.

All kinds of institutions now cannot tell us about their services, including the most piddling change to them, without also telling us that they are "contemporary, innovative and forward-looking" and "committed to continuous improvement" – as if the decision to raise their rates or change their phone number can only be grasped in this "context-sensitive" way.

To help us all get going in the same direction they might give the context a name, like "Growing Together" or "Business Line Plus", or "Operation Decapitation", where the service is a military one.

"Managerialism", a name for various doctrines of business organisation, comes with a language of its own. Even if the organisational principles of management or marketing were well suited to politics and education, managerial language is not. Marketing, for instance, has no particular concern with truth. Management concerns are relatively narrow – relative, that is, to life, knowledge and possibility. This alone makes marketing and managerial language less than ideal for a democracy or a university. In addition, it lacks almost everything needed to put into words an opinion or an emotion; to explain the complex, paradoxical or uncertain; to tell a joke. If those who propagate this blather really believed in being "context-sensitive", they would understand that, in the context of ordinary human needs and sensibilities, this language is extraordinarily insensitive. It enrages, depresses, humiliates, confuses. It leaves us speechless.

Public language that defies normal understanding is, as Primo Levi wrote, "an ancient repressive artifice, known to all churches, the typical vice of our political class, the foundation of all colonial empires". The politicians, the managers, the consultants, the facilitators, the economists will tell you it is in the interests of leadership, management, efficiency, "stakeholders", the "bottom line" or some organisational imperative, but public language is, in essence, the language of power. It has its origins in the control of one person by another. In all societies "To take power is to win speech".

It will not always be obvious, of course, but intimidation and manipulation come as naturally to public language as polite instruction and enlightenment. Lies and distortion also come naturally, even among the well-intentioned. The complex is rendered simple, the simple complex. Sordid and self-interested deeds become examples of selfless heroism; true heroes are overlooked or airbrushed out. Cynics and pragmatists are made into people of high purpose, people prepared to make "hard decisions". Myth, legends, fantasies and lies are the traditional stuff of public language. That is why vigilance is needed: an argument concerning the public language is an argument concerning liberty.

*

To Levi's list of obfuscating types we could add many sociologists and deconstructionists, including some who design school curricula and courses with the word "studies" in them. For blighting the world with years of pious variations on "access and equity", "gender equity", "rich multicultural diversity" and other clichés of the left, political correctness has a case to answer. When the politically correct meets the managerial – usually in civil service departments – horrors are born in the language. People are likely to establish an EOWA Women in Management Tools Module 5, and go about saying that "increased energy for improving employment outcomes for women can be obtained by engaging a broad range of men as EO partners"; that what they need most is "quality participation opportunities and sustainability"; that they must "implement and achieve enhanced values"; and that "a focus on outcome targets without an emphasis on improved employment practices will not deliver support from men and will not result in sustainable changes to improve gender equity outcomes".

But the politically correct do not deserve all the blame. Eight years ago, the Australian prime minister, John Howard, came to office denouncing political correctness and encouraging free expression among those who had, he said, been silenced by left-wing "thought police". Disaffected xenophobes and racists took advantage of the offer and Australian politics turned sharply to the right. Critics of government policy were labelled "elites", "chattering classes" and – most devastating of all – "latte drinkers". After a few years, John Howard declared his mission accomplished: good citizens who had been cowed by these urban elites were saying what was on their minds, he said. Mr Howard had liberated his people from political correctness, or at least from the left-wing version of it. But he had not liberated the language. The language is much worse than it was when he started.

Political correctness and its equally irritating twin, anti-political correctness, economic rationalism, dope-smoking, Knowledge Management – wherever fashion and cults exist the language inclines to the arcane or inscrutable. This is no bad thing of itself, but it's obnoxious in a democratic or educational environment. Among Druids, Masons or economists we expect the language to be unfathomable or at least unclear or strange. They speak in code. This can only be because they do not want us to understand, or do not themselves understand, or are so in the habit of speaking this way they have lost the ability to communicate normally. When we hear this sort of language it is, therefore, common sense to assume there is a cult, or something like a cult, in the vicinity. And what if everywhere we read and hear people saying: "The team, whether or not it is acceptant of the change, now puts itself on the curve"; or, "major change drivers impacting on the sectors"; or "enterprise and sector strategies to address the impact of the strategies"; or, "penetration, development and expansion of the vertical market segment and strategic close of high impact deals"? We must assume that the cult has taken over.

While English spreads across the globe, the language itself is shrinking. Vast numbers of new words enter it every year, but both our children's and our leaders' vocabularies are getting smaller. Latin and Greek have been squeezed out of most journalists' English, and "obscure" words are forbidden unless they qualify as economic or business jargon. You write for your audience and your audience knows fewer words than it used to and hasn't time to look up unfamiliar ones. The language of politics is tuned to the same audience and uses the same media to reach it, so it too diminishes year by year. "Downsized", business would say. Business language is a desert. Like a public company, the public language is being trimmed of excess and subtlety; what it doesn't need is shed, what is useful is reorganised, "prioritised" and attached either to new words or to old ones stripped of meaning. In business, language is now "productivity-driven".

What of the media, whose words we read and hear every day? The code of conduct of the International Federation of Journalists is categorical: "Respect for the truth and the right of the public to truth is the first duty of the journalist". There can be no respect for the truth without respect for language. Only when language is alive does truth have a chance. As the powerful in legend turn the weak or the vanquished into stone, they turn us to stone through language. This is the function of a cliché, and of cant and jargon; to neutralise expression and "vanish memory". They are dead words. They will not do for truth.

Therefore, to live according to their code, journalists must choose their own words carefully and skilfully and insist that others do the same. The proper relationship of journalists to the public language is that of unrelenting critics. It is their duty to see through it. But we cannot rely on them. Norman Mailer once wrote on behalf of writers like himself that "the average reporter could not get a sentence straight if it were phrased more subtly than his own mind could make phrases". They munched nuances "like peanuts", he said. True, it happens and it's maddening, but weak prose is still journalism and roughly meets the requirements of the code. It is something else, however, when journalists ignore abuses of the public language by people of influence and power, and reproduce without comment words that are intended to deceive and manipulate. When this happens journalism ceases to be journalism and becomes a kind of propaganda, or a reflection of what Simone Weil called "the superb indifference that the powerful have for the weak".

The war in Iraq provided a case in point. The military provided brand names for its tactics – "Shock and Awe", for instance – and much of the media could see nothing but to use them. Each day of the campaign the media was briefed in the language of the Pentagon's media relations people, whereupon very often the journalists briefed their audiences in the same language. The media centre in Doha was always "on message", and so was the media. When the military said they had "degraded" by 70 per cent a body of Iraqi soldiers, this was what the media reported. Few said "killed" and only the Iraqi minister for information in his daily self-satire said "slaughtered", which was a more honest word but a blatant lie because he said it of American soldiers, not Iraqi ones. One journalist, who knew something about the effects of Daisy Cutter bombs, said "puréed". And no one showed any pictures of the bodies. To be "embedded" with the Coalition forces, or to be an "embed", was to be embedded in their language and their "message". It turned out that "embedded" just meant "in bed with" in the old language. If the military said they had "attrited" an enemy force, generally that was what the media said, and it was the same if it said "deconflicted".

All this was a sad retreat from both the journalists' code of conduct and the noble achievements of twentieth-century war reporting. Just as significant was the way the media's language spoke for the willingness of journalists to join the military in denying the common humanity of ordinary soldiers – especially the largely conscripted cannon fodder – on the opposing side. Here was another retreat – from war reporting standards going back to Homer.

The public language will only lift in tone and clarity when those who write and speak it take words seriously again. They need to tune their ears to it. Awareness is the only defence against the creeping plague of which this is a microscopic specimen: "The inquiry may allow for relevant businesses or industries to be identified and for investigation into the possibility that certain regional or rural areas of the state would be more affected than others." No doubt in the place from which these words came, they were judged competent. But they are not competent in the world at large. They are not competent as language. They represent an example of what George Orwell described as anaesthetic writing. You cannot read it without losing a degree of consciousness. You come to, and read it again, and still your brain will not reveal the meaning – will not even try. You are getting sleepy again. Read aloud, in a speech for instance, an audience hears the words as they might hear a plane passing overhead or a television in another room. We can easily make it sound less like a distant aeroplane by the simple expedient of saying it as if we mean it: "The inquiry will decide which businesses are relevant and which parts of the state will be badly affected". It's just one sentence. But we have to begin somewhere.

We must keep things in perspective, of course. The decay of language is not of itself life-threatening. It can be an aid to crime and tragedy; it can give us the reasons for unreasoning behaviour, including war and genocide and even famine. Words are deadly. Words are bullets. But a word is not a weapon of mass destruction, or a jihad or unhappiness. Like a rock, it is not a weapon (or a grinding stone) until someone picks it up and uses it as one. We should be careful not to sound too cranky or obsessive about words. You can't eat them or buy things with them, or protect your borders with them, and it will not do to make an exaggerated display of our concern. Make too much of a fuss and you will be quickly told that worse things are happening in the world than the decay of public language; that the *bottom line* is that language is not a *core issue*.

You might also be told that you are a kind of Luddite and must learn that resistance is futile. And this is true to the extent that managerial language is to the information age what steam engines and belts and pulleys were to the industrial. It is mechanised language, or language as an assembly line. It is full of "change drivers", "core values", "strategic implementation" and "continuous improvement going forwards". It has no provenance and no memory. Like a machine, it removes the need for thinking: the uniquely human faculty of thought is suspended along with all sense of what feeling, need or notion inspires your activity. Like assembly lines, managerial language is insensitive to human needs, including the need to have some control over what one is doing. People who are compelled to write and speak this language every day will tell you they are never certain they know what the task is, or what the point of it is. The language seems designed to screen them from the meaning of their work, so they are never quite sure they know what they are trying to say or what is being said to them. Managerial language is an abuse of human rights. It robs people of their senses, their culture and their tongue.

To the extent that it is moulded and constrained by opinion polls, marketing and media spin, and is infused with much of the same organisational doctrine, political language is the cousin of the managerial and just as alienating. To speak or be spoken to in either variety is to be "not in this world". It is to deal in a dead language. Ten years ago, when she received her Nobel Prize, the American novelist, Toni Morrison, described it this way:

A dead language is not only one no longer spoken or written, it is unyielding language, content to admire its own paralysis. Like statist language, censored and censoring. Ruthless in its policing duties, it has no desire or purpose other than maintaining the free range of its own narcotic narcissism, its own exclusivity and dominance. However moribund, it is not without effect for it actively thwarts the intellect, stalls conscience, suppresses human potential. Unreceptive to interrogation, it cannot form or tolerate new ideas, shape other thoughts, tell another story, fill baffling silences. Official language smitheried to sanction ignorance and preserve privilege is a suit of armour polished to shocking glitter, a husk from which the knight departed long ago. Yet there it is: dumb, predatory, sentimental – exciting reverence in schoolchildren, providing shelter for despots, summoning false memories of stability, harmony among the public.

If I deface a war memorial or rampage through St Paul's with a sledgehammer I will be locked up as a criminal or lunatic. I can expect the same treatment if I release some noxious weed or insect into the natural environment. It is right that the culture and environment should be so respected. Yet every day our leaders vandalise the language, which is the foundation, the frame and joinery of the culture, if not its greatest glory, and there is no penalty and no way to impose one. We can only be indignant. And we should resist.

Introduction, *Gobbledygook* (*Death Sentence*, UK edition), 2004

Iconography

IMAGINE FOR A MOMENT THAT George Orwell was right when he said that words have precise and specific meanings and we should do our best to stick to them when we speak or write. Orwell argued that "slovenly" language made it harder to think clearly, and, as clear thinking is a precondition of enlightened and functional democracy, language is not a frivolous concern. Let's say we took Orwell seriously for a moment. *Only* for a moment, because the time we spend on taking language seriously is time we cannot spend on taking "real issues" such as "Aussie values" seriously. It "mitigates against" them, as they say sometimes on the ABC. But spare a non-frivolous moment for the language and think about the way we use the word "icon".

Two or three days after Steve Irwin died, I heard a man behind me in an airport queue say to his companion that Germaine Greer had "tried to gut an Aussie icon". His companion was astounded to hear that anyone should be so insensitive. "I mean," said the man, "I wasn't a big rap for the bloke, but he was an icon and you have to respect that. You don't go gutting an Aussie icon".

Language proceeds by imitation and it's a safe guess the traveller thought of Irwin as an icon because that is the cliché everyone in the media had chosen. They did not call him a naturalist or a blowhard, and he had got beyond "celebrity". Some stressed he was a "family man". But above all he was an "Aussie icon".

Back in 1946, when Orwell wrote *Politics and the English Language*, icons did not wrestle with crocodiles and pythons. Icons were still, as they had been for the previous two millennia, sacred images, usually of saints, venerated by Christians, especially in the Eastern Church. They were mute and inanimate *representations*, though granted they spoke plainly to the faithful.

The sorts of people who are now called icons were once called national heroes or stalwarts or giants or lions, or citizens much loved and looked up to. Explorers, soldiers, political leaders, entertainers, scientists, sportsmen, horses and dogs: the world was not short of what are now called "icons" just because that was not then the word for them. Take Field Marshal Montgomery, for instance, or Edmund Hillary, Albert Einstein, Winston Churchill, Eleanor Roosevelt, Douglas Bader, Don Bradman, Gary Cooper, John Landy, Jane Russell, the Queen, Phar Lap or Rin Tin Tin. For some people, Orwell was one. Stalin was another, for some people. It was more than admiration. They represented to us something elevated, if not perfect; and in them we saw ourselves as we would like to be. They embodied our ideals.

We went some way to making icons of them if we had a photo or poster above our beds, or a little bust on the mantelpiece; but the person and the representation were kept distinct. A pepper shaker was not Winston Churchill, nor had it any of his powers, just because it was in his likeness. This was for the same reason that Winston Churchill was not a pepper shaker, and had none of a pepper shaker's powers. There must have been some general intimation that there was peril – and possibly madness – in failing to distinguish between the reality and the representation. Some people might hold that a little gilt-framed, hand-painted image of St Anthony and a photo of Stalin are both icons. But even if we accept that questionable proposition, we are not therefore obliged to believe that St Anthony was in his own person an icon of Christianity and Stalin an icon of communism. Andy Warhol knew that he was making icons of Marilyn Monroe and Campbell's soup, not making Marilyn and the soup icons.

There is another reason for taking Orwell's advice and reserving "icon" for its original and accepted meaning. Photos of Hitler and Stalin and the badges of Mao were created in imitation of icons to encourage quasi-religious veneration. They were mass-produced facsimiles designed to invest the Führer, the Great Leader and the Great Helmsman with perfect wisdom and seeming divine powers. This was Orwell's very point: slovenly language and slovenly thought live in permanent and dangerous embrace.

The American Heritage Dictionary of twenty years ago defined "icon" as a representation or symbol. The latest one includes two new meanings: the picture representing a file or program on a computer screen and "One who is the object of great attention and devotion; an idol". Most, though not all, other dictionaries have done something similar. The English language is forever changing, of course, often for the better and just as often for the worse. In both cases, as followers of Orwell would know, it is all but futile to resist.

Yet we might as well mark the changes. Before those popular heroes became icons, we had, in addition to a language with more variety and life in it, a more general freedom to dissent. One did not have to like Don Bradman or Winston Churchill in the way it seems one has to like these modern "icons". They were legends in their ways and it was common for bits of myth to attach to them. But our attitude was not religious. In the end they were what they were, and if they were transcendent it was only as a cricketer transcends the demands of that game, or a general an enemy with the high ground, or a nurse septicaemia, or a horse the limitations of most horses. There was no heresy or threat of damnation in ignoring them.

Still, it is hard to put a finger firmly on the difference. Three-quarters of a century ago almost a quarter of Melbourne's population turned out for the funeral of Sir John Monash. No one called him an Aussie icon. Or even a war icon; or an engineering icon; or a Jewish icon. Is it possible that they mourned him as an icon while thinking him a mere national hero, or a good man who had served his country very well?

It is more likely that our democracy had not evolved to the point where, for want of a local monarch, messiah or patron saint, the people grant themselves the same sovereignty by means of these "icons". What are "Aussie icons" if not likenesses of the people at large? And from what do they derive their authority – not to say, majesty – if not from "Aussie values"? The very alert will notice the switcheroo: where the old icons reminded the faithful of their relative weaknesses, in the new Aussie icons Aussies see confirmation of their strengths. The Aussie icon is, as one would expect, an enhanced icon.

Let no one – no one who does not wish to be nailed by the ears to a gum tree – suggest that this phenomenon runs in any way parallel to that observed in the United States by H.L. Mencken: "As democracy is perfected," he said in 1920, "the office [of the president] represents, more and more closely, the inner soul of the people … On some great and glorious day the plain folks of the land will reach their heart's desire at last and the White House will be adorned by a downright moron". We can ignore Mencken, like any other bitter old curmudgeon. He was a notorious elitist, blind to democratic progress and could not tell an Aussie icon from a catfish.

But we are trying to honour Orwell here, and all the others, including Mencken and William F. Buckley Jr, who say that although language is by nature inexact, we should strive for exactitude. With "icon", the heart of the difficulty is the matter of representation. Even computer science keeps the original sense of "icon" as an image or symbol of something else. But the Crocodile Man, though an idol, remains himself and not a symbol in the sense that an icon is. It was the same with St Anthony. That is, we do not make the saint an icon; we make icons of the saint.

And here is the opportunity for Kim Beazley. The following proposal could in a single stroke do a service to plain English, make a lasting contribution to Australia's national security and dig him out of a hole. Let us make a real icon of Steve Irwin, a framed engraving or photograph with a crocodile, much as St Patrick is with a snake and St Agnes with a lamb. Make another of John Howard and of a random third, and let our customs officers show them to all visitors and intending immigrants. Demand either that they name all three or, by some non-verbal means such as kissing or weeping or pressing to their brows, prove their respect for the Aussie values these icons symbolise. A simple test and those who pass it will enter with our blessing. Those with whom it draws a blank shall be turned away.

The Monthly, October 2006

The conservative crusade
against the ABC

FOR MILLIONS OF AUSTRALIANS, THE ABC is all at once a homely
source of intellectual and spiritual nourishment, a reliable source of news
and information, and an ungainly emblem of the country's character. In
some measure, it satisfies both their national pride and what remains
of their Anglophilia. For millions more, insofar as they are conscious of
its existence, the public broadcaster is an irrelevant item of megafauna.
On these broad lines the country divides: what is a sort of indispensable
national house cow for one large portion of the population, another
portion of comparable size scarcely knows and doesn't give two hoots
for. Like the two ventricles of the heart, they pump away in peaceful
coexistence.

Then there is a third cohort, possibly numbering in the thousands,
who believe the ABC is run by "leftists" and crusades on "leftist" causes
such as "boat people, same-sex marriage and global warming". One of
the chief spokespeople for this extra ventricle, Andrew Bolt, recently
asked readers of his blog to "imagine if every single one of the main
ABC current affairs shows" were hosted not by the "leftists" who presently host them but by him and "fellow conservatives Janet Albrechtsen,
Gerard Henderson, Tim Blair, Miranda Devine, Piers Akerman, Tom
Switzer and Rowan Dean".

So close your eyes and imagine ABC current affairs programs, including Radio National's venerable *The Science Show* (Robyn Williams is numbered among the bad), being hosted not by the present "caste" of competent broadcasters but by these "conservatives". What do you see? Fox News? What are they saying? Anything? If in this imaginary world no one at the ABC "crusaded on boat people, same-sex marriage and global warming", as our outraged correspondent insists the present lot do, it seems possible that their replacements might have nothing left to talk about.

They would crusade on "free speech, climate scepticism and free markets", he says. How strange, then, that they have crusaded against the ABC for letting the public know what Australian governments were up to with our neighbours, and for presenting information on boat arrivals that the government has been denying us. If free speech is their thing, how come they are for Scott Morrison and against Edward Snowden?

Oh, where are the conservatives of yesteryear, with Orwell and Oakeshott at their side, and the "open society" forever their objective? Now, it is a commonplace that open societies depend upon the individual's right to scrutinise government policy. Why, then, are these self-styled conservatives so down on the free flow of information and so happy to defend government secrecy? Tell us again how the ABC is less than patriotic for reporting the stories of refugees in the face of the Navy's determination to say nothing at all about what they have chosen to call, with Orwellian panache, "on water" matters. In the interests of free speech, will we swear to take the military at its word and question the patriotism of any civilian – or public broadcaster – who dares to quote a different view? Especially civilians who are "not even Australian", as the minister for defence so sagely put it.

Yet I doubt that even disgruntled ABC viewers and listeners would charge the ABC with insufficient dedication to free expression. Or free markets. I don't recall any of the named hosts – even the one who once worked for that stalwart of the socialisation objective R.J.L. Hawke – doing much crusading against free markets. Nor do I remember their extensive advocacy *for* same-sex marriage, but how refreshing to imagine an ABC crusading against it. As refreshing as imagining a show about science being hosted by an anti–climate science crusader.

*

You have to feel for the government in this. Much as they might wish to imitate their friends and supporters in what they like to call the "free" – as opposed to "government-owned" or "taxpayer-funded" – media, they can't paint the government broadcaster as a chilling Orwellian nightmare without seeming to betray a liking for the genre. Pity, that: it would make a good speech. Like the one James Murdoch made in Edinburgh in 2009. He described the BBC in just those terms, and who cared if Orwell was spinning in his socialist grave at the gall of it? That's the thing about the "free" press: "their money; their free speech", as our blogger says. Free, that is, to traduce the living and the dead, posture madly, peddle influence, be parasites, ignoramuses and (*vide* Murdoch and son) epic hypocrites. There is no dog to bark at them – well, a couple of very small and all but toothless mutts, perhaps.

And there's the rub. Most of those millions who value the ABC might in other circumstances be satisfied with the children's shows, sport, music, arts, religion, farming, nature, nurture, history, philosophy, language, science, sociology, drama, emergency services and Stephen Fry. They might make do with an evening news service, if they thought they could trust commercial media for the rest of their current affairs. But they *don't* trust them. It's possible they find the very thought demeaning. They don't like their news and opinion mixed in with advertising and coloured by the need to chase revenue through unrelenting noise and vehemence. They don't like the tone of commercial media. It's a matter of taste – or snobbery, if you prefer.

For the same reason, a lot of viewers and listeners would not complain if the public broadcaster stepped back from the popular melee. Some no doubt perceive bias or a lack of balance, but very likely just as many are peeved because they think it ill becomes their ABC to imitate the public riot. And this might be why the likes of such a right-wing caste are not likely to ever take over the organisation. A true conservative "eyes the situation in terms of its propensity to disrupt the familiarity of the features of [their] world". By this definition (Michael Oakeshott's), the ABC is in essence a conservative institution: old, familiar, pervasive and habit-forming, bearing the nation's heritage and beliefs, speaking for the pluralist complexity of the country. It does none of this perfectly, but it is pretty well alone in doing it at all. By the same definition, the so-called "conservatives" who berate the ABC are not conservatives but heretics, radicals and vulgarians, and no amount of Dvořák – or Lou Reed – will cure them.

What is curious is where the obsession stems from. Even if the "massive power" alleged of the public broadcaster were real, it is hard to think of an election result that the ABC decided, or of political leaders cosying up to the ABC in the way they perennially do to Rupert Murdoch and used to do to Kerry Packer. Who does the British prime minister, David Cameron, most want to be his friend? Rupert Murdoch or Chris Patten, the former Conservative Party chairman and present chief of what the Murdochs reckon is a rampant and menacingly "authoritarian" BBC? Who does Tony Abbott think more important? Murdoch or Mark Scott, a former adviser to a Liberal government and the present managing director of the equally menacing ABC? Is it that these national broadcasters have no power worth pursuing, or that in the main they use it responsibly and cannot be bought? Or that they are institutions woven so thoroughly into the fabric of national life that no amount of normal political harassment and interference can much change them? Whatever the case, true conservatives must at least half-heartedly rejoice.

Not these anti-"leftists", however. No doubt, as James Murdoch made clear, the "free" media resents any inroads public broadcasters are making on their commercial territory, but that's at best a partial explanation for the journalistic Tea Partying. More likely it's some species of projection. Never has the ideological difference between the major parties been narrower. So general is the liberal-pluralist consensus, the parties must search for something to believe in. Increasingly they find it in the dark corners of talkback radio (or the lighter ones of Q&A): not in reality, but in beat-ups and the excrescences of populism. There is a little bit of Putin in all sorts of politicians now.

Conservatives have their open society. They have a market economy, freedom of speech and pervasive liberal values. For some, so many victories were bound to prove unbearable, the more so, perhaps, because a lot of them occurred without their participation. They have inherited the spoils but, with one or two exceptions, have no claim on either the struggle or the moral and intellectual tradition. For all the unlikely power granted them by modern media, it is their fate to feel marginalised, denied, unfulfilled: when all's said and done, like fringe dwellers excluded from something essential at the centre of Australian life – namely, as the blogger reveals, the ABC.

The Monthly, March 2014

There it is again:
Or a short history of cant

Cant. n. . . .

3. A whining pretension to goodness, in formal and affected terms . . .

4. Barbarous jargon.

—Samuel Johnson, A *Dictionary of the English Language*

Once he had been dragged into the bush, the lion with its coarse tongue would lick off his skin, drink his blood, and then, leisurely, usually starting with his feet, eat him.

—Peter Beard, *The End of the Game*

AMONG ALL THE WAYS TO leave the world — ways not invented by humankind, that is, *natural* ways — to be eaten alive must be just about the worst. And imagine you're one of the poor blighters working for peanuts on a railway in southern Africa, lying out on the veldt at night, not knowing when the "abominated jaws" might seize you. Did human ears ever hear a more terrible sound than the ravening lions' roar?

Neuroimaging carried out on animals early this century showed that fear activates the midbrain — the parahippocampus, the thalamus and so on — while *de*activating much of the frontal cortex, the hypothalamus and other regions. Among the parts activated by fear are those which are also switched on by dire need for air and water, the primordial parts; the parts *de*activated were in general the parts that make reasoning possible. Anger, naturally enough, seeing that it's a primordial emotion, showed up in a pattern very like that of fear.

Sixty years ago when unlit towns spread no light into the landscape and country nights were darker, the westerly ripped up the valley and battered the old weatherboards of our house on the hill. At other times, the air was still and the drizzle drifted down in silence. Thalamus glowing, frontal cortex kaput, I lay in the perfect blackness of my bedroom and listened for man-eaters.

The critical moment, the one that might decide our fate, is that which falls between the first sign and the second: the first tells us something may be there, the second tells us that probably it is there – which leaves us to decide *what* it is and what to do about it. For excellent reasons of survival, fear reaches a rat's amygdala in twelve milliseconds, and I doubt it took longer with me. How is one to judge in an instant what is commonplace and what not, what harmless and what deadly? How to be prudent but not timid; brave but not stupid? Of such deliberations my childhood was made. And so, possibly, were *homo sapiens*.

Of course that footfall I heard outside my window was not a lion come to eat me alive. Nor was it the Demon of the Abyss, or some rival clan planning to kill me and kidnap my sister. But it might have been a couple of demented escapees from the prison on French Island twenty miles away, or town delinquents on a killing spree. That voice in the whistling wind and the creaking branches of the cedars was likely just the bull bellowing his desire, unless it was God calling me to be his evangelist – not calling, *demanding* with menaces. If none of those parties, probably it was some repulsive thing just arrived from space and eating people whole.

We need fear. It's necessary for our survival, and therefore an engine of our evolution. Before stepping into a thicket the more sensible early humans imagined a man-eater lurking there, and thus survived. Before they lit a fire in a cave, and round it gave birth to a greatly enlarged frontal cortex and civilisation, some of them must have imagined how nice it would be to sit and warm their hands and talk. But when the fire had died, they must have imagined – as I did when ours had – the enemies that prowled outside. Fear and imagination are of a piece. The stuff of nightmares is the same stuff that keeps us alive and gives us a taste of both wisdom and baloney.

The solution – though fallible and often dependent on negotiations with the gods (another offspring of fear, surely) – was to identify patterns.

(It so happens, at least according to Freud, that our first fear is that of being born, and it is heralded by a pattern of contractions.) Our hearing, vision and sense of smell were feeble compared to those of predatory animals. We were slower, weaker; pathetically inferior in tooth and claw, as we were in climbing and burrowing. But we had a brain with which to learn the habits of our enemies and prey. We learned to distinguish the sound of a lion padding about at the cave's entrance from that of a passing ibex or angel. In the same manner we could separate familiar voices and friendly footfalls from threatening ones, and the screech of a curlew from an enemy imitating it to disguise a message to his colleagues. We learned to read the signs. A sign being "something by knowing which we know something more", we stood a chance of getting to know how to overcome our woeful inferiority and exercise dominion over all the fangs of Nature.

Before exercising my own dominion over them, I learned to cope with fear by silently reciting *The Owl and the Pussycat*; and if that didn't work, the *Apostles' Creed*. As if to a drumbeat I would chant my way through Kipling's *If*, a framed copy of which gathered dust on the dressing table, or the words of *Galway Bay*, all of which I find I still know. It was another tactic to tell myself a story in which I was the hero, a person of exemplary courage and flair, and not the trepid child quaking between the blankets. To make myself a worthy member of the human race, I made myself up. Thus I discovered the usefulness of cant.

It must have been the same in the cave. To drive out fear they sang or chanted as people do in cathedrals and the animals do in *Animal Farm*. The art of song was born. And at day's end they told stories. From what happened on the hunt, the things they saw, the frights they got and the fear they conquered, they made what Yuval Noah Harari calls the "narrating self" – a delusional and dreadfully destructive animal, and the only one to believe in things that do not exist outside its imagination. We are ourselves a kind of invention, a primitive form of artificial intelligence soon to be replaced by a more sophisticated form. For Harari says the great journey of *homo sapiens* (lasting about ten seconds on the evolutionary clock) is about to end, and the era of robots about to begin. It is a telling reminder of our true nature and of our origins, that this kind of information, like that relating to global warming or the prospect of nuclear war, activates scarcely a thalamus while a bump in the night still lights them up everywhere.

As usual we can only wait and see if those with the finest frontal cortexes, including the many who design the things that point to our annihilation, will be smart enough (or *inclined* enough) to save us. But as we wait for the end, if the end it is to be, some people may be tempted to look away from their smartphones for long enough to ponder their beginning. While the study of palaeontology will help, there is another way. Much as scientists can "hear an echo" of the big bang fourteen billion years ago and through giant telescopes see its faint glow in microwave background radiation, we might hear echoes of humankind's beginnings in language.

Listen to the affectations and numberless deceits of politics, commerce and the media; the dumb certitudes, the posturing, the simpering apologias, the cant that "stop[s] up the mouth of enquiry". We might wonder if the daily flood of self-narration – the "narcotic narcissism", in Toni Morrison's words – does not faintly reverberate with the ancient effort to keep fear at bay. Stay listening, and in your mind's eye (your primary visual cortex) you might see dimly the ancestral bully who first turned the lion outside into his own instrument of terror, and still rules us with it when he can.

In Chekhov's short story *Ward No. 6*, Ivan Gromov finds the familiar, banal and crushing patterns of daily life suddenly becoming signs of imminent persecution and imprisonment. The story goes to show how fine the line is between the common interpretation of things and the heretical or mad, and, seeing that Gromov ends up in the living death of a lunatic asylum, how much is at stake. Anyone who tries to write about society or politics can profit from this example. One at least starts from the premise that the truth is only sometimes in appearances. There are patterns beneath the patterns, and that's where we'll find the best story and possibly the real one, if not the evolutionary design itself. But remembering that one is part of the same design, and, as much as every human being and the birds that sing in the morning, as prone to cant, we should leave some room for laughing.

From *There It Is Again*, 2017

Freudenberg:
A time to remember

What survives the wreck of time is the force of the imagination and the power of expression.

—Lewis Lapham

LONG BEFORE HE DIED, GRAHAM FREUDENBERG had entered the Labor pantheon. He was one of very few to get there by means other than a parliament or trade union. Graham floated in on the graces of his sentences and the synthesising powers of his mind. He was Labor's great articulator, its poet.

Australians first heard of him around the time of the 1972 election when it was reported that he had written Gough Whitlam's mighty Blacktown address — one account adding the romantic detail that to compose some of it he had taken a room in the Hydro Majestic Hotel at Medlow Bath, in the Blue Mountains.

Historian that he was, he would have known that a kilometre or two up the road the great prehistorian and one-time Labor adviser and speechwriter Vere Gordon Childe had fallen from Govetts Leap — it is reasonable to suppose that he killed himself. The author of the 1923 classic critique *How Labour Governs*, Childe had recently returned to Menzies's Australia, and despaired at the lack of social progress. He told a Melbourne audience that their suburban culture was in substantial ways inferior to tenth-century Iceland.

Fifteen years later, there was Graham Freudenberg writing the manifesto for an Australian social democracy. Labor would seize the chance to "recreate" Australia, "liberate the talents and uplift the horizons of the Australian people" and "revive in this nation the spirit of national cooperation and national self-respect". Labor would do this and more through "the most carefully developed and consistent program" ever offered to the people. This last, the speech assayed at length. A saviour had arrived and Labor was alight with hope. Modern Australia was about to be born.

Graham's belief in Labor was unbreakable. It was his church. For all the flaws of its machinery and the corruption of its personnel, all the failures and contradictions that Childe had trenchantly analysed, Labor still held the keys to that immanent but elusive prospect of social justice and the fulfilment of national possibility.

For nearly fifty years Freudenberg wrote speeches for Labor's cause. The ideas and arguments he made articulate and persuasive over half a century were Labor's. The policies and prospects described in speeches for Calwell, Whitlam and Hawke were Labor's. But his purpose needs to be separated from his achievement. Those speeches were laid before the nation. His triumphs lie in the realms of Australian politics and Australian history. He belongs in the national pantheon.

It is well known that Freudenberg and Whitlam had an uncanny affinity, but his speeches did not need Whitlam's distinctive rendering. The plain, sinewy phrasing of a speech he wrote in May 1965 retains its power on the page and just as uncannily summons the voice and persona of Arthur Calwell from otherwise faint memory.

With calm precision this speech put before the national parliament the case against the Vietnam War. It proposed an alternative to the government's strategic view. It predicted a bloody quagmire from which the United States would eventually retire humiliated. And, in a passage explicitly directed to Calwell's Labor colleagues and the party rank and file, it faced the consequence of "doing our duty as we see it":

I offer you the probability that you will be traduced, that your motives will be misrepresented, that your patriotism will be impugned, that your courage will be called into question. But I also offer you the sure and certain knowledge that we will be vindicated; that generations to come will record with gratitude that when a reckless government wilfully endangered the security of this nation, the voice of the Australian Labor Party was heard, strong and clear, on the side of sanity and in the cause of humanity, and in the interests of Australia's security.

The speech pays rereading, not only for the force of the argument, but as an early example of the writer's art. Freudenberg did not set out to take audiences soaring on rhetoric to another plane but, as Lincoln did, to fasten them to an idea.

A command of reasoning and evidence is essential to this, as it is to a newspaper article, or any argument. Something like a poet's imagination helps. But what distinguished Freudenberg's speeches, and gave them force, was the poise of the words and the dignity they granted the person speaking them. They were seemingly compelled by nothing but their own logic and the rhythm of the language.

And then there is Blacktown, 1972, and the speech dedicated to the men and women of Australia:

> The decision we will make for our country on the second of December is a choice between the past and the future, between the habits and fears of the past, and the demands and opportunities of the future. There are moments in history when the whole fate and future of nations can be decided by a single decision. For Australia, this is such a time.

Language technicians might be able to tell us what made the cadences so effective, why when we heard Whitlam utter those words our hearts thumped, and even when later in the speech he was talking about bringing sewerage to the outer suburbs the tears had not dried in our eyes.

The mechanics aside, the speech cashed in on the sense that one era was passing and another beginning. History was the element in which, intellectually, Graham Freudenberg lived, and from which his thoughts and sentences flowed. His big speeches never wandered far from his awareness of the flux of time, and it was this as much as his technical mastery that gave them the gravitas and drama to stir an audience.

If it did not quite live up to the memory of 1972, at least for those who thought Labor's time had come again, the party's campaign launch this year was galvanising. What Bill Shorten's speech lacked in poetry was balanced by the combination of policy weight and cordiality calculated to reflect the Labor family's outward empathy and inner harmony. As a performance piece it worked.

The whole show wanted for nothing – except a sign that people were listening. For all the excitement in the Brisbane room, at home in front of the television one felt very alone; worse, one fought a palpable sense that Shorten might as well have been spruiking non-stick saucepans while the rest of the country watched *My Kitchen Rules*. It was no fault of his: what we sensed was not the failure of a speech, but the death of *the* speech.

The news cycle began to kill it thirty years ago. Now governments and Oppositions must feed the monster twenty-four hours a day – not with speeches but with messages, for which read, mainly twaddle. Meanwhile, trillions of tweets and images have licensed lies and stupidity, allowed thugs and ignoramuses to prosper, bigotry to flourish, triteness and shallow optimism to replace even cursory analysis.

Kevin Rudd's apology to the Stolen Generations aside, it is hard to think of a speech any politician has made this century. It's not for want of good speechwriters – there have been plenty of them, including Bill Shorten's. It's because speeches have little value in the political culture. The media has no need for them, and the public no appetite, nor probably the attention span. The political speech has been all but reduced to a meaningless bow in the direction of tradition.

With the overthrow of the speech much else is overthrown, including the experience of feelings such as those generated by Whitlam in 1972, or Lenin in 1917, or any number of others, for better or worse, including some written by Shakespeare. So much connective tissue is lost: argument, irony, imagination, knowledge – the confluence of past and present. The story is lost. The loss of the speech is a loss to politics, and to human culture. Childe might have noted its disappearance from both realms.

It's been missing for so long we hardly notice it anymore, but that was the other thing missing from this year's Labor policy launch. Bold policies demand a compelling narrative to bed them in. Labor did not have one.* Either it saw no advantage in declaring a philosophy, or years of messaging have left it without one worth declaring. In truth, at no time

---

* Labor's campaign slogan, the moth-eaten cliché "A fair go for Australia", is a symptom of the problem. The term "fair go" does not appear in the Blacktown address, which shows a speech can be written, and Labor can succeed, without it.

in the past twenty years has the party effectively laid before the people a form of words to give voice to its ambitions, the national sentiment it wishes to foster, the community and nation it wishes to create – nor convincing evidence that, thus armed and directed, its time has come.

It says a great deal for Graham Freudenberg that a speech he wrote nearly fifty years ago still resounds today. It says less for Labor. Any number of reasons will be given for the devastating defeat this year. It's unlikely the people investigating will decide that, before doing anything else, the party should steel itself against the cultural trend, look hard towards the horizon and find an eloquent way of saying what they see. But if they did, and found themselves believing in a social democracy for these times, they would honour Graham Freudenberg and do something to dispel the current despair.

The Monthly, September 2019

"Use your brains"

I THINK IT IS THE custom on these occasions to offer words of inspiration: to encourage you to believe that, in one way or another, you should "follow your dream". As if, once you dream of circumnavigating the earth in a bark canoe you are already halfway there.

I'm sorry, but I can't offer that assurance. These few words are for those among you whose dreams are more like mine: mine defy interpretation most of the time, and those that I can understand are not the sorts of dreams anyone would *want* to follow.

Another version of the inspirational message is that "you can be anything you want to be". I don't think so. I wanted to be a fighter pilot in the Battle of Britain, and I've never really got over the disappointment. I wanted to be Louis Armstrong – what good was that? Set goals, people say, but, in my experience, a lot of the people who say this do *little else* but set goals. I've never found much in common with goal-setters.

Here's another inspiring cliché of our times: "Live in the moment". This is good, so long as the moment is good, but in the course of any life there are many moments in which one would sooner *not* live: moments when we would rather relive a less painful or frightening past, or imagine ourselves in a happier future. What is more, millions – hundreds of millions – of our fellow human beings are born to lives in which pretty well all the moments are miserable, and any notions of living the dream or following the dream or being anything you want to be are cruel jokes.

A version of a graduation speech given to students at Monash University in 2010.

It's the spirit of the age, I know, and perhaps a person should not set himself against it. But I can't recommend as a universal guide to living, an idea that only makes sense in a country as lucky as this one and in these luckiest of times. Try telling a child in Darfur to "live the dream", or the parents of a child with incurable cancer to "live in the moment". It is a little like my telling my father, who had no education and no choices, that he could have been anything he wanted – if only he'd written a mission statement.

So what can be recommended? As far as I can tell we live a little in the past, a little in the future and a little in the present. We spend a lot of time dreaming and a lot of time doing what we find pleasurable, or believe to be necessary, or have no choice *but* to do. We spend a lot of time sleeping. And a lot of time … wasting time.

I grew up about forty miles away, on the other side of these hills, and I spent all my school holidays about ten miles from here. It seems about a week ago – not fifty-odd years. It seems to me now that I've wasted roughly half those years – and the best advice I can think of giving you is to try not to do the same.

It's a lot of time to waste. Of course, I find various ways to forgive myself. For instance, I tell myself that it is in the nature of human beings to not do much. In many societies they seem to just sit under the trees most of the time – the men in particular. Or they play cards all day in smoky cafés. Or smoke hookahs and stare idly into the middle distance trying to fathom the mysteries. That's one excuse – the comparative anthropology excuse.

Another one is physiological: I can tell myself that I'm predisposed to addiction, programmed to it. Addicted to social life; addicted to sport; addicted to television shows; addicted to ease or pleasure.

All of these are very human responses to life. But none of them pacifies the frustrated sense that I've wasted too much time. So what possibly can I offer you by way of a guide to living? I can only say this: use your brains.

Here's a funny thing. We human beings are not very strong – gorillas I think are ten times stronger. We are not very fast – a kelpie is much faster, and a kelpie has a far better sense of smell. We don't climb very well. We can't fly. We're ungainly in the water compared to fish or platypus, and we can't breathe under it. We're hopeless burrowers.

Our domination of the world is consequent entirely on our brains. Yet most of us will do almost anything to avoid using them. Have you seen what's on cable television?

The most popular entertainments in the world – the Olympic Games and football – are staged around the efforts of human beings to perform feats of strength, speed and dexterity at which other species would laugh – if they could laugh. (That is one thing we can do that they can't – but again it's only because of our brain.)

The other entertainments – Hollywood's for instance – generally concern physical beauty. And a lot of Hollywood people are gorgeous, of course. But have you ever seen a panther – in the wild? I'm hoping I will before I die.

There is also shopping, surfing the internet, watching TV (including reality TV), worshipping celebrities – and going to work.

Fine. Except in most if not all of these cases the script is largely written for us – by corporations, advertising and marketing companies, media companies, our employers. Not all of them are cynical and shallow, but some of them very cynical and very shallow, and all of them are very good at manipulating us – even down to using a language which disguises or blurs meaning, simulates thought while making it impossible, presents itself as knowledge while it crushes imagination, and leaves us effectively brain dead.

The marketeers and knowledge managers know it is very important to encourage us to believe we are exercising our free wills, but the choice we exercise as consumers is not the same as the choices open to us as citizens or as human beings. To choose between different brands of breakfast cereal or sneakers is not really the same as making a moral choice, a political choice or any choice dependent on reason, character and imagination.

Yet even our education system in the past twenty years has felt obliged to treat education as a product and students as consumers, which means that we learn, that we use our brains, for the *commercial* purpose of acquiring the product, rather than for the human purpose of satisfying our curiosity. Learning how to think and how to choose might take all our lives – but it's better than being a slight advance on sheep.

Even politics has been invaded. Tony Abbott advertises Speedos and seems to be saying that to lead the Opposition he needs a resting pulse of forty-four or less. When Barack Obama was running for president, his stocks went up when he casually threw a basket from long range on a military basketball court, and they went down when he went tenpin bowling and his ball went in the gutter.

I'm not against sport, or making money. I have been addicted to horse racing and football since I was four. Sport and money make us happy, no doubt about it. They create a feeling of wellbeing, and are probably good for our health. But using our brains well has a similar effect: here's something I read the other day in an article by the American writer Lewis Lapham:

> Neuroscientists remark on the sensation of joy produced by the chemicals in the brain when the mind is being put to creative and imaginative use, a phenomenon they associate both with the pleasure of sexual orgasm and with the endorphin high experienced by athletes in the zones of effortless performance.

If your education has not provided you with moments like this, ask yourself why – and start again.

I read a new book about President Obama this year. (It's called *The Bridge* and I recommend it to you.) Now there is a man who used his brains. He could have settled on his emotions. Being black, abandoned by his father – such a childhood might explain failure, or futile rage and despair. Obama rejected those, and when he graduated from Harvard he also rejected the chance to be a very rich lawyer. He went to work among the black community in the South Side of Chicago. He chose public life over private life, personal responsibility over personal angst and self-indulgence, and raw human experience over the cultivated kinds you find in big law firms. He chose his identity – he would be black and be Barack, not Barry. He was at crucial times carried by circumstances and he was lucky that they were never too strong against him, but his career was built on his knowing how to think and choose, how to wed ideas and experience, how to use his brain. He read. And he thought. As all his contemporaries say, he was always thinking and always learning.

This is not to hold Obama up as your role model – though if you're looking for one, why not? He's a very good act to follow. But there's a personal anecdote I want to relate, because in a subtle kind of way it helps to illustrate my theme.

Barack Obama's father came from Kenya. In the early 1960s he went to the United States to study. The old empires were breaking up and the US government was keen to see that the postcolonial governments in Africa had in them people well disposed to the United States. Barack Obama's father went home with a degree, full of hope that he would find an influential place in a government led by a man who was the great hope of Kenya – Thomas Mboya.

Now just as the United States pursued its interests in Africa with scholarships, so did the Soviet Union. In 1968, with half a dozen other students and an American history lecturer from La Trobe, I went to the Soviet Union, and in Leningrad we met a group of young men from Kenya, Tanzania and other countries who were studying for a six-year master's degree. So while Barack Obama's father learned capitalist economics in the United States, these students learned Marxist economics in Russia. The one we got to know best was a very witty, clever and engaging man – and full of hope for Kenya. When we left we asked him what he intended to do – and he said, "Why of course, go home and build the new Kenya with Mr Thomas Mboya". Just like Barack Obama's father.

In 1969 Tom Mboya was assassinated. Over the next twenty years Barack Obama Senior slid steadily into self-indulgence, dissolution and despair. I don't know what happened to my man from Leningrad.

I met him more than forty years ago, and for the last thirty I have not been able to remember his name. But when I read about Obama's father, this second time, it came to me. I typed it into Google and put Nairobi after it – and there it was in the white pages: Musinde, Dickinson A.W. I've written to him – and I'm half-hoping that it will turn out that I end up going to Nairobi to see him again and find out how his life has gone. Not, I hope, like Barack Obama's father's.

Now it's a wonderful thing that one can draw up a name from the Nairobi phone book in a matter of seconds; and it will be even more wonderful if he answers my letter. Not wonderful in any grand sense, but in the sense that's it's wonderful when the thread of our life intersects with another, with something we had never thought of, or which seems unconnected.

It might also be awful, of course. But even then it will be a story. Food and reproduction aside, nothing is more attractive or more necessary to human beings than a story. They reassure us, excite us, stimulate our brains, give our lives meaning and comfort. To have a story and be part of a story is like having the sky above and just as indispensable.

Now, if I catch up with this man again it will be because I didn't play cricket that summer in 1968 or hang out in Carlton bars. I borrowed the fare and went to the Soviet Union instead. That was the start of it, and it has come to life again for only one reason – I read a book. And in the book found a connection that triggered something in my brain which has opened up a little door to perhaps … who knows … I may at last see a panther in the wild.

And even if I don't catch up with him, it remains that I was able to connect an experience in my life with someone else's experience; indeed, with a moment in history. It is not that these things make us feel more important, but that they make us feel more *conscious* – which is to say more alive to our humanity and our potential. These things never happen while watching TV. Laboratory tests have proved it. I don't think they happen when we're twittering or texting either.

So that's my inspirational message. No need to dream the dream, or vision the mission or any of that claptrap. Read books. Do things. Learn things. Don't let anyone else write your story – not the marketeers, not the sloganeers, not the media, not your employer (don't let them write your language either), not mateship or any other fad. Teach yourself to recognise the manipulators' signs. Use your brain – even if it's not a very good brain, it's the best thing you've got and to waste it is a crime against yourself.

Remember what Plutarch said: "The mind is not a vessel to be filled but a fire to be kindled".

Graduation address, Monash University, Gippsland, 2010

AUSTRALIAN
HISTORY

Stories light and dark

FIRST BASE FOR ALL THOSE who are despairing at the near demise of Australian history might be to recognise that people live well enough without it. History is optional. I lived pleasantly enough for more than forty years without knowing that a passenger on the Second Fleet, a fifteen-year-old "unfortunate" girl who belonged to a gang of crooks from Covent Garden, and a man on the Third Fleet, an East End hanky thief, were my ancestors. Of course I am glad now to have this juicy fact in my pocket – I take it out occasionally and wonder if guilt or shame played any part in keeping it a secret for all that time – but it is probably just as well I did not know earlier. Young people seduced by their ancestry are too often impervious to life's other mysteries, and bereft of imagination. History infarcts them. They prize their facts like other kids defend their marbles. Clichés tumble from their mouths, they fall prey to fantasies of lost fortunes or gentility, they imitate their fathers when they should be defying them, they dress too old, go a bad colour and repel all but fellow pedants from their circle. They become the dreary caricatures of history, the subject's mummies, its shrunken heads, its totem poles. The whole and the living recoil from them and, on their example, from the subject which consumes them. Yet, unthinkable as it seems, they have been known to find their way into history and education "departments". The places where history is most influentially taught and written have often harboured history's own worst enemies.

No one who values verifiable truth would ever say this of the department in the University of Melbourne. The Melbourne school of history is the place from which nearly all the most famous Australian historians have sprung. Much of the history of Australia has been conceived and written there. In our intellectual life its influence is phenomenal. Scott, Crawford, the Fitzpatricks (Kathleen and Brian), Clark, Blainey, Serle, Turner, Inglis, Macintyre – there is hardly a heavyweight of note who did not pass through the Melbourne school.

Not surprisingly, there was always an Olympian tone about the place, a sort of tweed wall. It was an attitude problem, more shadow than substance, though some would say it had substantial effects – that, for instance, had Geoffrey Blainey been employed early in his career and Brian Fitzpatrick late in his, Australian history might read quite differently. More than good old Melbourne snobbery was involved. The exclusive tendency is endemic to the discipline. Historians everywhere are prone to think of themselves as keepers of the Grail, guardians of the sacred, or at least the ones with the big bag full of facts; it is just a small step from there to the conclusion that anyone seen approaching from another angle is a brigand.

If this somewhat defensive tendency is least apparent among the best historians, it is presumably because they know that writing history, writing the story of the past as if it were the truth, is an act of considerable presumption and, for anyone attempting it, humility is the appropriate attitude to strike. The best historians set themselves tasks which require more imagination, passion and skill than mere fact grubbing. Historians are at their most arrogant when they are most narrow in their inquiry. Often they are least persuasive when they are most certain.

I am not talking here about history's subjectivity, but rather its difficulty, its uncertainty. On this recognition history's potential depends; by this recognition it escapes from both pedantry and its reputation in certain philistine quarters as a "soft" subject – soft being a pejorative, meaning easy, not requiring algebra, calculus or any other serious conceptual effort. Fifteen years ago colleagues of mine, lecturers in urban studies, used to tell new students that history was a soft subject. Anyone could teach history, they told me.

At that time arts degrees were being awarded to young people who did not know World War I from World War II or what the Holocaust or the Gulag was. Many of them could not write a paragraph of coherent historical narrative or read one with understanding; or name half a dozen significant historical events (let alone analyse them). Some of them did not know why or when their immigrant parents had left their own countries. Many of those whose families had been in Australia for three or more generations could not say whether they were of English, Irish, Scots, Welsh or any other descent. They did not know what the United Kingdom comprised. History and the United Kingdom were equally inessential to them. I began insisting that they go home and find out how they got here. We spent two or three weeks looking at a single paragraph from someone like Tawney – someone who wrote about concepts in plain and elegant English. It was impossible for many of these students to understand a single sentence of the theory they were being given in some other subjects. Huge areas of common historical knowledge were unknown to them, but assumed by their lecturers. To compensate they plagiarised, chronically and blatantly.

In these lean times Australian history is experiencing, the temptation might be to make history as "soft" as possible; it might be expected to have more appeal – and more utility – in its primitive, bag of facts form. We might drum it into the buggers. To do this, however, especially if it were to be linked to some notion that students must be taught a positive lesson, would be the intellectual equivalent of a tariff wall. The subject would wither behind it. History should never adopt such a tactic.

If we are to embark on a revival of Australian history, this might be a good starting point. History is vast and protean: don't demean it. We would all be glad if young Australians knew more of the facts of their history. We tend to believe that knowledge of these facts would have an improving effect on their character. We all despair at ignorance, indifference and cynicism and think we must teach them that the past can be known, that even in this subjective world there is such a thing as objective knowledge. But much as we would like them to know the dates of Federation, the names of the explorers and who won the wars, and to have it all uncluttered and free of doubt, history will not reduce to a recitation of agreed important facts. We can recite them and the timorous and pedantic of our offspring will recite them back to us. But don't call it "history". Call it general knowledge, but don't put history in the same tomb. Pretending there is certainty, of a moral or empirical kind, where there is none, will not make our children more enthusiastic or better citizens, or wiser ones. The smart ones won't believe you and the rest won't be listening.

Much of the fascination of history derives from the knowability of the past, but some derives from the unknowable or the almost knowable, or the fleetingly knowable. Some history lies buried, some – it seems to me – shimmers in the air. It vanishes and reappears. Echoes and fades away. Historians may settle for what is in the ground and tangible, for what the bones themselves reveal. This is fascinating and useful. Historians can also try to make sense of what is in the air – to give the bones a life above the ground. This is dangerous. It is also essential if history is to maintain its attraction and, in the Australian case, recover it.

Australian history came to me principally through an inescapable awareness of the pioneering past. It was in the walls of the house. Under cypresses. In faces. And on the mantlepiece where, like New Age crystals, a little pyramid and a sphinx from Egypt locked up the family's part in the legend of the wars. Why was sugar called "a bit of sook"? Why say "common tally voo", even when saying goodbye? We never asked and no one ever told us that it had come back from the Somme. We learned a lot of history at school, but nothing lasts as long as the past we only sense – the unspoken, untaught past. We interpret and reinterpret it forever. It expands in size and meaning. Without being a Freudian, a Jungian or a structural anthropologist, it is reasonable to assume that this is because it has invaded – even formed – the structure of our minds.

The first time I came in contact with that term I rejected it entirely. My grounds were not intellectual: I simply didn't recognise it for what it was. I forgive myself for this: it happened in my final year as an undergraduate at La Trobe University and Greg Dening and Rhys Isaac (later a Pulitzer Prize winner) were the teachers. To ordinary history students in the era of the Vietnam War they were foreign countries. They taught history from the perspective of ethnography, anthropology, the sociology of knowledge. They were interested in the structure of the mind and myth. They were looking for signs and the meaning behind words when the rest of us were looking for facts, or general laws, or some means of fulfilling our ideological desiderata. Dening called his subject "reflective history": we thought sometimes that it was indulgence and quietism. We stared at him, impatient, sullen and uncomprehending. One day – I swear I didn't dream this – he picked up his briefcase and threw it across the tutorial room in frustration.

I don't think I understood a word he said from beginning to end, and I will venture that the casual history reader would find him difficult now. People who want to get the drift of his thinking should read his collection of essays published as *Performances*, or an earlier book called *Mr Bligh's Bad Language*. Here he is in *Performances* summing up the behaviour of the Hawaiians who killed Captain Cook:

> They were not slaves to the structures of their minds. Their stories and rituals of Lono did not predict how they would act. But when they explained to themselves what was happening, and then what had happened, they had nowhere to turn to but their own mythic consciousness. The meaning of what happened then became more important than their experience of what happened.

It is less that these words do not readily reveal their meaning, more that the concepts are foreign. Mythic consciousness, indeed! Structures of minds! While listening to Dening speak at a seminar, Alfred Deakin's biographer, the late J.A. La Nauze, is reputed to have murmured loudly, "We have an enemy among us". By then Dening had taken a chair in the history department at Melbourne. It seemed a strange place for him to be. Melbourne didn't even have a school of sociology or anthropology. After *Mr Bligh* was published, someone described Dening as "magical realist". Someone else charged him with the killing of history.

The fog of that final year was truly awful. I suppose it gave us some idea of what it feels like when history is out of reach: when the past is silent, rituals meaningless, culture and landscape without provenance, language indistinct, democracy beyond one's grasp. Dening and Isaac put before us works by the American historians Bernard Bailyn, Kenneth Lockridge and John Demos, and the sociologist Peter Berger, and asked us to see in them more than our assumptions, training, maturity and patience allowed. I felt like a cretin. I might easily have gone delinquent. Later I came to believe that Dening was the best influence anyone ever had on me. Not only did he let into the discourse of history the ideas of sociologists and ethnographers, but he also opened the way to psychology. He did what historians are supposed to do – he made everything in the world curious (he might have said "problematic"). Despite many indications to the contrary, he greatly expanded the potential of narrative by pushing history into new realms of interpretation. He made it possible to find stories within stories.

History is an improving pursuit, unquestionably. We should be in no doubt about its potential for good. But if we are embarking on a revival of the subject we should not think that history is the place where any well-adjusted child will start. Much as we might like them to seek their identity in what we tell them they are, or what we are, it seems the much more common impulse is to seek it in what they can be. They seek it in their imagination – every great storyteller knows that, as should every historian – they seek it in the future, even if they later find it in the past.

Heaven help the students whose spirits are so low that they feel their worth derives from the experience of their elders; or the parent or teacher who comes to them bearing history as a catechism or heavy weapon to keep them all in order. History is romance, adventure and wisdom – and pedantry, cliché and myopia. History has within it the seeds of its own destruction. We can make it what we like, including dead.

The second point might be this: if historians are going to take the responsibility for reviving Australian history they had better start by recognising their responsibility for bringing it so close to obsolescence. Blaming philistine outside forces is easy and understandable –politicians, postmodernism, the media, state schools, the decline of religion and average attention spans, or the speed of technological and economic change. But historians can never escape responsibility for history's fall.

After all, they begin with a great comparative advantage. They deal in a highly valuable and seductive commodity. What would you prefer to sell door to door – sociology or the story of humanity? History – storytelling at least – is the second-oldest profession in the world and very likely was born just a few minutes after the oldest. History is irresistible. And once the taste is acquired it is a lifetime addiction. It doesn't recede with age or familiarity; it dogs us, shadows us, looms up in front of us.

History deals with everything which is fundamental to every life. It deals with sex and violence, the body and the mind, the left and right sides of the brain, the greatest hopes and the basest instincts, the most banal necessities and the most wondrous follies. History sells – even Australian history, if you ask Robert Hughes. Along with sex and beauty, it is Hollywood's staple. Shakespeare did well out of it, and Hollywood is doing well out of Shakespeare. A historian's canvas is vast: it includes the seas and continents, the mountains and rivers, the forests and plains. There is nothing that has ever happened on a battlefield or in a kitchen or in a mind or a heart, that historians cannot at least attempt to understand and describe.

Why is it necessary to state the obvious about history? So that we are properly impressed by the local profession's most recent accomplishment – to have made Australian history so dull and seemingly irrelevant that our children do not want to study it.

As it turned out, in a desperate last circuitous fling at the subject, which I think involved Marx's *The German Ideology* and something by Durkheim, I grasped just enough of Greg Dening's meaning to scoot through into an unlikely career in academia. But I almost lost my feeble grip just a year later when Alan McBriar, the historian of the Fabians, all but demolished me at a seminar by saying in his kindly way that this sociology of knowledge I was spouting seemed to him just some refurbished variety of historicism. He did not mean historicism in the sense employed by Karl Popper in his famous critiques of Hegel, Marx and others who talked about general laws in history – and in whom Popper discerned the intellectual foundations of modern totalitarianism. That would have been flattery. There was no flattery in the McBriar corrective. He meant historicism in its earlier, near-opposite sense, which holds that historical events can only be explained in the context of the values and ideas prevailing at the time – and in which we saw the intellectual foundations of mean-spirited empiricism and political quietism.

There has been a great deal of postmodern and poststructuralist water under the bridge since then and many people would take it to confirm Alan McBriar's scholarly observation, or the judgement of the person who said that Dening was killing history. I suspect most Australian historians are still inclined to treat excursions into other disciplines, with the possible exception of economics, as a kind of folly. And if they feel tolerably comfortable in halfway houses like historical anthropology, or find they can ignore ethno-historians like Dening, they hold full-blown postmodernism in the same contempt as most postmodernists hold historians. In some quarters even irony – surely postmodernism's most endearing quality – is on the nose.

Here the endemic arrogance of history poses the greatest threat to it. Who else but historians, whose concern is human behaviour, could ignore what is known (or even speculated) in other disciplines? Why should they? To defend the big bag of facts? To uphold the general laws? To protect from scrutiny what Murray Kempton called in his last published essay, the "ragbag full of myth"? (Not that a Murray Kempton would be likely to mess about with Freud, Lacan or Barthes. A wry, liberal and worldly journalist, and a peerless student of politicians and crooks, he was concerned with the more practical things which drive them – like envy, weakness, ambition, their role models, their mothers.) However we choose to look at it, from the most arcane theoretical position or the most prosaically practical, we can no more pretend that history is immune to psychology – or the postmodern – than we can that women are not part of it. In politics the word is nearly always followed by the word "bullshit", but politicians practise psychology, manifest psychology, and play to it in the electorate. Like football, politics is a psychological game. The only thing as remarkable as a politician denying psychology is a historian denying it: as if psychology is not at work in war, say, or, as if a single man on a remote frontier is not prey to memory and emotion; as if envy has no role in history.

It is equally futile to imagine that the media can be left out of the equation. It is fine for journalists to have no knowledge of history – it probably suits them – but historians can't have the compliment returned. The media is part of the context with which historians have to deal. It is not the fourth estate, it is the game itself. Every moment of political life is governed by media imperatives. The meaning behind words and actions is inextricably tied to the media's moods; policy is to varying degrees governed by it, political fortunes are made and broken by it as never before; even the character of politicians is shaped by it. All this before we come to the business of grasping the ways in which public perceptions are formed by the media. It is quite impossible to work in a modern political environment and imagine history being written or taught without treating the media as an insatiable, omnipresent player. It is like writing about Napoleon without noticing he was in Europe.

A postmodern person once asked me what it felt like to be a historian these days. She meant it must feel very odd, because it seemed to her a very odd thing to be. The question irritated me, but not as much as the laugh that went with it. The laugh meant it was genuine. I even wondered if I looked like a historian. And the longer I worked in politics the more I wondered if a historian might look extinct.

Of course the historians who think postmodernism is the problem can make an eloquent case. If you deny the possibility of finding truth and objectivity, who will seek it out? If you debunk humanism and pull the rug on the notion of progress, who will believe in anything? If you then find a generation with little knowledge of facts, and disinclined to believe they are knowable, and you also find a retreat from science and reason – the finger tends to be self-pointing. It is almost possible to persuade yourself that the line which describes the passage of the postmodern runs parallel to the one which marks the decline of political idealism and engagement. Not a few people might argue that next to those two lies can be drawn another, showing the decline of history in our education system.

This train of thought has its seductions. What made me love history in general and Australian history in particular was not Greg Dening's "reflective history", but the politically impassioned teaching of idealists and romantics like Peter Cook and David Johanson, who drew their inspiration from humanism and socialism. In different ways both of them had been encouraged to think passionately about history by Manning Clark. Both were left-wing, much more left-wing than Clark, and much closer to Marxism without being Marxists. Neither of them published as much (or lived as long) as he should have. But, like Manning Clark, they were great teachers: they believed in human capacity and human progress – almost desperately so – and that is how they made us believe in history. Not with theory or reflection, but with a kind of heroic, life-threatening conviction. If other teachers, like John Hirst, nagged away at our assumptions and pricked our pretentious balloons, all the better.

That is the third point. Australian history will not be revived by proscribing certain varieties or closing the door on new ways of approaching it. That applies to Greg Dening and equally to Manning Clark. The vilification of Clark destroys more than his reputation. By attaching personal slander to (arguable) critique, Clark's worst critics threaten to put all his work beyond our reach, and with it a conception of history which gave birth to our best historians, a sustained period of excitement about the story of this country and an unexampled six-volume history – which, for all its flaws, continues to enlighten and threatens no one. The assault is not only on Clark and his work, but on history itself.

Clark began with the premise that we could best understand Australia by understanding the three great ideas in the minds of Europeans who settled it – Protestantism, Catholicism and the Enlightenment. It happened that these pillars of his history eroded with the general faith in them; the central conceit of the first volume could not be sustained to the last. But, eccentric as this variant on the idealist conception of history might seem now (and seemed then to Marxists and others), it had virtues which will undoubtedly outlive the present chaos.

There is a rough parallel with the American historian Perry Miller. Miller began his studies of early New England society with the premise that his subjects could only be understood by knowing how they perceived their relationship with God. Since his death more than three decades ago, a generation of revisionists has greatly enlarged and altered our understanding of that society. And what's more, as Edmund Morgan has pointed out, "by conferring intellectual respectability on the Puritans, Miller also prompted explorations of colonial society that owed little directly to his own work". The same can be said of Clark, and in some ways more so. Not only did he confer intellectual respectability on the minds of representative men like Samuel Marsden, William Charles Wentworth and John Joseph Therry, he conferred it on Australian history. He added immeasurably to the interest in it. No one in his time gave the story such a push and with it a raft of storytellers. A decent society might acknowledge this. A decent community of historians might have acknowledged it with conviction.

That is surely the fourth point: historians will have to defend their discipline against philistine political assault. Take the term now blithely put about it as if to suggest some similarity with modern dictators – "rewriting history". Take, for example, the common charge that Paul Keating tried to "rewrite" Australian history and that his model for this was Manning Clark. Clark these days is described variously as a Marxist-Leninist and a "black armband" historian, which means, according to John Howard, a historian who sees history as nothing more than a story of imperialism, racism, sexism and so on. Now if we can just find a historian willing to say that Keating is a Leninist who believed Australian history was all run through with sexism then we will be on to something very radical indeed. Of course if we can't find one, we might have to declare that a real "rewriting" of history – in the sense of deliberately propagating a fallacy – has been attempted by the very people who are so freely alleging it of people they believe to be political opponents.

The charge that Keating deliberately propagated a fallacy when he said the British betrayed Australia at Singapore is silliness of another order. It is possible to believe that Churchill was a great man – and that Britain is a great country – without believing that either is flawless or incapable of self-interest. It is also possible to express a view about history which differs from the orthodox, or indeed from any other, without perforce "rewriting" it. It would, of course, help the present debate if politicians and journalists recognised that it is in the nature of history to be rewritten; and that most of the rewriting of Australian history has occurred within the walls of history departments. It would be reasonable to expect that historians might help them recognise it.

It would also help if in the continuing assessment of Manning Clark the public was allowed for a moment to separate his work from his bizarre declarations of admiration for Lenin. With historians of the twentieth century we simply have to. It may count for a good deal in any judgement of Clark's character that as late as 1970 he went beyond most Leninists in singing Lenin's praises. But that does not make him a Marxist-Leninist any more than it makes him a Soviet agent of influence. It does not nullify the work he did as a writer and teacher. If it did, what are we to do with Hobsbawm, Christopher Hill and E.P. Thompson? What will we do with the twentieth century? In the early 1960s, when Australian history was booming and beyond political reproach, when Henry Bolte was premier of Victoria and Robert Gordon Menzies was prime minister, Victorian matriculation students were required on pain of failure to read Russel Ward's *The Australian Legend* and a long article on the history of the labour movement by Robin Gollan in Greenwood's *Australia: A Social and Political History*. Until the anti-Clark campaign revived I had almost forgotten that Russel Ward and Bob Gollan had done more than express admiration for Lenin; admittedly they did not compare him with Christ, but unlike Clark, who did, they had both joined the Communist Party. The case rests – our current attitude to history is a form of regression.

These thoughts are in part prompted by reading a recent book by John Demos (the same John Demos served us by Greg Dening and Rhys Isaac twenty-five years ago). The book is *The Unredeemed Captive: A Family Story from Early America*. The subtitle is really very droll, given the brutality and unimaginable hardship, suffering and sadness of the tale he tells. It concerns the capture of the daughter of a prominent Puritan minister by Indians in 1704. Similar things happened on other frontiers, including our own. This one is a little different because the girl stayed and, refusing every entreaty to return to her father, married a Mohawk, had children and converted to Catholicism. From relatively sparse evidence, Demos reconstitutes three cultures, describes the structure and operation of the Puritan mind down to its last tic and reminds some of us at least that we have not entirely escaped from its grotesque inhuman fantasy.

Demos writes with consistent ease and grace. He evokes the radically different French, Indian and Puritan cultures and describes gruesome and heart-rending events with a complete absence of sentimentality, without explicit moral or political judgement, and with no sign of the theoretical foundations on which the study rests. The jacket offers this extract from a review by Hilary Mantel:

> John Williams [the Puritan minister] wrote: "God can make dry bones, very dry, to live". So can historians; that must be their job, and it is seldom performed so successfully as here. Demos made the bones live by taking the tools of his revisionism and applying them to old fashioned narrative.

Demos writes in a preface, "As a child in school, I had been drawn to history by the stories". But narrative, he reminds us, was in "deep eclipse" when he was a young historian. Then, in middle age, story crept back. In *The Unredeemed Captive* he "resolved to yield to it fully".

This can be the fifth point: history needs everything it can get from other disciplines, but it will win more friends in the form of story. Notwithstanding the Minister for Foreign Affairs' reported objection that Clark's history is too much like a novel, story is history's best weapon and irresistible embrace. Stories can relate the most profound truth and express the most dire uncertainty. The silliest thing historians ever did was give them up; the best thing they can do is relearn the art of telling them.

Raymond Carver wrote a story about a group of ordinary American men on a long-awaited fishing trip who discover a woman's body snagged in the river near their campsite. They decide not to spoil their trip by driving back to report it, persuading themselves that nothing practical will be lost by leaving her there until they have had the good time they promised themselves. Principally the story concerns the wife of one of them – her repulsion and his guilt and anger. John Howard should read the story. Carver's fishermen behave as he would have historians behave. He asks them not to report felonies, to be dumb, to ignore truth when it is inconvenient. It is not easy to decide which is the bigger folly – to ask them to do this, or to believe that they can? To want to hide the truth, or to believe that by this means guilt is washed away?

The most dangerous part of the assault on so-called "black armband" history is not the suggestion of political proscription which hangs about it, or its persistent traducing of historical work and even sometimes the character and loyalty of historians: the biggest threat is to history itself. Even if this reactionary interregnum proves to be a long one, historians are unlikely to shy away for long from subjects and methods of approach which might be called "black armband". But if the history curriculum is sanitised, history's decline will be terminal. Carried to its logical con- clusion it would put *The Unredeemed Captive* beyond our reach. After all, Demos could easily be charged with cultural relativism and even politi- cal correctness, and most certainly with multiculturalism. What is more, large sections of his work describe behaviour and events, and character traits of the founding fathers which are not, to use a word favoured by the enemies of black armbanditry, "uplifting".

We are obliged to ask why the campaign singled out Australian history for correction – why should European, Asian, American and African historians be free to tell the whole story, while Australian histo- rians are hogtied? Why should historians of the Soviet Union be allowed to instruct their students in the Gulag, while Australians are encour- aged to keep within the boundaries of political convenience or some new national taste? It is easier to find answers to these largely rhetorical questions than it is to explain why historians – Australian and others – have not in any concerted way publicly defended their profession. Why should literature, art and cinema studies be free to study the dark, while history is confined to the light?

Forget the wars and massacres; forget, for now, even the loss which history almost always describes, if it cannot repair; forget the function, the meaning and the potential of history; forget the truth. Forget it all and you still have to answer the question – how do you tell a story with only light? Take it out of the stories we tell our children and we'll lose them. Take it out of John Howard's Protestant intellectual inheritance and he's lost himself. No Bible, no *Kidnapped*, no westerns – no Captain Cook, no Lawson, no Barbara Baynton, no Steele Rudd – no Robert O'Hara Burke. No *The Australian Legend*.

That is the sixth point: even if it could be justified on moral and intellectual grounds (which it simply can't be), leaving out the grisly and sad bits is precisely the thing to do if you want to drive kids away from history. Without them they won't believe you, for a start. Without the bad they won't believe the good – and they won't believe in it either. Without it, you deny everything we know about the structure of human minds. Without it, you make history that infantile disorder described at the beginning of this article. Without it, you may as well join up with the politically correct who also want to instruct the young in pieties rather than realities.

Political correctness did become a disease of the Australian history curriculum. It also became a disease of the public service. It infested language and institutions like borer which meant in some the effects will hang around after the disease has passed. It stifled talent and, in some cases, justice. Worst of all, it debilitated thought and action. Politically correct thought is anathema to liberalism and to history. And very often it is its own worst enemy.

In history we see it in anachronistic judgements and polemical over-kill, particularly when the subject is Aboriginal Australia, but in other areas as well. There is no question that political correctness invaded high school and university curricula for a while, as did certain methodological fashions which made learning history a nightmare of tedium and confusion. There is no reason to doubt that some politically correct historians were motivated by those things the anti-politically correct allege – including guilt. We should be wary of the judgement of people for whom atrocious acts in the past justify some political need or a craving in their unconscious. Political correctness is silly, hostile to imagination, and inimical to the interests of both history and social improvement. It will be very good for the country when it has gone. And it will be just as good when its opposite has gone as well. Deep loathing for political correctness does not put us beyond the reach of history, and history's judgement. If the facts are there and can be found they should be found – and they should be known. Of course, among those facts we will find a number of earlier examples of political correctness on both sides of politics. An earlier form of political correctness possessed John Hewson the day he rushed outside to protest after Paul Keating put a protective arm around the Queen and told her that Australia was going its own way in the world. It was at work in those governments which for so long censored literature. The Victorians knew a thing or two about it. Arthur Phillip was at it within a few days of sailing into Sydney Cove.

That is the seventh point, then: from whatever side of the political divide it comes, any effort to make history a source of certainty in an age of uncertainty is bound to fail. The risk for history curriculum-makers is that in searching for new standards of objectivity they set new standards of irrelevance and indifference; by seeking to correct a perceived political imbalance they narrow history's potential and stifle its mystery and appeal.

Those two convicts of mine – victims of political correctness they might have said – help to make the point. If the present debate had any substance to it, there would be just two ways to write their history. The non–black armband version would have us concentrate on the "positive" side: that is, the side which instructs us in the benefits which transportation ultimately brought to these convicts and their descendants, including me. Black armbandits, of course, would be drawn to the social evil which produced them, the inhuman penal code which sentenced them, the misery of the voyage, the Aboriginal community they displaced. They would count the scars on their backs. Of all the inherent absurdities in the present debate the greatest is to imagine that history cannot accommodate the whole story.

In fact the lives of those two people can be approached in a dozen ways. They might cast a little light on both stories. After all they are representative not just of Australia's penal origins, but two of Geoffrey Blainey's famous theses – the tyranny of distance and his idea that Norfolk Island, to which the two of them were immediately dispatched, was a major reason for British settlement of Australia. Their lives might tell us something about coping with exile at the bottom of the world or why their descendants through six generations kept this convict stain from view. They might tell us something universal about the immigrant experience, and this might help us weigh not just the gains, but what loss has meant in our historical development. Our very recent experience of the *Bringing Them Home* report suggests that this is a kind of understanding we have been lacking. In fact it suggests, at best, an astonishing myopia among Australian historians of all varieties. It even suggests that it is on the black armband side that our deficit lies.

It is not that we cannot understand these things. We erected our finest monuments to the soldiers we lost in war, and no one has ever been under the illusion that their loss was not permanent, that it did not go further than the loss of lives, and that it was not passed on to succeeding generations. The Australian War Memorial remains not just a monument to the dead but, as anyone who has spent an hour there knows, a consolation to the living. History has this among its uses – it can console. As Kerryn Goldsworthy pointed out at a recent seminar, the wearing of a black armband (like a red poppy?) says, "I remember the dead, I care about the dead, I don't want to forget the dead" – which are hardly sentiments historians should abhor.

History may not have the capacity to heal, but it is a worthwhile aim. We are not the first generation to learn that so long as we do not confront the realities of our historical relationship with Aboriginal Australia we will lack a mature understanding of ourselves. We can find voices offering this advice through all of the 210 years since the British decided to put a settlement here. There were legal and paramilitary interventions; there were religious and scientific exhortations. Men made observations of a psychological kind 160 years ago which were never stored in the collective memory, but perhaps now should be. Take, for example, Baron Charles von Hügel, who in 1833–34 wrote of the Aborigines:

> I was often even astonished at their power of feeling. But what is to become of a poor, uncouth and indolent people who never hear one sensible word, or anything suggestive of either intellect or sensibility, from an Englishman? Whenever he sees a New Hollander ... the jokes go on until the Englishman can't think of any more.

When we ignored the dark side of the frontier – in fact ignored the concept of the frontier itself – we ignored much more than the implications for the dispossessed. We ignored the moments of our creation. And creation, we surely know, *always* has a dark side. We now confront the practical issue of native title and human dispossession in almost universal ignorance, in a void where history should have put a drama. We turn against immigration with the same absence of knowledge and sentiment. There is still no defining, widely read history of the White Australia policy. For the story of immigration we turn to a handful of personal memoirs, not to the work of historians, yet immigration is one profound historical experience all Australians in some sense share. If historians choose to pursue the melancholy themes of our history in the story of the frontier, the emigrant ships, among women, in the loss of the natural environment, in the story of the suburbs or the selections, it just may turn out that the "guilt industry" is a very productive, useful and even "uplifting" one.

The last point might be this: if Australian history is to revive we will have to devise courses which frankly acknowledge the modern student's weaknesses and lack of interest without compromising history's strengths. The essential balance is always between ideas and the capacity of the audience to understand them. It will be no use to substitute for history what Stuart Macintyre has called the spectacle of historians talking among themselves. It will not do to regress to a bag of facts, or some notion of what is good for young people, or some pretence that history is objectivity's last redoubt in a wickedly subjective world. History will die an ugly death if, under pressure, it holds out against people who come to the parapets with ideas. But when they come wailing "black armbands!", "guilt industry!", "not sufficiently uplifting!", rain down Bibles and bellow back the words of Pascal:

> It is dangerous to prove to man too plainly how nearly he is on a level with the brutes without showing him his greatness; it is also dangerous to show him the greatness too clearly apart from the vileness. It is still more dangerous to leave him in ignorance of both. But it is of great advantage to show him both.

The Australian's Review of Books, 9 July 1997

Manning Clark

There is no life of a man, faithfully recorded, but is a heroic poem of its sort, rhymed or unrhymed.

—Thomas Carlyle

PERHAPS IT WAS ONLY IN Melbourne, which appeared to have come unstuck without our being able to find anyone to credibly blame, that the mood of depression this time seemed ineradicable: for once not even the simultaneous coming of a brilliant spring and the great Australasian racing carnival lightened the locals' hearts. Then, to top it off, Darren Millane, a Collingwood footballer, a hero, a great man of the proletariat with a look of indestructibility, ended a bender of heroic proportions by driving his car into the back of a semitrailer. The press coverage of Millane's funeral exceeded by far the deaths in recent years of the country's greatest novelist, Patrick White, its greatest surgeon, Victor Chang, and its greatest historian, Manning Clark. Those who mourned Millane and those who wondered why there was so much mourning for him probably did have something in common – presumably it crossed some recess of the minds of both that this was the end of the road.

That was the worrying thing – we got the feeling that this was not just an economic recession, but the end of reasonable hope for the place. Remember, it was not a corrupt government which had lost the bank and the building society and unheard of amounts of public money. This was a prudent, honest, hard-working government, a government with imagination, a government which saw a great future ... and yet. They might as well have been corrupt, for the result was the same.

With no one to hold responsible in a way that satisfactorily released the anger (and guilt, because hadn't everyone run up a little debt of their own?), it began to seem as if there might be a new reality to face. A reality more daunting than free market economics, or the greed of our entrepreneurs, or our helplessness in the face of international tariffs and plummeting commodity prices – it was that we were not good enough. Not up to it. There was a feeling that in the overview Australia had stepped onto the world stage around 1890 and, for about one hundred years, performed a passable imitation of a country with a reason for being, if not a great destiny, and now, for want of any further inspiration or energy, was slouching off, like Henry Lawson to the pub.

Manning Clark was almost excessively fond of quoting the Karamazov brother who said he wanted to be there when suddenly everyone understood what it had all been for. Well, in October 1991 it was not hard to imagine that as citizens walked the incredibly empty streets of Melbourne they were saying to themselves, "Who cares, it was for nothing".

Perhaps it was only in Melbourne that people were quite so glum, but there were similar reports from Perth, a general strike in Sydney and the worst drought for a generation in Queensland and northern New South Wales. It was also eerily like the last decade of the previous century. There were no visible signs of leadership – in fact, so rudderless was the ship of state, guided as it was by a caricature of a contemporary Australian reminiscent one minute of Billy Hughes and the next of Cranky Jack, that two old stagers, Gough Whitlam and Malcolm Fraser, emerged from the political morgue to stand on the same stump and rail against the way things seemed to be going.

Manning Clark died wondering not only about the big existential question, he wondered also if Australia was finished, whether it would "peter out". Was there an Australian culture, a point of view, a sense of direction of sufficient strength to see the country through? Or had we run out of fuel and begun drifting towards a destiny not of our own making? He suspected that we had. Clark was making more than a melodramatic point. Dostoyevsky was haunted by the belief that, if the Christ story wasn't true, life was no more than, as he put it, a carnival of devils; it required just a short leap of the imagination for Clark, the man who chose to make Australian history the reason for his being, to ask what if the Australian story wasn't true.

Manning Clark's *A History of Australia* is not a carnival of devils but there is something in the phrase which helps describe the canvas he created. It is painted with fallen angels: men and women with souls which joined them to all history, all societies, all creation. That was the central conceit which enabled Clark to choose Australian history instead of British, or German or any of the other branches which self-respecting scholars of his day chose. That very simple idea, that the story of Australia, as much as any other story, was the story of the human heart, got the whole thing going. The three great ideas he set up to encompass all the players in Australian history – Catholicism, Protestantism and the spirit of the Enlightenment – were just three ways of understanding what the heart tells us. This much-criticised construction was in fact the source of excitement for his Australian readers and students. It helped and often inspired them to believe in both the subject and the place. Clark's work thus addressed the key issue in Australian cultural life. The same one addressed in different mediums by his contemporaries Nolan and Boyd, White and Barry Humphries: how do we invest this empty, philistine place with meaning? How do you project a big idea onto small minds – how do you see a big idea in small minds? Or as the first European preachers who came here put it: how shall we sing the Lord's song in a strange land? Clark's great achievement was to show how, at least figuratively speaking, it could be done.

In football Clark saw metaphors for life bravely and brilliantly led. He saw, as all lovers of the game do, the varieties of humanity and human experience. Footballers lifted themselves above drabness and dullness, they aspired to immortality. In Clark's Kingdom of Nothingness they made something of themselves.

In Clark's *History* the same theme persists. Everyone is someone (hence the constant use of the honorific Mr and Mrs), everyone believes something, everyone is like someone or something, everyone has a place in the universal taxonomy of the human species, everyone is seeking the moment of glory or imagines one in the past. The Kingdom of Nothingness demanded Clark's idealism. Into the hearts and minds of convicts and gold diggers, politicians, petty officials and minor poets he stuffed all the great passions and follies. He gave them Christ, or his absence: either way Clark was relieved of the burden of judgement, and he wanted that, because Christ had said "Judge not".

Clark made every one of his characters either a seeker after the mystery at the heart of things, or part of that mystery. He armed them with one of the three great European faiths and floated them off onto the great river of life. The act of genius was to convince a cynical audience that the river flowed through the desert of Australia. In this scheme of things everyone is elevated or at least puffed up, and so everyone is brought down. It is democratic levelling not by legislation but by Nietzschean irony. Cook is undone by hubris, Macquarie by self-righteousness, Sturt by impotence, Hughes by hate, Menzies by arrogance. The list goes on and on: Manning Clark never felt constrained to understate a theme.

Nor to undersell himself. The three-piece blue suit and the hat were as emphatically theatrical as a Barry Humphries disguise. They made him an instantly recognisable figure in the landscape. The melancholy voice and the grave face – "full of great oaths and bearded like the pard", as Brian Fitzpatrick once quipped – were a mask for a remarkably warm, funny, earthy and tolerant man, and one more at peace with suburbia and the vulgarities of Australian life than his admiring public probably imagined. He liked an audience. He was forever "opening a country dunny in Woop Woop", as Patrick White is alleged to have said. No doubt there was a lot to be learned from these trips into the interior, but he was also taking the Word to the benighted inhabitants. And one suspects that to a degree he was addicted to public performance. There was always a high degree of self-consciousness: he knew his *History* was making history and that he was one of the characters in his own story. It followed that he did not want to end up like George Reid, swept from the great river of life into a billabong.

So what sort of performer was he? A tragedian, an ironist, sometimes a satirist. If one believes with Carlyle, as Clark undoubtedly did when he began, that the "history of the world is but the biography of great men", the history of a society of second-hand Europeans is always going to run closely parallel to farce. Australians worshipped as heroes those who, like themselves, had fallen from the heights of (European) civilisation, or from grace, or faith. They are almost all people who came unstuck. That is why Clark's tone, though not his style, is often as Swiftian as it is Carlylean: sometimes it becomes, like satire, "a sort of glass, wherein beholders do generally discover everybody's face but their own". But it is history, and even if the writing occasionally takes on a fantastic quality (the opening paragraphs on the gold rush are quite a bizarre example), and if the "eye of pity" with which he always tried to regard his subjects was often as sardonic as it was pitying, it is nearly always redeemed by his love for the place and for the people in it. Although they are frequently emblematic vehicles for Clark's preoccupation with human folly, his Macquarie, Wentworth, Parkes and Deakin, to name just four of the more substantial ones, are not satirical characters for the simple reason that we know they lived in the same place as we do.

With his huge work Clark erected a tower for himself and, as he must have anticipated, it has been shot at every day since. Now that he is dead his opponents will redouble their efforts. The complaints will be the same: the errors or the absence of facts; the sometimes gross repetitions; the sentimentality; the incessant irony; the lack of political sophistication; the hopelessly old-fashioned idealism; the failure to pay sufficient attention to the common people, to women and Aboriginal people. They will continue to see his work as an assault on Australian pragmatism, as investing the past with faiths which do not presently exist. They will continue to deny what Clark believed with Carlyle, namely that "in every sense … a man's religion is the chief fact with regard to him".

His critics will be right and wrong at the same time. They will be right to see faults because Clark's work has many of them. They will never run out of ammunition. But they will be wrong to think that the tower can be shot down. It can't be for many reasons, but a perfectly sufficient one is the fact that Clark's *History* is now as much a part of the national story as Burke and Wills. It inhabits the same country of myth and legend, universal drama, white dreaming if you like. That is the great strength of Clark's brand of history. It goes on living. And who can confidently say, at the end of this or any other century, that the idealist conception of history which underpins his tower is wrong? That those theories which discount envy and greed, madness, good and evil are more likely to be right?

And who can really say that the Clark taxonomy was wrong? The case of Darren Millane is testimony to "the madness of the human heart", "the thunder in the trousers", the "can't put the cork back in the bottle" type of man, and all the other debilitating conditions for which Clarkisms can be found. And there is something to say for the argument that these things are more universal and comprehensible than working-class consciousness, or race or gender consciousness, or economics: in Central

Australia, a month after Millane's death, a fifty-year-old Aboriginal man who had spent the previous two days instructing a group of students on the Dreaming told me how shattered he was by the news. His people understood Millane, he said; as far as he was concerned, Darren Millane was one of them.

Because he was a great historian as well as a great romantic, Manning Clark knew that what seemed to be the logical and proper outcome of history was never the same as what actually happened. The storyteller lives with disappointment to help others to live with it. If what Clark sensed in the last years of his life turns out to be the case, if the great revival does not occur, probably it will again only be irony which saves us: for one of our main comforts will be one of the few clues to the discovery of what it has all been for – the story which grew out of the huge labour and love of Manning Clark.

Scripsi, vol. 7, no. 3, 1992

Geoffrey Blainey

Geoffrey Blainey would be a rare historian if nothing else distinguished him but the fact that his books are read. No Australian historian has matched his sales. More than just read, *The Tyranny of Distance* remains a publishing phenomenon. It is now in its umpteenth edition, the "twenty-first-century edition" no less, with a new chapter addressing the prospect that after thirty-five years his famous thesis might have run its course.

It is no surprise that he finds for the defendant. Blainey is more than Australia's most loved historian; he is a political force, a man of power and influence. He is still held to be a villain in some quarters, but in not so many these days. Recently he has seen his fellow historians come forward to make peace. That soft, insistent, measured tone of his will haunt some of his colleagues for the rest of their lives, but the great majority of his fellow Australians, both plain and influential, will continue to read, listen and admire.

The Tyranny of Distance was the main foundation of his reputation. It was a brilliant book by any standards and unquestionably one of the half-dozen most influential of our last century. The great force in Australian history, he said, was distance, or isolation, he sometimes called it. The great aim or interest, therefore, has been to conquer distance. This central premise was brilliantly simple and boundless in its applications, as fruitful in its way as *On the Origin of Species*. It is the equivalent in Australian historiography of Fred Williams's or Sidney Nolan's landscapes. It is as if fitted with its own screw propeller.

Methodologically, Blainey hopped over the redoubts constructed by his predecessors. His approach was the antithesis of Manning Clark, his old teacher, friend and only rival in celebrity. Clark was the idealist, the recorder of angst. Blainey was the recorder of progress. His nearest local kin were Brian Fitzpatrick or Noel Butlin, the economic historians. But *The Tyranny of Distance* was both more radical and more gripping. In his "materialist conception" there were hints of masters like Fernand Braudel and even Marx, but there was much more of a businessman's or a Methodist's regard for utility and common sense. In the end, Blainey was Blainey and he owed nothing to anyone.

He did for Australian history much as Elizabeth David did for English cuisine, and did it about the same time. He made our history as she made Mediterranean cooking – approachable, palatable, doable. For inexpert readers, he replaced academic stew and amateur adventure with beguiling stories expertly told in simple, muscular prose. For academics there was alarmingly little scholarly apparatus on show and few outward signs of condescension, yet Blainey's work was equally free of writerly embellishment.

And like David's recipes, Blainey's formula worked. To read him was to understand not just what had happened but how it had happened, the chemistry of it. In the modern idiom, he empowered his readers (especially those who were teachers and students) by giving them the priceless ability to make sense of their country's history, to see the drama in it and in the drama a richer context for their own lives. He did it mainly by writing it in terms most readers understood, and this he did by making the first principles of his history self-interest and utility. He came not as a historian weighed down with the ordinary lode of methodology and wisdom, but more as a farmer comes to an intractable animal, or an alchemist to the elements, or a capitalist to his bottom line.

He wrote memorably about what it was like to have lived on a whaling vessel, to sail steerage to the gold rushes, to navigate through icebergs, to be carried on the "brave west winds" south of the 40th parallel. I cannot think of another book that describes so well the creative force of wind and weather. Blainey was always looking for the patterns in history, the force fields, the unseen equivalents of tides, winds, monsoons, the earth's rotations. The people in his books were governed by these forces, and by like things: specifically their interests national, financial, corporate, individual. Blainey's governments and people follow their interests rather as mutton birds follow whatever it is that leads them to fly from Bass Strait

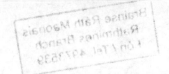

to Alaska and back each year. And like mutton birds, there is no significant sign of religion or ideas. Sometimes their interests become like a religion, and sometimes they are shipwrecked or beached.

Consider refrigeration, on which Elizabeth David also wrote at some length. It is the mid-nineteenth century; we have meat and we have a market for it, but we don't have a means of bringing the two together. Distance again stands in the way of self-interest, creating necessity, the parent of invention, which leads to progress and greater public good. Refrigerated transport means a huge increase in the wealth of the Australian colonies, especially for those with the broad acres to grow mutton and beef, and better health for the folk of Britain and Europe, though not for James Harrison, the Geelong printer who did much of the pioneering work. Harrison went bankrupt; beached, like George Bass was in Peru (or did he sink in the Pacific?). He succumbed to the tyranny of distance, like Burke and Wills, Kingsford Smith, Hinkler and HMS *Sirius*, whose story is as good as any of them.

Largely because of Blainey it is now widely accepted that the decision to send the First Fleet to Sydney Cove owed less to the need for a new convict dumping ground than to the requirements of the British Navy and British interests in the Pacific and Asia, including an interest in thwarting French ambitions there.

It was Blainey who showed us how, for the first half-century, the settlement concerned the sea much more than the hinterland, that whaling was a more significant industry than sheep and remained so long after a route was found across the Blue Mountains. The primary purpose of the places of secondary punishment dotted round the coast was to protect the sea lanes for British shipping. The delay in settling New Zealand is explained by the simple fact that New Zealand had no place in these interests, just as the delay in settling the fertile coast between Port Lincoln and Cape Otway can be explained by the fact that it arcs away from the southern shipping routes, and Melbourne's foundation was delayed for half a century because the mouth of the Yarra was too far from the strait to be useful for reconnaissance. The pattern of these events changed only when Australia's raw materials became valuable to Britain.

Scarcely a page of *The Tyranny of Distance* does not contain some revelation of this kind. They pile up on top of each other. The colonies' isolation from Britain and Europe relative to North America obliged governments to subsidise migration. To meet the cost, land was sold at higher prices; by the 1860s, it was eighty times higher than in the United States. The high cost of land meant debt, to which may be attributed in varying degrees the Kelly Gang, the *Bulletin* school, the Australian sense of humour, the presence of up to three banks in every country town, the omnipresence of governments in economic and social affairs (because they are cashed up by the high price of land), the depression of the 1890s and therefore some of the motives of Jack Lang, who never got over his father going broke in it and who had, of course, some influence on our previous prime minister, which suggests that the high price of land in 1862 had a bearing on the career of John Howard. That some of these speculations are mine rather than Blainey's only goes to show that once the notion gets a grip you cannot say where it will lead.

On the upside, as Blainey says, the length of the voyage and the need to run migrant ships as something like little floating welfare states had their own influence on the character of the society. Perhaps we may in part ascribe to the long voyage everyone made the Australian predilection for "big government", the sense of entitlement and propensity to whinge, or even some part of the collectivist ethic expressed in mateship and trade unions. Perhaps, with our ancestral memory of the little picture of a boat we tend to shy at bigger human vistas. Perhaps it retains some hold on our conception of a social model, our instinct to huddle.

Through mining, wool, paddle-steamers and trains, well into the twentieth century, the Blainey thesis remains compelling and productive, like one of James Harrison's machines popping out iceblocks from nowhere. It opens windows onto the wars, industry, the relationships with Britain and America, postwar immigration, pretty well everything. Of White Australia he writes intriguingly that having been thoroughly connected with Asia in the first decades of its history, Australia was able to cut itself off only in the last decades of the nineteenth century because the majority of the population lived in the south, where it was universally agreed that coloured labour was a curse. In the north, however, it was viewed as a necessity.

So Australia achieved racial unity; and the gains of that unity were obvious. The price of unity was that many Asians later resented a nation which discriminated against Asians. A less obvious price of that unity was to retard the using of those few scattered resources in northern Australia which seemed capable of supporting many people at an Asian standard of living and few at an Australian standard of living.

This is one of the relatively rare moments when Blainey talked about possibility lost. Another one was the country's refusal to accept the supersonic Concorde. When he wrote about this in a later edition, there were strange signs of irritation, almost as if the people's refusal had been an affront to his thesis. On the other hand, he expounds at length on the peculiarly Blaineyesque observation that "Some of the most revealing and important facets of Australian history came from events which did not happen". It is true, of course, even if it one is left thinking that it would be just as true if the word "French" or "Icelandic" were substituted for "Australian".

With Blainey, for every dozen blinding revelations there is a statement of the bleeding obvious. For instance: "Distance contrary to the title of this book is not always a tyrant". Of course it's not; in fact the book's primary achievement is to demonstrate how thoroughly distance has been overcome. The title could as well be *The Triumph Over Distance*. So when he says more than once in the final chapters that distances are shrinking, or that Australia by 1956 was not "impossibly far away", he seems to be competing with his own argument.

In his conclusion to this "twenty-first-century edition", Blainey declares that, while the world is "shrinking", distance is not dead. The internet, mobile phones, jumbo jets and other modern miracles have failed to kill the effects of isolation, and sometimes only magnify our sense of lost time and the need for personal contact. They also give us jet lag, deep vein thrombosis and, who knows, brain tumours. So long as there is QF1 and Heathrow at the end, and people still have to go to Perth, distance is not dead. And just as well: the time we still need to travel is often the only time in business and politics for rest and peace.

My difficulty with Blainey's answer to the question is not that he is wrong but, these things being relative, I cannot see how anyone, with the possible exception of Doctor Who, could reach a different conclusion. What is more, I think it very likely that if the question had been put, let's say, to the inveterate nineteenth-century traveller the Rev. John

Dunmore Lang, after his first voyage on a steamship, he would also have replied: "Tamed but not dead".

The more recent the events, the harder it is to write about them and we should not be too hard on Blainey if, having done a fair impression of a stump-jump plough for a dozen chapters, the clutch begins to slip in the last couple. But there are signs that the closer he gets to his own time the more randomly he projects and defends the Australia he has defined. In pursuit of his thesis he has allowed to go unremarked such popular human concerns as religion, psychology, literature, ideology, modernism, doubt; as if they were swept past on the westerlies, destined to wash up on the shores of some unfortunate magic realist republic. There are remarkably few people in Blainey's book, few moral dilemmas, few minds and fewer doubts. Historians going down these paths he tends to treat as harmless.

But historians who weigh the balances of development differently, or, on a conscientious reading of the evidence, come up with different views about the frontier, the wars or Asia, can expect Blainey's catty reproval.

One of the great virtues of Blainey's *Tyranny* is its portrait of Australia's vigorous and essential early engagement with the subcontinent, Asia and the Pacific. After demonstrating how close to Asia the infant colony was, how it was virtually a "satellite" of India, strange that in his more recent chapters Blainey should traduce the efforts of Australian governments to take up the challenge anew. He says these politicians have insisted that Australia is "part" of Asia; in fact, they have much more often insisted that, while Australia is "in" Asia, and that its future substantially lies there, it is not Asian and never can be.

To his opponents Blainey takes some of the old Melbourne history school style, meaning he tends to assume exclusive ownership of both facts and interpretation. But Blainey has more than airs, Blainey has teeth. He has an agenda. Threaten or question it and one may expect to come under heavy fire. He may present himself publicly with the diffidence of a conscientious, slightly aggrieved schoolboy, but Blainey operated as he writes – as a man without the afflictions of doubt. It might be, as Manning Clark and Kathleen Fitzpatrick speculated in their published letters, that the acid springs from a youthful grievance with the Melbourne school itself. Whatever the reason, Geoffrey Blainey is a jealous defender of his own fort.

These days we can see in *The Tyranny of Distance* something more than a brilliant interpretation of Australian history. There are also some of the underpinnings of contemporary orthodoxy. No one had a sharper, less equivocal and more generally persuasive view of how Australia was made and what it meant. It is not too much to say that this view has since taken on some of the characteristics of a prescription for the nation's life. Essentially, Blainey defined Australia as a British place modified by the workings of self-interest and utility. Far from being dead or tamed, *The Tyranny of Distance* and Geoffrey Blainey have never been so alive.

The Age, 19 February 2002

Brian Fitzpatrick

I do not seek, however long the conflict may last, a muzzled opposition.

—R.G. Menzies, 1939

IN 1953 THE AUSTRALIAN LIBERAL conservative Frederic Eggleston lamented the lack of an antipodean equivalent to Edmund Burke:

> We want more than political leadership. We need intellectual leadership on all great issues. We miss, in Australia, the publicist, the man detached from politics but able and well-informed, in whom the public can trust, and who will speak plainly and fearlessly.

Eggleston, of course, did not count Fitzpatrick for the same reason that he chose Burke rather than, say, Hazlitt, as his archetype. But if Fitzpatrick was not detached from politics (and surely neither was Burke), for a large section of the Australian political and intellectual community he embodied all the values Eggleston found lacking.

Fitzpatrick's "ideals" or guiding values were never clear. He combined a respect for almost aristocratic Old World graces with an affection for the working class and a notorious propensity to be socially "difficult". He called himself a socialist, yet his beliefs were more akin to libertarianism. He loathed narrow empiricism but he also scorned "high theory" and was never a systematic thinker. He was a cold-hearted Marxist and a soft-hearted liberal. He was a utopian and pragmatist.

Even if they were reconcilable, these categories would not entirely capture either the man or his significance in the Australian intellectual community. This significance to his generation emerged at the testimonial dinner given him in 1964. Here tributes were paid by an astonishing array: from Sir John Latham to representatives of the extreme left. One speaker, the Labor senator Sam Cohen, remarked, "You don't talk about 'people like Brian Fitzpatrick'". There was more in this than mawkishness. Fitzpatrick simply *was* sui generis. For this, his extraordinary energy was partly responsible – a quality which is not readily explained.

Fitzpatrick was unique because he *acted* at the same time as he thought. When most of his generation were merely resenting, Fitzpatrick was organising. More generally, Fitzpatrick's unique standing stemmed from his reflexive reaction to authority. He was fundamentally a rebel: a libertarian first, a socialist second. He could therefore be logical and rational but he could not be sufficiently consistent or predictable to satisfy either a party leader or a sociologist.

Fitzpatrick did have one persistent ideal, and that was his wish for an enlightened community. This was hardly an uncommon hope for an intellectual. Most Australian intellectuals have accommodated that hope in political parties, in an acceptance of pluralism or, occasionally, in a bohemian elitism. In the last two cases, effectively, the intellectual builds his environment in isolation, but Fitzpatrick's wish existed in the – largely Melbourne – milieu of humanism, rationalism, meliorism and Protestant non-conformism. In this, Fitzpatrick was "like" countless others – he was part of the "tradition". But while he was "like", for example, Vance Palmer in his humanism or Jack Barry in his Irish sense of injustice, neither Palmer nor Barry was "like" him.

The intellectual and political characteristics of the "tradition" had roots in the eighteenth and nineteenth centuries and it also found justification in the "Australian legend". There *was* a link between the Irish convict rebellion at Castle Hill in 1804 and Fitzpatrick's twentieth-century rebellion, if only because he *thought* there was. It is of more than superficial significance that Fitzpatrick was always likely to break into "Faith of our Fathers" or "Kevin Barry" in the pub or on the tram on the way home. Obviously, Fitzpatrick's activity was also sustained by the twentieth century, which seemed set on a course at odds with his ideal – it seemed, to him at least, to have maximised inhumanity, irrationality and conformity. However unique, Fitzpatrick was very much a product of his age. There is something in Manning Clark's recent remark (apart from a failure perhaps to appreciate Fitzpatrick's cussedness and the pleasure he got in earning his stigma and notoriety):

> It was the poet and the puritan in Fitzpatrick which attracted him to the wild duck's loft: it was our Philistines who left him with the ravaged face.

Fitzpatrick had resented the parochialism and the philistinism of the 1930s. In the 1950s, the publicly unlamented, virtually unacknowledged death of the brilliant (socialist) scholar V. Gordon Childe or the jailing of the painter Albert Namatjira for providing his people with alcohol, like the spectacle of H.V. Evatt's perpetual frustration by the unenlightened or party hacks, suggested that little or nothing had changed. Australia remained in the grip of the philistine. To resent this was not uncommon, but to devote one's life to opposing it with so little compromise was unique.

It is not easy to assess Fitzpatrick's influence and possibly futile to try. He was, of course, unlikely to change the direction of Australian history. The Labor leadership, to cite but one example, did not take much notice of his demands for an independent foreign policy and seemed incapable of realising that foreign economic and military interests were likely to make profound political demands.

Fitzpatrick would have welcomed the election of the Labor Party in 1972 and applauded many of its domestic and foreign reforms. But he may have been a little less stunned than most of the ALP and its supporters by the manner of the government's defeat in 1975. After all, he had always pointed to the potential abuse of powers and assumed that if they were there they might well be used.

But he had some influence: his writings defined the outlook of a significant body of Australians for a generation; he changed the thinking of countless people, even, from time to time, some "prominent" people; he simply helped many more. Like John Anderson in Sydney, he came as close as anybody else to being a key figure in a city's intellectual life for a generation. And he went closer than anybody else towards embodying intelligent opposition to the dominant Australian political culture of the middle years of the twentieth century.

In 1965 Fitzpatrick was still researching Australian history and railing against its contemporary course. He went to Sydney, late in August, to work in the Mitchell Library. On 3 September he died in his sleep at Bondi. The newspapers acknowledged his death much as they had V. Gordon Childe's, though Harold Holt granted him the virtues Eggleston had sought. As one Melbourne historian said:

> Any community with a sane sense of values would have accorded him the honour he amply deserved while he lived, and saluted him when he died ... with an adequate sense of national loss, respect and affection.

But such communities, of course, would have no need of radicals.

Epilogue, *Brian Fitzpatrick*, 1979

Liberalism, capitalism – and revolution?

TWENTY YEARS AGO STUDENTS OF the United States lived in the relatively sure knowledge that Woodrow Wilson was a moralist whose occasional demonstrations of realism were but aberrations; it was also known that he was a liberal, albeit with conservative tendencies; and he was unquestionably an idealist, with just a passing interest in political economy. This was common knowledge. Then Martin J. Sklar from *Studies on the Left* pointed out that Wilson's puritanism was a worldly doctrine which, reinforced by a diet of Smith, Bright and Cobden, underpinned his faith in the American political and economic system, just as F.J. Turner's "frontier thesis" provided him with a rationale for American imperialism. In other words, Wilson the starry-eyed idealist and champion of the little man was a character merely complementing Wilson the conservative and champion of the large corporation. What would we be asked to swallow next? That Thomas Jefferson owned slaves?

But equally as important as these iconoclasms were the motives and methodology from which they were derived. Sklar began with the assertion that the greatest source of historical misconception about Wilson was the compartmentalisation of his mentality into paradoxical categories – the "moralistic" and the "realistic" (or "commercialistic") – as if they were mutually exclusive. Sklar and his associates, among them W.A. Williams, James Weinstein, Eugene D. Genovese and Gabriel Kolko, embarked upon a full-scale critique of American liberalism based on the theoretical premise that historians had for too long separated ideology (and intellectuals) from the fundamental reality of American society – the capitalist mode of production. This was to be history with a political purpose: the editors of *Studies on the Left* saw as their primary target "a flexible and developing liberal ideology [which] has been a mark of the sophistication and consciousness of American corporate leadership acting in its own long-range class interest".

For more than a decade now in Australia, what used to be called the New Left has been engaged in a similar critique. Here the main target has been, in one form or another, the labour movement which, as Richard Gordon and Warren Osmond wrote eight years ago, "has always been able to preserve the illusion of its being a genuinely oppositional force when in fact its basic goals and historical assumptions have been such as to compound the hegemony of the dominant, bourgeois culture and its underlying social structure". Tim Rowse's *Australian Liberalism and National Character* may be seen as the latest and most sophisticated attempt to show how and why Australian society and politics operates within a fundamental liberal consensus.

In theory at least Rowse's book marks a significant advance in the project. Rowse sets out to reform what we have been innocently calling Australian cultural history (innocently, because, like Woodrow Wilson's head, our history cannot be compartmentalised):

> The only way to make sense of the tradition of writing about Australia and the critical responses to it is to recognize in it the protean influence of liberal concepts and ideas. Liberalism is a discourse capable of a range of political inflections within a constraining conceptual framework. Moreover it is hegemonic ideology, it articulates the theory and rationalizes the practice of a certain intellectual ordering of society, the dominance by a ruling class over subordinate and fragmented social classes.

Thus the ideas of G.V. Portus, or W.K. Hancock, or Lloyd Ross, or Donald Horne should not be treated in isolation, either from one another or from the relations of production. Intellectuals, Rowse says, are "ideologues involved in a class struggle of a different kind". Their writings are responses to developments in Australian capitalism and, if their prescriptions seem to conflict in many important ways, the differences should not be allowed to obscure the salient fact that none of them has seriously questioned the capitalist mode of production; therefore, all of them are producers of liberal hegemony. He sees a consistent pattern in the discussions of Australian society undertaken by intellectuals since World War I — a consistent liberal ideology, flexible enough to cover exigencies as they arise from contradictions within the ruling class and the state, but consistent nonetheless. "Liberalism", Rowse says, "is an extremely simple doctrine, whose application has nuances of endless complexity".

Commencing with an analysis of liberalism as ideology — it posits the capitalist state as "the neutral bearer of common interest" instead of the "structural guarantor of a continuing class dominance" — Rowse examines a succession of Australian intellectuals who have endeavoured to explain our society or redirect it since the turn of the century. From H.B. Higgins and the "secular evangelists" of the Workers' Education Association he describes the pattern of "new liberalism" — liberalism which saw Deakinites and respectable Labor converge in their attempts to temper the harsher winds of capitalism by state intervention on the one hand, and encourage (as Woodrow Wilson did) the enlightened corporation on the other. The project foundered on the class struggles which followed the Great War; the concept of arbitration took a turn towards the ruling class, and W.K. Hancock in 1930 published *Australia*. Rowse devotes a chapter to this seminal work. He sees it as a corrective to the naivety of the New Liberalism. New Liberalism was a product of capitalism in an age of optimism. Reflecting harder times, Hancock is seen as calling those optimists to heel — away from state interference and towards market forces in the economy, away from intellectual laziness and jingoism and towards the higher standards of European civilisation in the culture.

In his examination of the reconstructionist ideals of World War II, Rowse again finds consensus where conflict or incoherence have always been assumed. Essentially the manufacturers and the ALP policymakers agreed on "the need for new legitimating ideologies".

> History had shown that a consensus resting purely on the motives of economic individualism was not viable. Some kind of non-materialist ethic was needed. Sir Herbert Gepp predicted the downgrading of profit and the upgrading of social responsibility as a motive in the business world; Lloyd Ross wanted to see profits legislated away altogether.

Even before the failure of the 1944 "Powers" referendum, some Labor intellectuals were beginning to doubt the virtues of the state-managed society they had previously seen as the model for the new order. There was something of a return to the ideal of the independent citizen as opposed to the planners: doubts about social control fused with cold war fears to create the slogans for Menzies's return and the ideology for a long period of capitalist prosperity.

Finally Rowse peruses the writings of the "New Critics", the Hornes and Colemans and Pringles, who in the age of affluence and anti-communism were able to steal the Australian ethos from the left with their ambivalent celebration of the middle class, while the left floundered in the consumerism and "classlessness" of Keynesian capitalism. The language of both left and right was liberal, often populist, and couched in terms of immanent national identities — be they Barry Humphries's or Stephen Murray-Smith's.

This summary is, of course, too cursory, but Rowse's argument does not lend itself to précis: it reduces to a nutshell or it does not reduce at all. But we now have a generally coherent overview of the ideology of Australian capitalism, a convincing critique of aspects of Labor ideology and a much-needed corrective to some of our well-worn myths — particularly the populist ones, which nowadays may be best observed nightly on TV current affairs programs and each morning in Rupert Murdoch's newspapers. Rowse's writing is, if nothing else, hard-nosed. More importantly, the ideas are located consistently, if sometimes tendentiously, in Australian history.

Rowse's argument contains many little surprises and one big unsurprise. It is surprising, for instance, to see the Institute of Public Affairs paraded under the same banner as the Labor Reconstructionists. But, Rowse says, the differences were ultimately inconsequential: neither corporation management nor state management "sought an end to the basic material social relations of capitalism". On the other hand it is surely no surprise to learn (only to be told) that the dominant ideology of liberal capitalist society is liberalism — that revolution has not been the aim of non-revolutionary intellectuals. Where is the problematic? Rowse says Australian commentators have always presumed oppositional politics where there was basic consensus: the real facts have been obscured by a mythology of egalitarianism and by our intellectual failure to see the capitalist mode of production as central.

One could complain about the patches of tendentiousness; the rather too facile rendering of Ian Turner and others, or (and it is not an unimportant consideration) the indigestibility of some of the prose in Chapter I. It could be argued against Rowse that if a Marxist has obligations to historical specificity, if the justification for a book about liberalism in Australia is that it took a uniquely Australian form, then there is an equal obligation to be historically accurate in one's definitions. Were not Evatt, Palmer and Fitzpatrick "liberals" of an entirely different colour to the "industrial psychologists" Muscio, Northcott and Mayo? The former being hostile to the corporation, the latter its advocates? Isn't it invidious, even ludicrous, to place Lloyd Ring Coleman, of the somewhat sinister (in 1944 at least) American advertising agency J. Walter Thompson, in the same basket as Lloyd Ross and H.C. Coombs? What sense can be made of Australian history if we treat its major ideological antagonists as merely nuancing the same central idea? The answers, of course, depend on one's own ideological outlook. If one believes that change in Australia can only be gradual, then, while one might find some stimulation of an academic nature in Rowse, the manner and implications of his argument are likely to seem either preposterous or meaningless. Ultimately, to accept Rowse's thesis, one has to have a revolutionary perspective for Australia; for only a revolutionary perspective can reconcile the people and the ideas he sees as consensual. That is a fact about this book which simply cannot be dodged.

Yet it seems to me that those revolutionaries like Rowse who are presently engaged in the philosophy of praxis have both to face and take responsibility for the implications of their social theory – in terms of both its immediate pragmatism and the realisation of the ideal. If "in the one case we have a social praxis, which as societal synthesis makes insight possible; in the other case, a political praxis which consistently aims at overthrowing the existing system of institutions", as Jurgen Habermas says, then Rowse and his colleagues must confront the realities of revolution as rigorously as they confront the realities of capitalism. If not, they should accord to liberalism the virtues its proponents accord it.

"In times of adversity", Rowse writes, "the liberal intellectual too easily bemoans the 'treason of the people', and adopts a pessimistic view of his or her own fate". But disillusionment has not been exclusive to liberals: communists too have despaired in droves, partly because they have concluded that devotion to revolution in society with the most minimal preconditions for revolution is time ill-spent if opportunities for piecemeal advance are squandered, and partly because they found the *illiberalism* of a revolutionary party insufferable, or inconsistent with the idea of human emancipation. There is a real sense in which the revolutionary weakness of liberalism is also its moral strength.

Without revolutionary prospects, a revolutionary perspective is likely to provide the basis for no more than an alternative academia. Rowse and his colleagues, particularly on the Melbourne journal *Intervention*, enjoy – and may even have earnt – a singular status in the Australian left: more sophisticated than the Maoist barbarians but with more (Althusserian) balls than the humanist eunuchs, they need partake of neither action nor liberal agonising. "The crisis", Gramsci said, "consists precisely in the fact that the old is dying and the new cannot be born: in this interregnum a great variety of morbid symptoms appears". Until such time as the "new" can be born, Rowse and his colleagues run the risk of earning far more academic respectability than revolutionary progress. The irony would then be twofold: they would have become another beneficiary of liberalism's unique flexibility and another of Gramsci's morbid symptoms.

If Gramsci is right, Tim Rowse (and morbid symptoms like myself) is lucky to be living in the long liberal interregnum. Not because it is grounds for quietism – far from it. It is not because we need do nothing that we are lucky, but because just now we don't have to do anything if we don't wish to. Somewhere in America, Martin J. Sklar is teaching history.

Meanjin, vol. 38, no. 1, April 1979

A Highlander on the
Australian frontier

*How amiable does the design appear of withdrawing the poor and
humble from the miseries incident to their situation, amidst the cold
selfishness of an advanced period of society; and transplanting them to
a new country where the same odious distractions do not meet them,
but where they will all find themselves equal in being dependent only
on nature and their own exertions for their support and enjoyment.*

—Earl of Selkirk, 1806

*How shall we behave ourselves after such mercies? What is the Lord
a-doing? What Prophecies are now fulfilling? Who is a God like ours?
To know His will, to do His will are both of Him.*

—Oliver Cromwell, 1561

GIPPSLAND IS THE SOUTH-EASTERN EXTREMITY of the Austra-
lian mainland. Like so much of the rest of the continent it is subject to
droughts, floods and fires on almost cataclysmic scale. But the climate is
also benign. Mountains to the north feed rivers which wash vast stretches
of pastureland before they spill into the coastal lakes lying serenely at the
end of a windswept beach ninety miles long. These days, those inhabitants who choose to earn their livelihood in competition with the natural
environment raise sheep and cattle, fish for scallops, lobsters, abalone
and sharks, or work on the oil rigs offshore in Bass Strait. The others,
the vast majority of the population, make a living in the towns – in small
businesses, butter factories, on the roads and railways, all of them living

off and serving the hinterland and the summer tourists. They elect conservative MPs in Gippsland; if they attend church at all it is as likely to be Catholic as Protestant since there have always been plenty of Irish there and since the last war Italians have joined them; the businessmen join Rotary Clubs and organise things, encourage "pride in the community" and build monuments to their own public-spiritedness; the others play cricket and football and go fishing for mullet and bream in the rivers, or on the sheltered lakes in small boats with outboard motors. It's not paradise but one could do worse than live in Gippsland these days.

It was undeniably a good deal closer to the Western conception of paradise in the thirty thousand years before 1838 when an Aboriginal population inhabited it exclusively. The Aborigines fished the lakes and estuaries, hunted the marsupials for their flesh and hides, and gathered the fruits the bush offered. They grew no crops, raised no animals (except a dog, the dingo, which ate their refuse and kept them warm), built no permanent dwellings, no houses, churches or prisons, stayed in no place long enough to exhaust its resources. The Aborigines paid no wages, exploited no labour, accumulated no capital. To regenerate its growth and so guarantee their food supply they set fire to the bush from time to time, but in this, as in every other aspect of their existence, they were not just in harmony with the environment but a part of it.

The Aborigines were not of course some inverted version of the hyperboreans. The vagaries of the climate no doubt inflicted dreadful hardships. They practised infanticide, homicide, wife (and prospective wife) beating and, probably, but by no means certainly, cannibalism. It is impossible to resist saying that life in Gippsland's state of nature could be nasty, brutish and short. But not so short as it became after the arrival of the Europeans.

Although it had been seen from the sea for years, Gippsland was not settled until the first Europeans chased their pastoral interests over the Australian Alps to the north. The first of them arrived in the 1830s – precisely when is not clear because they were not anxious to tell potential competitors about the land they had found. In Gippsland, as in most other places on the Australian frontier, exploration was the direct result of the need and greed of squatters – those who began illegally grazing their sheep on the outskirts of the settlement and ultimately won both title to the land and a preponderance of political power. Between the time of occupation and the granting of tenure to the squatters, the conflict between the whites and the Aborigines was a brutally one-sided one in which the Aborigines, with no hope of victory, only lost the more by resisting defeat.

Now, while they considered their civilisation to be incomparably superior to the Aborigines', the English demanded of the first Governor of Australia that he treat the blacks with "amity and kindness". In Tasmania, Governor Arthur complied by issuing a poster which made it clear to the whites at least, that they would be as readily hanged for shooting a black man as an Aborigine would be for spearing a white. The Aborigines who saw the simple drawings posted around the settlement presumably got the message about English justice, although they may have found it hard to understand how one man could cold-bloodedly hang another. Possibly they were also repelled by the English habit of flogging wrong-doers – in 1837, an average year in the convict settlement, 5916 strokes of the lash were inflicted on the backs of 18 per cent of the population.

As the frontier expanded in Australia, the Aborigines' traditional hunting grounds vanished along with the sacred sites which bound each tribal group to its past and the environment. Tribes which had lived in harmony with each other for thousands of years were now forced to compete for food. As a result, internecine warfare took its toll. But the Aborigines were neither skilled nor experienced in wars of conquest and a far more destructive factor was the separation from their traditional land and society. The Aborigines were detribalised and in turn demoralised. More than one observer noted that collectively they seemed to have lost their will to live. Contact with white society had appalling consequences all over the frontier. They were devoured by disease, perhaps most horribly by congenital syphilis. It was estimated in the 1850s that two-thirds of the tribe occupying the area where Melbourne now stands were infected with venereal disease. It is difficult to conceive of the brutality of the Australian frontier. A settler in southern Australia wrote in the 1830s:

> Several of the men lately on this establishment are now very ill with native pox which shows how they acted with the Blacks ... I am told it is no uncommon thing for those rascals to sleep all night with a lubra and if she poxes him or any other way offends him perhaps shoot her before 12 next day.

Alcohol had equally disastrous effects. In fact it was possibly the most important catalyst in the catastrophe.

But the devastating effects of culture contact should not be allowed to obscure the less palatable fact that white settlers – decent pioneering Christian folk that they were – frequently indulged in wholesale massacres of Aborigines, usually because they threatened or seemed to threaten their livelihood, but sometimes because the blacks got "cheeky". Or simply for sport. For instance, at Myall Creek in 1838 three men bound together thirty Aboriginal men, women and children, slaughtered them with guns and swords and then burnt the bodies. To the horror of the white community the men were found guilty of murder, having pleaded that they did not know that it was a crime to kill Aborigines any more than it was a crime for a man to shoot his dog. The largest petition in the history of colony to that stage failed to save them and they were hanged. The Myall Creek affair demonstrated the contempt in which blacks were held. It also meant that, in future, whites would be much less inclined to boast about their massacres.

It was in the year of the Myall Creek massacre that Gippsland's discoverer arrived in Australia. Angus McMillan was born at Glenbrittle on the Isle of Skye in 1810, the fourth son of a sheep farmer on Macleod lands. The family was of tenuously independent means and Angus was not the only member of it to seek better fortune in the colonies. However, if Angus's piety can be taken as typical of his kin, the McMillans had a staunch Calvinist faith to support them in the very worst of times. And the times could hardly have been worse than they were on Skye in 1837.

While it is clear that the old clan system had supported only a spartan existence in the Highlands, the Clearances which followed the rout and defection of the clan chiefs caused misery and chaos on a scale which rivalled the suffering of the Aborigines during the white conquest of Australia. The effects of the Clearances are well known and one example from the *Inverness Courier* of 1838 makes the point: "Bad weather", it was reported from Skye, "had destroyed the peats and, unable to buy coals or wood, they drew lots to see whose hut and cottages should be used for fuel". Angus McMillan left a society which was chronically incapable of feeding, housing and clothing its members. It was also a society which tortured the souls of its weaker members with Manichean bribes and threats, and their bodies with public hangings and floggings, mutilation, stocks and ducking stools, and jails. Take three examples from the *Inverness Courier*. Elspeth Hayes was to be humiliated and detribalised. She was "ordered to be incarcerated in the tolbooth of Elgin for the space of one year, and to stand in the pillory thereafter with a label upon her breasts denoting her to be a Notorious Thief, and at the expiry of her sentence to be banished from Scotland for life". Alexander Gillon's body was never to return to the earth, for "after your execution you shall be hung in chains until the fowls of the air pick the flesh off your body, and your bones bleach and whiten in the winds of Heaven, thereby to afford a constant warning of the fatal consequences which almost always attend the indulgence of passions". Fanny Manson might therefore have been lucky to be sentenced to only one year's jail for concealing her pregnancy.

And those who did not meet these various fates, those who found redemption in work which was never rewarded with a full stomach, were exploited by their landlords until such time as they became a "clear superfluity", and then they were bodily removed to places such as Australia where their labour was needed.

Angus McMillan was probably not forced to leave his homeland, but economic circumstances no doubt pushed him to that decision – but once made it rapidly became in his mind a manifestation of God's will. The diary he kept on board the *Minerva* from Greenock to Sydney records his fanatical Calvinism: he ranted at the passengers who danced and sang as the ship left port – they should have been praying. He ranted at the captain who killed a sheep on the Sabbath. Life was a daily prayer to know God's will and to be shielded from calumny – and life was filled with calumny.

It was not surprising then that he passed very quickly through seamy Sydney on his way to the pastoral country, He soon became manager of a station owned by a fellow Skyeman, Lachlan Macalister. This was the hungry age of Australian pastoral capitalism. By the time it was over – which is to say by the time of the 1850s gold rush – up to two hundred separate Aboriginal communities had been virtually annihilated and much of the Australian environment had been changed beyond recognition and beyond repair. One of Macalister's more sensitive neighbours described it this way:

The most spirit-stirring sight which the sportsman can witness is the first view of a new pastoral district; and to the lover of the picturesque perhaps this is the most beautiful scene that Australia can afford ... Plains and "open forest", untrodden by the foot of the white man, and, as far as the eye can reach, covered with grass so luxuriant that it brushes the horseman in his saddle; flocks of kangaroos quietly grazing, as yet untaught to fear the enemy that is invading their territory; the emu, playfully crossing and recrossing his route; the quail rising at every step; lagoons literally swarming with wildfowl ...

Then mark the change that follows upon discovery. Intelligence of the new country reaches the settled districts, and countless flocks and herds are poured into the land of promise ... To some the regions bring wealth, to others disappointment, while Anglo-Saxon energy at last triumphs over every obstacle. But Nature, as if offended, withdraws half her beauty from the land; the pasture gradually loses its freshness; some of the rivers and lakes run low, others become wholly dry. The wild animals, the former peaceful denizens of the soil, are no more to be found, and the explorer, who has gazed on the district in its first luxuriance, has seen it as it never can be seen again.

Fresh from the starvation on Skye and Barra, this was to be Angus McMillan's experience.

McMillan soon learned from the Aborigines that good land lay on the other side of the Alps, and Macalister, whose flocks were in need of new pasture, sent him to find it. By now McMillan believed that the discovery of the new land was both his God-given mission and his God-given financial opportunity, and he was not daunted by the prospect of finding a route across unknown and extremely rugged terrain which must have taxed his nerve to its limit. No one could question the courage of Angus McMillan.

The Aborigines had called the land to the south Cabone Benel. McMillan called it Caledonia Australis. It was, he declared, capable of feeding "all my starving countrymen"; but until they arrived he was determined that he at least would be well fed, and he established five substantial sheep runs.

Once a port had been established and a track across the mountains blazed, the squatters moved in. Among them the Scots were legion, particularly men from Skye. The main town was named Bairnsdale by Archibald Macleod of Bernisdale, Skye. Another was called Orbost. The place names are a curious mixture of Aboriginal and Scots. On the track to McMillan's main run, five settlements were named successively Castleburn, Cobannah, Culloden, Briagolong and Boisdale. The first settlement was called Ensay. To the north of it lies Doctor's Flat, after Dr Alexander Arbuckle of North Uist. Not that McMillan did not pay his dues to England: the two great lakes he named Victoria and Wellington, and the port was called after the ubiquitous Albert.

The one name that did not stick was Caledonia Australis. A self-titled Count Paul Edmund de Strzelecki, a flamboyant Pole with an interest in science rather than sheep, passed through the area shortly after McMillan and staggered, starving, into civilisation to announce that he had discovered magnificent country which he had named prosaically but shrewdly after the governor, Sir George Gipps. Strzelecki's appellation stuck and he was made a fellow of the Royal Geographical Society, while McMillan chased sheep in his Caledonia Australis and cursed the "foreign impostor".

It was not always sheep which McMillan chased. There were probably about three thousand Kurnai Aborigines in Gippsland when the first whites arrived. By the mid-1850s only a few hundred remained, most of them recipients of church and state welfare. The Kurnai had resisted fiercely from the start, attacking both settlers and stock, including McMillan's. The white "reprisals" were devastating.

Between 1840 and 1850 McMillan and his countrymen took to the Aborigines with the murderousness of an old Highland regiment. The motives varied. Massacres at the aptly named Boney Point and Butchers Creek followed Aboriginal attacks on settlers' sheep. In another instance, up to 150 Aboriginal men, women and children were driven into a waterhole and slaughtered in retribution for the murder of Lachlan Macalister's nephew. The discovery of Macalister's body had led McMillan to form a "Highland Brigade" with which he rampaged through the Aboriginal community for months – legend had it that Dr Arbuckle was the brigade's piper as well as its field surgeon. In 1846 an observer wrote:

No wild beast of the forest was ever hunted down with such unsparing perseverance as they are. Men, women and children are shot whenever they can be met with ... these things are kept very secret ... some things I have seen that would form as dark a page as ever you read in the book of history.

Gippsland was distinguished by another grotesquerie – a classic Victorian melodrama with a Gaelic twist. It had been rumoured from the earliest days of settlement that a white woman who had survived a shipwreck off the coast had been captured by the natives and thereafter forced to suffer their beastly ways. No one was more convinced of the woman's existence than Angus McMillan, who claimed that he had found European clothing and a dead white baby in an Aboriginal camp. He also believed – though it is hard to understand how he came to the conclusion – that the lady spoke Gaelic. Here was a terrible combination of Christian self-righteousness, Highland nostalgia and, doubtless, sexual fantasy. In 1846–47 a series of expeditions were mounted in search of the mysterious "White Woman of Gippsland". At the end of it, the administrator of the province, who was convinced that the woman was no more than a figurehead from a ship, testified that at least fifty Aborigines had been killed in defence of her honour.

But, colourful as this episode was, it was an exception to the rule of massacre on the Australian frontier. The fundamental conflict everywhere was over land ownership and use. For the whites, greed soon became necessity and necessity, in turn, often became God's will. Christianity rationalised the destruction of Aboriginal society in an age before social Darwinism. The notion of the Aborigines as a race doomed by evolution was that of a later generation largely innocent of the massacres, random shootings and poisonings their forbears had carried out.* If Angus McMillan was representative, or the Rev. William McIntyre of Snizort who arrived in the same year, the Highland settlers sought not

---

* Although there are no recorded cases in Gippsland, the practice of poisoning Aboriginal food supplies was common on the Australian frontier. The poisons used ranged from strychnine to plaster of Paris.

only the land but to serve the Lord, to raise not only sheep but the "Altar of God", to establish not just Caledonia Australis but Zion. The land and God's will were indissoluble.

In this scheme there was no place for the Aborigines. They offended on a dozen counts. Not only did they steal the Highlanders' sheep but they refused to conform to Christian ideas about how a savage should behave. They were ignoble in their savagery, discerning rather than orgiastic in their cannibalism, calculating even in their infanticide, and stealthy (like the Viet Cong) in their warfare. They did not live as natives ought to live. They appeared incapable of appreciating the pure reason of Calvinism.

By 1885 the remnants of the Kurnai had become dependent on government or Church relief. A couple of hundred had been herded into a mission station, where they were taught much the same catechisms that were taught to children on the Isle of Skye. Some of the Aborigines may have found comfort in this. A missionary proudly declared that one of his black flock had said, "I can see Jesus" moments before his soul departed to the realms of bliss, to be forever with the Lord. But few of them can have comprehended that they were "gaining a victory through the blood of the Lamb" – they had been shot for having that blood on their hands. The Rev. Hagenauer was simply missing the irony when he discussed his triumph in a book enchantingly titled *Black but Comely*: "The grain of mustard seed began to grow, and the eye of faith saw like the prophet of old, the little cloud arise, which should pour out the Lord's blessing over the poor Aborigines in God's time".

Nor were the Highlanders struck by the irony of their actions. Or if they were, it did not stop them from destroying with guns and sheep and Calvinism a society that stood in their way merely because their own society had been destroyed in much the same way by the English. The Lord's blessing seemed to be squarely with the whites, so much so that in the 1850s Angus McMillan, ex-leader of the Highland Brigade, was made "Local Guardian" by the Central Board for the Protection of Aborigines. In this capacity he was responsible for the distribution of supplies to those fortunates who had survived the pillages of the previous decade.

Although he never recognised the fact, Angus McMillan was well served by history. He could obscure parts of it from the enquiring minds of travellers passing through. In later years he wrote some of it himself.

Then, when he was made responsible for the Aborigines' food, the sight of large numbers of natives gathered near his homestead was interpreted as evidence of beneficence. There is a photograph of McMillan, taken towards the end of the 1850s, which shows him sitting between two Aborigines whose release from prison he secured. No one seems to know just how he managed to get them a pardon, but such actions no doubt earned him the admiration of humanitarians, in addition to gratitude of those local inhabitants for the suppression of the Kurnai in the 1840s. The photograph speaks for both sides of Angus McMillan: the Aborigines' hands are grasped firmly by his; he looks at the camera with an almost insufferable piety; they look helplessly cowed. No doubt to a mid-Victorian audience only the virtue was revealed.

And so it has remained. These days Gippsland is dotted with roadside cairns to mark the trails McMillan blazed – his bonneted head embossed beside the words "Angus McMillan passed this way". An electorate, a college, a mountain, a strait, an annual memorial lecture, a motel or two and other oddments bear his name. He was and is ubiquitous and ineluctable. He is also a major repository of the community's past, not only through the granite symbols, but through potted local histories, local newspapers, the education system and the church. McMillan has been described to each generation in the same warm terms – "friendly", "public spirited", "deeply religious", "generous". He would have made a fine Rotarian. But in his day it was probably the Caledonian Society McMillan founded which played the role of assigning worth and respectability to citizens.

Now McMillan had some marvellous qualities. He was an indomitable bush-basher, forever on all fours, penetrating the impenetrable for someone else's benefit; he was a colourful and eccentric Celt and, it seems, generous to a fault. In some ways he was also a tragic figure: he died destitute, having lost everything to bushfires, droughts and bad financial management. He seems to have been changed by his colonial experience, to the extent, at least, that his housekeeper bore his two children before they were married, and that he left a large unpaid bill at his favourite bar when he died. He was, if nothing else, less puritanical in his colonial maturity. But posterity bestowed only respectability, of course:

in becoming a symbol of pioneering courage McMillan also became a paragon of how a civilised person ought to behave. The pity is that in losing the dark side of the man's character we also lost his tragedy.

New Edinburgh Review, 1981

Caledonia Australis revisited

MY ANCESTORS WERE PIONEERS, FIRST settlers in a forest – a quite stupendous forest in the hills between the riverine plains of Gippsland and the swamps of Westernport in eastern Victoria. In 1840, the Polish explorer and philanthropist Paul Strzelecki, the pastoralist and bunyip aristocrat James Macarthur, and a small party, including the almost-legendary Aboriginal guide Charley Tarra, had clawed their way through the forest and nearly perished. The pioneers came thirty years later and, as pioneers are wont to do, soon accomplished a feat of labour which to modern minds is beyond imagining. Modern minds are also prone to think that it was a shameful thing to destroy such a wonderful natural creation as that forest; the modern heart might almost stop at the dimensions of it. But the minds of the pioneers were full of dreams of cow yards and cream cans and paddocks full of rustling maize, and with God on their side their hearts were unstoppable.

A century after these ancestors of mine ventured into the forest with saws and axes and cut down their first hundred-metre-high mountain ash the shape of my cultural inheritance became clearer to me. The gist of this inheritance seemed to comprise a work ethic and a sense of irony, yoked together like two draught horses – or two brothers, or husband and wife, or a father and son – one grunting and cursing as he labours, the other making grim jokes through clenched teeth. At first glance the two look mutually – even murderously – hostile and out of step. But patient watching reveals a kind of unity, as if mighty labour and mockery

---

First published as the introduction to the 2009 Vintage Classics edition of *Caledonia Australis: Scottish Highlanders on the Frontier of Australia*.

feed off each other. In truth it seems to be that Hard Work and Wry Humour – like good and evil, life and death – are the inseparable and inescapable partners of pioneering and have been at least since Job.

For imprinted on the psyches of all pioneers is the knowledge that the Lord and Nature sometimes resist and even mock our efforts to know them or defy them. This is useful and essential knowledge. It makes toil, misfortune and loss bearable. Irony is seeing the joke that the unseen hand is playing – and sharing it. Irony is the informal conversation the pioneer has with God. It is the means by which we forgive him and ourselves.

Our pioneering heritage taught us that the labour of men and women can move mountains, and be defeated by the caprice of a dog. They can tame a wilderness and lose it all to rabbits. As often as not we learned about our heroic forebears as if they *were* comic figures: through stories of their frustration and failures, their eccentricities and their inability to master animals, trees, machinery and other elements in the pioneer's natural environment.

The serious side was much harder to get at. It tended to come sanitised and in the form of myth and cliché, the two being indistinguishable to young minds and having much the same stupefying effect upon them. The education system taught us that the feats of the pioneers were heroic and beyond question or reproach; and the pioneers' descendants taught us little more than this. The pioneers themselves, when they found a moment to reflect, were not inclined to boast or wonder. Pioneers are nothing if nor taciturn (talking wastes energy) and humble (vainglory is a notorious incitement of divine wrath). So it came to pass that clichés, having the virtue of modesty because they have no known author, and economy because they can be used again and again, were the order of the day. Clichés are the verbal equivalent of darned socks and reheated stew and, to a pioneer, just as indispensable.

The words we heard so often still echo in the deeper gullies of our brains: "things were very different then"; "there were none of the comforts, of course"; "people made do with what they had – because there was nothing else they could do when it was all said and done"; and "truth be told, they were happier than we are with all our creature comforts". This was the pioneering past: this, and local histories which were only sometimes reliable and nearly always written in the same Panglossian vein.

We were very conscious of these pioneers, but it was only a rare glimpse we got of what their eyes had seen and, rarer still, what their hearts and minds had made of it. We certainly did not see it in those roadside cairns and statues – the clichés set in stone looking out at the landscape, unseeing and unthinking.

I began researching these pioneers after attending the funeral of my grandmother. The project grew into something quite unlike the original conception, but the idea of scouring the pioneering legend for signs of life occurred to me while I stood among the weather-beaten old bodies – stiff-necked people, as the Bible says – gathered round her graveside. This grandmother was one reason why I knew my debts to the pioneers and even had some notion of what a blessing this heritage was. However, we also knew that with her we had buried knowledge of ourselves. As the day wore on this became a matter of general regret. "Another one gone", they said. "Soon there will be none left." They gathered to drink their tea and eat their cake and scones and speak of cattle markets and illness; they uttered the familiar homilies about the good innings she had had; and, as the chooks settled on their roosts and the magpies fluttered into the cypresses at dusk, they drove off to their homes in the hills where dogs and the TV news were waiting. Someone really should get them down on tape, quite a few of us said, and I don't think there was anyone there who did not feel that these people had more to tell than they had told, or had ever been told about them.

They were selectors, or at least their parents had been. Some of their parents had begun life in Australia working for the squatters, making their own way by phenomenal labour when the selection Acts made land available to them in the 1870s. They were the product of an attempt to create an Australian independent yeomanry and, if they were not in every sense what the Victorian legislators had in mind, they were at the very least proof that selection had authored more than the hardship and horse thieves which Australian legend tends to assert. They had survived the odds in peace and war and remained upright, conservative, patriotic, productive – and silent.

But these were characters from the second act. They had taken on the leftovers, filling in the gaps on the map of settlement at the end of Australia's "squatting age" and, in their sober and penurious ways, providing a perfect contrast to the less restrained egos of the pastoral frontier.

The pastoralists had grabbed huge tracts of land, amassed large, if unstable, fortunes, and built monuments to both their courage and their vanity. That, at least, is their story at the first reading. This book is by way of a second reading. Its concern is with the ambiguities, the unanswered and perhaps unanswerable questions about a moment in our history when some men suddenly found themselves with no witness except God and, God giving them no signs other than the approval implied in vast holdings and many sheep and cattle, they just as suddenly found themselves with the light of Providence smiling on them so brightly and manifestly: everything spoke of their good works, everything pointed to the future they had created, and certain events of the past were made a dark corner into which no patriotic citizen would ever shine a light.

Any study of a frontier is likely to ask more questions than it satisfactorily answers. Inevitably, this book is at times impressionistic, speculative and fragmentary. It offers descriptions of the Kurnai tribes who lived in Gippsland and the culture and experience of those who routed them, but it is far from the last word on either subject. It describes events that certainly happened, though in many cases we can do little more than guess at causes, consequences and the order of them. Like most frontier diaries those to emerge from Gippsland are incomplete and written long after the events took place, yet in this form they help describe not just the frontier but the way a country's history is written.

In particular, it is a study of one man who – half steering his way, half being blown – arrived in the new province and from that moment seemed to embody every paradox the frontier could throw up: making its history and being made by it, writing its story and engineering its secrets, living through all manner of triumph and torment and leaving a legend which put his life beyond our reach, ending up a cliché, a block of stone.

My personal interest in pioneers forms part of the context in which this book was conceived. The rest derives from developments in Australian historiography twenty years ago: namely, a renewed interest among historians in Aboriginal history and in exploration.

Exploration had a minor renaissance among Australian historians in the late 1970s, I think primarily because of Ray Ericksen's work on Ernest Giles and, somewhat later, Elsie Webster's monumental (and undervalued) study of Ludwig Leichhardt. Ericksen not only told an epic tale, he reminded us that exploration had cultural and political dimensions which the "explorer as hero" phase of history writing had neglected. Ericksen's Giles is both a hero and an agent of private interest. Australian explorers were almost always thus: with few exceptions they were sent on missions to extend the realms of sheep and cattle, and science – and even glory – simply followed in their train. Exploration was the ritual preliminary to the main event – the act of settlement and the accumulation of wealth.

Yet before the pastoral interests sent in the flocks and herds and retainers, and convicts and Native Police, and before the state sent in commissioners and magistrates, and the churches their ministers and missionaries, the explorer made his own kind of conquest. By naming the rivers and hills and rocks after the icons of his own culture, he began at once to paint out the past and with it the culture and legitimacy of the land's original inhabitants. Naming those lakes and waterfalls and canyons after Wellington and Victoria and the heroes of antiquity, or some wealthy benefactor or great aunt, was an act of stunningly simple effect: with a few strokes, writing the history of the place according to the lights of the explorer and his masters, substituting his ancestors for Aboriginal ones, and establishing permanent and familiar symbols, he eased the passage of new settlers from the old world to the new, from the frontier to civilisation.

While Ray Ericksen led in these directions, Elsie Webster's painstaking deconstruction – and reconstruction – of the Leichhardt story delved into the place of myth in Australia. Webster showed how hearsay, bad reporting, envy, prejudice, rumour, greed and intellectual fashion swallowed Leichhardt as completely as the desert did, and regurgitated him and swallowed him again – bending and twisting the myth, but never breaking or burying it.

Exploration and myth are inseparable and both depend upon an opposing force. There could be no exploration without the natives, no more than there could be anthropology or missionaries or heroism, to name just three Victorian fashions; there could be no white women in *durance vile*, to name a fourth. There could be no frontier without someone on the other side of it. The Australian Aborigines attacked Giles, Eyre, and Stuart, harassed Warburton, and frightened Mitchell into shooting them. They killed Kennedy and almost certainly Leichhardt. They played their part in the Burke and Wills saga, saving King while Burke died refusing the food they offered him. Giles came to respect Aboriginal knowledge and habits and even adopted some of them. Eyre became their protector. Mitchell ended up an admiring student of their culture and industry. At every step in the history of Australian exploration, the Aborigines were there; in fact and imagination, in reality and myth.

They were in schools too. Contrary to much opinion now, long before the groundbreaking work of Michael Christie, Lyndall Ryan, Judith Wright, Henry Reynolds, Roger Milliss and others inspired some conservative elements to claim that a "black armband" school of history was invading the national consciousness and poisoning young minds, Australian secondary school and university students were being taught enough about the conflict to write essays full of umbrage at the terrible things that had been done. As a marker of matriculation history exams and as an academic in the 1970s, I read hundreds of papers which dripped with moral outrage, but were almost devoid of anything which might be called historical knowledge. History teachers brought all the usual applications of logic and evidence to the convicts and the gold rush, squatters and selectors, Federation and World War I, but the subject of Aborigines was treated as a different exercise – a moral one, a good workout for young consciences. Indeed, much as they had been at the end of the encounter on the frontier, in our education system the Aborigines were handed over for spiritual instruction.

This was what the new writing on Aboriginal history changed: it put the subject into the realm of fact and interpretation where it properly belongs. And it introduced, as never before, the idea of the frontier. It may have been because they judged there to have been relatively little conflict in the settlement of Australia that some Australian historians were so loath to employ the concept. Some doubtless recoiled as they would from any abstraction, or any subject whose evidence was not strictly reliable. It could even be that the doctrine of *terra nullius*, whose literal meaning was a denial of the Aborigines' very existence, had played upon their minds. Whatever its causes, this strange oversight put the Aborigines at the same disadvantage in the writing of our history as it put them in the battle for the land. The loss, however, was on both sides: the Aborigines lost, with so much else, their proper place in history; and white Australia lost its perspective on the moments of its creation.

That is one reason why those people who in recent times have talked about Aboriginal history as part of a "guilt industry" have got it so lamentably wrong. They talk as if there had never been a frontier, or as if it was a moral and material void before we made it one. This is both bad history and bad psychology. "As far back as I can remember there were all sorts of tales in connection with this killing business, and it seemed to me that everyone was more or less ashamed of the affair", wrote a Gippsland pioneer to the Reverend George Cox early in the twentieth century. If any feelings of collective guilt now exist it is surely because they existed then. And if it makes us face them, far from being debilitating, the study of this history is perhaps the only effective therapy available.

It is not, presumably, because they want to establish a "guilt industry" in Japan that, fifty years after World War II, some Australians feel entitled to tell the Japanese to confront their past; rather it is because they want them to acknowledge the responsibilities that flow from the facts. Perhaps in anger some Australians do want to see the sins of the Japanese fathers visited on Japanese children. In that case they should have no difficulty understanding Aboriginals who want to see the same thing happen here. But the purpose of acknowledging the reality that our forefathers, men just like ourselves except they were more God-fearing and very often more respectable, massacred innocent people and hid or burned the bodies – the purpose of *history* in this case – is the very opposite of recrimination or vengeance. The purpose is to let the children into some of the secrets of their own natures and perhaps spare them the guilt of previous generations.

The publication in 1981 of Henry Reynolds's *The Other Side of the Frontier* did not turn the tide, but it did make a difference. At one level, Reynolds's book was a scholarly study of evidence which hitherto had mostly been ignored; at another, it was a contemporary polemic urging Australians to reassess the history of white settlement and recognise, at the very least, that if the Aborigines had regularly required shooting and incarceration, logic demanded that they be accorded something in history more honourable and adult than the role of passive and innocent victims.

For Reynolds and others, establishing the undeniable fact of widespread Aboriginal resistance would shift the foundations of the contemporary debate. Among other things, it meant that the words "conquest" and "invasion" would be more readily substituted for European "settlement". The High Court of Australia's 1992 determination that *terra nullius*, the doctrine that the Europeans had occupied an empty continent, was a legal fiction and that a native title did exist, and the subsequent implementation of the *Native Title Act 1993* make Reynolds's work a landmark study in Australian history.

Reynolds was not the only historian to fill in the picture of an extended struggle on the frontier of Australia. In addition to others I have mentioned, Judith Wright's magnificent (and too little read) *The Cry for the Dead* should have put the broad question of resistance and brutal repression beyond doubt. In his massive *Waterloo Creek*, Roger Milliss provides us with the crimes, the motive, the characters, the psychosis and a superabundance of forensic detail proving coordinated acts of extermination in New South Wales in the 1830s. *Waterloo Creek* (all one thousand pages of it) was a monumental and ultimately irrefutable addition to the record, but it did not invade the nation's consciousness. The same can be said of Phillip Pepper and Tess De Araugo's *The Kurnai of Gippsland*. Written after this book (*Caledonia Australis*) and not always agreeing with it, *The Kurnai of Gippsland* established beyond doubt that the claims made here in fact understated the case: the resistance was more concerted and so was the effort at extermination. I missed some of the most crucial evidence. There were more massacres than I acknowledged and there is more evidence for them than I found. Peter Gardner and Patrick Morgan have continued to dredge up documents in the past few years, and Gardner's relentless research is gradually yielding a pattern of behaviour which might well apply right across the Australian frontier.

That is something for historians to bear in mind: behaviour on one part of the frontier was often governed by the experience of another part – not to say by experience in the lands from which the frontiersmen came. It was not difficult to see that the deeds done in Gippsland were kept quiet because the Myall Creek criminals had been hanged, or to draw a faint line between the attitudes which produced those events and the attitudes and events in Gippsland. Milliss, though he scarcely mentions Gippsland, makes the faint line unmistakable and in doing so makes it much harder to deny the rumours of widespread killings in that province. In *Waterloo Creek*, Milliss paints a picture which Australian history has still not adequately registered – of *calculated* and *systematic* savagery towards the Aborigines. This was two years before the Highlanders of this book rode down from the Monaro into Gippsland. That the Aborigines would lose the battle was inevitable; that they would be all but annihilated was not so certain. But it helps our understanding to learn from Milliss that Lachlan Macalister, the godfather of Gippsland, was recommended by the Sydney establishment as the man most likely to do the sort of job which was ultimately done by James Nunn at Waterloo Creek. As much as common attitudes, common methods may have been at work. At Myall Creek in 1838 the blacks were roped together and cut down with cutlasses and sabres. P.D. Gardner's *Gippsland Massacres* tells us that, around the turn of the century, Mr W.H. Thomas, a schoolmaster at Woodside near Warrigal Creek in Gippsland, together with a Mr Lamb, uncovered "a quantity of human bones and skulls of men, women and children, even to very young children". And "as a result of careful examination of these it was disclosed that all the skulls were fractured, a piece being broken away at the base of the skull, as though caused by a blow from a tomahawk".

Caledonia Australis emerged from this sort of historical (and political) debate. It was, to that extent, a book of its time. And so, inevitably, when the New Right turned on what they took to be a Left interpretation of Australian history, this book tended to be thrown in with the others as a work from a school of historians who hated their own past, morbidly highlighted the worst in it and ignored the best, broke the rules of historical inquiry by applying contemporary liberal norms and values to people of another age, and sought under the guise of scholarship to relieve the guilt they felt about the treatment and condition of Aborigines.

A great deal could be said about the motives and reasoning behind this long campaign. To begin with, we can be sure that some people who wrote about Aboriginal Australia were, in various degrees, guilty of the sins alleged – including the sin of guilt. There has been no shortage of anachronistic judgements and polemical overkill in the writing of post-European Aboriginal history in recent times. Some of it may even fall into the category which would be thoroughly loathsome if its opposite were not generally far worse – "political correctness". But the expression – or affectation – of a deep loathing for political correctness does not put any of us beyond the reach of history, and history's judgement. If the facts are there and can be found they should be found – and they should be known. We might reasonably distrust the judgements of people for whom atrocious acts satisfy political needs or the cravings of their unconscious, but that is no reason to trust those who hide such things or hide from them. It can hardly hurt a mature society to know that its founders were capable of evil as well as good. An immature society can only benefit.

My ambition with this book was always to make a crack in the deep encrustation of myth which surrounds the settlement of Australia. Not because I loathe the people who made the myths or of whom the myths were made – on the contrary. Aren't we meant to love them? The myths not only keep these people from me but are, what is a greater frustration, inadequate to what I know or imagine about them. It is not that there should be no myths, not that we can live without them, rather it's that we need better ones to fill the void. If only a handful of young Australians now study their own history it is possibly at least in part because our myths no longer feed them and were never real enough, or big enough, to reproduce themselves.

I still look forward to the day when someone with the stature and subtlety of John Wayne steps onto the Australian screen and, with a look around the mighty landscape, confronts *himself.* That is not to abandon historical verisimilitude. It is not to forsake either the pioneers or the cause of modern Aboriginal Australians. It is not to abandon the irony which, of all the frontier's legacies, appears to have lived the longest. It is only to state the obvious; namely, if we don't confront the possibility of evil as well as the good in creation we are left with a moral and aesthetic void – a great hole where a drama should be.

That is what is most wrong about this charge of "black armbands": it is based upon a puerile and offensive assumption that to write about these dark events risks losing our respect for the builders of modern Australia. For some advocates of the theory it even seems to follow that those who write about them love their country less than those who pass them by. If these were my motives in writing this book I was not aware of them. I set out to give a more sympathetic portrait of the pioneers than any I had ever encountered. I wanted to give them blood as well as bones – religion, motives, choices, memories, identity, ancestors, an inheritance of their own. My ambition (instinct might be the right word) was to fill the void. I suspect the same is true of much revisionist history, which is, after all, invariably an attempt to find a deeper contemporary meaning in the past.

This book's most fervent advocate could not say it did much to either fill the void in our history or offer some inspiration for improvement. But rereading it now I can at least say that it proves there was a bigger story to tell about Gippsland than had been previously told, and even a new footnote to be written about Scotland. It does remind us that, while nothing governed the settlers' actions as much as the material ambition and financial necessity they shared, their behaviour on the Australian frontier had other origins – in culture and ideology, religion and memory – and that they had only some of these in common. If the result for the Aborigines was the same, we might say that it hardly matters if Lachlan Macalister seems to have justified his behaviour by one means and Angus McMillan and Patrick Coady Buckley by others. But of course it does matter, both to history and the modern debate. We might easily distance ourselves from the military mind of Macalister or the brutalised Buckley – but it is harder with McMillan. The harder we look at McMillan the more we see the patterns of our collective experience and the elements of our contemporary dilemma. The harder we look at him the more signs we see of the kindness and brutality, self-interest and charity, memory and amnesia, decency and hypocrisy that have characterised public and private dealings with Aboriginal Australia from the beginning to the present day. And the harder we look at the society McMillan came from the more we see how the dispossessed everywhere tend to follow the same path to material and spiritual poverty: in the nineteenth century, the Australian Aborigines were not the only ones to be first cast as dangerous and unruly savages, then left stranded between pity and contempt, and then thrown still further adrift from humanity by social Darwinism.

Common sense demands that we judge the behaviour of men and women according to their circumstances and the mores of their times, but it does not compel us to assume that all men and women will respond identically to those circumstances or observe the mores in equal measure. Difficult as it is to resist them sometimes, the purpose of recognising that people behave differently for different reasons is not to enable us to make comparative moral judgements. It is, rather, to make historical ones: to find the drama where the void is, to see how like us they are. "Men of their time" they were – just as the cliché goes – but Angus McMillan was one man and Henry Meyrick another and though they lived at the same time and were squatters on the same frontier, they thought very differently. Meyrick railed against the atrocities he knew his fellow squatters were engaged in, yet the same Meyrick said he would shoot Aborigines down like dingoes if he caught them killing his sheep. McMillan committed the atrocities, yet the same man felt constrained in the last years of his life to be the Aborigines' protector. To understand the frontier and what we have inherited from it we need to understand both men, and to do that we might do well to listen to another man of his time, George Dunderdale.

Dunderdale settled in Gippsland in the 1850s. He watched first hand as frontier history was written, and he wrote, often with wry judgement, about the irony of it all. Only once or twice does he sound mildly passionate. We live in an "age of whitewash", he says: "There is scarcely a villain of note on whose character a new coat has not been laboriously daubed by somebody, and then we are asked to take a new view of it. It does not matter very much now, but I should prefer to whitewash the Aboriginals". How could George Dunderdale know that by the expression of this simple sentiment he put himself among the category of chroniclers which a century later are labelled guilt mongers?

Introduction, *Caledonia Australis* (2009 edition)

Memory and imagination

Australians used to know the other side of the world much better than their own. They were raised on British and European history, and they were overwhelmingly of British and Irish stock. They saw themselves as an outpost of British civilisation and, with inevitable and largely admirable variations, as consanguineous bearers of British values.

Even the Middle East was more familiar to them than Java or Borneo or Papua – the Holy Land was still a wellspring of the culture. This might be why so many of the volunteer soldiers who went to war in Europe and the Middle East in 1914–18 spoke of it as an adventure. No one spoke of the war in South-East Asia as an adventure. They walked into the nightmare on their doorstep, and when they came back looking like skeletons, and with terrible stories of cruelty and privation, the sight of them confirmed our fear of what lay on the other side.

History chooses some and neglects others. In this way, it tends to create hierarchies. Gallipoli was a creation myth even before the battle was over. It became the centrepiece of the Australian legend and the battles waged later in France and Belgium and the Middle East were arrayed around its shining glory. Members of the First Australian Imperial Force who fought and died in these places were immortalised, most obviously in the memorials built in Australia's cities and in the obelisks, statues and other monuments erected to their memory in nearly every country town.

Some of those who returned ended up half-starving on soldier settlements in the country or eking out livelihoods in the cities, and living with injuries and memories and grief of a kind which, since Vietnam, we know is often beyond the reach of the most intensive counselling. But even the most unfortunate World War I veterans and their descendants had the comfort of knowing that the First AIF had earned a place in Australian history that bordered on Homeric. They were the immortals and all those memorials in all those little towns tell us why: count the names of the dead and living inscribed on them and the statistic takes shape – one in five of those who went did not come home.

With few exceptions, the Second AIF was never raised to the heights of the First. Perhaps because the war to defend Australia was so complicated by the drama of competing affections, history tended to make as much of the home front as the battlefields. The towering figure of Lieutenant Colonel Ernest Edward "Weary" Dunlop aside, in the pantheon of World War II no soldier or sailor or airman of any rank has risen above the name of wartime prime minister John Curtin, a fact which would grieve Curtin deeply.

Then there were the Americans. The Americans saved Australia – almost literally in the Battle of the Coral Sea – which left Australians with that much less to claim, whatever they had achieved or endured. General Douglas MacArthur's ego by itself attracted more historical limelight than any number of battalions could muster for themselves.

When the war was over, the tide of mass culture and domestic politics was also against the Australians: the American and British film and television industries offered up countless stories from the war, none of them Australian, naturally enough. Publishing houses filled Australian bookshelves and young Australian minds with British books about the war, and a few from the United States. It was no hardship to read them and a small price for the freedom and prosperity those countries had in various way bequeathed us, but after the war, as before it, Australians still had fights to win if they wanted to be truly independent and have their own stories told and known. Sometimes they were not helped by their own masters: in Australian schools in the 1950s and 1960s, Australian history was studied only up to World War I. It was called British History. No one learned about the war in Asia and the Pacific. Simpson and his donkey we knew, but it was forty years before we heard of Weary Dunlop.

Only recently have stories surfaced of a number of remarkable engagements, some triumphant, some tragic, involving Australian soldiers, sailors, airmen and nurses. Milne Bay, Timor, Ambon, Malaya and Borneo may never challenge the battles of the Great War in the realms of myth. Indeed, despite the commemorations of recent years, numerous articles and at least two feature films, they have scarcely registered in the national consciousness. But, once broached, history's well is inexhaustible and, as these stories are drawn from it, Australians might begin to find inspiration and enlightenment in them.

One day, they might see the dead of the Sandakan march, the guerillas of Sparrow Force in Timor, the airmen who inflicted the first defeat on the Japanese at Milne Bay or the sailors of the *Armidale* (and other ill-fated ships) as figures in an early chapter of their own story – as Australians who risked all not just in the front line of battle, but in the front line of nation building. As the country's destiny becomes more closely tied to Asia and the Pacific and many of the old ties to Britain fade, they might even be seen as the first soldiers of the modern Australian nation.

A series of drawings by Melbourne artist Jan Senbergs commemorates one of those forgotten engagements, an almost unknown incident in an almost unknown chapter of World War II. In peacetime, an event such as this would create a media storm. The survivors would be made heroes and paid large sums of money for their stories. Thousands of memorable images would be generated by journalists and photographers, and one or two replayed so often that our minds would be imprinted with them. But the sinking of the *Armidale* left hardly a trace. The survivors spent a few days in hospital and resumed the war. The only images were in their minds.

Not that they expected much more. They were men on active service in a war which killed at least fifty million people. Only in peace do simple acts of bravery or extraordinary feats of survival get turned into fame and money. Yet the *Armidale* survivors might wonder about the imperfections of history: they had lived through a terrible and freakish tragedy, the stuff of myth and nightmare, a moment from the *Odyssey*. They had endured it in the service of their country in the hour of its greatest peril and it had all happened just a few hundred kilometres off the Australian coast.

Nothing could have rendered the reality of Australia's geography and its future with more intensity than the events of those ten days towards the end of 1942 after the *Armidale* sailed out from Darwin. But everything conspired to keep the story in deep shadow.

On 1 December 1942, the corvette HMAS *Armidale* was sunk in the Timor Sea by Japanese aircraft. In company with HMAS *Castlemaine* and *Kuru* (HMAS *Kalgoorlie* sailed separately), the *Armidale* had left Darwin two days earlier, intending to land Javanese commandoes under Dutch command at Betano on the southern coast of occupied East Timor. They were then to embark Portuguese women and children and 176 Indonesian troops. The Japanese spotted them as they left Darwin Harbour, and before they reached Betano they came under heavy air attack. The corvettes sought shelter in heavy rain squalls sweeping the sea, an action which delayed the beachhead rendezvous. When the ships arrived, no one was waiting. Fearing the possibility of putting the troops directly into the hands of the Japanese, the ships withdrew without landing them.

The next day the British commander in Darwin, Commodore Pope, ordered the *Armidale* back to Betano, advising that "air attack is to be accepted as ordinary routine secondary warfare". The *Armidale* tried again and was again unable to make the landing. The time it took to make the second attempt proved fatal. Pope recalled the ships, but only three of the four returned.

There were eighty-three crew and sixty-six soldiers on board when Japanese torpedo bombers and Zero fighters finally sank the *Armidale* after a two-day battle. Seventeen-year-old gunner Ted Sheean went down with the ship, wounded, but strapped to the Oerlikon gun and still firing.

The men who survived the sinking clung to whatever they could in the oil, blood and brine: drums, a Carley float, a motorboat, a broken and submerged whaler, painters' planks that sailors had collected in various ports and strapped to the ship's side rails because they knew they might find themselves in the sea. Covered in oil, many of them badly injured, they began to lash the flotsam into a raft. Japanese aircraft returned and strafed them with machine-gun fire. Sea snakes swam about their heads. Sharks circled, brushing past their dangling legs and feeding on the dead and injured.

They got the motorboat going and loaded seventeen injured men into it. Though they could see the mountains of Timor, they made for Darwin, preferring the perils of that voyage to the prospect of capture or death at the hands of the Japanese. The men clinging to the wreckage devised a tactic against the sharks. They watched as the fins circled them and they yelled in unison and furiously thrashed the water when the attacks came. "Bar a few horrible incidents, it seemed to work", Col Madigan, a survivor, wrote later. Madigan was twenty-one years old. A lot of his comrades were younger.

The Australians grew wary of the Javanese soldiers, who carried side arms. There was "friction" between the two groups. The Javanese were given the Carley float. They drifted away with their Dutch commanders and were never seen again.

The raft kept breaking up. The sun blazed down. On the fourth day, by a remarkable feat of ingenuity and strength, they managed to raise the ship's whaler, dock it to the raft and repair it with canvas. But who would board the whaler and who would be left on the half-submerged make-shift raft? Somehow the officers chose twenty-nine men for the boat. On 5 December, the men in the boat farewelled the men on the raft and began rowing towards Darwin, 470 kilometres away.

On the same day, the *Kalgoorlie* was sent out to search for the *Armidale*. An RAAF Hudson spotted the motorboat and, at 8.15 p.m. on 6 December, the *Kalgoorlie* picked up the survivors. Permission to continue the search was refused. The *Kalgoorlie* returned to Darwin.

In the whaler, the food and water began to run out. The men drank urine and tried to catch fish and seagulls in their hands. Their skin burned in the tropical sun. Ulcers ate into their flesh. They began to suffer delusions. On the eighth day, as if the gods had intervened, it rained. And just as miraculously, on the same day, an RAAF Catalina appeared in the sky above them. Earlier, the men on the raft had seen the plane, and the Catalina had seen them. Photographs had been taken from the plane of the men waving up at them. On the ninth day, a Hudson bomber dropped food and water to the whaler, and soon after, the *Kalgoorlie* found them.

Twenty-seven survivors and two dead men were taken aboard. When they lifted the whaler from the sea, it broke apart. Somehow they had paddled it 217 kilometres. As they lay in blankets on the mess deck of the *Kalgoorlie* they heard the ship's sirens and then gunfire. Two Japanese planes were strafing and bombing the ship. But the *Kalgoorlie* survived.

Some survivors were unrecognisable to their friends. They were "badly disorientated and had little recollection of what had happened or was happening", one of the *Kalgoorlie*'s crew recalled. Fifty years later, one of the men from the whaler said that not a day of his life had passed without his recalling some moment of the ordeal. The men spent several days in hospital in Darwin, and then those who were physically able went back to the fighting – without fanfare or even recognition. It was as if their experience had been exactly as Commodore Pope described the mission: "ordinary routine secondary warfare". No decorations came forth. Ted Sheean received no posthumous Victoria Cross. No Australian sailor has ever received a VC.

The men on the raft were never found after the Catalina spotted them. Not a trace. It was a mystery like Ludwig Leichhardt's disappearance in the desert; or they were like Burke and Wills, who also reached the point of deliverance and had their lives snatched away. Japanese aircraft may have found them. The raft may have broken up. Their comrades who survived hoped they might turn up at the end of the war in one of the prisoner of war camps. But they had vanished.

Towards the end of his memoir of these events, Col Madigan asks: "Was there a heart to this matter or just a conglomerate of individual impressions?" One answer might be that the heart of the matter is in the impressions. Those of us who weren't there depend on the memories of those who were; and even then we depend on our imagination to tell us what it was really like. If Madigan is asking if there was a meaning to it all – something to which the rest of us can cling and better know ourselves – it can only be what this meeting of memory and imagination throws up. That is what stories do. It's what history is meant to do. Or in this case, art.

Introduction, Col Madigan and Jan Senbergs,
Armidale '42: A Survivor's Account, 1999

Cassocks among the tussocks

I'd sooner we got married at New Norcia, like Mum and Dad.
Though I ain't really a Catholic.

—Jack Davis, *No Sugar*

THERE ARE NOT MANY MONUMENTS to the Big Ideas in Australia. There is Canberra, which is a monument to the idea of Australia, but it does not convince everybody. There are numerous monuments to Mammon or Enterprise, depending on your point of view, but these are not so much ideas as ways of life. The monuments to God are like others elsewhere and mainly empty these days, while the monuments to humanity can only be found by those who know what they are looking for. But there can be no question about the Benedictine monastery at New Norcia on the Victoria Plains, 160 kilometres north of Perth. It is singular, uncompromising, unmistakable. It is a large lump of Gothic among the gum trees, monks among the wheat farms.

Before you go to New Norcia you should go to Northam. Northam is a "historic town", like York to the south of it, but do not let this put you off. The Avon River flows through both of them, blue in a brown summer landscape. Both towns have more than their share of pleasing stone buildings converted into cafés and museums. But I would not spend too long in either of them; a picnic perhaps, or a browse in the Anglican bookshop of York.

Northam's interest, I suspect, lies mainly in its unwritten history, or at least that history which is not presented to the tourist. In 1933 eighty-nine Aboriginal people were arrested and trucked off to a camp on the Moore River. They were arrested for scabies. They were supposed to be "rotten with scabies". In fact they were not: there were no more scabies among them than there would have been in a working-class white suburb. But the Premier of Western Australia, Jimmy Mitchell, wanted to keep his seat in Northam. He thought the white population would forgive him for the Depression if he kicked the blacks out. Mitchell lost his seat, which was some kind of justice. But the blacks, of course, lost a great deal more.

When you travel to New Norcia from Northam you are travelling on an old trail. On the way you will pass through Toodyay, another "historic town". The jail has been restored to the rather lovely little redstone building it was when it took in its first black prisoners, and Moondyne Joe, the bushranger. Black schoolchildren have scrawled on the walls inside, "Noongas rule".

You sail through Bolgart, "historic Bolgart", by the silos. A cricket match is played on a baked oval. The batsman on strike has a stance uncannily like Geoffrey Serle's. It is good to remember the eastern states. Bolgart has a population of 150 or so, including a chiropractor. Every town in Western Australia seems to have a chiropractor. In Perth, they flourish like revivalist churches. In the country – at least the wheat country, where backs are under terrible pressure – it is common to see signs saying "479 Geraldton" pointing in one direction and in the other, "Chiropractor".

Onwards. Dead goanna, small dead snake, dead kangaroo, foot-long dead lizard (*Moloch horridus*), dead magpie, large dead snake, dead parrot, dead parrot, large black snake (alive), dead parrot. Green parrots bob and weave before the windscreen.

Not all the plains are sown with wheat. There are large patches of natural vegetation distinguished, of course, by the most ancient and novel order of plants, *Xanthorrhoea*, which the Aborigines call *balga*. To the rest of us they are blackboys. They are a marvellously useful species, yielding gum, grubs, material for torches and thatch, cattle fodder and firesticks. *Xanthorrhoea* have survived all this exploitation and bushfires – indeed they thrive in bushfires and scorn hardship. Still they stand in thousands, pointing their fingers at the sky. Sometimes they bend them in Leunig-like curls. Occasionally, with unnerving effect, they form question marks.

In this setting you see a great variety of wildflowers in diaphanous and furry extremes and the colourful kangaroo paw – some short ones mimic perfectly an all-but-buried marsupial. White ants tirelessly clean up and build their heaps, monuments to the work ethic. A cicada splits the air and is answered by several others. Goannas scuttle and cavort. Smaller lizards eye the sun. Snakes sleep. The Victoria Plains are very old.

Across these plains in 1846 came Rosendo Salvado and Jose Maria Serra, Benedictines from Spain. At least they were accustomed to heat. Serra was Catalan; Salvado, who became the dominant figure in their enterprise, was Galician. They hoped to bring the benefits of their civilisation to the Aborigines, as St Benedict has brought them to the northern tribes of Europe, by bringing them a refuge and a faith. Pope Gregory had personally blessed the priests' endeavours, but they depended as much on hard work and money.

Salvado's approach to missionary work differed from all of his contemporaries. He insisted that his mission confer the advantages of civilisation as well as the work, so he not only taught the skills of farming but paid wages. He was a very practical man as well as a good one. His school for Aboriginal boys offered not just an education but two bowls of excellent soup a day.

He saw common ground in Aboriginal magic and ritual, encouraged music and play and made no secret of his respect and admiration for Aboriginal culture, which he went to great lengths to understand.

Salvado had some notable early successes. His crops grew and his stock multiplied. The wine was good. A bushfire one day was turned back after Salvado placed in its path a painting of Mary the Immaculate. Salvado took two Aboriginal boys to Rome. Francis Xavier Canaci and John Dirimera fanned the face of the Queen of the Two Sicilies and were clothed in the monastic habit by Pope Pius IX. Francis excelled at his studies, become fluent in Latin and then fell ill and died four years after his arrival at the age of seventeen. John Dirimera died in Perth at the age of fifteen.

Years later, Daisy Bates said that the story of these two boys was yet further proof that Aborigines could never receive higher education and could never live in European society. We might ask why they would want to live in European society, and what specimen of European society she had in mind.

Salvado proved that Aborigines could be educated because he knew that they had been educated once before. He proved it when it was easier to believe the reverse. He proved, as well, that they could and would work, when the common wisdom had become that they could not and would not. However chauvinistic, it *is* salutary to measure the Aboriginal response by European standards; remember that it was Bates who decided that it should not be. Of course they worked – there were squatters and Crown Lands commissioners all over the country who knew this because they depended on them. But history wrote itself differently. It is the rare virtue of New Norcia that history's detail and complexity are retained. Its story supports an Aboriginal case for exhuming the body of Daisy Bates, and hanging the skin in the National Museum.

One gets the impression from Salvado's memoirs that he knew something about the scope of his task. Perhaps he had an inkling that the one truly extraordinary thing about the continent – the one great human phenomenon – was the ancient civilisation of the Aborigines. It is no slur on white civilisation to say that it remains so. Where, for someone like Salvado, was a majesty to match his church's? In the mean townships and runs where spiritual life was dim? Or in Aboriginal society where souls resided on the twigs of trees?

Aboriginal girls from the Victoria Plains were sent to the Sisters of Mercy in Perth. The first of them, an abandoned six-year-old, was taken there on Salvado's shoulders. Sister Ursula, of the convent, lamented that although they all "received the sacraments regularly and with great devotion … civilisation seemed to be more than they could bear. They all died young". Could it be that the constantly reiterated promise of eternal happiness was too great a temptation?

Salvado had his failures. Back at New Norcia, Aboriginal people were coming to the mission not for the liturgy or the promise of life after death, but to escape murder. For all the attractions of Christianity and Catholic ritual, New Norcia, for a while at least, functioned chiefly as a safe house, as much a refuge from European civilisation as the embodiment of its virtues.

These days that civilisation is on display at the New Norcia museum and art gallery: the fabulous monstrances and other paraphernalia of the church (most of which is quite unfathomable to this Protestant); a considerable collection of seventeenth-century paintings, including a Titian, which depicts a Pope's narrow but marvellous escape from assassination; and an extensive collection of artefacts from the local Aboriginal culture.

To spend some time in the museum is both affecting and unsettling. It is a cocoon of civilisation. It pronounces charity, care and the fraternity of humankind. It reminds you, too, of what is outside.

There is, necessarily to pay for the Honeywell security system, a museum shop which is a combination of a Pellegrini Catholic shop and an airport souvenir bar. You may buy New Norcia T-shirts and base-ball caps, tea towels and spoons with the Virgin Mary on the stem, and a wide range of Monastique cosmetics which are manufactured by the Carmelite Sisters.

If you stand on an anthill and look over the monastery fence at seven o'clock on a Sunday morning you will see monks bustling about in their green garden. The Falcons of wheat-farming families are parked outside the chapel. At the Mission Hotel a large breakfast is served. Dinner is by candlelight as you look out on the plains and watch the yellow-tailed black cockatoos retiring for the night.

In the bar you might see, as I did, a wheat farmer fall off his stool and onto his head. "Can't hold their liquor", the Aboriginal patrons think. The Mission Hotel is strongly recommended for ambience and food.

You will return to Perth via Mogumber, which is close to where the Northam Aborigines were sent in 1933. Like so much of Australia's his-tory, you cannot see it from the road unless your eye is very educated. The best thing to do on your return is to stand in a piece of blackboy scrub. You might find yourself thinking of the entire continent and how oddly you sit upon it. Of Spanish monks driving bullock teams, or perched on Lanz Bulldog tractors. Of Rosendo Salvado with a six-year-old girl on his shoulders, trudging to Perth. Of eighty-nine Aboriginal men, women and children being trucked across the land and out of sight several years before this became a pattern in Europe.

Consider the lizard: the speckled *Moloch horridus*, one of which Salvado once accidentally trapped for three months. Having had only earth to eat, it was remarkable that it was still alive, he said, but its colour was much dimmed. And look again at the blackboys. Salvado noted one more capacity of their stumps. When burnt, he wrote, a blackboy stump casts a light so bright he often read his breviary by them when camped in the bush at night. The scrub giveth and the scrub taketh away.

The Age, 4 January 1986

INJUSTICE AND
IDEOLOGY

The "war" on terror

THE WAR ON TERROR WAS resumed in London this week when four – possibly five – terrorists failed in an attempt to blow up themselves and hundreds of others on the public transport system. It seems that, like the successful suicide bombers of a fortnight ago, these young men were British Muslims. In Egypt, suicide bombers managed to kill at least eighty-nine local Egyptians and foreign tourists and injure hundreds of others. To this point, the identity of these bombers remains unknown, but three groups have so far claimed responsibility on the internet for the atrocity. Of course, in Baghdad and other places in Iraq, as in every other week, suicide bombers killed and maimed scores of people. In various parts of the world George W. Bush, Tony Blair and John Howard expressed their sadness at the loss of life, their loathing for the killers and resolute determination to win the "war on terror".

What they didn't get round to was telling us who or what, precisely, the enemy is. In Iraq they are generally called "insurgents". Elsewhere they are terrorists. Wherever they are, President Bush likes to call them people who hate our freedom and way of life. We know that they are not all "insurgents" in Iraq: the people who captured Douglas Wood were simple criminals, although one would have thought from the reporting that they were driven by the same demons that possessed the four suicide bombers from West Yorkshire. Among the ones to whom the term "insurgent" might sensibly apply, there are local Sunnis, foreign revolutionaries and disaffected leftovers from the Saddam Hussein regime. And doubtless there are others engaged in violent resistance for different motives and beliefs, including resentment of the occupation.

The point is we don't really know who it is we're fighting in Iraq.

Dick Cheney or Donald Rumsfeld or George Bush might know. It's possible that Blair and Howard know. But if they do, they have not told us in a way that is believable. We are saving the government there; and we are keeping faith with the brave Iraqi people who voted in the elections: these seem like good reasons, but they are also old and notorious reasons for occupying armies to stay on and on until there is nothing left to defend and face is all there is to save. Some people might connect the events in London with the scenes of John Howard in Iraq among Black Hawk helicopters in a helmet and body armour. Others might make a connection with Vietnam.

As it did for so long in Vietnam, in this "war" any old thing will do. The lies that made it possible, the tens of thousands of civilians killed, the damage to the United States' reputation, the fact that the occupation daily incites the rage of young Muslims everywhere and that while it has been fought at such obscene cost Osama bin Laden has gone free – all this ought to make journalists hyperactively sceptical and probing. But no: this week in London, though Paul Bongiorno tried bravely, the rest of the pack were either overwhelmed by five minutes of artful and passionate vapidity from the prime minister, or they were too confused to care.

It's the word "war". From the moment the "war on terror" was declared, everything went fuzzy. Australians persuaded themselves that refugees from terror might be agents of terror. American soldiers went to fight in Iraq believing they were avenging 9/11. The whole world was conned into believing Saddam had weapons of mass destruction. The consequences of these now well-known delusions are still with us and compounding. No one responsible for creating them has been punished or has paid the smallest price and it seems unlikely that they ever will.

So long as it is a "war" on terror we are easily persuaded to do and think all sorts of other things that in normal times we'd shun. It's a war so we'll put it down as collateral damage. We will give up civil liberties as Philip Ruddock says we should. We will find reason where there is none to speak of, and cling to beliefs despite the evidence against them. We'll condemn suicide bombers as subhuman filth who kill civilians, but we won't condemn stealth bombers, which also kill them. We will render our enemies monolithic and insensate like a thing, rather than pathological like human beings; we'll flaunt our own anger but never recognise theirs. We'll conceive of them as cowards or at best poor deluded fools and never think that wars have always required young men to give their lives in battle and young men have always done it. It is war and nothing can compromise our righteousness.

We'll call it a *just* war, which of course is what the terrorists believe it is, and so we'll join them in the folly of forgetting that there is no such thing. There are just causes and necessary wars, but no war is just. Read Homer. Ask the dead. Ask the family of the young Brazilian held down by British plain clothes police and shot eight times in the head. And then ask if Simone Weil did not have a point when she said that force – which is war's stock in trade – "petrifies the souls of those who undergo it and those who ply it".

The "war on terror" is a convenient brand, but it is also hard to think of a better way to elevate the enemy's self-regard and, in the long run, through lies, hubris, monstrous acts, eroded rights and self-deceit, lower our own. The British fought the IRA's bombers without doing them the honour of calling it a war. Better to say we're just defending ourselves and the things we believe in.

New Matilda, 27 July 2005

WHEN ABU MUSAB AL-ZARQAWI WAS killed on 7 June 2006, US military officials first said that he was dead when they found him, which is no less than one would expect after two five-hundred-pound bombs landed on the house he was in. Two days later, however, the same officials told journalists that the Iraqi police were the first to reach the site and that they found the terrorist alive: he "mumbled something but it was indistinguishable" and "attempted to turn away off the stretcher", they said. "Everybody resecured him back onto the stretcher, but he died almost immediately thereafter." The military spokesman told how soldiers washed the blood from Zarqawi's corpse before taking photographs: "Despite the fact that this person actually had no regard for human life, we were not going to treat him in the same manner".

As the US military offered this revised account, an Iraqi witness told a different story. A man identified as Mohammed or Ahmed Mohammed told Associated Press reporters : "We put him in the ambulance, but when the Americans arrived they took him out of the ambulance, they beat him on his stomach and wrapped his head with his dishdasha [robe], then they stomped on his stomach and his chest until he died and blood came out of his nose".

In view of Zarqawi's atrocities and the part he played in what is at present called the "insurgency", we might ask if it matters how he died. The man was a vicious thug. Spare a thought, perhaps, for the two women and the child who also died in the air strike, but Zarqawi killed many more than that and doubtless would have killed more still. It is just as fair to ask why we should believe an Iraqi witness – especially one who, it seems, lived near Zarqawi's hideout – before we believe the American military.

The problem with the first of these two apparently reasonable points of view is that so many civilians have now been killed and wounded – at least fifty thousand have died since the invasion began – that the word "atrocity" as aptly describes American conduct as Zarqawi's; if not for us, then surely for those on whom the phosphorous bombs are being dropped. As for the second, such has been official American deceit about the war in Iraq that by now we might as well believe the most partisan bystander as their military – or their administration, or much of their press.

Or their president, who declares and believes himself a war president in a "war paradigm" – which is to say, in a situation where normal democratic standards, including standards of truth, may be suspended in order to deal with the (unending) emergency. And the press fall into line "in this very serious time" (*The New York Times*), and describe his lies as "the president just being the president" (CNN).

The alleged massacre by US Marines of twenty-four civilians at Haditha on 19 November 2005 is one more case in point. The dead included a seventy-six-year-old in a wheelchair and four children aged under five. Within twenty-four hours of the shootings, the Marine Corps said a Marine and fifteen civilians had been killed by a roadside bomb. Soon after, they said the civilians had been inadvertently killed in a battle with insurgents. The cover-up lasted until March this year, when *Time* magazine broke the story with compelling evidence from eyewitnesses; a cover piece followed in June. The military did not act alone in the cover-up: Al Jazeera ran the story of Haditha on the day that it occurred and shared its information with the Western media, but the Western media ran the Marines' story and went on running it for four months.

At least fourteen US soldiers are serving sentences for killing or abusing prisoners in Iraq. There are now investigations into a dozen or more incidents involving rape, murder and "voluntary manslaughter" of civilians. Four were announced in June, including one into the premeditated rape and murder of a woman and the murder of her family.

After the Haditha story broke, retired Air Force colonel Mike Turner, a former planner at the Joint Chiefs of Staff, offered this interpretation: "What we're seeing more of now, and these incidents will increase monthly, is the end result of fuzzy, imprecise national direction combined with situational ethics at the highest levels of this government".

"Situation ethics" seems not to have reached Australia yet. Not officially. We're a practical people and never did like doctrine. If you've not heard of it, it's a theory first proposed in the mid-1960s by Joseph Fletcher, an Episcopal minister, in his book *Situation Ethics*. The argument, in essence, is that the ethics of any course of action depend much less upon an external code than the state of things at the time. Just ask yourself whether you should bear false witness when the truth will cost your life or a loved one's, and you have the gist of it.

Proponents of situation ethics insist that it is nothing like moral relativism. Moral relativism is a notorious nonsense of liberals who recognise no moral truth at all. Nor are its proponents to be compared to folk who justify foul acts by reference to revolutionary, as opposed to reactionary, truth; or to any other species of fanatic or Machiavel, including Richard Nixon, who ever found in doctrine a convenient justification for committing crimes. There is nothing wrong with situation ethics per se: the problem began, as Colonel Turner seems to have decided, when, rather like Marxism, it fell into the wrong hands.

It was inevitable that Haditha should arouse memories of the massacre of Vietnamese civilians at My Lai in 1968. Twenty times more were killed at My Lai; it was a village, not just three houses, and rape, torture and mutilation accompanied the killing. Regular soldiers did the business, not the venerated Marines. But then, as now, the affair was covered up by the army – the "investigation" was led by (then) Major Colin Powell – and the administration and the press joined in the whitewash. Then, as now, patriotic Americans (and many like-minded Australians) tended to see the men responsible as the real victims: victims of a war in which very often the enemy could not be distinguished from the civilian population; men under extreme stress; men for whom normal standards of judgement and behaviour had, with good reason, broken down.

At Haditha it was "purely shooting people", the Democratic congressman and Vietnam veteran John Murtha said, after being briefed "at the highest level" by the Marines. "Our people overreacted because of the pressure on them, and they killed innocent civilians in cold blood", he said; and thus, in a single sentence, both condemned and – as if ordinary ethical considerations did not apply in their situation – excused them.

This is no redneck's view, and it wasn't when My Lai was in the news. Then, as now, the men responsible were either a few bad apples, or they were good men made momentarily bad by bad situations; and if they were guilty, so were the men who sent them. Sympathy for the soldiers went far and wide, and to the top. William Calley, the only man convicted of murder at My Lai, served just three years – not in jail, but under house arrest. During his trial, banners demanding clemency hung in streets all over the country. Calley claimed he was just doing what he was told to do: "Nobody in the military system ever described them as anything other than Communism. They didn't give it a race, they didn't give it a sex, they didn't give it an age. They never let me believe it was just a philosophy in a man's mind". The public thought this a reasonable defence. Richard Nixon said the telegrams were five hundred to one in Calley's favour, and so he pardoned him. You'd swear they had all been reading *Situation Ethics*.

More people would have been killed at My Lai had not a US helicopter pilot, Chief Warrant Officer Hugh Thompson Jr, risked his life and career to forcibly bring it to halt. For this most soldierly action Thompson was persecuted by the army, vilified in the media and before Congress, and shunned and threatened in his home state of Georgia, where Governor Jimmy Carter urged citizens to drive with their headlights on to show their support for Calley.

Thompson was shot down five times in Vietnam, the last time breaking his back. When he died, aged sixty-two, in January this year, the media replayed a distressing interview he had given a year and a half before. He wept as he told the interviewer about what he saw at My Lai, and his subsequent treatment by his army and his country. But the most telling thing he said was this: "I wish I was a big enough man to say I forgive them, but I swear to God I can't". For Thompson, the situation did not change the ethics: soldiers do not murder, he said.

Simple as that – and the same as the old generals Grant and Sherman said. Situation ethicists might say that love led him and his crew to stop the massacre, but it seems much more likely that it was an external code, a belief in something unshakeably true.

The idea of situation ethics had not long been born when Calley's ethics were judged to be situational and Hugh Thompson unethical in his reading of the situation. But something (the situation or the ethics?) must have changed, because in 1998 the men who had stopped the slaughter at My Lai were given medals for valour. The military changed its rules and made it unlawful for a soldier not to intervene if he came upon unlawful acts. Thompson spent the last years of his life giving talks to young soldiers on "doing the right thing". Before he died, he said he felt ethics were now "all but tattooed on their foreheads".

And then there was Abu Ghraib. Thompson, by now a hero of sorts, said that by their obvious unconcern the soldiers in the photographs revealed that they were acting with the sanction of their superiors. The situation was not of the soldiers' making. And we know that to be true: the situation was the making of people higher up, as high as the US attorney-general, Alberto Gonzales, who said, "the new paradigm renders obsolete Geneva's strict limitations on questioning of enemy prisoners", and abandoned any attachment to an external code. As high as Donald Rumsfeld. As high as the president.

Now, in contrast to My Lai, the US military is sending offending soldiers to jail. It is insisting on the application of a code. In recent weeks there has been talk of the death penalty.

Maybe it's not the same thing, but situation ethics doesn't seem to work very differently from – or much better than – moral relativism. This might be because it's the president and the military and the cabal around them, and the press embedded with the cabal, with the "war paradigm" and the lies it sanctions, who decide what the situation is and what it's not. After that, stuff happens.

The Monthly, August 2006

The East Timor problem

BACK IN THE EARLY '90S I could find out about East Timor just by going shopping. The struggling supermarket across the road was run by an East Timorese man and his wife and teenage children. He had fought in the resistance to the invasion and remained a part of it in Melbourne. So long as the Indonesians were there, to go back would be to die. He was a cheerful character with a quick smile, but most times I saw him he told me how the people of East Timor were being terrorised; that they were being executed, tortured, starved; that a lot of people he knew had disappeared; that people who went into hospital in East Timor did not come out. Many of the things chronicled in the report of the East Timor Commission and related in Mark Aarons's harrowing article in the April 2006 issue of *The Monthly* this man said to me in the supermarket aisles. It was genocide, he said.

This is how I knew. But one way or another, every Australian did. How much we knew depended not on whom we talked to, but how much we wanted to find out. All through the Indonesian occupation we knew. And knowing, we were happy to trade with Indonesia, go there as tourists, and, without demur, vote for governments − and in my case, work for governments − that wanted to be friends with the Suharto regime. Nothing we knew about East Timor persuaded us that we should take a less accommodating approach to Indonesia.

The man from East Timor knew I worked for Paul Keating, who was then the prime minister. He admired Keating more than he did any other politician in Australia, but he could not understand how such a smart man, and a man with his sympathies, could be so wrong about Suharto. Then again, Suharto was a smart man as well. Maybe too smart for Keating, he thought. It's possible that he was right about this – or, if Suharto was not too smart, then too intransigent.

Either way, it's irrelevant. The fact is that Suharto did not have to outsmart anyone. By the early '90s, when this East Timorese man was running his supermarket, among the policymakers in Canberra no one who believed his sort of stories could recount them and expect to be heard. The policy was as the resurrection is to the Roman Catholic Church: the belief that pursuing close and friendly relations with Suharto was the only sensible way to pursue Australia's interests was the first article of faith.

The second, following from the first, was that our relationship with Indonesia must not be made hostage to events in one of its minor provinces. Around this dogma layers of seemingly self-evident truth accumulated, and through them no countervailing thought or evidence could seep. A believer in the policy was like any other believer, including old communist believers. All evidence that could be denied was denied; all that could not be – corpses, for instance – was duly deplored, but as something aberrant rather than typical of a vicious regime. And then there was the old maxim, the one about history's often brutal course with which no wise person argues. The minds washed clean by historical inevitability are numberless.

The relationship was important because Indonesia was the most populous Muslim country in the world. It was a developing country offering numerous "complementarities of interests". A successful relationship was a precondition of successful Australian engagement with Asia. Immeasurable economic and geopolitical benefits would come of advancing it, and none would come of retreat. In speeches, the ways we'd profit were recited like a catechism, and listeners were left to reflect upon the costs of not living by the faith. But East Timor was as good as any other measure of the dictum: the more we talked to Suharto, the more trust and mutual dependence we established in Jakarta, the more the future of the two countries became entwined, the more chance we had to have some influence on the way the place was governed.

For people who said that "engagement" really meant "appeasement" there were several standard replies. Would they prefer a military invasion? Anyone for a Bay of Pigs? Would they make a case for sanctions? Or did they recommend no policy except moral suasion? Inertia plus outrage:

to which Suharto would return his impassive stare, or leave the room, or read you his non-aligned nations speech on comparative national development, pointing out that there were no journalists and photographers making the case for human rights when Western countries were colonising the world, including Indonesia, and slaughtering, exploiting and brutalising large numbers of its inhabitants. Indonesia did not lecture Australians on their treatment of Aborigines. Indonesia did not question the integrity of Australia's borders. And so on. It was not beyond the general, the man most responsible for the deaths of hundreds of thousands of leftists at the advent of the New Order, to outflank the left on the left.

Besides, the people for engagement said, unless the East Timor lobby had evidence that Suharto had designs on Darwin or on other parts of South-East Asia, the charge of "appeasement" was hyperbole, a convenient anachronism. Whatever else might be said about the realpolitik of approving the occupation, East Timor was not granted to Indonesia as Poland and Czechoslovakia had been to Hitler, to stem his appetite for more. While all exercises in the realities of power that do not end in full-blown war or perfect peace may be, to a greater or lesser extent, morally deficient, they do not all constitute appeasement. On the contrary: in an imperfect world decent people frequently do best by minimising the number of victims and the extent of their pain.

Life under a murderous occupation – though the policy would never have countenanced such a term – might be better than life in a failed state, albeit one perennially dependent on Australian aid and Australian policing. What was more, in an imperfect world, Suharto's Indonesia was a lot better than its critics were willing to concede, or able to see from their lofty, Pilgeresque perches. It was not so hard to make a case for the Indonesian point of view: in 1975 they had acted as any nation might when a communist insurgency was mounted in a territory adjacent to their border, an erstwhile shamefully neglected colony of Portugal. If the hypocrisy of Portugal's objections to its successors in East Timor did not, of itself, justify the Indonesian occupation, a sympathetic observer could see how it might have incited it.

Sympathetic understanding was the foundation of good policy. Where an unsympathetic observer saw Indonesia as closed and repressive, a sympathetic one saw that while it was not an open society, nor was it entirely closed or entirely repressive. True, from time to time, the TNI cracked a few heads in restive provinces. True, the local press was not what we might call free. And by Western standards the regime was corrupt – though the beneficiaries might say that nothing they were ripping from the national wealth could match the booty Europe had taken. With all its imperfections, this nation of eighteen thousand islands was home to 240 million people whose standards of health and education were improving and who were, for the most part, free to practise their various religions and live according to their various traditions. Indonesia was an advancing, relatively open, moderate Muslim nation. And above all, it was stable.

In this, another part of the argument lay. Paul Keating had always believed – and as prime minister publicly said – that Suharto's control of Indonesia had been of incalculable benefit to Australia. To understand him one only has to think of what it would have meant had Indonesia remained unstable after Sukarno fell in 1966. And it was not just the economic opportunities and the military savings generated by the pro-investment, anti-communist Suharto: there was a psychological dividend. For the longer those 240 million Asians on Australia's doorstep were kept in order by the general, the more peaceful became our sleep. We recoiled from the massacres of "communists", but we found ourselves more relaxed when they were gone and we soon forgot the manner of their going.

Suharto gave us nothing less than the chance to shed our ancient fears of Asia. He was not the reason we dropped the White Australia policy and began to take in Asian migrants, but he made it much easier to accept the change. It is more than a coincidence that the generation of Australians that took such pride in open immigration policies and that declared pluralism, tolerance and diversity among the country's defining characteristics corresponded to the rule of Suharto. And it is no mere coincidence that when Suharto fell and Indonesia began to register in Australian minds as it had in the old Sukarno days, as problematic and unreliable, the fear returned. We closed the borders, replaced the value of tolerance and diversity with chest-beating about Australian (and "Judaeo-Christian") values, and before you could say "Australia for the White Man" our leaders were proposing citizenship tests for migrants.

That our era of openness should be so brief is hard enough for liberals to swallow. Harder still might be the idea that liberalism in Australia profited from despotism in Indonesia; that what we took for our own courage and optimism was really just the profit on Suharto's ruthlessness; that at some deep level we were complicit. And isn't this the rub: that countries only get that sort of courage when, every now and then, despite their dread and the attractions of sophistry, they practise it?

It was good policy, no doubt; but never less than cowardice as well. This is not to say Australians don't deplore tyranny, but rather that we deplore it at our own convenience, and no more than the people of other countries and other times who, when it turned up on their doorsteps, notoriously turned their backs.

The Monthly, June 2006

A never-never land for sense

THREE AND A HALF HOURS westward from Gove, the half-dozen houses of an Aboriginal outstation lie baking in the scrub. At certain times of the year about eighty people live here. As well as the houses, there is an airstrip, two school buildings, a workshop and a phone booth: and a story attaches to each of them.

A couple of weeks ago, police arrived and searched the place for drugs. They had no reason to think they would find any and they didn't. When the place was established almost forty years ago the community banned all drugs, including alcohol and kava, and the rule has applied ever since. There is no gambling. And if the police were looking for signs of domestic violence or molested children, they weren't going to find them either. It's not paradise, but these things don't happen here.

They are Yolngu people. To judge by the rock paintings and mythology with which they identify, it is likely they have been on these lands for at least forty-five thousand years. As with other outstations, this one was set up to maintain the culture and language and the land from which they are inseparable. The white Australians of those times thought this was reasonable. The feeling was that enough damage had been done to these people, and that less might be done in future if they were given their ancestral lands and, as far as possible, allowed to live according to their customs and beliefs.

It is hard country and it has made them resilient. The chief custodian was raised in keeping with the laws and rites of his ancestors. He grew up nomadic and can give the Yolngu name to every species of plant and animal that lives there, every rock and every painting, every waterhole and every kind of fish. He is a tiny, impish man; alternately anxious and laughing. He also looks indestructible, and if he proves not to be in the next few years, it will be the tobacco and not the country that does it for him. Tobacco is the only non-medicinal drug allowed at the outstation.

The great objectives of the outstation movement were to protect the cultural traditions and pass them on to future generations, and to keep the young people away from the chaos of the larger settlements where drugs, violence and despair devour them. Go to one of these settlements and then go to the outstation and you can easily conclude that the objective has been met. The young people of the larger centres know little of their traditions and look unhealthy. The children of the outstation know more and look healthy and happy. The teenagers and adults carry no surplus fat. Their skin shines.

They would be even healthier if the contractors who put in the septic tanks and drains had done their work more conscientiously: a real septic tank, instead of the 44-gallon drum they used, and agricultural pipes to drain water away from the taps would have eliminated the pools of stagnant water where parasites gather. They would be healthier still if the health department had held the contractors to account, or if it had not taken the view that the people's rotten teeth should not be treated because then everyone else would want their teeth done, and if it had not excused its own neglect on the grounds that Aboriginal people can tolerate more pain than whites.

The people at the outstation go hungry sometimes. This is partly because the habitats of the animals they once hunted are being destroyed by exotic species. Cane toads have killed off the goannas and pythons that were once an important part of the people's diet. Water buffalo and pigs gouge the land, rip out vegetation and erode and foul the creeks.

They also go hungry because their supports fail them at nearly every step. The dozen houses are as if expressly designed to be unliveable in the sweltering climate and perfectly unsuited to the inhabitants' way of life. No breeze can blow through them. Most of the solar panels only worked for a few weeks after they were installed and no one ever came back to fix them. The tractor provided to maintain the airstrip is a Korean model without spare parts. For more than a year the people asked for someone to come and fix it. Three months ago a volunteer overhauled it, but it lacked two parts. It still does. The community generator was running the batteries flat. The community was blamed.

But the volunteer found that the person sent to repair it had assembled the alternator the wrong way. The daily life of the people is conducted in the shadow of this incompetence, waste and neglect. The stories are funny in the manner of Russian satire; but the reality, like the Russian one, is corrosive and dispiriting.

Dr Neville White is a biological anthropologist. He is also a Vietnam War veteran. He drove up to Gove from La Trobe University thirty-five years ago and has been there for months at a time every year since. He persuaded Rotary and other philanthropic bodies to put up the money for a school and a workshop, and he took up a team of other veterans to build it with the young men. When the workshop was finished, at a cost of several thousand dollars a bureaucrat flew out from Darwin to supervise the installation of an illuminated exit sign.

The vets teach the young men various mechanical and construction skills; how to repair houses, how to paint them. The young men are keen to learn. Until recently a teacher came each week from the regional college – a teacher with trade skills who could work with the teenagers and young men. Two young women from the outstation were trained to be assistant teachers. Enrolments at the school more than doubled. A second, larger school building was erected.

And then, after a few months, the trade teacher was taken away. The young men who had been learning how to repair Land Cruisers and plumb houses found themselves in class with six-year-olds being taught how to make pizzas. Enrolments halved. Most have gone to the centres where the drugs and chaos are. Some went because they were frightened by stories that the police and soldiers were coming after them. The Yolngu often use signs to communicate with each other: to signify police they cross their wrists, as if handcuffed.

The difference between the efficiency of the volunteers and the ineptitude of the bureaucracy is startling – as startling as the difference between the volunteers' generosity and the paltriness of the bureaucracy and the contractors. Next time Australians congratulate themselves on their work in Aceh or East Timor, or deplore the US response to Hurricane Katrina, they might reflect on the Northern Territory.

No white community would stand for it. But then, in general, white communities are not so heavily dependent on the government. Some are, of course; and some, like the Aborigines of the outstations, choose to live in remote and unproductive places. But the white people who do this are commonly esteemed as authentic, if not "iconic", Australians, and the passing of their way of life is reckoned a national tragedy. There was a time when it seemed possible the country would think this way about the Aboriginal people living on their homelands, but it now seems certain that this time has passed.

Even if the services intended for the outstation reached it, life would still fall well short of perfect. When the sun is setting and the kids are playing football or hanging from the mango trees, and the men are hunting and the women tending fires, and the bee-eaters are whizzing about and the old custodian is wandering up the airstrip on his nightly search for tracks and taking the odd pot shot at mudlarks with his shanghai, it comes close to *seeming* perfect. But of course it's not: it wasn't before the Europeans, it wasn't after them, and it's not now.

Yet it is so much better than the bigger centres. And it would be so much better still if the promises were kept; if the humiliations and disappointments were kept to a tolerable minimum and the people were not obliged to be always asking – like children – for their recognised entitlements. It is not just the impression of relative health and happiness: there is hard data to say they are healthier. And while government surveys never seem to ask the question, the people on the outstations will tell you that they feel healthier, happier and safer there.

The practical skills the residents want, and which the vets and the government teacher were beginning to provide, are precisely what the government says it wants. Being able to fix their own and others' vehicles would not only provide income and jobs, but also free them from the grip of town repairers who charge them what they like and do not hesitate to confiscate their cars if they cannot pay their bills. Local Yolngu work teams can maintain the buildings, machinery and roads at a fraction of the cost of contractors. Providing guided tours for scholars and students would make for useful jobs and income and maintain the connection with the land. Everything the people of the outstation want, the government says it wants for Aboriginal people. Everything the people have conscientiously shunned for thirty-five years, the government says must be shunned now.

So why would the government abolish the permit system that protects the land against degradation and the people against booze and drugs? No one seems to know if the system still applies or not, but tourists and hunters are assuming that it doesn't and are heading into the lands for the first time in forty years. Why would they cancel Community Development Employment Projects on these outstations? Why would they tell the people that they must be economically self-sufficient yet deny them the means they have chosen to do it? Why tell them – as the Yolngu say they have been told – that they must set up a shop and sell drinks and artefacts to the motorists that occasionally travel the Katherine road? Or dance for them at night? Why, when the hub towns are plagued with booze, dope and violence, force the outstation people back into them? These are not my questions: they are what the local administrators and educators are asking.

Whatever the particular merits of the present federal government intervention, there is no question that the big centres needed drastic action. They have needed it for years. But why starve the people out of the homelands? The old custodian speaks just enough English to make his view of these things clear. It's not for drugs or for children, he says. It's for mining. He has always said "no". But they never stop asking. And they'll win in the end.

That is one plausible explanation. There is another one which he cannot know: that they have put themselves beyond the reach of booze and drugs, but they could not escape the culture wars and the Carlylean tenet of their chief protagonist – that history is always right and just and the vanquished have no cause worth defending.

The Sydney Morning Herald, 20 October 2007

UNTIL FORTY OR FIFTY YEARS AGO, thousands of Australian children were educated in schools consisting of one room and one teacher. Classes of less than a dozen were common. That the schools were in remote areas did not matter. Australian children had a right to education regardless of where they lived. It was an all but universal principle: education bestowed benefits on individuals and society that easily outweighed the cost of providing it. Among other things, it was the means by which children might escape the poverty of their parents and raise healthier and more adept offspring of their own.

To this end, Australian governments made education free and compulsory and, as the logical proof of their good faith, built and maintained these little rural schools and trained, paid and housed the teachers.

Students did not leave these schools with much command of physics or the classics, but they were numerate and literate. They were not qualified for university. But they could read a newspaper or a book or a summons or a form from the government. They could write a letter or read one from their mothers, prepare an invoice, measure distances, add, subtract, multiply and divide and point to Sydney on a map. And having these abilities, should they wish, they could further educate themselves, and inevitably they did.

These things are proverbial and we are well past needing to mention them in any conversation about education or "education revolutions". But among Aboriginal communities in the Northern Territory, they are, for all practical purposes, unknown. Children on Aboriginal homelands grow up unable to do any of the things that eight years in a remote school fifty years ago taught kids to do.

At a homeland 250 kilometres west of Gove, the teacher sometimes comes three days a week, and sometimes only two. On the other days, educating the children falls to the Aboriginal assistant teacher who lives with her family next to the school. She is bright and dedicated, but very young and untrained and cannot exercise the authority of a qualified and experienced teacher.

So for half of most school weeks the kids muck about in the grass and dust outside the new school. You can feel their future ebbing away – like the water in the community tank, which has been leaking for two and a half years and empties itself every night. The children have spoken English vocabularies of perhaps fifty words. As each day the rest of Australia's children learn something new and build on what they learned the hour, the day, the week, the year before, these children learn nothing and have nothing to build on. They play and laugh, and the gap grows wider and hope fades by the minute.

It's not for want of a school. The old school, built with funds from Rotary, is still in good condition, and the new school finished just last year is cool and well-equipped. There's a new house for the teacher, a telephone, television, shower and flushing toilet.

It's not that the parents don't want the kids to go to school, or that the kids don't want to go. The new school was built by the Northern Territory government and opened by the then minister for education because for a while, two years ago, thirty-seven kids were attending the old one. At the same time, a dozen teenagers and young men were learning trade skills and English in a new workshop funded by Melbourne charities and built by volunteers and the homeland people. Education is what everyone wants on this homeland, and English – they are, they say, "trapped by the language".

It's not for want of a teacher. They have a teacher who receives a full-time salary to teach full-time at the community. And this, she says, is what she wants to do. But, by all reports, the college on Elcho Island responsible for the homeland is primarily concerned with national benchmarks and university entrance standards. No one on the homeland has any chance of meeting those. The college has decreed that homeland teachers will spend only five or six days a fortnight in the classroom, and the other days in classroom "preparation". We were told that the school principal believes doing more would "set a precedent".

While the schoolteacher comes barely half the time, the trade teacher no longer comes at all. He was taken away because the college insists that the workshop is not a bona fide educational facility. The young men who were learning skills and English have drifted away to join the wayward, lost and hopeless in the larger centres.

The homeland parents could move to one of these places. The nearest hub town to this homeland is one and a half hours away. There's a school there with teachers present five days a week. Perhaps the federal intervention will force them there eventually. But the parents do not want to go. The homeland is safer and measurably healthier, and in all ways, save education, better for children. So much better, parents in the bigger centres send their children to relatives in the homelands.

We might wonder why, if it does not intend to provide teachers, the Northern Territory government builds schools and ministers of education fly out to open them. The answer is, they're not schools. It's a sort of trick, you see. They're community learning centres. And CLCs don't get teachers in the way that schools do.

There's a lot of debate about education in the Northern Territory. In some places they can't get the kids to go to school, so politicians – including the federal minister – talk about forcing the issue by making money or food or work dependent on attendance. Everywhere, ideologues and educationists argue about whether lessons should be taught in traditional languages or in conjunction with English or in advance of it, or not at all.

Bureaucrats argue about who is responsible for education. A person from a federal body called the Indigenous Coordination Centre told us in the boardroom of an elegant new building in Gove that, while the aim of the centre was to see that money got to the "grassroots", her organisation was not responsible for education. Nor was it responsible for any failings of the Homeland Resource Centre, which means it's not responsible for roads, sanitation, machinery, fuel or food. Nor, although it boasts a "health solutions broker", does it give any sign of being responsible for health. So what are you responsible for, we asked? What do you coordinate? The "different buckets of money", we were told. They coordinate the buckets and the movement of people between them, it seems, and the impressive thing is that they do it from the new building with the internal security doors and the plasma TVs. Like the health solutions broker we met six months earlier, the ICC person had never seen the grassroots of a homeland.

It seems simple. The Northern Territory government ought to educate these people. Since it is not, the federal government should do it. And if it can't do it, it should outsource it to New Zealand, which seems to hold more strongly to its founding beliefs.

At Gove airport, a bevy of teenage schoolkids and teachers, all of them white, were on their way to walk the Kokoda Trail in Papua New Guinea. Among them was a man who looked very like the former minister for education who less than two years ago opened the new homeland school. He was wearing the same blue T-shirt as all the others, with the words "courage, endurance, mateship" – all the great Australian values – written across the back.

The Sydney Morning Herald, 5 July 2008

344

Revolutions past

"HE WHO GNAWETH A COW'S horn gnaweth in vain and shorteneth his life; for he grindeth away his teeth, yet his belly is empty." So said an Indian prophet, we are told. Astute as his observation was, to be fair to inveterate gnawers the example of a dog will tell you how hard it is to give the thing up once you've started in on it. It's not for nutrition that dogs go on chewing a cow's horn long after the last flecks of blood and viscera have gone, but for the narcotic effect of the chewing. I have seen them: a dog with a cow's horn falls into a kind of stupor from which no amount of shouting, whistling or clod-throwing can release it. I have seen the same thing – we all have – among the power elite.

For three decades now, the politicians and their advisers, economists in both public and private spheres, many of the media wiseacres, and pretty well all our business leaders, including the most egregious rent-seekers, have had their jaws jammed round the idea that free markets are in every way beautiful, and that government, even of the most democratic kind, is the market's natural enemy and tends always to the horrid – even towards "evil". Call it what you will – economic rationalism, neoliberalism, trickle-down economics, monetarism, Friedmanism, Hayekism – this is the cow's horn of the political culture.

How else has the doctrine survived the madness performed in its name? Put aside the full-blown atrocities of the ideology in practice that Naomi Klein describes in *The Shock Doctrine*. Forget the criminal tragedy of Russia that gave the world Vladimir Putin. Forget the grotesque inequality that gave it Donald Trump. Forget the 2008 financial debacle. Leave out altogether, if you will, the example of the United States, where the doctrine evolved in partnership with the long campaign by corporations and "libertarian" ideologues to reverse the New Deal and stamp out every other manifestation of Keynesian and liberal thinking. Forget the corporatisation and debasement of American democracy. As the American journalist Matt Taibbi said in a 2009 article about that "great vampire squid wrapped around the face of humanity" Goldman Sachs, "in a society governed passively by free markets and free elections, organized greed always defeats disorganized democracy". But ignore this: pay no heed to recent indications that Goldman Sachs is already having as much influence in Trump's administration as it had in Obama's. And, leaving aside the fact that our prime minister is himself a Goldman Sachs man, think only of the local example.

How are your wages compared to ten years ago? How's your power bill looking? How are you getting on with the banks? Assured, are you, by their commitment to Corporate Social Responsibility and balancing the needs of customers and shareholders? Is life much better since all your services became "contestable"? Not feeling a little gouged every time you walk through an airport or drive on a freeway or enrol in a course? How's your debt going? Keeping body and soul together? Any houses trickled down to you? Not feeling that despite regular smashed avocados you might be gently, almost imperceptibly, sinking into the realms of at least relative poverty? And politics: how's that looking? Dynamic, innovative, agile – or, in its pointless, inconsequential plots and bad acting, more like *Midsomer Murders* on 24/7 repeat?

Does anyone believe reducing the corporate tax rate from 30 per cent to 25 per cent over several years will yield all the "competitiveness" of which the PM speaks, or the jobs, or that it will benefit anyone but their senior executives? Does anyone think cutting penalty rates will make the world a better place? Does anyone believe giveaways to business and takeaways from wage-earners will lead to Jobs and Growth? If we find it puzzling that so much of the daily political story is made up of matters that concern hardly anyone outside the hoary little legions who depend on them for nutriment, it might be because the economic debate has lost all inspiration and credibility. We are to be satisfied with a daily regimen of "there are no quick fixes to the challenges we face", "there are no overnight solutions" and "it will take time to turn these issues around", and such occasional acts of less-than-electrifying dispatch as the government's recent instruction to the ACCC – to look into power prices and report back *in fifteen months*. Whereupon the government – should it be the *same* government in fifteen months – will consider what action, if any, should be taken "to ensure markets are competitive and energy consumers … can have confidence in the reliability, security, pricing and terms and conditions of supply".

Some of us recall the early days of economic rationalism, when it was a kind of religion, and converts spoke in economic tongues and apostates in whispers. To question the precepts of the new order was tantamount to confessing one's unworthiness. Parishioners and comrades who let it slip that they thought a political philosophy should draw on more fields of knowledge and experience than economics, and that not everything before the Great Economic Awakening lacked wisdom and intelligence, were self-evidently fossils of the *ancien régime*, counter-revolutionaries, infidels, Whitlamites. That is, until political necessity demanded some kind of compromise with doctrinal purity: a subsidy for the sugar industry to save a northern seat or two, something less than annihilation of the car industry to save them in Adelaide or Geelong. Here's a bit of drought relief; there's a bone for the environment.

The trouble with economic rationalists is not that they believe in free markets; rather, it's that, as fundamentalists, they cannot allow themselves to believe that anyone else does. In truth, pretty well everyone believes in them, but most folk also believe that societies, like life itself, are too complex, human needs too various and human nature too obnoxious to be left to private enterprise – commitments to the triple bottom line and Corporate Social Responsibility notwithstanding. As the examples of education and energy and employment go to show – along with child care, aged care, roads and roof insulation, to name a few of the responsibilities rendered corporate in recent years – some things just need regulation. Some, believe it or not, are better left in public hands. And to say that is not the same thing as saying you believe in a command economy – unless, that is, you think Bob Menzies ran a command economy.

It might be, rather, to say that the future belongs to the person or party who can offer up a compelling case for the *mixed* economy that in one form or another we have always had. To get things started, Labor could do worse than to announce in words no one can mistake that it is done with economic rationalism now and forever. Malcolm Turnbull's

conditioned instincts will tell him to call it crude and outrageous populism – it's the econocrats' equivalent of what Stalinists called "reactionary
tendencies" – and he'll add that it betrays Labor's great achievements
under Hawke and Keating. But they weren't pure and he's not either.
He should take one last look at the US election and then offer Labor a
unity ticket. Let them all note what happened when Trump and Bernie
Sanders both recommended letting go of the neoliberal bone. Trump
bowled over the candidate who had only pretended to let it go, and,
according to a Fox News poll, right now Sanders is probably the most
admired national politician in the United States. Fawning to popular
prejudice, quailing before opinion polls, inciting fear, encouraging delusions and hysteria, abandoning your principles to save your political skin:
populism has all these unattractive faces. And it has one other – sometimes it's an expression of righteous anger, of resistance. Populists, like
the people they appeal to, are capable of being right.

Quite apart from the prospect of pulling the debate back to what used
to be called the main game, and offering the prospect of finding a new
coherent narrative for the country, renouncing the doctrine, clearing it
out from the debate and the language, would actually free politicians from
the pointless, barely endurable hypocrisy and doublespeak that balancing
corporate and democratic ideology requires.

Let us take as our models for the new order two old dogs from the
existing one.

In late March this year, after the new ACTU leader, Sally McManus,
declared her belief that the neoliberal "experiment" had "run its course",
the chief political architect of that experiment, Paul Keating, said that
she was right. In earlier days "liberal" economics had dramatically lifted
real wages and personal wealth, he said, but since 2008 it has "run into a
dead end and has had no answer to the contemporary malaise".

A fortnight earlier, John Hewson, once the most zealous neoliberal
in the country, wrote a column that in 1992 would have made the basis
of a speech for Keating: the Keating who in that year made like a democratic socialist and with some justification painted Hewson as a heartless
and unreasoning fanatic. Too often the makers of public policy forget
that they "are attempting to improve our society, not just our economy",
Hewson wrote. "Do we want to build a society where we consciously
create an underclass ... a group of people who cannot hope to share in

the life, ambitions and achievements of the rest of our society?" Talk about a bleeding heart! Then he went after privatisation, the banks, the miners, monopolies, multinational tax dodging and unfair wages. In conclusion, Professor Hewson said he hadn't "suddenly woken up a socialist" but was rather "still basically an economist". And one who believed in markets. "But I want them to work for the greater benefit of our whole society, not just to benefit a few."

Sorry, John, but judged by your old neoliberal canons you *have* woken up a socialist, or at least a social democrat, or someone in the very broad centre of Australian public opinion since Federation, and at all events a natural fit for a Labor Party where you might be usefully set to work writing a manifesto for the new order. *Fightback* would be a good title.

The Monthly, May 2017

In revolutions everything is forgotten ... The side once changed, gratitude, friendship, parentage, every tie vanishes, and all sought for is self-interest.

—Napoleon, 1816

DESPITE THE NOISE OF POLITICS and many indications to the contrary, it is not outlandish to suppose that a healthy majority of Australian voters hold the most basic tenets of modern political economy in common. They generally agree that a market economy is far more efficient and productive than a command economy, and, no less generally, that a cohesive, just and good society depends on well-judged government regulation and activity.

Labor speaks of the Liberals' "top end of town", and the Liberals of Labor's "class war" and the "politics of envy", but these are sham refrains. Anachronisms. Were politics reset in keeping with the times, the parties would concede that it is not a contest between social democracy and a capitalist free-for-all, or "the light on the hill" and "the forgotten people", or even conservatives and progressives, but one in which the ghosts of organisations that once had some claim to represent these passions compete to prove themselves the superior financial managers.

No one now speaks credibly of an organised and conscious ruling class, or of a working class organised against it. The class war, like the Cold War, is long over and both sides of it have been decommissioned. The parties continue, but much as the Protestant churches do – either emptied of both parishioners and faith or reborn without the poetry.

Yet politics has never been more vicious. This is at least partly because the general consensus obliges the major parties to exaggerate their differences, traduce the other's policies, and fight phony (culture) wars. It is also because the parliament – the place where the civil war was continued by civil means – is no longer the principal battlefield. The media is, and the media needs blood. And loot. The more politics resembles *Game of Thrones* or a bad marriage, the more loot of every description. The parties, substituting for old armies, are too tame. It is not an accident that, in the early stages of impeachment proceedings in the United States, the president was retweeting his supporters' warnings of the civil war resumed.

It is equally no accident that a delusional celebrity with contempt for Congress and any form of democratic check on his ambition got to be president, or that another narcissist with scant respect for parliament became conservative prime minister of the United Kingdom. Australia has plonked for Scott Morrison, equal parts Barnum & Bailey and Ogilvy & Mather.

"The corruption of the best things gives rise to the worst", David Hume said. Sceptic, atheist and profound influence on American revolutionary thought, Hume's thinking goes to show that the definition of conservatism in the eighteenth century could be stretched to accommodate many different strands of thought, including classical liberalism, altruism and the notion that the origins of morality (and aesthetic pleasure) lie in human sympathy. It was why Robert Menzies could get away with calling his party Liberal. And it was what for the briefest moment Malcolm Turnbull seemed to promise.

But the ruling faction of the Liberal Party loathes liberalism, and is conservative only in confounding ways. They are for small government, and they are for big government surveillance regimes; for freedom of the individual, and for camps for the indefinite detention of innocent people; for freedom of the press, and for raiding the homes of journalists and sending whistleblowers to jail; for standing up for "dinkum" Australian values, and for being the White House hamster; for globalisation as it relates to capital, but not as it relates to the United Nations; for farmers clinging to their land, and for international agribusiness. One could go on.

We might think conservatives would see climate catastrophe as a threat to order and reason, not to mention self-interest. Not the modern strain. As spiritual descendants of landed classes and traditions of noblesse oblige, the desecration of the natural environment, the loss of productive land to urban sprawl, the degeneration of our river systems, the shrinking of country towns unto death, the loss of both beauty and function in the landscape, and forms of intensive farming that threaten the land's sustainability – all these should be a plague upon their souls. Not the present crew.

Conservatives of a certain stamp once held it almost as an article of faith that staggering progress in science and technology is not matched by improvement in human nature, and that the survival of civilisation required us to encourage the nobler instincts of men and women. Don't conservatives *by nature* value cultural memory, tradition, language, "the refuge of art"? ("And this is the only immortality you and I may share, my Lolita.") But there are none like these remaining.

Yet, forgive them their apostasy, as we will be obliged to forgive the Labor Party for theirs if, having lost the election, they renounce the policies on which they ran and the beliefs underlying them.

Paul Keating says the Labor Party lost last May because it failed to understand the "new middle class". Perhaps he's right, and perhaps it's also right to say that he and Bob Hawke created this new middle class – though when *Forbes* magazine recently reported that signs of a class fitting this description had turned up in figures published by US Bureau of Labor Statistics, they seemed to think the upheaval had something to do with technology and globalisation and the like. The new class comprised "healthcare workers, for instance, and technicians, service sector employees and lower-level managers" and, unlike the old middle and working classes, it was growing.

However it was created – by government fiat or a momentous lurch in history – it is not middle class in ways that would make a lot of sense to old residents of Camberwell or Mosman, or to old sociologists either.

We are not talking about the middle class that Marx and Weber tried to figure. Having just tumbled out of capitalism's revolutionary churn, the new middle class is bound to lack the timeworn habits of the old one. Being new, it has no roots in much beyond its own self-interest, and no values to call its own, except perhaps those picked up from management philosophy. Being middle class, Flaubert and his ilk would say, the thinking will be of a "low" kind. More likely it will reflect not just self-interest, but *rational* self-interest – so long as the sentiment is compatible with any irrational aspirations that might be governing them.

Being new, the new middle class is in part defined by the absence of ideology, or even of any consciousness of itself as a class. The prime minister, however, has quickly addressed this shortcoming by giving it – and any others happy to accept one – an identity. Or at least a brand. It is a very touching and powerful moniker, even suggesting a philosophy – or is quietude more of a faith? They have become the Quiet Australians, and now they know that self-interest and aspiration are the blessed states of Man.

It is the age of aspiration. Labor, its deputy leader says, must become the "party of aspiration". We thought it was. The shadow minister for communications says the party must "advance aspiration". We thought it did.

Debate about the party's direction as usual leads us to wonder if the ALP will remain a vehicle for the broader – and dare we say higher – aspirations of humanity. Will they add the high ground to the low ground lost to Morrison? Or try to take what conservatives have relinquished?

If that invites a contradiction, so what. Labor will never be without contradictions. No party ever is. And no party ever wins except despite them. This government is proof of that.

The Monthly, November 2019

SPORT AND NATURE

A demigod called Don

IN THE GALACTIC ERA OF my growing up, we dominated every sport that mattered. We won Davis Cups and Wimbledon, we ruled the pools, won gold and broke world records on the track. We had Hoad, Rosewall, Emerson and Laver; Cuthbert, Strickland, Matthews; Fraser, Rose, Konrads; Landy, Lincoln, Thomas, Elliott.

In cricket, meanwhile, we won many more than we lost and the team abounded with near legends such as Harvey, Benaud, Davidson and Grout. But there was a hole in the galaxy. Craig, O'Neill and Walters were all at some stage meant to fill it. They couldn't. No one could. It wasn't fair. In no other sport were such comparisons made. Only in cricket did the world await a second coming. In cricket no one escaped the memory of Bradman and the shadow it cast.

Of course, he was not God, but in a country where sport was a religion and the Ashes like a holy war, Donald Bradman was a God substitute. It makes no sense to call him a great player. Allan Border was a great player. Legend is the wrong word, too. Victor Trumper is a legend. Phar Lap, Bernborough and Ned Kelly are legends. Legends have something capricious at their centre – a fatal flaw in their character, a vulnerability to fate. It's in this, as much as in their ideal qualities, that we see ourselves. Unlike Bernborough, who always left his run to the last minute, and Phar Lap and Ned, who died leaving us wondering why and what if, Bradman left us very little to wonder about.

In the late '60s a racehorse called Vain did a fair imitation of Bradman. It won twelve of its fourteen starts, and but for human error would have won them all. It won its last three in the space of a week, leading from go to whoa and getting home by prodigious margins. Vain ran other horses off their legs. Bert Bryant, the great race caller, said after one race, "that's not a horse, it's a machine", as if the best transcended nature. He was onto something there. Vain was a horse of annihilating powers, of God-like invincibility and perfection. I developed a mild obsession with the animal.

There were greater horses than Vain, more legendary horses, horses which in their struggles against handicappers, injury and age gave punters a heroic view of their own lives. But Vain was no people's horse; Vain held out hopes of something beyond. That's where he met Bradman – on a celestial plane.

It is entirely possible that Australian horse worship expressed some kind of primal need which established religion and politics failed to meet. Australians have never been beguiled for long by charismatic religious or political leaders. Billy Graham seduced them briefly during a very dull patch in the '50s and, using similar techniques, Bob Hawke mesmerised them for a while in the '80s. The young Elizabeth, even more than Di, excited rapture and imitation.

But none of these – much less Deakin, Hughes, Curtin, Chifley or Menzies – was ever accorded transcendental qualities. Hinkler and Kingsford Smith got up there for a while but they both crashed.

As in our hearts we expected them to. As we expect everyone and everything to. Not that we don't admire them: they're all fit inhabitants of museums – but not of Olympus. The Australian Olympus is an empty, echoing place in which a few horses can be heard clattering about. And a ball hits a bat repeatedly and a solitary voice calls in a nasal twang: "Yes! No! Wait!"

In common with God, according to an old philosophical proof of His existence, Bradman was "something that which nothing greater can be conceived". It is the average which sets him apart. Take Bradman out of it and cricket is a game in which no test player can average more than sixty. Bradman's average is ninety-nine. A three-minute mile might be roughly equivalent. Anything comparable in the hundred metres – eight seconds for instance – we'd say must have been hand-timed by a close relation and assisted by a gale.

But Bradman's average was accumulated without assistance of any kind, and very often against the odds, over twenty years, all over the world. It is superhuman. And anyone who thinks the duck he made in his last innings was final proof of his mortality has got it arse about. Bradman's last duck was the most God-like thing he ever did. Any self-respecting deity – and anyone passingly familiar with the behaviour of the Almighty over the years – will know that to have scored the four runs he needed to push his lifetime average past one hundred would have been an unholy folly. It would have been a confession of mortality, a hint that he had something to prove. Jesus chided his disciples for harbouring similar thoughts.

Bradman was a sort of Cromwell among cricketers, a relentless, irresistible Protestant presence beating his enemies into dust – as if every bowler was the Antichrist and every ball a graven image he must dutifully pulverise. Every day was a Drogheda. In (Keith) Stackpolese, he played each ball on its merits and punished the loose one; but in Bradman's eyes hardly any ball had merit, hardly any deserved to escape punishment. He not only made extraordinary scores, he made them extraordinarily quickly. He regularly made more by himself in a day than we are accustomed to seeing whole teams make in a day and a half.

Plenty of players have matched Bradman's genius on their day, or have equalled his deeds across a season, but no one else has been invincible across a twenty-year career.

You don't have a Bradman until you add to the illimitable skills a stainless-steel mind. He did far fewer of the human things which undo batsman so regularly they become clichés: he played fewer careless shots; he did not seem to have bad patches, runs of outs, dips in form or confidence; he was less often distracted, including by his own reflection. Bradman's average tells us less about his skills than his relentless self-control, his will to dominate, the fanatical dimension of his psyche. West Indies' Viv Richards showed just how different he was every time he allowed his boundless talent to express itself in suicidal assaults. Bradman's genius encompassed an imperviousness to such self-destructive impulses. He never let boredom fill the gap between the game and his mastery of it, his skill and his opponents' inferiorities. Trick shots did not tempt him.

He was both an artist and the epitome of the work ethic: hard-working, ordered, methodical and shrewd; grasping everything that came his way, wasting nothing, deferring the gratification of a four for the safety of a single, accumulating – constantly accumulating – like a business entrepreneur. Leave nothing to chance. Show no mercy to rivals. He is at least an honorary member of the pantheon of twentieth-century Australian nation builders. BHP's Essington Lewis would make a congenial companion in eternity.

Yet Bradman's star also vied with Hollywood and Ealing Studios. It's difficult to say if the men and women who milled through turnstiles to see him bat harboured the same fantasies which Ronald Colman and Cary Grant inspired. Some women still glaze over when they remember Keith Miller at full stretch, but Miller might have been an exception. The sexuality of cricket is subtle, not to say quite absent in many cases. At least until recently the etiquette of the game did not encourage speculation about the contents of a man's creams. In Bradman's day all exhibitionist instincts were, like the wedding tackle itself, salted away in a box. But then that was Cary Grant's appeal as well. Cary Grant and Don Bradman both knew that narcissism and crude display are for mere mortals, that standing in front of a mirror makes it harder for others to admire you. Perhaps we cannot expect someone like Brad Pitt or Shane Warne to understand this. How could they, growing up surrounded by their own reflections? These days it is probably not understood by any-one with his own teeth.

Forty years ago, when John Landy lost the 1500 metres at the 1956 Melbourne Olympics, a cloud of darkness engulfed me. Yet the next day it almost felt right. Landy, after all, was not the God of running but of decency. He was the embodiment of what we took to be the greatest of virtues after mateship – sportsmanship. If athletes had been permitted advertising, John Landy would have had embroidered on his singlet the words framed on thousands of mantlepieces: "For when the one Great Scorer comes to write against your name, He writes not that you won or lost but how you played the game".

Today's pectoral-twitching cruds tend to make the heroes of those days look like innocence itself. They weren't innocent, of course. Lew Hoad, Herb Elliott and Dawn Fraser weren't innocent. Don Brad-man certainly wasn't. They were just brought up with no television and fewer mirrors. If they seem now to have been gloriously unaffected it was because they thought that grace was the natural and proper demeanour for people who habitually blitzed their opponents. It was part of being a hero. John Clarke once described to me how the great New Zealand middle-distance runner Peter Snell broke world records before crowds of politely clapping dairy farmers who had finished milking early. Snell would stand there sweating in his singlet at the end and thank them all for coming, no doubt aware that when they got home they'd have to feed the calves.

Australian cricketers used to be like that. Some of them, like Ken Mackay, played with a kind of world weariness. Lindsay Kline looked almost shy. Even the macho types – Benaud and O'Neill played with shirts undone to their navels – could never be accused of actually showing off. Perhaps it was because they were closer to the days when the Almighty watched with an unforgiving eye for skites, for anyone putting on the mantle of invincibility. Or perhaps it was because they knew Don Bradman was watching.

Bradman was not shy or, for a country boy, even particularly laconic. He was exploiting the commercial value of his talent when most of his contemporaries still hadn't seen the connection between the two – or had and thought it sacrilegious. He was certainly not modest, nor averse to publicity. He might not in all circumstances have stopped to help a fallen opponent as John Landy did. In some things he anticipated the brasher characters we have seen in the game since the '70s. Yet he could never be mistaken for anything other than a chip off the national block. He had the walk, the gimlet eyes – the look Steve Waugh took on – which, like his voice, made him unmistakably Australian. He played the right game too. Hubert Opperman was a phenomenon on a bike, Heather McKay a freak at squash; Lindrum was beyond compare at billiards; but none of these sports were of the same account. Beating the Poms at cricket was the one true national passion.

It was essential to our self-esteem that the First AIF had performed better than the British on the Western Front, that Monash outperformed their generals, that Melba showed them how to sing. Not necessarily true, but essential. It was essential that we beat them at all their own games. Above all, it was essential to beat them at cricket. A cricket game could straddle the extremes of the national sentiment – the loathing of Britain and the love of it, the strut and the cringe.

Bradman drove right down the middle, triumphant: proof that we could get the national rocks off without doing anything silly. His effect was immeasurably large. It helped that he came from the bush and that the Australian legend was alive and well. Bradman was perhaps the most persuasive evidence that something in the air and open spaces, the dust, sweat and eucalyptus, something in the experience of Australians, turned ordinary folk from the British Isles into matchless athletes, poets and sopranos – not to say soldiers, aviators, innovators and irrigators.

The experience of the half century which has passed since Bradman retired tells us that there will be no second coming. We will go on seeing hopeful signs in the genius of other players. People will always say, as they've been saying recently about Tendulkar, "That must have been how Bradman batted". But if Bradman were here, he would only have to point at the scoreboard. Tendulkar has already played more tests and he's made half as many centuries; his average is a little over half that of Bradman. For intimations of Bradman the best place to go is not to Test matches, but to the lower grades of cricket. Anyone who has played the game in its rustic or suburban forms has run into these characters; the ones who will not go out, who punish what by the lights of fairness and reason does not deserve to be punished, who have no sympathy, who take no visible pleasure in anything short of total annihilation. The ones who chat amiably about horses at teatime then stroll out and thump you again until dusk.

You'll find similar types among fishermen, hotel pool players, rose growers and ladies who play solo. You get intimations of Bradman whenever you meet the person who you can't beat.

We think of the gods when we contemplate Bradman because his deeds suggest the conquest of mortal limitations. He annihilated not just his opponents but the barriers between mind and body, science and art, prose and poetry. He took a cricket bat and with it forged a marriage between Australian pragmatism and something unconquerable and sublime.

The Australian, 27 August 1998

Steve Waugh: Why we loved the other PM

You know you don't have to act with me, Steve. You don't have to say anything and you don't have to do anything. Not a thing. Oh, maybe just whistle. You know how to whistle, don't you, Steve? You just put your lips together and blow.

—Lauren Bacall to Humphrey Bogart,
To Have and Have Not

TO JUDGE BY THE VOLUME of press reports, Steve Waugh's retirement from test cricket is the most important event of the year so far. Consider the other stories he knocked off the top of the news when he played his last innings in Sydney. Some of the fifty thousand or so victims of the earthquake at Bam were still being dug out of the rubble; the leaders of India and Pakistan were meeting to reduce the threat of nuclear war between them; refugees were still on a hunger strike in the compound in Nauru; an inquiry found that the White House systematically distorted the truth in making its case for the invasion of Iraq (not that this was news); and it was revealed that Princess Di once jotted something down about Prince Charles plotting to kill her. Typically, the London tabloids put this item ahead of Steve's farewell; but in Australia he buried it along with everything else, including the one about the crocodile man and his baby. Not bad for a batsman who didn't hook or pull.

Steve Waugh is famous well beyond Australia. In India taxi drivers can tell you that he has a wife, two daughters and a son, and what their names are. Being famous in a country with a billion citizens probably makes Steve Waugh the most famous Australian alive. And the most liked. There are billboards on Indian roadsides showing him with some of the orphans he cares for in Calcutta. In India he appears to be regarded as a "good man", and this summer's farewells suggest Australians feel the same way.

But why? True, no right-hander ever played a better square drive off the back foot than Steve. But his brother's cover drive was just as good, and one of the most beautiful things in the history of cricket. Steve's was like a shotgun blast.

We can't have loved him just for his square drive. That would be like loving Humphrey Bogart for the way he shot people. Come to think of it, there was something wonderful in Bogart's cold stare into the eyes of his adversary and the way he fired from just in front of his coat pocket, as if taking a man's life was just a variation on a handshake.

Waugh had that merciless gaze in common with all heroes of film noir. He had the swagger as well. His swagger was more like a duck's than George Raft's, but he was also the cricketer most likely to tell someone, as George Raft did in *Nocturne*, that if he didn't shut up he'd wrap a piano round his neck. You had to like his style.

As with all film noir heroes, the good lay half buried in the dark side. To like him, you had to look past the scarred, hard-boiled bits. And he *was* scarred. In his youth he played like a prince. After the Lord's test in 1988, the once-dashing English opener Denis Compton thanked him for reminding us how the game should be played. Compton spoke for the MCC, no less. But after he was dropped from the side, Waugh shed all the graces, until at times he looked plain ugly at the crease.

He became immovable and indestructible. Fearless. That was the attraction. He was Steve Waugh and you could take it or leave it. So he was the sort of man who wouldn't give you the skin from a grape: that's better than one who gives you the whole thing and thinks he's bought you with it. It's better than being a hypocrite, or a crawler, or a preacher, a pimp, a chump or a politician.

It was because he was Steve Waugh that we forgave him things we didn't forgive in other players; we justified them, or we decided that with Steve Waugh no justification was necessary. He claimed a catch that the cameras showed wasn't clean. He was an inveterate, unapologetic sledger. Even his most ardent fans suspected that once or twice he batted for his average. As captain he didn't discipline delinquent players. It seems he thought he was paid to solve the case, and it was no one's business how he did it. Did his critics want him to go soft? Was that how you won? Well, we could save our oil, as Alan Ladd once said. He didn't get where he'd got listening to clucks like us.

It has often been said that the captain of the Australian cricket team is the other prime minister: the one who expresses more of the country's prevailing character and who is better known abroad. Both prime ministers were at the Sydney Cricket Ground last week. The one on the ground was playing his last scene, and like the stars of film noir, he was playing it exactly as he always played it, by being himself. The other one was in the in the stands, method acting as usual at a game he shows few convincing signs of understanding.

In real life, of course, the one who looks less like Humphrey Bogart or Robert Mitchum, and more like the bit player who opens the safe at gunpoint and is left tied up and gagged, is the real prime minister and Steve Waugh is now a private citizen. And even as the PM cheered away it might have crossed his mind that he, the old bit player, was seeing off yet another star.

That's the joy in those old films: immortality depends not on the length of your life, or your success at it, but on what it stands for. Perhaps it was for his cricket that Steve Waugh was loved. But if it was also for his character, then truth is alive and there is still something good in sport. It means that artifice and narcissism are not essential, that blandness is only optional, and to feel something for the people of a very different country is not unpatriotic.

The Age, 15 January 2004

The turf

A FRIEND OF MY FATHER had a racehorse. He was a big chestnut gelding called Goldbao and in the winter of 1956 he won three races on end. The third of them was a two-mile event at Flemington. He won it by ten lengths. It was inevitable that my father's friend, whose name was Reg, dreamed about winning that year's Melbourne Cup, but Goldbao broke down. It was a year before he started again, and when he did it was at Yarra Glen. His trainer, Owen Lynch, said it was not worth backing him because he wasn't fit enough to win. But the horse, as they always say, never knows such things and Goldbao won at tremendous odds. Reg listened to the race in our kitchen and when Goldbao won, a packet of cork-tipped Turfs hit the wall beside the wood stove with great force and spilled bent cigarettes all over the place. Perhaps it broke the spell, because the horse did not race again. Reg bought another horse and called it Dlaniger, which is Reginald spelt backwards, and Dlaniger went in much the same direction.

Overall, Reg didn't have a lot of luck with horses, but in those six weeks when Goldbao was winning it was as if he had literally been touched by Fortune. He bought a big Ford Customline and bags of Violet Crumbles. Photos of Goldbao's victories hung on the walls in their sitting room. The one of him ten lengths clear in the Flemington straight and nothing else in the picture, R. Hutchinson perched quietly behind his pricked ears, made an impression on me that has lasted all my life.

Humans have been enchanted by horses since the Stone Age. They are engraved on the walls of the caves at Chauvet with leopards and bison. In a thirty-thousand-year-old chamber at Lascaux, Stone Age people imposed four horse heads upon each other to give the impression of a photo finish.

It is unlikely that anyone was riding them. The first convincing signs of equestrian humanity were found by archaeologists in the Ukraine in the Bronze Age grave of a horse now known as the Dereivka stallion. This 14.2-hand, six-thousand-year-old horse had been buried with two dogs and several clay figurines, such as one might expect to find with the remains of a notable warrior or prince. The Dereivka stallion was not only the first horse we know to have been ridden with a bridle, the figurines and dogs in the grave with him suggest he was also the first to be revered.

A racehorse is a kind of talisman for people who normally don't believe in them: like those riders on the Ukrainian steppes, owners hope that their horse might pass on some of its power and grace and the wild spirit inside. Failing that, a fat wallet and a good night out will do. With horses you can at least imagine crossing over. Goldbao's winter of success brought briefly into our lives and imaginations Pimm's, cocktail cigarettes and a shadowy racing man with a noirish, Camusian Robert Ryan look about him, who kept a form guide in one pocket of his gaberdine overcoat and in the other a jar of mussels in brine – the kind you used to see lonely and gathering dust on the shelf in fish and chip shops – and every so often would take a mussel from the jar and slip it down his throat whole. A child could not help but be impressed. These early childhood experiences are critical in our development, and in my case help explain why, since I was seven years old, form guides have been symbols of liberty unrestrained.

All my life I have browsed them, and all my life I have listened to the races, even in Japan where I could not understand a word. Once the habit forms you listen without listening. I heard Father Edmund Campion say in a Sydney pub one Saturday that hearing Johnny Tapp calling the races was like the national anthem. It is true: there is always that stirring arc between start and finish, and always the climax, hour upon hour, day after day. It grounds us, means life goes on. Race calls are for some of us what evensong is for Anglicans: a refuge, rather like the TAB is, or the stables at Caulfield on race day. There is something about these horse-connected places that restores human equilibrium.

Jockeys are unsuitable role models for boys that grow to normal size or fail to develop the smile of an assassin, and I could not go on forever wishing to be R. Heather or N. Sellwood. I transferred my allegiance entirely to the horses like Todman, Tulloch and Sailor's Guide. But jockeys can get a grip on your imagination. The two unforgettable faces of my child-hood were Peter Lorre and W. Williamson. And then there is the way they ride. The Ukrainian stallion no doubt felt like a winged arrow to his rider, but at seventy kilometres per hour a good thoroughbred is faster. Put twenty of them into a race together and you have a partly controlled stampede. It is one of the marvels of human competence to see a jockey, weighing all of fifty kilograms, spring onto one of these beasts and with ease command it. And then when the race begins, rate the horse's speed, conserve its energy and, keeping its rhythm even as it plots a course past slower and rapidly slowing horses, time its run to the finish. Watch them as, with their hands, their knees and thighs and feet, with the whip – with all these things at once – they search for whatever it is in the horse's genes that might get it to the line first. Men less than four feet ten are unlikely heroes, but jockeys frequently make a case. Watch Steven King on Fields of Omagh in last year's Cox Plate, or Frankie Dettori leading from begin-ning to end down the wavy mile-long straight at Newmarket and you will see skills that rank with any in sport. See a horse snap its leg and fall and watch the others come down over it and you can't question the courage of these small people – and even when you can, you can hardly blame them.

Naturally, a jockey's task is made possible by the horse's training, and that in turn is easier because, once out of the herd, horses like to bond. They will make an inseparable friend of the stable pony, or a cat or a dog or a rooster. Of course they will also mate up with the trainer, and the trainer, with a stick in one hand and lump of sugar in the other, makes the most of it. The smartest horse may be less smart than a border collie or a good parrot, but it is smart enough to learn who its friends are. It can also tell who is competent around horses and who is not, and will fre-quently make the incompetent pay. The extraordinary thing is the great differences between the smart and the less smart, the passive and the cranky, the beautiful and the plain. That some beautiful-looking horses can't gallop and some plain ones have been wonders of the turf is axi-omatic. It is just as true in reverse: among the legions of slow horses are countless plain ones, and among the few champions are such beauties as the black Octagonal and the golden Vain.

It is in the ability to gallop that the most astounding difference lies. With a few friends I have had an interest in several horses, and all of them by the standards of a Cox Plate field were hopelessly slow. But over two thousand metres the fastest of our horses would have beaten the slowest by half a circuit; though it has to be said that the slowest we had, a gelding with one floppy ear which lifted its feet as if it were stepping over snakes, would have been beaten by an elderly man on foot. R. Heather would beat him were he still with us. We whistled him one day from a hundred yards away and, though he came at a gallop, I had rolled a cigarette and lit it before he reached the fence.

On the other hand, the best of our horses, a grey mare who won six races in the country and twice was city placed, would have been lapped by two other grey mares, Emancipation (who was as plain as a horse can be) and Surround (who looked like Natalie Wood). Then there are horses which can run like the wind for a thousand metres and stop as if shot when they reach a thousand and fifty. And there are stayers that don't get up momentum until they've gone a mile or more. The real duds are very fast horses that only go for nine hundred metres, and stayers that never get going at all. But all these are revealed characteristics, and owners and trainers and punters can make allowances. So can handicappers and the people who devise races for horses of all classes except the supremely hopeless.

What are much harder to measure and understand are those innate characteristics of horses that no amount of human intervention can change. Herein is the mystique of the thoroughbred. Training regimes can increase a horse's stamina or speed, and teach it to conserve its energy, but only rare horses can do both and not even the best trainer can turn the others into what their genes insist they are not. Nor can training overcome the genes that make some good horses hopeless if the ground is wet or muddy, while some slow ones seem to go much faster in it. And no trainer could do for the attitude of a seventeen-hand horse we had: at the first of its two runs it threw the jockey in the mounting yard, savaged the clerk of the course's horse, and pig rooted most of the way round Cranbourne. With horses, as with people, some are just born evil.

The genes that determine attitude are the most important ones. Why do some horses with great ability never produce it in a race? Why do some always run well but not well enough to win, while others win every race until the handicapper beats them? Some horses give in easily or seem to beg other horses to pass them, while others – such as Manikato and Northerly – fight furiously all the way and refuse to let anything get past. Some are Chamberlains and some are Churchills. Then there are those like Better Loosen Up who repeatedly finished races like a train to win by the smallest possible margin.

The answers might lie in those herds on the Ukrainian steppes, where some horses were dominant and many more knew their place. By this reasoning, the squibs and the ones that could win but won't are imprinted with the thought that they're not supposed to, and for the same reason they never learned to put up with pain. In other words it is not always the fastest horse that wins, or the one with greatest stamina – it is the horse that is, genetically speaking, meant to and therefore has the will to do it. This is, I admit, a very poor guide to punting – but show me one that works.

The really telling fact about thoroughbreds is that, unlike humans, they are not getting appreciably faster. It is as if the dominant racehorses of each year are the equivalent of the horses that dominated in the wild, before thoroughbreds were invented. The mare that wins the race is the mare that would have led the stampede. It is probable that all the great and charismatic horses, the horses that people have revered, are great and charismatic because they are *by nature* dominant. This is the horse that all breeders try to breed, all owners hope to buy, all trainers want to discover in their charges.

The pity is they can't tell you. Good judges can see signs, but nothing's certain till they reach the racetrack, and that won't prove much until they're in a race, and most times it will take a dozen or more races before it's clear to everyone concerned that the horse just doesn't have it. Between that moment and his first morning in the trainer's stable, large sums of money go down the drain. On balance the horse with the floppy ear is the best kind of horse you can have, because it was clear from the start that he could not get out of his own way. It's the ones with a glimmer of ability that bring you undone. The merest sign it might be able to gallop and the pain begins.

If it is "forward" enough to race by the age of two, it is almost certain to go shin sore and have to be turned out again until it is three. Then it starts again. Horses' eyes provide almost 360-degree vision and are situated at the top of their long heads so they can see approaching wolves and sabre-toothed tigers and eat at the same time. This is essential in the wild but less useful in a race. It means they tend to see things everywhere; they get spooked by horses coming up behind them, or imagine a mammoth in the car park. If your horse shows these symptoms, the trainer will use blinkers on it. Horses can't see things immediately beneath their heads or just in front of them, so if yours starts looking for objects that might need leaping, the trainer might use a nose roll on it. The blinkers might work, but they might also have the effect of putting the horse into a kind of coma, or releasing more wild energy than any jockey can contain; and whatever the nose roll does to the horse's line of vision it's not proof against its imagination.

Once you have sorted out the equipment best suited to your own mad animal – and I have not mentioned lugging bits, tongue ties, half blinkers and other devices including bicarbonate of soda – experience will tell the trainer if the horse's potential lies in sprinting, staying or middle distance. More experience will tell you if the horse is the kind that likes to lead, sit just off the pace or come from behind. And yet more experience is likely to reveal to you whether your horse is the kind that does not like to go between other horses, or does not like other horses on the outside of him or on the inside of him, or is frightened of other horses, or is more interested in biting them than beating them. If within twelve months you have definitive answers to all these questions and have found the means of dealing with them you will have done well, especially as it means that your horse has not bowed a tendon, got a chronic mysterious cough, gone sour, died of colic or – as one of ours did – broken its neck on the wire stay of a power pole in a storm.

Your trainer has the horse as fit as man can make it, he's picked just the right race for it, worked out the right gear; it's drawn the kind of barrier that suits its style of racing, the going is of the right consistency. Still the chocolates are not yours. The horse might bang its head on the barrier and be scratched there and then. (This happened to one of ours.) The jockey gets it trapped in a pocket and only gets out when the race is over. (This happened to another one of ours.) It gets a check just when it's gathering momentum. (This happened just about every time our horses raced.) The jockey has taken a sling to lose the race. (We suspect this happened once.) Or the most likely thing of all – there is a better horse in the race. Slower than yours perhaps, but with something in its genes – or in its bloodstream – that yours lacks.

The possibilities are without number and should persuade any sensible person not to gamble on horses, much less own one. For all the science and knowledge that has gone into it, there is still enough of the stampede about most horse races to leave almost nothing that is not open to chance.

And therein is the attraction. There is no equivalent in golf to the Dereivka stallion. Nothing about Ernie Els connects to the wild in the way it did in Manikato or Might and Power. Very little in life does. I have never seen a golfer who looked half as interesting as W. Williamson, or as beautiful as Vain. And among those who follow golf – or football or poetry readings for that matter – you never see the variety of class, character and existence that you see on racecourses. Picture a man leaving a golf course. Now picture a man leaving Sandown on a wet winter evening, trying to convince himself that he didn't need the money. A battling trainer driving two hundred miles home with his horse that got held up for a run and was beaten by a nose. And the owners with the horse that won. Everyone who goes home from a racetrack goes home with a story.

Long after my interest in other sports has faded, I remain riveted by horse racing. Not everyone can understand this, but the same people would likely forgive Degas for the same fixation. For all his famous ballerinas, Degas painted at least as many jockeys and horses. For every painting in the Paris Opera there is one of the racecourse at Longchamp; and it was for much the same reason that he painted it – for life's spectacle. His pictures connect horse racing to the landscape and thus to sport's pastoral roots, and for this reason he might not have liked Randwick or Flemington quite as much. But everything else about the scene is essentially the same: the jockeys' insouciant grace, the owners representing all the species of vanity, hope and anxiety, the colour, the clip-clop, the smell, the punters and bookies and touts and experts, the ones in the know and those who know nothing – and those marvellous beasts.

Good Weekend, 22 October 2004

THE FOOTBALL ENDS, AND THE vanquished lie here and there on their backs, like blowflies after a spray of Mortein. It would make a telling coda to the season if the victors were allowed to go around stamping on them. Instead we are left this depressing spectacle and the cries of a triumphant army denied the right to rape or pillage. Allow the winning team to march away two or three players from their opponents' ranks, a trainer, their masseurs and massage oils; carry off their exercise bikes, their wives and girlfriends. For now, the final siren confirms the one thing which, for the sake of the industry, several million people have once more been persuaded to forget – that it's just a game.

And so the season turns to racing. The good horses come out, the not-so-good go to the spelling paddock, and the old and average look desperately for new careers in showjumping, or board a truck to the knackery. That's the difference between horse racing and all other legal sports: horse racing is for keeps. Racing is the meanest game, and not just because it's the only entertainment in which animals are whipped.

Of course the people who run the business pretend that glamour is the essence of it. You'll see the word "glamour" every day until the Cup is run. At the Melbourne Spring Carnival the cameras will churn through celebrities and socialites who wouldn't know a racehorse from an ant-eater. Like sparklers on a birthday cake, it is not that they don't belong there, just that they are the least part of it.

Great though the variety is, from the most taciturn to the most ebullient and showy, the most urbane to the most frayed and rustic, racing types all carry the thorns and gravel of an earlier, harder age. They have not fallen for the idea that we are born equal and have an equal right to thrive, or even live. Their horses tell them that: a great and unbridgeable chasm separates the midweek country horse and the Saturday city horse; between an average city handicapper and a weight-for-age horse the void is just as wide; and between a good weight-for-age horse and Black Caviar or Tulloch there is one as wide again. And those differences do not describe why, when they all descend from a tiny gene pool, one horse is a tractable, brave and kindly animal, and another fractious and evil-tempered; why one is sound and another fragile; one stout-hearted, the other a squib; one bursts her boiler trying to be first, and the other is equally set on proving her inadequacy; why the heart of yours weighs ten pounds and the heart of Secretariat weighed twenty-two pounds.

Then there is the fact often remarked by struggling trainers that the good horse is ten times more likely to be struck by lightning or a wayward piece of an aeroplane's fuselage than a slow horse, and that a horse which has excited connections with signs it is an athlete will find a way to break its leg while eating an apple in its stable, whereas if you tether a slow one to a railway line and leave it there for the night, the trains will go around it. Racing trainers – and owners and punters – must live with these brutal facts of Nature.

They also live with jockeys, the fifty-kilogram men and women obliged to perch on the withers of these five-hundred-kilogram animals and steer them in their "arc of flight" at anything up to seventy kilometres per hour, balanced on ankles not much thicker than a Coke bottle. To make their living, jockeys surely take more physical risks than anyone else in sport, including bullfighters. They are killed. They break their necks, their arms, legs, ribs and vertebrae as often as footballers sprain their ankles. They are regularly concussed and in comas.

The difference between top jockeys and average ones (and good rides and bad) is very wide, though not as wide as the difference between horses. Great jockeys are as much marvels to behold as any gymnast or footballer and deserve to make a pile of money and get kissed by Gai Waterhouse and whole syndicates of owners and to meet the Queen. No less essential to the sport, the less great and the wholly down at heel (a category judged to include the many who have lost their nerve or never had it) get paid a couple of hundred dollars to take the same risks on horses that, while slower, are just as big and just as likely to suddenly shy, falter or drop dead.

Not only do jockeys ride these horses, they also carry with them the expectations, prejudices and wagers of trainers, owners and punters. Good rides are not proof against the rage of frustrated hopes: but "butcher" the horse, and there must be times when, having passed the winning post, jockeys have wondered if they might clear the car-park fence and keep riding until sundown. With good reason it is alleged that sometimes they have also been known to carry the weight of intimidation, or something more than the standard fee, for finding a position in the field from which it is impossible to win, or riding a horse "upside down", or dropping the whip, or by some means causing their mounts to hang in or out or race like hobbled ducks.

I have co-owned or co-leased a dozen or so racehorses, of which perhaps four deserved the name (and another untried one might have if it had not died of a heart attack while cantering). My co-lessees and I remain confident that a jockey whose career was fading once nicked a plain, one-paced mudlark of ours at a meeting on a country course. Afterwards, in the cold drizzle, he sat on a bench in his singlet; thin, pallid, smoking a cigarette (I've always had half a feeling he rode the race stoned on something) while we stood round, wanting to take his neck in a throttle hold or throw him up in a tree, and yet unable to utter the accusation outright.

Low as we were in racing's pecking order, he was lower. There had been an atrocity (and of course it remains possible that nothing more sinister than incompetence had caused it, or some kind of allergy or migraine or an invisible willy-willy or something had pocketed our horse for six and a half of the seven furlongs they ran), but the indelible sense of that moment was that he was the real poor bastard and we were just another lot of bullies in his life.

The basic relationships in horse racing are feudal. This is necessary to provide a thread of certainty in the most uncertain of callings. No doubt it also attracts the sheiks and tycoons who put up the big money for the best-bred horses and send them to the top trainers – hundreds of horses, hundreds of millions of dollars. Time was when Australian racing some-how balanced the innate hierarchy of the profession with a larrikin and democratic spirit; an equation which, among other things, fortified the language with marvellous drolleries and made Australian race callers the unofficial poets laureate.

So long as the sport of kings was also the sport of the masses, train-ers of modest means could still look to Tommy Woodcock or Vic Rail and think it not ridiculous to hope for a nugget among the tailings – like Reckless or Vo Rogue.

In the first big day of spring racing, however, about three quarters of the several million dollars up for grabs at Flemington and Rand-wick went the way of a casino owner and Gai Waterhouse, and a sheik and Dato Tan Chin Nam got a slab of the remainder. Increasingly, imported horses – imported, that is, by local heavyweights – win the main middle- and long-distance races, and even the country cups. Thus our little prospects narrow and the dreams grow more outlandish.

So why would anyone of modest means and average good sense invest so much as a cent of his own money in or on a racehorse, or spend a minute even thinking about the caper, much less making heroes of horses or jockeys, as I have since I turned five? It could be that in an age now dim, a horse or like animal was the totem of my ancestor; and the totem became in time a God; and like the totem, the God was, as Freud declared, a father-surrogate; and the jockey is me, shrunk by guilt and longing, flogging it, clinging to it, "horse and rider as one", and trying to outrun it at the same time.

It could be this. Or it could be that like Damon Runyon I thought all life was six to five against but, being a mug, assumed that meant for everyone.

The Monthly, November 2012

Ken Hunter:
Like a vertical greyhound

TO FIND A FOOTBALLER LIKE Ken Hunter you would have to go to the country, and probably before the war. To places like Birchip and Coragulac, where legendary players came to training on their horses and frequently marked their own kick. In the VFL in the past twenty years Ken Hunter was a footballer like no other.

When he played on the half-back line with Bruce Doull you had two footballers like no others and quite unlike each other. Doull had a lot written about him when he retired – not enough, but a lot. He didn't look conventional, yet in many ways he was. His skills were fundamentally of the classical athletic variety – balance, vision, strength and ball handling. He had them all to such a high degree that he could do uncanny things, seemingly as a matter of course. He seemed to have so much more time than most other players.

Hunter did not have the same athleticism. He was truly unconventional. When you say that Hunter was uncanny you are really saying it was uncanny that he ever got a kick in league football. He had balance, but not in the way Jesaulenko or Raines or Hart had it. Hunter was hard to knock over because his legs gave way instead. Doull had legs like a moa. Hunter's were spavined, like a blue wren.

Hunter did not have Doull's peripheral vision, at least not so as you would notice. He seemed only to see the ball ahead of him and that was the place he ran to. He didn't have strength in a way you would notice either, but he was made of different material. He had strength in every fibre and in his mind. He had it right down to the tips of his fingers. He was built like a vertical greyhound, but he did not run like a greyhound. He ran like a bloke going after the cows. He looked like he *needed* a greyhound.

There was nothing wrong with his ball skills. I don't think I ever saw him drop a mark that was markable, and fumbling was just about unknown to him. But his ball skills weren't in the same realm as those of Rioli, Weightman, the Krakouers or a hundred other players. If there is a category for him it would be in the ranks of the Tucks and Hudsons, the type of footballer who gets by on the fundamentals of the craft – knowing where the ball is going and being in the best position to get it when it arrives. And yet he often got to where the ball was at the worst possible time, when a bloke, or several blokes, twice his size were there, too – waiting for him. He got there in the manner of an angel or a fire-man and usually just in time.

There was a spiritual quality to the way he played football. I don't simply mean that he played it with a moral air – although there never was a fairer footballer and few ever took such a vicious beating as he did in the days when the Essendon backline was manned by Cossacks and jackals. I mean he played as if possessed by a spiritual force.

The spirit of Anzac? He had courage of the heroic kind. He was for-ever leaping into the breach. He kept proving to us that we are always uplifted by the person who puts his life at risk for a cause, even more so by those like Hunter who do not appear to revel in the glory. He reminded the more sentimental among us of that wounded, blinded soldier coming back down the Kokoda Trail supported by his mates. He played as if possessed by an ancestral memory of deeds once done, values once held.

There was a bit of Bert Facey about him, as well as a bit of Batman. But in fact he played like a spirit. He tumbled around at the tops of packs and elevated himself at the most unnatural angles. He made of a hum-drum pack a figurative painting, by appearing on the scene flying with a leg pointing to the sky.

He was quintessentially human, even Australian human, but he was also a contortionist and a magician. He left us with Sendak-like images of grace in mayhem. He was also a spirit in this: he would beat an oppo-nent twice his size by fading the pressure of his body. By disappearing and appearing. As the ball was in the air, where the opponent expected a resist-ing force it was not there; where he expected a void he found resistance. He applied pressure by degrees. He was an acupuncturist of a footballer.

With the freakish things they do, some players thrill the eye, some the mind. Hunter did this. His marks were as consistently breathtaking as those of anyone who played in the past decade. But a very few players thrill the heart as well. Hunter did. He was not just an ornament to the game. He was an ornament to the soul.

It was not because Carlton fell down a hole this year that I stopped going to watch them. It was because the commentators were passing their final heartless, philistine judgements on Ken Hunter. And when they dropped him to the seconds the club did, too.

Sunday Herald Sun, 27 August 1989

Lingering memories of
monster kicks at Loch

THE PUNDITS OF THE BIG smoke, the legends, the tyros with mous-taches who chose careers in television instead of boundary umpiring, can say that football is on the decline. They can say it until we all abandon the habit of a lifetime and begin reading the front pages first.

Today's decline of League football is nothing. It is a mild dip, at worst. In time it will be seen to have left a small vacuum where a portion of the heart used to be. But it is nothing compared with a broken love affair, or even a punt on the neddies gone astray. It is easy to see why the crowds have fallen off – easier than seeing why everyone feels compelled to write about it. The fifteen-metre penalty, for instance, is a farce, and the change to metrics is only partly responsible. The game is played like a relay race for greyhounds; coaches have the charisma of commissars; Waverley is a historic boil on the nose of Victorian society; and the ABC recruits too many moralisers who judge a footballer not by the length of his kick but by his attitude to life.

It is true that the great players have gone. Not all of them, but far too many. Last year I saw Carlton run on the ground without Rod Ash-man, and felt sick. Ashman, who for years brought a Methodist revival to the team's last quarter. Ashman, the only man in memory to forge a path through Mick Nolan's legs, baulking his left by selling the dummy to the Gasometer's mother in the crowd on the right. Ashman was smart – chapel smart. No Ashman, no Barry Gill, no Robertson, Crane and Quirk.

It is like imagining Geelong without Hovey, Gazzard and Renfrey, no Haygarth, Walker and Devine, Norm Sharp, and many more. All of them wool classers, hence hands as quick as a concert pianist's, their refusal to work with wet balls, and their decisiveness – go for it or no, the judgement was breakfast to them.

Forget Geelong. I did when I saw Jesaulenko play. And Robertson. Robertson never received the acclaim he deserved. Ian Robertson was the longest kick in history. I once saw him put a ball through from the centre of Princes Park. It went through goalpost high and lace up. (The demise of the torp is another blot on the game.) Robertson had a broken finger when he kicked that goal. Next week he lined up with Footscray and, soon after that, with Oakleigh. I have seen Robertson bring Francis Bourke to his knees – to bring him any further would have required an elephant gun or the sudden appearance over Richmond of the Blessed Virgin.

Robbo came from Dalyston, a bleak village frequented by sheep farmers, garfisherfolk and mulleteers near the Borough of Wonthaggi. When the ANZ bank transferred him across the hills to Loch, Robbo signed up with us. We needed him at Loch. The permit player had not put in all year. His credit had run out at the pub, and there were unpleasant murmurings around the hotdog stand on the wing. Those old permit players were brave men; Pud Kees, Ray Poulter, Ron Carruthers, Don Scott (the first) came up our way for about ten quid a match. They stood in the goal square and were murmured at by dairy farmers from one week to the next.

Robertson was heaven-sent. He brought not only a reputation for scrupulous and convivial telling, but he could kick. Although he came from sandy country, he revelled in our mud. We trained with him in the preseason and thought the flag was ours. I remember the night the smoke went up from behind the showers on the Thursday before the first match. There were grins on all our faces.

I suppose the kick-to-kick sessions should have sounded the warning. Robbo ruined them. Our ground was not a long one. We spent all night retrieving balls. In the interest of engaging others in the marking contests, he was asked just to stab pass or handball.

Came the day of the first match. I think it was Glen Alvie we were drawn against. Glen Alvie was a tough side and, like Footscray, master of its own terrain – a hillside. The lambing season made the Glen Alvie players virtually unbeatable; no one could match their skills in the afterbirth. But we were drawn at home.

Our selectors had a problem with Robertson. Where to play him? Kicking towards Tuckfields Hill, centre halfback was reckoned most expedient. A deal was done with the proprietor; to have Ian's torps returned by the son, who looked like being an achiever. The southern end presented a greater problem. It was farcical to play your best goal kicker at fullback, but beyond the boundary at that end swirled Alsop's Creek. From any closer than the last line of defence Robertson's spiral punts would have ended up in Bass, and we had no desire to donate our balls to that mob. By midwinter, when the creek ran a banker, our prize recruit would be a curse. The selectors envisaged matches going on until ten, while teams of urchins with Aladdin lamps retrieved the pill in tin canoes.

In the end there was no alternative. On the Tuesday, Robbo was put on the train with a letter of recommendation from our president to Carlton's. Saturday night we saw him on *Pelaco Inquest*. Best on ground. No transfer fee.

Our club did not go into mourning, although there was plenty of regret. He was one of nature's gentlemen. Just kicked too far. In a way we were proud. With Richmond wizard Donny Davenport, he was our most celebrated export, although we always reckoned Willy Paterson was as good as any of them, if too light. Not that we got any credit for Robertson. It was always said he came from Dalyston, but we knew that it was Loch he left.

Still, Robbo's sudden and unforeseen departure coincided with a decline in fortune at the club; that and the premature retirement of Ray Humphrey, a peerless centreman in the mould of Whitten. At forty, or so, Ray hung up his boots, and I never saw a better footballer. His mother also was a lion of the club, and his father, with Lyle Davenport, breathed the life of yesteryear into the Loch Football Club. We might have won a string of premierships if the ground had been longer. But it's been a battle ever since. It's true what they say – things are never the same again.

It's an extended season of nostalgia we are going through, I know. It's the long post-urban and industrial disquiet in our hearts. There was nothing like the smell of saveloys wafting from the kero tin at three-quarter time in the thirds. There was nothing like the toot of horns when a goal was scored.

Perhaps our judgement is distorted. Perhaps country football is still the same. Perhaps Loch will rise again, or is, at this very moment, rising.

But when I hear my almost teammate, Ian Robertson, broadcasting from the Gold Coast, I think not. When I see the sign outside Victoria Park, saying "Collingwood v. Bris Bears", I can hardly think at all.

I wonder about country football; all kinds of non-League football. Are they playing the modern game? It doesn't matter really. It's other things that count. Mighty goals and missed ones, the failures of nerve and confidence, the grubbed pass in the last seconds of a cliffhanging preliminary final linger as long in our memories as they do in Swan McKay's. Only when one no longer hears the expression "the psychological moment", will the game really be in decline.

From *The Greatest Game*, edited by
Ross Fitzgerald and Ken Spillman, 1988

Seasonally adjusted

So, IT IS AUTUMN. To put us beyond the claws of winter we should be storing up and making mulch. Every leaf must be composted, every seed and shell, every fish head, coffee ground and teapot slop. Worms thrive on the leaves of books and also like old underwear. Centipedes grow huge and vigorous in socks. Good mulch makes the mouth water.

While they are still dry, gather bark and sticks and put them under the house – if you still have a house. Preserve the plums and make jam and brandy. The same with pumpkins. Steep your citrus and nuts. Turn the apples into cider. Stock the freezer with stewed stone fruits. Do these things now, unless you want to lose your beloved by August.

But at this time, when the sweat should be splashing from our brows, what does Nature do? She turns fetching. She slowly cools the air, softens the light, turns the world russet and pink. "Lie under the fig tree", she whispers to us, "and let the leaves land upon you and the grass grow round you and the sun shine on your nose". By every contrivance she says to us, be a flim-flam. And all the while the earth is growing cold. As Jack Frost approaches, Nature is testing our will. Deliberately, no doubt.

There are three ways to deal with this predicament. The first is the way of the ant – or Calvinist. The second is the way of the grasshopper – or sybarite. The third is to hire a man – or woman.

The first way you work like the devil, become dull and obnoxious to family and friends and spend the winter pretty well permanently alone with your stiff joints in front of the fire. The second way you dance and sing and drink the cellar dry and spend winter burning the wine racks for warmth, cursing your improvidence. The third way is by far the best, but do you know what help costs these days? The only acceptable way lies in a combination of the three: to find some pleasure in the work and get some help for nothing. This means doing the work of an ant with the soul of a grasshopper and putting the family on to the weeding. It goes without saying that what you have there is the bourgeois. The definitive suburban Australian. In short, the gardener. It is for him or her that the ride-on mower and the family were invented.

Let us be brutal about it: in many ways it is odious. Gardening is hostile to radical thought, to common endeavour, to creative intercourse, to café society. It loathes excitement. It breeds intolerance and tiny-mindedness and attenuates personal growth. It is a selfish, antisocial activity.

For all its fabled healing and redemptive powers, gardening causes considerable vexation, feelings of powerlessness and loss of sleep. When it is not the thrips it is the codling, when it is not the codling it is the bloody sparrows, when it is not the bloody sparrows it is the dog, which poops in the alyssum, bites the heads off the sprinkler system and thrashes about with blood poisoning in the azaleas. When it is none of these things, the boronia dies.

Gardening increases the level of personal debt: it swallows money as readily as it swallows water and fertiliser. Do you know how much a lemon tree costs? Do you know what percentage of them die in the first two seasons? If you have a garden you do not need any other worries.

Yet gardeners are sacred Australians and gardens are their shrines. No one may invade or trample their sacred soil. Children are put on the street rather than have them enter the garden. It is just the way we have turned out. Gardening is at once an expression of our individuality and a petty proof of our refinement. It exists in that part of the Australian mindset called "keeping up standards". Even Mrs Kelly grew a geranium and a few pumpkins for the boys up at Greta and if a copper had touched them Ned would have drilled him as surely as he would if ever a hand were laid on his Mum.

We believe our garden is our personal space and by rights is to be untrammelled. We can have what we like in it, including deadly things. There is no law to say one might not have a garden of black widows, wolfhounds or hobgoblins. One may set snares and traps, lay baits, and take to any intruding beast with a broom. There are two fairies in the garden next door, we think.

We may do what we like in our gardens: we can throw clods, use a shanghai, urinate, spit and barbecue animals. There is nothing to stop us indulging in idolatry. A man near us does a strange dance in front of his bird bath every morning. We may sunbake, smoke and use a chainsaw.

We may drink to any excess, abuse children and lay into the dog. We can commit the sins of greed, lust and envy. It is decreed by custom to be the one place where men and women may be unequivocally themselves.

We can sit naked in the fuchsias and read the Koran if we like. We may hold poetry readings. Lewd and riotous imaginings are permitted all year round. No one will dob you in for dreaming there.

But if you grow marijuana they will. If you grow one single plant of it they will turn against you. The police will be around with their dogs and handcuffs and quite possibly their television crews. Highly trained at weeding, they will leap your camellia, pick their way through your azaleas and pull your plant out by the roots. Then they will take it away and burn it, or most of it we may be fairly sure.

Fair enough, too. The stuff does not belong in gardens. It is an affront to everything they stand for. It belongs with criminals – and who ever heard of a criminal with a garden? But if you do happen to have it in your garden and you do not want a visit from the police, compost the leaves and put the flowers under the cumquats you have put in the brandy. You'll be pleased as Punch in August.

Sunday Herald Sun, 25 March 1990

THIS IS THE SEASON OF UNREGENERACY; the grass stops growing, the birds fly north, bears and snakes take to their beds, when all of nature does a ritual imitation of death – and we go about our business as if we are not of it.

This is the season when the daphne halfway blooms then hesitates, bulbs burst through the earth's crust and seem to change their minds, cars will not start without the choke – and we jog on the spot asking through our foggy mucous-laden breath, "If winter comes, can spring be far behind?" This is the annual, but not continuing, period of time in which our levels of contentment, seasonally adjusted in terms of the wider context, are not at their optimum.

We have ways of dealing with it, of course. Eucalyptus on the handkerchief. Plenty of carbohydrate to keep the fire going inside. We learn these things in childhood, and also how false comparisons can get us through.

What shivering child did not suffer the infuriating comparisons with winters elsewhere? In the suburbs, children were told as they got shuddering out of bed to think of the dairy farmers who were up in the sleet at five. On dairy farms, they were told to think of what it would be like in Tierra del Fuego. In Tierra del Fuego, it was the Eskimos they heard about. What were Eskimos told? How lucky they were not to live in Melbourne, quite possibly.

"Cripes, it's cold", we'd say through chattering teeth. "It's nippy, right enough", they'd say, "but it's a dry cold. It's not like that horrible damp cold" – as if we were meant to feel some sympathy for the people who went down with the *Titanic*.

Fifteen centimetres of frost lay down on the flat. The puddles were brown ice. Icicles hung from the dog's teeth. The chooks crackled as they walked. A magpie's warble lay shattered beneath the tree.

"We cannot ride to school today", we said. "Not across the flat! We'll freeze to death before we reach the second bridge." Frozen drizzle shredded our purple ears. You could see the bone in our noses. "Douglas Mawson, Sir Douglas Mawson, spent nine months down an Antarctic glacier, did you know that?" they'd say. "By the breath of God frost is given", they shouted as we pedalled off.

We hit the flat at forty kilometres per hour with our jaws locked in a mummy's grin. Cobwebs trailed from our spokes and eyes. We were screaming when we hit the bridges. Platypuses skated on the creek below. A cow that had bent to drink in the early morning had its head frozen in the water.

They did not believe this at morning talk, even though we were still stuck to our handlebars and stayed that way till playtime. "Stop shivering", the teacher garumphed: "The mean winter temperature in Novosibirsk is thirty degrees below zero. In 763 AD, the seas at Constantinople were frozen one hundred miles from the shore and to a thickness sufficient to bear a horse and cart, did you know that?" "Crumbs", we obediently said.

The elders were right. Winters do vary in their intensity, but we also differ in our apprehension of them. I have since been to Novosibirsk when it was forty-five below. You could write your name on your own breath. Yet it was not so cold as the flat when we crossed it on our bikes. It was pre-greenhouse then, of course.

Our parents were also right about the difference between damp and wet cold. I saw a wet bear hunter in Novosibirsk and he was dead on his feet. There is also windy cold, the type which gets into your spine and runs to the most nether points beneath it; drab cold which fills the flesh with a dull ache and brings on fits of melancholy; and the cold which, combining wind and rain and long periods of dull light, makes drizzle of the spirit.

Melbourne's winter has all of these. It is performed in four acts. The first consists of those few weeks when one wonders if it's going to come. There are leaves still on the trees and the sun shines daily. It is an Indian summer if you like. There is a pause. Soot falls down the chimney, the mice disappear, the lawn sighs and turns dun. Farmers talk of drought.

Then come the deluges. The roof and spouting leak and all the air turns grey. Another Indian summer follows. Late in July the weather is always good. Splendid in fact. Wattle blooms. The jasmine buds dark pink. We anticipate the smell.

The gales fly in while we're asleep and, with them, hail and sleet, train strikes, tax bills, council rates and your team drops out of the five. Only in the Northern Hemisphere can they talk of light in August. It is worse because one never knows when it will end. This is the very dead of winter and not infrequently it runs into September and even October. The first weight-for-age races of the spring calendar are often run on boggy tracks. The form is as misleading as the climate.

Yet in that long night something happens to Melbourne dwellers that sets them apart. We are held on the cusp of pleasure – the sun, the flowers, the horses – too long not to test the soul. August is the month when many among us give up. It is the month when a person of Melbourne is most likely to succumb to pleasure.

This pattern is well documented in all cold cultures of which the bawdy writings of Robbie Burns provides perhaps the best example. Burns could not help himself in a prolonged blizzard. Coldness is what gets the singer into trouble in the risqué and often proscribed North American song which goes:

She wept, she cried, she damn near died
Tell me, what could I do?
So I pulled her into bed
And covered up her head
Just to keep her from the foggy, foggy dew.

Love "proves the pleasanter the colder", Samuel Butler said. There is also the Mallee fragment:

In winter I think of Jacinta
The women I once had and lost
Jacinta! I wish I could mint her!
And pocket her when there's a frost.

In cold, we become heat-seekers. We find enclosed places and huddle there, taking comfort in the closeness of things. It is why Melburnians have always liked chamber music, recitals and reading, and equally the reason why very often you will see on their dour faces the odd sign of guilt.

The winter has shaped our history in subtle ways. In small congregations cut off from each other by rain and icy winds, envy and suspicion are bred. An unwillingness to communicate, except in the letter columns of *The Age*, makes of petty grievances immutable and historic loathings. Differences of opinion become factions – in art and letters, sport and politics.

The tendency to huddle may explain the groupers and even the disproportionate political and economic influence of the Melbourne Club over many years.

It is probably no accident that the Eureka Stockade occurred at Ballarat, where the cold is intense and damp and the storm clouds are blacker and more frequent than anywhere else in Victoria. I had not been cold until I was in Ballarat, a traveller once wrote. He was not the last to make the observation. If anyone was ever going to take up arms against the state it would be there.

Melbourne's winter gave birth to Australian Rules football, perhaps the most frantic of all games after ice hockey. In the many learned discussions on the origins of the sport, no one has drawn the obvious conclusion that it was a game for keeping warm. This, of course, is only true for players. The outer at Waverley is perhaps the only place in Victoria which is colder than Ballarat.

Yet when all is said and done there is something about Melbourne's winter that disappoints. It can be very cold and very wet and very windy. Snow falls on the Dandenongs from time to time. I have seen a few flakes in Heidelberg. It gets very miserable in Melbourne but in the end it is more functional than Gothic. One gets the feeling that winter comes upon us because it is obliged to. It is there because without it there could not be autumn and spring. We are all grateful for those seasons and so we should be grateful for winter. But winter does not paint a picture here. Like the people, it never truly abandons itself.

Cities being what they are, it is not likely in the future to take on some new grandeur. The world is warming up. We will have increasingly sullen and unsatisfactory winters as a result, damp winters – and not just here but on the dairy farms which now live in the city's glow. For a frost like the ones we used to ride through, we will have to go up to the high plains, or Tierra del Fuego. Or back into our memories.

"The winter is past, the rain is over and gone", went the Song of Solomon. "Rise up", it said. How would we ever get out of bed in the morning if one year it never came at all?

The Age, 1 July 1990

Possums, rabbits and the society of birds

LESSER SUGAR-TAILED GLIDER POSSUMS HAD big, green, staring eyes, strawberry noses and tousled manes. Males were greeny-black and no bigger than a matchbox; females were roan and about the size of a woman's second toe. Both genders were lascivious in spring, and as they sailed from tree to tree in the lilly pilly gullies of East Gippsland they blew the sound of distant muted trombones.

They are all but gone now: the third-last one was trampled by a naturalist in January. The remaining two are females, now sentenced to lifetimes without love or issue. The species lives as long as horses and the pair are reckoned to be young, but that is possibly more comforting to us than it is to them. When they die, Nature will give a little sigh in remembrance of one more of her children gone for ever.

It is profoundly sad to contemplate, and by no means just because these gliders had the sort of cuddly qualities which have always attracted humanity: Nature mourns equally the extinction of the comparatively ugly weak-kneed grebe and the hirsute spitting spider.

Dwell for more than a moment on the permanent departure of any line of creature – bison, moa, glider or spider – and a hole is rent inside us. We are consumed by nostalgia of a primal kind, the sort in which we feel as if we are both swallower and swallowed.

It is more than feelings of guilt, more even than a powerful whiff of our mortality, which the news of the gliders gives us: it is bottomless and unspeakable regret. It's the dread feeling that the world tends towards the abyss and the taking of life is more powerful than the giving of it.

We can feel the same, of course, about past human generations, including those two or so between Federation and the Melbourne

Olympics who are now as extinct as any thylacine or drongo. And as singular. They had about them the look of both the hunter and the hunted. Hunted they were, by war and depression. And hunters – of rabbits primarily, for they lived in the Great Rabbit Culture of Australia.

They hunted rabbits, ate rabbits, traded rabbits and kept in their handbags or hung from their rear-vision mirrors rabbit tails or feet as talismans. Women wore rabbit coats and stoles, or the same made from fox's fur. Foxes thrived in the rabbit plague. Men attached their tails to car radio aerials and wore them in place of neckties. From the furs of rabbits and foxes, slippers were made for both sexes.

And on every male head was a hat made of rabbit hides. Look at the photos from the wars and the Great Depression: on the heads of capitalists and communists alike, on lawyers, plain men and Fancy Dans – hats.

Look at the Petrov Commission: it is remarkable, isn't it, that people so ideologically dissimilar as Petrov, Menzies and Evatt should have in common the belief that at all times in this earthly existence a man should wear on his head ten rabbit skins composed in a hat?

These hats were both functional and adorning. They were thrown in the air in moments of exultation, hurled on the ground and trampled in anger or despair; they were used to carry home mushrooms, peas, eggs, even newly hatched chickens, to hold the seed when sowing lawns and fields; they were held to breasts in the observation of the sacred and when singing hymns and anthems; they were used to chase poultry, to head off stray animals, to kill flies and other insects, to trap grasshoppers and mice, and to shield the eyes of the innocent from violence and obscenity.

A man's hat was an extension of his physical and moral being. It defined his stance, his attitude, and his upbringing.

Hats were a major tributary of the language. I'd keep it under my hat if I were you, people would say. I take my hat off to you; you're talking through your hat; hang on to your hat! they'd say. They even talked about eating their hats.

They've all gone now, the people of the Rabbit Culture – every bit as vanished as the lesser glider, or the Pawnee and the Sioux.

Don't be fooled by those derisory bits of thatch called Panamas, or those broad-brimmed symbols of officiousness you see on parking officers and four-wheel drivers, or the American peak caps with advertising attached in which youths strut around: they are all symptoms of disconnectedness, alienation and cultural poverty and have nothing in common with the hats an older generation used to raise to every passing woman of fair repute.

When they said they'd eat their hats, they meant, of course, that they'd be buggered. It was prescient of them, as it turns out. It was as if they knew that one generation is very soon devoured by another.

And that's as good a reason as any for not allowing ourselves to be consumed by the loss of the gliders – apparently they've been down in East Gippsland for millions of years.

The Age, 31 March 1991

E.E. CUMMINGS PRAYED THAT HIS heart would always be open to little birds. My family, the maternal side especially, has always shared some of his sentiment. It goes back to the clearing of the forest. As the trees went, the little birds came and dwelt in the hydrangeas under the window. Fantails, wagtails, blue wrens, scrubwrens, honeyeaters, eastern rosellas, finches, silvereyes, robins, thornbills, mudlarks and thrushes: generations of us have watched them from the kitchen and talked to them as if to friends or children. If it is one of the last pagan associations in what remains of the rural Protestant, or has a more philosophical origin, I do not know.

I do know that Cummings's line does not ring quite true. Birds are less a matter of the heart than of the senses. We are not talking about commitment, but rather the pleasure a bird's shape and sound affords us, and the wonder of its aeronautics. These things might be surrogates for something deeper (try holding a grey thrush in your hand and see if it doesn't stir something) but the first conscious sensations that birds create are aesthetic ones. A hovering kite, an egret by the water's edge, a thrush singing by the window – in every bird's construction there is first an irresistible line.

Consider that thrush. It is a very ordinary flyer, yet in appearance it is at least as pure a bird as the swallow: a swallow, in truth, is such an aerial acrobat as to seem part bat.

"Whatever the bird is, is perfect in the bird", Judith Wright wrote. And no bird is quite as perfect as a thrush. In the same verse Wright also talks of parrots and kestrels, but I think it's a fair bet that a thrush – "round as a mother or a full drop of water" – inspired the line about perfection.

"Whatever the bird does is right for the bird to do", Wright says, and contrasts that happy state with her own, which is "torn and beleaguered". It's a beautiful line, but like the one of Cummings, as untrue as it is true.

This spring, whenever I opened the back door, a magpie took off from its nest in a gum tree half a kilometre away and came skimming over the grass, arcing over the fences, zooming beneath the branches down the drive and veering straight at my brow, before braking impossibly late and landing on the porch rail beside me. It all took about five seconds. I've no doubt the magpie was showing me how exhilarating flying is for the creatures that can do it. And then it carolled.

Another magpie with a nest on a higher branch always followed the first, but it did not fly with the same élan or straight at me, and it always pulled up a metre further away. It was a shyer bird and its carol was more guttural. The first took the meat from my hand, the second only when I put it down. Both flew straight back to their nests, fed their pleading young with my mince and came sailing back to the porch again.

The young have now left the nests. In the morning they follow their parents to my back porch and whine for food while the adults warble away in their mezzo-sopranos until I come out. No unprejudiced human being could fail to be improved by the presence of magpies. They are fearless, resourceful, amusing and melodious, and, above all – as all birds have to be – stoic. But they also contain complexities of character: not in the multitudes of some humans, perhaps, but not that many less than the average. And, just to go on the sample at my door, between one magpie and another there are differences as pronounced as they are between, say, the Three Tenors or two modern political leaders when there is an election on.

Last week on a local road I saw a kookaburra dive from a fence post on one side to the verge of the other, in pursuit of what I don't know, because in the instant that it dived, a man on a motorbike roared round the corner and the bird's head struck the front wheel. The collision killed the kookaburra: it bounced back across the road and lay there on its back, quite still. What Australian does not love kookaburras? To be truthful, in that moment I would have been no more dismayed if it had been the motorcyclist on his back and the kookaburra flying on down the road.

What this bird did was *wrong* for the bird to do. Yet it was only a minor departure from the normal drama of bird life. Watch birds for a while, and you begin to see that what is natural for the bird is perpetual menace, frequent terror and sudden death – much of it inflicted by other birds – and to all this they must find solutions.

Around midnight a couple of nights ago, a honeyeater of some kind crashed into the wire-screen door and clung there shuddering. There was an owl in the trees outside. If owls are wise, it must be only in the daytime. When darkness falls they are ruthless, havoc-creating monsters. The owl and the pussycat went to sea, and when night fell the owl tore the cat to pieces.

Every day in the society of birds down by the lake, harriers, kites, falcons and eagles glide among their fellows, brazenly looking for one to kill. Patches of feathers and down on the ground – all-white, pink and grey, red and blue, green and yellow – are all they leave of any bird they catch, and the proof of their efficiency. They are the SS of the lake. Like owls, they use not just the weapon of surprise, but that of terror. They hunt in pairs or trios: hovering over the marshes on the edge, or sweeping and swerving low over the gums and willows in the hope that their sudden appearance, or the equally potent effect of their shadow, will frighten something out.

They sail and soar and dive in accordance with their natures and our ideal of them. But they also concoct, invent and improvise. On windy days they let the air carry them wildly from tree to tree, as if to use unruliness as a disguise and to heighten the terrible effect of their shadows.

At dusk, when flocks of galahs, corellas and cockatoos go screeching home, the hawks station themselves in trees, or glide and swirl about looking for their chance. At the same time of the day, I watched a falcon stand for twenty minutes in the reeds by the edge of the lake. I thought it was counting on ducks or cygnets coming ashore, but when a flock of parrots flew overhead the falcon climbed into the air – and into the parrots – like a surface-to-air missile. On another occasion, it hid for a long time in the grass on one side of a low ridge, then suddenly soared into air and swooped down the other side and onto some creature it must have sensed was there.

In response to the raptors' ingenuity, the parrots have worked out their own defences, which amount to a kind of Resistance. They post evening lookouts in the trees and on the ground. They divide their flocks. They fly jagged, crazy paths. They communicate endlessly. No galah or cockatoo ever seems to move without screeching a message of some kind to every other galah or cockatoo within a kilometre, and none ever hears a screech without replying.

And they are served by other species: by the magpies and mudlarks that spend a good part of every day obeying their ferocious territorial instincts and driving raptors from their airspace, and by crows whose motives might be more subjective.

If there is one bird unloved even by those who love birds, it is a crow. (In fact they're ravens, but in the language they are crows.) Crows are hated because they are black and symbolise death and drought, because their cawing is maudlin and depressing, and because they are eaters of carrion. What is worse, they eat dying animals before they are dead. Unable to pierce the hide of feeble young lambs, they peck out their eyes and tear their mouths and tongues. For this cruelty – which is consider-able, but nothing to our own – they are abominated.

Here is something a crow did. One morning three brown falcons were hooning around and wildly diving at every living thing, includ-ing a colossal pelican many times their size. It seemed likely they were just enjoying the general commotion their antics were creating, but they must have had a serious purpose because eventually one rose from the banks of a small island with a little egret in its claws. The other two flew off with it to share the meal.

A dozen galahs went back to the dead tree in the middle of the lake where they nest and camp at night. Two others sat lookout on the branch of another tree, three hundred metres away; and a metre from the two galahs sat a crow – talking to them. Not cawing – but talking, in a low and irate voice.

It was still talking when one of the falcons returned, flying at great speed towards the tree where the dozen galahs had settled. The crow took off in hot pursuit, surging to a level a few metres higher than the other bird and then, as the falcon's approach panicked the galahs into the air, the crow dived and knocked it sideways. The falcon recovered its poise, but the crow struck again and again and drove it off the lake. The crow flew back to the two galahs.

Absurd as it may seem, I could only see the crow's behaviour as fulfilment of an undertaking he had given the galahs. It was conscious philanthropy. Later, it also seemed to me to be the antithesis of our ancient belief, alive still in such fables as The Fox and the Scorpion, that animals cannot act outside their (savage) natures. Not for nothing is that fable very popular with devotees of the free market.

A couple of weeks after the episode on the lake, I noticed a teal labouring on foot between two dams, when out of nowhere a falcon swept in to kill it. A millisecond before the falcon reached the helpless duck a crow reached the falcon and knocked it to the ground. Another crow followed up. Feathers flew. The duck fled back the way it had come. The hawk went home defeated. The crows hopped off into some cypresses. It was impossible to see what they had gained from the action, unless it had satisfied some charitable instinct or a subjective loathing for the other bird.

> Then I could fuse my passions into one clear stone
> And be simple to myself as the bird is to the bird.

Some birds, maybe, but not quite as the crow is to the crow. Or the magpie is to the magpie. Or the butcherbird with the beguiling song is to the butcherbird with the habits of a fiend. As I stood under a tree one day, a silvereye dropped at my feet. I took it in my hand and, as its chest heaved up and down, I looked up into the tree from which it had fallen. In the lowest branch a butcherbird was sitting, staring down at me and the bird that he had dropped. A butcherbird would fit in a beer glass, but that stare stood my hair on end. And as it stared, the silvereye's heart stopped beating.

Since then I've looked at many photos of butcherbirds, and none of them has a stare like that. The stare was that bird's and that moment's alone.

And then there is the kookaburra, the larrikin icon of Australia before Steve Irwin replaced it. *Laugh, kookaburra, laugh,* we used to sing. We have in the family a sequence of three photographs of a kookaburra perched in typical fashion on a fence. In the first you can see it has something large in its beak. In the second there is less of the thing. By the third, all that protrudes are a couple of webbed feet on scrawny legs. It's a duckling, a couple of weeks old. If they'd shown that before the Movietone News, this country might have a different view of itself.

The Monthly, December 2007

AMERICA

The 310 to Drippin' Springs

THANK YOU FOR HAVING ME. I am honoured to be asked to give this address to so many distinguished people. Some of you I know have just been elected, some of you have not; some have been elected and not elected within the space of a few recent days. Whatever your personal experience, it has all helped to give the room a fresh democratic atmosphere.

As I said, I am honoured, but I am also conscious of the risks I run. To begin with, I know that many among you are professional and expert, and I'm only a casual observer. And while there are bound to be as well a few amateurs like me, I am aware that there exists in Sydney, especially in the Labor Party, a species of obsessive US fact-grubber whose knowledge of our great ally is almost unnatural. But Sherman did not take Atlanta by sitting around wondering if he was up to the task or contemplating any other nicety.

Sherman's is an example I wish I had followed much earlier in life. Who will argue with a man who burned Atlanta, proposed a final solution for the Plains Indians and, as far as we can tell from the photos, combed his hair with a bayonet? The answer is, only a madman. So I will plunge on without much regard, as Sherman put it, for the humanities of the case.

A few years ago I wrote an essay about the relationship between Australia and the United States. I called it *Rabbit Syndrome* after the character in John Updike's quartet of novels, Rabbit Angstrom. During the

---

A version of a speech given at a United States Studies Centre event in 2017.

course of his life, Rabbit grows fat and wealthy almost despite himself. He has a good brain and is capable of thoughts and feelings beyond his own self-interest, but he is rarely able to exercise them or aspire to much beyond golf, Toyotas, the female pudenda and a sunken living room. The patterns of his thinking and the shape of his life never escape the patterns and shape of hedonism and consumerism, which for most people, let's face it, define what it is to be free.

I used Rabbit as a metaphor for Australia. I also said – and this seems to me the moderately tragic bit – that while Australia exhibits all the symptoms of this rabbit syndrome, the United States exhibited these plus many more – including near-surfeits of genius, altruism and civilised endeavour. We are, I suggested, the ersatz, imitative rabbits, while the United States is the full-blown, high-fructose, energiser battery, *future* rabbit: way out in front in consumerism, celebrity culture, corn syrup, crime and carbon emissions – but also in being the fullest expression of human freedom.

For no more than this, and for suggesting – almost seriously – that our interests might be better served by petitioning for our inclusion in the Union, Tony Abbott and Christopher Pearson declared that I hated my own people: that I was un-Australian. I only meant that we should consider the advantages of taking a seat at the table. Then, if the prime minister thought Barack Obama unfit to be president, or Dick Cheney thought it would be a cool thing for him to say, the PM could say it without making an international goat of himself.

Still, in those days, it was better to be called un-Australian than anti-American. I counted myself lucky. But the episode did go to show how, oblivious to notorious historical precedent, those protagonists of the culture wars appear to think that the only way to serve one's country and its alliances is to refrain from criticising them – and indeed to mythologise them.

Strange how the tough guys of the right spoke of their country as if it had a glass jaw. As if the general population was feeble-minded and couldn't live with contradictions. And it's strange that those purporting to be pro-American should be averse to paradox and anything containing multitudes. Averse to a republic, too.

But I want to leave the culture wars. I wish they had never started and, like George Miller, I am hoping they will end. They are the worst thing to come out of the United States since PowerPoint – and for those of you who feel the lack of that tonight, I'm sorry, but you will have to make do with sentences.

Eric Hobsbawm wrote recently that he been going to the United States for forty years, yet when he stopped in Portugal on his way back to Britain, for a brief holiday in a "small, poor, linguistically incomprehensible seaside town", he felt like he was back in civilisation. I know what he meant. It's the absence of basic services in America, the belligerence of the media, the blatant inequality, the unrestrained consumerism – and the parochialism.

And yet I went to the United States in May 2005, on a book tour, and when I came back I realised that its effect on me had been as it always was – the effect of exhilaration. Italy has charms. So has Sydney for that matter – and so has Tasmania. The United States is light years removed from all of them. I don't mean better – only that there is no place on earth that even remotely approaches the experience of America.

May was before Katrina, and George W. Bush was still polling in the forties. When I went back in October, he had entered a serious slide. Katrina was one of the reasons. So was Iraq. Bush was changing the rhetoric on Iraq, but on one thing he was consistent – he kept talking about freedom. I'm sure you'll recall Bush's promise that "we will see freedom's victory". And how he was forever saying that terrorists "hate our freedoms".

Because it is such a cliché of American rhetoric, we're not inclined to take much notice when American politicians talk about freedom – even when we know that Americans have died in their tens of thousands for it. It shows the annihilating powers of a cliché. In any case, we think, it's less for the freedom that they hate you and more for the hegemony. "Our enemies hate us for our power and influence", would have been closer to the truth – and in truth not much would have been lost by putting it in those bald terms.

And yet if you travel round the surface of America – I went by train and car – the cliché begins to shed its carapace. Migrants with only broken English and no papers in Washington, DC, the descendants of slaves driving battered taxis in Jackson, embittered ex-soldiers in bars, Palestinians in Los Angeles, the proprietors of struggling Midwest motels, hedge fund managers who began with nothing and now

have views right across Central Park, men running scams on the highways – they will all tell you what they think is wrong with America, but
the one thing they think is right is freedom. America *means* freedom.
And if you say that there are other places which are free they will either
show no interest at all or, as a barman and former marine in San Anto-
nio told me, "Oh well, they didn't tell us that at school".

It's easy to grow impatient with American parochialism. It's a standing joke. On a train from Fort Worth to Austin, the twenty-stone Texan
locomotive driver beside me asked me where I was from.

"Melbourne, in Australia", I said.

He took a beat or two to answer.

"Thought you was from Drippin' Springs", he said.

"No", I said.

"'Bout thirty mile out of Austin. Nice out there. You take the 310.
Least I think it's the 310 ..."

He called to his friend across the aisle.

"Get to Drippin' Springs."

"Three ten", his friend called back.

"That's right. Thought so. Take the 310. They got pretty well every-
thin' out there."

You get used to it. You even come to enjoy it. And you learn that the
parochialism also begins with the idea of freedom – not the idea of it,
the fact of it. Because if you think you are free, as free as a person can
be, nowhere else matters. Even if you are an outcast, or a prisoner, or a
deserter: "even he, the man stripped of all values, on whom all earthly com-
pulsions press – there is no man exposed to the breath of the Eternal who
does not once see the star of freedom rising in the night of his isolation".

We can't put it all down to ignorance of other places, and the
freedoms and pleasures to be enjoyed in them. In fact, despite every
unconscionable insult to my social democratic sensibility, I love being in
America because of the tangible sense I have when I am there that I can
do whatever I want. It's like going to the races on a weekday – there is
a sort of guilty pleasure in it. I can grow absurdly rich; I can hunt a wild
animal; I can buy anything I want; I can harbour the most absurd ideas;
I can shoot someone; I can commune with God; I can pay someone $5
an hour to drive me around or prepare my meals; I can be whomever I
like; and, who knows, if God wills it as he wills everything in this world,

one day I might wake up famous. If I can do – or at least dream – all the things that it is in my nature to do or dream, I will much sooner forgive the things my country does that are *not* in my nature or my dreams.

As I said, I know what Eric Hobsbawm means. The statistics are outrageous: on income inequality, poverty, health, wages, working conditions, crime, violence, prisons, energy consumption, the plain ugliness of much of the urban environment. And that's before you get to the political system, which some old observers will tell you is corrupted beyond repair by money and special interests. Or the press – the appalling belligerent brain-numbing media.

And then there's the religion: the numbers who believe in the literal truth of heaven and hell, in the Mosaic account of creation rather than in evolution; and the growth and proliferation of fundamentalist churches and the takeover of others such as the Baptists by right-wing theocrats. Mark Twain was an agnostic, if not, by the end, a full-blown atheist, but he believed there was a need for a religion, if only to maintain order. So long as it was a not an Established Church – he liked the idea of contending Protestants. About forty churches he thought appropriate. But in towns of fewer than twenty thousand souls in the South and Midwest you'll find one hundred and forty.

The statistics will also show that a great many Americans believe in monsters, aliens, Satan and supernatural beasts – not least among them, the Beast of Revelation. I know I'm ignoring the sane worlds of Garrison Keillor and Charles Schulz, but Borges had a point when he said that when you look at American history and popular American belief you see what we often forget – it is, in the end, America, and has something in common with the culture of the countries to the south. It is, for instance, a country in which a great many people live their religion as pretty well no one has lived it in Europe since the Middle Ages – that is to say, with the Bible alive in their minds, with Satan alive and omnipresent and at war with the Lord.

When Katrina hit New Orleans and the Gulf Coast we saw the bad, mad side of the United States in microcosm. And remember, New Orleans is a serious place. This is the mouth of the Mississippi. After New York and Los Angeles, it is possibly the most famous American city. But the calamitous scenes we saw, the disastrous aftermath, might have been from one of the failed states of South or Central America. That is what one of the reports said: the response had most of the characteristics of a failed state. How could this happen in the greatest democracy on earth, everyone asked? How could it happen in a developed country?

There are all sorts of answers to this which are specific to the times we live in and the philosophies that now prevail – but the more general answer, I think, is that "developed" doesn't come into it. Not in the way it comes into Europe or here. America is a very sophisticated first-world country, but it doesn't seem to me "developed" in the way that Europeans and Australians generally think of it. That's because as much as it's a developed country, it's a frontier country – an inexhaustible frontier, with certain frontier values.

And it's a religious country in which many people – from the president to the volunteer workers in New Orleans – see the hand of God in everything. The God who put all those questions to Job, including: "Who provideth for the raven his food when his young ones cry unto God?" The answer, of course, was God – God provides. Not the state – unless He ordains it. Not even McDonald's, unless He orders it.

Tocqueville said that American democracy seeks to "keep [the people] in perpetual childhood … and spare them all care of thinking". Combine that view with religion – which both Tocqueville and Twain thought essential to it – and you have a pretty good recipe for deep quietism and avid consumerism.

The mistake – my mistake at least – is to expect America to be "like" other places. I travelled I think it was thirty thousand miles in America and at the end realised the truth of what Tocqueville called American exceptionalism. God does live there as he lives in no other first-world country. It *is* his chosen land.

America doesn't respond to the Whig interpretation of history. It's not about progress to some higher form of society, but about an endless churn – the capitalist churn invested with divine favour. The present strident anti-liberalism will probably die down, the Democrats will be returned, but America will not start behaving like us as a result, and I suspect if Eric Hobsbawm went back in another fifty years he'd find that nothing much had changed to his satisfaction. The socialist republic of Santa Monica will not spread much beyond its present boundaries.

And in general I'm inclined to be grateful for this. I don't think it's just al-Qaeda that hates American freedoms. I think a lot of the developed world is uncomfortable with them as well. I even think President Bush, at least in his subconscious, means this whenever he makes the statement. But when I ask myself why America intrigues and exhilarates me more than any other place, including this one, the answer comes down to this intangible – at least *almost* intangible – quality of freedom. It produces bluster on Fox News and elsewhere, it produces chaos and social failure, but it also produces a quality of forthrightness and self-possession and articulateness – "a keen practical sagacity, a bold freedom of self-assertion", as Henry Adams describes it – that is lacking in other places. It is blessedly without mateship, yet people are open, hospitable and generous and have an entirely different attitude to success – they actually delight in it, men like David Letterman and Larry King grow teeth just to smile and delight in it. That is why Americans who can afford them grow such teeth – to delight in success.

American freedom also produces, of course, the most astonishing scientific and cultural achievement. I remember driving through New Mexico one day and on this particular day a rocket was to be launched to Pluto, and at Los Alamos they were working on a nanotube elevator to take people and supplies to space, and someone was talking about the prophecies of Isaiah, and Tammy Wynette was singing "I wrecked the car and I was sad / And so afraid that you'd be mad", and I drove through the town where Kit Carson penned up the Navajo with the Apaches, and the town where Billy the Kid shot two men and escaped from jail, and the town where Lew Wallace wrote *Ben-Hur*, and the place where the first atom bomb was tested, and I came to Roswell where those aliens came to earth after the war. And on the same day, I think, Wilson Pickett died. Nowhere else does this happen. Nowhere else could this happen – certainly not in Portugal.

And there's another thing that happens there, at least when you travel around on the surface, and which I never see here. You actually see grace sometimes – not bourgeois gentility, drugged serenity or states brought on by aromatherapy, nor sanctimony of any kind – but startling, tear-inducing unselfconscious acts of grace that seem to me possible only when something primitive and childlike and raw is left in the culture. That's the thing: much that represents itself as unformed in the United States in fact goes to something much older and deeper than anything in the European countries. If you don't know what I mean by grace,

Marilynne Robinson's *Gilead* or Willa Cather's *Death Comes for the Archbishop* give some idea of it. The United States is the only place on earth where my atheism sometimes wavers, and I can only think it is because in the United States the meaning of life so often seems to be, as it was in the beginning, a religious meaning.

We might wish for a new Administration, a less hubristic foreign policy, a better health care system, fewer guns, fewer prisoners and much else that we associate with developed nations – but it would be a horrible thing for the world if we woke up one morning and found that America was on a path to be like us.

As for anti-Americanism, I grew up, by day, inspired by Davy Crockett, Groucho Marx, Louis Armstrong and Robert Mitchum, and, by night, by Gloria Grahame and Marilyn Monroe. And as their frontier was mine and their portraits of good and evil were mine, and as I thought of President Eisenhower in the same fond way as I thought of my Uncle Herb, whom he very much resembled, and as this connection has only grown stronger as my life has proceeded, I believe I am half-American and therefore to be anti-American would be a form of self-loathing.

I'm for loving America: so long as we think of it as Nelson Algren thought of Chicago – that it is "like loving a woman with a broken nose". In fact you might consider making it this new institution's motto, in Latin, beneath the flags of our two countries.

Speech to the United States Studies Centre,
Sydney, December 2007

Faith, freedom and Katrina

Also it is very important that time is allowed for Mr Brown to eat dinner. Given that Baton Rouge is back to normal, restaurants are getting busy. He needs much more than 20 or 30 minutes. We now have traffic to encounter to get to and from a location of his choice, followed by wait service from the restaurant staff, eating, etc. Thank you.

—Email from FEMA director Mike Brown's press secretary
to colleagues ahead of Brown's arrival in New Orleans,
31 August 2005

Oh my God!!!! . . . Just tell her that I just ate an MRE and crapped in the hallway of the Superdome along with 30,000 other close friends so I understand her concern about busy restaurants.

—Email response from Marty Bahamonde, a FEMA
official on the ground in New Orleans, 31 August 2005

CUTTING THROUGH NEW ORLEANS ON the freeway that runs above the tattered rooflines, the Superdome looms out of the dusk, a monument less to Hurricane Katrina than to the bewildering paralysis that preceded and followed it. The press had arrived two days before the marines, the marines before the head of the Federal Emergency Management Agency (FEMA), and five days passed before the president visited the region. Because a significant part – the poorest part – of the city had not been evacuated, large numbers of people had died. More died because help was so late arriving. The president, when he finally showed up, made a point of telling Mike Brown, the old buddy he had appointed to head up FEMA, that he was doing "one heck of a job". Then, standing in Jackson Square with civic authorities and press all around, he declared that the rebuilding of New Orleans would be "one of the largest reconstruction efforts the world has ever seen".

Two months later, there is only one lane open on the bridge out of New Orleans across Lake Pontchartrain. The traffic slows to a crawl. We sit and watch an orange moon climb into the night sky and drop a dozen shimmering reflections in the water. As it rises, so does a smell: of something like sewage but less organic and fouler. By the time we've crossed the lake to Slidell the moon's turned pearly – "soft and copious", as Walt Whitman called it.

Another forty minutes down the road we turn off Highway 10 into Pass Christian, Mississippi – population, until two months ago, seven thousand. The New Orleans gentry kept substantial houses in Pass Christian for 150 years. One of those houses is now jammed under the awnings of a Shell service station. Large houses rest on top of smaller ones. There are houses without roofs, and roofs from under which the houses have gone, leaving them spread-eagled on stumps. It is a work of magical realism: here, one night not long ago, houses roamed around scuttling buildings like Confederate raiders.

Katrina's wind ripped large trees from their trunks three feet from the ground and left jagged stumps as proof of its brutality. It made houses disappear. Yet clusters of smaller trees are standing and for every half-dozen houses in pieces, as if by an arbitrary exercise of will, or the grace of God, a flimsier structure has survived the wind. But nothing survived the sea surge. Pass Christian is ten feet above sea level. On the night of Katrina it was several feet below. When the sea came ashore it moved concrete slabs, washed asphalt roads away, flattened buildings made of brick and flooded every building.

Refrigerators line the streets, all of them taped up because the smell which was intolerable inside the houses polluted the air outside as well. Rubbish mucked out of the houses and stuffed in plastic bags lies on the roadside like heaps of innards. Signs are painted on the walls of the houses: a circle with quadrants indicates the day a house was inspected, the organisation that inspected it, the number of human corpses found within, as well as the number of cats, dogs or other pets found dead.

Somewhere along the road a light glows under awnings stretched across makeshift kitchens and trestles loaded with groceries. In the tents and vans around the awning, volunteers and refugees are sleeping. The vans wear the badges of churches from Florida to Minnesota. One says "Pastor and People, one in the spirit seeking a more excellent way". Another says "Thank God I'm Episcopalian". The light is on for security, but it is also the light of American Christianity.

Biloxi, Mississippi, is twenty minutes up the road from Pass Christian. It's easy to miss on the highway strip of fast-food franchises, Walmarts, Walgreens, real estate outfits, drive-in banks, mortgage houses, credit agencies and churches, all in much the same architectural style and all set on profligate amounts of land. The strip runs for miles along the Gulf Coast and it makes you wonder why on the night of Katrina the Holy Comforter didn't take the opportunity to make a more comprehensive town-planning statement. Some of the big signs are still bent at 160 degrees, but corporate America is indestructible and the really big ones like Walmart, Wendy's and McDonald's replaced their tattered roofs and straightened up their signs within a fortnight.

Evangelical America is no less indomitable. Katrina had hardly blown out to sea before a wave of volunteers of all denominations from all parts of the country descended on the coast. At eleven p.m. in the Lutheran Church only a half-dozen of sixty-five volunteers are awake. The rest are sleeping on camp stretchers and inflatable mattresses on every bit of floor that is not taken up with makeshift doctors' surgeries and donated supplies: breakfast cereal, toilet paper, AAA batteries, canned fruit, mops. When I ask who made the donations I expect her to say Walmart or Dixie but the lady says, "God. God our Guide". Next morning God made the pancakes as well. "He works through our hands", the lady said as she mixed them. Beside her the polystyrene cooler is marked "The Lord is Life".

In April 1960 black Americans protesting at segregation were driven from Biloxi's beaches by a gang of white folks. Those days are over, and if the descendants of those protesters still live in Biloxi, chances are they work in one of the massive sky-scraping casinos. Biloxi's big thing is gambling. But Mississippi's lawmakers don't hold with gambling and they made the operators build the casinos on concrete barges in the water, spitting distance from the beach. They employ thousands of people, about half of Biloxi's residents – or they did until Katrina came ashore.

Most of them won't open for a year, but when they do at least they won't have to be in the sea anymore. The storm surge drove them as far onto the land as they had previously been off it. Recognising necessity, or perhaps sensing a Biblical dimension to this jaw-dropping phenomenon and seeing no other sense to make of it, within a fortnight the city fathers made the casinos' new onshore location legal.

Naturally, the sea that drove the casinos onto land also surged into the residences of those who worked in them. It first knocked down the more opulent houses along the beachfront. The brick walls and everything inside them have gone, leaving only the swimming pools and the crazy paving. Massive oaks lie hundreds of yards from where they grew. They say there used to be a couple of grand antebellum houses, but there is no sign of them. Down by the casinos, an area still cordoned off by the army, a green fishing boat is hard up against one of the walls from the old part of town. Look down towards the water and you can see the path its skipper took when the surge picked him up and hurtled him towards the shore: through a two-lane driveway under the casino, past the five-storey-high guitar of the Hard Rock Cafe and a quarter of a mile inland, till it hit what might have been the post office. In the rubble between the boat and the Hard Rock Cafe a waitress from the nearby Waffle House found a Fender guitar signed by Johnny Cash. Hard Rock headquarters in Florida promised to pay the shipping costs if she sent it back.

In the hours that Katrina raged along the coast, sea birds turned up hundreds of miles away in the car parks of Tennessee supermarkets. They stayed for the day and then went home. But the people have no homes to go to. A lot of them never will. Drive around the streets of Biloxi and you can see why.

Once it got past the bricks, the water surged unrestrained into the weatherboard bungalows behind them, which housed black and Vietnamese communities. Every house was inundated. Of those that survived, most have been mucked out. Piles of plasterboard, floor linings and furniture are heaped beside those houses that are still standing. The air is full of mould and then, as you feel the temperature rise in the mid-morning, the other incomparably worse smell rises with it. For every three houses there are two useless, abandoned cars, grey-brown with salt and dirt. There are tens of thousands of useless cars on the Gulf Coast. Like the houses in Pass Christian, the houses in Biloxi have signs painted on the front wall indicating whether corpses were found inside them. That story is not over – in the last week eight more bodies have been discovered, including two children. No one knows how many more they'll find, or how many were sucked out to sea when the surge retreated.

No one really knows where everyone's gone. More than a million people have left the coast, many more than fled the Dust Bowl in the 1930s. They are living in hotels and motels, temporary shelters, trailers, state parks, with relatives and friends. Birmingham, Alabama, has organised accommodation for 3000. The schools took in the children. The local chamber of commerce found 3000 jobs. In total, Alabama registered 22,600 evacuees, but authorities think the real number is at least 60,000. It is the same with the 26,000 registered in Baton Rouge and the 150,000 in Houston – the actual number of evacuees is thought to be much higher.

Each of the 419,000 registered families has been given $2358 by the government. The money is to keep them in food, clothing and rent, if they can find an apartment or a motel room. But life's hard in America without a car, a credit card, a computer or cash. Cities that used their own resources to accommodate Katrina's victims can't sustain the effort forever. They expect evictions to start this month. They say some of the trailer parks are becoming ghettos. Utilities are breaking down. Only a fraction of the trailers needed for evacuees have been provided. And winter is coming. No one questions the generosity or the resourcefulness of communities across the United States. And of course no one questions the churches. But just about everybody questions the federal government.

Loaded with bottled water, nurses and supplies the Red Cross van crawls around the streets like Mr Whippy, looking for people. Whole blocks are deserted. Then a spectrally thin woman appears on a porch. The volunteer driving the van is a handsome grey-haired Vietnam War vet from New York whose father was in the landing at Guadalcanal. He has a brittle military courtesy. He stops and says through the window, "American Red Cross. Is there anything you need, ma'am, anything we can help you with?" "Batteries", she says. "We've got batteries, ma'am", he says. And his assistants get out of the van and fill a box with flea powder, apples, bananas, crackers, chocolate, a mop, vacuum packs of Alaskan salmon, toilet paper, diarrhoea formula and batteries. Another woman appears and a young man. "Y'all need anything?" asks the New Yorker, adopting the local style.

Over the next couple of hours the Red Cross van finds about twenty people living strangely dignified lives in the mess. It's a great coming together. A volunteer nurse who drove down from Connecticut replaces the dressing on a young man's wounded foot, while another one from South Dakota watches on. A woman caring for a diabetic multiple amputee describes her devotion to the Lord and the understanding of His ways that her mother taught her, while a young man from Phoenix, who is serving ten months in what remains of one of Bill Clinton's national youth programs, ferries groceries into her trailer. A soft-spoken, immaculately groomed woman who looks about thirty-six takes what she is offered reluctantly. She says "Yes" when she is asked if she has children, but "No" when she is offered an armful of soft toys: one of her children is thirty and the other twenty-five. Her sister-in-law is much more enthusiastic and bounds into the Red Cross van to kiss the people in it. There are smiles and hugs and blessings all round until the groceries run out and the van goes back to the church on the highway. It was a good day, says the team leader, "we emptied the van"; and it seems churlish not to share his sense of satisfaction, or allow any doubt about whose souls – ours or theirs – had been ministered to that afternoon.

In New Orleans alone there are twenty-two million tons of debris to clear. The devastation along this part of the coast must have produced at least that much again. It is a monumental task. And yet it does seem strange that after two months these people are still living in mounds of rubbish. Could someone not bring in a bulldozer and clear their streets at least? You sense paralysis. And you wonder why they are being given snack food and not generators and coolers and meat, barbecues. Why they get diarrhoea medicine and not portable lavatories. Why, when doctors are expecting an outbreak of scurvy, people are being given Honey Smacks. In an almost palpable atmosphere of faith, hope and charity you don't want to be critical, but you can't help wondering.

The saying goes in Louisiana and Mississippi that if you're a Lutheran you must be from somewhere else. But Katrina has done a bit for the Lutheran profile: or, as the pastor's wife insists, God has done it through Katrina. Not only did He bring together so many people in a spirit of Christian love, He created missionary opportunities for the Lutherans.

So while groceries and medicine have been dispensed and teams from their little church alone have mucked out thirty houses, there has also been the opportunity for what she calls "mission fill". When God sent Katrina, He sent miracles, she says. She wants to stay and talk but has to leave for the first meeting of Interfaith, a body representative of all the denominations working in the disaster areas which has been established to decide who gets what from federal government funding.

On public radio, a leader of a Louisiana church with 250,000 members also speaks of the opportunities created by Katrina. Far from weakening faith it will strengthen it, he claims. What if fear knocks on your door and faith does not answer? Martin Luther King Jr said that faith *must* answer, only faith *can* answer. The Louisiana minister agrees. He thinks Katrina might be the beginning of an ecumenical awakening and an opportunity for his church and the more traditional evangelicals to take back some ground from the religious right. In the face of such need he believes churches might find common cause and recognise that they must resist hypocritical governments that, claiming to be Christian, give $50 million with one hand, and with the other, in the name of fiscal responsibility, take $50.6 billion from health care, housing and other programs that assist the poor.

People from countries where religion long ago retreated to the background might be surprised to find evangelical churches in the front lines of disaster relief. But religion is in the front lines of everything in this country. The first people to be consulted about Supreme Court nominations are religious leaders, and the first question to be asked of nominees concerns the separation of church and state. It's a country where God is in both the storm and the pancake batter. He is present at rodeos, where successful contestants give thanks to the Good Lord for protecting them and "helpin' me hold on" to bucking bulls. "All credit to Him", they say. He's in football stadiums, where national teams, in breach of their Lord's injunction to pray privately and without display, go down on their knees and pray together. He's in the White House, as we know, and in congressional, gubernatorial and every other kind of election many of the candidates also go down on their knees.

There is certainly anger at the failure of government to carry out its responsibilities or even accept them. It is a disaster as great as Katrina itself, one national newspaper said last week. Another commentator said that in the government response one could see "all the symptoms of a failed state". Marty Bahamonde, the sole FEMA representative in New Orleans when the hurricane hit, called it a "systematic failure at all levels of government". It didn't help that the president, criticised for his slow response to Katrina, was on the ground with his sleeves rolled up within hours of Hurricane Wilma going through Florida eight weeks later.

The critics have not been mollified by the release, in recent days, of emails sent by FEMA director Mike Brown and his press secretary, Sharon Worthy. The emails give the impression that Mr Brown, his wife and staff were less concerned with the emergency than they were with the shirt he chose for television, its sleeves rolled up to show he meant business. As people drowned or waited to be rescued from attics, Bahamonde was in the Superdome, emailing Brown on his BlackBerry, telling him they were running out of food and water, that many would not survive the night, that the situation was "past critical". Brown replied, "Thanks for the update. Anything specific I need to do or tweak?"

Even before these emails made the news, if you asked four Americans what they thought about Katrina, chances were at least one or two would pour forth the rage and shame they felt at the time it took George W. Bush to even seem to notice what was happening in New Orleans. But these days ask Americans to recall *anything* about George W. Bush and you will get much the same response.

And yet the anger is tempered by the common belief – much older than the modern free-market fashion – that sensible citizens should not expect very much of governments. It helps to remember that, in general, where there is more faith in God there is less faith in government, and less reliance on it. As Tocqueville put the equation 170 years ago, "If faith be wanting in him, he must be subject, and if he be free, he must believe". Tocqueville said it and so did Walt Whitman: democracy is inseparable from religion. "At the core of democracy is the religious element", Whitman said, and he meant "all the religions, old and new". That is the sense one had among all the religions old and new on the Gulf Coast, and in the meeting of social justice and religious ecstasy in the Biloxi church. In experiencing Christian fellowship and purpose, they were experiencing America as a place that filled needs beyond the self. And in experiencing this, it seems reasonable to think, those people felt they were experiencing democracy as God intended it in their country.

The churches are carrying so much of the responsibility in part because they never ceded it to government and they are big and strong and fervent enough to fill whatever vacuum the government leaves them. It is as if Katrina recreated the original ground for Christianity: God rained on rich and poor alike, on the just and the unjust. Divided on false lines, they can now unite in the common cause of human need. When everyone's lost everything the words of the old spiritual apply to everyone:

I got shoes, you got shoes
When I get to heaven I'm gonna put on my shoes …
And walk all over … heaven.

If for the churches Katrina is a kind of cleansing, a chance to see in the murk and devastation a light of opportunity, for many in the secular end of town it's a great moment of truth. There are people who say Katrina will have a more profound and lasting effect than 9/11; that it laid bare all the fault lines of American society: race, inequality, energy, the environment. That might explain the seeming paralysis in the place where decisions about such things are made – the federal government. Everything since the dim-witted insouciance of the president in the first few days of the disaster suggests that Katrina created problems beyond the federal government's reach and comprehension. It might wish to leave as much as possible to the churches, state and county authorities, and the good will of communities, but it cannot escape all responsibility. For one thing, it built the levees that collapsed. Two months later, no one has decided what is to be done: about the levees, about the rubbish, about the evacuees, about what sort of rebuilding there should be and, in much of New Orleans, if there should be any rebuilding at all.

There is no leader. On television last week, John Barry, the author of a book about the 1927 Mississippi floods, remarked that Herbert Hoover, the president during that crisis, evacuated three hundred thousand residents in the time it took President Bush to get Mike Brown into New Orleans after Hurricane Katrina. People who know about disasters and people who know New Orleans and the environment of the Gulf Coast cannot understand why a "czar" has not been appointed – a Giuliani or a Bloomberg for instance. Why the Academy of Science has not been called in to work with such a "czar" and the US Army Corps of Engineers. Why no one in government seems to be addressing the questions that are addressed in the opinion pages and letters columns of newspapers every day. The church speaks of grasping opportunities that Katrina created, but the government, when it speaks at all, speaks increasingly of retreating from the big promise made by the president in Jackson Square. Will it take the opportunity to rebuild the regional ecosystem from the ground up or just rebuild the levees but sink them deeper this time? Will it make a Venice of New Orleans as some writers have suggested or, as another wrote to the Birmingham paper, "a slum of the future ... hastily and shabbily reconstructed on sinking earth ... prepared for suffering souls to live out their lives, periodically casting their votes for morsels that promises entice". Conservative Republicans now say that the parts below sea level should not be rebuilt at all. Suddenly they're worried about the deficit.

Newt Gingrich was on television the other night telling young people at a business school that wherever government went on the Gulf Coast there would be failure. He asked his audience to imagine New Orleans if Fedex were in charge. Or McDonald's. Or Travelocity, an internet travel company. It's easy to see that it's been a long time since Newt made his own bookings – and easy to point out that companies generally go where there is profit rather than need. Gingrich, however, was making a different point: US government departments and agencies don't work, he said, because they are built on obsolete models that go back to civil service regulations devised in the 1880s and revised but not fundamentally changed in the 1930s. Government in his view is now constitutionally incapable of providing the services people need.

Gingrich's student audience, it goes almost without saying, were all ears and among them not one could think of a single thing to say in favour of government at all. You wondered what they might think if they had heard a ghostly voice saying that the citizenry "must effectively control the mighty commercial forces which they themselves have called into being". If out of the blue they heard it call for "a far more active government interference with social and economic conditions in this country". What outrageous liberal would they think was behind such words? Paul Krugman? Susan Sarandon? In fact, the words come from the old tiger of American individualism and imperial can-do, Theodore Roosevelt. Obsolete model or not, it's hard to imagine the rubbish would still be lying in the streets if Teddy Roosevelt was in charge of the government. Or F.D.R. or L.B.J., for that matter.

What no one seems to be able to decide is if the government is incompetent because it's a government, or because it has been put in the hands of incompetent people – or cronies. The debate does not always divide along the familiar ideological or party lines: conservatives and Republicans have been among those arguing that government failure with Katrina goes much further than cronyism or the inexplicable slug-gishness of the White House, that it is a symptom of general decline in the status and abilities of government over the past twenty-five years. They wonder aloud about such a government's ability to cope with a bird flu pandemic.

That feels much closer to the truth, perhaps because it is where the failures of the White House and the bureaucracy converge – in the appar-ent absence of will, of purpose, dispatch. After Katrina it is impossible to imagine a modern US government of either stripe having the capacity for a New Deal or even a Great Society. It is easier to imagine that these were aberrations which the last three decades of government, intent on satisfying the wants of the white middle class, have been determined to pull down. Katrina was not a failure of government per se, but a failure of a government that has been compromised, run down and badly led. It was the failure of government in an era when government is out of fash-ion. Perhaps the whole story is contained in one article that appeared in a Gulf newspaper recently: in it a local contractor complained that every day he looked around and saw what he could be doing with his fleet of bulldozers, but he can't get a tender. How come Halliburton can get them, he asks, and I can't?

Downtown New Orleans and the French Quarter are functioning again. The hotels have pumped out their basements and got the worst of the stink out of the elevators. Not that it is easy to get a room: they're full of insurance assessors and FEMA people. It's only when the train pulls out and gets beyond the Superdome that you see the full meaning of Katrina and the statistics it's produced. Nearly half a million people lived in New Orleans before Katrina; almost three months later there are only seventy thousand. Mile upon mile of gutted houses, useless cars, empty streets.

Here and elsewhere on the coast it seems incredible that the country which took Baghdad in a fortnight and nearly forty years ago landed two men on that soft and copious moon can't move the rubbish.

There is a black man on the northbound train with his five-year-old daughter. The mother left when she was six months old. His house in Slidell was washed away and all he owns is in the US Navy duffle bag on the rack above him. He's going to Maryland, where a couple of old friends think he might be able to get a job. In front there's a poor, white extended family of eight. Seven feet of water went through their house. They're going to start again in New York, or maybe New Jersey. An old black couple tells them that New Jersey is better for bringing up kids. None of them is ever going back.

Good Weekend, 24 March 2006

Once upon a time in America

Each day in Zanesville, Ohio, a coal train headed for the local power station rounds the bend in the line at the bottom of Main Street and grinds towards the rusted rail bridge across the Muskingum River. It makes the turn at a tortoise pace, and the symphonic, transfixing howl of the wheels could be a kind of tone poem for the decline of Zanesville. The rail bridge stands parallel to the road bridge: the locally famous Y-Bridge that spans the Muskingum's confluence with the Licking River. The left arm of the bridge runs into ruin – a gas station, an abandoned car yard, vacant lots – the right arm, into buildings a little less desolating to the eye, if not to the spirit. In the grey, polluted water below, every day two or three black men are fishing. A sulphurous odour wafts from the old and blackened "egg products" factory half a mile upstream. Three blocks back up Main Street, in the heart of downtown Zanesville, you can pick up a four-storey Victorian store in good condition for $90,000. The streets are empty, abandoned. Commerce is a ghost. And nothing can dim the suspicion that this place might be a fair measure of the country's future.

The people who built the interstate highways in the 1950s might have done worse to Zanesville: they might have put it right through the centre of town. They could have knocked over the magnificent old four-storey courthouse and straddled the spires of the churches. They could have run the pylons right down Main Street and the Y-Bridge and, who knows, they might have if the hills on either side of the rivers had been differently aligned. Instead, they built Interstate 70 four blocks north of Main Street, along the fringe of downtown, past the Art Deco John McIntire library (a bequest of Andrew Carnegie) and two-thousand-seat Art Deco

419

Secrest Auditorium (a bequest of the New Deal), so motorists heading west to Columbus or east to Wheeling, West Virginia, needed only veer a little to land themselves in the middle of the town. The road builders leapt the Muskingum and the railway line, chopped the end off Maple Avenue, cut Linden Avenue in half and created two Zanesvilles: North, which leans Republican, and South, which prefers the Democrats. Downtown Zanesville, a noble grid of mainly red-brick commercial buildings and improbably handsome churches, lies sad and vacant in between, the lights at the street corners changing all day and night, imposing imaginary order on largely imaginary traffic.

As he steers his Buick under the roaring highway and past the cluster of motels and chain restaurants, Mayor Howard "Butch" Zwelling explains that Interstate 70 makes Zanesville an ideal distribution centre and he points to the Pepsi establishment right by Exit 154. We drive out to the East Point Industrial Park where, on old farmland sites, amid glowing remnants of the Appalachian forest, Dollar General has a massive warehouse, Avon is building an even bigger one and, in a whopping dun-coloured monolith, a wholly-owned subsidiary of the fast-food chain Wendy's makes a few hundred million hamburger buns a year.

The Zwellings have been in Zanesville for a century. Butch Zwelling is a graduate of the town's schools and Muskingum College; he was an attorney there, for more than twenty years an elected judge, and mayor since 2005. He remembers the days when the streets of downtown Zanesville were thronged, when those stately buildings housed thriving local businesses, when the famous potteries were just about the backbone of the town's economy, when a couple of passenger trains and dozens of freights came in every day, the skating rink and Tom's Ice Cream Bowl were buzzing, the old churches were full on Sundays and three synagogues served the city's 160 or so Jewish families, of which the Zwellings were one. In those days Maple Avenue was lined with maple trees so resplendent that the scene appeared on postcards. One national magazine declared Zanesville pre-eminent among model American cities. These days the avenue is a perfect (treeless) example of the gruesome shopping strips that became the new model for American cities in the last half of the twentieth century. Early in October this year *Forbes* magazine declared Zanesville the seventh-most vulnerable town in the United States.

Naturally enough, Butch is having none of it. *Forbes* quoted the following figures: 8.9 per cent unemployment; 16.2 per cent below the poverty line; only 18 per cent with an associate's degree or higher. But Butch quotes the record enrolments at Zanesville's higher-education centres, and the new corporate investment the city is attracting. A Time Warner call centre is about to open. The city has a great airport with a classy lounge for the business traveller. And he's hoping to announce a new $28-million development built around a state-of-the-art theatre just south of the I-70.

And some great shows are coming to the Secrest, including, on Friday night, *Celebrate America* – with Johnny Cash's niece Kellye, who was Miss America 1987, and Karissa Martin, who is Miss Ohio 2008. The same Miss Ohio is singing at the new Primrose assisted-living community's Open Day. She is a slightly built brunette and she sings sweetly enough to please a crowd of budding retirees invited to consider the limitless comforts on offer. Dave Joseph, a local tenor, is also at both functions, and at both he sings "The Star-Spangled Banner" – and then an Elvis song.

There's a bar, a branch of Tom's Ice Cream Bowl and even a cinema, playing *Casablanca*, with a popcorn machine and a Republican girl from Illinois serving the stuff. True, Zanesville might never recover the glory days of half a century ago, but sitting in his office with a photo of his Romanian grandfather in an American World War II military uniform on the wall, and a Bill Clinton talking doll on the bureau behind him, Butch says Zanesville has a great future – and he's such a charmer, you find yourself nodding and saying "Gee" and "Wow", even though you're not convinced and wondering how much good can come to a city forced to play a zero-sum game with giant corporations, how much wealth and energy can accrue from the low wages they pay and the minimal benefits they provide their workers, how the fabled entrepreneurship of Americans can take back an economy in their grip. Or take a measure that really counts: American TV markets are rated 1 to 210. New York is a 1. Zanesville is a 203. Butch presses the button and the Clinton doll says, "I never had sex with that woman"; and then, "It depends what your definition of 'is' is".

In a crude sort of way, politically speaking, as Zanesville goes so goes the country. Like Ohio itself, roughly equal numbers reside either side of the political divide. Butch Zwelling is a Democrat, and in New Concord, a few miles east, the ace pilot, astronaut and 1984 Democratic presidential candidate and former senator John Glenn has lived most of his life. Drive the suburban streets and the Obama–Biden and McCain–Palin signs populate lawns in about equal proportion, sharing the turf as they must with prospective senators, sheriffs, judges and the like, and various "propositions", all to be determined on the same day as the vote for president takes place.

Like Zanesville in reverse, Ohio divides between Democrat Cleveland in the north and Republican Cincinnati in the south. Columbus, a sort of sampling of the nation itself, is the undecided middle. Zanesville is south-eastern Ohio, which begins and ends roughly where the glaciers of the last Ice Age ended. The dividing line between the ice and the moraine is easy to see twenty or so miles west of the city, even when barrelling along the I-70. Zanesville's hills are the moraine. It is west Appalachian by geography, and in many essential ways by culture and temperament. "Gripped with an ungentle sense of religion and fate", Susan Orlean wrote about the south-east of her home state. In truth it belongs in West Virginia, she says, and belonging there – even in a good year like 2006 or this one – makes Zanesville and the county of Muskingum hard going for modern Democrats.

Depending on how you look at it, Zanesville is a city chronically divided, or a near miracle of unity and healing. In the Weasel Boy bar, a scientist from New Concord tells me the region is curious for hosting species overlapping at their most southern and northern extremes. As in nature, so in Zanesville: part southern and part northern; part Appalachian and part, almost, Midwestern. And all those churches testify to godliness and vice in equal proportion. Likewise, to unyielding faith and intellectual enlightenment: the signs of glaciation might be obvious to the scientific mind, but not to those enrolled in Zanesville's creationist schools.

Pre–Civil War, one side of the bridge was pro-slavery and the other, centred round the Presbyterian church of Harriet Beecher Stowe's brother, William Beecher, was abolitionist: the town was part of the Underground Railroad, a haven for runaway slaves. The slavery side had been settled from what became West Virginia, whence came Zane Grey's ancestor Ebenezer Zane, in 1797; the abolitionist side – called Putnam – was settled by people from Connecticut. The story goes that resentment between the two towns sometimes led to violent confrontations on the bridge.

This strand of Zanesville's history still has a way to run. The Ku Klux Klan rallied in the town less than a decade ago, and people say there is still an active local chapter. Officially, segregation no longer exists, but in certain real ways the old story continues. The great majority of black residents of Zanesville live in one ward, the third. Another community, a local lawyer explains, lives on the fringe of town in a place called Coal Run Road. For decades these people asked to be connected to the town's water supply, but the water stopped where the black folk started. Too expensive, they were told. Not enough pressure. But two hundred yards up the hill, white residents had town water. Water was finally connected in 2004 and, after the Ohio Civil Rights Commission found the people of Coal Run Road had suffered racial discrimination, they were awarded $11 million in compensation. The past is not always visible to the present. When the Lind skating rink opened in Linden Avenue, in 1948, it was decided that Mondays – and only Mondays – would be the day for black residents to enjoy the facility. Tom's Ice Cream Bowl started up a few doors away the same year. Not wanting black people coming from the rink to his parlour, on Mondays Tom shut up shop. The Bowl moved round the corner, Tom is long gone and the Civil Rights Bill was signed almost half a century ago, but one half of the tradition continues: Tom's Ice Cream Bowl is still closed Mondays.

Two weeks before the election, the national Poll of Polls had Obama five or six points in the lead. The debates were over. Obama had won them all, the last resoundingly. Colin Powell had just given him an eloquent endorsement to add to Oprah Winfrey's. McCain had made a mess of the financial meltdown, in the course of it offending David Letterman, and Letterman had given him a terrible drubbing. Palin had made a fool of herself on television. McCain had been obliged to reprimand his own supporters. Everything was breaking Obama's way.

For about a week after the Republican convention, McCain had seemed comfortable enough; but in the debates he had looked cranky, resentful and, strangest of all for an old campaigner, confected. He looked like a man out of his skin, which only made Obama look even more at home in his. McCain looked hot; Obama, cool. McCain looked jerky; Obama, fluid. McCain sounded snide; Obama, gracious in proportion. McCain had Palin running for him – but just as often, it seemed, for herself and the pagan fertility cult she had brought from Alaska. Earth mother, wolf-hunter, mystic, maverick: whatever she was, she touched something in the groin of the country and made it okay to be stupid again – or, as the pundits put it, she energised the Republican base. The problem for McCain was that the more she energised, the more he fossilised. All she could find to say about him was that – like a lot of folks' grandpas – he had been a hero a long whiles back, before you was born. And, by the way, he knew "how to win a war". Which war, we wondered? Joe Biden was not half as raunchy or attention-grabbing – but then, he wasn't running for president.

Obama had Michelle, whose skin might have disturbed racists even more than her husband did, but in everything she was gracious, whole, *un*disturbed. McCain had Cindy. David Foster Wallace watched her during McCain's run in 2000, "brittlely composed and smiling at the air in front of her and thinking about God knows what". Eight years later nothing had changed, except that she looked much older than her fifty-four years and less composed than masking a desire for vengeance.

One was in the prime of life; the other was on the way to assisted living. It showed up in the media. Plugging away in the McCain corner, Bill O'Reilly, Sean Hannity, the always-alarming Charles Krauthammer and the rest of the faded Fox News gang resembled ducks as lame as the president they had cheered for so long. They were unwitting parodies of right-wing zealots. But the liberals they scorned were real, as real as their parodies of the zealots. And though it might have been a flight of fancy, it did seem that Jon Stewart and Stephen Colbert on Comedy Central, Tina Fey and the satirists of *Saturday Night Live* and, above all, the almost gung-ho lefties on MSNBC were not only younger and funnier and cleverer than the Fox crew, but more influential. It was like a dream, some nights – America was liberal again.

But nothing Obama did for himself, and nothing the media did for him, was half as good for his campaign as the financial crisis. The financial crisis gave him purchase: it proved his case and disproved McCain's. There was Alan Greenspan telling the House of Representatives Oversight Committee that this "once-in-a-century credit tsunami" had forced him to recognise there had been a "flaw" in his thinking or, as he put it, in "the critical functioning structure that defines how the world works". Was he saying that Adam Smith's "invisible hand" was prone to mischief? That capitalism itself was "flawed"? He looked like Moses might have in his one-hundred-and-twentieth year and, hearing him utter these words, Henry Waxman, the committee's chairman, could not have looked more surprised if the walls of the House had cracked and the ceiling fallen in. The "ideology" had not been "accurate", Greenspan said, which suggested that his sociology might be as flawed as his economics.

Obama did not have to engage his academic mind, of course. The word "greed" did well enough for him. In a country where the minimum wage is $6.55 an hour and tens of millions have no health insurance, the spectacle on Wall Street gave his message of change what every message needs – concrete meaning. It is the strangest thing to an outsider: how optimism is almost a necessary condition of US citizenship. You can spell out the deficiencies of the society, the statistics pointing unmistakably to decline, and they won't question them – but they will say they're *optimistic*. Probably it was this reflex that led McCain to say the fundamentals of the economy were sound; and when he realised they weren't, to say that he had faith in the American worker. American workers didn't need his faith, they needed help – and things were such that at last some of them were prepared to admit it.

But a black man? With a black wife? And black children running round the White House? And the middle name Hussein? They still needed persuading.

The financial crisis should have decided the issue and, in retrospect, it probably did. But two weeks out, that wasn't obvious in Ohio. In Ohio, just one or two points separated the candidates. That was the disconcerting thing: with the country going down the drain, and McCain's campaign a patent mess, by what perverse reasoning were 47 or 48 per cent of voters determined to vote Republican?

The Obama campaign headquarters set up on the abolitionist side of the river, in Putnam. A philanthropist – the executive director of the Muskingum County Community Foundation – made the building available, and in doing so confirmed the suspicions of Zanesville's Republican elites. It's a splendid location by the river, beneath Putnam Hill all cloaked in the colours of the fall, and beside Muddy Misers, Zanesville's best restaurant ("You could be in Connecticut", one patron said), which is owned and managed by a Republican with an absolute mania about his parking spaces. People say they have pulled down mansions in Zanesville because some bigwig couldn't get a park outside the bank.

Obama's people first decided which states were battlegrounds. Then they broke those states into precincts, and the precincts into neighbourhoods, and to each neighbourhood they appointed a leader. Ohio was broken into 1231 neighbourhoods. Where John Kerry had five organisers in a county, Obama had more like twenty-five. Where Kerry had twenty organisers in a state, Obama had more than two hundred. Kerry, as the saying goes, hunted where the ducks are. Obama hunted for undiscovered ducks, timorous ducks, ducks that did not know, or could not admit, that they were ducks. The first task was to register voters – Democrat voters. The second task was to make sure they voted – Democrat. It meant knocking on doors and phoning everyone in the neighbourhood, not just once but several times, right up to election day. It meant braving abuse and menaces and dogs; having doors slammed in your face, phones slammed in your ear. It meant organising teams to drive people who could not drive themselves to the polling booths; and teams of lawyers from all over the country to attend these polling booths and make sure no dirty tricks were played and every vote was counted.

A young woman from Iowa – a Harvard graduate – has been sent to Zanesville as field organiser. Another young woman has been sent in to be her deputy. They have organised several hundred volunteers: from women in their eighties to teenagers; trade unionists, artists, lawyers, mailmen, musicians, students, teachers, people from California and New York, black and white, Christians, Jews, patriots and sceptics. Some of them say this is the best thing they have ever done.

Sending leaders from outside was a good idea, not only because it assured a coherent and consistent message, good management and leadership; but also, it seems likely, because it kept to a minimum the inevitable yammering in an organisation whose members were drawn from every corner and every layer of the community and every reach of local history. Volunteers they are, but this is not to be confused with a Sunday working bee or a church fete. The mood is sombre, driven: as if there was no choice about it, as if they were building levees to save the city from a flood.

"I serve as a blank screen on which people of vastly different political stripes project their own views", Obama wrote. Not entirely blank, surely: change; hope; belief; cool, single-minded resolve – for his followers, Obama projects half a dozen qualities that add up to "Yes, we can". But the big message is unity, binding a divided nation with a sense of common purpose. A blank screen he may wish to be, but there is no denying that he is also a saviour, not a preacher; a figure to believe in and around whom the sad and angry can congregate. People talk about how his campaign has revitalised not only democracy in America, but communities as well. You also get the feeling that, for the duration of the campaign at least, he is revitalising lives, souls.

In the Weasel Boy bar, Tim, a hundred-kilogram mailman with no hair and a black T-shirt that says "I didn't come here to lose", drinks beer with a lawyer whose Republican friends think Obama is a socialist and that to vote for him is close to un-American. The campaign has shone a pale light on the town's dark side. The mailman knows how to handle dogs, which is useful for a political canvasser. What he's not so used to are the opinions of some of the people whose mail he has delivered for years. Canvassing for Obama, he's discovered bigots where he thought there were reasonable people. At this time of the year, people go out into the woods to hunt deer with bows and arrows. Tim goes not to hunt but to watch the deer, the bald eagles, the minks and the beavers from his kayak on the river. He was sitting there in the dark before dawn one time when a blue heron landed on him by mistake. On election night, he says, he intends to paddle his kayak across the ponds where the old open-cut mine used to be and sleep out under the stars.

It must take a bit of courage to knock on doors in a city like Zanesville and a county like Muskingum. Among those doing it is a man from Brooklyn, a writer, sixty years old. He grew up in one of Zanesville's old Jewish households, and left forty years ago. He could have watched this campaign from Brooklyn with all his liberal friends, but succumbed to a great notion that he should come back to his hometown, where he might make a difference. He's been knocking on doors for three weeks.

The Jacksons are also canvassing for Obama. They moved to Zanesville from Cleveland around 1970. He was a star basketball player. She was an academic. They tried to rent a home in a middle-class district, but the owners or agents always found a way to deny them. When at last they managed to buy a house, they found one of their dogs with its head cut off. Then the other one was shot. They had two ponies. Both were shot. A neighbour warned them that a petition was going round demanding that they be forced to leave. The neighbour urged them to stay. They did, and now they both teach and live what seems to be a very comfortable life. They are restoring the home of a runaway slave who started a business and prospered in Zanesville. Zanesville, they say, has always been a place to take in the outcasts of society.

If racism is the first of the prejudices Obama provokes in places like Zanesville, religion is the second. Muskingum County has something in the order of 130 different religious congregations, 40 per cent of them mainstream Protestant. The next biggest group are the evangelicals, who easily outnumber the Catholics, despite the two huge Catholic churches separated by a block downtown. Zanesville, I heard someone say, is "evangelical ground zero". Not all of them will think he is a Muslim, a terrorist, a child-killer or the Antichrist – but some will. And then there are the super-patriots and Second Amendment fanatics. The county is home to at least two militias, or "patriot groups": the Ohio Defense Force and the Ohio Defense Force Home Guard – and some kind of neo-Nazi organisation is also rumoured to exist. There are a lot of guns in town, and doubtless even more in the hills. They are not all in the hands of sociopaths – the decent, the amusing, the civilised, the sane, even liberals own guns in America: multiple guns. But there are plenty who think Obama is determined to take their guns away; and that, they think, is tyranny. The NRA doesn't help: its magazine, *American Rifleman*, says Obama will be "the most anti-gun president in American history". And that Sarah Palin will be nothing less than "a stellar new voice for gun owners in Washington".

A scale replica of Washington's Vietnam Veterans Memorial Wall is travelling the United States this year. In Zanesville, they set up in a big car park between the I-70 and the Secrest, a power station to the side. It was not beautiful, and not a lot of people gathered under the marquee to hear Butch Zwelling speak of the sadness the wall inspires. Dave Joseph sang "The Star-Spangled Banner" again; a baritone country singer wearing black jeans and a black moustache sang "We Made it to Arlington": "Dust to dust / Don't cry for us / We made it to Arlington". And together

they sang "Proud to be an American": "I'm proud to be an American /
Where at least I know I'm free".

Before three uniformed buglers played "Taps", a quiet, articulate man
on a cane stepped to the microphone. His name was Jim Warner, and
he had been a POW in North Vietnam with John McCain. He told the
story, related by Livy, of the man who for love of his country allowed his
captors to burn off his hand. John McCain was that sort of man. And
Warner wanted us to know that it had not been in vain. The Vietnam
War, he said, had "exhausted worldwide communism", and it remained
for "Pope Jean-Paul, Lady Thatcher and Ronald Reagan to come along
and push it off the cliff".

John McCain came to Zanesville two Sundays before the election. Determined to not hand the day to him, in the morning two dozen Democrats
and the local media gathered by the school. They stood there with their
placards while the lieutenant governor of Ohio told them that, being a
swing city in the swing state that decided the last election for the most
powerful office in the world, no other city in the world was more important than Zanesville was just now. What the people of Zanesville decide
might decide the future of the planet.

It was easy enough to get a ticket for McCain from the Republican
headquarters on Maple Street. Butch Zwelling was not invited and, waiting outside the school gymnasium where McCain was due to speak, you
could hear the mayor a couple of blocks away mowing his lawn. State
troopers patrolled the surrounds. A man rode up on his bicycle; in his
early fifties and an Obama voter, he was a long-distance runner with no
fewer than a hundred marathons under his belt. He was the odd man out,
the one person in Zanesville who was not optimistic about the future of
the United States. He thought the country was in terminal decline. The
mayor and a couple of other people had expressed the hope that Obama
might come to Zanesville before election day; this man said it would
never happen, not so close to the election – Zanesville was too dangerous.

As the afternoon began to fade, we saw the flickering lights on the
motorbikes as they roared down Blue Avenue, powering up to the inter-
sections where two would stop, while half a dozen more rode on. It was
an American show, a mesmerising stage routine. The big black SUVs

followed the bikes; then came the great brown bus – the Straight Talk Express – with blacked-out windows, but you could see a little light burning at a table inside: so it was both a bus and a log cabin on wheels. Then the van with the security men, all its windows open, including the back ones; armed men inside in darks suits, their heads swivelling all around, scanning the parks and the big grey Faith Methodist Church opposite the school, but seeing only the troopers in their brown uniforms and the little family gathered to watch in their charity-store clothes, the mother in a camouflage jacket, about sixty, blowing big pink bubblegum bubbles and waving as the candidate passed.

There were two thousand people inside and they'd been waiting for two or three hours. Now they were being warmed up with some heavy metal, and when the McCains came on the roar was visceral. Cindy spoke first. She said that between the McCains and the Palins, they had five young men serving abroad. This the crowd also approved. Lindsey Graham, the senator from South Carolina and McCain's devoted friend, introduced the candidate, but not before saying Cindy was "classy, one heck of a mother, a devoted wife and a great businesswoman", and she would make "a heck of a First Lady". The crowd may not have looked like they had a heck of a lot in common with a classy businesswoman, but they went for it. When he got to McCain, Graham stuck to the military script: "For a navy guy, this is as good as it gets", he said. "A beautiful wife who owns a beer distributorship; four children, two in the military." He whipped up the passions with a story about General Petraeus – suddenly the unimpeachable hero of the patriotic American – over in Iraq, winning the war, looking after our troops, and how liberals at home were undermining him, and Obama had "hid in the Democratic cloakroom rather than defend General Petraeus". They were outraged.

"Forty-one years ago today, John McCain was shot down over North Vietnam", Graham said. "And forty-one years later, he's still fighting! When it comes to our enemies out there, John McCain is watching for you." Enemies? Which enemies? It didn't matter; they waved those little flags.

And McCain walked on in the tumult, thrusting his arms forward because his captors left him unable to raise them above his head. Jim Warner was right to quote Livy: there *was* something Roman about it. No doubt McCain knew his audience, and the patrician in him thought it pointless to give them more than would satisfy their basic instincts. But even by the generally lamentable standards of a stump speech, this one was miserable. McCain is more than a military hero; he is an original wit. Watch him in other contexts and you see how he is attracted to the comic in things, that he can't resist the confrontational thought. In another life he could do stand-up. Not here, however. The speech was typical of his whole campaign: the man did not look or sound like John McCain – or anybody else, for that matter.

Joe the Plumber had been useful for a week or so, but something about him seemed to please McCain's whimsy long after he had worn out his welcome. He seemed to find the comedy irresistible. *Saturday Night Live* portrayed Joe as John's little friend, the imaginary one he kept in a box and talked to whenever he was lonely. If you closed your eyes as McCain talked about him in Zanesville, you could have sworn you were hearing the same sketch.

He had only a couple of points to make. First, Obama wanted to "spread the wealth". Every day he said this, several times in each of anything up to five speeches; and each time he made the quotes with his fingers. Mimicking the gesture became part of Jon Stewart's daily comic routine. Stewart got laughs. McCain got equally satisfying boos. "Boo!" they went in Zanesville. "Boo!" And John McCain grinned and behind him Cindy allowed herself a sphinx's smile. So long as this and other benighted camo-wearing crowds – many of them on welfare, many relying on schools and charities to feed and clothe their kids, all relying on Walmart – somehow contrived to think that spreading wealth was bad, the man with seven homes and thirteen cars would say it was. "I want to strengthen our defences and lower taxes", he shouted, and they roared and shook their flags, maddened at the paltry $611-billion defence budget, incensed that marauding tax collectors were stifling entrepreneurial spirit in the forests of Appalachia.

"We've got to drill offshore! We've got to drill now!" And that, along with forty-five new nuclear-power plants, was the energy problem taken care of. They cheered.

Then he talked about "Joe the Biden", who had warned that America's enemies would test Obama in the first six months of his presidency. Why vote for the untested when he, John McCain, had "already been tested"? For all the cheering, thereafter the speech ground along like a Leopard tank in low gear. "I want to bring our troops home in victory and hon-our", he said, and with that jab at the old Vietnam nerve, shamelessly leveraged his war record. "I have the scars of war … I'm not afraid of the fight. I'm ready for it … I will fight for you, my friends … I've never been the kind to back down." And so on. They were words to inspire frenzies in this and similar gymnasiums all over the country. But they also seemed beneath him. He walked off pumping his arms forward the familiar way, as the band played "Johnny B. Goode". He'd convinced them, but he must have known they didn't need convincing. Outside a man selling McCain–Palin–Joe the Plumber badges was calling out, "Handmade by Americans, laser-printed, not made in China".

In the end, Obama didn't come to Zanesville. The next Sunday, he appeared in beautiful sunshine outside the State House in Columbus. Sixty thousand people showed up. The queue to get through security snaked back through the streets for a mile or more – until the square was packed and they told people to simply mill on the fringes. Otis Redding and Aretha Franklin boomed over the loudspeakers. Security guards stalked the tops of the buildings with rifles and binoculars. Michelle Obama introduced her husband. The audience was charged. Obama had only to light the fuse. But here, as everywhere in the campaign, he stopped short of that. I heard only one King-like line – a "righteous wind of change" was blowing at their backs: it was hardly enough to sug-gest that this was an angry black man running for president. He was cool: so cool and so determined to cover the policy ground that the audience fell into strangely extended silences. When his criticisms of McCain pro-voked booing, he said, "Don't boo – just vote". It was a masterful little routine, and every night on TV you could see him using it somewhere.

The sum effect was an improbable calm. He had kept passion sim-mering, but seemed much more intent on keeping their minds clear, on reminding his audience that the reasons for voting in Barack Obama were not merely emotional, but logical. He would not take them to euphoria. As stump speeches go, it was unusual for having many of the qualities of a lecture, and just enough of a sermon. The congregation went home feeling, I suspected, rather like footballers who have been told by their coach to take things one week at a time.

*

In Fourth Street, between the offices of the Zanesville *Times Recorder* and the Zanesville Police Department, DJ serves espresso and good sandwiches and bagels at Ditty's Downtown Deli. A sort of glowing ember in the ashes of downtown, the tiny shop fills up from seven a.m. with policemen, plumbers, journalists, the mayor … it's what the town once was. DJ is a prince: a Democrat, very likely the biggest elected member of Zanesville's city council and the only one with a ponytail. He loves music and guns, and so do his wife and twelve-year-old daughter. He talks about the depression people felt after the 2004 election. They could not believe the result – literally. They felt sure they had been cheated.

The day before the election, it preys on everybody's minds. Two weeks earlier, on Obama's turf in Chicago, a black bookseller told me he was sure "they" wouldn't let Obama win. "They" would find a way to cheat him out of it. A taxi driver the next day said the same thing: they would rig the vote and come up with a scare tactic to make people – the "stoopidest people on earth" – vote against their own best interests. Now, the polls still show something close to an Obama landslide. They show a win in Ohio. At an elementary school just beyond the city limits, a dozen ten-year-olds say what makes the United States great is freedom. People in other places are not free. In England, for instance, the king cuts your head off if he doesn't like you. With an axe. It's the same in France, but it's sharper. Eleven of the twelve want Obama to win. (Gas prices, they say.) The odd one out who wants McCain reckons Obama has it in the bag. Grown-ups are nowhere near as sure – recent experience and the chaotic American voting system do not permit much confidence.

On the Monday evening, Joe Biden comes and delivers his last speech for the campaign. About eight hundred people walk up Putnam Hill to see him. In a red dress, his wife Jill performs the introduction with perfect ease and a charming smile. Oh, for American teeth! For Joe Biden's teeth! Joe the Biden wears a bright blue tie that makes his skin glow like the autumn leaves and when he flashes that smile, he seems to belong to one of those overlapping species. Joe's a master. He pulls every particle of focus, yet it feels like he's just another guy at the picnic. He praises Obama for his "steely nerve", his "composure" and his "wisdom". It's the last speech and the crowd is small, but he doesn't spare himself and for a long while afterwards he mingles, doling out kisses and handshakes and mock punches on manly jaws and poses for photographs that will sit on mantelpieces for a century. Before he leaves, he wanders over to the look-out alone and gazes down on Zanesville. At the door of the bus, Mayor Zwelling waits to get his ear.

Down at Obama headquarters, the volunteers are still on the phones, long lists beside them. *Are you going to vote tomorrow? Who will you be voting for? Can we help you get to the polling place?* It is remarkable how people can train themselves to be resolute and cool and never take offence. Don't boo – just vote. The next night, in the same hall, they have their reward. Over dinner on the way there, a young waitress says "apparently" Obama's father was a terrorist. The "guys in the kitchen" told her. "It's scary", apparently. But Obama wins; Ohio goes Democrat; the Republicans win in Muskingum, but by only half as much as last time.

In hotel foyers, bars and airport lounges three days later, Fox News was still belting away, but surely only because they had been there as long as the curtains, and no one noticed them anymore. It might have signalled the end of the Vietnam War, and not just for John McCain. Those people for whom Vietnam created an oedipal crisis that only Ronald Reagan could solve are now going grunting into retirement or jail; or, like George W. Bush, to some barren corner of the country where they can commune with God and ghost their memoirs. The game is over. Their enemies, the baby-booming liberals, might crow for a while, but they must know their days are darkening too. Of all the pleasurable sensations Obama's victory and his glorious victory speech provoked – the blind will no longer lead the blind, sentences will be whole again and truth will reign in them, Butch is right and Zanesville will be born again – this was the best of them: we don't have to listen to the sounds of our own generation anymore.

The Monthly, December 2008

Enemy within

I.

I am proposing, as it were, that the nations should with one accord adopt the doctrine of President Monroe as the doctrine of the world ...

These are American principles, American policies. We could stand for no others. And they are also the principles and policies of forward-looking men and women everywhere, of every modern nation, of every enlightened community. They are the principles of mankind and must prevail.

—Woodrow Wilson, 1917

US policy is thus definitively approaching a stage of madness ...

—Slavoj Žižek, *Living in the End Times*

EVERY FOUR YEARS THE PEOPLE of the United States of America choose the person they think most likely to keep them free and safe; and best placed to decide what their country's interests are and how they should be pursued. Among those interests are the interests of national security, which means they are in effect choosing the person who will decide who should be spied upon, selectively bombed or invaded, and who left alone; who should live and who should die; if life on the planet should continue or pretty much cease. Well, if they don't do it, who will? Actual voting is for American citizens only: while recognised as people by the US Supreme Court, corporations wholly or partly owned by foreigners cannot vote, but may contribute as much money as they like to the candidate of their choice. On election day, across the country about 130 million of the 230 million who are eligible turn out to vote, some of them with marvellous knowledge of affairs, and some in bottomless ignorance of everything; some with the tiny part of the brain that enables them to reason and judge, and some with the evolutionary accumulations of instinct and fear that lurk in the other 98 per cent of it.

"We have never been just a collection of individuals or a collection of red states and blue states", Barack Obama told the crowd in Chicago the night he was elected in 2008. The words were just the thing for the occasion, of course, but every day since has given the lie to them. Obama was doing in this speech what all the best American speeches do: laying the stress on the egalitarian and the communitarian, as if the qualities recommended by the Reverend John Winthrop for his Christian colony of Massachusetts four hundred years ago remain the qualities that set the United States apart. But, of course, if any country is a collection of individuals it is the United States. Otherwise all that talk about rugged individualism and the American Dream and doing it "my way" would be so much hogwash. It has to be a collection of individuals or advertising wouldn't work.

Americans are divided on party lines as never before. The lines between red and blue states, counties and communities have never been so clearly drawn. Of course, there are purple states as well as red and blue ones: "battleground" states, meaning states where the contest is tight, where the ducks are, the ducks being the ones hunted by the candidates, the relative handful of people who decide those questions that a presidential election decides for the world. In purple states the differences that divide one state from another divide the state itself. Check the electoral map of Pennsylvania: in 2012 Obama won in just twelve of that state's sixty-seven counties, but he took the state and its twenty electoral votes because he took Philadelphia and Pittsburgh. Since 2008 the whole country has come to resemble a battleground, albeit one, like the Somme for long periods, in stalemate. And 2008 was another age: back then there was only one red party and one blue party. Now there are two of each.

The United States is a miracle of an ever-evolving pluralist democracy and, in the absence of any other candidates for the role, still the last great hope of humankind. It is a wonderland of invention, a marvel of freedom and tolerance, and by most measures the greatest country on earth.

"We are, and always will be, the *United* States of America", Obama said. He surfed on the cheering, and in that moment some of us almost joined in. God bless them, we almost said.

But to think of the United States as a place, or even as a state, is probably the first mistake. While their political leaders will forever say there is more to unite than divide them, in fact the citizenry is divided by cultural, historical, racial, ethnic and ideological differences that every day – every *minute* in the media – make the platitudes laughable. Democrats say there is more to unite them – as they divide them with identity politics. Republicans chide the Democrats for their identity politics while they dog-whistle to bigotry and preach nostrums they learned at the feet of Ayn Rand.

Some of these tears are visible and categorical: in the suburbs and the cities, for instance, where the dividing lines are so abrupt you can find yourself in a different world in the space of a few absent-minded steps. Some are invisible or subterranean: on the highways you cross them, like songlines, without knowing. There are fractures going back to the Civil War and beyond, forces for good and ill generated in now forgotten times that nevertheless impose themselves, even as the politicians declare their "boundless confidence in America's promise" and implore the people to think of tomorrow. The state has been so deeply fractured for so long that only national crises, real or imagined, and their associated eruptions of fear and loathing of an external enemy can bring it together. We talk of Americans wrapping themselves in the flag: they *bandage* themselves in it. The yard signs of the election season are polite disguises for the underlying truth: the United States is a concatenation of sulky tribes, provincial, ignorant and seething with ambition, frustration and resentment.

The first days of June were great days for Hillary Clinton. She had just won the California and New Jersey primaries. In a prerecorded video released by the Democratic Party, Barack Obama had endorsed her as the most qualified candidate for president ever. Elizabeth Warren was busy endorsing her all over the place, including on Twitter. And at last she'd driven off the old wolf who had appeared on the landscape out of nowhere and dogged her wagons every day for months. True, Bernie Sanders was holding out, and Hillary's supporters were unbecomingly narky and impatient with him. But Sanders was thinking of his own supporters: how to keep them believing and wanting to vote, and, before her election platform was agreed, how to bargain as much radical Bernie into routine Hillary as he could. Bernie's crew were going to take some convincing. "Hillary is a bad aunt", an eighteen-year-old girl told me. "What's Bernie?" I asked. "A cool uncle", she said. She was *very* cool, a cool millennial. "Bernie *represents* millennials", she said. "Hillary tries to be *like* them." There was more in that observation than symptoms of a first political crush.

On 10 June Hillary Clinton spoke to the Planned Parenthood Action Fund in Washington, DC. Planned Parenthood had endorsed her way back in January. These were her people. We expected her to be exultant. She was brilliantly not so. As the cheering died down, she offered a history lesson. When Planned Parenthood was founded, in 1921, as the American Birth Control League, women could not vote. In most states they could not sit on juries. It was a crime to offer information about birth control, let alone provide it. Today half of all US college graduates are women and women make up nearly half of the paid workforce. There are twenty women in the Senate. There are women on the Supreme Court and women in leadership positions in Congress. Three women, including Hillary Clinton, have been Secretary of State. And now, the last pane in the glass ceiling, a woman was the Democratic nominee for President of the United States. She resists the applause.

In a steady conversational tone she reminded her audience of the part that Planned Parenthood played in this progress. She thanked them. It was in large measure a result of their efforts, she said, that fifty-one years ago the Supreme Court legalised birth control – for married couples – and soon after, in *Roe v. Wade*, recognised the right of women to have abortions. Planned Parenthood can take credit for the dramatic drop in maternal mortality in the United States, and for the fact that there are fewer unintended pregnancies than ever before, fewer teen pregnancies and fewer abortions.

Clinton drew the links between the work of the organisation and broader realms of public health, economic growth and opportunity, the strength of families. In thanking them, she was doing more than acknowledging the advances they have made for women; more than thanking them for endorsing her. She was also demonstrating that whatever the bitter and often bizarre state of current US politics, the country can change, and not only through technology, or start-ups, or economics of any description. Her paean to Planned Parenthood was to recognise progressive thought as a defining element of American politics, and to acknowledge the grassroots battlegrounds where politicians – Clinton, Obama and Sanders included – earn their chops. Organising around an idea or a cause, networking, lobbying, educating, publicising, protesting and pushing into representative politics to change the world from within – these are American democratic traditions. Hillary Clinton wrote her senior thesis on the subject. Denied the higher offices, grassroots organisations have long been women's political arenas. This was true of both major parties until the election of Ronald Reagan (in the words of a Republican woman) "buried the rights of over one hundred million American women under a heap of platitudes" and handed the women's vote to the Democrats.

Planned Parenthood occupies deeply contested territory. In the most recent physical attack, in November 2015, a religious maniac shot dead three people, including a police officer, at a Planned Parenthood office in Colorado Springs. Nine others were wounded. A lot of people who are not religious fanatics also dislike Planned Parenthood. Jeb Bush wants to defund it. So does the Heritage Foundation, and the largest Protestant body in the country, the Southern Baptist Convention. And of course for most of the ninety-five million evangelical Christians in the United States, some of whom might be called fanatics, Planned Parenthood is anathema.

Donald Trump has called women fat pigs, dogs, slobs and disgusting animals. He says Elizabeth Warren has a "fresh mouth"; in the old B movies that was usually followed by a whack in the kisser. For asking him difficult questions, he said of the Fox journalist Megyn Kelly, "You could see there was blood coming out of her eyes. Blood coming out of her wherever". Pregnant women he called an "inconvenience" for employers; he has said women who have abortions should be punished; that if women want equal pay, they should "do just as good a job as men". When Clinton says Trump will defund Planned Parenthood and appoint justices who will overturn *Roe v. Wade*, she is telling the truth.

One would expect Clinton to shine in this forum, and she did. It was a gem of a speech, and Clinton herself was compelling. One watched thinking she should never leave the conversational lower register in which her intelligence and knowledge are palpable. She's at her best when she speaks as if at Bible study or a Methodist camp meeting. "We love eloquence for its own sake, and not for any truth which it may utter, or any heroism it may inspire", Thoreau wrote. With Clinton talking, truth seems at least in prospect; when she orates, it is more distant. But then, is this what she's up against? Men can hector and bellow as much as they like, but women never? Women must not be shrill?

That's the thing about modern news channels: you can tune out and examine your thoughts, even order another beer, knowing that whatever you just saw or heard will be replayed constantly for the next hour or so, and if it's important, half a dozen pundits – including one or two ideological thugs – will be there to tell you why. And if you can't hear it over the din in the bar or the gym, you can follow it on the supers at the bottom. Though the image might remain, as quickly as the words enter the mind they fade from it, and are replaced by something else. *Is that what Sean Hannity looks like? What's that gorilla doing with a toddler in a pond? Which one is Megyn Kelly? Looks like Muhammad Ali is about to die.* The stupefying loop in which we trap ourselves on news channels might owe something to P.T. Barnum's circus: just inside his crowded tents Barnum had a sign saying, "This Way to the Egress". Thinking they were going to see a curious animal, customers found themselves outside the tent and had to pay to get back in again. And while we're outside, consider what an American election is worth to the networks: for the political advertising that super PACs can finance so abundantly, and from advertising around coverage of the circus itself.

Switch to CNN – it's Hillary. To Fox – Hillary's on half the screen and four heads are waiting to talk on the other half. History is not news. The substantive points of policy, the links she's making, the implications for the country – not news. The news is part of what over fifty years ago Daniel Boorstin, writing about American culture in general, called the "thicket of unreality which stands between us and the facts of life". News is making what he called "a pseudo-event" – or rather a series of them – out of a real one. Elections are news made in the same way. The pundits are not there to judge the quality of thought or action, any more than the candidates are there as authentic, spontaneous beings. An election is a horse race and no one cares what horses are thinking. The pundits are there to judge the quality of a thought or the truth of a remark by the political measure only. It may be a shallow thought or an outright lie, but will it work?

Donald Trump understands the news channels better than they understand themselves. He is a walking, talking pseudo-event, a compilation of them. His "outrageous" tweets push people towards the media and the media towards him. He dominates the news. He wins every day. Even when he loses, he wins. He's turned the whole thing inside out and made the media his lackey. Most people see the news rather than watch it. They see it as they move around: in subways, bars and cafés, the back of taxis, in gyms and hotels. Trump doesn't need to be saying anything much. The shallower the better: his *best* thoughts are shallow ones, he says. He doesn't say the people are shallow, or their perceptions are shallow, though he knows they are. Just as long as he's there. The more he's there, the more people might think he's worth a shot.

As Clinton was speaking to her natural constituency, Donald Trump was about to address one that he needs to make his own. Trump having knocked Ted Cruz out of the race, who else can the Faith and Freedom Coalition turn to? The Faith and Freedom Coalition, one more lobby group that man has made of God, is pro-life, pro-marriage, pro-family, pro-economic growth. "Restoring America's greatness and founding principles" is the banner under which the members march. They like to quote Tocqueville: "The safeguard of morality is religion, and morality is the best security of law and the surest pledge of freedom … The Americans combine the notions of Christianity and of liberty so intimately in their minds, that it is impossible to make them conceive the one without the other". It remains hard to decide which is the more remarkable: the way Tocqueville saw into the American mind, or how, after nearly two hundred years, the American mind is so little changed.

Faith and Freedom is run by Ralph E. Reed, a political associate of the corrupt lobbyist Jack Abramoff. In 1983, while Reed was drinking in the Bullfeathers pub in Washington, DC, the Holy Spirit approached him and demanded he come to Jesus. He did: he joined the Assembly of God by public phone that very night. It was not an agreement that required him to break off the relationship with Abramoff. According to Reed, the Faith and Freedom Coalition is the twenty-first-century version of the Christian Coalition of America, the creature of Pat Robertson, an evangelical media mogul who numbered among his many business associates the Liberian dictator, war criminal and harbourer of al-Qaeda terrorists Charles Taylor. To Trump's audience, the story of Planned Parenthood that Clinton so admired was an outrage to God and a disgrace to their country. She might call it "giving women control of their own reproductive cycles": they call it denying "the ['God-given and unalienable'] right to life of all innocent persons, from fertilization to natural death". (The threat is contained in the "innocent".) Faith and Freedom asks members and visitors to its website to sign a pledge calling on Congress to "defund Planned Parenthood immediately".

A week earlier, speaking in San Jose, Clinton had attacked Trump as "temperamentally unfit" to be president. The pundits judged it a significant move, possibly a good one. Trump tweeted: "Bad performance by Crooked Hillary Clinton! Reading poorly from the teleprompter! She doesn't even look presidential!" Every day, he tweets something about "Crooked Hillary". For half the country it's her name.

In 1999 Donald Trump gave an interview in which he said he hated abortion, but was – and he was emphatic about it – pro-choice. There was a time when the first President George Bush and Mitt Romney were pro-choice too. They changed their views in time to run for the White House. Who can blame them when more than one in four of the population are evangelical Christians? The evangelicals can't: what's the point of evangelising if not to bring about a change of heart? The religious right hates Planned Parenthood and Donald Trump needs their votes, so now he hates them too. That's okay with the religious right.

Trump's enemies can't help but mock the way he looks. But they mocked Ronald Reagan too: his face, "in repose, suggests the work of a skilful embalmer", Gore Vidal said. But as with Reagan, so with Trump: what about his appearance is not American? The improbably perfect, pearl-white teeth? The glowing skin? The invisible nips and tucks? The coif: I have been told that his hair seems to lead such a mesmerisingly independent existence because science has contrived to attach it to his head by what amounts to a system of guy ropes – each strand actually fixed to his scalp has another six grafted onto it. So Donald Trump has worked on his appearance. What American who wants to succeed has not?

He doesn't have the family with him today. Sometimes he lines his blonde women up like prisoners stolen from a rival beauty pageant. He has a teleprompter, and he looks awkward with it. But he begins with just a few notes, and his pitch is impeccable, if a little ingratiating to some tastes. Some tastes might be to violently gag, but this audience is used to ingratiating. They take his imitation of a God-fearing Christian as the sincerest form of flattery. He thanks Ralph Reed: "He's been just an amazing — just an amazing guy, an amazing support, a terrific man". "I happen to be Presbyterian", he says with a demure smile, and draws applause. "There's about three of you out there", he says, coyly again. Calvin and Knox gave rise to this? Droll Donald.

Yet Trump is speaking to Tocqueville's observation: Christians, evangelicals in particular, but others as well, demand presidents who believe in God for the assurance it gives them that the covenant will be observed. "It is you yourselves who have called us to this office", John Winthrop said; "and, being called by you, we have our authority from God". In Winthrop's hands, at least, it's not an entirely nutty proposition, even if it takes nutty forms and nutcases often proclaim it. As much as it is the people's will to elect their governors, it is God's will to have them do so: a guarantee of obedience, up to a point. But there can be no covenant with a non-believer, and no assurance of God's favour, if the office has not "the image of God eminently stamped upon it". The essentially Calvinist notion gathered force in an elemental union with patriotism, which developed through the nineteenth-century revivals and declared the meaning and purpose of the United States to be God's meaning and purpose. "Patriotism should constrain us to evangelize this nation", the Home Missionary Society insisted in 1842, when they were a force.

Americans want a president through whom God can act. But as well as the right president, it must be the right god. Trump understands this too. Lacking a little in the way of theology and bereft of the faith that "electrifies the whole man", he electrifies them instead with a burst of popular cant: "Radical Islamic terrorism is … taking over and we can't let that happen. We cannot let that happen!" He is yet to refer to the "Islamo-progressive axis of evil" or declare that the Muslim Brotherhood has infiltrated every reach of government and is "'weaponizing political correctness' to shield themselves from criticism and keep us blinded to their ultimate objectives": perhaps his speechwriter missed it on the Faith and Freedom website. "It's happening all the time", he says.

Now he's back talking as if he has the wafer on his tongue and is wondering when he should swallow it. How good the Christian community has been, he says. What wonderful support he's had from the "wonderful Christian leaders and Christian voters". How wonderful faith is. "For not he that commendeth himself is approved, but whom the Lord commendeth." He didn't say this, but he might have. How wonderful. How wonderful that anyone can believe he's sincere. But they do.

"Okay", he says and looks towards the prompter. "It's an honour to speak here today and discuss our shared values." "Here are the goals. And I … put some of these together … just the other night, because of this [meeting]. I wanted them to come from *me*, from my heart." Of course we were not expecting one of those revivalist sermons that took the American soul (and the American language) to heights of the sublime, but his goals came across sounding less heartfelt than talking points some management-trained campaign hack had written out and Trump was seeing for the first time. "We want to uphold the sanctity and dignity of life." Cheers. "Marriage and family as the building block of happiness and success." More cheers. He reads carefully and emphatically, but the words are peculiar: "The people who go to church, who work, and work in religious charities, these are the foundations of our society. We must continue to forge our partnership with Israel and work to ensure Israel's security." Cheers and whistles. He makes a mess of whatever he was meant to say about the freedom of religion and race and the colour of people's skin, maybe because he choked when he got to the bit about freedom of religion and remembered what he'd just been saying about Muslims. He escapes into cliché: the country is divided and "we're going to bring our nation together".

Then he's into "Crooked Hillary". He tells them that she wants a 500 per cent increase in Syrian refugees. Boos. A young woman stands and shouts, "Refugees are welcome here", and goes on shouting while three giant bull-necked bouncers haul her out of the room, and the faithful chant, "USA! USA! USA!" Then two more young women stand and shout over the chant, "Build bridges not walls!" They too are dragged out as Trump says, "What's happened in our country is so sad. We are so divided … By the way, these are professional agitators, folks. They're sent here by the other party".

Now, with his Mussolini pouts and grimaces, he escorts them round the panoply of Hillary's base intentions: federal funding of abortion on demand, up to birth; "Obamacare" – bureaucrats making decisions about your health; abolition of the Second Amendment (the NRA, he reminds the crowd, has just endorsed him – "Wonderful people"); her "Wall Street agenda will crush working families"; she'll put bureaucrats, not parents, in charge of our lives; she'll destroy our inner cities, trap children in poverty, "raise your taxes tremendously", "plunge our poor African American and Hispanic communities into turmoil and even worse despair. Believe me. You look at what's going on".

And then the emails: "Hillary Clinton jeopardised national security by putting her emails on a private server, all to hide her corrupt dealings. This is the reason she did it, folks". "Bill and Hillary made $153 million giving speeches to special interest groups since 2001". (Fact check: it was $153,669,661.00.) Hillary's donors "own her". "Bernie Sanders was right about that." Trump spent $55 million of his own money to win the primaries, and he did it for you. Yep. He's going to put America first …

But the networks have to cut him short because down in Dallas shots have been fired at Love Field, a domestic airport. All the networks have now gone to Dallas. A video has been posted on Instagram. There's a voice – presumably a policeman's – shouting, "Get down! Get down!" The policeman seems to be backing out of the terminal with his gun aimed at something on the floor. He seems to fire at whatever it is. Nine shots. The networks put the video on loop and it rolls for the next hour while their experts speculate. Is it a terrorist attack that's "unfolding"? It doesn't look like it. But if you have the technology to be there and bring it to us as it breaks, what else can you do but speculate aloud? Just wait and see?

It turns out the man being shot at was armed, but only with a rock. He was African American. He'd been trying to smash the windows of his girlfriend's car, first with a traffic cone he'd picked up off the road, and then with rocks from the verge. She had dropped him off at the airport and dumped his luggage on the pavement – you can see it all on the CCTV footage the airport released later. Love gone wrong is all it is. They shot him when he made for the airport door. They shot him again when he was half inside.

But that's not what people see when it's "breaking news". They see an unseen menace. A gun extended. Excited shouts. Shots. People hurrying out of harm's way. "Oh, my God!" they say. The anchors listen in their earpieces for new developments. Is it a terrorist attack? "It's happening every day", didn't Donald Trump just say?

2.

There is always a philosophy for lack of courage.

—Albert Camus

*I became far better at arguing my point of view and far more satisfied with
my political positions once I became a conservative, because I realized I
was correct. It's the same thing a lot of people have when they convert to
Christianity. They suddenly become very committed and dedicated to it,
as opposed to the ambivalence they had about their former atheism.*

—Mark Belling

It is easy enough to find the East and West Coast liberals, and the southern and Appalachian rednecks, and the battered and embittered working
class of the rust belt. Just follow the money, the assault weapons or the
electoral maps. I was looking for a place that was not one thing or the
other, a normal sort of place. I thought the Midwest, the farming states,
the heartland. Wisconsin is the state of big dairy farming – the most
"normal" farming of all. Wisconsin combines farming, industry and a
great university. It's a model of American moral seriousness, Yankee
patriotism, political pragmatism and steadfast values. The "nation's
ballast", one writer called it. In other places it's called "America's Dairy"
and "Cheeseland", for Pete's sake. That sealed it.

It is possible to conceive of American national identity as consisting
of two dominant affects: one communitarian, the other individualistic;
one surrendering to church, community or state, the other masterless;
the steady farming family and the restless wanderer; the town lawyer or
teacher and person of ideas, and the rancher, the man of action; the east-
erner (James Stewart) who thought he shot the devil Liberty Valance,
and the man of the west who actually did (John Wayne). Wisconsin, like
the rest of the Midwest, is a product of both ideal types. The wild and
hairy trappers gave way in the mid-nineteenth century to respectable
homesteaders, many of whom had given up their stony blocks in upstate
New York and New England for the 160 stone-free acres on offer further
west. The settlers craved independence and saw it offered in the land.

In his 1860 election campaign Abraham Lincoln adopted a slogan that had been doing the rounds with radical reformers – "Vote Yourself a Farm". The people did and the *Homestead Act* passed two years later.

In Wisconsin these people of gumption and courage repeated the community-building patterns of the places they had left. They dominated Wisconsin's commercial and political institutions long after they created them. The same morally upright, improving values of the nonconformist churches came with the next wave of settlers, from northern Europe and the British Isles, and laid the foundations for a century of progressive politics.

But you can't fly anywhere – not even to Cheeseland – without going through security. You arrive in the United States and they tell you to put your hands up – that's after they've told you to stand in a glass booth. In Los Angeles a week earlier I made it to the queue for security an hour after joining the queue for customs – with an "express" card. It's the same at LaGuardia. Getting to the other side without screaming, barefoot and possibly with your trousers round your knees, is mainly in the breathing. Once you're through you can sit down and chill out watching Fox, and marvel that the fear is now so universal you never hear a word of complaint.

We fly in over ice-blue Lake Michigan. Squatting on the south-west shore, Milwaukee's gleaming skyline looks brave and prosperous. The inhabitants endure one of the country's toughest winters, but the cold gives them character. Milwaukee is a byword for hardiness, as it is for industry. Many of the city's residents are descendants of nineteenth-century European migrants who came looking for land and wound up factories and breweries – Milwaukee used to be one of the biggest beer-making cities in the world. German Poles gave Milwaukee brewing, bratwurst, precision engineering and socialism (in days past it elected socialist mayors), and their traditions, although a little faded now, continue in religion, festivals and food. Most of Europe is represented in the white population: Italy, Ireland, Serbia, Sweden, Norway, Greece, Russia; Catholics, Lutherans, Christian Orthodox and Jews. Milwaukee was for a long time the "most foreign city" in the United States.

Milwaukee is both a model twenty-first-century economy and an echo from the days when industrial enterprise went a long way to defining the United States and its heroic, well-paid, hardworking citizenry.

The same citizenry were immortalised after a fashion in *Happy Days* and *Laverne & Shirley*. The city's manufacturing tradition continues, even though professional and service industries now create more wealth and employment, and give the renovated downtown modern ambience. Briggs & Stratton and Harley-Davidson still have their headquarters there. Milwaukee still makes high-quality power tools, mining and agricultural machinery and X-ray equipment. They still have Rockwell Automation and one or two other Fortune 500 companies. Given that jobs in US manufacturing fell by 29 per cent in the first nine years of the twenty-first century, on the surface Milwaukee has not done so badly.

But look closer and you see one of those subterranean divides. Milwaukee is rust-belt USA: surviving, but much changed. In 1960 it was a city of 740,000 people: now it's less than 600,000. The white proportion of the city's 2010 population was just 37 per cent, about half what it was in the mid-twentieth century. Seventeen per cent now identify as Hispanic or Latino, more than four times the number of fifty years ago. African Americans make up 40 per cent. In a state with an abolitionist, Underground Railroad history, it is the most segregated city in the country. The almost exclusively white surrounding suburbs hived off from what a Republican official in 2014 called "the colored section".

When African Americans came to Milwaukee in the 1960s the city had begun to decline. There were no jobs that could not be filled by white workers drifting down from the fading lumber industry in the north. No black middle class arose, and no leaders. They began as an underclass and remained so. Now four out of five black children in Milwaukee live in poverty. In a country with more people in prison than anywhere else on earth (China possibly excepted), Milwaukee has the highest rate of incarceration of any city. Forty per cent of the Milwaukee male prison population are there for low-level drug offences: mandatory "three strikes and you're out" sentencing tripled the Wisconsin prison population between 2000 and 2008. The state now spends more on its correctional system than it does on its education system. In public schools, the "achievement gap" between white and black students is the widest in the country.

That noble skyline is a lie. Milwaukee is one of the four or five poorest cities in the United States. Among many other signs of what that means, sixteen thousand adults and children are evicted from their rental properties each year. *The New Yorker* reported on "sheriff squads whose full-time job is to carry out eviction and foreclosure orders … moving companies [that] specialize in evictions, their crews working all day long, five days a week". That's what a model twenty-first-century economy can do for you.

Milwaukee votes Democrat: 67 per cent of them voted for Obama in 2008, 15 per cent more than the state as a whole, and in 2012 the figures were exactly the same. But leaving the city on the I-94, you pass through the suburbs of Waukesha County, a creation in the main of "white flight" and a Republican voting bloc without equal in the United States. Waukesha is the seat of Wisconsin's governor, Scott Walker.

The son of a Baptist preacher and educated at Marquette, a Jesuit college, Walker believes he was called by God to politics. "God has told me I'm chosen to cut taxes and stop killing babies", he once said. He is backed by business, the religious right and, crucially, by two right-wing radio jocks, Charlie Sykes and Mark Belling. Sykes and Belling have shows on the same station that combine into a conservative "SykesBelling" force. Their audience, the ex-urban blue-collar "septic tank belt", "married women at home with kids" and "old white men", form the base of the Republican Party.

Both Sykes and Belling started out as liberals and converted to what they call conservatism. Both are zealous supporters of Scott Walker and, by most definitions of the term, racist. This from Belling concerning a black Congresswoman, for instance:

> What do you think the chances are she was sitting on the toilet? … Maybe Gwen was sitting there on the crapper and this was one that was not working out too well for her or something. "Blew-ee!" "Congresswoman, you've got to vote." "I am sittin' on de toilet!"

Walker and his Republican-controlled state legislature have cut budgets for programs that might help the African American population, pushed for private-school vouchers that undermine public education, with great thoroughness and finesse gerrymandered the electorate for the next decade, stripped collective bargaining rights from unions and introduced voter ID laws that are calculated to disfranchise anything between 200,000 and 350,000 underprivileged voters.

Wisconsin Democrats will tell you that Walker has divided the state to an unprecedented extent, and overturned a tradition of cooperation between the major parties. With the prolonged civil upheaval that his labour laws provoked in 2010–11, the old divides became polar opposites, "different planets" which Republicans characterise as "makers versus takers". Reading a racial dimension into the phrase is optional. It is not just a matter of different parties: social researchers find entirely different worldviews. As a consequence, they say, the will to find answers to big problems dies on the ideological battlefield. Wisconsin, the nation's ballast, is now a fair measure of its predicament.

In a Buick, courtesy of a splendidly successful government bailout of General Motors, I drove the sixty miles west to Madison. Madison is a progressive, liberal, Democrat university town. I read that someone once said Madison was "thirty square miles surrounded by reality". So I was driving through the reality: looking for it in the green and fallow fields and the homey-gothic farmhouses of purest white with their porches and verandas, on immaculate oak-shaded lawns. They perch their homes on low rises, as if to memorialise their triumph over the land and human weakness. Something in their pristine ethereality whispers God or an uneasy element contesting with Him.

Flags flew in the towns, but rarely on the farmhouses: was some Puritan horror of icons at work? The Holstein cows did not graze in pasture but milled round the regulation red barns of the American Midwest, waiting to give up their milk, quite possibly to undocumented Mexican workers, thence to one of the mighty conglomerates of a consumer market that grows ever more concentrated. And ever more irksome to Senator Elizabeth Warren: "It was one of the basic founding principles of our nation", she says. "Concentrated power anywhere was a threat to liberty everywhere". Even cows are tethered to the dictums of the founding fathers.

The shock jocks seemed not to be broadcasting. The rental car was tuned to a Christian evangelical station and I left it there. In fact it was not so much a Christian station as an anti-Muslim one. The preacher's solemn exegesis of Paul's Second Letter to the Corinthians seemed but an excuse for the denunciations of Islam that every five minutes interrupted it. Paul's letter could be taken to recommend a little tolerance and humility: "But we will not glory beyond our measure, but according to the measure of the province which God apportioned to us as a measure ..." The station announcer was having none of it. Love thy neighbour as thyself – phooey! The Christian god and the god of Islam are not the same, and it is a dangerous liberal fallacy to think otherwise. Islam exists to destroy Christianity. Christians are engaged in a war for survival. The US government has been infiltrated. So VCY America waged war in the bucolic calm while the Holsteins (each one generating $34,000 in economic activity, according to a Scott Walker press statement) moped and the green grass swayed and glistened in the sun. "The media, our schools and even our financial institutions are being infiltrated through covert tactics designed by Muslim leaders years ago. Their goal is simply to create an America dominated by Islam", the station website says. Substitute "communist" for "Islam" and "Muslims", and every word could have been uttered by Joe McCarthy in the '50s.

In his famous book published on the heels of the McCarthy era, Richard Hofstadter discerned a "paranoid style in American politics". McCarthy might have been the main target of his investigation, but he found in US history examples of the same "style" among left-wing populists, including the early twentieth-century trust-busters. At other times, paranoid waves have been fed by imagined Masonic conspiracies, Protestant conspiracies and Catholic conspiracies, Jacobin conspiracies, slave-owner conspiracies and international banker conspiracies. Today Hofstadter might find elements of the same style in Bernie Sanders's insistence that the country is being run for the all-but-exclusive benefit of Wall Street's billionaires and millionaires. But he would find the paranoia is deepest where he found it in his own day, on the right wing of American politics among the Tea Party people, the birthers, the Trump supporters. In 1964 he wrote:

> But the modern right wing ... feels dispossessed: America has been largely taken away from them and their kind, though they are determined to try to repossess it and to prevent the final destructive act of subversion. The old American virtues have already been eaten away by cosmopolitans and intellectuals; the old competitive capitalism has been gradually undermined by socialistic and communistic schemers; the old national security and independence have been destroyed by treasonous plots, having as their most powerful agents

not merely outsiders and foreigners as of old but major statesmen who are at the very centers of American power. Their predecessors had discovered conspiracies; the modern radical right finds conspiracy to be betrayal from on high.

It's a generally accepted theory that the modern American right came out of the south in the '60s after the passing of the Civil Rights Bill. There's another theory that its origins lie in California in the '30s, when big business jacked up against Roosevelt for empowering unions. Roosevelt had the quaint idea that by raising wages and living standards, unions might help the economy revive. The theories no doubt are good ones. Yet when you're among the grassroots right they don't talk about unions or civil rights for African Americans. They talk about freedom. At the Tea Party rally I went to in 2009, the local Republican baritone sang, "I'm proud to be an American / Where at least I know I'm free", and everyone who took the microphone talked about the people "on high" who were eroding their freedom by taking away their assault weapons or imposing Affordable Care on them. They talked too of the people who had died defending freedom. Their banners read: "I'll keep my guns and my liberty. You can keep the Change". "Less taxes. Less government. More freedom." The Kochs might have written them. *Really*, they might have – they finance the Tea Party, including their advertising.

Of course, they will also talk about the threats from *Roe v. Wade*, the federal deficit, Islam, atheism, evolution, homosexuality, the United Nations, trade deals, the military-industrial complex, and Hillary Clinton and other politicians from both sides who have sold them out and want to take their guns. At some point they will put their hands on their hearts and look up at the flag as someone sings "The Star-Spangled Banner".

But freedom is the thing: they speak of it as God-given and guaranteed by the Constitution, and therefore as if it exists only in the United States. It must be a tic passed down from the Revolutionary War. They think that nothing's changed in Europe since 1778. It's useless to tell them that people are free in many other countries as well, and free from worrying about freedom so much, many of them. In America, the rest of the world drops out of sight.

American political analysts have written millions of words in explanation of the Tea Party phenomenon. But the novelist and Christian essayist Marilynne Robinson might come as close to truth as any of them. In an interview this year, Robinson spoke about "a glacier of fear ... creeping toward the culture". In an earlier essay she wrote: "First, contemporary America is full of fear. And, second, fear is not a Christian habit of mind". She sees fear in the way the right talks about immigration, for instance; on Fox News, in the "commodification of anxiety and hostility through media"; in attempts like Scott Walker's to reduce voting rolls in Wisconsin; in "Americans ... now buying Kalashnikovs in numbers sufficient to help subsidise Russian rearmament"; in the snake's nest of conspiracy theories, be it that the president is a radical Muslim born in Kenya, or the United Nations has a plan to conquer the whole world, including Texas. She would see fear now in the bizarre dehumanised riot gear in which phalanxes of police confront Black Lives Matter protesters on suburban streets.

By way of explaining how a self-professed Christian country could be gripped by fear, Robinson offers the example of a sixteenth-century French citizen on his way to slaughter Calvinists: he "would no doubt have said that he was taking back his city, taking back his culture, taking back his country, fighting for the soul of France". The ghastly massacres of that era were incited by fear: "by the thought that someone really might destroy one's soul, plunge one into eternal fire by corrupting true belief even inadvertently".

To "fear hobbyists", Robinson says, fear is addictive, a stimulus, and an incitement very often to violent and terrible acts. For Robinson this marks a change in American values and aesthetics. Fear has never been an admirable human trait, particularly in a country that draws much of its self-image from the frontier, and much of the remainder from the example of Jesus. Yet Americans, who once admired courage above all human qualities, now seem to get high on fear. Not that we see them trembling; but we see and hear fear's most common disguise, belligerence. From the very beginning that was the Bush administration's response to 9/11, and it is what we have heard from the Republican Party ever since. It was the mood of the Tea Party. Not the quiet courage once personified on the screen by Gary Cooper or Spencer Tracy, or the real-life self-effacement of General George Marshall, but the belligerence whipped up and exploited by Donald Trump, and the preening self-aggrandisement (and self-enrichment) of General David Petraeus.

Robinson makes a point familiar to viewers of old Hollywood films, that much of the far west and the Midwest was settled not by gunslingers but by communities, very often *religious* communities, descended in spirit from the Puritans. Communities much like the ones through which this highway I was travelling passed: where people once lived out their winters in sod huts, where courage was a close relation of humility and grace, of turning the other cheek, of generosity and sacrifice, and – Native Americans aside – of a mutual obligation to provide liberally for all. Something of the same order is implied in the preamble to the Constitution.

Yet for every dozen Hollywood westerns in which a good community was terrorised by a dreadful individual, there was one in which a community gone to the bad was put right by a good individual. Communities have within them the seeds of horror, as Robinson knows very well. Perhaps her fellow Americans are less inclined to burn witches. Very likely, fewer of today's fearful believe in the eternal fire, but listen to swathes of them and you could be forgiven for thinking they feel their very souls are threatened. And why not, when so many of them continue to believe that their country, no less than the early religious communities, is ordained by God, has "His image stamped upon it" and, when it is not betrayed by government or threatened by axes of evil, walks the path He has chosen. No other nation so relentlessly pores over its founding documents as if, like the Scripture they also pore over, they contain the sacred and inviolable truth and any breach of their tenets is a blasphemy and a threat to existence. While it might recede from time to time, the fear – and the anger and aggression – will remain as long as this exceptionalism is the nation's creed.

Noble and creative as it has often been, provider of an essential thread in the best of the American ideal and source of a rare grace one encounters only in the United States, American Christianity also disguises fear and feeds ignorance, paranoia and prejudice, along with a readiness to smite enemies with weapons of unspeakable destructive force. This too is American exceptionalism.

3.

On, Wisconsin! On, Wisconsin!
Champion of the right.
"Forward", our motto
God will give thee might!

—Anthem of Wisconsin, verse 2

Corporations and individuals allied with corporations were invited to
come in and take what they would . . . I determined that the power of
this corrupt influence, which was undermining and destroying every
semblance of representative government in Wisconsin, should be broken.

—Robert La Follette, 1897

One feels the might of the ice sheets in Wisconsin much as one senses the vanished sea in the Australian inland. The Wisconsin Glacial Episode, which ended eleven thousand years ago, left not only the lakes and the landforms, but a spectre. The frontier is long gone but you sense it. Even in summer you sense the winter, and find yourself wondering at the qualities men and women brought to bear to make the wild landscape into seeming gentleness. Glaciers made Wisconsin's rich and porous soils. They made the flatlands, the wetlands, the low rounded hills and the lakes. Their retreat created the rivers in which beavers flourished, with pelts adapted to the glacial cold. The European beavers having been hunted to near extinction, from the mid-seventeenth century, French, Dutch and English trappers came to Wisconsin to catch and skin the American beavers to make hats for European heads, both secular and clerical, meanwhile corrupting and blighting with disease and alcohol the indigenous Ho-Chunk as a prelude to dispossessing them entirely.

Downtown Madison was a marsh when the Sauk warrior Black Hawk crossed it with his starving band in 1832. Seven hundred and fifty US soldiers were hot on his heels, among them Abraham Lincoln, Jefferson Davis and several men who later became congressmen, senators, governors and the like: the marriage of military service and politics is as old as the country itself. The war ended with the Battle of Bad Axe on the banks of the Mississippi, where a gunboat cut down Black Hawk's people "like a scythe through grass". Many of those who escaped were later killed by rival tribes who had thrown in their lot with the US troops. That was the end of not only the Black Hawk War, but of resistance east of the Mississippi. Black Hawk was captured, given a celebrity tour of the east coast and died in 1838, by which time the land around Madison was being cut up and sold to eastern speculators, and two hundred Europeans had begun to build a city.

At one end of downtown Madison today stands the Capitol, a splendid Beaux-Arts rendition of the familiar sight in US capital cities; a gilded bronze nearly five metres tall stands atop a mighty sixty-metre white granite dome. From the ground it might be Athena, but she's actually "Wisconsin": in robes, an eagle perched on a globe in one of her hands, the other raised as if urging all below to live up to the state motto – "Forward". On her head is a helmet topped with a badger.

Not a mile from the Capitol, at the other end of the city, is the 370-hectare campus of the University of Wisconsin–Madison. With more than forty thousand students and colossal research endowments, UW is one of the great public universities in the United States. (It places ahead of every Australian university except Melbourne in *The Times Higher Education World University Rankings*, and above Melbourne in other surveys.) Charles Lindbergh, Frank Lloyd Wright and Joyce Carol Oates went there. So did Dick Cheney.

In the clear, crisp air of the evening, a pretty girl sang country music in a little amphitheatre. Young people promenaded, rode bicycles, ate empanadas and ice cream and sipped chai lattes at sidewalk tables outside cafés, bars and bookshops. A smart set had assembled in the new art gallery. It was a short walk to the shores of Lake Mendota, where university students were frolicking and drinking beer as the sun set gloriously over the water. A Republican governor named Lee Sherman Dreyfus said Madison was not reality. He was right. A visitor can't walk around the city without thinking how unlikely the whole thing is. A quarter of a million people living in sparkling amenity; one end dedicated to learning and research ("continual and fearless sifting and winnowing by which alone the truth can be found"), and the other to democracy and justice. In between them, an opera company, a symphony orchestra, a ballet company, a theatre company and a chamber orchestra that plays in the evenings on the lawns of the Capitol. It has a museum of art, a museum of contemporary art, half a dozen community theatres, a historical museum, a children's museum, a veterans' museum and a Centre for Film and Theatre Research. It has music festivals, film festivals and beer festivals. It is regularly named the best city to live in in the United States; the best for college sports, and the healthiest. It has buildings by Louis Sullivan, Frank Lloyd Wright and Cesar Pelli. On Saturdays it stages the biggest farmers' market in the country.

So why, in a country as rich as the United States, are there not more cities like Madison? The link between UW's research and entrepreneurial businesses, together with the assured skills base and the city's general amenity, virtually guarantees Madison's prosperity. Anyone tired of Silicon Valley and wanting to see the sort of city an American future might hold would do well to see Madison.

It didn't happen by accident. The city – and the state of Wisconsin, for that matter – has a long history of progressive politics. The communitarian values of the foundation settlers, centred on church and school, local cooperatives, and traditions of mutual aid laid the foundations, as they did in much of the rural United States. The pattern of boom and bust culminating in the bruising depression of the 1890s, the human costs of industrialisation, the corruption that came with the railways and the corporations, the inequality and abuses of power, generated popular resistance across the country. That old canard, satisfying to many Protestants and Social Darwinists alike, that poverty was the fault of the victim and wealth a reward for virtue, and that both were the natural order of things, lost purchase on the public mind. In Wisconsin it was overthrown. Progressivism became the dominant political ideology and progressives the dominant politicians.

There is a bust of Robert Marion La Follette in the Capitol's rotunda. He has a prodigious head of hair swept back, a broad and resolute jaw, eyes that gaze beyond the general ruck. Born poor in (truly) a log cabin, a teenage farm labourer supporting his fatherless family, La Follette took himself to the University of Wisconsin, thence to the law, Congress, the state governorship and the Senate. According to a 1982 survey of historians, with Henry Clay he was the most effective and influential senator in US history. At UW in the 1870s, La Follette was influenced by the president of the university, John Bascom, a New

England Protestant theologian and sociologist. Much less troubled by Darwin and evolution than he was by the "gospel of wealth" and the inequality and corruption of morals to which it gave rise, Bascom believed the state had to take on the social duties once left to the churches. "Fighting Bob" La Follette gave his life to that cause. In 2011, when thousands rallied at the Capitol to protest Scott Walker's anti-union legislation, La Follette's bust was draped with the sign: "Fighting Bob would fight the bill" and "Long Live La Follette".

In his early years in politics, as much as La Follette brought ideas of social reform to the people, the people brought them to him. He found them everywhere, not least among dairymen and other farmers, especially the Norwegians, whose language he spoke, and the professional classes, many of them emerging from the university. A brilliant and tireless speaker and a campaigner of astonishing energy and stamina, he turned latent grievances into political force: which is to say, he was the definitive populist. The word is often a pejorative, especially in this country: we have "shameless" populists, and people who "resort" to populism, as if it's about as low as a politician can go. Despite the triumph of "meritocratic" ideology, which is neoliberalism's specific antidote for the disease, in the United States populism on both the left and right remains legitimate. In the United States there are articulate liberal commentators who actually recommend populism. In theory, after all, there can hardly be a purer interpretation of democracy: the uncorrupted people's voice against the self-serving elites. Michael Young, the English sociologist who coined the term "meritocracy", despised the fashion for it: first, because it is largely a smug fantasy perpetuated by those who sit at the top of the social pyramid; and second, because it bestows on those at the bottom the slur that they are there because they have no merit. Even feudalism spared the poor that insult: their lowly station was an accident of birth. While the underclasses in an alleged meritocracy might be reluctant to acknowledge the wound to their dignity, the elites should not be surprised if it adds a savage streak to popular resentment.

Robert La Follette took on the elites for forty years. He took on the railroad trusts, the lumber bosses, the corporations, the party bosses, Woodrow Wilson and the political tide that swept the United States into World War I. He allied himself with farmers and trade unions alike, Democrats and Republicans according to their worth; he pursued war profiteers and defended persecuted dissidents. He blasted the Versailles treaty and the League of Nations as a high-sounding farce erected on the same fatal mix of imperialism, nationalism, racism, exploitation and greed that, he said, led to World War I. He stood for an expanded democracy, guarantees of civil liberties, state ownership of the railways and utilities, the rights of workers to form unions, farm credit and plebiscites before any declaration of war. He stood against monopolists, imperialists and "any discrimination between races, classes and creeds". In his run for president, he won a sixth of the vote nationwide.

Wisconsin was the most progressive state in the union. It went into the statutes of the university and became known everywhere as the "Wisconsin Idea": the university would seek wisdom from all the people of the state, and share its knowledge with them. It was "a poem of faith in mankind", a member of the UW Board of Regents said in 2013 when Governor Walker tried to do away with it.

While no single initiative defines the Wisconsin Idea, an abbreviated list of legislation passed in Madison in the first fourteen years of the twentieth century gives a sense of what it meant: women and children's labour laws; laws regarding industrial safety, public health and food standards; conservation laws; workers' compensation. Laws governing campaign spending and lobbying; direct primaries and referendums on citizen initiatives. A tax commission, an inheritance tax, insurance and banking laws, a trade practices act. In addition a first-class education system was established. Progressives came up with what became known as the "Madison Compromise". Concerned that their city lagged in industrial assets and production, but just as worried that industrial growth would have destructive social and environmental consequences, they decided that Madison would have only "high-grade" industries that hired skilled and well-paid workers. In the ten years from 1910 to 1920, both industrial output and factory employment increased by 280 per cent.

This is ancient history, of course: or rather, it would be if La Follette's influence stopped with his death in 1925. It didn't. His program was taken up in other states, and by Upton Sinclair when he ran for governor in California in 1934. Fiorello La Guardia brought his ideas to New York City. More significantly, much of Roosevelt's New Deal can be traced to La Follette: Harold Ickes was an adviser to both men and an architect of the New Deal, which made the United States more socially progressive than any country in Europe. For half a century after Roosevelt's election, tax on incomes over a million dollars averaged 82 per cent. US estate taxes of 70 to 80 per cent were twice those in Germany and France. Wisconsin was a state as progressive as any in the world, and the South aside, the United States did not lag so far behind. Yet by the mid-1980s it had been decided that these rates and a federal minimum wage, which had coexisted with the most sustained era of prosperity and social mobility in US history, were an unbearable burden on free enterprise and the American way.

The mayor of Madison these days is Paul Soglin, a Democrat. In the '60s at the University of Wisconsin–Madison he was a campus radical. He appears in a photo taken during a student occupation at UW in 1967. The hood of his sheepskin coat is pulled up over his head, and it neatly frames his young face and the "impishness and charisma" a girlfriend of the time described. All the other students in the front line are caught in a moment of elemental fear, because just behind the photographer the police are advancing with tear gas and truncheons. In what otherwise could be a still from a 1950s horror movie, Soglin looks almost serene: calm enough to have pulled the hood up to protect his head and neck, and to gaze at the advancing cops as if trying to find their historical context. A minute later, he was getting belted on the floor with the others. The Madison police were not progressive. Six months after the occupation Soglin was a Madison city councillor. Six years later, aged twenty-seven, he was mayor. Not long ago he suggested making "Madison – seventy-seven square miles surrounded by reality" the city's motto.

Paul Soglin agreed to meet me on a Sunday morning. Now seventy-one, with greying hair swept back like La Follette's and a matching moustache, he long ago converted his university activism into progressive municipal politics conducted by orthodox democratic means. He was radicalised by the war, by the counterculture and by a heavyweight history department that included William Appleman Williams, the critic of American exceptionalism, the legendary lecturer and left-wing activist Harvey Goldberg and the "spellbinding" liberal George L. Mosse. For transforming young minds there is probably nothing more powerful than history in the hands of a charismatic teacher. Soglin also found inspiration in the semi-sacred texts of American thought: William Lloyd Garrison, the abolitionist; and Henry David Thoreau, whose *Resistance to*

Civil Government has been a thousand times quoted in support of causes on both the right and left of politics. Brutal police actions can also have a powerful effect in the formation of ideology.

Mayor Soglin hasn't forgotten the old slogans. Long ago Mao Zedong said, "Whoever controls the countryside controls the cities". The mayor says these days, "Whoever controls the sewers controls everything". Because in Madison the left used more intelligence than is often the case, and took control of traditional politics, Ronald Reagan never took hold, he says. The city has held true to its progressive traditions. After his 2008 campaign visit was a massive success, Obama came back in 2012 for the biggest rally of the campaign.

Nine times Soglin has been elected mayor, the last in 2015 with more than 70 per cent of the vote. He can take a lot of the credit for Madison being the good city that it is. The mayoral biographical note, however, describes his philosophy in decidedly modest and unromantic terms: "balanced investment in human capital and appropriate municipal infrastructure" and a "focus … on equity and developing a tax base that can support human services". A rough translation from the managerial would be: "Madison is no accident". The city is the result of a much assailed and greatly debilitated, but unbroken American tradition of democratic socialism.

Paul Soglin supports Bernie Sanders. When I spoke to him, Sanders was still in the race and rated an outside chance to win the nomination. That prospect passed soon after, but Sanders's supporters were sustained by the belief that the strength of his campaign would leave Clinton with no choice but to head in their direction, and the party establishment would have to follow suit. On the face of it they were right. Soglin has known Sanders since the late 1970s, when they worked together on reforms to state and local government. Although it is a much smaller city than Madison, Burlington in Vermont has the same combination of a post-industrial service economy, a university and an airport, and as mayor in the early '80s Sanders steered it in much the same direction as Soglin in Madison, and with the same lasting effect. They are two of a handful of radical progressive mayors who have confronted the prevailing pattern of development and established highly liveable alternatives to high-rise ugliness and social decay. Soglin introduced Sanders to a crowd of eight thousand when the senator came to Madison in 2016.

He came twice more and eventually won the Democratic primary with 56.6 per cent of the vote.

In Paul Soglin's view the modern Republicans are not a true conservative party, but are merely manipulating the angry dispossessed – an assessment to go with that of the former Republican congressional staffer who said they were "becoming less and less like a traditional political party in a representative democracy and becoming more like an apocalyptic cult, or one of the intensely ideological authoritarian parties of 20th century Europe". In the contest with this dark force, Soglin believes Sanders has done most of the heavy lifting and offers a chance for the Democrats to pick up the old populist thread. Millions of young voters can re-energise the party, so long as the party moves with them. There have been three lasting realignments in US politics: after the Civil War, with F.D.R. and with Reagan. Soglin says there is now the prospect of a fourth, and it rests with Sanders and Clinton.

4.

We come back to the magic words, and they all depend upon "community".

—Perry Miller, *The Life of the Mind in America*

Let's drop the domestic stuff altogether . . . I mean, who gives a shit if the minimum wage is $1.15 or $1.20 compared to something like [Cuba]?

—President Kennedy to his speechwriter, before his inaugural address, 1961

It is one of the curious things about Bernie Sanders's campaign that, both here and in the United States, commentators have characterised his ideology and objectives as, in some way, exotic: if he calls himself a democratic socialist, he must be doing something Scandinavian. In fact, the roots of Sanders's philosophy are firmly in the United States. They reach back as far as the reality to which they are opposed – namely, social inequality and the corruption of politics consequent on the ruthless and unrestrained pursuit of self-interest known as capitalism, or sometimes as greed. They go back to the War on Poverty in the '60s, the GI Bill of the '40s, to the New Deal of the '30s, to the trust-busters, progressives and Eugene V. Debs socialists of the early years of last century. In fact, they go back to the founding fathers. Thomas Jefferson wanted primogeniture done away with. Tom Paine wanted a pension for people over fifty, funded by an estate tax, and a leg-up payment to people trapped in poverty. John Adams favoured property qualifications for voters, but believed pretty well everyone should own property. Those freedoms that Americans are forever insisting are guaranteed in the founding documents were, according to the authors of the documents, dependent upon equality.

Given the shape of the United States economy, the deep failures of the social system and the unwillingness of Barack Obama and the Congress to make anyone pay for the delinquencies that led to the Great Recession, it would have been much more surprising – and disquieting – if no one had come forth. And yet, with the fading of the Occupy movement, that seemed likely. Imagine, a First World country founded on egalitarian principles in which the top 20 per cent of households have 84 per cent of the wealth, while the bottom 40 per cent have 0.3 per cent; and one family, the Waltons, owns more than the bottom 40 per cent of US families combined; and the ratio of CEO salary to unskilled worker is 354 to 1 (fifty years ago it was 20 to 1). A minimum wage of $7.25 per hour, which is 34 per cent less than workers on the minimum were getting in 1968. More than 20 per cent of children in the United States live in poverty, more than twice the rate of any European country. With a quarter of totalitarian China's population, democratic America has about the same number of people in jail.

These are a few bare facts of modern US capitalism: inequality is worse than in any other Western democracy, and there is less social mobility than in the others. And, as Thomas Piketty argues, with growth unlikely to get beyond 1 to 1.5 per cent in the foreseeable future, the return to (those with) capital will continue to outstrip it by 4 per cent or more and compound the inequality. Piketty is surely right to say that this is "incompatible with the meritocratic values … fundamental to modern democratic societies"; though of course it may not be incompatible with ever-deeper belief in those values among the people with the capital. The task that Piketty set for governments three years ago was to "go beyond growth and help democracy retake control of capitalism".

So what was the appeal of Bernie Sanders? Watch the ovation as he stepped onto the stage in Philadelphia, and the faces in the crowd as he spoke to them. What absence in their souls does the old codger fill that makes twenty-somethings cheer and weep? It's mainly his message, but there's more to it. Could it be that before Bernie Sanders they had only seen "pseudo-events" and never an authentic one on their political screens, much less an authentic Jewish working-class socialist? Sanders never had to worry about an "image problem", because he didn't have an image. When he appeared on television he did not look like a man in search of a camera; more like one who had been teaching school for fifty years and, having just retired, stumbled in on a talk show. But he was not without stage presence. You can try to manufacture charisma with a haircut and a face-lift, or you've just got it. Sanders was stooped, his face wore every one of his seventy-four years, but he could talk! His beliefs came forth not as mere words, but as unbridled urges. He sweated. His face turned red. He spoke in short concrete sentences with anger not far beneath the surface of them. No epic Lincolnian flourishes, none of Obama's rhetorical music, no cant, no jingoism, no echoes of the preachers. Instead – the facts. And – "We can do better than this". For once the word "passion" fits.

People say he's a grouch; that he's "abrasive" and "combative", and has little or no sense of humour. But politicians don't need humour anymore. There are professional comedians to do it for them. Probably the burden of this responsibility is what has made the comedians by now so very good at it, and some of them outstrip the politicians – and the pundits – for popularity and influence. For politicians who have decided that in worldly matters "one sinks by levity and rises by gravity" (as Lewis Lapham said), there is a twofold risk to this: first, that the comedians begin to be taken more seriously than the politicians; and second, that the politicians forfeit entirely this dimension of their humanity through failing to exercise it, and become ever less attractive to voters looking for a person of ordinary human complexity.

Sanders has escaped that fate. Let Larry David do the humour. At the Democratic convention he offered reassurance. Thanks to his supporters, Hillary Clinton will go to the election on the most progressive platform in the party's history, he said. Thanks to them, the radical work can continue through a new grassroots outfit called "Our Revolution". Not every diehard was satisfied, some no doubt because they hate Hillary, or just don't trust her, or think the Clintons have long been part of the problem, or because they believe Trump will beat her. But even those who saw him swallow the awful pill of capitulation and accepted his reasons for doing so will forever mourn the fact that Bernie Sanders won't be president. It has a lot do with what he said, but it is also the *symbolic* weight of the office he failed to win. He offered something grounded and authentic, and if he promised to do no more or less than give meaning to that part of the preamble to the Constitution that says "promote the general welfare", this was much more than his rivals could be relied on to do. The son of Jewish immigrants seemed to be not only the most genuine of the candidates, but also the one most genuinely descended from the nation's moral and intellectual ancestors.

"I infer that the sovereign, original and foundation of civil power lies in the people", Roger Williams wrote in 1644. In the first half of the seventeenth century Williams, who founded the settlement at Providence, Rhode Island, endured banishment and risked execution by advocating the separation of church and state. He believed in free thought, the abolition of slavery and generous treatment of Native Americans. That was the first time the ideal of civil power was uttered in America. You do not have to believe it could ever be made wholly real to wish for someone to wholly embody the ambition. Sanders would ennoble the country as well as improve it. That's why he was so hard to give up. He would represent their power, not steal it from them by pretending to be like them.

Surveys taken over the years since the global financial crisis suggest that most of the citizenry don't see it Sanders's way. The American Dream and political supineness go together. Ground that should be good for progressive politicians turns out to be fertile for regressive ones. If only objective self-interest was the sole motivation. But instead we find these people who depend on government loathing government on principle; people who would applaud the view that their country must not become "a politically correct neofeudal fiefdom of monolithic, paternalistic government" (or other modern Republican formulations of Burkean thought) and boo anyone who tries to tell them what side their bread is buttered.

Just about everyone, including Republicans and the wealthy, favours more equal distribution of wealth, but one study also found that only 5 per cent of them think inequality is a major problem. The average American does think the gap between CEO salaries and average workers is too great: they think a ratio of seven to one is about right. They guess it's about thirty to one just now, which is not a tenth of the real figure. Asked to guess how much the richest fifth owned, they reckoned around 60 per cent. Would it were so. Pew found that while six out of ten Americans think the system favours the wealthy, six out of ten also believe that hard work will take you to the top. When the primatologist Frans de Waal put two capuchin monkeys in adjacent cages and gave each of them a piece of cucumber, they were content. When he gave one of them a piece of cucumber and the other a bunch of grapes, the one that got the cucumber threw it at de Waal. Every time he repeated the experiment the victim of unequal treatment got wilder. Capuchin monkeys have no faith in America; they hold to no dream.

America has "never been a nation of haves and have-nots", this year's failed Republican candidate Marco Rubio declared in 2011. "We are a nation of haves and soon-to-haves, of people who have made it and people who will make it." The young Republican may be less inclined to believe it since Donald Trump shattered his dream in this year's primaries. In any event it was not merely because he believed it that Rubio made this apparently puerile claim: it was also because he knew Americans believe it, or at least want to believe it. Late in 2013 Barack Obama said, "the combined trends of increased inequality and decreasing mobility pose a fundamental threat to the American Dream, our way of life and what we stand for around the globe". Then he went a little quiet on the subject and started talking instead about raising the middle class. Commentators thought he changed tack because stressing inequality is too pessimistic a view and offends the faith of a lot of ordinary folk whose votes the Democrats need. The Republicans are happy to take what *The Economist* called a "semi-Burkean" position: to treat inequality as inevitable and concentrate on the opportunity to rise. It might be an illusion, but it's a "pleasing" one, and "pleasing illusions",

Burke believed, make "power gentle and obedience liberal".

All things are forgiven those who prove the Dream's alive. Bernie Sanders won a lot of people with his talk about the power of billionaires and the favours they buy, but another lot of struggling people prefer to believe in the billionaire. So they believe Donald Trump's credentials as an "economic manager" despite his record of bankruptcy, failure, fraud and non-payment of bills and wages – and despite what most economists think of his economic policies. Spend some time talking to folk in rust-belt USA, and you will find they don't speak much of inequality. Hardship a little, unfair treatment a little, Washington elites, yes; but to speak of inequality comes too close to heresy. Believing in America is not optional. If the times should test your faith, then believe in *other* times – times when America was great – and vote for the guy who vows to make it great again.

It might be what they're taught to think. You cannot know what ignorance or dogma, your *perspective* – patriotic, religious, racial or any other – does not permit you to see. You might not see, for instance, that up to the time of L.B.J., and even into the Nixon presidency, the United States could accommodate its fanatical attachment to individual freedom with progressive social legislation. Equally, miserable as your circumstances are, you might not know *how* miserable relative to other Western countries. There is that miserable minimum wage, for instance, and average hourly earnings for 80 per cent of the population are not much better. No statutory minimum annual leave. Minimal job security. No equal pay for women. Millions still without health cover. Even when they're angry, the Tea Party people only know the half of it. If they knew the whole of it – if they let themselves know – *then* they might be angry. Still, as *The New York Times* panjandrum David Brooks said in 2010, the American system "leads to more exciting lives". He said this near the end of a recession that saw nine million jobs lost, five million houses foreclosed on and $13 trillion in family wealth wiped out. Between 2007 and 2010 alone, Latino wealth fell by 40 per cent and African-American wealth by 36 per cent; and according to a Harvard study, forty-five thousand Americans died each year for want of health insurance.

5.

Squealing over the possibility that the military may call him up, Cassius makes as sorry a spectacle as those unwashed punks who picket and demonstrate against the war.

—Red Smith, on Cassius Clay

He simply refused to be afraid. And being that way, he gave other people courage.

—Bryant Gumbel, on Muhammad Ali

On a Saturday morning I drove north up to Green Bay as the tributes to Ali flowed in. One station devoted the whole morning to this radical Muslim. Well, he was radical when he started. In the '60s he was the greatest radical in the United States. George Foreman spoke for a while. He said he knew he was in trouble at the end of the third round of the fight in the Kinshasa. He had hit him with everything and Ali was still standing. Early in the seventh round, he hit him hard on the jaw: Ali drew him in and whispered in his ear, "That the best you got, George?" Foreman loved him. Was he the greatest? Well, he didn't have the biggest punch, or the best jab, and he wasn't the quickest – but, yes, he was the greatest. "He was like an eclipse of the sun", said Foreman. He was the greatest human being he ever met. "And, dammit, he was pretty!"

This was the early '60s: it's hard to imagine the courage a black kid needed to change his name and declare he was a Muslim; and demand to be called by his new name and have his belief respected. Then he stood up to the United States army, to the United States itself, and in doing this gave up what would have been the prime of his career. At an age when the rest of us were struggling with history and sociology essays, a black boxer had seen through the whole edifice, and knew just where the answer lay. At first, when he said he was the greatest, Red Smith and pretty well everybody else thought he was only talking about boxing. But being the greatest boxer was not even half of it: he was also saying he was greater than segregation and discrimination, greater than America itself and every myth and platitude then sustaining it.

Many of the people who had known Ali talked about his ability to "transcend": to transcend boxing, to transcend race, politics, religion. Listening to George Foreman, and remembering that fight and the one with Joe Frazier in Manila, we might decide that what Ali transcended above all was fear. As a boxer Ali never got much credit for courage. Perhaps it was the pretty way he fought, or because no one could see behind his boasting – "I've handcuffed lightning, thrown thunder into jail" – to the fear his courage overcame. If every boxer who gets in the ring has to overcome his fear, getting into the ring with Foreman and Frazier was surely to know terror. The violence would be terrible, the pain terrible. And even when it's at its worst – especially then – the boxer has to hold his form; keep boxing, not flailing; maintain his self-possession, be who he is, not what the other guy is trying to make him, which is wreckage.

It seemed possible that, being Christians, the people in Wisconsin's farmhouses might have seen something familiar in this interpretation of Ali. To overcome one's fear, endure suffering, speak truth to power. But it's unlikely they were listening. Did they hold Ali up as a model of courage and proof that the Dream was alive? Was he one of their great Americans? Not likely. Not across that wide canyon. The American mind is segregated; broken into facets of belief, culture and identity. Most of them you can enter by turning the knob on your radio, but you can't listen to two at the same time.

I turned into Ripon (pop. 7700 or so) for fuel and came across the Little White Schoolhouse nestled among trees. In 1854 a local man, Alvan Earle Bovay, called a meeting in the schoolhouse to rally opposition to a bill that proposed extending slavery beyond the limits of the Missouri Compromise. Fifty-three people turned up. "We went into the little meeting, Whigs, Free Soilers, and Democrats. We came out Republicans and we were the first Republicans in the union", Bovay recalled. The Republican Party – the anti-slavery party – was formally constituted at a meeting attended by Abraham Lincoln and Horace Greeley in Pittsburgh two years later, but the Little White Schoolhouse in Ripon is called the birthplace of the party.

A Republican think tank called the Ripon Society was established in 1964 with the intention of turning the party away from its disastrous Goldwater diversion and towards moderation. On Saturday afternoon, Ripon was moderation itself: a quiet and pervasive seriousness that a lot of Midwest towns have. The modest churches and public buildings and the lawns all impeccably kept. And there is Ripon College, established in 1851 and now providing a thousand "high-achieving" students from nearly every state and countries around the world with a "rigorous liberal arts and sciences curriculum and an active residential campus [that] prepares students of diverse interests for lives of productive, socially responsible citizenship". The prose bears little resemblance to hers, but it might have been a scene in one of Marilynne Robinson's novels. In the sunshine by the school in the good little town out on the grassy plain there was scarcely a sound, and not a soul in sight. Nothing to fear. Or is there? "An horrid stillness first invades the ear / And in that silence we the tempest fear."

Oscar Wilde thought socialism was a nice idea, but he could not see it working because he doubted people would be prepared to give up their evenings. Out near the Green Bay airport, in the foyer of the Radisson, the Wisconsin Democrats were at least giving up their Saturday morning. They could have been in the casino, just a step away, through the sliding glass doors. The casino is owned and operated by the Oneida Nation, a New York tribe, some of whom took up land in Wisconsin when it was offered to them in the 1820s and '30s. At ten in the morning in the dark, smoky nowhere, hundreds were playing the machines. Nothing beats gambling when you want to push life aside. Politics, which is just as addictive, is gambling's reverse: politics buries you alive in life, other people's in the main, until their lives become yours. The Democrats of Wisconsin sat behind tables ready to push an idea, or a book or a badge, to anyone who ventured near. The speeches were being given in the auditorium, to which I was refused entry until a guest accreditation could be arranged, by which time the speeches were over. So instead I bought a "Forward with Bernie" badge as a memento, and spoke to former state senator Tim Cullen, who was selling a book he'd written.

Governor Scott Walker had described Cullen as "kind of one of those guys who, he really doesn't care, he's not there for political reasons, he's just trying to get something done … but he's not a conservative. He's just a pragmatist". Tim Cullen had made a name for himself as a man who, in keeping with Wisconsin tradition, could cross the party divide. Walker, he reckoned, is the very model of the toxic modern Republican: the base tribal politician. He found that Walker tried to use him; that he didn't want the divide crossed, but widened and intensified. He took a "happy and united state" and set out to "angrily divide its citizens in order to advance his own political career". It might not be all down to Walker, but the state is certainly divided: not so long ago pollsters found 20 per cent were in the "persuadable middle", but now it's 5 to 6 per cent. Cullen quoted Jefferson – most do at some stage – "Great innovations should not be forced by a slender majority". That, he said, had been the guiding philosophy of Wisconsin politics: negotiate compromises, find common cause, keep the people informed and consult with them. But Walker, the conservative, has broken with tradition.

Tim Cullen comes from Janesville (pop. sixty-three thousand), on the Rock River fifty minutes south of Madison. Paul Ryan, the Speaker of the House of Representatives and the man most likely to be the next Republican president, comes from the same small city.

I drove into Janesville on a weekday morning. It was the usual long strip mall ending in a missing downtown. Paul Ryan's office was easy enough to find. Directly opposite, a plaque commemorates the spot where Abraham Lincoln made a speech in October 1859. We do not know if the Speaker of the House draws inspiration from it; does he wonder, for instance, if Lincoln would have endorsed Donald Trump? Ryan has a bit of the dark and gloomy look of Lincoln. He endorsed Trump, but the pundits say it is only to protect the Republican position in Congress and take some of the heat out of the party's divisions. I went to Janesville on the rough chance that, if not Ryan himself, someone in his office might be able to explain his thinking. His office, tucked into a sort of arcade, was closed and the lights were off.

Janesville's public buildings, both the old and the relatively new, are massive. In the quietness of the place their grandness looks a bit like collective overreach. Like so many old downtowns, downtown Janesville is not entirely deserted but it feels that way. The commercial buildings that once housed bustling businesses are now tired homes to law firms, barber shops, old wares shops and dimly lit bars that no one seems to go to. The Sons of Norway Lodge. Grafft Investments: property developers. There's a dreamlike sense of life no longer lived. No doubt all the action is in a mall somewhere. The rules of commerce ate the heart out of the heartland cities. Who can say that abandoning all that shared public space was good for American democracy? That it didn't make the polis that much more divided and neurotic? Who can say that this wasn't one of the ideas behind it?

Janesville had a General Motors plant but it closed in the Great Recession and the town is still recovering from the shock. George Parker invented his pen in Janesville around 1910 and they were made in the town for seventy years, until the company went to Gillette in a leveraged buyout and vanished. At eleven in a small café where I was the only customer, a blind man and his dog and a lady who looked like she might have been a vicar sang and played a kind of country dance on a ukulele and another stringed instrument. I was reading an article I'd copied from *Collide* magazine. It referred to "late capitalist services that turn the patterns of our world into information that can be sold back to us". Los Angeles, it said, is for "people who are comfortable with a certain level of cultural chaos and mixing and ambiguity and lack of boundary ... In LA there's no real right way to be". "You bet", as they say in Wisconsin.

"That was a nice biscuit, thank you", I said to the proprietor.

"You bet", she said.

"Did you make it?" I asked.

"You bet."

Across a deserted street I took a snap of a mural illustrating Janesville's heroic pioneering history and noticed a lady had stopped her car twenty yards back so as not to spoil it. For this extravagant act of civility I waved and called out, "Thank you". I didn't quite catch it as she drove past with a radiant smile, but probably she said, "You bet".

In a bar – I was killing time in the hope that someone would live up to the message on the answering machine and turn up at Paul Ryan's office – the three big news stories were rolling on the television. I was the only customer again and the barmaid was on her phone, so there was no choice but to watch Muhammad Ali lighting the flame at the Atlanta Olympics and knocking out Foreman in the Congo for the hundredth time in three days. It was all happening elsewhere. In other news, Trump had declared a judge could not fairly try a case against him because his parents were born in Mexico. Paul Ryan, among many others, had been appalled. They were still showing the gorilla towing the four-year-old boy wildly through the water – before television we went to bars to escape the trials of existence. Bernie Sanders came on and said that after all these years of people fighting racism and bigotry in America, Donald Trump being the Republican nominee for president was "incomprehensible". He said "incomprehensible" several more times, and one began to wonder if the word was comprehensible to people who leaned towards voting for Trump. Not that they would not know what it means, but rather that they would not use it. They might say "Beats me" instead. An election processes reality into platitudes. Even the images become platitudes. It grinds all the tendons and marrow and flesh of history, and all the cultural overlays of Los Angeles, and the ukuleles and "You bets" of Janesville, into something universally digestible. Hearing a word like "incomprehensible" in the middle of it is like finding a bone in a fish finger.

Janesville has its Tea Party. You can watch the early demonstrations on YouTube. The boards say things like "Defending our Constitution and Taking Back Our Government" and "Honk if You Love Freedom". The Janesville Tea Party endorsed both Paul Ryan and Scott Walker.

A few years ago, in the woods bordering a town in Ohio, I saw men building what I thought were tree houses. I learned from their fellow townspeople that they were "hides", and when the season opens the hunters get inside them and skewer any deer that moseys past within range of their bows and arrows. A former Republican Congressman, Scott L. Klug, told me Paul Ryan hunts deer this way. While it might not strictly qualify as ancestor worship, it seems likely that these men imagine they are connecting to something deeply American in their being.

Scott Klug has the assurance, good looks and glow of a TV presenter, and it turns out that's what he was before he became a Republican congressman. He went to Washington in 1991. Newt Gingrich drafted him into presenting the resolution that ultimately led to the federal government shutdown of 1995 and 1996. It's the general view that the shutdown got Bill Clinton a second term. Klug stepped down in 1999, and in the years since he's gone into the publishing business, written a thriller, and co-chaired Rudy Giuliani's unsuccessful bid for the Republican nomination in 2007–08. As of early June he would be voting for Trump.

With that record, people like me, who struggle with the complexity of US politics, might take Klug for a right-wing Republican. In fact he sits on the centre-right, the "sensible" conservative side. I met him over lunch in a room at the Nakoma Golf Club, which is out in the leafy suburbs of Madison's west. There were six others there: two of them, the editor of the *Wisconsin State Journal* and the past president of the Greater Madison Chamber of Commerce, were centre-right; two others, the managing editor of the *Capital Times* and the founder of a public affairs firm with long experience managing election campaigns, were centre-left; and the remaining two, a former Chancellor of UW and his wife, a retired Government Affairs vice-president at the university, were described to me as "centrist" in their politics.

To me, the remarkable thing about the meeting was that it was held. The former publisher of the *State Journal*, Phil Blake, whom I had only met a day before the lunch, arranged it for me without my asking. He seemed to have no difficulty persuading these people to give up two hours of their Sunday for some blow-in from another country, albeit a most dutiful ally. And even if their natural hospitality inclined them to come, there are few less enticing prospects than sitting round a table with one's political opponents in the middle of an election campaign.

One did not expect plates or food to be thrown, of course. All the same, the bitter political struggles of the past quarter-century have not been fought between the recognised radicals of either side, but people of this civilised stripe. It did not take far-right Republicans or far-left Democrats to shut down the government and impeach a president, or to give the centre-right reasons to do it. It was surely an extreme measure to invade Iraq, but those who decided on it were not political extremists. So moderate is the president who made that decision, he and his entire family boycotted this year's Republican convention, and as of today one of the Democrats who voted for the war is reckoned a "safe option" for the presidency, with a 92 per cent near-certainty to win. The long-running deadlock in Washington has its origins in Tea Party extremists, but they haven't done it on their own. A centrist administration used taxpayer money to bail out the banks that brought about the Great Recession and chose not to prosecute a single person. "Too big to fail" is the radical doctrine of moderates. There are no Tea Partiers on the Supreme Court, but the Citizens United decision, which granted corporations untrammelled rights to fund political campaigns through political action committees, could be judged extremist – or certainly *contributing* to extremism, whether through the potentially corrupting activities of the corporations, or through the disenchantment with regular politics that the appearance of corruption occasions. Paul Ryan is rarely counted on the extreme right of American politics, but he is – or was until recently – a neoliberal devotee of Ayn Rand's *Atlas Shrugged*, and a statistical analysis of Ryan's record when he was Romney's running mate found him substantially to the right of every vice-presidential candidate since the Civil War. It does not take extremists, just tribal politics and the view that beyond declaring war and recruiting young men to fight them, nothing government does can make for better lives and better places.

Four years ago, two experienced Washington analysts gave up pretending that the failures of US politics could be sheeted home in equal measure to both parties. The Republicans had to take most of the blame:

> The GOP has become an insurgent outlier in American politics. It is ideologically extreme; scornful of compromise; unmoved by conventional understanding of facts, evidence and science; and dismissive of the legitimacy of its political opposition. When one party moves this far from the mainstream, it makes it nearly impossible for the political system to deal constructively with the country's challenges.

Yet in the American worldview, individualism and communitarianism, conservatism and liberalism, have long coexisted, in politics and in individuals, and we can presume that, in one combination or another, all are present in any room at any time. Maybe that was what Jim Wood (of the Democrat PR firm) was talking about when, before we started on our Waldorf salads, he said slowly and emphatically, as if to make sure I understood a fundamental truth about his country, "America's genius lies in solving problems, and that's what the Democrats and Republicans will do". His words might be taken to reflect that same *Weltanschauung* – a belief, of an almost mystical character and amounting to a faith, in the unique ability of the United States to find the answers to any problem.

Not for a moment could anyone deny the genius. But if applied only to domestic "problems", the claim is contestable: the problem of racial segregation and discrimination, for instance, Milwaukee's problem, remains manifestly unsolved. And while to list them might be un-American in its negativity, there *is* the problem of inequality, the corruption of politics by money and rent-seeking, poverty, mass incarceration, gun violence and the general malaise that finds expression in one statistic: more than six out of ten Americans think the country is heading in the wrong direction. Or what might be a bigger problem: the unwillingness or inability of the powerful to approach these problems with anything more useful than a bucket of money and restatements of the faith. If applied to the projection of US power abroad, the faith is even less convincing. The Middle East comes to mind.

6.

I love leverage.

—Donald Trump

Fascism, it should be unnecessary to add, was no ideology in the traditional meaning of that term, but a faith which could not be explained solely in rational terms.

—George L. Mosse, *The Fascist Revolution*

The dominant semiotic weight of a Star of David over a pile of money is not a sheriff.

—Rick Wilson, Republican media
strategist, 5 July 2016

Michele Bachmann says Donald Trump has been "handpicked by God". But saying he has "1950s sensibilities" is the more telling of her judgements. Looking for dog whistles is a sure route to madness, but this could be one. The 1950s was a time when no white male needed to doubt his predominant place in America. For black Americans, then one in eight of the population, the 1950s was living with discrimination, persecution, poverty and terror. If you were a woman you were almost certainly living at a serious disadvantage, and if you were gay the only safe course was to hide the fact. That left white heterosexual males in charge. Of course, by "1950s sensibilities" Bachmann might have meant beauty pageants, political incorrectness, being the world's tough guy, Billy Graham and family television. Who knows what she meant? But it is true that one of the big changes since the '50s has been, as Hendrik Hertzberg puts it, that "the default position is not middle-aged white male".

Trump does outstandingly well with this group, and he pitches straight at them. It's not just the poor white male and the uneducated white male: two polls, one by Pew, one by *Washington Post*–ABC News, found male college graduates support Trump over Clinton 49 to 42 and 49 to 44, respectively. Graduate women back Clinton 57 to 35, a six-point lead overall that in most polls hides the attitude of the men.

This might have something to do with the changing nature of college education: graduates of the increasingly numerous bottom-tier colleges may not be doing any better than non-graduates and may share their white working-class resentments. There are two ways of discovering what these resentments are: we can look at the polls or we can look at what Trump has been saying. Trump knows that in the last half-century redistributive policies have brought about a substantial shift in income, power and status from the formerly impregnable white males to women and minorities. Everywhere they look they see women and African Americans, Latinos, lesbians and gays with wealth, celebrity and influence. He also knows that when the Reagan years handed the women's vote to the Democrats, the Republicans got the men's to about the same degree. So Trump insults women and Mexicans and singles out black men in his audiences and (while promising, after Orlando, to be the best defender the LBGT community ever had) opposes gay marriage.

Poll numbers among Republican men – graduates and non-graduates – provide a compelling picture of Trump's rusted-on base: for instance, 64 per cent of college-educated white Republicans and 75 per cent of those without a college education support Trump's idea of a fence along the entire border with Mexico. The reason is simple: they believe immigrants are a threat to both American jobs and "American values". A majority of Americans believe the increase in imports is "taking away US jobs" and a majority (among whites 59 per cent) believe that "trade with other countries" causes a net loss of jobs.

It is not, as they say, rocket science. Millions of Americans feel they have been robbed of their birthright. The country's wealth, history and traditions have been subverted or gifted to others. The American future is not theirs. They were losing long before the Great Recession, and since it hit they've lost even more. The greatest country on earth is becoming someone else's: that's if it still is the greatest country. Hell, when did they last win a war? An actual shooting war? Grenada?

Democrats should look to themselves for the answers. This is what happens with identity politics. It's also what happens when you "embrace globalisation", as all good liberals have done for the past thirty years. Liberals – the well-off ones at least – love globalisation for all the excitement and sophistication of it: and, loving that about it, they love immigration, multiculturalism and social inclusiveness. They can truly say these things enrich their lives. But what enriches one tribe impoverishes and threatens another. Globalisation has swallowed jobs, communities, unions and pride. It even takes patriotism: and sends it back relabelled as bigotry and racism. Ordinary prejudices are "inappropriate"; old forms of speech are "inappropriate". Common understanding of the differences between men and women is inappropriate. Political correctness is an attempt by the Puritan communitarian affect to crush the Jacksonian individualist one. Clint Eastwood says Trump gained support because "secretly everybody's getting tired of political correctness, kissing up. That's the kiss-ass generation we're in right now". You don't have to like Clint Eastwood to acknowledge that he has a political point, at least. You can loathe Bret Easton Ellis, and everything he says about feminists, objectified breasts and the male gaze, and still recognise that they're probably not a first-order issue for people who have lost their jobs or their roots in the country, or grew up thinking that gazing was harmless.

In an era when the New Left used the term loosely, George L. Mosse was at pains to find and preserve what the word "fascism" meant. Not much he saw in Madison in the 1960s would qualify. But Donald Trump might be different. Reactionary politics lives off "normative threats".

Reactionary politicians instinctively know how to exploit them. European fascism is a case in point. Nationalism and xenophobia; a stress on law and order; the glorification of war and violence; anti-intellectualism; anomie and alienation; impatience tending to disdain for democratic politics; ditto for corrupt big cities (even while practising corruption and dealing with the corrupt): these dispositions Trump's core followers share with fascism. Some of them are as old as the United States itself, and some would describe the outlook of millions who could never be called fascist. That does not mean Trump cannot call them up to his cause and "leverage" them.

George L. Mosse found the fascist temperament was at the heart of communitarianism. Fascism was a "scavenger doctrine" that pulled together old threads of community, picked up on prejudices and affections that people scarcely knew they had. Fascism posits a heroic, even mythic, past that portends the true destiny of the people and the nation. Often it sees the values of that past and the prospect of that destiny as betrayed, and promises a return to greatness. It values nationalism and militarism above all other virtues. Fascism rejects individualism, but absorbs its power in the collective, "each through the power of his own will". Mosse described fascism as a "civic religion," or the "people worshipping themselves".

Little here is inconsistent with the politics of Trump. Watch the Tea Partiers performing the rituals of their religion: in the uniforms of the disfranchised, the non-elites; hands on hearts gazing up to the flag, joining in the anthems, repeating the oaths and the nationalistic platitudes; calling out the treacherous enemies. Mosse found an occult thread in fascist ideology. It might be stretching a point to call some varieties of the born-again churches "occult" or even the near-worship of the tendentiously read founding fathers, but it's possible that they serve the same psychological purpose. If fascism makes scapegoats, Trumpism has them in abundance. If it advances a story of betrayal, manipulates the truth with lies and exaggeration, plays to the emotions more than the intellect, bullies and struts, promises to eliminate the nation's enemies at home and abroad, sets up "counter-types" to the national (or racial) aesthetic, plays on fear (Bolshevism in the 1930s case, Islam now), artfully uses the media as an instrument of mass persuasion while avoiding all serious scrutiny and indulges in spectacular display, Trumpism does that too.

If, as Mosse insisted, with all fascisms there is a unifying aesthetic, watch the Republican convention.

According to Gwynn Guilford, who went as an ethnographer to Trump rallies in Ohio this year, in each case, in the long wait before Trump arrives, the crowds are told over loudspeakers to look out for pro-testors in their midst, but not to touch them. Instead they are to chant "Trump! Trump! Trump!" until security arrives. "This happens repeat-edly ..." Until Trump turns up, they are constantly reminded that their community is threatened by saboteurs and non-believers, which means that when he finally arrives their devotion is at emotional breaking point. The press, meanwhile, have been corralled in a "cattle pen" at the back of the room. At various points in the speech Trump "scowls" at them and calls them the "most disgusting" and "most dishonest" people he's ever seen, pantomiming his disdain with an elaborate sneer before goading his supporters to turn and glare too. On cue, the crowd turns and boos. The orchestrated hate-filled rally was the primary grass-roots weapon of European fascisms.

"I alone", he said in his convention speech. If fascism pivots on the concept of the great leader with uncanny, almost supernatural instincts who alone can lead the nation from its existential crisis into greatness, Trump qualifies here as well. His hair qualifies him: it attracts attention, renders him singular, the one, the lone visionary. The choreography of his arrival at the RNC in the Trump helicopter, with the music from *Air Force One* booming out over the whirring of the blades, as the "Aryan" wife and children rushed forward to meet him, was fascist theatre, and it is hard to believe the performance was unconscious – unless it was unconscious self-satire. When the family are lined up behind him, you could think he was making a point about racial purity, and that the reified women are there to signify the duty their gender must perform – but it's probably more about the 1950s.

Yet, were he to win the presidency in ways resembling Hitler's or Mussolini's, it's inconceivable that Trump's next steps would resemble theirs. His brutish and ingenious destruction of the country club Repub-licans, and the capitulation of most of the remainder, are shameful and concerning, but even if this meant the end of the Republican Party, that is not the same as the end of US democracy. The Germans of 1933 had had a decade of democracy. The Americans have had a lot more than that.

The one condition on which fascism depends is a nation in deep economic crisis with nowhere else to turn. The United States is not in that condition. Far from going backwards, much of the United States is doing very well. Consider *The Martian*, a western for the globalised American elites. In keeping with the old western genre, it is an artistic expression of the Monroe Doctrine. The exceptional American in this case is played by Matt Damon, but it could have been James Stewart. Left alone on the frontier of space, our hero, having no instinct for philosophy, survives by combining traditional American can-do and the boundless possibility of American diversity. In the end he is saved not by his own dauntless courage and the help of, say, Walter Brennan or a big-hearted Lutheran dirt farmer, but by dauntless courage and a Silicon Valley hipster nerd, a number of scientists from the Indian subcontinent, a charitable act by the Chinese government, and a valiant, self-sacrificing female mission leader. And there was Trump saying he could not trust a judge because his father was born in Mexico.

Still, there is that unyielding poll figure: over 60 per cent of the population believe the country is heading in the wrong direction. Even as Obama's popularity has risen, and the economy has slowly recovered, the number has stayed the same. For this and many other reasons, Trump could win. If he does, it will not prove Mosse was wrong when he said European fascisms were unlikely to recur; rather, that he was right to say, "the fragments of our Western cultural and ideological past which fascism used for its own purposes still lie ready to be formed into a new synthesis, even if in a different way". Communitarianism, revivalism, populism, racism, messianic Christian faith, paranoia, provincial ignorance, patriotism, war, exceptionalism – the traditional forces in American life and politics combined with the deep divisions and the fear make that synthesis possible.

And if Trump doesn't win, will he walk away? Will his followers? He is telling them if he loses it means the vote was rigged. He doesn't need to be an actual fascist for the day after election day to be a worrying prospect.

7.

*"Look, Walter", Dulles told him, "I've got to get some real fighting men
into the south of Asia. The only Asians who can really fight are the
Pakistanis. That's why we need them in the alliance. We could never
get along without the Gurkhas".*

"But Foster", Lippman replied, "the Gurkhas aren't Pakistanis".

"Well, they may not be Pakistanis, but they're Moslems."

"No, I'm afraid they're not Moslems, either. They're Hindus."

*"No matter!" Foster replied, and launched into a half-hour lecture
about the dangers of Communism in Asia.*

—Stephen Kinzer, The Brothers

*The issue can be stated as a very direct proposition. If the United States
cannot accept the existence of such limits without giving up democracy
and cannot proceed to enhance and extend democracy within such limits,
then the traditional effort to sustain democracy by expansion will lead
to the destruction of democracy.*

—William Appleman Williams,
The Tragedy of American Diplomacy

If any of this year's candidates ever read William Appleman Williams,
there has been no sign of his influence. Hillary Clinton might have once
been seduced by his theories, but as secretary of state and now as the
Democratic candidate, she belongs firmly with the Arthur Schlesinger
school of triumphalists. Williams liked his history to make people "think
otherwise". That is to say he was a revisionist: "one who sees basic facts
in a different way and as interconnected in new relationships", to use
his own definition. The revisionist upends the *Weltanschauung* (how you
see the world and how you think it works). Though a radical thinker
and sympathetic to the social revolutions of his time, he was quick to
add that his argument was neither categorical nor treasonous. His readers should not "mistake a candid and searching re-examination of their
own mythology for a tirade of useless self-damnation", he said. Nearly

sixty years on, that mollifying line on the first page of *The Tragedy of American Diplomacy* is as telling as any in the book. Re-examining American mythology is the one thing that American democracy – and American foreign policy – has not been able to do.

For Williams, US foreign policy was an extension of US commercial need and ambition; more than that, it was governed by the same thinking and the same myths as governed the country's worldview. The myths were these, he said: the United States was isolationist until power was thrust upon it; except for a brief adventure around the end of the nineteenth century it was anti-imperialist; by "a unique combination of economic power, intellectual and practical genius, and moral rigor" the United States could be the world's beneficent policeman, without an empire to taint it. But the truth was, he said, the United States had been bent on expansion since Benjamin Franklin declared it necessary for the democracy. Half a century later, the country declared the Western hemisphere its natural domain. The problem of reconciling a republic with an empire was solved by deciding expansion was essential to the strength and virtue of the republic. There could be no freedom, no democracy – and no fulfilment of God's will – without expansion; be it west of the Appalachians, west of the Mississippi or west of the California coast. Freedom and the other great virtues of the republic were rendered inseparable from commercial interest. To "extend the sphere", in James Madison's words, was the only way the public could be good *and* wealthy.

The genius of US imperial policy was to expand American corporate and national interests without acting or looking like an imperial power, or feeling any need to confess it to anyone, least of all the American people. The so-called Open Door Policy meant an "informal" empire: doors that didn't open readily to American business interests were kicked in, but sheer economic power and muscular application of various inducements reliably forced the issue without the need for occupying armies. Unlike Rome, the republic remained, as did the old anti-colonialist strain, and there was just enough truth in the idea that American trade and influence was good for the underdeveloped world for Americans to feel that theirs was a "virtuous omnipotence".

But an empire it was and has remained. Anyone who doubts the proposition need only read Williams; and anyone who likes a good imperial yarn (in an American vein) should go to the story of those two great door-kickers John Foster Dulles and his brother Allen. Both sides of the Presbyterian character (or the two human responses to the doctrine of election) that are often found in one individual were here found discretely in two: Foster Dulles was a dire moralist and his brother Allen a rake and adventurer. The seventeenth-century Puritan and the frontier individualist joined in the glue of American exceptionalism. Both were hitmen for the cause of US world supremacy. There is astonishing venality, bastardry, deceit and hypocrisy in their story, along with the pitiless exercise of power. But what is more alarming is their misjudgement. In the 1930s, as evangelists for Wilsonian "liberal internationalism", the brothers led a crusade against "Bolshevism" of any stripe and for American business – including business that was crucial to German industrial strength. In March 1939, a week after German troops occupied Czechoslovakia, Foster told the Economic Club of New York, "Only hysteria entertains the idea that Germany, Italy or Japan contemplates war upon us". Two months after the invasion of Poland he had not changed his mind.

On the other side of the war, as Eisenhower's secretary of state and "global attack dog" for the wonderfully Puritan doctrine of containment, he did his best to make sure that the Russians were as paranoid as it was possible to make them, and Americans just as fearful. He took a collapsible lectern whenever he travelled and kept the people thoroughly abreast of his opinions, all of which reinforced their fears, assured them of their country's righteousness and persuaded them that the American Way should be the way of the world. A few doors away in the same street, Allen Dulles ran the CIA in lock step with his brother. They "turned the State Department and the CIA into a reverberating echo chamber for their shared certainties".

There were alternatives to the perilous course that postwar history took. Even if we believe that the United States was never the party that made it perilous, and that the alternatives were worse than the path taken, it remains deeply disturbing to think that on decisions taken by the Dulles brothers the fate of nations and all our lives depended.

Half a century on from the days of the Dulles brothers, observers noticed the same pattern of mutual reinforcement among the people gathered around President George W. Bush. These days it's called "groupthink". Groupthink means everyone pretty much agrees on everything and ignores evidence or logic that might point in another direction. The only thing this group was thinking of was invading Iraq. A "slam dunk", one of them said. As the groupthinking went on around him, Bush took up the banner of American exceptionalism with the eloquence of old – the "untamed fire of freedom will reach the darkest corners of the world". Here was groupthink for the masses.

If all America could do was reassert the ideology and policies of the past, rather than accept the limits of its freedom of action, it was doomed, William Appleman Williams said. In 1979, just before the seemingly endless Middle East wars got underway, President Jimmy Carter made a speech that asked US citizens to re-examine their thinking, to "think otherwise". For a millisecond he opened a different door.

The chief subject of the speech was the energy crisis, but Carter addressed something "deeper". "In a nation that was proud of hard work, strong families, close-knit communities, and our faith in God, too many of us now tend to worship self-indulgence and consumption", he said. Boiled down, Carter was asking Americans to change the way they lived and the way they thought about the world. The country had drifted into a "national malaise". He "invited Americans to rethink, in the most fundamental way, what it means to be a free human being".

Carter always subscribed to exceptionalism, and still does. He was not asking the country to renounce the creed, but to look again at its meaning. He was a devout Southern Baptist, an evangelical; the speech, said Hendrik Hertzberg, who was then his speechwriter, was "an exercise in national pastorship". It was a renewal speech, straight from Jimmy Carter's communitarian heart. Carter was speaking of something like another Great Awakening.

The "American malaise" speech might have caused William Appleman Williams to hope the *Weltanschauung* was up for reappraisal. Instead, Carter learned that no president was going to question the national mythology and get away with it. "He has said the malaise is ours, in the tones of a man who knows that it is his own", wrote Eugene Kennedy in *The New York Times*. How dare he "sermonize" to this "big muscular nation", wrote George Will. Self-interest, not self-sacrifice, was the nation's "bedrock", said Irving Kristol. Soon after the speech, the Soviet Union invaded Afghanistan. Then Iranian revolutionaries made hostages of fifty-three embassy staff in the uprising that overthrew the Shah installed

she tells the crowds on the campaign trail – the admirals and generals of the "world's greatest military". With Trump as her opponent, Clinton is doubtless the "safe" option: but she is also a fully fledged, and some would say dangerous, foreign policy hawk with no demonstrated ability to think beyond the doctrine of exceptionalism to which she subscribes as a matter of faith.

But of course, in an election, where foreign policy is concerned, every political speech descends (or rises, if bombast's your measure) into the same crowing, self-glorifying cant. Every political debate tends to come down to one side saying the country is the greatest on earth, and the other saying it used to be.

8.

You know what you did? You embraced the insanity you were telling us about.

—Don DeLillo, *Great Jones Street*

In the wake of the spectacular Democratic convention it seems unreasonable even to hint at the possibility, but if Trump were to win in November, Hillary Clinton might be the deciding factor. Such speeches! Such enthusiasm! Such ideals! Such drama and emotion! Such a pseudo-event! But a woman nominee – such a moment. And one to make Trumpland look ridiculous. Even that old lizard Bill Clinton was poignant in his way.

But Bill Clinton is the author of NAFTA and the president who ended Glass–Steagall. Hillary Clinton is going to the fight with Trump on a promise to at least look again at NAFTA and reintroduce an equivalent to Glass–Steagall to keep the banks in line. Thanks to Bernie Sanders, that's in the platform. So is a resolution to break up the banks that Congress bailed out – and didn't punish for their sins. Hillary is also now committed to scuttling the Trans-Pacific Partnership, which her new pal President Obama badly wants because it's a big part of his geopolitics. Hillary Clinton has a platform that really isn't hers. The Democrats are proceeding as one party, but in truth there are now two – one subscribes to neoliberalism and the other foreshadows its demise – and she has to represent both of them. Philadelphia was a beautiful and moving thing, and Democrats can only hope that all those tears of joy and love were enough to wash away the contradictions.

This might be unfair. Whether she was driven there by Bernie Sanders or has chosen to renew her old Methodist vows to the poor and meek, Clinton is running on a progressive ticket now, and she might decide to make that the colour of her presidency. She promises to invest heavily in the cities to lift people out of poverty; to invest in infrastructure, create jobs, revive manufacturing and raise the minimum wage. The platform promises comprehensive immigration reform, an end to student debt, paid family leave and much else. It *is* very likely what Sanders said it was – the most progressive platform in the party's history.

Listening to her now, you might think that after years as a member of the supply-side economics church, Hillary Clinton's joined the revived and steadily expanding demand-side one. Could she in eight years reverse the engines of inequality and corruption, bridge the divides and enliven the democracy? Could she desegregate the cities? Could she get her country leading the world by example to save the planet from global warming? Could she do something about the lobbyists, the power of money in Washington that is destroying American democracy from within? Take on Wall Street? Make the effort on behalf of public decency and ordinary justice that was not made after the financial collapse? Could she get the public interest represented in Washington again? Could she do something about guns? In Chicago on the Memorial Day weekend, sixty-nine people were shot. Six died. As of 1 August, 401 people had been murdered in that one city in 2016, 90 per cent of them with guns.

Are *any* of these things open to remedy? Probably not: the problems run too deep, but the effort would be uplifting and a more productive way to prove her country is exceptional than anything she might have in mind for bloodying foreign noses.

Could she get American troops out of Afghanistan, the fifteen-year war she mentioned not once in her acceptance speech in Philadelphia? That might be the most unlikely of all.

Nothing she says, old or new, will much impress voters who don't trust the Clintons, or think they reek of entitlement, lies and money.

The hole she's punched in the glass ceiling won't impress them. But the prospect of Hillary and Bill back in the White House might lift their loathing into realms of mania. It will feel like the ultimate corruption, the ultimate insult, the ultimate proof that the system stinks. You don't have to share this point of view to understand it. At the very least, her supporters could ask themselves what *they* would be making of the $153 million in speaking fees or the $1.8 million she collected from speeches to the banks, if they were pinned to Donald Trump – or to Mitt Romney or John McCain. Ditto the emails. The reasonable fear is that Hillary Clinton will be tempted to pacify the haters by the military expression of exceptionalism.

Clinton just *has* to win. If she loses, not only does the world get Donald Trump (and the US Supreme Court his appointments): the Democrats will have to live forever with their decision to make their nominee the most qualified presidential candidate in history, but also the person most disliked by the American public and possibly the only one that Trump could beat. And with the email business forever hanging about, it might get worse.

We can hope that from her example great numbers of American women will draw inspiration, and believe that both wisdom and opportunity will deepen with their influence on public life. It should have been a moment of pure celebration, seeing Elizabeth Warren on the hustings with Clinton early in June. But you could feel the hackles rising on every neck in every bar in every swing state across the country. Warren mocking Trump, trading insults – and the guys in the bar think she's mocking *them* and make a little resolution and write it inside their hats – "Vote this time". The triumph of one identity is the violation of another.

Trump says, Hand your fear over to me. Hand your loathing over too. I will deal with your enemies as I have dealt with mine. I will give you back your freedom, and your country. Your old lives will be yours to live again. I will halt the terminal decline. American exceptionalism, in which you all hold shares, will be underwritten by an exceptional American.

The Democrats scoff at Trump for wanting to take the country back to the past. But for many of the people whose votes will count in November, Trump's imaginary past is a more concrete thing to contemplate than the Democrats' imaginary present. Trump's also contains more hope, and it serves as a more believable American tomorrow. If, as seems likely,

Clinton wins, it will not be out of love, or even hope, but rather out of fear. She can win by simply letting her deplorable opponent lose. On the other hand, she's nothing if not adaptable, and she could yet see in these very favourable circumstances (the Republicans falling apart, negligible interest rates, a public appetite for radical reform) the chance to lead the nation's social and economic regeneration through, for a start, massive investment in education, renewable energy and infrastructure, and an equally massive legislative attack on inequality and political corruption. Call it a New Great Awakening or a New New Deal; it would owe something to both, and to Bernie Sanders as well, but also to her need to be more than the first woman president. Reawakening the old grassroots reformer deep inside could not only heap manifold blessings on the nation and consolidate a liberal Democratic ascendancy; it is surely also the best antidote to the dark forces now feeding on the country's malaise.

In the Branded Steer, men and women sat round the bar drinking beer and eating hamburgers. It's out near the Milwaukee airport, on a junction of two eight-lane roads, the only eating house within walking distance of the airport hotels. Sitting there among these people of prodigious girth, I was thinking of *The Deer Hunter*. The food was much as you'd expect in a place called the Branded Steer. The barmaid called me "darling" and wanted to know how my hamburger was. I thought if I sat there for more than half an hour I'd get maudlin. There was a malaise in the Branded Steer that I didn't want to catch.

But too late, I began to feel sorry for myself, and it wasn't just the hamburger. I would have to walk back across those absurdly wide roads, past those miserable chain "accommodations", to my own dark dogbox in the bar-less, café-less Holiday Inn. There to surf the never-ending news. "Shall I kill myself, or have a cup of coffee?" was how Camus put it. But the only coffee in the Holiday Inn was what you could get from a slot machine.

It happens in the United States. You can be feeling terribly alive and then you fall into a pit. What were they thinking when they built that Holiday Inn? From what concept of humanity, what manner of philosophy, what thousand-year tradition of hospitality did it derive? How did it come about that humanity's snug little bars and street cafés have ended up in the Branded Steer? And downtown Janesville now lives in an eerie silence. The answer is from no philosophy; no thought at all, except the thought of profit. Commerce "has no principle that can withstand a strong temptation to her insatiable cupidity", as the preacher said.

Ten years after Jimmy Carter talked about an American malaise, John Updike wrote an essay about the state of the union. He found dozens of things that made Americans feel bad: poverty (one in four children), homelessness, crime, industrial decline, racial and generational discrimination, lawyers, bankers, doctors, foreign takeovers, AIDS, environmental squalor and destruction, stalemate in the Middle East, obesity – it was a long list. He called it a "malaise".

The malaise would seem to be, if not permanent, certainly recurrent. In a recent piece on Donald Trump, the American writer Richard Ford used the term again. But Ford's take is slightly different. It's not contemplating the country's failings that brings it on, but something lacking in oneself. To be sure, Donald Trump seems inauthentic, phoney, less than actual; but "it's really we who're threatened with not quite fully existing. It's we who're guilty of not having something better on our minds. It's our national malaise with life that's become the problem".

The TVs flicker half-watched in the Branded Steer. They flicker in the foyer of the Holiday Inn and in the room to which I take myself. Clinton, Trump, the shooting in Dallas, Muhammad Ali's funeral in Louisville's Kentucky Fried Chicken Yum! Center. How do they turn it off? All those flickering impulses that the Donald Trumps can prey on? By taking up the Democratic slogan "America is already great"?

They need an Ali, a hundred million of them, or a president like him brave enough to think otherwise, or at least to think again.

Quarterly Essay, September 2016

American carnage

When Watergate investigators cornered Richard Nixon, he told them lies. In the Articles of Impeachment it adopted, the House Judiciary Committee noted these lies, along with other "false or misleading public statements" the president had made "for the purpose of deceiving the people of the United States". As if lying to the people were a crime! According to *The Washington Post*, which has been keeping a tally, as of April 3 this year Donald Trump's false or misleading statements since becoming president numbered eighteen thousand.

Trump's mountain of lies might constitute a new category of high crime or misdemeanour – something like "making false or misleading statements for the purpose of whatever". For the purpose of satisfying the toddler's monomania, for the purpose of enlarging the hoodlum's desperate insecurity and insatiable self-regard, for degrading political debate to a level that he can manipulate, for rendering the presidency a monetised family fiefdom or mafia lair, for leading the United States into the post-truth world of fake news and alternative facts where reality itself is a partisan judgement, for subverting democracy. For the purposes of ungoverned greed and power.

That Trump was guilty of the crimes for which he was impeached is beyond doubt. That he is guilty of many others is just as certain. He has used the office to enrich himself, his businesses and his family. He has replaced competent and dutiful civil servants with members of his family and business colleagues. He has surrounded himself with courtiers and lickspittles, sacked any who are less than recreant, and installed political fixers in powerful government positions. He has been unremittingly partisan. He has incited violence, intimidated witnesses,

threatened the press, uttered racial slurs and lent comfort to white suprem-
acist groups. He is a tax evader; he has paid thousands of dollars in hush
money to women with whom he had affairs, US$25 million in settlement
of three lawsuits relating to fraud at his sham university, and US$2 mil-
lion to settle claims relating to the misuse of funds raised for charity by
the Donald J. Trump Foundation. He has boasted of groping women, and
several women have accused him of sexual assault, one of rape.

No president in the history of the United States has proved so unfit
to hold the office, and nothing has exposed his unfitness so calam-
itously as the coronavirus pandemic. A disease that has so far killed
120,000 American citizens, 30,000 of them in his native New York,
and close to half a million worldwide, has not for a second shifted his
self-revering gaze. Trump dismissed it as a matter of no consequence
at first, and the delay cost unknown thousands of lives. Ever since, he
has offered lies, denial and baloney. Nixon lied to investigators; Trump
sacks them. Among the five inspectors-general (government watchdogs)
recently purged was the one investigating shortages of medical supplies,
and another was responsible for oversight of the $1–3 trillion stimulus
(nothing to see there). In nearly four months, not once has the president
been able to sufficiently subdue his power-seeking, self-aggrandising
instincts to show by word or gesture a convincing sign of sympathy for
the dead and dying, the suffering and the grieving. Nor has his wife or
any member of his family. And then, in the midst of misery and fear,
Trump staged his stunt with the Bible outside St John's Church in Washington, and threatened to call out the military to put down the protests
and riots that followed the killing by a policeman of George Floyd.

Yet, menace though he is, and fervent as our hopes might be that he
will soon be voted out, Donald Trump is not the most alarming thing in
the present American debacle. He will go, sooner or later, but whether
it's this November or four years hence, the divisions in American society will remain. And, so long as one of the two great factions has made
widening them its operating principle, they will widen. So long as it is
in the interests of money and the media to widen them, they will widen.
Trump is alarming, but when military helicopters flying at rooftop level
and police and national guard in battle gear are deployed to violently
clear a public park for the sake of a presidential photo-op, or on national
television the president suggests ingesting disinfectant as remedy for

coronavirus, it is more alarming that he is still supported by 40 per cent of voters. It is more alarming that, like the police who stood and watched as their colleague killed George Floyd, medical people, as if too much in awe of his office and too fearful of his vindictiveness, looked miserable or bemused but said nothing as he burbled out his fallacies. As he is now, the gruesome sideshow to a deadly pandemic, so he was in the beginning when any one of a hundred things he said and did should have been enough to give any voter pause, and ten of them sufficient to recognise him for what he is – a crook and a thug conducting a heist. But they voted for him. That's the most alarming thing. In electing Trump, American voters projected onto the presidency the mountainous social and economic evidence of a nation irretrievably divided and declining.

The Democrats have plumped for Joe Biden, a famous "hands-across-the-aisle" healer thought deserving after two failed cracks at the job and eight years being the cool Obama's warm Joe Sixpack deputy. Far from the most talented or commanding of more than twenty candidates, the old white man was judged a safer bet than a Jewish democratic socialist, a high-achieving gay Midwestern mayor, or any one of several women, including the formidable left-wing senator Elizabeth Warren and the former Californian attorney-general Kamala Harris. If Biden's mind and body hold up until November and, what is almost as desirable, if he can convince enough of the electorate that he won't be wheeled out of the White House and into assisted living before his term is up – to be succeeded by his vice-president, whoever she may be – he might win in November. The polls suggest he'll bolt in. But the dirty bit is just beginning, and in the showdown to come we can only hope that believing Biden can knock over Trump is not the same as believing James Stewart was the man who shot Liberty Valance. (It was really John Wayne, lurking in the shadows of Shinbone's main street.)

Still, it was the moral of that film: Without myth, great men cannot fulfil their destiny, nor great nations theirs. (Nor the press: "When the legend becomes fact, print the legend", as the newsman says when he learns the truth at the end.) And, as the film also made clear, there are *two* myths – two big ones at least, two founding myths. There is James Stewart, the man of progress, all for education, a free press, capital works, the Constitution and the law – the Northeasterner, the communitarian, spiritual descendant of the pilgrim fathers. And there is John Wayne, the man of the past, all man and all heart, no education nor much time for the idea of it, the rugged self-governing individual, his rifle a symbol of his self-reliance, and in his hands the last guarantee of the good – the Westerner, descendant of the vanishing frontier. In the film their destinies collide and, though Wayne gets much the worst of the love angle (that's progress for you), they reach across the aisle as it were, and the evil one, the hoodlum, is vanquished.

The history of the United States being substantially the history of these divides, American politics is always to greater and lesser degrees their expression. They are essential to the Democrats' self-definition and without them the wellspring of their rhetoric dries up. How else could they speak of "healing"? If they could not say there are "no red states and blue states, only the United States", of what could they speak? If they could not pursue their healing mission, they would be obliged to mount their campaign on policy. They have plenty of policies. But in the modern political culture, policy is as welcome as sand in a carburettor. It does not belong in the media narrative. The Gettysburg Address does not belong. Short as the speech was, it was still too long for a tweet, much too long for a grab, and too complex, too radical by far. Americans don't like that sort of thing. You can't have everyone sounding like Bernie Sanders. One of his speeches went for eight and half hours. Americans don't like long speeches. Or Elizabeth Warren. Sure, she's brainy. That's her problem. Or half of it. George McGovern was brainy, and left-wing like Sanders and Warren – a liberal. He won one state in 1972. One. That's why they set the party up the way they did – to keep people like McGovern and Sanders out.

The necessity – real and imagined – to conquer evil has been a uniting factor in the country's history; the general excitement of conquering has been another. In these and smaller enterprises it is no small thing to have God on your side. And there's the treasure, of course. And the buoyancy granted by economic and technological headway, and a superabundance of consumer goods. There's manifest destiny and the idea that at once justifies the empire and disguises it, American exceptionalism. There's the American dream. There's Dolly Parton. And the Constitution, which in general has prevailed. The things that unite them are indeed greater than the things that divide them, as Democrats often proclaim, but that is only to say there's at least one bandaid for every wound. It is true that the nation has survived the great divides, and just as true that the divides have survived the nation. Now, in one nation under God, the factions are irreconcilable tribes, with different value systems, different assumptions and ambitions, different notions of truth. The basis upon which the nation has held values in common – freedom, the anthem, the Constitution, truth itself – is no longer agreed. The primal myths that, in Hollywood, came together to banish hoodlums have not come together against Donald Trump. Instead, one faction has made him the infallible projection of their contempt for the other side. On their behalf, Trump usurped the throne of America's elective monarchy and now charges all his critics with *lèse-majesté*. For Trump loyalists the thrill of his transgression is visceral. He is the embodiment of their freedom and their truth, their revenge on the condescension of the meritocracy, the corruption of governments, and the faithlessness of the parties that walked out on them. For the other faction, used to the old rules of engagement and the veneers of civilised argument, the world has been turned on its head, and it all happened so quickly and at such odds with received wisdom, the hardest thing is to stay calm and try to think what Jed Bartlet would do.

The signs were there with Hurricane Katrina: the social and racial inequality, the decaying infrastructure, and the ineptitude and heartlessness of a federal government wholly unaccustomed to any problem that couldn't be left to free enterprise in combination with the churches. Katrina probably was the beginning of the end for George W. Bush, which means it was something of a beginning for the Democrats. They could make ground on the failings of the Bush administration, and, if only by default, earn the support of society's losers. Enter Obama with the sharp mind and shimmering rhetoric, and Hope as his catchword.

There are the measurable distinctions of race, ethnicity, gender and class, and there are these and other social groupings asserting themselves as "identities". Liberals find it hard enough to distil their beliefs into a consistent and intelligible creed. Their philosophy, if not their nature, lends itself to ambivalence and contradiction, which liberal rhetoric only papers over. Before Barry Goldwater steamrolled Nelson Rockefeller for the nomination in 1964, the Republican Party was liberal. The liberal case can be politically powerful and entirely feckless. Roosevelt's New Deal and Johnson's Great Society go under the rubric of liberalism, but where some citizens see in these programs a notion of moral economy consistent with liberal tradition, swathes of Americans who might otherwise call themselves liberals see such government incursions into the national life as inimical to freedom, individualism and the American way. Philosophically, liberals can't reasonably deny the case for identity politics, or the causes behind it. Nor can they deny it and pretend to be in tune with the motley of contemporary American life.

The Democrats' problem is that identity politics sharpens focus on social and political fragmentation, and no party wants to be the party of that. The problem becomes deeper when some identities speak louder than others, or worse, louder than the voice of the party – worse still, decide the language in which the party speaks, what it is acceptable to say and what is not. The Democrats will not win the people's hearts and minds by telling them what they can and can't have in them.

Among those who need persuading are people who are neither particularly liberal nor particularly reactionary, but perhaps live in the rust belt and the Midwest and have their own identity and their own needs, which, with some justification, they feel the Democrats neither respect nor understand. By "deplorables", Hillary Clinton did not mean these undecided voters, but they could hardly fail to draw the inference that not all identities are equal. From every cause, the political mill extracts an opposite: so "Black Lives Matter" soon runs up against "All Lives Matter". Identity politics, which began on the progressive side of the mainstream, becomes, on the reactionary side, the *white* identity politics that has been profoundly helpful to Donald Trump's takeover of the Republican Party and the White House.

In theory, it is the purpose of democratic politics to resolve by debate what might otherwise be resolved by civil war. For reasons of financial greed and public entertainment, debate in modern democratic politics must come as close to war as possible. A slide from a 2018 internal presentation to Facebook executives read, "Our algorithms exploit the human brain's attraction to divisiveness". It went on to say that without change the site would attract "more and more divisive content in an effort to gain user attention & increase time on the platform". No change has been made. Fox News did not need algorithms: it did it on instinct.

As war reduces everything to competing war cries, so does modern politics. When communism no longer made for a credible enemy, liberalism, the philosophy on which more than any other the nation was founded, took its place. In the thirty-six years since Ronald Reagan announced it was morning in America, liberals have spent much of their time ducking the "L" word and trying to prove themselves worthy participants in the American dream. Bill Clinton dodged the "L" word by getting himself elected as a New Democrat. New Democrats, like New Labour in Britain and Hawke–Keating Labor in Australia, combined an insistent rejection of trickle-down economics with the practice of it. Though nothing Clinton did in eight years came within a bull's roar of what Democrat Lyndon B. Johnson's administration managed in one (1965), there were some grounds for forgiveness. Johnson had a liberal Congress and Supreme Court, and Republican opponents who had yet to adopt the strategy of blanket opposition that Clinton ran into.

Still, Johnson got Medicare for the aged and Medicaid for the poor, the *Civil Rights Act* for African Americans, federal aid to elementary and secondary schools for the disadvantaged, a few billion for his war on poverty, and much else, including new national parks and wilderness areas, and national endowments to the arts and humanities. Who knows what else he would have done if Vietnam had not brought him down? The country might be like a workers' paradise.

Johnson had another advantage: polls at the time showed that most Americans had faith in their politicians and the state. The efforts of the New Left to dismantle this faith were nothing compared to those of Reagan and his platoon of hairy-chested tax cutters and draft evaders. By the time Clinton got the job, the state was as dirty a term as liberalism. By then, excepting a few isolated pockets, liberal, communitarian and egalitarian ideals had been airbrushed from American political discourse, and in conservative quarters from the annals of American democracy. It turned out that the country had been built pretty much solely by entrepreneurs – though no one has ever explained why such a seminal American concept should be known by a French word that a lot of Americans can't pronounce. The entrepreneur was the human – or political – embodiment of the Chicago school of economics (or public choice or trickle-down economics … it goes by many names). Suddenly no one much cared if the entrepreneur was a decent human being or a repellent one; a benefactor or an exploiter of humanity; George Hearst or Thomas Edison; Theodore Roosevelt or the corporate thieves he loathed. It was not the person but the principle that mattered. It became a commonplace that, for Americans in their natural and unspoiled condition, government and all forms of reliance on it was anathema to the soul.

The tech boom of the '90s put the wisdom of free-market economics so far beyond doubt that Clinton could not resist the urgings of Wall Street donors and took the free-for-all to a logical conclusion: in 1999 he repealed the 1933 *Glass-Steagall Act* that restrained banks from operating as both commercial and investment enterprises. Now everyone could join in the entrepreneurial riot. By the time Hurricane Katrina hit, the ordinary functions of the state were too depleted and compromised to be effective, which for the likes of Newt Gingrich only went to prove the case that governments were no good at anything.

In 2006, I met a wealthy investor on the beach in Santa Monica: ex-Harvard, ex-GOP, ex-Goldman Sachs. In his view all his old connections had gone to the dogs. He told me in detail what was going on in Wall Street, and why the biggest crash since 1929 was coming within a year or two. When I asked him what could be done, he said: "Buy gold". (I never got around to it, of course.) If he knew, how was it that no one else did? No one with the power to do something to prevent it? As chair of the US Federal Reserve, Alan Greenspan saw it as a possibility, but thought markets would self-correct, much as companies so famously self-regulated. Appearing before a Senate committee in 2008, he seemed genuinely shocked that this had not proved to be the case.

In 2006, Timothy Geithner, then president of the New York Federal Reserve, might have wondered if all those derivatives were safe, but he didn't follow it up. Lawrence Summers was the economist who advised Clinton to repeal the *Glass-Steagall Act*. Obama made Geithner secretary of the Treasury and Summers director of the National Economic Council. The story of the bailout that the Obama administration engineered during the Great Recession has been told often enough. Trillions of taxpayer dollars went to banks judged too big to fail, and within a few years those banks were much bigger. In 2000 the combined assets of the six biggest banks was equivalent to 17 per cent of US national GDP. In 2015 the figure for the four biggest was 52 per cent.

Why Obama chose the people he did is puzzling. Why he approved a response to the GFC that amounted to socialism for Wall Street and free-market capitalism for everyone else is even more puzzling. Why there were no prosecutions is also puzzling. He could have taken on someone with a more liberal and imaginative mental cast, a warrior less compromised by past and immediate associations, less technocratic in attitude and appearance. He might have put in a Joseph Stiglitz or Robert Reich. Whomever he chose, Obama could have made the millions of poor victims of the crisis the focus of his energies – and his rhetoric. He could have got a few dozen prosecutions under way. The country with more people in jail than any other country in the world could surely find cells for half a dozen bankers. Maybe he didn't want to upset Wall Street. He was new in the job and wanted a steady start. Maybe he didn't want to look like an angry black man. He looked like a cool black man instead, which might not have been any more helpful. But anger was needed. The Great Recession shone a light on the United States so bright it was impossible not to see the staggering inequality and outrageous imbalance of privilege and power brought about by neoliberalism and the self-justifying lie of meritocracy. To put it another way, the country was dying of greed. Obama missed the moment, a historic opportunity to change the nation's course.

The Tea Party protests began within weeks of Obama's election. No one who attended the first wave of them could have imagined that gatherings of a hundred or so gun-toting misfits chanting for Sarah Palin and demanding "freedom" would end up controlling the US Congress and clearing the way for Donald Trump's election. Funding from the Koch brothers helped, but the Tea Party's staggering momentum was only possible in the absence of a countervailing force. When another New Deal or Great Society initiative was needed, the Democrats were not there; worse, they seemed to be on Wall Street earning, as Hillary Clinton did, US$250,000 per speech, or bathing in the auras of celebrity.

Of course, the Republicans blocked Obama at every turn, and of course Fox and Breitbart gnawed away, but hardscrabble America did not need much urging from nefarious corporate and alt-right sources to think Washington and both parties had abandoned them. Why would they not respond to populists? Obama put his faith in building bridges to his opponents, but so long as they would not take a step in his direction, he was stranded. He extended their tax cuts, talked their talk about their deficits, appointed their kind of people. He ceded ground until, as one of his liberal critics said, he began to sound like an Eisenhower Republican – which still left plenty of room for Tea Party Republicans to attack him. For all his calm intelligence and decency, Obama never rekindled the fire he lit when he became president. He was essentially a manager. In a recent book, George Packer described him as a "technocrat disguised as a visionary". Sure, just now civilisation would likely settle for a technocrat disguised as Ivan the Terrible, but if we accept Packer's judgement – and it's hard not to – we have to accept the part that Obama played in Trump's success.

When the independent senator Bernie Sanders ran for the Democratic nomination in 2016 it was to occupy a space in the political landscape that the Democrats had vacated in the '90s, and had left vacant long after it became apparent that economic rationalism and globalisation was a deepening social disaster. Trickle-down economics had caused torrents of money to flow upwards. The top 1 per cent of income earners owned 39 per cent of the nation's wealth while one in six children lived in poverty. As the rich got richer, their tax rates went down, which made them richer still, and the richer they got the more power they had to influence the political system. As Jane Mayer and Nancy MacLean have demonstrated in their separate studies, the effort to turn the country into a plutocracy (some might say, restore it to this state) – with the likes of James M. Buchanan, Ayn Rand and Milton Friedman lending it respectable intellectual roots – was conscious, orchestrated and relentless. It began in response to the New Deal and has never stopped. But it had deeper roots in fractures as old as the country itself: in the racial divides, in the clash of free-market and communitarian myths, and, in the case of Buchanan, principal founder of "public choice" economics and the Koch brothers' favourite economist, the loathing of someone from Murfreesboro, Tennessee, for the Northeastern elites.

Since Reagan's election in 1980, the US economy has doubled in size while real wages – the element on which, above all others, social justice depends – have flatlined, and taxes have become dramatically less progressive. In many parts of the country, once prosperous manufacturing towns have gone into unstoppable decline as US companies with unembarrassed zeal moved their operations to countries where workers get a pittance. One can see this as the natural operation of free enterprise, just the way of the world, and tell folk that it means they get cheaper goods. You can tell them that they will find better jobs in the knowledge economy or the gig economy. But it's a betrayal just the same, and that's how a lot of them see it. Add to their betrayal the evidence of social collapse, visible in the empty streets, and measurable in the statistics for health, suicide, drugs, domestic violence, crime, education levels, personal debt, evictions. The simpler measurement, however, is the success of the Tea Party, and Donald Trump and that slogan of his.

Despite remarkable popular support, the Democrats rejected Sanders in 2016 and again this year. He was a "socialist" and a "populist", so of course he would have lost. In fact he was on Johnson's Great Society trajectory, and to believe he would have lost in 2016 means believing against all logic that he would have lost states that Hillary Clinton won, because he almost certainly would have won the three crucial states she lost: Pennsylvania, Michigan and Wisconsin. He would have won them because his alternative to "Make America Great Again" was not the grotesquely inept "America is Already Great" or a continuation of New Democrat policies, but a doubling of the minimum wage and health insurance for everyone. He would have won by appealing to both the interests of workers and the old solidarities of those states.

It is the great triumph of neoliberalism to have persuaded so many Americans, including many Democrats, that the profit motive and individual self-interest is all that has ever governed their thinking and behaviour. It might be that, where the political parties and the commentators have failed, the coronavirus pandemic succeeds in showing up the many fallacies underlying this belief. If nothing else, surely, the experience has cemented in a fair sample of the public mind a reborn respect for collective as opposed to entrepreneurial solutions, for the justice in paying wages commensurate with the value of work done, for a health system that like so much else about the United States, including its president, does not resemble the chaos of a failed state.

And if he wins, will Joe Biden return it to order and success? James Stewart first encounters Liberty Valance when Liberty holds up the stagecoach in which he's travelling to the town of Shinbone. "Stand and deliver!" the robber shouts. If Donald Trump is Liberty Valance demanding America give itself up to him and his gang of thieves, Biden must be

Stewart, and who can be John Wayne if not an honourable Republican (or several of them) who, when all hope seems fanciful, will cross the divide. The evildoer will lie in the dust and the nation will be indivisible again, there will be no red states and blue states ...

Turns out there's nothing to worry about.

The Monthly, July 2020

WRITING AND ART

Mark Twain:
The wayward tourist

IN THE LAST DECADE OF the nineteenth century, Mark Twain was the most famous man in the United States; the "most conspicuous", to use his own words. For conspicuousness *worldwide*, he had no rival except perhaps Gladstone or Kipling, but Gladstone and Kipling could not rival his other claim to fame. For not only was Mark Twain near enough the most famous man on earth, in general he was held to be the funniest. That he was known as a funny man did not always please him, and his wife and children were adamant that "humorist" was less exalted than their man deserved. But humour was his genius and his bread and butter and his way of coping with the gloom that dogged him. His writing amused millions and at times his public lectures generated something very like hysteria. In packed halls the slight man with the shock of hair (it was auburn in his youth) and big moustache stood quite still next to a small table on the stage and, by simply talking and looking and pausing, created unstoppable, roaring waves of laughter and groans from people with the stitch.

He could do it to roughneck audiences in California and to stuffed shirts in the east and to all the varieties of society in between. He could do it in London and in Paris, and he could do it just as well to the common and anonymous as he could to the most revered. After sitting through one of his speeches in Chicago, the formidably unsmiling Civil War general and US president Ulysses S. Grant told Twain he had made every bone in his body ache; and observing him from a distance over a shipboard dinner Mary Mason Fairbanks wondered what gift this man possessed to make "venerable divines and sage-looking men [convulse] with laughter at his drolleries and quaint original manners".

There was more behind the spell he cast than his genius with words. He was a performer, a performing artist. He refined and rehearsed his lectures until he knew each phrase and its intonation by heart and could perform them with ease in his magical – a genteel listener said "abominable" – drawl. He claimed his sight was "of the telescopic sort" and used it to fix on certain people in the hall – an eye Bret Harte said was "so eagle-like that a second lid would not have surprised me". He told what he called "humorous" stories, as distinct from the "comic" story which was English and the "witty" story which was French. Any fool, he said, could tell the English and French kinds because they relied only on the matter of the story, but the American form depended for its effect upon the telling, and the telling was "a high and delicate art". An artist knew the trick was to tell it "gravely" and "conceal the fact that he even dimly suspects that there is anything funny about it". The humorous story was a rambling thing and full of incongruities of the kind made famous by Mark Twain's legendary predecessor, Artemus Ward: "I once knew a man in New Zealand who hadn't a tooth in his head" (long reflective pause – then, dreamily) "and yet that man could beat a drum better than any man I ever saw". Pauses were essential, pauses of exactly the right length. Mark Twain had pauses of all lengths from short to the nearly unendurable that he would break with some drollery – his "snapper" – that released the tension and the tide of cackles. He *worked* his audience.

Half of it was in the technique, half in the content. Knowing himself, he knew that the true humorist was a serious person if not a downright doleful one and that his stories depended for effect on the audience sensing this about him. "The secret source of humor itself is not joy but sorrow", he said. "There is no humor in heaven." His public performances were never without moments of pathos. He might, for instance, read from *Huck Finn* the scene on the river when Huck decides not to send Jim back to slavery, and lumps would form in two thousand throats – all of them to be dissolved in the next, invariably funny, story. It is possible that by these seemingly effortless combinations Mark Twain led his audience to feel that they were in the presence of not just a great artist but a great soul and "every bosom returned an echo", as Dr Johnson said.

Mark Twain was America's first superstar, and he had a star's temperament. He threw tantrums like any other prima donna and then disliked himself for doing it. He was sensitive to criticism. Signs of disrespect, such as a patron leaving his hat on, could enrage him. But he delighted people and delighted in delighting them. One of the funniest things he ever wrote was an imaginary conversation between Elizabeth I, Walter Raleigh, Francis Bacon, Shakespeare and other Tudor luminaries. It was written in cod Elizabethan, and called *1601: Conversation as It Was by the Social Fireside, in the Time of the Tudors*, and among its main subjects were flatulence and sex. On their walks together Mark Twain and the Presbyterian Reverend Joe H. Twichell would read it aloud to each other and end up laughing and rolling on the ground.

To please his wife or mother, or a muscular Protestant of the Joe Twichell kind, he could pretend to religious belief, but only with difficulty and it never lasted. Mark Twain was a disappointment to religion. He knew his Bible: raised a Presbyterian by his devout mother, he learned it as the Word of God, and all his life he drew on it for both material and style. He had charisma and gifts of insight, observation and persuasion for which most preachers would give their teeth. But he came to think that the Word of God was mainly claptrap and full of obscenities, unprovoked malice and irresistible inducements, he said, to juvenile masturbation. The grace his talents sometimes seemed to give him was attended always by anger and disappointment in both God and humankind.

Nothing riled him like the hypocrisy of Christians. The motto "In God We Trust" he said, "is simple, direct, gracefully phrased; it always sounds well ... I don't believe it would sound any better if it were true". Though he hounded the churches he was not opposed to the *idea* of them. "We *must* have a religion", his hero says in *A Connecticut Yankee in King Arthur's Court*, but far better to have it "in a split-up and scattered condition". Such churches exercising an independent conscience made for a healthier republic, but churches that had become allies of worldly power and privilege were not only gross hypocrites but a threat to democratic society. As for an established church, "any established church is an established crime", he said.

> She [the Church] invented "divine right of kings", and propped it all around, brick by brick, with the Beatitudes – wrenching them from their good purpose to make them fortify an evil one; she preached (to the commoner) humility, obedience to superiors, the beauty of self-sacrifice; she preached (to the commoner) meekness under insult;

preached (still to the commoner, always to the commoner) patience, meanness of spirit, non-resistance under oppression; and she intro-duced heritable ranks and aristocracies, and taught all the Christian populations of the earth to bow down to them and worship them.

If the churches offended his moral and democratic sensibilities, as he grew older the very idea of God wounded his common sense and added insult to the injuries done to innocent people, he among them in his mis-ery after the deaths of his wife and children. After his first and favourite daughter died he wrote: "He gives you a wife and children whom you adore, only that through the spectacle of the wanton shames and mis-eries which He will inflict upon them He may tear the palpitating heart out of your breast and slap you in the face with it". It was less that he did not believe in God's existence and more that he could not forgive Him for His crimes. Twain was halfway between a modern existentialist and the first one, Job. But in the end he was less amenable to comfort than Job. In his last work he wrote as Satan, and by then he was calling the Beatitudes "these immense sarcasms".

Mark Twain was born (two months prematurely) Samuel Langhorne Clemens, son of Marshall and Jane, in Florida, Missouri, on 30 Novem-ber 1835, and grew up genteel poor in Hannibal, a port on the Mississippi. Missouri was a slave state and Sam's father, a Virginian by birth and hopeless with money, owned at least two slaves and his uncle several more. The perennially cash-strapped Marshall sold the last of his, Jenni, when Sam was about seven years old. Marshall died four years later, at which point, so Sam said on his seventieth birthday in New York, his son began smoking in public (before that he had been "discreet" about it). A feeble infant who was not expected to survive more than a few months, for the first seven years, he said, he lived "entirely on allopathic medi-cine", in particular cod liver oil. The family had come into nine barrels of the stuff when his father took a drugstore for a debt and "it lasted me seven years. Then I was weaned".

The place of Sam's childhood and youth lived in his mind for the rest of his life. Hannibal and the Mississippi provided the setting for *Huckle-berry Finn*, and much else in all the forms and branches of his work reveals the indelible imprint it made on him. Along with his eagle eye he had a hypersensitive ear: one, he maintained, that could not stand cuckoo

clocks, church bells, opera or the German language, but served him fab-
ulously in most other things. From his memory of those river days he
brought forth hosts of characters, incidents, scenes, smells, and, most
tellingly perhaps, sounds – among them, voices, especially the voices of
the slaves. As much as anything else it was his recreation of the American
vernacular that made his writing so distinctive and influential. Through
that acute ear he managed to make the world speak for itself, and do it
intimately. There was the world of white Americans like Huck Finn,
who begins his tale: "You don't know about me, without you have read
a book by the name of *The Adventures of Tom Sawyer*; but that ain't no matter". There was the world of black Americans, like the teller of the ghost
story he related hundreds of times, *The Golden Arm*: "Once 'pon a time dey
wuz a monsus mean man, en he live 'way out in de prairie all 'lone by
hisself, 'cep'n he had a wife. En bimeby she died ..." And there was the
grand assumption behind the method: that the United States was vast
and various and had to be represented in its own voice and on its own
terms: "You tell me whar a man gits his corn pone, en I'll tell you what
his 'pinions is".

And from the river came his pen name: Mark Twain means "mark
two", the "two" meaning "two fathoms", meaning, on a paddle steamer
of the kind that for a time the young Sam Clemens piloted, the river is
twelve feet deep, which was the safe minimum for navigation. In his first
novel, *The Gilded Age*, he quotes his own conceit: one of the leadsmen on
decks calls, "By the mark twain!"

It was a commonplace among those who knew him that Mark Twain
was able to say and do things that Sam Clemens was not. Later analysts
argued that, unintentionally or not, the name spoke for the contradictions in Sam's character, or his desire to escape from them, or from
realities he feared, despised or found unbearable. All his life it was but
a very short step between truth and fantasy, dream and reality. He was
impressed by R.L. Stevenson's *Dr Jekyll and Mr Hyde* for its exploration
of the dual personality of which he thought himself possessed. Reading
William James on consciousness strengthened his belief in the reality of
dreams, especially his own. He was "acquainted (dimly)", he said with
his "spiritualized self", which "can detach itself and go wandering off
on its own ... I know that it and I are one, because we have a common
memory". This is why it is often very hard to say which of his stories,

including those he told on the stage, were drawn from his memory of real events and which from those he dreamed. He was talking about the dual personality just hours before he died. By then he had pretty well decided all Creation was a kind of dream. Maybe "Mark Twain" spoke for that too.

Four million people in the United States, one in every eight, were slaves when the Civil War began. Strangely for a slave state, when the day came Missouri chose the Union side; stranger still in view of his later opinions, Sam joined a Confederate militia. Circumstance more than pro-slavery or secessionist conviction propelled him to the southern side; nonetheless, at twenty-five he was still as he had been raised and taught, a racist and a Southerner. His membership of the ragtag company was a bit like Coleridge enlisting in the navy, except Coleridge lasted just a night and Sam a fortnight. For the whole time they were engaged in retreating (always with wet feet and then they "ran out of umbrellas"), until the whole company "became so fatigued we couldn't retreat anymore".

He headed west to the goldfields of Nevada and California where he failed to find his fortune, but in the newspapers of California he did find his vocation and in the mining camps and bars another lode of writer's material. For the *Alta California* and other newspapers he wrote gems about mining life, street life, the life of crime and the lack of life in religion. He wrote about San Francisco's startlingly frequent earthquakes, and occasional brilliant hoax pieces, including one about a petrified man found in the mountains, "pensive" in attitude and welded to the rock he sat against for centuries. A Sacramento paper sent him to the Sandwich Islands from where he dispatched a series of articles and collected the material for his first series of lectures. He went back east, a "disreputable looking" figure on a cholera-stricken boat in 1867. He was thirty-one and well started on the way to being the famed Mark Twain, journalist, humorist and author of a story about a frog – *The Celebrated Jumping Frog of Calaveras County*.

Some writers, his erstwhile friend and lifetime rival Bret Harte among them, get on the way to fame and stumble. Sam Clemens was never going to let that happen. He had charms to match his talents, and he soon had friends and admirers where they mattered: in New York, in the New England elites, and at the "great barbecue of corruption" in

Washington, DC, where he worked for a senator and came away hating politics and convinced that the hypocrisy of the American political system rivalled that of the churches. Of these friends the most important was the editor and prolific author William Dean Howells. Howells did more than anyone else to secure the passage of Mark Twain into the higher reaches (if not the very pinnacle) of American literature, and that of Sam Clemens into eastern society. With Howells there for the next forty years he was much less likely to fall, and it is because he didn't fall that in the last quarter of the nineteenth century American literature took on its distinctive character: "a lean, blunt, vivid chronicle of American self-invention, from the yeasty perspective of the common man", in the words of Mark Twain's most recent biographer, Ron Powers.

The view was present in his first book, an account of a voyage he took to the Holy Land and semi-sacred sites of Italy and Greece with a shipload of mainly pious pilgrims. *The Innocents Abroad* was published in 1869, and with help from a warm Howells review in *The Atlantic Monthly*, it was an instant hit. More than that, it at once established the tenor of Mark Twain's new American voice. *Innocents Abroad* was a different kind of travel writing. There were luminous descriptions of the wonderful things they saw with none of the genre's usual mush. In places from which normally awestruck platitudes tumbled forth he came up with satires. In the Church of the Holy Sepulchre he said he wept when he came across the tomb of an ancestor, Adam. He said the copies he saw amateurs making of *The Last Supper* were better than Leonardo's original. And he made the road to Damascus an excuse for flaying his companions who would not travel it on the Sabbath.

It was both the first modern travel book and a kind of boisterous scouting of territory in which Henry James would soon pitch his gorgeous tent. The habit among New World travellers had been to bow down and write about the wonders of the Old World from an Old World point of view. Mark Twain wrote from a New World point of view. Wherever he went he took the same "yeasty perspective" that he took to California or the Mississippi. He was an American and saw no need to apologise for it. It was the Old World that had some explaining to do.

Over the next twenty years Sam Clemens carved out his place in American life. He was the pre-eminent rider on the wave of American popular culture that, driven about equally by greed, newspapers and high ideals, rolled across the country after the Civil War. He was more than a rider: he was its clear and distinctive voice. He gave shape and consciousness to the age, spoke for it and against it, was both critic and exemplar. He was on the one hand Mark Twain, the conscience of America and the repository of pre-gold rush memory. He reckoned what had followed was "moral rot", an age that had invented "a thousand useless luxuries, and turned them into necessities, and satisfied none of them; it has dethroned God and set up a shekel in His place". On the other hand, he was a practical man like Hank Morgan, his Connecticut Yankee, and nothing if not adaptable. If success required accommodations as well as genius he could make them.

In 1872 he published *Roughing It*, accounts of his adventures out west and in the Sandwich Islands. A year later there was *The Gilded Age*, a novel written with Charles Dudley Warner to satirise the hectic, greedy times in which he lived, and for a long while prospered. There followed in rapid succession a book of short stories, the novel *The Adventures of Tom Sawyer*, and books of reportage and memory, *Old Times on the Mississippi*, *A Tramp Abroad* and *Life on the Mississippi*, which some people, including Kaiser Wilhelm of Germany, told him was his best work. And all the while he kept up a steady flow of newspaper and journal articles, many of them excoriating corruption, exploitation, imperialism and racism, and many of them merely descriptive or funny.

In the course of this great creative flow he wooed, with unremitting and ingenious intensity, and finally married the frail, demure Olivia Langdon, his *Livy*. She was the daughter of Jervis Langdon, a self-made millionaire, political progressive and passionate abolitionist who, with his wife, had been among the brave people who helped thousands of runaway slaves make their way to freedom in the North on the so-called Underground Railroad. Sam Clemens's Presbyterian Church had been for slavery and contrived to find it sanctioned in the Bible. It was in revolt against this reasoning that Livy's family had abandoned the Presbyterians and set up an abolitionist Independent Congregational Church whose principal minister was Thomas K. Beecher, the brother of Harriet Beecher Stowe. While Sam never took to the Langdons' church, he found their politics agreeable: pro-slavery and unmistakably prejudiced in his antebellum youth, as Livy's devoted husband he was an unremitting critic of Jim Crow and racism pretty well everywhere.

Livy bore Sam Clemens a son (who died as an infant) and three daughters. She also bore his long absences, his explosions of rage and the troughs of his fortune. But she would not bear less than decorous prose. She was forever knocking the rough edges off him, and her daughters, who knew nothing of Missouri, tended to support her in this project. She ran her polite eye over every word he intended for publication and amended as she went. "I hate to have your father pictured as lashing a slave boy", she wrote in one margin. "It's out. And my father is whitewashed", he wrote back. She would not stand "He left in a sweat": he made it "He left in a hurry". She objected to "stench", "breechclout" and "awful". "You are steadily weakening the English tongue, Livy", he complained. But he changed them all. It was in part to satisfy her mannerly ambitions that he abandoned his distinctive voice in the novels *The Prince and the Pauper* and *Personal Recollections of Joan of Arc*. His children thought they were just about the best books anyone ever wrote. His public was less enthusiastic.

For all the Clemenses' collective efforts, the Brahmins never quite accepted him and the literary snobs continued to label him a "mere humorist". But his phenomenal book sales, astute management of publicity, great gift for public performance, and his investments in the booming postwar economy combined to make him very rich. Believing his publishers had exploited him, he started his own publishing company and it got off to a stupendous start with Ulysses S. Grant's *Personal Memoirs*. The great general had been at best a feckless president in a corrupt age, but Sam liked him. His terse, plain prose was much more that of the general than the president. They shared certain political views: Grant despised slavery and even more he despised the slave interests who persuaded what he called "the poor white trash" of the South that they had common cause. He had no more time for American imperialism: the Mexican War in which he won his military stripes was, he said, "one of the most unjust ever waged". It was "an instance of a republic following the bad example of European monarchies". It might have been Mark Twain speaking. Grant's book was a triumph for both of them.

Sam Clemens poured his new riches into a magnificent house in Hartford, Connecticut, and stocked it with the finest furniture and man-servants. He and Livy entertained the liberal-minded wealthy and famous in grand style. He installed a billiard table and a telephone – the first, he claimed, in New England. He preferred the table. "The billiard table is better than the doctors", he said. The phone was no more than a "time-saving, profanity-breeding, useful invention" and he didn't think it would catch on sufficiently to make it worth investing in the company. But in general, he could not believe his luck.

Grant's was one of two books published by Sam Clemens in 1884–85. The other was *The Adventures of Huckleberry Finn*. What Grant had done in war, Twain did in *Huck Finn*. He took slavery head on. He put a boy on a raft with a slave and let him learn the astounding truth that the slave was no less a human being than he was: that you could not lash him without his feeling pain; you could not part him from his family without his grieving; you could not take his freedom without his wanting to regain it; and you could not give him back to slavery without forfeiting your own humanity. Like Grant in the war, in *Huckleberry Finn* Mark Twain prevailed.

Louisa May Alcott said the book was not fit for children and if Mr Mark Twain could not write something more uplifting he should not write at all. Then the newspapers joined in the chorus of polite disapproval. And then, anticipating the high-minded progressives who seventy years later proscribed *Huckleberry Finn* for calling negroes "niggers", the high-minded traditionalists of the Public Library of Concord Massachusetts declared that the book was "trash ... more suited to the slums than to intelligent, respectable people" and they would not have it on their shelves. They have given it "a rattling tip-top puff", said Sam Clemens, and once he got it into the papers it would sell "25,000 copies". Broadly speaking, he was right. He managed the press superbly, as he nearly always did, and the book was a financial success. But for libraries to ban his story while keeping unabridged Bibles available for children was an irony of a very bitter kind. It didn't help that his wife and favourite daughter were ambivalent about his masterpiece. They would have liked something a little less colloquial and a little more civilised, and in this they may as well have spoken for the mandarins who would never properly acknowledge his literary achievement.

It took a later generation to see the glories of *Huckleberry Finn* and how it transformed American literature. With few exceptions, the best American writers of the next century acknowledged its pervasive influence. The most recent is Norman Mailer, who, in a less than subtle inversion, says that to read the book now is to imagine that he has borrowed from Sinclair Lewis, John Dos Passos, Steinbeck and Faulkner: that one can see the hands of Heller and Vonnegut in the irony and Bellow in the picaresque; that it has something of *Catcher in the Rye* and traces of *Deliverance*, John Wayne, Victor McLaglen and Burt Reynolds. And much of it he surmises might well be "lifted straight from Hemingway". To this long list Mailer might have added *The Simpsons* and *South Park*, and the "down-home" affectations of the current US president. In fact a United States without Mark Twain is inconceivable and probably intolerable. As for Hemingway himself, he said *Huckleberry Finn* was the "headwater of American fiction … There was nothing before that".

No local panjandrum in his lifetime was as odious as the foreign one, the English one, Matthew Arnold. Arnold first offended by scoffing at Grant's grammar in a review in a British journal. Mark Twain scoffed back, bringing down the house at a New York club by reading a flatulent passage of Arnold's and declaring Grant's book a masterpiece and Grant himself an imperishable American hero. A couple of years later Arnold wrote an essay called *Civilization in the United States*. Boiled down, his thesis was that no such thing existed, and never could so long as the Americans persisted with their "glorification of the 'average man'". He referred as well to what he called, their "addiction to the 'funny man', who is a national misfortune". Mark Twain began but never finished a reply. But he did finish a book in which England is annihilated to the last man by modern American inventiveness and weapons of mass destruction and it is possible Arnold was on his mind when he wrote it.

The book, published in 1889, was *A Connecticut Yankee in King Arthur's Court*. Though not a great commercial success, it's hard to deny that here was another "headwater" of an emerging American consciousness. Within a couple of decades of Mark Twain's death the *Yankee* was made into a film starring that other homespun chip off the democratic block, Will Rogers, and there have been at least half a dozen other versions, including one with Bugs Bunny as the Yankee. *A Connecticut Yankee* was satire, science fiction, burlesque, Marx Brothers farce, reminiscence — and, as always, a moral fable. It was also a statement of his bleak vision, even a prophecy of the cul-de-sac he imagined the United States, if not mankind, had entered.

As Sam Clemens was a man of the New World and loved America and democracy so did his character, Hank Morgan. Hank even liked the sounds Sam liked and put them to the same comforting use. Finding himself trapped in the sixth century he indulges his memories of the New Haven train: "this k'yar don't go no furder – ahh-pls, aw-rnjz, b'nanners, s-a-n-d'ches…" Hank converts King Arthur to the cause of liberal capitalist democracy and stands like Mark Twain and General Grant against the things that spoil or threaten its perfection: ignorance, superstition, privilege, greed, cruelty, poverty and racism. In their place he gives them science, humanism, know-how, patents, newspapers, bicycles, dynamite and marketing. He gives them irresistible progress. But just when the Stars and Stripes start billowing in every reader's heart the whole thing self-propels into the farce of Armageddon: a massacre staged by good people whose technical superiority has sapped their senses. As if mesmerised by the machinery he commands, Hank Morgan becomes a prototype of a later species of American; if not quite Dr Strangelove, then Donald Rumsfeld and other modern military spokespersons: "Of course we could not count the dead because they did not exist as individuals, but merely as homogeneous protoplasm, with alloys of iron and buttons", says Hank.

Clemens had a great fondness for the past but his imagination was modern. He could not resist mechanical things. He studied them, bought them and invested in them. He bought a typewriter and put two typists to work on the manuscript of *Huckleberry Finn*. He bought a bicycle. When his arm grew painful from writing he bought a phonograph and dictated directly into it before abandoning the thing because "it hasn't any gift for elaboration". He invested in dozens of new inventions. Not all of them were duds, but the one that really mattered was. For years he poured money into the development of a typesetting machine that the inventor had convinced him would forever change the printing business. He believed that, once perfected, every newspaper in the world must have one, and it would become for the inventor and himself a veritable money-making machine. But it sank and the Clemens fortune sank with it. The family moved to Europe and exile from the financial calamity. Then his publishing company sank as well and was declared bankrupt in April 1894. Though he was required to pay only part of the debt he told *The New York Times* he would be paying "100 cents in the dollar".

That is how Mark Twain happened to come to Australia in 1895 – to pay back his debts through a lecture tour. "I've got to mount the platform again or starve", he said. He signed up to tour countries on five continents and give 150 performances. He started with a couple of warm-ups in Cleveland, Ohio, and travelled by train to Vancouver, from where he caught the steamer *Warrimoo* for Sydney. He had companions: "Two members of my family elected to go with me. And a carbuncle". The family members were Livy and Clara, his second daughter. Both of them were depressed by his need to become a "mere humorist" again.

The *Warrimoo* anchored in Watsons Bay on 15 September. Soon after that the press arrived in a launch and an interview was conducted as the writer leant over the rail. A winch was operating noisily, so much that what was said by one party was not heard by the other, and vice versa, but *The Sydney Morning Herald*'s representative heard enough to report that when Twain was asked for his views on Australia, he replied, "I don't know. I'm ready to adopt any that seem handy". Even when they heard him clearly, it was sometimes hard to say what the great humorist had actually said and what the journalists permitted themselves to imagine Mark Twain might say.

He got off to a sticky start with the newspapers. When he said he favoured free trade they said he had insulted Sir Henry Parkes, who favoured protection. If Parkes took offence he did not show it and when the two men met he pressed on him a book of his notoriously bad poems. Then Mark Twain offered his now low opinion of Bret Harte, and the Australian press said that he had insulted all the Bret Harte readers of the colonies. He offered the view that there was some merit in the theories of Henry George, but he didn't think they would come to anything practical. This was also held to be bad form. So at the end of the second day he said, "Having thoroughly established my reputation for humor by talking of politics seriously, I shall stop".

Instead he cast a curious and generally benign eye on wherever he was taken and whatever he was told or given to read about the country. Australian readers hoping for something equivalent to Tocqueville's timeless observations on American democracy will be disappointed. Mark Twain did not overly extend himself or his readers when he wrote about Australia. But in the discursive, eccentric, intimate account of the journey he called *Following the Equator*, he glided around the colonies like a man on roller skates, and more than a century later his prose is still fresh enough to take his readers with him, including those in need of re-enchantment with their country's past.

The Clemenses were greeted – almost literally – like royalty, and the lectures, called "At Homes" were triumphs. Of the first one, at the Protestant Hall in Castlereagh Street, *The Sydney Morning Herald* reported: "The man's work and the feeling of it was endlessly in the hearts of his audience, who not only cheered but waved hats and handkerchiefs as he stepped out from behind the Stars and Stripes". In Melbourne, an archdeacon in a box seat laughed so much he "turned scarlet and banged his walking stick on the floor". There was the *Jumping Frog* sketch, *The Golden Arm* and, for seriousness, the moment in *Huckleberry Finn* when Huck saves Jim from slavery. The *Telegraph* said he was like "an old friend – a personal friend" whose appearance produced "a spontaneous expression of love and admiration". The organ of Australian radical nationalism, *The Bulletin*, was there and their reporter said Mark Twain looked like "an amazed gum tree". *The Bulletin*'s most talented contributor, Henry Lawson, the man who for a moment promised to be Australia's own Mark Twain, went to a performance and demanded a chair at the foot of the stage because he was deaf. It was reported that he cheered and beat his stick with enthusiasm, which only makes it seem sadder – and stranger – that there is nothing anywhere to say Lawson met him face to face. Of all the comparisons to be made between Australia and the United States at the time of Mark Twain's visit, none is more instructive or dispiriting than that between the American's passionate and supple democratic philosophy and the sentimentality and jingoism that were about to consume Henry Lawson – a comparison of their literary production is, of course, no less depressing.

J.F. Archibald, *The Bulletin*'s editor, did meet Mark Twain. He took him fishing and afterwards put around the story that he had employed a boy to wait out of sight on the rocks below them and attach fish to the visitor's line. In an article in 1992 Richard Hall argued it was Archibald who gave him the impossibly tall tale about Cecil Rhodes and a shark that Twain retold in his book about the tour. Mark Twain knew that the locals took it as their stern duty to pull the legs of foreigners, and it is hard to believe he would have taken such preposterous bait. But perhaps he was tired and his resistance was low. Another joker may have fooled him with the one about a Tasmanian sheep-eating parrot. Whatever it felt like then, to have made a fool of Mark Twain does not now inspire feelings of patriotic pride. Then again, in his youth Mark Twain had been capable of his own hoaxes and professed a "democratic" view of fact and fiction. "I could remember everything whether it happened or not", he once said. It is possible he might have thought that by repeating the story the joke was on them. It is even possible he dreamed it. Fascinated equally by science and spiritualism, his view of dreams and reality was also "democratic". Like his fictions his dreams were vivid and momentous. In Sydney he had one that he remembered for the rest of his days. In it he saw that the universe "was the physical person of God; that the vast world that we see twinkling millions of miles apart in the fields of space are the blood corpuscles in His veins; and that we and the other creatures are the microbes that charge with multitudinous life the corpuscles".

He was ageing, tired and in pain from the carbuncle. They still had thousands of miles to go – to New Zealand and back (all those "junior Englands"), to Ceylon, India (for more than two months) and South Africa. Wherever he went in Australia they loved him just the same, though the reports sometimes give the impression it was only partly for what he said. It was also for his consistent graciousness, and because he was Mark Twain. While he did not exactly "give them muck" as Nellie Melba once recommended to a fellow performer, he knew the proprieties and did not trouble his Australian audiences with social criticism or question with any vigour the direction the Australian colonies were taking. He arrived at the tail end of an economic depression, a drought, rabbit plagues and the great effort for Federation, and chose the rabbits for the immortal paragraph. He had missed the very worst of the worst economic depression in Australian history by only a couple of years, but it was the prosperity and success of the place he noted, and he warmed to the egalitarian spirit. Not that he was wrong to admire the public investment in civic buildings and services; the way a town of just forty thousand people such as Ballarat "has every essential of an advanced and enlightened big city". As for the labouring classes, it was as if the trade unions, which were at that moment recovering from withering defeats two years earlier, had misread their situation. "The workingman was a great power everywhere in Australia", Mark Twain wrote. He was right in this as well, though to say that in South Australia the worker was "sovereign" and that South Australia was his "paradise" was taking it a little too far. In his notebook he went even further: "Australia is the modern heaven – it is bossed absolutely by the workingman".

He did notice the effort for Australasian Federation and met some of the main players, among them Sir Henry Parkes. Federation had Mark Twain's blessing, but the man who so loved the American republic and loathed hereditary privilege, the established church and imperialism thought it would be "unwise" and unnecessary for the colonies to "cut loose from the British Empire". He had read the mood well. The Australian colonists were in general both pragmatic and loyal, and to the extent that they supported Federation they preferred it "under the Crown". The American colonists would have taken the same course if they had not been commercially oppressed, Mark Twain wrote. The truth is he loved England almost as much as he loved the English language. And Matthew Arnold notwithstanding, the English loved him, and he delighted in their approval. Rudyard Kipling got the Nobel Prize in 1905 but two years later Oxford gave Mark Twain a doctorate and chances are it meant as much to him.

It has always been the way and a great sadness to Australians of several generations: whenever celebrated writers, or celebrated anything, come to Australia they seem to be less interested in the people and their achievements than they are in the animals. It is surprising that Mark Twain was not photographed holding a koala. We crave his estimate of Alfred Deakin and instead find kookaburras, magpies, platypuses, boomerangs and the Melbourne Cup. Why Tasmania always gets the writers gushing forth, who can say? He spent no more than a few hours in Hobart, but this was enough for two chapters about the convict settlers and the cruelty of the system that sent them to the colonies for the pettiest misdemeanours. In Hobart he visited a home for the indigent and saw ex-convicts there: "a crowd ... of the oldest people I have ever seen". There are photographs of these survivors of the convict days. Not only do they look old, they look dead. They might as well be made of wax. It is not surprising that the visit seemed to leave a mark and made him think of "life in death". He saw no Aborigines, but he wrote more about them than everything else put together. By contemporary standards, his tone was grossly patronising and as often as not he had the facts wrong. But what he said about the "savages" was unfailingly sympathetic, curious and admiring and in this he ran hard against the local prejudice.

Perhaps inspired by Sir Henry's poems, at his third performance in Sydney Mark Twain came up with some verse. He said it was an example of how hard it is to write poetry when one knows nothing about it. It went:

Land of the ornithorhynchus
Land of the kangaroo
Old ties of heredity link us

Then he stopped. This was as much as he had with him, he said. He had composed three more stanzas but had given them to a man he met on the way to the hall who said he'd had nothing to eat for two weeks. The routine created one of those roaring waves of laughter, so he repeated it in several other places. It spoke sublimely for the traveller's dilemma and somehow captured the unequal and unresolved nature of the relationship between the two countries – and it was possibly the most brilliant thing he did in Australia.

Soon after they reached London the Clemenses learned that Susy, the eldest daughter and Sam's favourite, had died of spinal meningitis. "It is one of the mysteries of our nature that a man, all unprepared, can receive a thunderstroke like that and live", he wrote. Livy died a few years later after long, debilitating illness. Their third daughter, Jean, developed violent epilepsy and had to be placed in an institution. She died in her father's New York home a few months before he did. Sam thus outlived his wife and three of his four children. If he was America's "greatest and most embittered humorist" as William Safire chooses to describe him, there were these good reasons. There was as well what he saw as shameful American military imperialism and the complicity of Christians – and the Christian God – in the crime. In 1906 he wrote a Swiftian denunciation called "The War Prayer", but it was not published in his lifetime. He died in New York in 1910, the same year as Tolstoy, who might as well be called "Russia's greatest and most embittered novelist".

As a novelist perhaps Mark Twain does not measure up to Tolstoy, or to his countryman Henry James, or to the requirements of Matthew Arnold. Yet from the novels, stories and journalism of this "mere humorist" flowed all of American twentieth-century realism, and that influence of course went further still. Had he replied to Arnold's jibe at any time in the last thirty years of his life he could have said that the "funny man" was the clearest and most recognisable voice of his country, and more than those of any other writer his words and his imagination tell us what that country was like. Funniest or most embittered, he was also surely among the sanest Americans – and if he were alive now he would seem even saner. He was at once a critic of his country and its most loved citizen. That he had run away from the war that became the *sine qua non* of manly patriotism did not matter. That he lived for long periods in Britain and Europe did not reduce him in his compatriots' famously provincial eyes or dim his understanding of them. That he was a South-erner, a secularist, an anti-imperialist, an anti-racist and an ironist in an age when evangelical religion, the Monroe Doctrine, Jim Crow and un-diluted patriotism were ascendant creeds did not matter. He remained the essential American and the still small voice of the flimsy, paradoxical, eternal good in the democracy. For most of those who have read him he still is. The trick, as he said, was all in the telling.

Introduction, *The Wayward Tourist:
Mark Twain's Adventures in Australia*, 2007

Jan Senbergs

W<small>HEN</small> J<small>AN</small> S<small>ENBERGS WAS SIX</small> years old, he fled Europe's horrors with his mother and little sister in a horse and cart. They left behind his father who had just been shot and killed at their home in the Latvian forest. From Riga, courtesy of folk we now revile as "people smugglers", they took a boat in the night to a place behind the Allied lines in Germany. Then they walked. The next six years the Senbergs spent in various Displaced Persons camps. In 1950 they reached Melbourne.

Knowing this story, some of us see signs of it in Jan Senbergs's art: the monster machines, the ruins, the burned and broken bushlands, the contorted forests of habit and ambition, hubris and conformity, memory and invention that he makes of cities. Starting from the same premise, his dark, malevolent seas, heroic ships, cars scuttling on sinuous roads, bleak, abandoned mining sites, even the chaos and squalor of human settlement in Antarctica, all seem like variations on a theme brutally imprinted in his childhood. Where human beings go there goes an element of the beast, more or less rampant depending on circumstances.

Senbergs deals in menacing shape and inexorable force: his cities cling to the coast and bend and warp as if caught in earth's upheaving crust; his abandoned human sites are monuments to Time which is beyond our comprehension and the pathetically brief moment of humanity. His human beings are mocked both by Nature's grandeur and by the terrible instruments that their genius and flaws create. Their existence is implied by the technology with which they live, or the destruction they have wrought, but they are otherwise invisible. Those we do see occupy small corners, on meagre rations and furtive copulation.

Very likely Jan would reject all this as at least two-thirds tendentious hokum, and very likely he would be right. Even in the unlikely event that he thought it fair comment on his work, it misses the essential fact that grim and uncompromising as that work might be, he delights in the world he is depicting. God might be dead and the existential struggle hopeless, but there's glory to be had just the same. Senbergs meets indifferent Nature – including human nature – eye to eye, without sentimentality or pleading. He meets force with force. Paradox with paradox. Ambiguity with ambiguity. His dark signature line is his banner, sword and mind-bender.

Senbergs's paintings, prints and drawings can startle and incite something close to primal gloom and melancholy. Often enough they also chance upon a rare and original beauty, but never one he can be accused of seeking. That his work might ever be decorative, modish or gratuitously attractive, or didactic or moralising, heaven forfend! These are thoughts to haunt him. Irony he allows – indeed, thrives on – because irony is born of recognising our pitiful condition and is the natural means of managing it.

Senbergs does not tell the childhood story as if it were the thing that made him – his listeners retell it to themselves that way. To hear him tell it, one would think his life started when he got off the boat and, with barely a word of English, found a country congenial to his pagan taste. "Towns are excrescences", E.M. Forster said, "grey fluxions, where men, hurrying to find one another, have lost themselves". Not for Senbergs: a town was where he found himself, became a local and grew. The larrikin contrarieties of the landscape and its creatures; the rituals of football, horse racing, the punt, the pubs; the local insistence on not taking oneself or anyone else too seriously; the vernacular of Richmond and Fitzroy; the sun warming the democratic temper: he lapped them all up. A wog, a Balt or a reffo inevitably he was, but he was a very Australian one.

The streets of Melbourne and the bush beyond fed his imagination and his inquiring émigré's mind. So did reading, travelling, teaching, talking: there was the Melbourne art scene, the circle gathered round Rudy Koman, and he was also in time to angle his way into what remained of the old-left bohemian push that gathered at Tattersalls Hotel. By the time I met him twenty-five years ago, in addition to his reputation as an outstanding artist he had acquired an impressive formal knowledge of art, an assured grip on the Australian art world and an intimate acquaintance with local characters and haunts.

How the eleven-year-old Latvian refugee became this most generous, entertaining and obstreperous *bon vivant* might be called a miracle, were not these feats of creative adaptation proverbial among refugees when they are given any sort of chance. He was familiar with the paradoxical, overlapping worlds of Jorge Luis Borges *and* those of talkback radio. He read Calvino, Thomas Bernhard *and* the racing guide; listened to Schubert *and* the football; admired Max Beckmann, Soutine *and* William Barak; painted Antarctica and his studio and a kookaburra with equal bravura.

Many influences doubtless come together in his art, but minimalism is not one of them, or postmodernism. "Isms" don't appeal to him; or, if for a moment they do, he is quick to clear them from the decks before they get a hold. Students of his work see expressionism, surrealism and abstraction, but not to the extent that his name can ever be credibly linked to them. He is only comfortable as a maverick, an outsider, a dissenter like his Lutheran forebears. Originality is a faith with him, probably because he senses that to give it up will land him in banality or, worse, in fatal irrelevance; perhaps also because anything as prescriptive as a fashion or a "movement" might dampen a mind tuned to adapting. Survival is a creative enterprise.

As figurative artists tend to, Senbergs takes his inspiration where he finds it: in travels within Australia and abroad; in writers he has come upon, such as the American novelist Donald Barthelme and the Scottish poet Edwin Muir, and in familiar scenes and fleeting experience. Barcelona has inspired him, but so has a ship on Port Phillip Bay, or the asbestos mines in Western Australia, or a dead sheep in Tuscany. His fantastic elevated views of Melbourne and Geelong, including the brilliant *Geelong Capriccio*, drew inspiration from the picture maps of pre-Renaissance cartographers which gave shape to his own longstanding fascination with geography and place.

The set for *Blade Runner* might just as well have played a part in some of his wilder city paintings, but I doubt he has seen the film. I'm not sure that he has ever come across E.M. Forster's remark either, but people who have might be put in mind of it by those same paintings.

And that is the nub: even if we could show that at that moment in the Latvian forests, or at any other in his lifetime, his imagination formed like an atoll in the sea, he still had to *make* these images, and go on making them. To make them he had to have Jan Senbergs's indomitability, his acute and sympathetic eye, his curiosity, his joy and pessimism, his courage. If, as Simone Weil said, "Nothing can have as its destination anything other than its origin", then perhaps we are obliged to recognise that Jan Senbergs, artist, originated in his imagination and that's where he's been going all along.

Jan Senbergs exhibition catalogue, July 2013

Andrew Chapman:
Political vision

POLITICS IS NOT THE ONLY human activity where envy and pride, love and ambition meet every day as a matter of course. They meet pretty well wherever people go. But only in politics do these base elements of human nature meet daily with self-sacrifice, ideology, dutiful public service, high principle and patriotism; along with bastardry, humbug and betrayal, and the more mundane motives of superannuation, travel allowances and free tickets. Sometimes politics can seem to be little more than blather, an elaborate disguise for nest-feathering, a cynical charade and, for that matter, a tiresome one. It's a game that attracts all types and sometimes the dullards and cynics are the winners. As consuming passions go, politics can be pretty ordinary. But in a good patch there's nothing like it: the most fun you can have standing up, folk used to say.

Ambition is inescapable and so powerful in the human breast, Machiavelli decided, because Nature has made it possible to desire everything, but not to attain everything. Millions of corpses have wired us to fear ambition uncontained. The ambitious are wise to throttle down their inner drive, keep it commensurate with demonstrated abilities and usefulness, balanced by their altruism or anything that might pass for such a thing. Save the ambition for the savage moment of release, and then come forth sphinx-like and tell them you did it for the country, for democracy, for decency, for *them*.

Very often there's some noble truth in the midst of this dissembling, but that makes the business of politics no less savage. Politics is power: but what makes it different to power in, say, Hollywood films or the Old Testament, is that in politics power is denied. Richard Carleton's famous question to Bob Hawke on the night he deposed Bill Hayden riled

Hawke so terribly because it went to the naked fact of the matter, the fact of power: "How does it feel to have blood on your hands?" Carleton asked. How dare he suggest that power was involved, that blood was the inevitable consequence of ambition? Or take Sarah Ferguson's question to Joe Hockey on the night of his first Budget: "Is it liberating for a politician to decide election promises don't matter?" Hockey's wounded grimace inverted the truth of the relationship; as if Ferguson were the powerful one and the treasurer a mere servant of the people trying to do his best from a position of great disadvantage. So accustomed are we to this inversion, some of us almost felt sorry for him; and a fellow journalist commissioned to conduct an audit found insufficient respect had been shown the treasurer and the interview had the potential to "breach the ABC impartiality guidelines". So we demand respect and impartiality for the powerful, but not the truth from them.

Enter the photographers clicking away, poking their lenses ever closer to the pollies' noses, as if deep secrets might be hidden in their pores. In general the subjects are of no more mystery, goodness or beauty than you or I; but they are politicians and they contain riddles which democratic duty demands that we unravel. Hundreds of reporters and commentators are employed to extract the meaning from the circus, and thus counter the hundreds more who are employed to bend it to particular advantage. Then we ourselves, when making what we can of politics from what we read, hear and see, re-bend it through our own partisan lenses.

If new media technology has reduced their once singular importance, political photographers continue to offer a penetrating light. In the still photograph, as opposed to the moving image, there is nothing to distract us from the face, wherein it is alleged the mind's construction can be seen. We might also see something of the mind in the way a politician walks, or waves his hands about, or tugs at his ear, or twitches under pressure – but you don't need a video to see them doing it. The very different swaggers of Keating and Abbott are plainest in still photographs. You can see Keating's ambition in his cuffs and in his shoulders, Abbott's in his bandy legs. A good still image will always tell us as much as a moving one will, maybe more for being nearer to a distilled essence.

Look at Andrew Chapman's photographs of the men who ran the Coalition of the late 1970s. They speak directly of power. They have desired everything and now think they have attained it. Their fate awaits them. We see them before they are undone. Those who were there will be reminded in an instant, not only of the men but of an era, and of a drama whose last act had yet to be played out. Those who weren't there, but who want to know what it was like, will find in those photographs a fertile place to start.

Look at the photos of the young R. J. L. Hawke and the young Keating and see the perfect self-possession the best politicians always seem to have, and the rest of us can only wonder at. But then look at John Howard, and wonder how someone who so plainly lacks this quality could end up serving as prime minister for longer than either of them, longer than anyone else bar Robert Menzies. Look a bit longer and we might begin to see behind the oversized spectacles and the uncertain smile a desire just as fierce as that which drove his rivals, which fed on theirs and on their vanity. Look longer at the rivals and we might see traces of doubt.

Andrew Chapman has been photographing Australian politics for forty years. The record he has left is a marvel of acumen and perseverance. The acumen speaks through the effect of the photos on the viewer: whether his subjects are farmers in their blasted landscapes or politicians in theirs, his photographs testify at once to human ambition and what Susan Sontag called in a famous essay on photography "time's relentless melt". The perseverance is in what it takes to get a collection like these.

For all but a few players, politics is suffused with dreary repetition and inconsequentiality. Like life in the trenches, most of it is spent waiting. There are great dramatic moments and great characters; but some of Andrew Chapman's most telling photographs are surely the product of waiting through those political droughts described by John Button: "When nothing much happens ... people are constantly on edge, waiting for the first hint of a political development and terrified of missing it when it comes". Somewhere in that tense stillness hides the true nature of the political game, and by pointing his lens at it for forty years, Andrew Chapman has left us with a priceless insight into our modern history and ourselves.

Introduction, Andrew Chapman, *Political Vision:*
A Photographic Journey Through Australian Politics, 2015

Prometheus and the pen

You know the legend of Prometheus – there are several, but I mean the one in which Zeus binds him to a rock where each day his liver is eaten by an eagle. Were he an ordinary man, the agony would be brief, but Prometheus is an immortal, so his liver grows again, and the eagle comes to torture him each day. The story has fed the human imagination since a century or two before Homer.

But here's another story. Scientists in Japan have created working human-liver tissue, not with embryonic stem cells, but with adult cells coaxed into pluripotency – a beautiful word meaning the ability to become a different kind of cell.

No more ethical concerns about building cells from embryos. No need to fool the immune system into accepting new cells, because the cells are the patient's own. It's the first step to building a complex human organ from scratch.

There's a little way to go, but it seems conceivable that all humans might quite soon end up with livers like Prometheus's. And, indeed, who's to say that in time they won't be able to grow all the other parts and, if Medicare will cover it, make us immortal like him.

We might think that growing a liver, not to say the prospect of immortality, would be worth a column inch or two on the front page of the Fairfax website, but no – this story, including a Renaissance picture of the Titan tormented on the rock, occupied barely a page in a recent edition of *The Economist*, which means that most people will come across it two or three years hence in the waiting room of their accountant or periodontist.

For my own part, while immortality is superficially appealing, I just know I haven't the necessary improvement in me to make it worthwhile.

Who wants to be a writer of modest talent forever? Never to get within a bull's roar of Tolstoy or Dickens? That's the point of the myth, after all, isn't it? We'd each have our own eagles gnawing at us through the endless hereafter. I'd be very grateful if they could grow me a new neck for the time I have left to me, but immortality, no thanks.

To get back to the point – try to imagine the literary equivalent of this story. What book or play or poem in history comes close to this – *The Divine Comedy? Don Quixote?* The first performance of *Hamlet? The Owl and the Pussycat?* Is there anything a writer can do that compares to growing a new liver from bits of the old one's owner? I think not. Science dwarfs our imaginations, makes fools of us.

Some not so much, of course; which is why it took me twenty years or more to find the gall to say, "I'm a writer", when people ask me what I do. I still mumble it and say "scribbler". Tolstoy was a writer. George Eliot was a writer. Balzac and Kafka, Faulkner and García Márquez are writers. J.M. Coetzee, John Updike, Alice Munro, Margaret Atwood, Seamus Heaney, Les Murray, V.S. Naipaul – these are writers.

True, I used to be able to say I was a historian, but less because I wrote history and more because I taught it. Marc Bloch and Eric Hobsbawm are historians.

Then there's that humiliating term "public intellectual": it turned up on the sleeve of a US edition of a book of mine and caused me great embarrassment. A couple of American radio interviewers asked me what such a person was. I could smell the derision. I learned to say a public intellectual is a person with a platform and an opinion – like you, Homer, or you, Sean. Anyway, they liked the idea and shut up about it.

When I came back I found a poll had been conducted, ranking Australia's public intellectuals – one to twenty. It left out journalists such as Ross Gittins, Paul Kelly and Les Carlyon, but included me. I don't know why.

The difference between thinking journalists and public intellectuals I do not understand. The difference between thinking journalists and thinking writers I do not understand. Was George Orwell a writer, an intellectual or a journalist? H.L. Mencken? Claud Cockburn?

I don't quite know what makes an intellectual, let alone a public one. Freud was one, I know that. And Einstein was. Keynes. Those Japanese scientists strike me as being intellectuals. And this list alone confirms that I am not.

This is not modesty – false, real or calculated. It's no more modest than recognising that one is not a gum tree or a polar bear. I'm not particularly modest: at least not so modest as to be immune to the idea that I am a better writer than some others who follow the vocation, that I find much writing by others tiresome and even pointless, and believe it would be better for everyone if some of them just stopped. Survival in the profession depends on fighting off the thought, whatever the evidence for it, that I am one of them.

That there are writers like me and writers of a different order is something I must know if I want to call myself sane – which is more important to me than calling myself a writer. So I must know that I am not Mark Twain or Henry James either. Twain said he was "drawn to writing of a low order". I'd be happy to say that too – if it weren't that his low-order writing was of such a high order.

That's one reason for being a sort of reluctant writer: one's manifest inferiority to great writers, and the sense that, anyway, even the great writers are chaff in comparison to the people who discover DNA, see into deep space and grow livers.

It might have *something* to do with coming from among people for whom writing was a dubious profession – not a serious thing to be doing with one's life. A stupid sort of a thing to do with it, in fact. Maybe, once subjected to that sort of conditioning, we never entirely escape its effects.

So, I don't know about the other writers here, but I am not comfortable with being a writer. I have more than once felt that my membership of the profession will soon expire: I will wake up one day and find I've been on a thirty-year bender and don't know which side is up, and now must settle down and get a real job.

I am not even all that comfortable with the company of other writers, and surely that is true of most: we'd rather spend time with detectives, soldiers, sex workers, scientists – people we can write *about*. I mean, if you're a writer why knock about with other writers – even if you like them, you're not going to get much of a story out of them. I have travelled in the landscape with writers, and it was great fun, even if there was a lot of yawning. But I've also travelled with scientists and painters – and that was travel of a different order. *That* was marvellous. They're also better drivers.

My insecurity is not helped by the contemporary cult of writing, which requires the author – or *encourages* her – to be a performer, even a sort of celebrity. This applies in equal measure to very distinguished writers and writers of modest achievement. It's no bad thing, of course, but it has little to do with writing – and sometimes not much to do with performing. I wonder if there are people who are choosing to become writers for the lifestyle it seems to offer, the chance to perform at writers' festivals, to have a more distinguished public persona than what is possible in the public service or on Facebook.

I am very grateful for having been able to make a living from writing for thirty years – and also amazed by it – and I take more pleasure from reading the works of other writers than I do from anything else, except racehorses. But when it comes to assembling writers in a room, even just a mental room, I have to be reminded that a writing community exists, with common interests and potentially common ambitions – with anything in common at all really.

And writers are so often wrong. I don't mean juvenile errors of judgement. I'm thinking of the bigger things they've been wrong about. There have been heroic writers, of course, but in general their political judgement is terrible. In the twentieth century so many of them were terribly – all but criminally – wrong.

How *could* anyone not actually in the pay of Stalin, or in fear of him, say upon visiting the Soviet Union when millions were starving in a government-sponsored famine – "I have seen socialism and it works"? How did Manning Clark fall for it when he went there a quarter of a century later? George Orwell saw through it. Sartre didn't. Koestler saw through it. A lot of people with a lot less education and intellectual pretension saw the reality of Stalin before a lot of writers and intellectuals did. A whole generation of writers fell for it – and had I lived through the '30s I might have fallen too. Of course they wanted to believe: it is possible to understand *why* they did it, but surely a mistake to understand it so well that we can't judge them. To not judge them is unfair to the victims and to those with more sense and moral courage.

Three of the writers present at the beginning of the Australian Society of Authors were or had been pro-Soviet communists: Dymphna Cusack, Frank Hardy and Judah Waten. I remember meeting Judah Waten in the mid-1970s. A very charming, gentlemanly soul, sitting in front of a big poster of beautiful Lake Baikal. Not a corpse in sight. He told me how the United States was on the way out, and the Soviet Union had the answers. I think Judah was one of the few to join – rejoin in fact – the Communist Party of Australia *after* the invasion of Hungary. He seemed to think they had proved their mettle there.

Fortunately for the ASA more practical enthusiasts prevailed: Walter Stone, Dal Stivens, Jill Hellyer, Nan Chauncy, Betty Roland. The thing took shape despite the political nuisances and the abstainers such as Patrick White, who wrote to say writers should simply get agents; and Hal Porter, who said it was not his "nature or his inclination to belong to groups of any sort". And groups of writers? Well, writers were a "breed [he] held no brief for".

I can sympathise with that. I don't think Proust would have joined the ASA either. But the truth is, however disenchanted with the profession, or insecure in it, and however sceptical about the promise of collective action one might be, there comes a time each year – and it is nearly always a dire time – when the cheque turns up from PLR, or ELR or CAL, and I give thanks to the ASA and, with an image in my mind of Frank Moorhouse hovering over a martini in the Bayswater Brasserie, I send off my subscription and a small donation.

That is one thing I know I have in common with all other writers – the need to make a quid. And hard as it is now, it was much harder when the ASA was founded. It was harder twenty years ago, when you were lucky if you could get forty cents a word from the newspapers.

But, what else do we have in common, we writers? What other threads bind us? I can think of only one, and that is language. The medium in which we work. If scientists can regenerate a liver, even grow one from scratch, can a society of authors regenerate a language, or even just defend it? I doubt it. But, maybe, collectively we can demonstrate a care for it – its "sacred quality", as Barry Lopez put it. I wonder if the ASA might propose that the language be granted protections under a heritage listing.

Writing is difficult, and the more one does it the more difficult it becomes. That is one of the reasons – perhaps the main one – that, in this information age, the language in which we express ourselves and think has been reduced so quickly to a conveyor belt for cliché and messages. We writers have in common the knowledge that language is more than this, and with the knowledge comes some kind of duty to retain its glorious potential.

The truest thing about writing that I have ever read is this, by George Eliot:

> Examine your words well, and you will find that even when you have no motive to be false, it is very hard to say the exact truth, even about your own immediate feelings – much harder than to say something fine about them which is not the exact truth.

That seems to me the thread that binds all writers together: not just the difficulty of the craft, but *recognising* the difficulty. And it could be that in this lies the seed of a common ambition.

Address on the Fiftieth Anniversary of the
Australian Society of Authors, 2013

EPILOGUE

On indignation

AMONG MY FAMILY, MOST OF them descending from the Calvinist coast of Scotland, were many who had this much in common with the tribes of the Judean wilderness: they struggled to get through a week without taking umbrage at some piddling thing and wishing the offender one way or another to damnation. They did a good deal of internalising. They practised long silences. In subtle ways this constant exercise of pride probably held the family together – at least what remained of it when the unworthy had been banished. Anthropologists long ago observed the same principle in what used to be called primitive societies. It is functional after a fashion, and often funny after the event. But it is rarely fun at the time.

By way of example, while riding the five miles that separated his half-cleared hundred acres from the nearest town, a grandfather of mine convinced himself that a Mrs H. had just slighted him outside the general store. He already suspected the woman of flattering herself that the few sheep she and her husband ran put them in a rank above people like him who milked cows. Construing something "superior" in her expression when he had raised his hat to her that afternoon, very soon after he was at the mercy of his pride. As he rode home, the poison thickened in his blood, and by the time he got inside his house it had gripped him like a python. It is "a highly characteristic sign" of indignation, Charles Darwin wrote, when "the wings of the nostrils are somewhat raised to allow of a free indraught of air". No sooner had my grandfather sat down for a cup of tea, than his nostrils flared like a Jersey bull's and, with a great indraught of air, he slapped his hat back on his head and, telling his sons to get on with the milking, fairly flew out the door. For the boys watching from the porch that late afternoon, the sight of their father flashing between the gum trees as he galloped down the road that led back to town and the residence of Mrs H. became a permanent memory.

He was a soldier settler not long back from the Great War, and this was the strange part of it: after three years enduring everything the Axis and the northern European winter could throw at a man, including Passchendaele, Ypres, Mouquet Farm, Mont St Quentin and the Spanish flu, who would have thought he could be bothered by such a trifle? They say war changes a man, but it does not change all of him: nothing short of shell shock or physical brain damage will change whatever frames the self-possession demanded by battle. This is what survives of him at war's end. If Ulysses had one thing left when he got home it was self-possession, along with the indignation necessary to protect it. It was indignation – with the goddess Athena's connivance – that drove him to slaughter his wife's suitors.

Indignation is tied with very taut strings to the instinct for self-preservation. It is related directly to death in the same way that humiliation is. When Athena stirs it up, she demonstrates one of the pre-eminent affinities of our nature: between taking personal offence and taking lives. The Old Testament makes the same point repeatedly. Samuel, for instance, appears to find hacking Philistines and sacrificial animals to pieces no impediment to getting on with life and making a success of it. It comes naturally.

Those earlier members of my family did not actually hack at each other or their neighbours, but they often had them on their minds as day after day they hacked at weeds and routed trees and no doubt remembered the words of the Psalm: "Let their eyes be darkened, that they see not; and make their loins continually to shake. Pour out thine indignation upon them … let them be blotted out of the book of the living". The words which are said to foretell the instruction and fate of Jesus, in fact foretell the instruction of whole tribes and nations, and the fates of millions. Psalm 69 is the psalm for the indignant; the ones trapped in the chaffcutter of their own righteousness, whose zeal has created enemies exceeding the number of hairs on their heads, their mothers' sons among them. "O God, thou knowest my foolishness". It could have been our family motto.

Indignation is passed on through generations as surely as red hair or haemophilia. It is also contagious. The soldier settler's sisters were even touchier than he was, and their cat caught it. It glared and spat at every other living thing, which in turn made visitors indignant. In a similar vein, Mrs H., who I imagine had felt nothing but bewilderment when my forebear confronted her among the washing on her clothesline, was very soon gripped with indignation of her own. To accuse her of slighting him – it really was too much. To think that she would bother slighting such as he! She! What did he take her for? He! What did he take himself for? Him! Her! And so on. Having caught his indignation, as it were, they fought like scorpions to a standstill and he went home silent and exhausted.

It is doubtful if he had learned anything. Indignation is not a learning environment. But the truth, had his mood allowed him to see it, was that he liked sheep. Nothing would have made him happier than to have a couple of paddocks full of Romney Marsh ewes and wethers, as Mrs H. did. "Nobody lies as much as the indignant do", Nietzsche said: and often to *themselves*, he might have added.

For people who hate nothing more than giving offence to others and have no taste for strife, the difficulty is always to know what it is that will offend. There are more or less universal insults concerning the character of one's mother, the size of one's genitals, the gait of one's horse, etc.; but those and a few others aside, there are almost as many sensitivities in the world as there are people to offend them. While some can be read in the briefest acquaintance or just by looking at a person, at least as many are hidden from the most astute beholder, if not from the person herself. And then there are some – Don Quixote, for example, and also a great aunt of mine – whose mere appearance invites obvious insults, yet to these they are immune; while a mild remark about some seemingly unconnected thing will cause them to explode and demand a duel to the death. It depends, of course, on what the person imagines he is or most wants to be – of what he thinks his worth consists. The facts of this may be hidden not only from the person giving offence, but from the person taking it, and the fit of pique that follows – even one that lasts for years – might never be understood or explained by either of them. These hurts are as much like allergies as psychological conditions, but unlike both those common afflictions, have no cure outside opium or religion.

As with Don Quixote, who is a very knowing madman, the person prone to fits of indignation is frequently expert at teasing fits from others. Like those parasite birds that ride on the cow's back, the tease lives off the indignant: he whispers in their ears, baits them; like Satan or Athena he plays the Id. In my own childhood someone was always trying to get a rise, and someone was always stalking off in tears and slamming doors behind her; or marching out of the cowshed and down the hill as if determined that the rest of us would never see her again. "Huffs", they were called, or "scots". But the indignant very often walk into a void. They need resistance. And sooner or later they have to come in for tea. What then? What does it profit a man to throw his custard at the wall?

For the incurably indignant, one answer is silence, the complete fade-out: deep, long, infuriating, inexplicable silence. For the silent one, this is the equivalent of the prophets' sojourns in the desert. If he stays there long enough, he can imagine he has entered a higher state, perhaps even a state of grace, certainly a state beyond the reach of his own feelings that would otherwise be gnawing at his innards like so many rats. For those who have to cope with this style of protest, indignation does not begin to describe their feelings – they would happily kill them. Cain is a case in point. Jealousy – indignation at God's outrageous and, as usual, unexplained favouritism – might have driven him to murder his brother: but who ever heard that story without suspecting that Abel was a psychological martyr long before his brother whacked him and created the first real one?

I had uncles in the mould of Abel. And aunts in the mould of Cain. Uncles and great-uncles who though they shared the same roof exchanged no more than sighs for weeks on end; uncles who were cast out forever by aunts who for unfathomable reasons went lifetimes without speaking to other aunts.

It is not to deprive us of their wisdom and personal charm that they don't speak; it is to prey on our consciences. They will have us feel guilty. With silence they will grind us until we confess our wrongdoing. Hurl cow pats at me, they say; make me bleed; nail me up: I will not cry out. You will not have the satisfaction.

This kind of martyrdom is indignation's closest relation – the brother, if you like. It is both a weapon and a way of surviving the incipient civil war in families. It issues from the never-ending drama of the self, not least the self's innate capacity for fantasy, megalomania and envy. Indignation and martyrdom: those two were just about my chief inheritances.

Jesus – at least as he was taught to us – was to the Old Testament God as lithium is to hypomania. He tried to put a check on indignation, which might be one reason why He taught with parables rather than rules. The effect of the New Testament on the cosmology of my youth was irremediable confusion: chaos and hellfire and piety. One moment I was as if commanded by the inner voice to let fly in righteous anger like Samson among the Philistines or Jesus in the temple, the next retreating in the glow of the Beatitudes, murmuring, Turn the other cheek, blessed are the peacemakers, blessed are the meek, suffer the little children, don't be like your grandfather.

In my eleventh and twelfth years I lived equally impressed by God's awful power and the sweet possibilities of the Sermon on the Mount. Soon enough, however, I found that while I could do without loving my enemy I could not live without bouts of indignation. There is too much pleasure in it. I was drawn as if my body needed it as much as salt and carbohydrate. The Karamazov brother might have been feeling as I did when he said that he didn't want harmony. "From love of humanity I don't want it ... I would rather remain with my unavenged suffering and unsatisfied indignation ... Besides, too high a price is asked for harmony; it's beyond our means to pay so much to enter on it." It was not just the adrenaline rush or the perverse delight in chaos, or the even purer form of pleasure that withdrawal brings: it was my inability to imagine much more than boredom flowing from Christian serenity. I inherited, or had reinforced in me, a roughly equal measure of pious obedience and indignant revolt: a loathsome amalgam, especially in a child. Not that I recognised it, but I know I always felt better when my unconscious was decent enough to push me in one direction at a time.

Indignation is anger, but not quite the same. Anger has a less specific character. We feel indignant when we're jilted, deceived, betrayed, cheated, traduced, overtaken on a double line, suffer rudeness from a bank teller, impertinence from a dental hygienist: when we've had one too many lousy rolls of the dice. We may feel it if some remote extension of our being is insulted: our children or our dog, our car or refrigerator, our God, our horse. Jockeys say that it is safer to insult a horse's owner or tell him his wife is ugly than to tell him that his horse is slow or lacks heart. Some time in the future, by using advanced infra-red photography, it might be possible to map the emotional reach of every individual in a country town or suburb – or a school or penitentiary.

The feeling often fades as quickly as it flares, but it can last for years as well. It can poison the soul. It may seem to pass and then resurface much later, possibly in an unexplained tic or catatonia. It may grow into anger or rage: into force for that matter – into violence, murder and war. Castles and battleships, cannons and grenades are, in certain lights, physical expressions of human indignation. It has roots in fear, bitterness, shyness, desire and every unsatisfied need of the flesh and the spirit. Our indignation barks inside us; bursts forth and retreats like another personality, like Dr Jekyll's Mr Hyde. It can grow into psychosis – *Psycho*'s Norman Bates burbles with childish indignation.

Anger obliterates personality. Indignation expresses it. Indignation is full of dramatic, including comic, possibility; anger is never funny and whether it is real or feigned, soon becomes uncomfortable and drab to witness. Charlie Chaplin did indignation all the time, anger only rarely. It is the same with many of the great comic turns: Katharine Hepburn, Lucille Ball, James Stewart, Stan Laurel, Tony Hancock – they were all good at indignation. It is one of possibly two emotions on which Harrison Ford has built his stellar career.

Very likely it has something to do with the spectacle of a grown-up behaving like a toddler. As a two-year-old wails when some part of his world is taken away or it behaves in ways that he cannot control, the comedian wails when his pride is punctured or deflated, when his monomania meets reality. So, sometimes, does the theatrical gangster; like Edward G. Robinson when the end comes in *Little Caesar*: "Mother of Mercy, is this the end of Rico?"

The Puritan mind was much concerned with "training the will" of the child, beating down the stubbornness and pride it brings into the world. "*I*, when it relates to God, is expressive of His dignity … When used with reference to men, it expresses their pride", wrote an eighteenth-century Presbyterian. Nothing in human nature is more likely to oppose God's will than the individual will. It is obvious in the two-year-old who only knows gratification or indignation. Just as it learns to walk and talk and exercise its will, it encounters new threats to its control. It must surrender omnipotence and make do with some less satisfying notion, such as "God is present in each one of His creatures". The Puritans reckoned this was the decisive moment: train the child to walk God's path, speak God's word, do God's will, or let him will his own way to perdition. As the unbroken will stood between every child and submission to God's purpose, it stood, quite literally, between heaven and hell. Mrs Wesley was in no doubt that the success so clearly manifest in her godly sons, John and Charles, could be put down to her breaking their infant wills. Thereafter *righteous* indignation was the only indignation available to them.

Pride thus comes before the greatest of all falls, the fall from grace and into the arms of the devil. In the days when Puritans were holding witch-hunts, wilfulness – including indignation of the unrighteous kind – was one of the forms of behaviour likely to get a person into trouble. Among people who fear God and value peace and harmony, the chronically wilful represent the gravest threat. That they should risk their own souls by refusing to humble themselves before God is bad enough; but their wilfulness places the whole community in peril of His wrath. In such places those not doing God's work perforce must do the Devil's. The Puritans redrew in civil society the line long drawn in Christian religious establishments: between the righteous indignation of the Godly and the fiendish indignation of the wilful.

In an early episode of *The Sopranos*, the psychopathic Paulie Walnuts orders a coffee in what looks very like a Starbucks. Paulie's will, plainly, was not broken as a child. No self-respecting capo's was. There would be no show if their wills had been broken. An entire film genre would be lost. Paulie has never been in a Starbucks or any place like it before. He feels threatened: anything unfamiliar is a threat to Paulie Walnuts. The middle-class blonde girl taking orders for triple mocha supremes and espresso macchiatos issues from a culture as far removed from the Sicilian and the criminal as it is possible to be. The combustible Paulie looks around with his customary aggression. Everything about the place gets under his skin. We invented this stuff, he says: so how come these other people are making money from it? How come we didn't get into it? What's the matter with us? Within moments he's burning with the offence to his dignity and his family's dignity, and to what is just and proper. He puts a stove-top espresso pot inside his coat.

Honour and indignation are elements of the same environment. Money is another one. Money – the "points" – is the one thing that will keep Paulie's mood stable. So long as he's getting his "points" he's tolerably pacific. If he's not, only blood will console him. The relationship between money and pride is a perpetual theme of *The Sopranos*, as it is in most films about gangsters – and also in nineteenth-century novels and some of the plays of Shakespeare. It is a theme of human history, which is not surprising given that money – whatever form it takes or name it goes by – weighs the worth accorded to the person paid it. Whether it comes as ochre or diamonds, shekels or wampum or virgins, what we now call money has always been taken personally. Dollars could as well be called "indignants". Too little tribute will cause a war or signal the decline of the nation it is owed to; having too few "points" has the same effect on Paulie Walnuts – it plunges him into savagery and he goes forth with "the weapons of his indignation" (in God's case, an earthquake or boils; in Paulie's, a gun or baseball bat), and if satisfaction is denied him he declines into depression and superstition.

Like some of my own non-Sicilian ancestors, when Paulie is not being driven by his own indignation, he's trying to stir it in others. Rider Haggard wrote that Kipling once told him that this world had "every attribute of hell: doubt, fear, pain, struggle, bereavement, almost irresistible temptations springing from the nature with which we are clothed, physical and mental suffering, etc., ending in the worst fate man can devise for man, Execution!" This is what Paulie wants the world to know – that everyone must suffer, what happens to him must happen to them. Paulie's boss, Tony Soprano, lives on the same precipice of despair. The show is a study in the relationship between indignation and depression. Christopher, Junior, Johnny Sack, Phil Leotardo – they are all two-year-olds. All manic depressives.

Long before, when we were children and could not even imagine families like the Sopranos, much less laugh at them, Steele Rudd's *On Our Selection* was the funniest thing in the house. The Rudd family were struggling Protestant selectors and, before they were turned into buffoons for the screen, they were not far removed from small farming families like my own. It was the comedy, above all, that we recognised. The humour flowed from the meeting of Dad Rudd's noble nature and heroic intentions with intractable, inchoate and vindictive Nature: the droughts, the fires, the cockatoos and kangaroos, the feckless sons.

In one story, "When the Wolf Was at the Door", the family is penniless and has only pumpkin to eat. At the dinner table Dan asks Dave if he'd like some bread. "Damn your insolence!" cries Dad, leaping to his feet. "'Go!' said Dad, furiously, pointing to the door, 'leave my roof, you thankless dog!'"

It is an Old Testament moment, and no doubt a Freudian one as well. In our illustrated edition, Dad was shown standing at the head of the table with the family sitting meekly round it. His beard was white, like God's, his eyes wild and he was pointing to the door. It was the one story that wasn't funny. The superego can never be funny of itself, only when it's punctured: as when, with the banished Dan still unsighted after many months, Dad grows testy again, and again in the manner of a Bible story – this time at the man's insufferable lack of gratitude. "To leave me", he says, "just when I wanted help! After all the years I've slaved to feed him and clothe him …!" It is both a laboured irony and an expression of the way indignation serves as a mainstay of the oldest human stories.

The British psychologist Donald Winnicott saw a direct connection between the art (and religion) of adult humans and the most inexplicable and alarming of all slights on our being, our weaning as infants. The symbols and rituals of adulthood, like the dolls and bears and bits of blanket (the "transitional objects") carried everywhere by children, help us to live with that dreadful affront. Like any state of excitement, to be indignant is to be not one's usual self; and being a state in which one's real or presumed self has been threatened, it is to feel an all but irresistible need to get on one's high horse and brain the offender at once. But writing and thinking both take time and a rush of adrenaline is not always their friend. *Writing* indignantly is rather like slowly hitting someone with a brick, or slowly brushing a tarantula from one's cheek.

George Orwell was one of a rare species: a political creature with his sense of indignation so well governed it actually helped his writing. "When I sit down to write a book", he declared, "I do not say to myself, 'I am going to produce a work of art'. I write it because there is some lie that I want to expose, some fact to which I want to draw attention, and my initial concern is to get a hearing". His "starting point", he said, was "always a feeling of partisanship". In most writers a wound to their political or moral sensibility is likely to inspire the "purple passages, sentences without meaning, decorative adjectives and humbug generally" that Orwell deplored. But outrage had the opposite effect on Orwell. His best writing, he said, always had a political purpose; his worst "invariably" lacked one.

In their social intercourse, people cultivate masks, blank stares and verbal blinds of various kinds to defend their dignity and hide the rush of blood provoked by insults. For much the same purpose, offended writers put themselves at one remove by creating satires, burlesques and characters like Voltaire's Candide, Swift's Gulliver or Johnson's Rasselas: characters for whom naivety serves as the mask and allows them to get to the bottom of human folly politely and without losing their reason.

Not everyone can do it. Compare the sinewy clarity of Orwell's prose – he aimed to make it like a "window pane" – with the deep purple from Edmund Burke's philippic on British abuses of power in the eighteenth-century Raj: "… the foul, putrid mucus in which are engendered the whole brood of creeping ascarides, all the endless involutions, the eternal knot, added to a knot of those inexpugnable tape-worms which devour the nutriment and eat up the bowels of India".

Burke was not always purple, of course, and even when he was, the effect was often hair-raising. His "inexpugnable tape-worms", what's more, would do for, let's say, the Aboriginal experience of Northern Territory bureaucracy, and his "endless involutions" for any number of privately owned public utilities that plague our lives. The entire passage may apply to any remote power, including some close to us, like banks or call centres, that at once provokes and stifles indignation and in this way leaves us feeling less than human.

It was lucky for everyone that Burke's verbal resources ran as deep as his feelings. Such a phenomenon of sustained outrage as his years-long pursuit of Warren Hastings and the East India Company required equally phenomenal metaphors rendered in language of boundless variety – or else it would be brushed off as the ranting of a maniac or an Irishman. Burke once said that Hastings could not dine "without creating a famine", and his life would have been well worth living if that had been the only thing he ever said. While it is probably true to say that his savaging of Hastings aroused just enough sympathy for the man to get him acquitted, it also helped establish some new moral principles for colonial governance: new because until then, presumably, Englishmen had not thought Indians sufficiently human for the inhuman abuse of them to be worth getting indignant about.

"Indignation devours me", Flaubert said. He wanted to "purge" himself of it. The feeling consumed the last decades of his life. The bourgeoisie, the working classes, the peasantry, the intellectuals – every social category offended him. *Democracy* offended him. Mankind in its "irremediable wretchedness", in particular as it presented itself in the 1870 Paris Commune, offended him. Above all, stupidity offended him, and nearly everyone was stupid. "I can no longer talk with anyone at all without becoming furious, and everything I read by my contemporaries makes me quiver with indignation", he wrote to Turgenev. The only thing he was not indignant about was his own youthful behaviour, which, to be charitable, was nearly as stupid as anything he encountered in his mature years. And his intolerance of stupidity almost certainly had roots in his dire awareness of our inability to know very much about anything. The two idiots of his unfinished novel, *Bouvard and Pécuchet*, read an entire library and know infinitely less at the end than the nothing they knew when they set out. So with Flaubert: the more he learned the more he came to see that "We still know almost nothing and we would wish to divine the final word that will never be revealed to us". The stupid touched something very personal in Flaubert – namely knowledge of his own ignorance. The stupid came blindly trampling over the terrible secret. "O God, thou knowest my foolishness."

Even if it can't be said with certainty of Flaubert, it seems likely that the degree of our indignation is related to the degree of our guilt. To choose a topical example: if some decent people get indignant about pictures of naked children in modern works of art while others just as decent don't, is that because the second group are less decent in the matter of children, or because the first group are? Are the second lot simply insensible to the moral danger the first lot see, or are the first lot compensating for disturbing feelings the pictures stir in them?

I would number myself among those people who don't feel much offended by Bill Henson's photographs while conceding that they are not in every case morally vigilant or as strict with themselves as they should be. They do not feel themselves threatened by pictures of naked children, they do not feel their children are threatened by them and, perhaps because a bit of nakedness really never hurt anybody, they do not feel the child in the photograph is threatened. It might be for these reasons that the matter does not spark their indignation; it might be because they feel indignant about too much else, or because stupidity or cultural theory has left them without the capacity to feel indignant about anything; or it might be that they have an aversion to particular kinds of moral indignation – especially the kind which cannot coexist with ambiguity, a sense of humour, or any other sense that might grant us tolerance and self-awareness. There is always a sense with the morally indignant that their real aim is to console themselves.

"The voice of honest indignation is the voice of God", William Blake said. And that, on occasion, is the trouble with it. The morally indignant speak as if on His behalf. There is the righteous indignation of an Edmund Burke or an Emmeline Pankhurst or a Martin Luther King Jr, and there is the righteous indignation of people who confuse virtue with loathing vice and seeing it behind every door and shrub. There is the indignation of Jonathan Swift and the indignation of Barnaby Joyce. There is Aleksandr Solzhenitsyn's indignation and there is Jack Benny's schtick. One would think, given the extremes of human experience, God might have granted us some more specific mechanisms for dealing with it. There is indignation over the unnecessary suffering of millions, and indignation over a bad haircut. The related worlds of television, talkback radio and social media swarm with the indignant. There is the indignation of the victims and the indignation of the powerful and entitled who reckon resistance is a denial of their natural rights. There is indignation of the kind necessary to resist tyranny and exploitation, whether they are practised by a petty bureaucrat or a dictator, and there is the indignation used to justify them. There is real, feigned and imagined indignation. It is one of life's great conjuring acts for any human being to settle on the right kind in the right proportion.

Indignation might be viewed as the psychological equivalent of the body's immune system, which, when it recognises a virus threatening our equilibrium or existence, manufactures quantities of phlegm and mucus to protect us. Very often we speak as if the effects were the same when a slight invades us and we lack the eloquence to discharge our wounded feelings: we gag on them, become speechless. "Here he got choked by excessive indignation", Conrad says of one of his characters in *Heart of Darkness*. Winston Churchill recognised the syndrome when he called across the House to a noisy political opponent: "The honourable gentleman should not really generate more indignation than he can contain". In the same chamber in 1939, as Chamberlain propounded his egregious position on German territorial demands, an honourable member was reported to have thrown up, which seems to confirm Darwin's observation: "Extreme disgust is expressed by movements round the mouth identical with those preparatory to the act of vomiting".

In general, the immune system gets it right, but there are times when it protests too much and becomes more virulent — and more deadly — than the invading virus. It is called a cytokine storm and most of us have seen parallel symptoms in the aggrieved: outbursts out of all proportion to the offence, capable of causing lethal strokes and heart attacks in the offended and painful if not actually dangerous to bystanders.

Like the souls it seeks to defend, indignation is sometimes an ennobling spectacle and an agent of welcome progress, and just as often ugly and destructive. It is the natural stuff of politics, just as it is of gangster films: stuff with which to bolster oneself, reduce others and manipulate as many as possible. No one can master politics if she has not mastered indignation — her own, her supporters' and her opponents'.

Hitler's revolution, like those of other ideological stripes, was substantially built on indignation; and like the others, once established, maintained itself by projecting onto the minds of citizens myriad counterrevolutionary phantoms, subversive elements, enemies of the people, treasonous tendencies and so on — each of them not only a threat to stable government, but an affront to the ambitions and sacrifices of the people and their glorious leaders. In both Hitler's Germany and Stalin's Russia the language of indignation was used to *eradicate* feelings of indignation. The effect of this — combined, of course, with the threat of exile, torture and execution — was to create at worst surly complicity, but more often a collective raising of hackles. Indignation is not only contagious; it is also addictive, as most people who have lived in a family or played contact sports will know. After a while we need the adrenaline: it feels better than thinking, which might be why all societies seem to need some level of hysteria pretty well all the time.

If to be indignant is to stand on one's dignity, totalitarianism makes sure that nobody can. Anyone who has felt the invisible, "hypnotic force" invade him and "dissolve his will", Vasily Grossman wrote, will be "astonished that a man can rebel against it even for a moment". Possibly it was because the Soviet regime had crushed their dignity that the bulk of the Russian population could not muster much resistance when a band of the old oppressors filched their country's wealth; and why when a kleptocrat and thug came forth echoing both Stalin and the Tsars, they cheered. As if to restore their lost dignity he spoke of "Great Russia", and constructed a unique Russian worldview out of largely imagined "Russianness". Restoring their pride and identity enlarged their capacity for taking offence, and his for manipulating them.

Hitler's genius – and we only call it this because he had so much time to practise – was to keep his propaganda personal and concrete. Every good speechwriter knows this is the only way to do it: find some poor cove with a story of misfortune or modest triumph to tell, and run your admiration or your indignation through him. Make him your Stakhanov, your message made flesh. Among democratic politicians Bill Clinton made an art of it, and Eleanor Roosevelt came gently to the conclusion that her "interest or sympathy or indignation is not aroused by an abstract cause but by the plight of a single person whom I have seen with my own eyes … Out of my response to an individual develops an awareness of a problem to the community, then to the country and finally to the world". Hitler came to the same conclusion. He began with himself, and eventually had millions of other "single persons" at his disposal. He got them in the main by making sure their enemies were no more abstract than they were. The Jews, the Bolsheviks, the traitors of Versailles, the homosexuals, the unfit: all those for whom he felt visceral fear and hatred he moved his followers to fear and hate. Because all of them were threats to German dignity, all good Germans were perforce indignant.

From On Indignation, *2008*

On optimism

Life is contemptuous of knowledge; it forces it to sit in the anterooms,
to wait outside. Passion, energy, lies: these are what life admires.

—James Salter, *Light Years*

WHO KNOWS WHAT LESSONS WE will learn from the virus? Probably none: at least none secure from myth and misrepresentation. None able to withstand the appetites of self-interest and politics. The lessons will be whatever we are persuaded to accept or believe.

"Which way shall we turn to save our lives and the future of the world?" Winston Churchill asked in his last speech to the House of Commons. He was thinking of children and the new hydrogen bombs and wondering if God had "wearied of mankind". Sixty-five years later, cue mordant laughter.

Yet we're still here, still living amid the proof of humanity's bone-headedness and unmistakable evidence of genius; faintly aware that we are of Nature and at its mercy, and also of the extent of our dominion over it. But never like this. It's as if some freak thing has possessed our heads and made our world a stage to dramatise the great conundrum. We tread in such uncertainty and in such an altered landscape we dare not think too many thoughts.

Pity our poor leaders confronted with the new reality. In the first weeks they did what comes naturally: they gave us optimism. The Chinese began by pretending it wasn't there and shooting the messengers. The Brazilians said it was a "fantasy". The Italians said, "Go to the piazza". The Iranians said, "Go to Qom". The Australians said, "Go to the football". President Trump said go wherever you like, it's a Democratic "hoax", it will vanish "like a miracle", it's nothing to worry about, we have it under control, "we cannot let the cure be worse than the problem itself", etc. Optimism has killed thousands.

Hope is essential for human beings, but optimism is voluntary. George W. Bush and the neocons that ran him were optimists. It's a medium for fanatics, predators and cynics. It's the cake Marie Antoinette is alleged to have recommended. For a slogan, Barack Obama chose "Hope", but when he gave his country back to Wall Street, he chose Optimism – and the country got optimism's incubus, Trump.

Another deadly optimist, V.I. Lenin, said something to the effect that certain events in history are like lightning: for a moment they reveal the world not as it seems but as it really is. They revealed it to him perhaps, but the masses had to make do with slogans. Communism equals optimism plus slogans. Yet the metaphor retains some force. Dark as these times may be, the pandemic has cast rare light on the powers that govern us in ordinary times, and revealed them for what in the main they are: performative claptrap, lies, a waste of time.

Optimism is a refuge of the scoundrel, like its thug relation, patriotism. Boris Johnson called up British bulldog and the Blitz; the Italians, the evening aperitivo; Trump called it the "Chinese virus", the "foreign virus" and urged the view that the United States, being the United States, really didn't have a problem; in Australia they reminded us that we were "all in it together", and that people whose behaviour was not in keeping with this tenet were "un-Australian". Hoarding groceries was particularly un-Australian, which seemed strange since hoarding is a governing principle of a free enterprise society, and providing for one's family is recommended everywhere.

In any event, it at once became apparent that we Australians, like the Chinese, British, Americans and everyone else, are decidedly *not* all in it together. Cliché is another sanctuary from complex, uncertain reality, and just as base and useless as the others.

Australians with ready cash and credit, with superannuation, country houses, no rent or mortgages to pay and jobs that can be worked from home, are in a different boat to the legions whose livelihoods are precarious, including more than a million casual workers and migrant workers who will get nothing from the government bailout.

Those with the internet are better off than the two million without it. Lockdown for months in a big house with a yard is not the same as lockdown in a little house or flat without one. The countless variations on this score require minimal imagination or sympathy. Prospects for the elderly are not the same as those for the young, and each generation sees the COVID world, and the world after COVID, through a different lens. Life for doctors, nurses and hospital staff – many of them casuals and migrants – is infinitely more grim and demanding than it is for just about anyone else. We are no more all in it together now than we were before the pandemic – in truth we are *less* in it together, and likely will remain so when the crisis passes.

One lousy cliché is bound to spawn another, so we shouldn't wonder when we are served incessantly the one about being "at war" with the virus. Inevitably, the evil and obnoxious crook in the White House has cast himself as a "wartime president". The pandemic he downplayed a few weeks ago he now calls the greatest crisis in American history – and he, it follows naturally, must soon become greater than Lincoln and F.D.R. It is not – we trust – in our prime minister's nature to make such claims, but at least one national commentator has already declared he might yet be "Australia's most important wartime leader".

War metaphors infest the language at the best of times. In general it's just laziness, a haven from the strain of thinking. Yet it might be that people who inhabit the realms of power and influence, and come to assume that all life's important questions are answered in the language and manoeuvres of politics and money, find war the most congenial alternative because it leaves them in charge. In Operation Sovereign Borders, though a uniformed army chap stood adjacent at press conferences, the real general was the minister, Scott Morrison. Now, however, political leaders must surrender intellectual authority to science and its practitioners, and the moral high ground they scramble for to doctors and nurses. They have been overcome by truth and knowledge.

This is not a war. If pandemics bore any relationship to war, nations would prepare for them. War and preparations for it are incessant and obscenely expensive state activities and a lucrative trade for immense corporations. But this pandemic, though long predicted by scientists (and Bill Gates, among others), and portended by HIV/AIDS, Hendra, SARS, MERS and Ebola, arrived as if all of a sudden by spaceship from another universe.

The prospect of a pandemic – even the near certainty of it – has no purchase in spheres of power governed by such universally agreed imperatives as budget surpluses and winning elections. It turns out that until the pandemic was here in concrete fact it could not provide the kind of political and pathological payoff that war and the language of war does.

Irksome as the thought may be, whatever gratitude and praise we may mean to heap upon nurses and doctors and hospital orderlies and paramedics, we give them less than they deserve when we ascribe to patriotism or military precedent their care and compassion for the sick and dying. War might seem to elevate their selflessness, but once pushed into such exhausted mental territory it is diminished and falsified.

It is true that, like war, the pandemic requires discipline and a degree of regimentation, but so does learning a language or a musical instrument. So does education. The "enemy" in this crisis has been ignorance and untruth. This is the main difference: in wars, as they say, truth is the first casualty, but in the two months of the pandemic truth has steadily asserted itself and the casualty has been humbug. Knowledge has steadily replaced it. One by one the standard falsehoods and manoeuvres have been pushed aside, among them the ideological underpinnings of political debate in the past decade and a half.

The Budget would return to surplus as promised. The outrageous sums Labor threw at the GFC would not be thrown at the pandemic. Let there be no talk of wage subsidies and the like. Free child care – are you joking? But what had been standard Coalition talking points for years were suddenly as chaff before the wind. The government would be spending amounts of money that made Labor's outrageous sums look like a little light berley. It would spend a large proportion of it on wage subsidies paid to employers. It would spend as much as circumstances demanded.

The principles of Coalition philosophy are not the only ones contravened by the government's measures. A Labor government would have had to shed its own attachments to neoliberal economics, not to say the same political habits that afflicted the government's early response.

Having seen our decommissioned manufacturing industry struggling to produce face shields and masks for health workers – what would have

taken them a day four years ago took one car company more than a fortnight — and the inadequacy of global supply chains in a crisis, might
both sides of politics rethink their shared hostility to anything resembling protected industry? Will public investment in science become
respectable again? Will science itself become respectable? Having seen
the power of Nature, and recognised that bellicosity, denial and posturing are futile defences against it, and for the time being allowed that
scientific knowledge is humanity's best hope, will we take the lesson to
climate change as well?

Yet because they portend the old debates resuming, the old faces
taking up their old places to perform their hackneyed, cheerless scripts,
these questions don't have much appeal just now. Some of us have fallen
for the scientists, the knowledge flowing on our screens, the honest
reasoned arguments and, no less, the varieties of genuine humanity we
have been seeing. The citizenry has sprouted heroes, among them the
eloquent Senior Nurse and Disaster Manager at St Vincent's Hospital,
and the respiratory physician who sent shudders through ABC's *Q&A*
audience by telling them what this disease does to human beings. The
times are strange because they are uncommonly real.

For evidence of this reality, which the best spin and marketing can
never approach, go to the video made by the NHS respiratory team
in a Belfast hospital. It is the plainest and most moving of advertisements. They stand in the foyer and one by one beg their fellow citizens
to "please stay at home". It's just possible that when we're allowed out
again, some of us will be in no hurry to go.

The Monthly, May 2020

Acknowledgements

HERE ARE COLLECTED ESSAYS, COLUMNS, reviews, op-eds and occasional addresses from the past forty years. Most of the pieces are reprinted as they first appeared in journals and newspapers, with an odd error of fact or grammar corrected, an occasional tangle untangled, some paragraphs cut adrift. "On indignation" has been filleted from a longer essay. Forewords and afterwords aside, there is nothing from my books, nor any speeches written for other people.

The writing in this collection has been through the hands of more editors than it is possible to name, so I thank them all for their guidance and attention. Meredith Curnow graciously released essays from an earlier collection published by Penguin Random House. Chris Feik, the masterly editor of Quarterly Essay, chose the entries and found a way to arrange them on thematic lines. For this and essential aid in past endeavours I thank him. Also, Kate Hatch and Kirstie Innes-Will for assiduous editing; Sean O'Beirne and Erin Sandiford for locating articles. Finally, and for much more than the idea of this omnibus, my thanks to Morry Schwartz.

CPSIA information can be obtained
at www.ICGtesting.com
Printed in the USA
LVHW081910090221
678832LV00007B/211